Strategic Dynamics: Concepts and Cases

first edition

Robert A. Burgelman

Andrew S. Grove

with Philip E. Meza

McGraw-Hill Irwin

Boston   Burr Ridge, IL   Dubuque, IA   Madison, WI   New York   San Francisco   St. Louis
Bangkok   Bogotá   Caracas   Kuala Lumpur   Lisbon   London   Madrid   Mexico City
Milan   Montreal   New Delhi   Santiago   Seoul   Singapore   Sydney   Taipei   Toronto

**McGraw-Hill
Irwin**

STRATEGIC DYNAMICS: CONCEPTS AND CASES

Published by McGraw-Hill/Irwin, a business unit of The McGraw-Hill Companies, Inc., 1221 Avenue of the Americas, New York, NY, 10020. Copyright © 2006 by The McGraw-Hill Companies, Inc. All rights reserved. No part of this publication may be reproduced or distributed in any form or by any means, or stored in a database or retrieval system, without the prior written consent of The McGraw-Hill Companies, Inc., including, but not limited to, in any network or other electronic storage or transmission, or broadcast for distance learning.

Some ancillaries, including electronic and print components, may not be available to customers outside the United States.

This book is printed on acid-free paper.

1 2 3 4 5 6 7 8 9 0 QPD/QPD 0 9 8 7 6 5

ISBN   0-07-312265-3

Editorial director: *John E. Biernat*
Sponsoring editor: *Ryan Blankenship*
Editorial coordinator: *Allison J. Clelland*
Executive marketing manager: *Ellen Cleary*
Lead producer, Online courses: *Victoria Bryant*
Project manager: *Dana M. Pauley*
Senior production supervisor: *Sesha Bolisetty*
Senior designer: *Mary E. Kazak*
Developer, Media technology: *Brian Nacik*
Cover image: © *Photodisc*
Typeface: *10/12 Times Roman*
Compositor: *International Typesetting and Composition*
Printer: *Quebecor World Dubuque Inc.*

Library of Congress Cataloging-in-Publication Data

Burgelman, Robert A.
    Strategic dynamics: concepts and cases / Robert A. Burgelman, Andrew S. Grove, with
Philip E. Meza—1st ed.
        p. cm.
    Includes index.
    ISBN 0-07-312265-3 (alk. paper)
    1. Strategic planning. 2. Information technology. I. Grove, Andrew S. II. Meza, Philip E.
III. Title.
HD30.28.B828 2006
658.4'012—dc22   2005049135

www.mhhe.com

Table of Contents

This book has its roots in a somewhat unusual pedagogical collaboration: An academic (RAB) and a chief executive officer of a major high-technology company (ASG) getting together to find a way to integrate action-based but reflective executive experience with theory-based but grounded academic research for the purpose of providing a novel learning experience for MBA students.

Our collaboration started in the fall of 1988 when we wrote a case on Intel Corporation's exit from the dynamic random access memory (DRAM) business and the company's transformation into a microprocessor company. Teaching this case brought the executive into the MBA classroom to contribute to an existing elective course on the strategic management of technology and innovation at Stanford Business School. We did not realize this at the time, but this case, which opens this book, contained the empirical and conceptual seeds that would sustain our pedagogical collaboration for the next 17 years.

After three years of further documenting the story of Intel's strategic evolution and discussing it with bright MBA students in the classroom, we decided that it was time to develop a new elective course. The time was ripe. The early 1990s saw the rapid growth of the PC market segment in the computer industry and it was becoming clear that the microprocessor revolution would have deep impact on all segments of the computer industry. The title of the new course, "Strategy and Action in the Information Processing Industry," reflected this.

As we progressed with our course through the 1990s and early 2000s, the emergence of the Internet, networking, and other communications technologies spread the impact of information technology in ever-widening circles, leading us to write new cases about companies in industries that would have seemed far removed at the start of our collaboration. Many of these cases are made available in this book. We also increasingly understood that our course was really about strategic dynamics: the interplay between strategic action and the environment. Hence, the title of the book.

Putting together a book like this one requires significant support. In first instance, we want to thank the Stanford Business School for its sustained support of our field research and course development throughout the entire period of our collaboration. Initially Dean Mike Spence and since 1999 Dean Bob Joss, together with successive cognizant associate deans for academic affairs, have provided us with the resources necessary to pursue our course development objectives.

Over the years, many MBA students and several research associates have helped us in developing the case material necessary to keep our course at the leading edge. Not all cases and notes that they developed could be published in this book, but they all helped. We thank them all. Cases and notes published in this book involved the collaboration of George Cogan (Stanford MBA '89), Eric Marti (Stanford MBA '88), Ray Bamford (Stanford MBA '96), Jeff Maggioncalda (Stanford MBA '96), Frederic Descamps (Stanford MBA '03), Sweta Sarnot (Stanford MBA '03), Lewis Fanger (Stanford MBA '03), Cecilia O'Reilly (Stanford MBA '03), Christopher Wittig (Sloan '04), Sami Inkinen (MBA '04), and Jean-Bernard Rolland (Stanford MBA '04). Les Vadasz, formerly President of Intel Capital, helped write the broadband and voice over IP cases.

Since fall 1999, Philip E. Meza has been our valued research associate. He helped write a large number of the cases published in this book and also has served as teaching assistant of our course. We recognize his contribution by listing him as co-author for this edition of the book.

We thank several academic colleagues who served anonymously as reviewers of our first manuscript. Their incisive queries and helpful suggestions have had a significant positive impact on the final version. We also thank Ryan Blankenship, our senior editor at McGraw-Hill, whose early support, gentle probing, and continued encouragement helped us to further strengthen the manuscript. Our administrative assistants (Nanci Moore for RAB and Terri Murphy for ASG) and McGraw-Hill's editorial staff made sure the book's production process stayed on track.

Finally, many thanks to Rita Burgelman, Eva Grove, and Marjorie Qualey for their continued patience, understanding, and support.

Robert A. Burgelman and Andrew S. Grove
February 2005

This book is about strategic dynamics in information technology–driven industries.

What is strategic dynamics? Strategic dynamics describes the interactions between companies and their environments. Over time, these interactions strengthen or weaken the strategic position and the distinctive competencies of incumbent companies. All companies in all industries are affected by the results of strategic dynamics and many eventually succumb to them. (Just compare, for instance, the companies on the Fortune 500 list in 1950 with that of 2005.) But to study how strategic dynamics work it makes sense to do so in industries in which they can be observed to operate at a relatively fast rate and so for this book we have chosen to focus on information technology–driven industries.

Why information technology–driven industries? First, because we know them best; but beyond that because they are characterized by rapid changes in the business environment due to the constant evolution of technology, which in turn necessitates frequent strategic changes.

What are information technology–driven industries? They are, first, firms in the information technology industry proper, such as various hardware component (e.g., Intel), software component (e.g., Microsoft), original equipment (e.g., Dell), and service companies (e.g., IBM), whose fortunes are driven by the relentless advances of information technologies broadly defined. But increasingly, they are also industries in which incumbent companies' inputs, outputs, and distribution are radically transformed by digital technology. Think, for instance, of how digital technology has affected or threatens to affect companies that publish traditional animated stories (e.g., Disney), produce and distribute music (e.g., Universal Music Group), or provide telephone service (e.g., AT&T).[1] All of the companies in these industries have struggled to find the right strategies and associated set of strategic actions to meet the challenges faced by the information technology–driven changes. What are strategic actions? They are changes in the business, planned and executed by general management to shape the future of the company.

Who are we? One of us has spent a career studying the way strategy is formed by both top-down and bottom-up actions in organizations; another of us has worked in the information technology industry for 40 years.

The book offers the opportunity to study the evolution of several information technology–driven industries. The Introduction begins with a very brief overview of this evolution, starting with the maturation of the microchip, the technological driving force for most changes. It then discusses the confluence of compounding forces that have produced the Internet economy and e-commerce, and others that are currently reshaping the software industry. This is followed by different manifestations of the convergence and/or collision between different sectors of the industry that are the consequence of technological evolution.

The book also offers the opportunity to study three interrelated conceptual themes related to strategic actions. These are also discussed in the Introduction. The first of these, titled "strategic action and strategic dynamics," examines the role of strategy in companies' evolution and the dynamics that result from the interaction of the companies' strategic actions with their environment, which often changes. Of particular interest is the case when the environment changes as a result of the strategic action itself. The second theme studies the relationship between strategy as intended and strategy as reality. In particular,

---

[1]Other information technology–driven industries that we have studied but do not report on in this book include, for instance, financial services (e.g., Charles Schwab) and health care (e.g., Kaiser Permanente).

we examine what happens when alignment between the stated strategy and the strategic action diverges, as often is the case in rapidly changing environments. When the environmental changes are very large, they often create conditions that we call strategic inflection points, periods which represent the possibility of having to choose between alternative strategies, which can further widen the divergence between the possible paths of future development of the companies' evolution.

The third theme describes the ways different companies navigate such large environmental changes—we study corporate transformation, ways companies change in a major way what they do and how they do it. Such transformations require management to navigate and control chaos on one hand and rein in chaos on another, requiring exquisite leadership on the part of a top management.

The book's structure follows The Introductions' discussion of the evolution of industries driven by information technology, and each of its main parts contains cases that can be studied in light of the three major themes. Many of these cases illustrate more than one of the major themes, and the choice of which theme to emphasize is dictated by our judgment of what learning each case can highlight best. Wherever possible, we use a technique that we like to call critical comparative case analysis. This involves juxtaposing comparable situations in which there are differences in only a limited number of variables, while keeping most conditions approximately the same. By confining our cases to information technology–driven industries, it is possible to find opportunities for such comparative analysis.

We have found both studying and practicing strategic dynamics in information technology–driven industries very exciting and very much fun. We hope you will too.

PART 1

Introduction: Industry Context and Key Themes

Evolution of Information Technology–Driven Industries

Introduction

We view the evolution of information technology-driven industries through the lens of our field research, which has involved longitudinal tracking of the role of strategy in Intel's evolution (in real time since 1988) and of the role of Intel in the evolution of the personal computer industry.[1] Our field research has also focused on many other companies in the rapidly evolving information technology–driven industries since the late 1980s. The resulting cases and notes reflect the impact of relentless technological change, major deregulation, and increasing globalization of competition on the structure and evolution of these industries through at least two business cycles, an Internet boom and bust, and current slow recovery.

The Microchip Matures

In December 1997, *Time* magazine called the microchip the "dynamo of a new economy."[2] And indeed, during the 1970s and early 1980s, companies such as Intel, Microsoft, Motorola, Apple, Sun Microsystems, and Novell, among many others, had been able to open up new market segments in the computer industry based on advances in the relatively new semiconductor technology, which followed Moore's Law of continued rapid decreases in the costs of memory and computing power. During the 1970s and 1980s, Japanese companies had been able to defeat leading American companies (such as Motorola in consumer electronics and Intel in dynamic random access memory—DRAM)[3] and take away market segment share from IBM in mainframe computers, which raised some fears that the United States was losing its competitiveness in high technology. At the same time, however, microprocessor technology had enabled the development of desktop computers, which created new growth opportunities, but also strong competitive pressures for the established, vertically integrated mainframe computer companies such as IBM, minicomputer companies such as DEC, and specialized computer companies such as Wang Laboratories. While relatively new companies, such as Intel and Microsoft, thrived

---

[1]Grove, A. S. *Only the Paranoid Survive*. New York: DoubleDay, 1996; Burgelman, R. A. *Strategy Is Destiny: How Strategy-Making Shapes a Company's Future*. New York: Free Press, 2002. Burgelman, R. A. "Strategy as Vector and the Inertia of Coevolutionary Lock-in." *Administrative Science Quarterly* 47 (March 1994), pp. 325–357.

[2]Isaacson, W. "The Microchip is the Dynamo of a New Economy Driven by the Passion of Intel's Andrew Grove." *Time*, December 29, 1997, pp. 46–51.

[3]Grove, *Only the Paranoid Survive*; Burgelman, R. A. "Fading Memories: A Process Theory of Strategic Business Exit in Dynamic Environments." *Administrative Science Quarterly* 39 (1994), pp. 24–56.

and became driving forces in the new, "horizontal"[4] computer industry, many of the old giants withered in a wave of Schumpeterian creative destruction caused by "increasing returns to adoption"[5] that favored the winning horizontal players. By the late 1990s, however, the PC market segment growth (in dollars) was maturing and Intel and Microsoft were looking to find new avenues for profitable growth in enterprise computing, communications infrastructure, wireless communications, consumer electronics, online services, and other areas.

Compounding Confluence—Take 1: The Internet and E-Commerce

During the early to mid-1990s, a compounding confluence of forces including the emergence of the World Wide Web, the multimedia PC, and the first browser software created the opportunity for entrepreneurs to found Netscape Communications and gave birth to the Internet economy and e-commerce. This, in turn, affected the competitive position of incumbent companies in many industries including the online services companies and traditional media companies, and produced events such as the merger of AOL and Time Warner. It also helped spawn a plethora of new companies such as Amazon.com (Yahoo!, eBay, USA Interactive, and Google are other representative examples). During the late 1990s, the Internet created a "dot-com boom" of economic activity followed shortly thereafter by a "dot-com bust." Some of the new companies continued to explore and exploit the new business opportunities the Internet opened. But most newly founded businesses and their associated revenue models turned out to be nonviable and disappeared. At the start of the new century, failed Internet entrepreneurs and their disappointed investors in Silicon Valley and beyond had to work through a painful aftermath. Nevertheless, the revolutionary effects of the Internet on established companies' procurement, logistics, distribution channel, and customer relationship management strategies continued to exert themselves unabated. Many established companies, such as Intel, Cisco, Dell, Barnes & Noble, Wal-Mart, and GE successfully used the Internet to streamline their operations and offer customers more convenient ways of doing business.

Compounding Confluence—Take 2: Saving or Sinking Software

A second compounding confluence of forces, again including the Internet but also the open source software movement and the global availability of broadband connections, affected the software market segment in various ways. In light of the view emerging in the early 1990s that "the network is the computer," BEA Systems was founded on the insight that if the network is the computer then a new type of operating system is needed, leading to the development of "middleware," in particular application server software. With the Internet opening up the opportunity to provide Web services that would help simplify and reduce the costs of enterprise computing, major players such as IBM, Oracle, and Microsoft entered into the middleware fray. Almost simultaneously, the open source software movement was getting momentum with the wide availability of broadband connections, enabling

---

[4]Grove, A. S. "How Intel Makes Spending Pay Off." *Fortune,* February 22, 1993, pp. 57–61. Farrell, J., Monroe, H. K., and Saloner, G. "The Vertical Organization of Industry: Systems Competition versus Component Competition." *Journal of Economics & Management Strategy* 7, no. 2 (1998).

[5]Arthur, B. W. "Competing Technologies: An Overview," In G. Dosi (ed.), *Technical Change and Economic Theory,* New York: Columbia University Press, 1987, pp. 590–607. Arthur, B. W. "Competing Technologies and Lock-in by Historical Events: The Dynamics of Allocation under Increasing Returns." Paper WP-83-90, International Institute for Applied Systems Analysis, Laxenburg, Austria, 1983.

the development of the Linux operating system and other free software products in the server and desktop computing market segments. Soon companies like MySQL were founded on the belief that open source software would gain a prominent place in the enterprise software market segment as well. These developments posed serious challenges to traditional software companies such as Microsoft and Oracle, which saw the open source software movement as a potential threat.

Convergence or Collision—Take 1: Computing Meets Cellular Phone and Consumer Electronics

Throughout the 1990s, Moore's Law continued unabated to drive down the costs of computing. It became clear that the intelligence provided by microprocessors would become integrated in wireless communication and consumer electronics devices, possibly leading to the horizontalization of these market segments. This movement toward convergence—or collision—of the computing industry with the wireless communication and consumer electronics industries threatened vertically integrated companies in the wireless telecommunications industry, such as mobile phone new giant Nokia and old giants such as Sony and Philips in the traditional consumer electronics industry. Companies used to working in the low-cost horizontal structure of the PC market segment, such as Gateway, HP, and Dell, were poised to capitalize on the trend toward horizontalization, paralleled by the digitization of content, to enter consumer electronics market segments with a new approach centered on the so-called digital home of the future. Intel and Microsoft saw themselves as the facilitators of this development and hoped to create major new growth opportunities to compensate for declining ones in the PC market segment. Other semiconductor companies, especially Korean giant Samsung, also saw this as a major growth opportunity.

Convergence or Collision—Take 2: Do Digits Defeat Pen and Plastic?

Digitization of content and digital distribution drove the convergence—or collision—of the computing industry and the traditional entertainment and media industries. Digital video games originated around the same time as the PC but became a major new form of entertainment for young people with the arrival of Nintendo's console-based games. Nintendo's lead was soon followed by numerous video game producers, the more prominent being Sega, Electronic Arts, and since the mid-1990s, Sony. Not surprisingly, Microsoft has entered this large and fast-growing market segment as well. As noted earlier, the game console is now viewed as a contender for becoming the hub in the digital home. Video game characters (e.g., Mario) now compete with traditional characters (e.g., Mickey Mouse) for young people's time and attention. Digital animation companies, such as Pixar and Dreamworks, also have created new characters that compete with those created by traditional pen-based animation companies like Disney.

The unlimited capacity for increasingly high-fidelity digital transfer of music files offered to tens of millions of technology-savvy PC owners by Napster and other companies created havoc with traditional legal property right protection regimes in the entertainment industry. It also created a great divide and a fair amount of acrimony between technology and traditional entertainment and media companies. A well-known personalized example of this tension was seen between Disney's CEO Michael Eisner, who lobbied the government to force technology companies to develop means for limiting unauthorized transfers of content, and Steve Jobs, CEO of Disney's digital animation partner, Pixar, who resisted such moves.

Convergence or Collision—Take 3: IP Meets Telephony

Digitization of voice, data, and video drove the telecommunications industry and the Internet together. But this convergence—or collision—needs to be examined against the background and in the context of government regulation and deregulation and the emergence of a number of new technologies that were potent forces in the evolution of the telecommunications industry. The deregulation of the telecommunications industry started in the late 1960s and culminated in the Final Modified Judgment of 1984, which ended the monopoly of AT&T. It set in motion the first drive toward convergence between the traditional wireline telecommunications, emerging wireless telecommunications, cable, and computer industries. Further deregulation of the telecommunications industry in 1996 created a host of unanticipated consequences for incumbents as well as new entrants. The intent of the deregulation was more competition in the local exchange network. The result was more consolidation with fewer and more powerful incumbent local exchange companies. Where new entrants hoped to capitalize on the mandated access to the incumbent local exchange providers' copper wire networks (known as the "last mile") to deliver new broadband technologies such as asymmetric digital subscriber line (ADSL) to consumers, the incumbents successfully stymied their entrepreneurial initiatives through bureaucratic maneuvering.

The large increase in demand for bandwidth during the mid- to late 1990s stimulated by the rapidly growing use of the Internet motivated competitive local exchange providers to invest many tens of billions of dollars in optical fiber network infrastructure. But new technologies such as dense wavelength division multiplexing (DWDM) greatly increased the carrying capacity of existing optical fiber networks. This, combined with less than expected growth of consumer demand for bandwidth, led to an enormous bandwidth oversupply and the rapid demise of most of the highly leveraged entrants in this new market segment of the telecommunications industry. This, in turn, led to the implosion of demand for telecommunications equipment with catastrophic consequences for the suppliers. By 2005, the incumbent local exchange companies had begun to offer ADSL service widely but the rapid growth of voice over the Internet protocol (VoIP) created yet another challenge to their future growth.

Wireless voice communications had grown tremendously during the 1990s, creating new giants such as Nokia and offering other companies, such as Samsung, very large new growth opportunities. Digitization of both voice and data offered the prospect of high demand for third-generation wireless services and the emergence of the wireless Internet. These prospects led major telecommunications companies in the United States and Europe to bid tens of billions of dollars for access to wireless spectrum. As demand for these services failed to materialize during the early 2000s, they ran into financial problems, which in turn drove further consolidation. The emergence of substitute wireless technologies such as Wi-Fi and MiMax was posing potentially serious competition for the existing wireless infrastructure and its major suppliers.

Three Key Themes

Introduction

As noted earlier, we study the evolution of information technology–driven industries in terms of three interrelated key themes that together form an analytical lens. The first theme—strategy and strategic dynamics—raises the question of how companies can gain, sustain, or regain profitable growth in the face of various types of strategic dynamics. The second theme—strategy and action—is based on the observation that in rapidly changing environments it is quite difficult to maintain alignment between stated strategy and strategic action and examines how companies can regain such alignment. The third theme—industry change and corporate transformation—recognizes that industry-level change inevitably requires a company to fundamentally rethink its strategy and business model. It must transform itself in terms of *what* it does and, even more fundamentally, *how* it does it.

Theme I: Strategy and Strategic Dynamics

Strategy

Theme I examines the role of strategy in a company's evolution and the dynamic interplay between strategy and the environment. Strategy is concerned with a company's efforts to maintain profitable growth in its environment. To facilitate our analysis, we call such a focal company P and its environment E, which includes market and nonmarket forces. The extent to which each force creates dependence of P on E or supports P's control over E needs to be examined. For instance, P needs to determine how dependent it is on particular customers, suppliers, or partners versus how much influence it can exert in these relationships. The most important of these forces determine the overall degree of dependence or control P experiences. Many times one or a few forces dominate in importance; these are the ones we try to identify and study. A framework for such analysis is shown in Figure 2.1.

Situations characterized by low influence and low dependence (strategic indifference) are the least interesting from a strategic management point of view because P's strategy is largely irrelevant. They are perhaps most illustrative of the classical economic model involving atomistic players that cannot change the conditions they face.

High influence and low dependence mark situations of P's strategic dominance. Many company leaders would think of this situation as the "holy grail" of strategic management. The great success stories in the history of business usually involve companies (e.g., Ford, DuPont, Kodak, Polaroid, Xerox, IBM, DEC) that were able to dominate their environment for an extended period of time. Low influence and high dependence characterize situations of P's strategic subordination. These situations are of course undesirable and usually come about, as we will discuss further below, because E changes in fundamental ways without P being able to prevent it.

High influence and high dependence produce situations of strategic interdependence between P and the other players in E. In a rational world all players will seek to gain and

FIGURE 2.1 | A
Framework of
Possible States
Facing *P*

		P's Dependence on *E*	
		Low	High
P's			
C			
O	LOW	Strategic Indifference	Strategic Subordination
N			
T			
R			
O			
L			
O	HIGH	Strategic Dominance	Strategic Interdependence
F			
E			

Source: Adapted from Strategy Is Destiny: How Strategy-Making Shapes a Company's Future by Robert A. Burgelman. Copyright © 2002 by Robert A. Burgelman. Reprinted with permission of The Free Press, a Division of Simon & Schuster Adult Publishing Group. All rights reserved.

maintain control of their destiny. Their chances to do so improve as they become better informed and more strategy-wise, and as they command more resources. Hence, *P* is likely increasingly to face situations of strategic interdependence. This requires *P* to look for both cooperative and competitive ways to interact with other players in *E*. The stability of strategic alliances, partnerships, ecosystems and other forms of collective strategy depend on the parties involved simultaneously seeking to maintain interdependence and strengthen their relative bargaining power. Companies in the information technology industry, in particular the market segments that have moved from vertical to horizontal structures (see below), experience strategic interdependence.

Having identified the forces that affect *P*'s ability to grow profitably in *E*, strategy serves to change them to *P*'s advantage, or, if they cannot be changed, to find out how they work and to use them to its advantage. Efforts by the various players to reduce unwanted dependencies and exert more control where possible—seeking to become more valuable (more scarce) to the other parties—produces various forms of strategic dynamics.

Strategic Dynamics[6]

As discussed so far, *P*'s strategic actions interact with *E*. While *E*'s boundaries are relatively well defined at any given time, in a dynamic world other industries or newly emerging environmental segments may potentially affect *E* at some time. To facilitate the analysis we call these other industries or emerging segments *e*, and we consider (*E*, *e*) the relevant environment for some parts of our further discussion of strategic dynamics.

Both *P* and other players in (*E*, *e*) most of the time engage in rule-abiding strategic actions: actions that are consistent with the prevalent power relationships among the industry

---

[6]Burgelman, R. A., and Grove, A. S. "Let Chaos Reign, Then Rein in Chaos: Nonlinear Strategic Dynamics in Organizational Evolution." Unpublished Manuscript, Stanford Business School, January 2005.

FIGURE 2.2 | A Typology of Strategic Dynamics

(E, e)		**P's Strategic Actions**	
		Rule-abiding	**Rule-breaking**
	Rule-abiding	Limited change	P-controlled change
	Rule-breaking	P-independent change	Runaway change

Source: R. A. Burgelman and A. S. Grove, "Let Chaos Reign, Then Rein in Chaos: Nonlinear Strategic Dynamics in Organizational Evolution," Working Paper, Stanford Business School, December 2004.

players and with the industry recipe (the pattern of executive judgments about key success factors) that determines how P and the other players in (E, e) compete and that guides them toward achieving a relatively stable industry equilibrium; or they can seek to turn the basis of competition decisively to their advantage by engaging in rule-breaking strategic actions. We view rule-abiding actions simply as conventional (expected) and rule-breaking actions as unconventional (unexpected). Figure 2.2 presents a typology of strategic dynamics produced by P's and (E, e)'s strategic interactions.

Strategic dynamics involving P and (E, e) are *nonlinear* depending on whether they materially change the structure of E; that is, P's (or other players' in (E, e)) rule-breaking strategic actions lead other players (or P) to take actions they otherwise would not have, which multiplies their impact. Nonlinear strategic dynamics affect different players' share of potential industry earnings (PIE) in ways that are difficult to reverse.[7]

Limited Change: Linear and Stable   Most of the time P's strategic actions play by the rules governing the basis of competition in E because P does not have the resources necessary to try to change them or because P anticipates that the other players will respond in kind. For the same reasons, the other players in E most of the time also engage in rule-abiding strategic actions. The interplay of P and E's rule-abiding strategic actions produces limited change, which basically leaves the existing industry structure intact. While limited change can be highly dynamic, it is linear and stable: The equilibrium among the various industry forces is not materially altered and the distribution of PIE is fairly predictable over time, with small shifts one way or the other that are reversible. Some scholars have called this "Red Queen" competitive dynamics,[8] as it evokes the image of the *Alice in Wonderland* character running as hard as she can just to stay in the same place. The pattern of mutual adaptation over time between P and E may become increasingly difficult to change and lead to strategic inertia at both the company and industry levels of analysis.

P-Independent Change: Nonlinear and Disruptive   Sometimes, major changes in E— "10X" changes—are directly and immediately the result of the independent rule-breaking strategic actions of players other than P and/or involve exogenous technological, regulatory, political, cultural, financial, or natural shocks. P-independent change is nonlinear and

[7]Saloner, G., Shepard, A., and Podolny, J. *Strategic Management.* New York: John Wiley & Sons, 2001.

[8]Barnett, W. P., and Hansen, M. T. "The Red Queen in Organizational Evolution." *Strategic Management Journal* 17 (Summer Special Issue, 1996), pp. 139–157.

disruptive: The rule-breaking actions by other players materially change the equilibrium in E and have a multiplicative negative effect on P's share of the PIE relative to that of the rule-breaking players. Sometimes major changes in E come about indirectly, having started in e. Most e are initially small and many turn out not to be viable, but some do and offer players the opportunity to engage in rule-breaking strategic action outside of P's purview and the competitive pressures exerted within E. If e is successfully explored and exploited, it may grow to complement E or turn into a substitute potentially threatening E. Such e are sometimes initially explored autonomously by executives within P, but who fail to convince P's top management to fully support them. Disruptive technologies,[9] which are further discussed later in the chapter, are an example.

P-Controlled Change: Nonlinear and Complex   Sometimes the confluence of industry forces offers P the opportunity to break the rules while the other players in E continue to engage in rule-abiding strategic action. Through radical innovation, acquisition, political influencing strategies, and/or taking advantage of changing industry regulation, P is able to fundamentally alter the basis of competition in E. P-controlled change significantly increases P's bargaining power in the network of relations with other industry players. P-controlled change is nonlinear and complex: P's rule-breaking actions create a 10X change in E forcing the other players to respond in accordance with P's actions, which multiplies their effect and creates nonlinear increases in P's share of the PIE. P-controlled change requires P to try to control numerous cause-and-effect relationships involving many agents, which are difficult to categorize and analyze, in order to pursue a "market-driving" strategy. A market-driving strategy goes beyond a time-paced strategy[10] because P cannot simply impose its strategic intent on the product-market environment unilaterally. Rather, such a strategy depends on P's understanding of the new complex patterns of behavior in the industry created by its rule-breaking strategic actions. These dynamic patterns determine the critical event horizons for P's strategic actions; for instance, the normal technology adoption cycles of customers and technology development cycles of partners.

P-controlled change may be planned or unplanned. Planned P-controlled change directly and immediately changes the competitive dynamics in E. Probably more often, P-controlled change arises as an opportunity from the confluence of forces in a more or less fortuitous way. These opportunities can often be traced back to "autonomous" initiatives[11] (initiatives that were outside the scope of P's strategy but were nevertheless supported by P's top management) in some e rather than E. In that case, capitalizing on the opportunity for rule-breaking action will depend on P's capacity to recognize the strategic implications of fortuitous consequences of strategic actions *after* they are already in progress but *before* others realize their implications, and on its ability to correctly assess the critical time horizon for deliberately taking advantage of these insights. Understanding

---

[9]Christensen, C. M. *The Innovator's Dilemma: When New Technology Causes Great Firms to Fail.* Boston: Harvard Business School Press, 1997; Christensen, C., and Bower, J. "Customer Power, Strategic Investment, and the Failure of Leading Firms." *Strategic Management Journal,* 1996.

[10]Gersick, C. J. G. "Pacing Change: The Case of a New Venture." *Academy of Management Journal,* 37 (1994), pp. 9–45; Brown, S. L., and Eisenhardt, K. M. "The Art of Continuous Change: Linking Complexity Theory and Time-Paced Evolution in Relentlessly Shifting Organizations." *Administrative Science Quarterly* 42 (1997), pp. 1–34.

[11]Burgelman, R. A. "A Model of the Interaction of Strategic Behavior, Corporate Context, and the Concept of Strategy." *Academy of Management Review* 8 (1983), pp. 61–70.

the causal link between action and outcomes allows P to solidify advantageous emergent patterns of behavior in (E, e).

Runaway Change: Nonlinear and Chaotic   Sometimes, both P and other players in (E, e) engage in rule-breaking strategic actions, causing a 10X change created by P to combine with a 10X change caused by the other players. Other players' rule-breaking strategic actions may be delayed reactions to P's strategic actions or vice versa. P and other players in E sometimes act simultaneously, for instance as a result of both having anticipated each other's intentions. Still another possibility is the spillover of rule-breaking strategic action started by some players in e into E and confronting or triggering P's rule-breaking strategic action or response, causing convergence or collision of these other industries with E. We call this runaway change. No single player controls runaway change, which basically destroys and not just loosens the existing industry structure. Runaway change is nonlinear and can be characterized as chaotic: Changes in the other forces in (E, e) do not change in accordance with P's rule-breaking action but rather interact with these actions in uncontrolled ways.

Here, P (and the other players as well) faces the challenge that, in contrast to complexity, chaos manifests no visible relationships between cause and effect, and new patterns do not necessarily emerge, which prevents P from effectively pursuing a market-driving strategy. The law of unanticipated consequences makes it quite difficult for P's internal selection environment to correctly take account of the confluence of forces and for its executives to rely on their capacity for strategic recognition and correct assessment of critical event horizons to foresee the outcomes for P and the other players in (E, e). Runaway change leads to a new industry structure within which new and newly reconstituted companies will have to establish a new equilibrium. P's ability to capture a growing share of the PIE becomes unpredictable, and it is unclear whether P's rule-breaking strategic actions will eventually be to its advantage.

Learning from Rule-breaking Strategic Action

Changing E—the "rules of the game"—to the strategist's advantage is an old idea. But what are the lessons that can be learned from rule-breaking strategic actions, which often are taken by leaders unconscious of their eventual momentous impact? Rule-breaking strategic action, by definition, ignores or violates the rules that are generally understood to be necessary (if not sufficient) for success. If it succeeds, however, it may possibly reveal *new* rules or principles that can become part of fundamental strategic doctrine. Any such understanding is about *past* rule-breaking strategic action and there is a certain danger associated with it. Perhaps this is why the generals are always well prepared for fighting the last war. The best we can do is to examine the underlying logic of rule-breaking strategic action and the conditions under which it is more likely to succeed.

Theme II: Strategy versus Action

Theme II is based on the premise that the reality of P's strategy resides in its strategic actions rather than in its strategic statements. Strategic action is consequential: It involves binding trade-offs in resource allocation and commits P to a course and direction that cannot be easily reversed. While good luck or bad luck almost always will play a role in determining P's performance, strategy serves to reduce the potential impact of bad luck and to capitalize on good luck. This requires in the first instance developing a clear understanding of the external and internal forces that shape P's performance.

FIGURE 2.3 |
The Extended
Industry Analysis
Framework

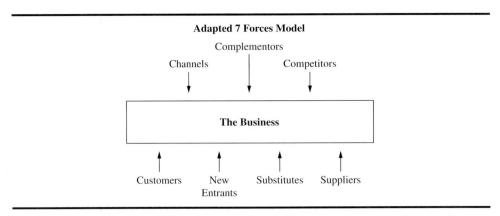

Source: A. S. Grove, Lecture material, mid-1990s.

Market and Nonmarket Forces

External forces that affect *P*'s performance and evolution include market forces—the five forces framework of traditional industry analysis[12] and complementors[13]—as well as nonmarket forces associated with technology and government regulation.

Market Forces   Market forces encompass the traditional five forces, as well as complementors and distribution channels, which are particularly important in the information technology industry. Figure 2.3 shows the extended industry analysis framework.

Each of these forces raises important strategic questions.

Customers   Are there many of them or few? How demanding are they? How knowledgeable are they? How stiff are the competitive challenges they face?

Channels   How good is access to distribution channels—original equipment manufacturers (OEMs), value-added resellers (VARs), system integrators, retail chains, online? What is the relative importance of each of the different channels for reaching end customers? How is their bargaining power evolving? How much is the company locked in with any particular channel?

Competitors   How powerful, vigorous, and competent are they? Are there many or few? How well funded are they? How strongly are they focused on your market segment?

Suppliers   How powerful, vigorous, and competent are they? Are there many or few? How aggressive are they? Are they opportunistic or do they take the long view in building customer relationships?

New Entrants   How powerful, vigorous, and competent are new or potential competitors? How well are they funded? What novel strategies and competencies do they use to compete?

---

[12]Porter, M. E. *Competitive Strategy.* New York: Free Press, 1980.

[13]Brandenburger, A. M., and Nalebuff, B J. "The Right Game: Use Game Theory to Shape Strategy." *Harvard Business Review,* July–August 1995, pp. 57–71.

Substitution   New techniques, new approaches, new technologies can upset the existing ways of building or delivering a product or service. Such changes fundamentally change the basis of competition in an industry, or worse, may reduce its relevancy altogether. The key question is how likely are such new approaches to emerge?

Complementors   These are other companies whose products and/or services complement a particular company's products and/or services; that is, they enhance the value of that company's products and/or services in the eyes of the customer. This is not a novel force. Gasoline suppliers, for instance, complement automobile manufacturers and so do bun manufacturers the manufacturers of hamburgers. As explained further (see systems versus component competition below), however, in the information technology industry complementors have become a very potent force.

Nonmarket Forces   In addition to these seven forces, government regulation and various aspects of technological change also may affect P.

Regulatory Change   Regulation and deregulation can significantly affect the dynamics of an industry. Regulatory change may dramatically change acceptable strategic behavior in E and provide conditions that stimulate the emergence of new entrants. Simultaneously, incumbent players may attempt to take advantage of regulatory change or adopt the new technology and begin to compete with the new entrants before they have been able to secure strong strategic positions in the industry. These two types of races play an important role in determining a new industry order. In the middle of these races, however, strategies of both incumbents and new entrants may be unclear, and senior managers will face high uncertainty regarding the effects of their strategic actions.

Technological Change   Technological change also may differentially affect the competition among incumbent companies and/or lower barriers to entry in existing industries. Sometimes technological change stimulates the birth of altogether new e. Technological change is a particularly potent force in the information technology industry, and its effects manifest themselves in a variety of ways. First, the strategic implications of vertical or closed system versus horizontal or open system industry structures are important in the information technology industry. Companies that offered their customers complete and proprietary systems dominated the mainframe and minicomputer industries. IBM, for instance, vertically integrated a large number of hardware and software components in its proprietary mainframe computers and managed the evolutionary trajectories of multiple proprietary technologies as well as their coordinated deployment in new product generations. In this closed system industry, customers became locked in with their proprietary mainframe systems vendor.

The desktop computer industry, which emerged in the early 1980s and grew rapidly, followed a different, horizontal model. Different P specialized in different hardware and software technologies. In this horizontal industry, open standards prevailed and market forces determined which hardware and software components were combined by original equipment manufacturers (OEMs) to offer end-user systems. Winning the dominant market segment share in their layer was the strategic imperative for the various P in the new computer industry, because players in other layers wanted to work with these winners. The ability of P to garner support of many producers of complementary products led to the emergence of so-called ecosystems.[14] Intel and Microsoft are perhaps the best-known

---

[14]See, for instance, Moore, J. F. "Predators and Prey: A New Ecology of Competition." *Harvard Business Review,* May–June 1993.

examples of winners in their respective horizontal layers that have created large ecosystems around their technologies. Other examples include Cisco and SAP.

Second, "increasing returns to adoption," is a new and important dynamic that manifested itself perhaps most forcefully first in the horizontal desktop computer industry but is now manifesting itself in other industries as well as they become more horizontal. Increasing returns to adoption means that a technological platform, like Intel's x86 microprocessors, becomes increasingly valuable as more people use it. This creates a virtuous circle and may lead to a "winner-take-all" competitive regime in E. Increasing returns can arise from several sources.

Third, "disruptive technology" is another new and important concept that manifests itself forcefully in the information technology industry. A product is usually characterized by multiple performance metrics. At any given time, P's customers demand performance improvements along some of these metrics, such as speed or cost. At some point a new product may appear that emphasizes a different performance metric, for example, form factor versus speed or cost. Existing customers of P may initially show a lack of interest in this new performance metric. As a result, P will stop resource allocation to the product with the new performance metric. However, a new class of customers may place value on this very performance metric. Over time, this new e, usually addressed by new firms, may grow and the new product may also begin to improve on the original performance metric, making it attractive now to the customers of P in E. As a result, what looked like an astutely managed company may lose its leadership position.

Dynamic Forces Driving Company Evolution

P's evolution is determined by the combination of external and internal dynamic forces. The framework of dynamic forces driving firm evolution shown in Figure 2.4 captures this.

Official Corporate Strategy   Official corporate strategy concerns top management's statements about P's intended strategy: the business(es) it wants to be a winner in and its intended competitive advantage.

Basis of Competitive Advantage in the Industry   The basis of competitive advantage that P faces depends on its chosen product-market position. Most industries, though not all, contain several viable positions that companies can occupy. The external market and

FIGURE 2.4 |
Dynamic Forces
Driving Company
Evolution

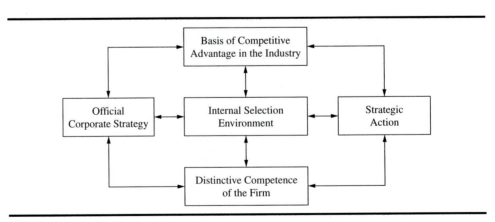

Source: From R. A. Burgelman, "Fading Memories: A Process Theory of Strategic Business Exit in Dynamic Environments," *Administrative Science Quarterly*, March 1994, p. 31. Reprinted with permission.

nonmarket forces discussed earlier determine the basis of competition that governs success in each of these positions. As any of these forces change in major ways the basis of competition—the external selection environment—changes as well.

Distinctive Competence Distinctive competence concerns the differentiated skills, complementary assets and routines that P possesses to meet the basis of competitive advantage in the industry. Distinctive competencies are viewed as intrinsic to P's identity and character. For instance, they very much determine the type of corporate strategy, for example, differentiation or cost leadership, that a company will pursue. They are not easy to change.

Strategic Action Strategic action is what P actually does. Strategic action in large companies is usually distributed over different levels of management and different, specialized groups. Leaders' strategic actions respond to external and internal selection pressures as well as to the stated official strategy.

Internal Selection Environment   An established P differs from start-ups by the fact that it can to some extent substitute internal selection for external selection. This implies the centrality of the internal selection environment in P's strategy-making process. The internal selection environment mediates the link between official corporate strategy and strategic action and between industry-level sources of competitive advantage and firm-level sources of distinctive competence.

Strategic Inflection Points

In dynamic environments the alignments between strategy and action and between basis of competition and distinctive competence—illustrated by the arrows connecting these concepts in Figure 2.4—are likely to come under tremendous pressure. Like rubber bands, the arrows in the figure stretch in different directions, indicating that the forces are no longer in alignment. Divergences between P's stated strategy and strategic action and/or between distinctive competencies and the basis of competition signal a "strategic inflection point" (SIP): a critical period during which major threats as well as new opportunities come about. Figure 2.5 illustrates this idea.

Following the types of strategic dynamics discussed earlier (Theme I), most of the time P's strategic actions respond to relatively small changes in E, which do not cause a SIP (limited change). Sometimes market and nonmarket forces that are not under P's control cause a SIP. Initially a change in one of these forces is usually small, but it may grow to become an order of magnitude—10X—stronger than it was before. This may lead P to have to move away from an unfavorable E (P-independent change). Occasionally P can change E, which creates a SIP for the other players (P-controlled change), or potentially for everybody involved (runaway change). Clearly, it is beneficial to see a SIP coming sooner rather than later. Unfortunately, the signals are usually ambiguous and conflicting in the beginning. SIPs, however, generate what we call "strategic dissonance" in the organization. Strategic dissonance refers to signs of distress that signal that fundamental change is at hand. Top management can take advantage of the information generated by strategic dissonance to develop new strategies and lead P through the turbulence and uncertainty associated with SIPs.

P's ability to prevent the rubber bands from breaking and to find new ways to reestablish alignment between the dynamic forces depends on several key characteristics of its internal selection environment. First, whether the internal selection environment is

FIGURE 2.5 |

Strategic Inflection
Point

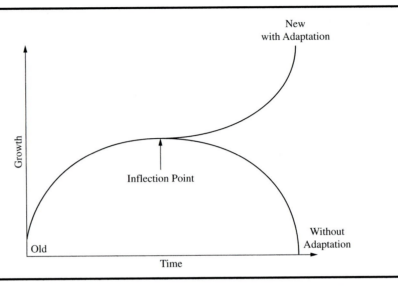

Source: From R. A. Burgelman and A. S. Grove, "Strategic Disonance," California Management Review, Winter 1996, page 6. Copyright © 1996 by The Regents of the University of California. Reprinted from the California Management Review, Vol. 38, No. 2. By permission of The Regents.

able to take quick and accurate account of the *confluence of forces* (often independently and unexpectedly coming together); second, whether it has put into positions of leadership executives with *strategic recognition* capacity (the ability to quickly recognize the strategic implications of the confluence of forces); and third, whether its senior and top executives are able to assess *critical event horizons* (the time horizon within which strategic action needs to be taken to be effective). Such an internal selection environment depends on a culture that values dissent and encourages open debate. Developing and nurturing a management culture that values strategic debate at middle and senior levels but is also able to bring the debate to a conclusion that realigns stated strategy and action as well as the basis of competition and distinctive competence is a key task of top management.

Theme III: Industry Change and Corporate Transformation

Building on Themes I and II, Theme III further develops the idea that a company's adaptive capability depends critically on its strategy-making process.

A Framework of the Strategy-Making Process

Figure 2.6 provides a conceptual framework that indicates how *P*'s strategy making actually works and the various ways in which *P* can adapt.

The framework presented in Figure 2.6 offers more detail about the linkages between official corporate strategy, strategic action, and the internal selection environment that are part of the rubber band model discussed earlier in this chapter (Figure 2.4). Figure 2.6 suggests that a *P*'s strategy making encompasses induced and an autonomous processes.

Induced Strategy Process   The induced strategy process (the lower loop in Figure 2.6) resembles the top-driven view of strategic management. The *concept of corporate strategy*—the official corporate strategy—reflects what top management has learned about

FIGURE 2.6 | A
Framework of the
Strategy-Making
Process in
Established
Companies

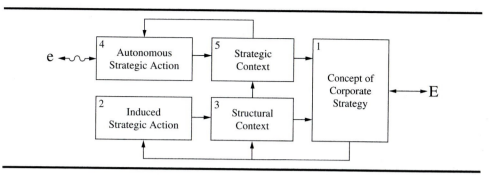

the basis of P's past successes in terms of what it is good at (its distinctive competencies), where it can win (its product-market position), what it stands for (its core values), and what it strives to achieve (its objectives). As top management continues to learn, the concept of strategy evolves over time. At any given time, it expresses top management's strategic intent and induces strategic action on the part of operational and middle-level managers. *Induced strategic action* is oriented toward gaining and maintaining leadership in P's core businesses. Examples of induced strategic action are efforts to increase market penetration, new product development, new market development, and strategic capital investment projects for the existing businesses.

When P is small, the link between strategic action and the concept of corporate strategy is readily maintained, simply because there are few key players, communication loops are fast, and strategic iterations work rapidly. As P grows, strategy making becomes increasingly distributed over many groups (functional, product, geographical) and multiple levels of management. This provides an important source of internal variety of thought, as individuals who possess different data, ideas, motivation, and resources all strive to undertake strategic initiatives. It also implies that unless P is able to establish mechanisms to maintain coherence, corporate strategy will eventually become unrealized.

Structural context comprises the administrative and cultural mechanisms that top management can use to maintain the link between strategic action and the existing corporate strategy. Organizational structure, planning and control systems, resource allocation rules, measurement and reward systems, recruitment, development, and promotion processes, as well as socialization processes including more or less explicit principles of behavior, are elements of structural context. All these elements should complement each other to facilitate effective and efficient strategy implementation.[15] Structural context is a key part of the internal selection environment.

P's induced strategy process interacts with E (Figure 2.6). Through this process top management may proactively influence E to P's advantage. This is reflected in the causal arrow going from the induced strategy process to E. More frequently, the causal arrow goes from E to the induced strategy process. Top management's role is to use the induced strategy process to maintain alignment between official corporate strategy and strategic action. The induced strategy process maintains P's character, and P continues to successfully upgrade itself in E. In a sense, the induced strategy process is the expression of P's "genotype"—the

---

[15]For a discussion of "complemenatrities" in strategy-making see Roberts, J. *The Modern Firm,* Oxford University Press, 2004.

way it adjusts and renews itself while maintaining its genetic inheritance and makeup. A strong induced strategy process is also likely to be accompanied by strong strategic inertia. While resistance to change has long been described in the organizational literature, it is important to realize the difference between the continuity and persistence associated with the induced strategy process, which up to a point can be helpful, and simple resistance to change, which often is not.

Autonomous Strategy Process   The autonomous strategy process (the upper loop in Figure 2.6) is less well understood. *Autonomous strategic action* involves initiatives of individuals or small groups that are outside the scope of *P*'s corporate strategy at the time they come about. Autonomous strategic initiatives are significantly different from induced strategic action, for instance in terms of technology employed, customer functions served, and/or customer groups targeted. They typically involve new combinations of individual and organizational competencies that are not currently recognized as centrally important to *P*. They often emerge fortuitously and are hard to predict. They often come about because *P*'s competencies are fungible, offering the possibility to pursue new businesses that may be more or less related to the company's core business. Autonomous strategic initiatives may turn out to be complements or substitutes from the perspective of the core business, but this is not always clear at the time they emerge.

If "genotype" is a metaphor for *P*'s makeup expressed through its induced strategy process, "mutation" is one for the outcomes of its autonomous strategy process. Like most mutations, most autonomous initiatives do not survive (most new ideas are bad ideas) because they will not continue to obtain resources. But like some mutations, some autonomous initiatives turn out to be important for *P*'s continued evolution. They typically respond to *e* (Figure 2.6). Many of these *e* never grow to become important, but some do and may eventually threaten or even replace *E*.

Initially, top management is not sure about an autonomous initiative's strategic importance and whether *P* has the capabilities to successfully pursue it. To resolve such indeterminacy, the *strategic context* for the autonomous initiative must become defined. A key function of the strategic context is to link autonomous strategic initiatives to the corporate strategy, thereby amending it. Lacking these created linkages, autonomous initiatives may be able to linger on for some time in the shadow of the core business but they will become resource starved and forgo the opportunity to demonstrate their full potential. When it has become reasonably certain that an autonomous initiative is viable, top management amends the concept of corporate strategy. Such an amendment integrates the autonomous activities with the induced strategic process. Both processes involve the activities of multiple levels of management. The willingness of managers at operational and middle levels to engage in autonomous strategic action is influenced by their perception that their views will be considered and their assessment of the likelihood that the combined strategic processes will result in an outcome that allows *P* to win.

Strategic context determination or dissolution is part of the internal selection environment. Strategic contexts will change as autonomous strategic action leads to new business opportunities competing for limited resources with existing ones. This internal competition may lead to new businesses replacing existing ones (strategic context determination), causing strategic business exit through abandonment or divestment (strategic context dissolution).

Autonomous strategic initiatives explore and potentially extend the boundaries of *P*'s competencies and opportunity sets: They provide the opportunity to learn about variations in markets and technologies. Through such initiatives *P* can also enter new niches (*e*) opened up by others, which might eventually pose a threat to the current strategy. On the other hand, autonomous initiatives can potentially have a dissipating effect on *P*'s distinctive competencies. Resources can be spread thin if too many autonomous initiatives are supported, perhaps at the expense of the mainstream business. Distinctive competencies can also be diluted or lost if an autonomous initiative is not supported and important talent decides to leave the firm. Most dangerously, autonomous strategic initiatives may undermine P's existing competitive position in E without providing an equally secure new one.

Keeping Induced and Autonomous Processes in Play Simultaneously   Relying on only the induced strategy process or the autonomous strategy process is unlikely to lead to good results over time. Continued adaptation requires keeping both induced and autonomous processes in play simultaneously at all times, even if one process or the other may be more prominent at different times in a P's evolution. This balancing act is one of the most difficult challenges faced by top management.

Strategic Inertia, Adjustment, and Transformation

P becomes an established company only if it survives the selection pressures of E over an extended period of time. P must then continue to compete effectively for customers and serve them profitably. To do so P continues to develop specialized distinctive competencies and routines that allow it to be predictable, reliable, and accountable. These attributes are key to continued survival. But these very attributes also carry the seeds of strategic inertia in the face of more radical changes in E (P-independent change). Several systemic and psychological sources of inertia have been identified.[16] For instance, if P's competitive success has been based on a strategy of differentiation or product leadership, it will face significant difficulties if changes in E cause the basis of competition to favor companies employing a strategy of cost leadership or operational excellence. The converse also holds. Inertial tendencies do not preclude strategic adjustments, which involve small changes at the margin that leave P's overall strategy in place and may temporarily result in improved performance. However, inertia can hinder and even prevent the implementation of the type of changes that are called for in the process of strategic transformation.

Transformation involves rapidly and radically changing P's strategy and supporting structural context. This is potentially risky because it eliminates the existing organizational learning captured over time by the induced strategy process—it sets back the clock so to speak—and subjects P again to the liabilities of newness. It often means "betting the company." Even if successful, it requires management to lead the organization through a difficult and uncertain period, what we call a "Valley of Death."[17] Note that strategic renewal through the autonomous strategy process, on the other hand, is helpful if it starts before radical, companywide strategic change is necessary. It explores new e (usually relatively small in the beginning) and offers the possibility of developing new distinctive competencies. Internal experimentation can reduce the risks inherent in transformation.

Traversing the Valley of Death

To make it through the "Valley of Death" associated with a transformation poses tough challenges for top management. Top management can pursue basically two different strategies that are somewhat related to the forms of adaptation discussed above. These are illustrated in Figure 2.7.

---

[16]Burgelman, R. A. "Strategy as Vector and the Inertia of Coevolutionary Lock-in." *Administrative Science Quarterly* 47 (March 2004), 325–357.

[17]Grove, A. S., *Only the Paranoid Survive,* New York, DoubleDay, 1996.

FIGURE 2.7 |
Strategies for
Crossing the Valley
of Death

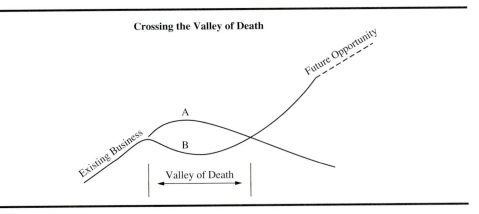

Source: A. S. Grove, Strategy and Action in the Information Industry Course, Final Lecture Material, Graduate School of Business, Stanford University, mid-1990s.

Strategy A in Figure 2.7 is based on top management's belief that the strength and momentum of *P*'s existing business model may carry the company—allow it to jump so to speak—all the way across the valley. This requires adjustments but no radical changes in the corporate strategy until the valley has been crossed. It assumes that the company can manage transformations quickly, moving discontinuously from one corporate strategy to another, once it decides to do so. The dangers with this approach are twofold. One danger is that the momentum may slow down and the organization may not make it to the other side (e.g., demand drops precipitously and the company runs out of cash). The other danger is that the momentum turns into inertia and even though the company gets to the other side (demand, while diminished, sustains sufficient generation of cash) it still cannot change its strategy, or cannot do so fast enough, and faces severely reduced prospects.

Strategy B in Figure 2.7 involves adaptation to a new business model and the development of supporting competencies associated with a new corporate strategy to cope directly with the changing environmental demands, before *P* enters the valley. This strategy involves early radical strategic change. The dangers are twofold. If the transformation is sudden and forceful it may drastically undermine or damage *P*'s existing business model and thereby again lead to a cash crunch before the other side of the valley is reached. If the strategic change progresses through the slower process of experimentation and selection associated with day-to-day strategic renewal, the danger is that top management will not be putting the full support of the company behind the new strategy and will fail to reach the other side of the valley.

Let Chaos Reign Then Rein in Chaos

The rubber band model and the framework of induced and autonomous strategy processes suggest that the optimal strategy-making approach top management should use to navigate strategic inflection points requires balancing the perennial tension between chaos and order. At such times a company's existing strategic intent is losing relevance and the forces that drive a company's evolution are no longer aligned. Unfortunately, in dynamic environments it is not immediately clear what the new relevant strategic intent should be and how the forces can be effectively realigned. In order to find out, a period of experimentation is necessary because only stepping out of the old ruts will bring new insights. So, top management must let go for a while and "let chaos reign" as different executives pursue different directions in search of a new viable one.

But chaos cannot be the friend of organizations very long. Eventually, top management must "rein in chaos" and bring the forces back into alignment. This requires top management to become clear about the company's new direction and strategic intent. It includes describing what the company will pursue as well as what it will *not* pursue. This new resolve must be followed by changes in resource allocation and may have to involve changes in senior leadership positions. Such strategic leadership on the part of top management requires courage to follow through on a new conviction even though not everybody shares that conviction yet. Such courage should be based on insight into the external and internal strategic situation facing the company. Creating a strategy-making culture in which both top-down and bottom-up internal voices are strong—allowing constructive confrontation among the best informed views of middle and top executives—provides the foundation for objectively analyzing both the external and internal strategic situations. Maintaining the strength of the bottom-up voice is one of the most important contributions to a company's culture that top management can make, and it is the most important way to enhance the productivity of the strategy-making process.

Conclusion

The three interrelated key themes of strategy making and related conceptual frameworks introduced in this chapter offer the opportunity to gain insight about the evolution of companies in information technology–driven industries as discussed in Chapter 1. The proof of the pudding is in the eating, however, and the cases and industry notes presented in the parts of the book that follow this introduction provide instructors with the opportunity to examine for themselves, with the help of their students, the real-life situations that illustrate that evolution.

With this is mind, let the learning process start.

PART 2

The Microchip Matures

The Microchip Matures

"Intel Corporation (A): The DRAM Decision," focuses on the decision Intel's top management faced at the end of 1984: whether to exit the dynamic random access memory (DRAM) business. Intel was the successful first mover with DRAM products in the early 1970s, yet found itself with an inconsequential market share at the end of 1984 in the face of strong competition from Japanese new entrants. While at that time some Intel executives still believed that DRAM was critical for Intel's future, DRAMs actually played a minor role in Intel's product mix during the first half of the 1980s. Electrically programmable read only memory (EPROM) products were still important at the time of the case, but logic products had already replaced semiconductor memories as Intel's biggest business by 1982.

Important discussion topics for this case are (1) the forces that drive industry evolution, (2) the forces that drive company evolution, and (3) the coevolution of the industry-level and company-level forces and (4) corporate transformation. In terms of our three key themes, the case offers a classic example of *P*-independent change; it illustrates how strategic action can diverge from stated strategy; and it provides an opportunity to examine how industry change in combination with internal change (favoring new specialty products over commoditizing products) may lead to corporate transformation.

"Intel Corporation in 1999" describes how Intel became the preeminent supplier of microprocessors for the PC market segment during the 1990s and the challenges that the company faced in the late 1990s. These challenges involved increased competition in the core microprocessor business (for desktop, mobile, and enterprise computing), as well as difficulties in managing new business development to secure future growth in the face of declining growth opportunities in the PC market segment.

Important discussion topics for this case are (1) turning luck into a strategy, (2) the role of increasing returns to adoption and ecosystem development in the horizontal computer industry, (3) managing environmental dependencies and exerting influence, (4) overcoming potential inhibitors of profitable growth, and (5) strategic inertia associated with extraordinary success. In terms of our three key themes, the case offers a classic example of *P*-controlled change; it documents how strategic leadership can link strategic action extremely tightly to the stated strategy and what the advantages and disadvantages are of such tight linking; and it provides an opportunity to examine how industry change may require an extremely successful company to transform itself yet again in order to find new growth opportunities.

"Inside Microsoft: The Untold Story of How the Internet Forced Bill Gates to Reverse Course" describes the events leading to Microsoft's somewhat slow embrace of the Internet as part of its corporate strategy toward the end of 1995, in spite of early efforts of lower-level employees to alert top management to its strategic importance for the future of the company.

Important discussion topics for this case are (1) the anatomy of strategy-making, (2) complements versus substitutes, (3) the "silver bullet" question, which asks who your most dangerous competitor is, and (4) cycle time of strategic change. In terms of our three key themes, the case is a classic example of a situation of *P*-independent change morphing eventually into runaway change; it provides insight in the stages of the strategy-making process in a highly dynamic context (raising awareness, strategic dissonance, and strategic action); and it offers the opportunity again to examine how industry change may force a company to transform itself to meet a competitive challenge.●

Case 1.1

Intel Corporation (A): The DRAM Decision

Introduction

In November of 1984, *Andy Grove,*[1] Intel's chief operating officer, stood in his office cubicle gazing out at Silicon Valley and thought about his company's future. The semiconductor industry Intel had helped create 16 years earlier had entered what looked to be a prolonged cyclical downturn. Some operations had already been trimmed, but Grove believed the company would have to react again soon (see company financial data in Exhibit 2). The recession hit the company's memory components division particularly hard. For much of the previous 5 years, memory components had been suffering under competitive pressure from the Japanese.

Since 1980, Intel had been losing its market position in *dynamic random access memories (DRAMs)*[1] as the industry average selling price per chip had declined much more rapidly than the 20–30 percent per year that was customary. The Japanese had taken the lead in unit sales of the latest generation of DRAMs, the 256-*kilobit* (256K) version, but Intel was fighting back with a program to "leapfrog" the Japanese in the product's next generation. Its $50 million 1-megabit (1 Meg = 4 × 256K) research project was soon to produce working prototypes. Intel managers estimated they were ahead of the Japanese in the 1-Meg device. Still, a debate was growing within the company about whether Intel could continue to compete in the commodity market of DRAMs. Grove was formulating his personal position on the matter.

It seemed clear that if Intel chose to continue with the DRAM product line it would have to commit to at least one $150 million state-of-the-art *Class 10 production facility.* On the other hand, Intel's other businesses were much more profitable than memories; in an ROI framework, the microprocessor business deserved the majority of Intel's corporate resources. It was difficult for both Grove and *Gordon Moore,* Intel's chief executive officer, to imagine an Intel without DRAMs. The memory business had made Intel, and was still by far the largest market segment in integrated circuits. Not the least of Grove's worries was how the investment community would react to Intel's decision to cede such a large market segment to the Japanese.

Company Background

Early History

On August 2, 1968, the Palo Alto *Times* announced that *Bob Noyce* and *Gordon Moore* had left Fairchild to form a new company. Andy Grove, who had been Moore's assistant director of research at Fairchild, also left to complete what the company's historians have called the "triumvirate." The three were key technologists in the emerging solid state electronics industry. Noyce had invented the integrated circuit (simultaneously with Jack Kilby at Texas Instruments), and Intel was the first company to specialize in making large-scale integrated circuits.

In mid-1969, Intel introduced its first product, a *bipolar static random access memory (SRAM)* with a 64-bit storage capacity. The chip itself was less than a quarter of an inch on a side and contained nearly 400 *transistors.* While the SRAM had some small markets, Intel had set its sights on the growing computer memory business, then dominated by *magnetic core* technology. To attack the magnetic core business required at least a 10-fold reduction in cost per bit.

The Intel managers decided early on to pursue a new process technology in addition to the relatively proven bipolar process. The *metal-oxide-semiconductor (MOS)* process promised to lead to increased transistor density while simultaneously reducing the number of fabrication steps required to make a working chip. The process had been published in scientific journals, but serious manufacturability questions remained. MOS transistors consumed only a fraction of the power of a traditional bipolar transistor and thus could be more densely packed on the chip. But they were also very sensitive to trace amounts of impurities in processing, raising the question of whether their performance characteristics would remain stable over time.

Les Vadasz headed the MOS team of several engineers. In contrast to the bipolar effort, the MOS effort

---

[1]Note: All italicized names appear with biographies in Exhibit 1; all italicized words appear with definitions in the technical appendix.

This case was prepared by George W. Cogan, MBA '89, under the supervision of Associate Professor Robert A. Burgelman as a basis for class discussion rather than to illustrate either effective or ineffective handling of a management situation.

© 1989 by The Trustees of Leland Stanford Jr. University.

EXHIBIT 1 | Biographies of Key Intel Personnel

Jack Carsten joined Intel from Texas Instruments and has held various high-level management positions since then. In 1985 he was senior vice president and general manager of the Components Group.

Dennis Carter is a Harvard MBA with an engineering background. He has worked in several areas of the company and is currently assistant to the president.

Sun Lin Chou received his BS and MS degrees in Electrical Engineering from MIT and his Ph.D. in Electrical Engineering from Stanford University. He joined Intel in 1971 and has managed the DRAM technology development group in Oregon since then.

Dov Frohman joined Intel from Fairchild in 1969. He was responsible for the invention of the EPROM. He currently manages Intel's design group in Israel.

Edward Gelbach joined Intel from Texas Instruments in 1969. He is currently senior vice president of sales.

Andrew Grove was born in Budapest, Hungary. He received his BS from CCNY, and his Ph.D. from Berkeley. After working at Fairchild Camera and Instrument for 5 years, he joined Intel in 1968. He has been president and chief operating officer since 1979.

Ted Hoff joined Intel as a designer in 1969. He headed the group that invented the microprocessor. Hoff left Intel in 1983.

Gordon Moore was born in San Francisco. He received his BS in Chemistry from Berkeley, and his Ph.D. in Chemistry and Physics from the California Institute of Technology. He worked as a member of the technical staff at Shockley Semiconductor for 1956–87, and founded Fairchild. He founded Intel in 1968 and is currently the chairman and CEO.

Robert Noyce was born in Burlington, Iowa. He received his bachelor's degree from Grinell College and his Ph.D. from MIT. He was a research engineer at Philco from 1953–6, a research engineer at Shockley Transistor, and a founder and director of Fairchild Camera and Instrument. He is credited with co-inventing (with Kilby at TI) the integrated circuit. He founded Intel and currently serves as vice chairman of the board.

Bob Reed received his bachelor's degree from Middlebury College and his MBA from the University of Chicago. He joined Intel in 1974. He was appointed chief financial officer in 1984.

Ron Smith received his bachelor's degree in Physics from Gettysburg College and his Master's and Ph.D. degrees in Physics from the University of Minnesota. He joined Intel in 1978 as a device physicist in the Static/Logic Technology Development Group. In 1985, he was manager of that group.

Dean Toombs joined Intel from Texas Instruments in 1983 with the express purpose of running the Memory Components Division.

Leslie Vadasz joined Intel in 1968 and has held a variety of senior management positions since then. He is currently senior vice president and director of the Corporate Strategic Staff.

Ron Whittier holds a Ph.D. in Chemical Engineering from Stanford University. He joined Intel in 1970. From 1975 until 1983, he managed the Memory Products Division. In 1983, he became vice president and director of Business Development and Marketing Communications.

Albert Yu was born in Shanghai and holds a Ph.D. in Electrical Engineering from Stanford University. He joined Intel in 1975.

moved slowly. The primary problem was to develop a stable transistor threshold voltage in order to avoid *threshold drift*. After a year of frustration and setbacks, Vadasz's team produced the first commercially available MOS SRAM, the 256-bit "1101." The successful processing sequence had several proprietary aspects which put Intel in the forefront of semiconductor technology development. Vadasz commented that at this early stage of development, the processing sequences had proprietary aspects, but were not always well understood.

Since the market for SRAMs was young, Intel had difficulty selling the new device. But the successful MOS process was immediately applied to the existing market for *shift registers* among mainframe computer makers. Shift register sales provided the company with a war chest of cash needed to weather its first semiconductor recession of 1970–1971.

Development of DRAM

Another technical innovation followed the 1101. Intel worked closely with Honeywell engineers to design and develop the first DRAM in 1970, the 1-Kilobit "1103." While the SRAM required 6 MOS transistors per memory cell, the DRAM required only three transistors. With fewer elements in each memory cell, the 1103 contained more storage capacity in the same silicon area. While the new design allowed increased memory cell density, it also required a significant

EXHIBIT 2 | Selected Intel Corporation Financial Data (year ended December 31)

	1976	1977	1978	1979	1980	1981	1982	1983	1984
Sales	226	283	400	663	854	788	900	1,122	1,629
COGS	117	144	196	313	399	458	542	624	883
Gross Margin	109	139	204	350	455	330	358	498	746
R&D	21	28	41	67	96	116	131	142	180
SG&A	37	48	76	131	175	184	198	217	315
Operating Profit	51	63	87	152	184	30	29	139	251
Interest and Other			(1)	(3)	2	10	2	40	47
Profit before Tax	51	63	86	149	186	40	31	179	298
Income Tax	26	31	42	71	89	13		63	100
Net Income	25	32	44	78	97	27	31	116	198
Depreciation	10	16	24	40	49	66	83	103	114
Capital Invest	32	97	104	97	152	157	138	145	388
Cash and ST Invest	26	39	28	34	127	115	85	389	230
Working Capital	93	81	67	115	299	287	306	608	568
Fixed Assets	30	80	160	217	321	412	462	504	778
Total Assets	156	221	356	500	767	871	1,056	1,680	2,029
LT Debt	0	0	0	0	150	150	197	127	146
Equity	109	149	205	303	432	488	552	1,122*	1,360
Employees	7,300	8,100	10,900	14,300	15,900	16,800	19,400	21,500	25,400
ROS	11.1%	11.3%	11.0%	11.8%	11.4%	3.4%	3.4%	10.3%	12.2%
ROA	24.3%	20.5%	19.9%	21.9%	19.4%	3.5%	3.6%	11.0%	11.8%
ROE	33.8%	29.4%	29.5%	38.0%	32.0%	6.3%	6.4%	21.0%	17.6%

Note: The first and second quarters of 1985 showed revenue of $375 and $360 MM and profit of $9 and $11 MM, respectively. The first and second quarters of 1984 showed revenue of $372 and $410 MM and profit of $54 and $50 MM, respectively.

*Includes $250 MM proceeds from sale of 11% stake to IBM.

Source: Intel Annual Reports.

amount of external circuitry for *access* and *refresh*. An advertisement placed in computer trade journals in early 1971 announced: "THE END. CORES LOSE PRICE WAR TO NEW CHIP."

In spite of the price performance advantage, customers had to be taught how to use the new device and convinced of its reliability. *Ed Gelbach,* VP of Marketing, remembered 1971:

> We could never find a customer that used them and yet we were shipping literally hundreds of thousands of them. They were all testing them and putting them in boards . . . but it seemed like none of the customers ever shipped machines with the part. My recurring nightmare was that all of those chips would be returned over a single weekend.

In order to speed the adoption of DRAMs, Intel started the Memory Systems Operation (MSO), which assembled 1103 chips along with the required peripheral controller circuitry for OEM sale into the computer maker market. Soon MSO was responsible for about 30 percent of Intel's business. By 1972, the 1103 was the largest selling integrated circuit in the world and accounted for over 90 percent of Intel's $23.4 million in revenue.

Gordon Moore called the 1103 "the most-difficult-to-use semiconductor product ever invented." Ironically, that may have helped in its market success:

> There was a lot of resistance to semiconductor technology on the part of the core memory engineers. Core was a very difficult technology and required a great deal of

engineering support. The engineers didn't embrace the 1103 until they realized that it too was a difficult technology and wouldn't make their skills irrelevant.

New DRAM Generations

From its early days, Intel was fighting a battle with processing yields. The early 1103s were produced on 2-inch diameter silicon wafers, each containing about 250 devices. Of the 250, early 1103 runs produced an average of 25 fully functional devices, or an overall yield of 10 percent. *Ron Whittier,* general manager of the Memories Components Division from 1975 until 1983, said that throughout a product's life cycle, wafer yields increased continually as process improvements were developed. The productivity of the factory was also increased by changing the size of wafers whenever silicon manufacturers developed techniques to grow larger silicon ingots and equipment manufacturers developed machines that could handle larger wafers. In 1972, *Albert Yu* headed a team that converted the bipolar process from 2-inch to 3-inch wafers, effectively doubling capacity.

In the early days, Vadasz recalled, MSO developed another strategy for increasing yield. Since it only took one defective memory cell (out of 1024 in the 1103) to make a chip dysfunctional, it seemed inefficient to throw away all defectives. MSO's scheme was to compensate for a defective memory cell using creative peripheral logic circuitry. The peripheral circuitry was designed to bypass the defective cells within each memory chip so that rejected 1103s could still be used. Since the scheme required extra 1103s in each system, Intel referred to the concept as "redundancy."

Soon after Intel's early success, competitors entered the market for DRAMs and began to erode Intel's MOS process technology lead. By the mid-1970s, Intel was one of several companies vying to be the first at introducing the new generation of DRAM memories. Every 3 years, a new generation with four times as much capacity as its predecessor was developed (See Exhibit 3).

Vadasz recalled that even at the 4K and 16K level, Intel was struggling to keep up with its competitors. During the formative years of the DRAM market, the chip design was in rapid flux. A startup company, MOSTEK, was able to take market share from Intel in the 4K generation by incorporating the peripheral circuitry required to manage the memory on the chip itself. Vadasz recalled: "the first DRAMs were not very user friendly, and MOSTEK came out with a better product." Mostek

introduced the concept of on-chip *multiplexing,* which allowed a smaller number of output pins to address the entire memory. Multiplexing started a trend in DRAMs towards user friendliness.[2]

Vadasz commented:

> Even though you have invented the product, sometimes it is easier for new entrants to seize an opportunity and beat you to the punch. They are not encumbered by the same things you are. . . . The real problem in technological innovation is in anticipating the relevant issues. Once a technological "box" has been defined, it is easy for a team of great engineers to optimize everything in that box. Choosing the box is the hard part.

Intel's first 4K DRAM was redesigned to include the internal multiplexing logic. *Sun Lin Chou,* who was involved in the 4K DRAM development, said that in the revised version, Intel also implemented a one-transistor DRAM cell that became the industry standard. While more challenging from a process technology standpoint, the reduction in the number of transistors allowed for a smaller chip size. The revised 4K version sold well, but time was short before the next generation.

Dennis Carter described Intel's early strategy as "staying ahead of the experience curve[3] using process technology." According to Sun Lin Chou, a successful DRAM company participates in the early phase of each generation when low competitor yields and high demand support high prices.

> In fact, for the first two years, the demand for DRAMs to the first market entrant is semi-infinite. As soon as the leading vendor makes a new DRAM, he can crank his capacity to the maximum and he will be guaranteed of selling all his output. This is not true for more complex products such as a logic product with a new function where the customers have to first learn how to use it.

Each new generation required a quadrupling of the number of transistors contained on a chip. The driving force behind increased density was the ability to define patterns of ever narrower dimensions (functional

---

[2]Eventually Intel sold MSO since the value added had been integrated onto the chip itself and the majority of MSO's customers had learned how to use DRAMs.

[3]The experience curve referred to the declining nature of industrywide manufacturing costs over time due to experience. The semiconductor industry had a 70 percent experience curve (costs reduced by 30 percent for each doubling in cumulative volume). Companies that were not ahead of the curve for a particular product or generation suffered erosion of margins or market share.

EXHIBIT 3 | Product Introduction Timelines

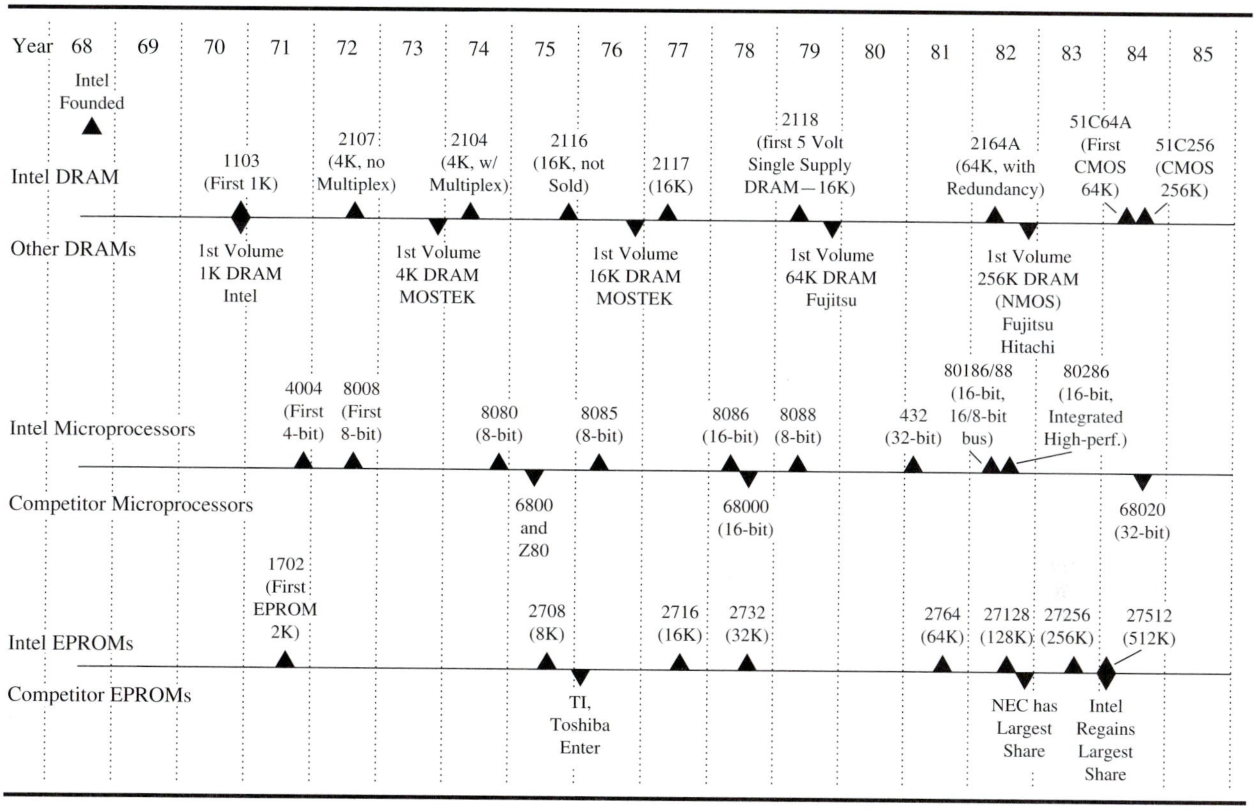

Year: 68 69 70 71 72 73 74 75 76 77 78 79 80 81 82 83 84 85

(68) Intel Founded ▲

Intel DRAM
- 1103 (First 1K) — 70
- 2107 (4K, no Multiplex) — 72
- 2104 (4K, w/ Multiplex) — 74
- 2116 (16K, not Sold) — 75
- 2117 (16K) — 77
- 2118 (first 5 Volt Single Supply DRAM—16K) — 79
- 2164A (64K, with Redundancy) — 82
- 51C64A (First CMOS 64K) — 83
- 51C256 (CMOS 256K) — 85

Other DRAMs
- 1st Volume 1K DRAM Intel — 70
- 1st Volume 4K DRAM MOSTEK — 73
- 1st Volume 16K DRAM MOSTEK — 76
- 1st Volume 64K DRAM Fujitsu — 79
- 1st Volume 256K DRAM (NMOS) Fujitsu Hitachi — 82

Intel Microprocessors
- 4004 (First 4-bit) — 71
- 8008 (First 8-bit) — 72
- 8080 (8-bit) — 74
- 8085 (8-bit) — 76
- 8086 (16-bit) — 78
- 8088 (8-bit) — 79
- 432 (32-bit) — 81
- 80186/88 (16-bit, 16/8-bit bus) — 82
- 80286 (16-bit, Integrated High-perf.) — 82

Competitor Microprocessors
- 6800 and Z80 — 74
- 68000 (16-bit) — 78
- 68020 (32-bit) — 84

Intel EPROMs
- 1702 (First EPROM 2K) — 71
- 2708 (8K) — 75
- 2716 (16K) — 77
- 2732 (32K) — 78
- 2764 (64K) — 81
- 27128 (128K) — 82
- 27256 (256K) — 83
- 27512 (512K) — 84

Competitor EPROMs
- TI, Toshiba Enter — 75
- NEC has Largest Share — 82
- Intel Regains Largest Share — 84

Note: *6800 and 68000 are Motorola products.* Z80 is a Zilog product.

Source: Intel Documents, Dataquest.

---

equivalent of wires and components in a circuit) on the silicon wafer, to invent creative ways of reducing the required number and size of components per memory cell, and to make larger chips without defects. Each new generation reduced the minimum line width by a factor of about 0.7, from 5 μm at the 4K generation. The minimum line width was controlled primarily by the accuracy of the photolithography process, while the maximum chip size was determined by the ability to control the number of random defects on the wafer.[4]

While competition was tough even at the 4K level, a series of process innovations kept Intel among the memory leaders through the 16K DRAM generation (see Exhibit 3). Gordon Moore developed the strategy of using DRAMs as a technology driver. The latest process technology was developed using DRAMs and later

transfered to other products. Early on in the company's development, Intel managers decided to merge the research and manufacturing functions. Gordon Moore had been dissatisfied with the linkage between research and manufacturing at Fairchild. As a result, he had insisted that Intel perform all process research directly on the production line. Moore commented:

> Our strategy optimizes our ability to make fast incremental process technology improvements. We don't have a central corporate research lab. We tend to evaluate other research advances in light of how they will affect our businesses. For instance, while Texas Instruments has been funding a research effort in *gallium arsenide,* we have been watching gallium arsenide develop for the past 20 years. We're still silicon believers.

During the 1970s, Intel competed by developing new processes that were used to enhance product features or to enable new product families beyond memories. The *HMOS* (high-performance MOS) process enabled Intel to introduce the first 5-volt-single-power-supply 16K

---

[4]The size of the chip defines the area of the wafer that each process-induced defect can potentially damage. If the chip size is too large, yields are unacceptably low unless the defect level can be simultaneously reduced.

DRAM in 1979. Earlier offerings, including Intel's two previous 16K DRAMs (2116 and 2117), required that the user supply three separate voltages to the chip. The new product, the 2118, greatly simplified the user's design and production tasks. While Intel had lost market share with the 2116 and 2117, it was all alone with the 5-volt device and captured a price premium of double the industry average for three-power-supply 16K DRAMs in 1979 (see Exhibit 4). The DRAM technology development group focused a significant amount of its resources on developing Intel's third 16K DRAM offering while competitors concentrated on the 64K generation.

Intel management decided to focus on the single power supply 16K DRAM for two primary reasons: they projected a relatively long life cycle for the 16K generation due to the technical challenge in achieving the 64K generation; and they believed the one-power-supply process would eventually dominate the memory industry. They considered it too risky to tackle both the 64K DRAM generation and the single power supply technology in the same product.

The drive towards smaller and smaller geometries was achieved through improvements in both processing methodology and processing machinery. Dennis Carter explained that in the early years some processing steps were considered black magic and defined a company's competitive edge. As time went on, the movement of engineers between chip companies and the involvement of suppliers and equipment manufacturers in process development efforts led to a general leveling of process capability among Silicon Valley firms. Sun Lin Chou commented about the trends in processing:

> Process technology and equipment have become so complex and expensive to develop that no vendor can hope to do better than his competitors in every process step. The key to innovation is to be on par with your competitors on every process step, but to select one or two or three process features with the highest leverage and focus your efforts to gain leadership there. In DRAMs we focus on high-quality thin *dielectrics*.

The Invention of the EPROM

Albert Yu, vice president of development and general manager of the Components Division said he usually associates the invention of any important product with one person. The EPROM (electrically programmable read only memory) was invented by *Dov Frohman*. Yu said Frohman not only invented the product, but he also described the physical effect, saw that it could be applied

to a memory device, designed the first part, and fabricated the first device.

Frohman's story has become legendary at Intel. As a recent hire from Fairchild in 1969, Frohman was assigned to help understand and remedy a strange phenomenon that was causing reliability problems with the MOS process. The problem involved the silicon gate structure. Frohman saw that the phenomenon could be explained by the existence of an unintentional *floating gate* within the MOS device. He realized that if a floating gate were intentionally constructed, a new type of programmable memory that would permanently store information could be built.

Frohman designed the first test devices and assembled a demonstration for Gordon Moore. According to Frohman:

> We put together a 16-bit array with primitive transistor packages sticking out of the 16 sockets, an oscilloscope, and pulse generator, and we carted all this into Gordon's office. There were red bulbs to indicate the bits. This was all new to us, and we were thrashing around. We showed Gordon that by pushing the button you could program the device, and we demonstrated that it would hold a charge.[5]

Later, it was discovered that ultraviolet light could be used to erase the memory. Moore committed the company to the production of the EPROM even though no one could tell where the device would have applications. Recalled Moore:

> It was just another kind of memory at the time, and people saw it as a research and development device. Today, the likelihood of someone killing an effort like this one is very high, because we require a well-defined application to a market from the outset. This is especially so because we are not lacking in opportunities. There is still a lot of evolution left in the current technology. If you consider the possibilities for reducing line width, you can see another 12 years of evolution along the same curve.

The Invention of the Microprocessor

Ted Hoff invented the microprocessor. Intel had been hired by the Japanese firm Busicom to design and build a set of chips for a number of different calculators. Busicom had envisioned a set of around 15 chips designed to perform advanced calculator functions. Hoff suggested building a simpler set of just a few general

---

[5]D. Manners, "Intel's 20th Birthday," *Electronic Weekly*, July 20, 1988:15.

purpose chips that could be programmed to carry out each of the calculators' instructions.

He was the architect of the chip set that Federico Faggin and a team of designers implemented. The set included four chips: a central processing unit (CPU) called the 4004, a read only memory (ROM) with custom instructions for calculator operation, a random access memory (RAM), and a shift register for input/output buffering. It took nearly a year to convince Busicom that the novel approach would work, but by early 1970, Intel signed a $60,000 contract that gave Busicom proprietary rights to the design. The CPU chip, 4004, was eventually called a microprocessor.

While Intel produced chips for Busicom that were successfully made into 100,000 calculators:,[6] a debate within the company developed about whether Intel should try to renegotiate the rights to the chip design. Hoff believed that Intel could use the devices as a general purpose solution in many applications ranging from cash registers to street lights, and he lobbied heavily within the company.

Eventually, Intel decided to offer reduced pricing to Busicom in exchange for noncalculator rights to the design. Ed Gelbach remembered the management decision: "Originally, I think we saw it as a way to sell more memories and we were willing to make the investment on that basis." Busicom, in financial trouble, readily agreed to the proposal.

The 4004 was introduced in 1971. It contained 2,300 MOS transistors and could execute 60,000 instructions per second. Its performance was not as good as custom-designed logic, but Intel believed there was a significant market for it. Early on, it became apparent that Intel would have to educate its customers in order to sell the 4004. As a result, Gelbach's group developed the first of Intel's development aides, which were programming tools for the customer. By 1973 revenues from design aides exceeded microprocessor sales.

In tandem with the 4-bit 4004, Intel developed an 8-bit microprocessor, the 8008, which was introduced in April 1972. The 8008 was designed with a computer terminal company in mind, but was rejected by the company because it was too slow and required 20 support chips for operation.

In the meantime, Intel's advancements in static and dynamic RAMs had provided a new process technology that promised increased transistor switching speed. Intel had created an *NMOS* process that was applied to the 8008. In addition, much of the functionality of the support chips was integrated into the new microprocessor, the 8080. As a result of process technology, the 8080 could execute 290,000 instructions per second. In addition, the 8080 required only six support chips for operation.

The introduction of the 8080 in April 1974 heralded the beginning of a new age in computing. The market for microprocessors exploded as new uses were developed. Intel was one year ahead of Motorola's introduction of the 6800 and eventually took nearly the entire 8-bit market. Even though the 6800 used an architecture more familiar to programmers, Intel offered more effective development aids and support systems. Several integrated circuits companies were licensed to produce the 8080 so that customers were assured of a second source of supply. Ed Gelbach remembered the mid 1970s as the good old days. At an initial selling price of $360 per chip, Intel paid for the 8080 research and development in the first five months of shipments.

Motorola and Zilog[7] continued to apply pressure in the 8-bit microprocessor marketplace (see Exhibit 4). But Intel's 16-bit microprocessor, the 8086, again was first to market by about one year when it was introduced in June 1978. Intel management decided that that upward compatibility would be a critical feature of the 16-bit chip. While the 8086 could operate software developed originally for the 8080, it employed a new architecture that required new software for full exploitation. An 8-bit *bus* version of the new architecture, the 8088, was also introduced. For two years, Intel did not meet its sales forecasts for the 8086 family as customers purchased only sample quantities and worked on a new generation of software. In the meantime, Motorola introduced its own 16-bit microprocessor, the 68000, and appeared to be gaining momentum in the field.[8]

Recognizing that the 68000 represented a critical threat that could lock Intel out of the 16-bit market and potentially the next generation as well, Intel created a task force to attack the 68000. The project was called operation CRUSH. The project leader said: "We set out to generate

---

[6]The casewriter noticed a Busicom calculator on Gordon Moore's desk. Moore also wore an Intel digital watch that he called his 15-million-dollar watch, referring to Intel's ill-fated venture into the watch business. He said: "If anyone comes to me with an idea for a consumer product, all I have to do is look at my watch to get the answer . . ."

[7]Zilog had been formed as a start-up by three Intel design engineers. Andy Grove commented that the loss of those engineers set back Intel's microprocessor program by as much as one year.

[8]Motorola won the Apple computer account with the 68000. The 68000 architecture remains Apple's standard.

EXHIBIT 4 | Market Information for DRAMs and Microprocessors

Product	1974	1975	1976	1977	1978	1979	1980	1981	1982	1983	1984
Worldwide Unit Shipments of DRAMs (in thousands)											
4K	615	5,290	28,010	57,415	77,190	70,010	31,165	13,040	4,635	2,400	2,250
16K 3PS*			50	2,008	20,785	69,868	182,955	215,760	263,050	239,210	120,690
16K 5V*						150	1,115	5,713	23,240	57,400	40,600
64K					1	36	441	12,631	103,965	371,340	851,600
256K									10	1,700	37,980
Worldwide Yearly Average Selling Prices of DRAMs ($/unit)											
4K	17.00	6.24	4.35	2.65	1.82	1.92	1.94	1.26	1.62	2.72	3.00
16K 3PS*			46.39	18.63	8.53	6.03	4.77	2.06	1.24	1.05	1.09
16K 5V*						17.67	7.38	3.84	2.23	1.98	2.07
64K					150.00	110.14	46.26	11.00	5.42	3.86	3.16
256K									150.00	47.66	17.90
Tot. Mkt.	10,455	33,010	124,163	189,559	317,932	562,339	961,785	621,775	950,506	1,885,745	3,593,242
Intel DRAM Market Share											
4K	82.9%	45.6%	18.7%	18.1%	14.3%	8.7%	3.2%	2.4%	2.3%	1.9%	1.4%
16K 3PS*			37.0%	27.9%	11.5%	4.4%	2.1%				
16K 5V*						100.0%	94.0%	66.5%	33.1%	11.7%	12.3%
64K							0.7%	0.2%	1.5%	3.5%	1.7%
256K											0.1%
Est. Rev.**($M)	8,667	15,052	23,643	37,976	40,479	32,882	28,139	25,534	33,109	68,238	58,607

*16K 3PS refers to the industry-standard, three-power-supply DRAM. The 16K 5V model requires only one power supply.

**Sales of 1K DRAMs were negligible by 1977. Estimates are created by assuming Intel prices at average selling price. Casewriter estimates that by 1984 Intel DRAM sales were closer to $100 MM.

Losses to gross income due to DRAMs in 1984 were estimated by the casewriter to be between $20 and $30 MM.

Microprocessor Sales History by Architecture[†]

	Architecture (% units sold)	1976	1977	1978	1979	1980	1981	1982	1983	1984
8-bit	Zilog (Z80)	2.2%	5.8%	12.4%	17.0%	21.1%	22.7%	23.4%	37.4%	35.1%
	Intel (8080,8088)	22.8%	36.6%	34.6%	38.9%	27.1%	19.7%	19.1%	22.3%	33.5%
	Motorola (6800,650X,680X)	15.0%	13.0%	17.2%	20.8%	18.8%	21.1%	17.9%	14.8%	14.0%
	Others	60.0%	44.6%	35.8%	23.3%	33.0%	36.5%	39.6%	25.5%	17.4%
	Total 8-bit (MM units)	n/avail.	n/a	n/a	12.5	22.4	33.8	47.9	67.8	75.1
	Average Selling Price	n/a	n/a	n/a	$6.03	$4.60	$3.32	$3.18	$3.25	$4.06
16-bit	Zilog (Z8000)				1.4%	4.5%	3.4%	5.1%	5.8%	6.2%
	Intel (80186/286,8086)			6.7%	14.0%	28.9%	31.7%	26.6%	32.1%	59.1%
	Motorola (68000)						3.9%	5.8%	10.8%	20.2%
	Others			93.3%	84.6%	66.6%	61.0%	62.5%	51.3%	14.5%
	Total16-bit (MM units)	n/a	n/a	n/a	0.5	0.8	1.8	4.1	7.1	10.0
	Average Selling Price	n/a	n/a	n/a	$30.29	$38.00	$16.96	$15.29	$14.25	$28.90

[†]Architecture refers to company who originated design, not to manufacturer. For example, while Intel's designs captured 33.5% and 59.1% of the 8- and 16-bit segments, Intel's actual unit sales of microprocessors accounted for only 14.5% of total market sales in 1984. Licensing agreements with other vendors accounts for the remainder. Next to Intel, NEC was the second largest unit shipper of microprocessors at 13.5% of total units. Motorola captured fifth place behind Zilog (8.9%) and AMD (7.4%) with 7.3% of microprocessor unit sales in 1984.

Source: Dataquest.

100,000 sales leads and get that down to 10,000 qualified leads resulting in 2,000 design wins in 1980." SWAT teams of engineering, applications, and marketing people were mobilized to travel anywhere in the world whenever a design win was threatened.

The CRUSH campaign emphasized Intel's systems approach, and produced 2,500 design wins in the first year. The most notable win was IBM's decision to use the 8088 in their first personal computer in 1981. IBM planned an open architecture personal computer, and Intel's 8086 family defined the software standard. Intel sales representatives knew they won the IBM account several months before it was made public when the IBM Boca Raton office started placing orders for Intel's ICE-88 development systems. In 1981, 13 percent of Intel's sales were to IBM.

The project to develop the next microprocessor generation began in 1978. The 80186 and 80286 were designed to be upwardly compatible with the 8086, and to offer increased integration, internal memory management, and advanced software protection (security) capability. The 80286 was designed to operate with as few as four support chips. The 286 team developed product features through extensive field interviews and created a list of over 50 potential applications ranging from business systems to industrial automation. Ironically, the applications list did not include personal computers, which later became the single largest application.

The 80286 was the most ambitious design effort ever undertaken at Intel. The chip contained 130,000 transistors (versus 29,000 for the 8086). Intel's computerized design tools were stretched to their limit. Four separate computer systems had to be used just to store the design. Design verification (a tool that checks that mask design correctly reflects schematic design) took four days of continuous computer operation. Several crises arose throughout the development period.

The 286 logic design supervisor recalled:

> At least once a year we went through a crisis that made us wonder whether we would get there or not. One was the chip size crisis. At one point, it looked like the chip would be as big as 340 mils on a side. That was so big that people outside the design team would roll on the floor laughing. They kind of enjoyed our misery. Chip designers love to hear that someone else's chip is too big, but when it happens to you, it's really serious stuff.

The design team of 24 people worked feverishly for three years to develop the first prototype. That device was fabricated in 1982 at Fab 3 in Livermore but did not operate with high enough speed. Gradually, all the bugs

were worked out, and only one hurdle remained: developing the methodology to test the chips as they came off the line. Production was ready to start making the 80286 six months before the testing procedure could be developed. Intel had to develop computer tools in order to design the tests. The chip was introduced in 1983, 18 months later than originally planned.

In the meantime, Motorola was gaining momentum. Dennis Carter, who worked on marketing the 80286, said:

> The 68000 came out after the 8086 and it was having some success in the marketplace, but we weren't particularly concerned because we knew the 186 and 286 were on the horizon. We believed we would announce the 286, and everyone would flock to our door. But when we introduced it, the world perceived the 286 not as a powerful monster machine, but as a slight continuation of the 8086. It also seemed that a lot of start-ups were using Motorola, and that was real scary, because that's one indication of where the future is going to be.

Project CHECKMATE paralleled the earlier project CRUSH in concept. CHECKMATE task force members gave a series of seminars 200 different times to 20,000 engineers around the world. Rather than emphasizing performance specifications that Motorola could also use to advantage, the seminar stressed features that had been included at the request of the marketplace in 1978, such as *virtual memory addressing* and *multitasking*. Carter recalled:

> As a result, the design wins completely turned around. When we went into CHECKMATE, some market segments were three or four to one in favor of Motorola. By the time we finished, it had turned around the other way.

Synergies between EPROMs and Microprocessors

No one foresaw that microprocessors would create a booming market for EPROMs. The original four-chip design for the 4004 was general purpose except for the ROM chip which had to be customized (at the factory) for each application.

Although it was developed separately, the EPROM substituted for the ROM and provided two advantages: The designer of a custom product could develop and revise his ROM-resident microprocessor programs quickly; and smaller applications that could not afford the expense of a custom ROM could substitute off-the-shelf EPROMs. Ed Gelbach commented:

It made sense to be able to reprogram the microprocessor instead of buying fixed ROMs for it. You could change your system overnight or every five minutes with EPROM.

Intel had a competitive advantage in the EPROM process and retained a majority market share until the late 1970s. Competitors had trouble imitating Intel's "floating gate" process. *Ron Smith,* manager of static/logic technology development said:

> If a device physicist were confronted with the EPROM out of the blue, he might be able to prove it won't work. The EPROM process has as much art as science in it, not only in the wafer fab, but in the packaging, testing, and reliability engineering.

In 1977, Intel introduced the 16K EPROM, 2716, which was compatible with any microprocessor system. All alone with the floating gate process, Intel enjoyed a boom in EPROM sales for two years.

By 1981, the industry faced a cyclical downturn, and Intel's virtual monopoly on the EPROM market was challenged by several competitors, including the Japanese. The industry average selling prices for the 16K EPROM dropped by 75 percent in 1980. Intel management responded by accelerating the introduction of the 64K EPROM.

In the midst of a semiconductor recession, Intel decided to retrofit the brand new Fab 6 at Chandler, Arizona, with a new photolithography technology: *stepper alignment.* Fab 6 had just come online and was idle (see Exhibit 5 for more detail on Intel facilities). The gamble was significant: "new process, new product, new plant, and new people." The 64K EPROM (2764) team met very aggressive yield goals, and Intel was again leading the world in EPROM sales. By mid-1981, Fab 6 had produced hundreds of thousands of 2764s, and output was doubling every quarter.

Technology Development

The 2764 had been used by Intel's Santa Clara Technology Development Group to develop stepper alignment. Steppers allowed smaller feature definition and smaller die size,[9] but the capital equipment was an order of magnitude more expensive than conventional projection aligners. Because of the trend towards more expensive equipment and the growing need for a new generation of equipment for each generation of product,

Intel modified its traditional philosophy of developing processes on fabrication lines.

From early on, Intel had divided its technology development into three groups that represented the three major process areas: EPROM, DRAM, and Logic. Competition between the groups for scarce resources in the Santa Clara facility had led to the decision to separate the groups geographically. By 1984, the three separate technology development groups were in three cities: EPROMs in Santa Clara, California; microprocessors and SRAMs in Livermore, California;[10] and DRAMs in Aloha, Oregon. While development of each technology was independent, management insisted on equipment standardization. Periodically, the groups got together, pooled information on equipment options, and agreed to purchase the same equipment.

Gordon Moore commented that resource allocation did not necessarily parallel the market fortunes of the process families:

> Allocation of resources to the different technology development groups is centralized by Andy and me. We want to maintain commonality. Also, we are old semiconductor guys. Ideally, one of the groups starts a new technology and the others follow. But for stepper technology this was not true; they all did it simultaneously.

The three groups each developed a distinctive style and distinctive competencies that related to their product responsibilities (see Exhibit 6). The Santa Clara group was responsible for the EPROM and *EEPROM* (electrically eraseable programmable read only memory) products. They focused on the processing steps most critical to EPROMs, for example the double polysilicon process used to create the floating gate. Similarly, the Livermore group concentrated on processes critical to logic devices.

The DRAM technology development group led the company in line width reduction. For example, the DRAM group was developing a 1 μm process while the logic group was developing a 1.5 μm process. Two key factors made DRAMs suitable as a technology driver: large demand for the latest DRAM generation (early high-volume manufacturing experience), and simplicity of integrating design and testing with process development.

Process specialization in all three technology areas limited the direct transferability of processing modules from one area to another, but DRAMs still provided a convenient vehicle for leading-edge process

---

[9]Smaller die size leads to higher yield and lower manufacturing costs. If die size is reduced by 25 percent, manufacturing costs are typically reduced by *at least* 25 percent.

---

[10]The Livermore site was also a production facility in 1984.

EXHIBIT 5 | Intel Facilities in 1984

Intel's Wafer Foundaries

Fab Area	Location	Year First Opened	Original Wafer Size	Current Wafer Size	Technology Development	Primary Production Focus
Ex Fab 1	Mountain View,	purch. 1968	1″	closed		
Fab 1	CA	1977	3″	4″	EPROM	Small number of EPROMs
Fab 2	Santa Clara, CA	1971	4″	4″	no	Logic
Fab 3	Santa Clara CA	1973	3″	4″	Logic, SRAM	Logic and SRAM (was DRAM)
Fab 4	Livermore, CA	1979	4″	4″	no	Microcontrollers and EPROM
Fab 5	Aloha, OR	1979	4″	4″	DRAM	pilot and DRAM
Fab 6	Aloha, OR	1980	4″	4″ and 6″	no	Logic, EPROM, Microcontrollers
Fab 7*	Chandler, AZ	1983	5″	6″	no	EPROM only
Fab 8	Albuquerque, NM	sched. 1985	6″	6″	no	EPROM
Fab 9	Jerusalem, Israel	sched. 1986	6″ plan		no	under construction
Fab 10**	Rio Rancho, NM	held at shell				
Fab 11**	Rio Rancho, NM	held at shell				
	Rio Rancho, NM					

*First 6″ fab area in world. Original 5″ facility used DRMs for shakeout. 1981–82 recession delayed production and allowed installation of 6″ equipment. Process transfer to 6″ wafers was unexpectedly difficult and took over one year.

**These fab areas could be loaded with facilities and equipments and started in about 2 years.

Intel's Other Worldwide Facilities (Excluding 50 sales offices)

Location	Date Started	Product Focus	Operation
Penang, Malasia	1972	broad	Component Ass'y and Test
Manila, Philippines	1974	broad	Component Ass'y and Test
Haifa, Israel	1974	Logic	Design Center
Barbados, West Indies	1977	broad	Components Assembly
Tsukuba, Japan	1981	Logic	Design Center
Las Piedras, Puerto Rico	1981	Systems, DRAMs	Systems Ass'y, Component Test
Singapore	1984	Systems	Systems ass'y

Source: Intel documents.

learning, and the DRAM group was highly regarded. Ron Whittier said:

> In 1984, the memory technology development group represented Intel's best corporate resource for process development. People like Sun Lin Chou are a scarce resource in a technology-driven company. Sun Lin's group understands and executes process development better than any other group at Intel.

Dean Toombs described the DRAM group as different from the others because of the relationship between design and process engineers:

> The DRAM designer is a specialist and more a device physicist than other designers. He focuses on the

memory cell and has to understand where every electron in the structure is. There is more of a connection between the designer and the process engineer. The design and the process are developed together. In contrast, a logic designer is not as concerned with the details of a transistor's operation. The process is critical, but not as interactive with the design.

Intel Product Line and Situation in Mid-1985

By the end of 1984, logic products (including microprocessors, *microcontrollers,* and peripherals) were the dominant source of Intel's revenue (see Exhibit 7). The company offered over 70 peripheral chips that worked in tandem with its microprocessor lines. The

EXHIBIT 6 | Technology Development Groups

	DRAM	EPROM	Logic/SRAM
Location	Portland, OR	Santa Clara, CA	Livermore, CA
Product Focus	Moderate, undertakes some basic research	Strong, little basic research EPROM and EEPROM Development	Strong
Process/Design Interface	Design engineers highly specialized in DRAMs with device physics focus. Process and design development are highly interactive and in parallel.	Process and design less tightly coupled.	Process and design loosely coupled. Design engineers focus on circuit design. Process engineers focus on shrinking line-widths technologies.
Key Distinctive Technical Competence	Thin dielectrics and pushing photolithography limits. Tend to lead Intel in geometry reduction. DRAMs are seen as technology driver. Currently the only group with a 1-micron technology	Problems specific to EPROM and EEPROM. Expertise in developing polysilicon and passivation processes. Also focused on pushing technology to 1 micron.	Processes to shrink existing products and increase yields. Currently developing new process for 386 microprocessor. Developing expertise in double layer metalization.
Number of Personnel	120	120	120
1985 Budget Allocation*	$65 MM	$65 MM	$65 MM
Other Comments	DRAM technology development group considered by many to be the most competent group. Major effort in 1-Meg DRAM development. Facility has low turnover.	Relatively high turnover to competing companies in Silicon Valley. Has successfully maintained Intel lead in EPROM technology.	Technology development takes place on facility used for production of logic products. Major project in developing 386 process.

*Casewriter's estimate.

80186 and 80286 were tremendously successful. In addition to the IBM PC business, Intel had locked up the IBM PC clone business with customers such as Compaq, who purchased microprocessors either from Intel or from one of its licensed second sources such as Advanced Micro Devices. The only serious 16-bit architectural competitor was Motorola,[11] although *Electronic News* had reported that 10 companies including NEC, Hitachi, Mitsubishi, Fujitsu, and Zilog were developing proprietary 32-bit products, and National Semiconductor had already introduced its 32-bit offering. NEC's proprietary design effort was par-

ticularly interesting since NEC also supported Intel's microprocessor line as a second source.[12]

Intel had also developed a line of microcontrollers that integrated logic and memory (both SRAM and EPROM) to provide a self-sufficient, one-chip computer. One Intel manager suggested that integration of EPROM technology with logic was an effort to lift EPROMs from a commodity status. The microcontroller business had products in the 4-, 8-, and 16-bit market segments that were used to control everything from house fans to

---

[11]Motorola's 68000 has a 16-bit bus, but actually uses a 32-bit internal architecture.

[12]*Electronic News*, 2/18/85. The article also reports that Fujitsu did not confirm rumors that it had a proprietary 32-bit design. Instead, Fujitsu indicated its development efforts were still centered on second source agreements with Intel.

EXHIBIT 7 |

Composition of
Revenues

Source: Dataquest.

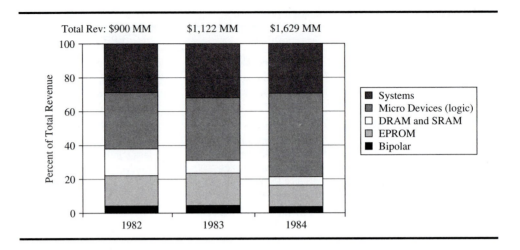

complex satellites and had prices ranging from one to several thousand dollars per chip.

Scheduled for introduction in late 1985 was the successor to the 286, the 32-bit 80386™ microprocessor.[13] According to one Intel manager, "once again, Intel was betting the company on a new product." With 270,000 transistors, the 386 was even more complex than the 286. Intel had invested heavily in computerized design and simulation tools that made the design task run more smoothly. In 1984, Intel believed it had the best chip design capability in the world. However, Motorola had developed a strong 32-bit product, the 68020[14] and was already in the marketplace winning designs, locking customers into its architecture.

The 80386™ was scheduled to be one of the first products made with the new *Complementary MOS (CMOS)* process (the 80C51 microcontroller and the 51C64 DRAM had both used versions of CMOS). It was also the first microprocessor to use stepper alignment, *double metalization* and *plasma etching*. Development of the 386™ process was taking place in parallel with a new SRAM process at Livermore under the direction of Ron Smith. Ron Smith explained:

> Our group was called the Static/Logic Technology Development Group and our charter was to develop *scaling improvements*[15] for the logic and SRAM lines. SRAMs were to lead the company in scaling. We saw

the SRAMs not only as a product line but as a vehicle for microprocessor development. The SRAM is an indispensable tool in developing any new process. It is much easier to debug a process using memory components because they are easier to test. That's why Intel traditionally uses memory products to develop a new technology.

In 1984, the Livermore group was developing two distinct processes, since the performance requirements for SRAMs and microprocessors differed. Although Intel had a good position in the low-volume, high-speed SRAM segment, it did not participate in the largest SRAM segment that demanded higher density (more storage capacity).[16] The high-volume SRAM segment demanded a new 4-transistor cell design and process. By contrast, the high-speed SRAM and the new 80386™ microprocessor both demanded a 6-transistor CMOS design.

The high-volume SRAM process required a complex *polysilicon resistor* technology that was giving Smith's group difficulty. Smith described the environment as it had evolved in mid-1985:

> Eventually, we decided to drop the poly resistor process and go with a 6-transistor CMOS SRAM product so that we could focus our attention on the 386 development. Basically, we sacrificed the high-volume SRAM for the 386™.
>
> To get an idea of the complexity of the 386™ development, compare it to the 286. The 286 team was really comprised of only six people. When it came time

---

[13]80386 is a trademark of the Intel Corporation.

[14]Introduced in sample quantities in September 1984.

[15]Scaling improvements allowed Intel to reduce the chip size of existing products without expensive redesign. The reduced chip size led to reduced manufacturing costs.

[16]Intel's overall SRAM position had diminished significantly over the years as Japanese manufacturers gained market share.

to develop the 386™, we had to come up with a double metalization process while at the same time reducing line widths to 1.5 μm (from 2 μm) and implementing the CMOS process. The 386™ process team had about 60 people: specialists in plasma etching, stepper alignment, chemical etching, and diffusion. If you compare the mask design for the 286 with the 386, you'll be able to tell how much area we saved by going to a double layer metal. Lots of the 286 area was taken up with the routing of metal.

Gordon Moore described a linkage between market and technology development that may have contributed to the loss of a competitive SRAM product.

> Product designers want to see their product in high volume. So, it is important to have volume in a product line to get high-quality designers on board. For instance, SRAMs received less attention for that reason than I wish they had. We had a strong position in high-speed SRAMs, but we gave it up without really making a conscious decision.

The systems business at Intel had continued to grow with the company and by the end of 1984 represented the same 30 percent of revenue that MSO had represented in 1973. While a great deal of the systems business comprised development products aimed at microprocessor and microcontroller users, Intel also had vertically integrated into software development systems and single-board computers so that it could offer its customers options at several levels of integration.

Manufacturing and Process Fungibility

While tolerating some process proliferation within plants, Intel took great pains to standardize each facility as it expanded its manufacturing base. In 1973, Grove was pictured in a snapshot at his desk with a foot-long mock chip package. On its side was printed the McDonald's Golden Arches logo with "McIntel" substituted. Each Intel chip would "look and taste the same no matter which facility produced it."

As larger diameter silicon wafers became available, Intel developed a process on one line and then transferred the technology to its other facilities. For example, a process for four-inch diameter wafers was first developed at Fab 3 in Livermore, California, by a team of three people. The team leader then supervised the start-up of Fab 5 in Aloha, Oregon, which was dedicated to four-inch wafers. In 1983, after delaying start-up due to the '81–'82 recession, Intel was the first semiconductor

company to use six-inch wafers at Fab 7, Rio Rancho, New Mexico (see Exhibit 8).

By 1984, Intel had seven fab areas in the United States, all within a two-hour flight of headquarters in Santa Clara. Due to more stringent manufacturing standards, the cost of a fab area had risen dramatically since the 1970s. A new fab area fully equipped cost between $150 and $200 million and took about two years to construct. The first overseas fab area had just opened in Jerusalem, Israel. *Jack Carsten,* senior vice president and general manager of the Components Group, commented in retrospect on the decision to locate in Israel:

> Around the time we were deciding to put up a fab in Israel, I supported the idea of building a fab area in Japan. I had actually obtained leases on Japanese soil so that Intel could locate its first overseas fab area in Japan. That plant would have provided some insulation from currency fluctuations, but the Israel plant had tremendous government subsidies and a good labor market. A Japanese plant would have also put us into the pipeline of Japanese equipment vendors, and linked us into the Zaibatsu network. We could have tapped the expertise of Japanese DRAM technology development, silicon makers, mask makers, and the infrastructural support. This is what Texas Instruments did, because they had a commitment to local manufacturing. Eventually, we chose Jerusalem, largely because of the subsidies. This is not to say that the Israel facility is bad. It is a fine facility, but it certainly can't offer currency hedging against the Japanese Yen.

Nearly all (97 percent) manufacturing capacity was devoted to MOS devices. Within MOS, the majority of processing was NMOS, but there was a trend towards increased CMOS. Each production facility was more or less dedicated to a particular process family (DRAM, Logic or EPROM), although some facilities manufactured more than one family. Within each family, some process sequences were sometimes customized to accommodate particular product performance needs. While the equipment within any fab area was similar, different fab areas had different generations of equipment, and some processes required more of a particular machine for line balancing. Gordon Moore commented on proliferation of process technologies:

> Over time, there has been a tendency to get more and more processes and that complicates manufacturing allocations. In the past, we solved the problem by brutally

EXHIBIT 8 | Sample of Cost Accounting Data for Selected Intel Products in 1984

Product	Process	Raw Wafer Cost ($)	# Mask Layers	# of Act.	Cost Per Act ($)	Line Yield	Cost Per Wafer ($)	Die Per 6" Wafer	Wafer Sort Yield	Total Cost Per Die ($)	Package/Test Cost Per Die ($)	Yield at Test	Total Cost Per Chip ($)	Average Selling Price ($)	Contribution Margin Per Chip
64K DRAM	NMOS DRAM	60	8	30	72.00	90%	2,467	1900	90%	1.44	0.45	90%	2.103	2.05	–2%
64K DRAM	CMOS DRAM	100	10	38	72.00	84%	3,376	1806	85%	2.20	0.45	90%	2.944	3.08	4%
256K DRAM	CMOS DRAM	100	10	38	72.00	83%	3,417	922	60%	6.18	0.65	90%	7.585	16.27	53%
64K EPROM	NMOS EPROM	60	12	48	72.00	79%	4,451	1582	75%	3.75	2.65	90%	7.112	8.15	13%
256K EPROM	NMOS EPROM	60	12	48	72.00	78%	4,508	756	60%	9.94	2.45	90%	13.764	21.00	34%
80286	LOGIC	60	10	40	72.00	90%	3,267	172	70%	27.13	2.00	85%	34.273	250.00	86%
80386 (samples)	1.5μm LOGIC	100	13	50	72.00	90%	4,111	131	30%	104.61	15.00	85%	140.716	900.00	84%

Key

Raw wafer cost: Raw wafer cost differs depending on whether or not process is CMOS.

mask layers: Refers to the number of times the wafer goes through the photolithography step.

of activities: Refers to the number of times the wafer is physically altered in the process.

Cost per activity: An average of worldwide manufacturing costs, including depreciation, materials, labor, and other facilities costs.

Line yield: Ratio of wafers started to wafers completed.

Cost per wafer: # of activities times cost per activity divided by line yield.

Die per 6" wafer: Number of devices on a 6" wafer (function of die size).

Wafer sort yield: Number of "good" die divided by total die after all processing is complete and before wafer is sawed and devices are packaged.

Total cost per die: Cost per wafer divided by number of good die per wafer at wafer sort test.

Package/test cost: Cost of packaging and testing one device.

Yield at test: Number of devices entering packaging divided by number of devices which pass final test.

Total cost per chip: Total cost per die plus packaging and testing costs all divided by yield at test.

Source: Casewriter estimates.

getting out of businesses. But the customers didn't like that. For instance, we abdicated share in microcontrollers because we had to clean out somewhere to do other things.

While each facility could not produce every family of products, there was some fungibility between products and facilities. In times when demand was strong and capacity constrained sales, Intel division managers would get together monthly to decide how to load the factories. Chief Financial Officer, *Bob Reed,* described the process as being one that maximized margin per manufacturing activity:

> Basically, there are three main process areas: fabrication, assembly, and test. Assembly is usually not a constraining factor—you can ramp it up as fast as you need to. Similarly, test can be ramped up in the short term. Fabrication (the front end of the process) is usually the bottleneck in times of tight capacity—it takes long lead times to increase capacity. Since fabrication is the constraining resource, fabrication is the key variable for assigning cost to products.
>
> Each process sequence (EPROM, Logic, or DRAM) is assigned a total amount of manufacturing activity based on the number of steps it requires. Total company manufacturing costs are then allocated to products on the basis of manufacturing activity. For each product, the overall yield (number of good die at final test versus total number of die on starting wafer) is applied as a divisor to the process cost to arrive at a total cost per good part. The sales price per part is then used to calculate margin per part, and margin per activity (see Exhibit 8).

According to Reed, sometimes the numbers told a compelling story about the DRAM business. The difference between margin/activity for DRAMs and for the highest margin products could be an order of magnitude. Ron Whittier, general manager of the Memory Components Division from 1975 until 1983, felt that the system for plant allocation was a very good one:

> Some companies really went too far by selling capacity to the highest bidder within the company. At Intel, a minimum production allocation would be assigned based on how much we needed to produce to maintain our long-term market position. Basically, we used our independent distributors as buffers. In times when DRAM production was pressured by other products, we tapered sales to independent distributors while maintaining sales to large account customers.

Grove commented that since the distributors never accounted for more than 20–30 percent of Intel's DRAM business, they could not really account for the levelling in Intel's DRAM sales (see Exhibit 4).

Whittier also noted that DRAMs had at one time been the single largest product line and thus could not easily be entirely displaced by other products unless total capacity was decreased. The finance group thought of DRAMs as a "low ROI, high beta" product line. Bob Reed insisted that the DRAM manager sign a symbolic check equal to the margin foregone whenever high margin products were bumped by DRAMs.

Ed Gelbach explained why Intel had stayed with the DRAM even though it looked less profitable than other products:

> I was in favor of keeping DRAMs from a marketing strategy standpoint. A full line supplier has a basic advantage in any sales situation. When you're competing with full-line suppliers, it helps to be able to offer a comparable line. Since customers often pay particular attention to their highest dollar volume vendor, it also pays to offer the commodity product since it is generally purchased in high volume. A more subtle reason boils down to reputation. Intel had been known to drop unprofitable products, sometimes leaving customers high and dry.
>
> In board meetings, the question of DRAMs would often come up. I would support them from a market perspective, and Gordon [Moore] would support them because they were our technology driver. Andy [Grove] kept quiet on the subject. Even though it wasn't profitable, the board agreed to stay in it on the face of our arguments.

Environmental Forces

Bob Reed realized the entire U.S. semiconductor industry was in trouble even during the boom year of 1984.

> Even though ROS for the industry was relatively high in '84, asset turns were decreasing and ROA was low. The business had become too capital intensive. An astute observer could see that the U.S. industry as configured couldn't provide its investors with an adequate return when a new plant cost $150 million and took at least two years to build. Intel was virtually alone with a respectable ROE.

In 1985, the semiconductor industry was expected to enter into another in a series of cyclical downturns, which seemed to occur every 5 years. The cause of the cyclical recessions was a classic case of oversupply and softening demand. Since 1980, a large amount of worldwide semiconductor fabrication capacity had been added, and learning curve effect (increase in yields, decrease in chip size, etc.) added another 30 percent per year to worldwide capacity.

In the previous recession, Intel had been one of a few companies not to cut back its production workforce. While Intel did not have a no-layoff policy, during the 1981–82 recession, Andy Grove had instituted the "125 percent solution." In that program all salaried employees were asked to work an additional 10 hours per week without additional compensation to accelerate product introductions. When the 1980 recession proved to be longer than expected, Intel instituted a 10 percent pay cut in addition to the 125 percent solution.

Intel had several groups of competitors (see Exhibit 9). The first were other U.S. full-line digital design and supply houses such as Motorola, National Semiconductor, and Texas Instruments (TI). Motorola had made the transition from a tube manufacturer in the 1950s to a diversified semiconductor and electronic systems manufacturer in the 1980s. It offered a full line of products competitive with Intel's, including DRAMs, microcontrollers and microprocessors, and was Intel's only serious challenger in microprocessor architecture. TI, while not renowned for its microprocessors, also had a complete product line, including a facility in Japan which was fabricating DRAMs.

The second category of competitor focused on process technology as opposed to design. That group was represented by AMD. While AMD produced a full line of component products, a significant portion was manufactured under license from Intel and others.

The third group included foreign competition, particularly Japanese. Japanese competitors included Hitachi, Fujitsu, NEC, Toshiba, and others. They had concentrated primarily on DRAM and SRAM products, although each also had a significant share of the EPROM market and served as second sources to U.S. microprocessor and microcontroller suppliers. Intel had second source agreements for its microprocessor line with Fujitsu and NEC.

Several U.S. DRAM makers had accused Japanese manufacturers of dumping DRAMs at prices below cost throughout the early 1980s.

Industry observers saw that Japanese firms under the direction of MITI had targeted semiconductors as a strategic industry and were investing for the long term. In the years between 1980 and 1984, U.S. firms invested a total of 22 percent of sales in new plant and equipment while Japanese firms invested 40 percent. The result was that by 1983, Japanese total investment in semiconductors exceeded U.S. investment. Production yields of Japanese semiconductor companies exceeded those of U.S. producers by as much as 40 percent.[17]

DRAMs were not the only product under siege by the Japanese. *The Wall Street Journal* published a story in June of 1984 that reported on a memo sent by Hitachi to its U.S. EPROM distributors. The memo said: "quote 10 percent below their price; if they requote, go 10% again; don't quit until you win."[18]

Intel had been wary of Japanese semiconductor companies for some time and had sued NEC in 1982 when it alleged NEC copied its 8086 product without license. Peter Stoll, an 8086 designer at Intel realized his chip had been copied when he discovered that NEC's 16-bit microprocessor had two transistors that were disconnected from the rest of the circuit at exactly the same place where he had disconnected them in a late revision of the Intel mask set.[19] This was considered evidence that NEC copied the chip without even understanding its design.

Bob Reed emphasized the importance of Intel's ability to protect its intellectual property:

> If our primary value added is in our design capability, we've got to protect that with vigilance. We have a strict policy of pursuing anyone or any company that appropriates our intellectual property—design or process.

In this highly competitve environment, managers at Intel and other companies often had to consider the problem of spin-off companies. Key engineers had sometimes left Intel to form their own companies with venture capital help. Their departure would stall research at a minimum, and according to Gordon Moore, could be seen as diluting the U.S. industry's ability to compete. Spin-offs were sometimes accused of taking technology with them.[20]

---

[17]"While the best U.S. companies obtained yields of 50–60%, the best Japanese were getting 80–90%," from Prestowitz, Clyde, *Trading Places,* 1988, p. 46.

[18]*The Wall Street Journal,* 6/5/85.

[19]Prestowitz, Clyde, *Trading Places,* 1988, p. 48.

[20]Intel had sued SEEQ for taking a technology for Electrically Erasable PROMS (EEPROMs). Excel, a spin-off from SEEQ was later sued by SEEQ. Note: Intel continued to pursue its own EEPROM process, but eventually decided not to participate in that market because it was too small. A second engineering team left Intel on friendly terms to found Xicor. In 1985, Xicor and Intel were negotiating a joint research project.

Dram Situation in 1984

Loss of Leadership Position

By the end of 1984, Intel had lost significant market share in DRAMs (see Exhibits 4 and 9). The first real difficulties had come with the 64K generation. In 1980, Intel's 5-volt 16K DRAM was still a market success due to process innovations, and work was continuing on the 64K generation. DRAMs traditionally led the company in new technology development, and the 64K DRAM was no exception.

Ron Whittier said that to make the 64K version, the memory cell size was reduced, but the actual die size still had to be increased significantly. The DRAM group calculated that given current defect levels in manufacturing, the required die size would be too big. Based on the number of defects per square centimeter normally experienced in fabrication, the projected yield on the 64K DRAM would be too low to be acceptable. In order to boost yield, the group decided to build in redundancy at the chip level.

Whittier described the redundancy technology:

> Essentially, you have a row and column addressing system on a memory chip. The periphery of the chip contains logic and refresh circuitry necessary to control and update the DRAM. In the 64K version, Intel added an extra column of memory elements so that in the event of a process-induced defect, the auxiliary column could be activated. There was a physical switch or "fuse" built in to each column which could be addressed by the tester machinery. When a bad element was detected, current would be passed through the switch and would blow a "fuse," inactivating the defective column and kicking in the auxiliary column. In this fashion, a defective memory chip could be "reprogrammed" before shipment, and overall yield could be improved.

Dean Toombs, general manager of the Memory Components Division after 1983, had worked on DRAMs at Texas Instruments (TI) before coming to Intel. Toombs said the discussion on redundancy was industry-wide. At TI, engineers had concluded that at the 64K generation redundancy would not be economical and had deferred the discussion until the next generation. For the 64K generation, TI ultimately chose to focus on reducing the defect level in manufacturing.

Intel's redundancy program started out successfully. Two 64K DRAM projects were carried out in tandem, one nonredundant and the other redundant. Prior to production

commitment, the redundant design was a clear winner, with yields over twice that of the nonredundant design.

Success quickly turned to failure as a subtle but fatal defect in the redundant technology showed up late in development. The fuse technology was less than perfect. The polysilicon fuse would "blow" during testing as designed, but a mysterious regrowth phenomenon was detected during accelerated aging tests. Sun Lin Chou commented:

> The failing fuse problem was simply a case of not having done enough engineering early on. We just didn't fully characterize the process technology and the fusing mechanism.

The result was that the switch eliminating the defective column of memory cells was not permanent. In some cases, the device would revert to its original configuration after being in the field for some time—meaning the defective cell would again become a part of the memory. Errors would occur in which the device alternated randomly between the two states, meaning that at any given time the location of data stored in the memory became uncertain. In either case, the failures were not acceptable, and Intel could not develop a quick fix.

In the meantime, Japanese competitors were throwing capacity at 64K DRAMs and improving the underlying defect density problem, which Intel's redundancy program had meant to address. Between July, 1981, and August, 1982, Japanese capacity for 64K DRAM production increased from 9 million to 66 million devices per year.[21] Whittier took a one-week trip to see Intel sales engineers[22] and explain that Intel's 64K DRAM would be late:

> The sales force was very disappointed in the company's performance. Any sales force wants a commodity line. It's an easy sell and sometimes it's a big sell. That trip was perhaps the most difficult time in my whole career. When I announced we would be late with the product, the implication was that Intel would not be a factor in the 64K generation.

While the development team eventually fixed the fuse problem and was the first to introduce a redundant 64K DRAM, the 2164, its introduction was too late to achieve significant market penetration.

---

[21]Prestowitz, Clyde, *Trading Places,* 1988, p. 44.

[22]Intel sales engineers sold Intel's entire product line, but were supported by applications engineers in a ratio of one engineer to every two sales representatives.

EXHIBIT 9 | Selected Competitor Data for 1984

FY 1984 (in $MM)	Intel	Nat'l Semi.	Texas Inst.	Adv. Micro Devices	Motorola	Hitachi	Toshiba	NEC	Fujitsu
Semiconductor Sales	1,201	1,213	2,484	515	2,319	2,051	1,516	2,251	1,190
Total Sales	1,629	1,655	5,741	583	5,534	18,528	11,003	7,476	5,401
COGS	883	1,146	4,190	276	3,206	13,632	8,182	5,117	3,346
R&D	180	158	367	101	411	898	597	391	(incl.)
SG&A	315	247	491	108	1,064	3,367	2,758	1,443	1,453
Other	(48)	1	168		387		(1,106)	673	335
Profit	299	103	525	98	466	631	572	367	523
Profit After Tax	198	64	316	71	387	709	250	189	297
Depreciation	113	115	422	43	353		627		374
Capital Expenditure	388	278	705	129	783		1,192	883	747
Total Assets	2,029	1,156	3,423	512	4,194	7,997			5,699
LT Debt	146	24	380	27	531	1,379	1,830	1,524	915
Total Equity	1,360	619	1,540	278	2,278	6,118	2,191	1,728	1,935

Semiconductor Market Share in 1984	Bipolar Digital	EPROM	DRAM and SRAM	MOS Micro-component	MOS Logic	Linear	Discrete	Opto-electronic	Total ($MM)
AMD	5.4%	10.5%	0.5%	1.8%	0.1%	0.4%			515
Fairchild	8.6%		0.1%	0.5%	0.7%	2.9%	1.3%	0.3%	665
Fujitsu	6.4%	11.1%	7.8%	3.7%	3.0%	0.8%	0.8%	4.3%	1,190
Hitachi	4.7%	17.4%	15.1%	3.7%	2.2%	3.7%	8.6%	4.3%	2,051
Intel	0.7%	16.0%	3.4%	23.0%	1.2%				1,201
Mitsubishi	2.6%	13.3%	4.0%	4.8%	0.4%	2.1%	3.7%	1.1%	964
Mostek			7.1%	1.7%	1.8%				467
Motorola	9.5%	1.1%	6.1%	9.0%	10.4%	5.5%	12.2%	1.6%	2,319
National	6.1%	4.2%	1.1%	3.6%	5.9%	8.9%	0.9%	1.2%	1,213
NEC	2.6%	5.8%	13.0%	12.7%	8.3%	5.9%	7.6%	2.8%	2,251
Philips	12.3%		0.7%	3.2%	3.7%	4.8%	4.4%	1.5%	1,325
TI	22.5%	10.5%	10.8%	3.6%	2.9%	8.4%	1.2%	4.1%	2,484
Toshiba	0.8%	3.6%	7.1%	2.2%	8.7%	4.7%	8.4%	8.8%	1,516
Others	14.4%	6.5%	21.3%	21.9%	50.3%	51.8%	50.9%	70.1%	10,900
Total Market ($MM)	4,783	1,319	4,906	3,229	3,493	4,888	4,986	1,221	29,061

MOS Microcomponent: microprocessors, peripherals, and microcontrollers

MOS Logic: gate arrays, custom logic, application-specific IC's

Linear: operational amplifiers, comparators, and other analog devices

Discrete: single transistors, diodes, and thyristors

Optoelectronic: LEDs, semiconductor lasers, and solar cells

Source: Dataquest and Annual Reports.

Attempts to Regain Leadership Position

Having assessed that they were behind in the 64K DRAM product generation, the DRAM group took another gamble. The development effort was shifted from NMOS to CMOS. The advantage of CMOS circuitry was lower power consumption and faster access time. Intel defined a set of targeted applications[23] for the CMOS DRAM technology. Whittier's strategy was to introduce the CMOS 64K and 256K DRAMs in 1984.

---

[23]One such application was laptop computers, which place a premium on low power consumption chips.

The notion was that by creating a niche market with premium pricing, Intel could maintain a presence in the DRAM market while accelerating forward into a leadership position at the 1-Meg generation.

Dean Toombs said that by the time he took over the Memory Components Division in 1983, things were "clicking along." Demand was in an upswing, and Intel seemed to have a technology strategy that could lead to dominance in the 1-Meg DRAM market. Many of the 2164 sales in 1983 went to IBM, and in addition Intel sold IBM the 2164 production and design technology. Toombs recalled that in late 1983 and early 1984, the silicon cycle was on an upswing and memory product demand was at an all-time high. The memory components division's bookings exceeded its billings.

During the boom of late 1983 and early 1984, all of Intel's factories were running at capacity. Allocation of production capacity between products was necessary. The question facing the memory components division was how to effect the transition from NMOS to CMOS. Toombs said the "hard decision" was made to completely phase out the NMOS line. All DRAM fabrication was consolidated in Oregon's Fab 5. Toombs suggested that the decision to "go CMOS" was consistent with Intel's general philosophy: to exploit new technology and create a lead against competitors based on proprietary knowledge.

The development of the CMOS 64K and 256K DRAMs took place in a facility adjacent to the Oregon production facility. While the development was not on the production line, there was a fairly smooth transition into manufacturing. The CMOS technology was more complex, requiring 11–12 masking steps versus 8–9 steps for NMOS. This resulted in a higher manufacturing cost for the CMOS process (see Exhibit 8).

The CMOS DRAM products were introduced in 1984 and priced at about 1.5 to 2 times the prevailing NMOS price. Intel management developed a niche strategy: Differentiate the product from other offerings and sell it on features. In addition to the CMOS feature, Intel offered an alternative memory organization that provided performance advantages in some applications. Intel sampled the products broadly to many customers and made many "design wins," particularly in situations where other DRAMs had inadequate performance. The 256K chip was well designed and executed. Sun Lin Chou commented:

> The 256K CMOS DRAM was the first DRAM product which did not have to go through some sort of design or process revision before or after going to market. With

this product, we felt we were regaining our lead in DRAM technology after three generations.

The CMOS DRAMs started as a winning product family. Unfortunately, the market softened as 1984 went along. The price of NMOS DRAMs fell by 40 percent in one three-month period from May to August, 1984. In the scramble and upheaval of the semiconductor market, Toombs said that Intel's differentiation message got lost. All suppliers were pushing product into the market, and Intel's superior product specifications seemed like just another ploy to get volume.

By late 1984, Intel's ability to make profits, and, more importantly, to project future profits in DRAMs was limited. Said Toombs: "In a commodity marketplace, your staying power is a function of the size of your manufacturing base." According to Toombs, by late 1984, Intel was down to less than 4 percent of the 256K DRAM market and had lost its position entirely in 64K DRAMs.

On the other hand, the technical strategy seemed to work, since the first prototype of the 1-Meg DRAM was expected in March 1985. However, as Sun Lin Chou indicated, Intel's technology strategy for the 1 meg had been different from that of previous generations:

> Our advanced capability in thin dielectric has allowed us to focus on reducing the minimum feature size to one micron instead of changing the entire cell design. Some memory leaders have chosen to scrap the traditional capacitor design, and are trying to move to a smaller "trench" capacitor, which requires an entirely new generation of equipment and processing. While they are still at 1.2 to 1.5 microns, we've pushed the photolithography technology further. We may have to go to the trench capacitor in the next generation [4 megabit], but by then we will be able to take advantage of their learning.

Toombs believed that the DRAM technology development group had provided Intel with a unique product capability:

> The 1-Meg DRAM will be a technically outstanding product, at least one and a half to two years ahead of any competition in application of CMOS. But the handwriting is on the wall. In order to make the DRAM business go, major capital investment is required and the payback just isn't there. The issue for 1985 is how to survive.

Jack Carsten believed it was critical for Intel to stay in the DRAM business. But in case the company was no longer willing to dedicate facilities to DRAMs, he felt a technology transfer deal should be made with a Korean chip manufacturer:

> The play I am proposing is to stop manufacture of the DRAMs, and to form an alliance with a large Korean company who has state-of-the-art capacity installed. We now have a functional 1-Meg DRAM. Basically, Intel could support the business through an R&D alliance and be the technology leader.

To be fair, you have to realize that the Koreans have state-of-the-art equipment,[24] but are not yet expert at using it. In order to make the technology transfer work, we would have to transfer 20 or so of our crack engineers to teach the Koreans how to make the 1 MB DRAM. Apart from the technology risk, there is the risk that we would create a new competitor. History is rife with examples of how technology transfers have backfired, and we've certainly been burned before. But, maybe there's some truth to the logic that the enemy of your enemy is your friend.

---

[24]Note: In February of 1985, Intel was to enter into an agreement with a Korean firm to transfer technology for two Intel parts. The technology had been developed at Intel to introduce the 8048 microcontroller (same generation as 8085 microprocessor) and the 2764 EPROM (see Exhibit 3 for time line). While those processes required 3- to 4-micron geometries, the 1-Meg DRAM product required 1-micron geometries. The Korean company had annual semiconductor sales of about $10 MM in 1984.

Options for DRAM

Grove could see several distinct options for the DRAM business: (1) drop it altogether; (2) stay in the business as a niche player; (3) license the technology to another company; or, (4) invest in DRAM capability at the 1 MB level and commit to a low-margin business.

As he reflected on the situation, he thought about how Intel had arrived at its current position:

> At the 16K level, we were leading in both EPROM and DRAM products, but capacity was tight. We reduced our committment to DRAMs in what was in effect a capital appropriations decision. Margins and customer dependence were both important in causing us to shift our focus to EPROMs.
>
> Then came the lackluster 64K design. We stumbled and it was a burning embarassment. Our market position was at 2–3 percent. You just can't win like that.
>
> Gordon [Moore] is probably right when he says the only difference between DRAMs and EPROMs is that EPROMs never missed a turn. If you miss a turn, the game is over.
>
> The bright side is that we might have lost a lot more if our 64K generation had been a success. Texas Instruments is probably losing more than five times what we are.
>
> We have been trying to find a clever way to stay in this business without betting everything we have, but maybe there is none.
>
> The key question is should we really commit to being a leader? Can we be? What is the cost if we try? What is the cost if we don't?

Technical Appendix

Access   In this context, access refers to the circuitry that allows the dynamic RAM user to read and write to specific locations of memory. Access time is a critical performance feature of DRAMs and refers to the amount of time it takes to read or write a bit of memory. Often DRAMs offer two different access modes, one that is bit by bit, and one that writes or reads large amounts of data. The bit-by-bit rate is typically slower.

Bus   Bus refers to the communication "backbone" of the microprocessor. An 8-bit bus can transfer 8 bits of data at a time between the microprocessor and the outside world (memory or other peripherals). The 8-bit-bus version of the 8086 actually has a 16-bit internal bus. Each cycle within the chip can handle two cycles of data input.

Bipolar   Bipolar refers to a generic type of transistor and to the family of processes used to make it. The bipolar transistor consumes more power than the MOS transistor, but can be made to switch faster. Excessive power consumption limits the density of bipolar products. The bipolar process is a relatively complex semiconductor process.

Capacitor   A capacitor is a circuit element (transistors, resistors, capacitors) that consists of two metal-like layers separated by a thin insulating film. In a typical integrated circuit the silicon substrate (wafer) acts as the first metal-like layer. The silicon surface is oxidized to form the insulating layer (silicon dioxide) and then a polysilicon layer is deposited over the oxide to form the second metal-like layer. In the context of DRAMs, the capacitor acts as an information storage device. When a positive charge is placed on one surface of a capacitor, a negative charge is induced on the opposite surface. The capacitor "holds the charge" for a limited period of time, and the presence of the charge indicates the a "bit" of information. The ability of the capacitor to store charge is related to its area and the thickness of the insulating film. The thinner the insulator and the larger the surface area, the more charge a capacitor can store. (See trench etched capacitor for more information.)

Chip   Chip refers to the actual integrated circuit which is cut from the wafer after fabrication. Typical chips are 100–400 mils on a side and can contain several hundred thousand transistors. The chip is put into a package where microscopic wires are attached to the die and brought out of the package in larger pins that can be soldered into a printed circuit board.

Class 10 production facility   Semiconductor fabrication plants are perhaps the cleanest areas ever created by man. Airborne particulates such as dandruff, pollen, and other forms of dust are a major source of semiconductor manufacturing yield problems. One particle of dust settled on a silicon wafer is enough to ruin an entire chip. The "class" of a facility refers to the amount of particulate in the air. Class X means that one cubic foot of air on average will contain X or less particles. A class 10 fabrication facility is designed with advanced air filtering designed to eliminate turbulance. Operators wear specialized clothing and enter clean rooms only through air showers that remove contamination. To give a sense of the cleanliness, a typical hospital operating room is between class 1,000 and 10,000.

Complementary MOS (CMOS)   CMOS refers to a semiconductor process that can produce a specific configuration of transistors which include both NMOS and PMOS devices. A group of six transistors fabricated in CMOS form the fundamental building block for Intel's latest generation of logic circuitry. The six-transistor cell is a bistable cell that is either in the "on" or "off" state. CMOS has the advantage of very low power consumption, since none of the transistors ever draw current except during the time when the six-transistor cell changes states from on to off. Laptop computers use exclusively CMOS integrated circuits.

Die   See chip.

Dielectrics   Dielectrics are insulating materials. In semiconductor processing they include silicon dioxide, silicon nitride, silicon oxynitride, and others. Dielectrics are used in several areas of integrated circuits. In DRAMs they are used for storage capacitors. In MOS transistors, they form the gate insulator.

Double metalization   Until the 80386, all of Intel's circuits employed only one layer of metalization. The design of logic circuitry (where interconnection between groups of transistors appears to be random) is greatly simplified by adding a second layer of metal. Although the processing sequence is complicated, double layer metalization allows chip size to be reduced.

Dynamic random access memory (DRAM)   A variety of RAM that maximizes utilization of silicon "real estate" and minimizes power consumption per storage bit. Each "bit" of information is stored as a charge on a capacitor driven by one transistor. Since the charge dissipates rapidly even when power is constantly supplied to the device, the information within each memory location must be rewritten (refreshed) hundreds of times a second. While the "refresh" function was originally taken care of by external circuitry, the latest DRAM chips have "onboard" refresh circuitry. DRAMS are available in 8K, 16K, 64K, 256K, and most recently in 1Meg sizes. K stands for Kilobit and refers to the chip's storage capacity. See kilobit definition.

Electrically eraseable programable read only memory (EEPROM)   A variety of ROM that can be erased and programmed at the user's factory. The device is similar to the EPROM except it can be erased electrically (without ultraviolet light).

Electrically programable read only memory (EPROM)   A variety of ROM that can be erased and programmed at the user's factory. The classical EPROM comes with a quartz window in its package so that ultraviolet light can be used to erase its contents. Then each memory location can be programmed to permanently contain desired information. In applications where low volume or time constraints prevent the fabrication of a custom ROM, or where the user may intend to make future modifications to his "nonvolatile" memory, EPROM devices are used. Sometimes EPROMs are supplied without quartz windows (cheaper). Since ultraviolet light cannot get in to erase these devices, they are programmable only once.

Floating gate   The floating gate is the structure in an EPROM device that allows a memory cell to be programmed and later erased. The floating gate can be charged by applying a relatively high voltage to the region surrounding it. Electrical traps in the floating gate store electrons that reach the floating gate. The trapped electrons can be sensed by surrounding structures. When ultraviolet light is directed at the floating gate, the light has sufficient energy to excite the trapped electrons out of the floating gate, and the memory is erased. See EPROM definition.

Gallium arsenide   A semiconductor material with properties considered by many to be superior to silicon's. The fastest switching transistors are made with gallium arsenide. Difficulty and expense in device fabrication as well as constant silicon device improvement, have led to a relatively small market for gallium arsenide products.

Gate oxide   The gate oxide is a critical part of the MOS transistor that is typically formed by oxidizing the surface of a silicon wafer (to make silicon dioxide) in a high temperature (1,000°C) furnace. The gate itself is typically formed out of a deposited layer of polycrystalline silicon. See definitions for threshhold drift and MOS.

HMOS   An Intel acronym standing for high performance MOS. HMOS is an NMOS process, with small geometries. See NMOS definition.

Kilobit (1K) 2^{10} or 1024 bits. Each DRAM generation has four times as much capacity as its predecessor. Since computers operate in binary code, the actual memory contents are multiples of 2. Thus the 1K generation has 2^{10} bits, the 4K generation has 2^{12} bits, the 16K generation has 2^{14} bits, the 64K generation has 2^{16} bits, and so on.

Magnetic core   A form of random access computer memory utilizing ferrite cores to store information. This technology was made obsolete by silicon devices.

Megabit (1MB) 2^{20} or 1,048,576 bits. See definitions for kilobit and DRAM.

Metal oxide semiconductor (MOS)   MOS refers to a generic type of transistor (see definition of transistor) and to the family of processes used to maket it. The switch in an MOS transistor is caused by the action of the metal (or polycrystalline silicon) gate on the "channel." MOS transistors come in two polarities: n-channel (NMOS) or p-channel (PMOS). To turn on a p-channel device, a negative voltage is put on the gate. The charge on the gate induces an opposite charge in the channel that completes the circuit between the source and the drain. When the voltage is removed, the channel no longer conducts. The n-channel device turns on with a positive voltage applied to the gate. The MOS process typically requires fewer processing steps than the bipolar process. The turn-on speed of MOS devices is controlled by fundamental physics (the mobility of electrons and positive charges in silicon) and the geometry of the device (as devices get smaller, they get faster).

Microcontroller   A microchip that integrated logic and memory functions.

Multiplexing   Multiplexing is a generic term used in many areas of electronics. In the case of the 4K and later DRAM generations, multiplexing refers to a scheme adopted to economize on the number of output pins required to address each memory location. Instead of using one pin for each column and each row in the matrix of memory cells, multiplexing allows the 4K memory to be addressed with just 12 pins (it contains 2^{12} bits).

Multitasking   Multitasking in this context refers to a microprocessor's ability to manage more than one task simultaneously. Multitasking is not simply a software feature. The ability to employ multitasking is embedded in the chip's architecture.

NMOS   See MOS. Several generations of logic were built on NMOS circuitry. A cell of six NMOS transistors replaced Intel's traditional PMOS logic family. NMOS transistors are faster than PMOS devices due to fundamental physical properties.

Plasma etching   Plasma etching is a process that is used to define patterns on the silicon wafer during the fabrication process. Until the early 1980s, all etching was done with wet chemicals. Plasma etching improves control and line width accuracy. It takes place in a partial vacuum chamber. Gaseous chemicals are introduced into the wafer chamber and ionized using radio frequency power. The ionic species selectively etch different materials used to build the integrated circuit. Plasma chemistry is a new discipline that has been brought to bear on semiconductor processing in order to achieve smaller line widths and better etching control.

Polycrystalline silicon (poly, polysilicon)   is a material that can be used as a conductor. In the wafer fabrication process, polycrystalline silicon is deposited on the wafer surface (usually in a low-pressure, high-temperature process) and etched in patterns to form connections between transistors. It is also used to form the "gate" structure of a transistor (the gate turns the transistor on or off), the "floating gate" of an EPROM cell (which stores the state of the EPROM cell), and one side of the storage capacitor that makes up a DRAM cell. Its main advantage as a material in processing is that it serves as a conductor while also being able to withstand high-temperature processing. While other conductive materials (such as aluminum) cannot withstand the high temperatures required by wafer processing and must be applied only at the end of the process, poly can be applied in the middle of the process and subsequently be covered by other layers.

Polysilicon resistor   By varying the conditions under which polysilicon is deposited on a wafer, lines of polysilicon can be used to form resistor elements. The poly resistor process was difficult for Intel to execute.

Random access memory (RAM)   (formerly called direct access memory). Family of information storage devices in which specific memory locations can be accessed (to retrieve or store information) in any sequence. This is distinct from "sequential access memory" in which data must be retrieved or stored in a specific order or sequence (example: magnetic tape memory, CCD memory, bubble memory). RAM is usually "volatile" memory. Thus a constant power supply is required in order to retain stored information. Several processing technologies have been used to produce the two generic varieties of RAM, DRAM and SRAM.

Read only memory (ROM)   A variety of memory that contains a fixed set of information that cannot be altered, often referred to as "nonvolatile" memory. Within a typical computer system, ROM contains a sequence of data that has been embedded in the chip at the factory. Thus ROM chips are custom made for each application. Only one masking layer in a 10-layer fabrication process needs to be altered to change the information stored in a ROM.

Refresh   Since a dynamic RAM will hold data only for a fraction of a second before it is lost (the charge on the capacitor holds only for a fraction of a second before it leaks away), a useful DRAM must contain circuitry that can continually read and update the contents of each memory location. This circuitry is referred to as refresh circuitry.

Scaling improvements   Scaling improvements refer to the general process of decreasing line widths in integrated circuits. In the early 80s, Intel's static/logic group focused on taking existing products and shrinking them to improve yield and increase manufacturing capacity. Devices would be shrunk proportionally (nearly), so that chip design would not have to be changed significantly.

Shift registers   Shift registers are a common type of sequential access memory used in computer systems to manipulate strings of data.

Static random access memory (SRAM)   SRAM is a RAM memory device that does not require refreshing as long as power is constantly applied. Each memory cell includes either four transistors and two resistors or six transistors. In comparison with DRAMs, fewer memory cells can be packed into the same area. SRAM memory can be made with faster access times than DRAM. The process for SRAM more closely resembles the process for logic devices. As a result, the on-chip memory contained in microprocessors is often SRAM.

Stepper alignment   The latest generation of photolithography processing is carried out on stepper aligners. The photolithography step has two key goals: to align the current mask layer to all previous layers and to transfer the narrowest possible line widths to the wafer. With traditional projection alignment, the pattern for the entire wafer is exposed at the same time. As wafer diameters increase and minimum geometries decrease, the alignment task becomes more difficult. The slightest thermal expansion or warpage will cause the devices on the edge of the wafer to be misaligned even when those in the center are aligned. Stepper aligners expose patterns across the wafer in several steps so that the "run off" at the wafer edges can be minimized. At each step, the mask and the wafer are realigned. Stepper aligners are very sophisticated optical and mechanical devices, costing upwards of $1 million per unit.

Threshold drift   Threshold drift refers to a phenomenon that causes the "turn-on" voltage of an MOS transistor to change over time. A certain critical voltage must be applied to the gate of an MOS transistor in order to turn it on. If the oxide insulator that separates the gate from the channel is not free of mobile ionic contamination, the threshold or turn-on voltage will drift or change over time making the device useless. One source of mobile ionic contamination is common table salt.

Transistor   First invented at Bell Labs in 1948, the transistor is a solid state device that can be thought of as an electrical switch. It is a three-terminal device: Voltage applied to one terminal opens and closes the circuit between the other two terminals. Transistors are the fundamental building block for electronic and logic circuitry. Configurations of transistors can execute logic functions. The first transistors replaced vacuum tubes and were fabricated one at a time by fusing three material layers together in a "sandwich" structure. Bob Noyce (Intel) and Jack Kilby (TI) invented the "planar transistor," which allows fabrication and interconnection of many transistors on one substrate. While many variations exist, two basic types of transistors dominate the current market: bipolar and MOS (or FET) transistors.

Trench etched capacitor   A traditional capacitor is formed on the surface of the silicon wafer (see capacitor definition) and occupies a significant portion of a DRAM cell's area. A trench etched capacitor conserves silicon surface area because it is oriented perpendicular to the wafer surface. Vertical trenches are formed using a relatively new technique called reactive ion etching in which the wafer is exposed to a plasma in a strong electric field. Some manufacturers have chosen to adopt the trench structure in order to produce the 1-Meg generation of DRAMs. (Note that another method of maintaining storage capacity while reducing area is to reduce the insulator thickness. This has been the traditional method, but has become more difficult in recent generations. Thin oxide capability is considered a key technological advantage. Current oxide (insulator) thicknesses are about 100 angstroms (one-hundred-millionth of a meter), considered to be near the limit of current manufacturing methods.)

Virtual memory addressing   This microprocessor feature allows the microprocessor to handle many users at the same time without confusing each user's tasks. More specifically, it refers to the microprocessor's ability to use its own protocol to keep track of memory locations regardless of the physical configuration of memory. For example, Intel's 80286 can assign up to one gigabyte of virtual memory addresses to different users. Those virtual memory addresses are then mapped into the physical memory addresses.

Wafer   A wafer is a slice of silicon that serves as the substrate for integrated circuits. Each wafer contains up to several thousand "chips." The first silicon wafers used in production were 2 inches in diameter. Most recently almost all of Intel's fabrication takes place on 6-inch-diameter wafers. In some processing steps such as diffusion, wafers are processed in batches of 25 to 50. Other processing steps such as photolithography take place on individual wafers, one at a time. As processing technology has become more and more complex and wafer size had increased, additional steps are carried out on individual wafers as opposed to batches.

Case 1.2

Intel Corporation in 1999[*]

"A common thread in all of Intel's success has been technology. Technology has tied it all together across the epochs."

—Gordon Moore, Chairman Emeritus, 1999

Introduction

By almost any measure, Intel Corporation has been among the most successful companies in history. According to *Time Magazine,* "the microchip has become—like the steam engine, electricity, and the assembly line—an advance that propels a new economy . . . Intel is the essential firm of the digital age."[1]

Since its founding in 1968, Intel's corporate strategy has driven, or in other cases adapted to, a rapidly changing technology and industry context. Intel's history can be divided into three prominent epochs: "Intel the Memory Company," which lasted from 1968 until about 1985; "Intel the Microprocessor Company," which lasted from about 1985 until today; and "Intel the Internet Building Block Company," which was beginning to unfold in 1999. The three epochs correspond, to a large extent, to the tenure of the company's top leaders. Robert Noyce and Gordon Moore, Intel's founders, directed the company during Epoch I. Gordon Moore and Andy Grove ran the company during Epoch II. And Andy Grove and Craig Barrett were leading the transformation to Epoch III. Exhibit 1 summarizes some of the key events in Intel's history.

Throughout its history, Intel's strategy has been centered on technological innovation and leadership. In Epoch I, Intel was a broad-based semiconductor supplier that primarily focused on developing and selling memory products. In Epoch II, Intel became a focused microprocessor company at the center of the PC revolution that eventually came to drive the PC industry. The transformation between Epoch I and II clearly changed Intel's substantive corporate strategy (from memory to microprocessor company), however the company's generic corporate strategy remained intact (differentiation through product leadership). The characteristics that make Intel's organization highly adaptive enabled it to successfully navigate from Epoch I to Epoch II.

As Intel entered Epoch III, the company faced several strategic management challenges: (1) exploiting opportunities in and addressing challenges to its core business, (2) pursuing new opportunities outside the core business, and (3) balancing the relative focus on (1) and (2) over time. A key issue Intel management has continually faced is identifying when a new opportunity or challenge is truly of epoch proportions.

Intel in 1999

In early 1998, Craig Barrett was named CEO of Intel and Andy Grove became chairman. In 1998, Intel's revenue grew 5 percent to $26.3 billion (after 20 percent growth in 1997), while net income fell 13 percent to $6.1 billion. Intel's gross margin percentage fell in '98 to 54 percent, from 60 percent in '97 and 56 percent in '96. Intel operations generated $9.2 billion in cash during 1998. In late 1998, Intel's market capitalization exceeded $200 billion for the first time. Exhibits 2–4 provide financial highlights of Intel Corporation for the period 1987–99. In the mid-1990s, according to *Forbes,* 80 percent of Intel's revenue, and almost all of its profits, came from microprocessors (see Exhibit 5[2]).

In 1999, Intel continued to aggressively pursue opportunities in the microprocessor business. At the same time, Intel top management questioned whether the company could sustain its record of outstanding revenue and profit growth without diversifying and developing new businesses.

Craig Barrett had strongly urged Intel's senior managers to think of their businesses in the context of the emerging Internet economy rather than the PC industry. In April 1999, Barrettt observed:

> The industry that we're in has changed. We made a transition from the 70s to the 80s from being an integrated circuit company to being a microprocessor company. Now we're transitioning to an Internet building block company. If you look at our mission statements, you'll see that they reflect this transition from being a microprocessor

---

[*]This case is an abbreviation of Robert A. Burgelman, Dennis L. Carter and Raymond S. Bamford "Intel Corporation: The Evolution of an Adaptive Organization," Stanford Business School case SM-65, July 1999. Copyright © 1999 by the Board of Trustees of the Leland Stanford Jr. University. All rights reserved. Third-party names and brands are the property of their respective owners. StrongArm is a registered trademark of ARM, Ltd.

[1]*Time Magazine,* December 29, 1997.

[2]Source: *Forbes,* May 3, 1999.

EXHIBIT 1 | Key Events in Intel's History

1968	•	Intel founded by Robert Noyce (CEO) and Gordon Moore (EVP)
1969	•	Intel introduces its first product, 3101 64-bit Schotky bipolar RAM
	•	Intel introduces the 1101, the world's first MOS static RAM
1970	•	Recession forces company to lay-off employees for the first time
	•	1103, world's first commercially successful DRAM, introduced
1971	•	Intel moves into its own building in Santa Clara
	•	Late List instituted
	•	1702, world's first EPROM, introduced
	•	Company goes public at $23.50 per share, raising $6.8 million
	•	4004, world's first microprocessor, introduced
1972	•	2102 1kB static RAM, company's first NMOS, introduced
	•	Company enters digital watch business, acquiring Microma
	•	8008, first 8-bit microprocessor, introduced
1973	•	Intellec 4-40 microprocessor development tool introduced
1974	•	8080 industry standard 8-bit microprocessor introduced
1975	•	Bob Noyce elected chairman of the board
	•	Gordon Moore elected president and CEO
1976	•	2147 static RAM, first HMOS product, introduced
	•	8085 8-bit microprocessor introduced
1977	•	Intel enters bubble memory business
1978	•	Intel phases out of the Microma digital watch business
	•	8086 industry-standard 16-bit microprocessor introduced
1979	•	Gordon Moore elected chairman of the board
	•	Bob Noyce elected vice chairman
	•	Andy Grove elected president and COO
	•	8088 industry standard 8-bit microprocessor introduced
	•	Bob Noyce awarded National Medal of Science by President Jimmy Carter
1980	•	Intel introduces the first math coprocessor, the 8087
1981	•	iAPX 432 microprocessor introduced
	•	Intel's sabbatical program begins in the U.S.
	•	IBM announces its first PC, based on Intel's 8088 microprocessor
	•	Intel's "125% solution" launched
1982	•	80186/80188 16-bit embedded processors introduced
	•	80286 16-bit microprocessor introduced
	•	First LAN coprocessor, the 82586, introduced
	•	*Wall Street Transcript* names Gordon Moore the outstanding CEO for the semiconductor industry the second year in a row
	•	IBM announces plans to purchase 12% of Intel for $250 million
1983	•	Intel imposes pay freeze/salary cuts in face of poor business conditions
1984	•	Gordon Moore and Bob Noyce named to IEEE Hall of Fame
	•	IBM announces PC AT based on Intel's 80286 processor
1985	•	Intel announces first layoffs in 10 years
	•	Intel/AMD/National Semiconductor file joint antidumping petition with U.S. government against Japanese EPROM manufacturers
	•	Intel decides to quit the DRAM business
	•	Intel 386 CPU introduced
	•	Bob Noyce inducted into National Inventors Hall of Fame

(continued)

EXHIBIT 1 | Key Events in Intel's History (cont.)

1986	•	Court rules that microcode can be copyrighted and that Intel's copyright is valid, in response to lawsuit brought by NEC
1987	•	Andy Grove elected CEO
	•	Bob Noyce receives National Medal of Technology from President Ronald Reagan
	•	Intel launches Knockout campaign
	•	IBM sells the last of its shares of Intel stock
1988	•	Employee cash bonus announced
	•	Late List ends
1989	•	i860 processor introduced
	•	Intel 486 processor introduced
	•	i960 CA processor introduced for embedded applications
1990	•	Craig Barrett becomes executive vice president of Intel
	•	Bob Noyce dies
	•	Gordon Moore receives the National Medal of Technology from President George Bush
1991	•	Intel announces it will exit EPROMs in favor of flash memory
	•	Intel launches Intel Inside® program
1992	•	Intel announces OverDrive processors
	•	Court rules that AMD does not have the right to copy any Intel microcode
1993	•	Craig Barrett named COO
	•	Intel introduces Pentium processor
1994	•	Intel introduces ProShare videoconferencing systems
	•	A mathematics professor discovers Pentium processor bug, leading to the Pentium processor flaw crisis
1995	•	Intel introduces Pentium Pro processor
1996	•	Oracle, Sun, and IBM announce the network computer
1997	•	Intel introduces Pentium processor with MMX technology
	•	Intel introduces Pentium II processor
	•	Sub-$1000 PC market gains momentum
	•	Craig Barrett commissions a course on "Growing the Business" for the top 100 managers in the company
	•	Andy Grove selected as *Time Magazine's* "Man of the Year"
1998	•	Intel Celeron processor introduced
	•	Intel introduces Pentium II Xeon processor
	•	Craig Barrett elected CEO
	•	Andy Grove elected chairman of the board
	•	Gordon Moore elected chairman emeritus
1999	•	Intel introduces Pentium III and Pentium III Xeon processors
	•	Intel acquires Level One technologies for $2.2 billion
	•	Intel announces plans to launch Intel Data Services

company to being an Internet building block company. Every third word makes a reference to the Internet.

Intel's 10Q-Report of May 1999, for instance, stated: "Intel's goal is to be the leading supplier of building blocks to the connected computing industry worldwide."

At a meeting of Intel's top management in mid-1999, Barrett described Intel's strategy to become the building block supplier to the Internet economy by focusing on four areas: client platforms, networking infrastructure, server platforms, and solutions and services. Barrett said, "The world changes and the center of gravity shifts. We need to shift with it. We want to be the center of gravity in each of these four areas."

Of these four areas, Intel's core business already addressed client and server platforms. Additionally, by 1999, Intel's networking business had become much more prominent both from a financial and strategic perspective. And to address Internet solutions and services, Barrett had

EXHIBIT 2 | Intel Financial Highlights, Revenue and Profit

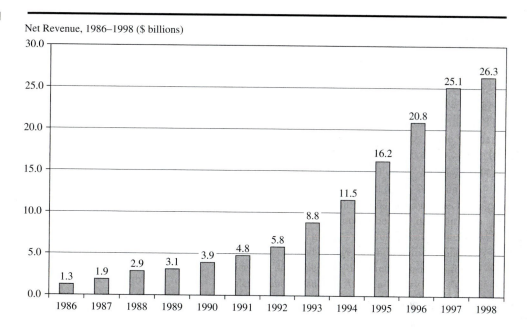

Net Revenue, 1986–1998 ($ billions)

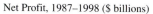

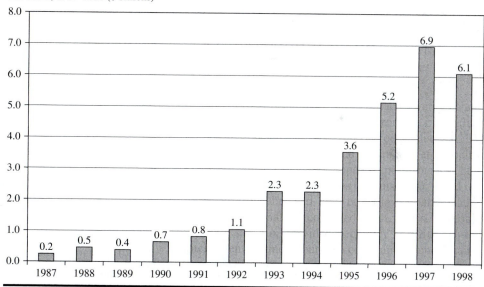

Net Profit, 1987–1998 ($ billions)

organized a new business group that would focus entirely on developing new businesses.

Reflecting on the strategic situation in 1999, Chairman Andy Grove said:

> Intel is undergoing an adaptation today that is a different version of the adaptation that occurred in the mid-80s. And it's almost as dramatic. The adaptation today is to the connected computer universe . . . It remains to be seen how well our senior management is tuned to that. I have

some concerns. We have a number of people that were very competent in the 2nd epoch of Intel. Right now the actions are not convincingly in tune with the new epoch.

Intel's Organization in 1999

In 1999, Intel was organized in a matrix structure that consisted of both product and functional groups. The product groups included the Intel Architecture Business Group, which had responsibility for Intel's industry-leading

EXHIBIT 3 | Intel Financial Highlights, R&D and Plant, Property, and Equipment

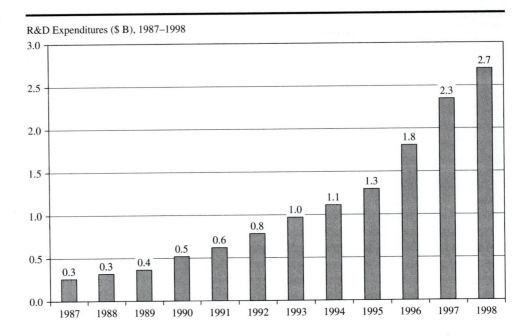

R&D Expenditures ($ B), 1987–1998

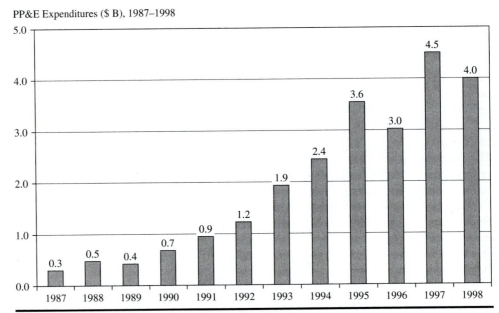

PP&E Expenditures ($ B), 1987–1998

microprocessor franchise; the Computing Enhancement Group, which produced chipsets, StrongARM processors, and flash memory products; the Network Communication Group, which developed products that provided network and Internet connectivity; and the New Business Group, which focused on growing opportunities in new and emerging market segments. The functional groups included Sales & Marketing Group (SMG), Corporate Business Development (CBD), Technology & Manufacturing Group (TMG), Microprocessor Products Group (MPG),[3] the finance group, and the legal group. Exhibit 6 shows Intel's organization chart

[3]Note: MPG performs the technical design and development for all of Intel's microprocessor groups.

EXHIBIT 4 | Intel Financial Highlights, Market Capitalization

($ billions, 1987–1999)

and Exhibit 7 lists Intel's officers. Intel's management ranks were deep, and 29 of the top 30 officers had been with the company for over 15 years.

In the third epoch, Intel's finance group continued to be a very strong part of the company's organization. The finance group was organized to mirror the operating groups, with most of the general managers or division heads having a dedicated controller as a counterpart. All finance personnel have a solid reporting line to Andy Bryant, CFO, and a dotted line to their respective operating groups. The finance group balanced the interests of shareholders, finance, and the operating groups. According to Andy Bryant,

> I tell the finance people that their first job is to look after shareholders, the second job is to look after finance, and their third job is to look after the operations. Their proximity to operations means that 80 % of the influence comes from the operations. I worry about the proximity overweighing their perspective . . . They should complement the skills of the GM, and . . . play a broker role. They have to be willing to tell me that I'm wrong, or that the GM is wrong. Always, they must look at what creates the best cash return to the company.

Key Strategic Challenges in the Core Business in 1999

In 1999, Intel was still the leading player in the microprocessor industry, and one of the most influential companies in the computer industry. However, the microprocessor business was becoming more segmented and its growth appeared to be slowing. Also, the Internet, rather than the PC, had become the driving force in high technology. Furthermore, there was a widely held belief frequently reported by the press that processor power was not important for Internet browsing. The combination of these

EXHIBIT 5 | Intel Revenue by Product Category, 1996

Microprocessors	$14.9 B
Chipsets	$1.4 B
Motherboards	$1.2–2.0 B
Networking	$1.0–2.0 B
Flash memory	$950 M
Embedded controllers	$530 M
Video conferencing	$33.5 M

Source: *Forbes,* May 3, 1999.

EXHIBIT 6 | Intel Organization Chart, 1999

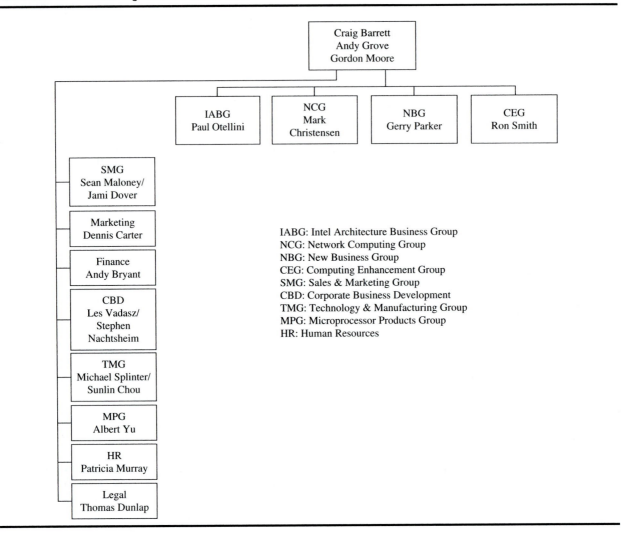

IABG: Intel Architecture Business Group
NCG: Network Computing Group
NBG: New Business Group
CEG: Computing Enhancement Group
SMG: Sales & Marketing Group
CBD: Corporate Business Development
TMG: Technology & Manufacturing Group
MPG: Microprocessor Products Group
HR: Human Resources

events could add up to a significant shift in the consumption of high-end processors.

The PC Market Segment By 1998, low-cost PCs had captured a significant percentage of consumer sales within the highly visible retail channel. Many of these machines initially used low-cost microprocessors from AMD and Cyrix. As a result, AMD's market segment share of Intel-based microprocessors grew from 6.7 percent to 16.1 percent between the fourth quarters of 1997 and 1998, while Cyrix's grew from 3.5 percent to 5.8 percent over the same period. Intel's overall market segment share dropped from 86.2 percent to 76.1 percent

during this period.[4] On the other hand, PC manufacturers such as Dell and Gateway who sold direct via the phone or the Internet continued to focus on high-end PC sales and were gaining market segment share away from the retail channel. Nonetheless, financial analysts reported that the growth of the low-end market was putting tremendous downward pressure on the average price of desktop microprocessors. Speaking to his class at Stanford Business School, Andy Grove said, "The 2nd law

[4]Source: Mercury Research, as quoted in *The Wall Street Journal*, 2/17/1999.

EXHIBIT 7 | Intel
Officers, 1999

Executive Officers:

Gordon E. Moore, Chairman Emeritus of the Board
Andrew S. Grove, Chairman of the Board
Craig R. Barrett, President and Chief Executive Officer

Corporate Officers:

Michael A. Aymar, Vice President and General Manager, Internet Data Services
Andy D. Bryant, Senior Vice President and Chief Financial Officer
Louis J. Burns, Vice President and General Manager, Platform Components Group
Dennis L. Carter, Vice President and Director, Strategic Marketing
Sunlin Chou, Vice President and General Manager, Technology and Manufacturing Group
Mark A. Christensen, Vice President and General Manager, Network Communications Group
F. Thomas Dunlap, Jr., Vice President, General Counsel and Secretary
Kirby A. Dyess, Vice President and Director, New Business Development
Carlene M. Ellis, Vice President and Director, Education
Patrick P. Gelsinger, Vice President and General Manager, Desktop Products Group
Hans G. Geyer, Vice President and General Manager, Flash Products Division
D. Craig Kinnie, Vice President and Director, Intel Architecture Labs
Sean M. Maloney, Senior Vice President and Director, Sales and Marketing Group
John H. F. Miner, Vice President and General Manager, Enterprise Server Group
Patricia Murray, Vice President and Director, Human Resources
Stephen P. Nachtsheim, Vice President and Dir. of Operations, Corporate Business
    Development
Paul S. Otellini, Executive Vice President and GM, Intel Architecture Business Group
Gerhard H. Parker, Executive Vice President and General Manager, New Business Group
Ronald J. Smith, Vice President and General Manager, Computing Enhancement Group
Stephen L. Smith, Vice President and General Manager, IA-64 Processor Division
Arvind Sodhani, Vice President and Treasurer
Michael R. Splinter, Senior Vice President and GM, Technology and Manufacturing Group
Leslie L. Vadasz, Senior Vice President and Director, Corporate Business Development
Ronald J. Whittier, Senior Vice President and General Manager, Intel Content Services
Albert Y.C. Yu, Senior Vice President and General Manager, Microprocessor Products Group

of thermodynamics, applied to the computer industry, is that everything gets commoditized eventually. Grove's Law is that the last one to get commoditized wins."

Many analysts were predicting that the PC was entering its twilight years. According to Paul Horn, senior VP of IBM Research,

> After more than 15 years as the center of the computing universe, the PC is about to give way to a new breed of . . . [specialized] devices that will dramatically change the way people communicate and share information.[5]

Other industry analysts expected annual PC sales to peak at around 100 million units, only slightly higher than 1999 levels.[6] Although it was a widely held belief that appliances would eventually replace PCs in at least some applications, there was not yet evidence of this happening. Exhibit 8 shows desktop PC unit shipments.

The Internet The Internet was causing revolutionary changes in the computing industry, and these changes presented both threats and opportunities to Intel. In 1999, the primary driver of PC sales was the demand

---

[5]"Low Cost PCs Forge New Mainstream," *CNET,* 1/21/1999.

[6]Source: SiliconValley.com, February 21, 1999.

EXHIBIT 8 | Desktop PC Market, Unit Shipments (000s of Units, By Price Range)

	Q1 1994	Q2 1994	Q3 1994	Q4 1994	Q1 1995	Q2 1995	Q3 1995	Q4 1995	Q1 1996	Q2 1996	Q3 1996	Q4 1996	Q1 1997	Q2 1997	Q3 1997	Q4 1997	Q1 1998	Q2 1998	Q3 1998	Q4 1998	Q1 1999
$3000+	7%	8%	8%	8%	6%	6%	7%	8%	7%	9%	11%	13%	14%	14%	7%	4%	2%	2%	2%	0%	0%
$2000–$2999	38%	32%	39%	39%	47%	54%	56%	60%	62%	64%	64%	66%	68%	41%	47%	41%	33%	33%	31%	13%	6%
$1000–$1999	51%	56%	50%	53%	47%	40%	37%	32%	28%	24%	22%	17%	17%	43%	46%	55%	63%	63%	65%	72%	76%
$0–$999	3%	3%	1%	1%	0%	1%	1%	0%	2%	3%	3%	3%	1%	1%	0%	1%	2%	2%	2%	15%	19%

Source: Dataquest, 4/99

for Internet connectivity. It was widely held that processor power was not important to a user's Internet experience, and this trend threatened to devalue desktop processing power. But there was a potential opportunity for Intel as well. The Internet caused more processing power to be needed in high-end servers that distributed content and processed online transactions, and this was a potential growth market for high-end Intel processors. According to Renee James, former technical assistant to Andy Grove,

> We have struggled for the last 2 years with how to make an impact on the Internet . . . This is one of Intel's biggest long-term strategic challenges. There has been a view that the Internet is happening without us.

Strategy and Action in the Core Business in 1999

Intel's core business consisted of both client platforms and server platforms. Intel's long-term strategy was to introduce ever higher performance microprocessors tailored for the different segments of the computing market. The company did so at a relentless pace. Between 1989 and 1997, Intel launched members of the 486 family, the Pentium processor family, the Pentium processor with MMX™ technology, and the Pentium II processor. (Exhibit 9 shows the evolution of Intel's microprocessors over time.) Moore's Law predicted that processor power would increase geometrically over time. This process had in the past resulted in tremendous improvements in the value delivered to PC users. For example, a Pentium® III

EXHIBIT 9 | The Evolution of Intel's Microprocessors

Processor	Date of Release	Clock Speed (MHz)	# Transistors (millions)	Typical Uses
4004	Nov 1971	0.108	0.002300	Busicom calculator
8008	Apr 1972	0.200	0.003500	Dumb terminals, bottling machines
8080	Apr 1974	2.0	0.006000	Traffic light controller, Altair PC
8085	Mar 1976	5.0	0.006500	Toledo scale
8086	Jun 1978	5.0–10.0	0.029000	Portable computing
8088	Jun 1979	5.0–8.0	0.029000	IBM PCs and clones
80286	Feb 1982	6.0–12.0	0.134000	PCs
386 DX	Oct 1985	16–33	0.275000	Desktop computing
386 SX	Jun 1988	16–33	0.275000	Entry level desktop & portable PCs
386 SL	Oct 1990	20–25	0.855000	Portable PCs
486 DX	Apr 1989	25–50	1.2	Desktop computing and servers
486 SX	Apr 1991	16–33	1.185	Entry level desktops
486 SL	Nov 1992	20–33	1.4	Notebook PCs
Pentium processor	Mar 1993 to Jun 1996	60–200	3.1–3.3	Desktops, notebooks, and servers
Pentium Pro processor	Nov 1995	150–200	5.5	High-end desktops, workstations and servers
Pentium processor with MMX technology	Jan 1997	166–233	4.5	High performance desktops & servers
Mobile Pentium proc. with MMX technology	Sep 1997	200–300	4.5	Mobile PCs and mini-notebooks
Pentium II processor	May 1997	233–450	7.5	High end desktops, workstations, and servers
Mobile Pentium II processor	Apr 1998	233–400	7.5–27.4	Mobile PCs
Celeron processor	Apr 1998	266–466	7.5–19.0	Low cost PCs
Mobile Celeron processor	Jan 1999	266–400	18.9	Low cost mobile PCs
Pentium II Xeon processor	Jun 1998	400–450	7.5	Midrange & higher workstations & servers
Pentium III processor	Feb 1999	450–550	9.5	High end desktops, workstations, and servers
Pentium III Xeon processor	Mar 1999	500–550	9.5	Business PCs, 2-, 4-, and 8-way servers and workstations

Source: Intel

processor–based system selling for about $1500 in early 1999 had roughly 10 times the performance of a comparably priced Pentium processor–based PC circa 1994. That rapid increase in value and performance had made it possible to offer tailored processors for different segments of the computing market.

Market Segmentation Strategy

In response to the changes in the computing industry, Intel reorganized its microprocessor line with new products and brands in each of the major market segments. The Intel® Celeron™ processor was targeted at the low-cost, entry-level part of the market, the Pentium II and Pentium III processors were targeted at performance desktops and entry-level servers and workstations, and the Pentium II Xeon™ and Pentium III Xeon processors were targeted at midrange and high-end servers and workstations. All these processors were derivatives of Intel's P6 microarchitecture. This segmentation allowed Intel to maintain a huge pricing range, with Celeron processors selling for about $63 each and high-end Pentium Xeon processors selling for about $3700 each.[7] This strategy had helped sustain

[7]Source: *Forbes*, May 3, 1999

EXHIBIT 10 | Average Sales Price, Intel Microprocessors

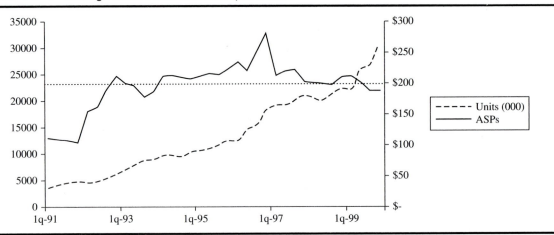

Source: NationsBanc Montgomery Securities LLC

Intel's historical average sales price for microprocessors (see Exhibit 10). Intel's product breadth made it more difficult for competitors to pursue niche strategies by exploiting holes in Intel's product line. Exhibit 11 shows projections for IA microprocessor unit growth and market segment share for desk-bound PCs, mobile PCs, servers and workstations, and upgrade processors.

Client Platform Products   The Celeron microprocessor, optimized for the low end of the market, was introduced in April 1998. The Celeron processor design was optimized to reduce manufacturing costs, whereas the Pentium processors were optimized for performance. The Celeron chip was the result of Andy Grove's recognition, alarmed by the idea of "disruptive technologies,"[8] that the low-end market had become a major potential threat to Intel's strategic position. Intel reassigned a number of engineers in 1997 for a crash effort to accelerate Celeron's development. Celeron was priced far more aggressively than the Pentium processors, and it had slowed Intel's market segment share losses on the low end.

Intel's Pentium II and Pentium III microprocessors remained the core of Intel's business. The Pentium II was Intel's largest volume microprocessor in 1998. In February 1999, Intel launched the Pentium III microprocessor, which the company positioned as being ideal for Internet

users. As part of the launch, Intel offered owners of Pentium III processor–based systems a free online service, called Intel® WebOutfitter[sm] Service, that offered plug-ins that were optimized to provide improved Internet performance.

Intel developed specialized versions of its microprocessors that were targeted at the mobile computing market segment. These processors were modified versions of the Celeron, Pentium II, and Pentium III processors, but had lower power consumption and size requirements compared to the standard processors.

The market for digital appliances, such as cell phones, handheld computers, cable set-top boxes, and automobile PCs was rapidly taking shape in early 1999. These products were relatively inexpensive, and generally required processors that cost around $20 or $30. Intel competed in these markets with both Pentium and StrongArm processors. The Pentium processors targeted at these segments were generally several generations old. StrongArm, acquired as part of a legal settlement with Digital Equipment, was noted for its high performance, its low power consumption, and—with a price between $21 and $33 in volume—its low price. These characteristics made StrongArm well suited for many applications within this market segment.

Some analysts were skeptical about Intel's resolve to compete in these markets. Craig Barrett admitted,

> Over the next three to five years our main focus will be on traditional computing devices, including more powerful workstations and servers. There may be some overlap, but we still think the main processor market

---

[8]Note: "disruptive technology" is a phenomenon discovered by Clayton Christensen; see *The Innovators' Dilemma*, Harvard Business School Press, 1997.

EXHIBIT 11 | Market Segment Share of I-A Microprocessors

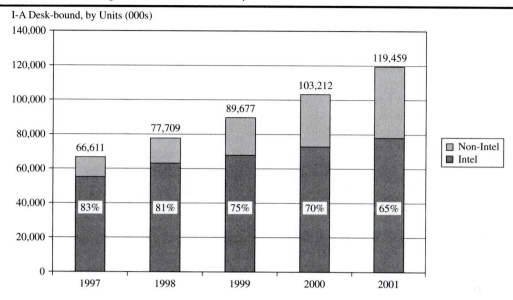

I-A Desk-bound, by Units (000s)

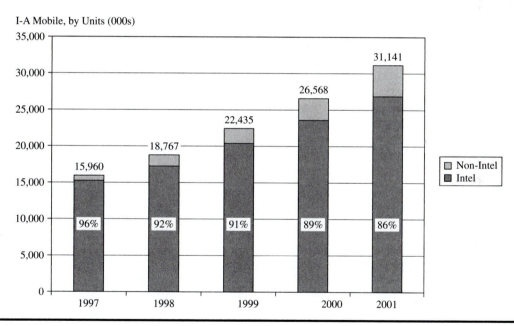

I-A Mobile, by Units (000s)

(continued)

will be for a computer that has the ability to do a wide variety of tasks.[9]

Speaking of the appliance market, Les Vadasz said,

> We'll compete, but this is not a major growth area for Intel. There's not that much silicon value and no segment will match the PC in volume. The appliances

market will consist of many smaller categories rather than singular winners.

Server Platform Products On the high end, Intel was increasingly targeting the computers that ran corporate data centers and the World Wide Web. The company believed it could establish a standard processor design in this segment, much like it had years earlier in the market for PCs, and more recently in the market for workstations

[9]Source: SiliconValley.com, February 21, 1999.

EXHIBIT 11 | Market Segment Share of I-A Microprocessors (cont.)

I-A Servers & Workstations, by Units (000s)

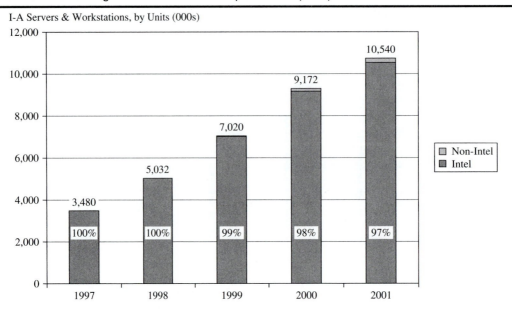

I-A Upgrades, by Units (000s)

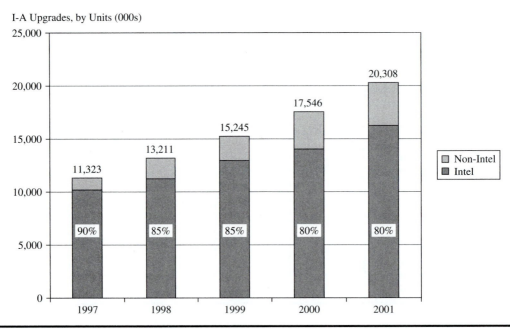

Source: Dataquest, 4/1998

and entry-level servers. The Pentium II Xeon microprocessors targeted at this market segment offered improvements in performance, reliability, and security, and were
designed for use in multiprocessor systems. In 1999,
50 percent of Intel's development dollars were being spent
on servers and workstations, despite the revenues in these
segments being much less than 50 percent.

Product and Technology Development

Technology leadership had been central to Intel's strategy
throughout its history. According to Andy Grove, "Intel
has pursued a technology driven strategy, which we've
executed relentlessly." In 1998, Intel spent $2.7 billion
for R&D, up from $2.3 billion in '97 and $1.8 billion in

'96. Intel's R&D spending allowed it to design multiple generations of new microprocessors concurrently. In 1998 and 1999, Intel continued its tremendous pace of product development. In 1999, Gordon Moore spoke again about the future applicability of Moore's Law and the industry's ability to continue making technology advancements and line-width reductions:

> We can still see 12 years down the road. I can generally see three to four generations ahead. Beyond that, it always looks like we will hit a wall, but we've been fortunate so far. As we move along, because of the physics of semiconductors, we will eventually hit one. Matter is made of atoms, and eventually we'll reach the limit of what the technology can do. It's amazing that the technology has been able to go this far . . . I think we'll move on more or less the same curve until about 2010 or 2020. Then we'll be approaching the limits of the atomic nature of matter. It will take a tremendous investment in technology to continue the advance.

Intel had also strengthened the quality of its product designs as a result of the highly publicized Pentium processor flaw issue of 1994.

Intel increasingly incorporated greater amounts of functionality into its microprocessors, allowing it to add more value and capture a higher percentage of industry rents. Gordon Moore addressed this issue in general:

> One of the really amazing things about this industry is that we assimilate the value add of our customers and give it back to them for free. The ones that recognize this force do well. The ones that don't, and try to protect their little niche, get steamrolled. The technology is phenomenal in terms of the economics. It commoditizes everything.

In February 1999, AMD introduced its K6-III processor, a rival to the Pentium III processor. AMD had dramatically reduced its time to market disadvantage—in earlier years it had taken AMD as long as 4 years to match Intel's new product releases. Even so, AMD had often come up with microprocessor designs that theoretically matched Intel's performance, only to fall short in the transition from the lab to the factory floor.

Intel had partnered with HP to develop the technology for 64-bit microprocessors. The first of the IA-64 product family, code-named Merced, was expected to be available in sample volumes in late 1999 and initial production volumes in mid-2000. In addition to running Microsoft's Windows NT, the Merced processor would also run most of the major versions of Unix, including HP-UX, Solaris, AIX, and Linux.

Intel faced challenges in penetrating the high end market segment, and Merced had been delayed several times. According to Paul Otellini,

> Overreach is our biggest challenge. We were working on the IA-64, the Xeon processor, and 8-way systems,[10] but were running behind schedule. We're moving this forward, but we've encountered technical challenges. This is truly rocket science, and there are very few companies who do this well. No one has successfully commoditized the high end.

Microsoft had similar ambitions to Intel with its Windows 2000 operating system, but it too had been delayed by more than a year. As a result of the delays with Merced, HP, and SGI had both decided to extend the lives of their own chip architectures.

Manufacturing and Production

Intel was renowned for its ability to manufacture its chip designs, and the company had developed the practice of optimizing the manufacturing process for a given chip, and then rolling out that process to Intel's other fabs in a process called "Copy Exact." In addition, Intel had closely integrated product design with process development. According to Albert Yu, senior vice president of Microprocessor Products Group,

> Having in-house manufacturing is very important. Design engineers in MPG work very closely with TMG (Technology and Manufacturing Group) to incorporate the design and manufacturing process. . . . This is a key element to success—the heart of the business. This is important to our ability to get the most into the smallest chip. If you look at our competition, the ones with their own manufacturing have chips that are compact and well designed. Competitors who don't (have their own manufacturing) have bigger chips.

Gordon Moore spoke of the importance of manufacturing and process technologies:

> One of the amazing things about our industry is that the next generation of technology is always much more cost effective than previous generations. Making things smaller makes everything else better simultaneously. That's a pretty unique characteristic with important implications. If you stop spending during a slowdown, it's a big drawback if you get behind. We have a saying:

---

[10]Note: "8-way" referred to a single system that used eight microprocessors.

"you never get well on your old products." We've been able to continue the march forward. Other companies have been in the same vein of technology, but nowhere near as successful. Over the years, we have made more profits than the whole industry combined.

Intel competitor AMD had traditionally had great difficulty in transferring its processor designs from the lab to the factory floor. On the other hand, IBM's manufacturing capabilities were generally considered world-class and IBM had recently announced several developments that put it at the forefront of manufacturing technology.[11]

Intel continued to invest heavily in state-of-the-art manufacturing facilities, spending $4 billion on capital additions in 1998, compared to $4.5 billion in '97 and $3.0 billion in '96 (see Exhibit 8). Most chip companies shipped prototype designs to potential customers before committing to build, and many others outsourced manufacturing rather than build their own fabs. However, according to one analyst, "Only Intel builds [manufacturing] capacity before it creates demand."[12]

Complementors

Though the so-called "Wintel" alliance remained strong, Intel's relationship with Microsoft had changed significantly, particularly on the low end and the high end. On the low end, Microsoft had released Windows CE, which targeted handheld PCs and other information appliances. Unlike other versions of Windows which were closely integrated with Intel processors, Microsoft initially ported Windows CE to several non-Intel processors. On the high end, Intel's Merced and future IA-64 processors were designed to work not only with Microsoft Windows NT, but also with each of the major versions of Unix.

Intel continued to work actively with development partners, providing them early access to new technologies so that Intel's new products would have strong applications that supported them at launch.

Corporate Business Development (CBD) performed an important function within Intel by doing acquisitions or making equity investments in strategic companies. Since 1996, Intel had invested about $2.5 billion into 200 companies, making it one of the largest venture firms in the United States. Some notable success stories included Inktomi, Broadcom, eToys, and Broadcast.com.

By 1999, CBD was making significant investments in Asia, Europe, and Latin America to support Intel's international growth objectives. In May 1999, Intel established a $250 million venture fund targeted at hardware and software companies that supported Merced. Speaking of CBD's role, Les Vadasz, senior vice president and director of CBD commented,

> CBD seeks to accelerate the creation of new market ecosystems, in part by using our financial resources . . . [For example], we've made a number of investments in hardware and software companies to accelerate their plans to adapt their products to the new Intel platforms.

Relationship with OEM Manufacturers

Through its brand strength, its influence over design standards, and its vertical integration into chipsets and motherboards, Intel became far more central to the PC industry. Some analysts likened the OEMs more to distributors than technology companies. According to Tom Yuen, cofounder of PC maker AST Research, "You no longer buy a Compaq computer, you buy an Intel computer from Compaq."[13]

According to Paul Otellini, "In a sense, PCs are now commodities, because most of the intellectual property is now tied up in the microprocessor."[14]

Since the early 1990s, Intel had been a major player in the market for chipsets and motherboards. This allowed Intel to support OEM manufacturers who were less competitive in these areas, improving their time to market, reducing their R&D requirements, and allowing them to focus resources in other areas. This leveled the playing field among OEM manufacturers, it reduced the value-add provided by OEMs, and it offset some of the power and competitive advantage of the major OEM manufacturers.

Intel's ability to influence design standards impacted the balance of power in the industry. Case in point: Intel's entry into the server market segment. In 1996, Compaq earned 27 percent of its sales—and all of its profits—from server sales, based on the success of their unique system designs. These systems cost between $10,000 and $20,000, and add-on processor cards cost about $16,000 more. When Intel entered the server market segment with proposals for comprehensive system design standards, the playing field quickly leveled. By 1999, dozens of OEMs using Intel technology offered multiprocessor servers

---

[11]Note: For example, IBM had introduced chips with copper wires, and had ramped to the 0.18 micron process.

[12]Source: Mercury Research, as quoted in SiliconValley.com, 2/21/1999.

[13]Source: SiliconValley.com, February 21, 1999.

[14]Source: SiliconValley.com, February 21, 1999.

EXHIBIT 12 | Intel Microprocessor Pricing

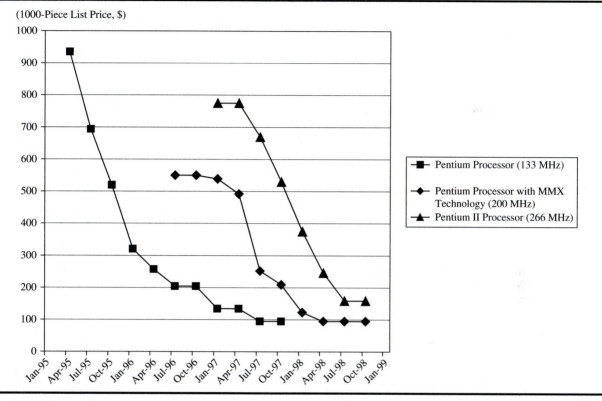

(1000-Piece List Price, $)

Legend:
- Pentium Processor (133 MHz)
- Pentium Processor with MMX Technology (200 MHz)
- Pentium II Processor (266 MHz)

Source: Intel

between $5000 and $10,000, with add-on processor cards at about $2500.[15]

Sales and Marketing

International markets had relatively low PC penetration and were viewed by Intel as an area of major potential growth. In 1998, more than 50 percent of Intel sales were outside the United States. Craig Barrett had focused significant effort on growing international sales, opening new sales offices in a number of countries.

Intel's technology leadership and time-to-market advantage allowed the company to recoup its R&D investments. Intel's practice was to aggressively reduce prices over time, especially as competitive products were introduced, which allowed the company to maintain market segment share and stimulate market growth. This pricing strategy also put enormous pressure on Intel

competitors. Exhibit 12 shows Intel's microprocessor pricing for several products over time.

Intel's outbound marketing efforts had become a key driver of its microprocessor business. Since launching the Intel Inside campaign in 1991, Intel had invested heavily in marketing, advertising, and promotions. For the Pentium III processor launch in early 1999, Intel spent about $300 million in advertising, more than double its investment on any previous chip launch.[16]

Competition

In early 1999, Intel's primary competitors in the desktop microprocessor market segment were AMD and Cyrix. Other competitors included Sun (Sparc), Compaq (Alpha), and Motorola (PowerPC).

AMD   Between 1997 and early 1999, AMD had design wins with HP, IBM, Compaq, Gateway, Sony, Toshiba,

---

[15]Source: SiliconValley.com, February 21, 1999.

[16]Source: *The Wall Street Journal,* February 17, 1999.

and others. In January 1999, for the first time ever, AMD chips outsold Intel chips in the U.S. retail desktop PC market segment, with a 43.9 percent unit market segment share,[17] based on strength in the sub-$1000 market segment. However, AMD suffered significant operating losses in 1996, 1997, and 1998 ($253 million, $91 million, and 164 million, respectively), as well as in the first quarter of 1999 ($128 million). In June 1999, AMD announced second quarter operating losses of $173 million.[18]

Cyrix   Cyrix helped launch the sub-$1000 PC market segment in early 1997, and in July 1997, National Semiconductor acquired Cyrix. In May 1999, after making significant market share gains in 1998 and early 1999 but also suffering steep operating losses, National announced that it would exit the PC chip business. In June 1999, National announced that Cyrix would be acquired by Via Technologies, a Taiwanese developer of chipsets that already had a clone of Intel's Celeron processor in development.

RISC Competition   In the high end of the microprocessor market segment, Intel faced stiff competition from the established RISC/UNIX systems from Sun, IBM, HP, SGI, and others. Despite gains by Windows NT and Intel systems in the low end of the workstation and server markets, these RISC/UNIX systems continued to hold market share on the high end. In particular, Sun Microsystems was perceived by many as the leader in the Internet server segment. However, according to Tom Lacey, "Sun has done a great job of marketing and hyping their association with the Internet. McNealy says that 'we're the dot in dot.com.' But there's a big difference between perception and reality."

Strategy and Action Outside the Core Business in 1999

The Creosote Bush

Outside the core business, Intel focused on developing business around both networking products and Internet services and solutions. Intel's singular focus on the microprocessor had been a critical factor in the company's success during the second epoch. However, Craig Barrett did not believe that the company's historical

---

[17]Source: PC Data, as reported by CNET, 2/26/1999.

[18]Source: AMD financial statements.

growth rates and profitability could be sustained solely with microprocessors. According to Barrett, "Microprocessors by themselves will not be the growth engine that they've been in the past."

During the second epoch, Intel's business focus on microprocessors had made it difficult for new ventures to thrive inside Intel. Craig Barrett likened the company's microprocessor business to the creosote bush, a desert plant that poisons the ground around it, preventing other plants from growing nearby. Although much of Intel's R&D investments went into technologies that complemented the processor and thereby offered opportunities to launch other new business units, the company rarely attempted to do so. Even when it did, the creosote effect made it difficult for the new business to thrive. The reason for this was simple. Any technology advance that enriched the PC environment was likely to create more demand for microprocessors. Thus, it was generally more valuable for Intel to give away technology and quickly disseminate it in the market, rather than try to build a business around it.

Faced with the changes being caused by the Internet and what appeared to be a new epoch, Barrett began actively pushing Intel to diversify into new businesses. In 1999, the most prominent manifestations of this diversification strategy were the Network Computing Group (NCG) and the New Business Group (NBG).

The Network Computing Group (NCG)

During Epoch II, Intel's networking group struggled to get resources, was not considered strategic by senior management, and was prevented from making acquisitions. As a result, the networking business had not grown as rapidly as it might have. Despite its slow start, by 1999, NCG had become a sizable and strategic business for Intel, with sales of approximately $1.2 billion. Since 1991, Intel's networking business had grown 58 percent per year and was expected to grow another 75 percent in 1999. NCG consisted of four distinct businesses: home networking, network adapters, small to medium-sized systems for business, and communications silicon. According to Mark Christensen, vice president and general manager of NCG,

> Looking forward, every segment that we play in is different. We have different competitors, different channels, different customers, etc. We're taking a targeted, segment by segment approach, and we've developed a unique strategy for each of these segments.

Christensen continued:

> Craig came up with the creosote bush image to illustrate to the company the challenge of trying to grow new businesses in one of the most highly successful companies of all time. He encouraged people to develop new businesses rather than just supporting "Job 1." The creosote bush was deep here . . ., [but] we've gotten lots of support from Craig and have now made significant progress in growing several new areas.

Craig Barrett discussed the charter of NCG:

> The charter of Christensen is to be the silicon building block supplier, not just to the LAN, but also to the WAN, and to also be a network building block supplier to the home and small business. This ties into the vision of a billion connected computers. We want to have the hearts and brains of the clients, servers, and some of the networking components. We're not into competing with the Ciscos and Nortels. . . . We want to supply the Nortels, Ciscos, Lucents, etc. with building blocks.

Home Networking   In 1999, the home networking market segment was still developing, but Intel expected it to become a $1 billion market within a few years. Intel had recently introduced a product called the Any Point™ Home Network that allowed consumers to use the phone line in their home to connect computers and printers together, and to provide Internet access to any PC in the house through a single ISP account. The Any Point product combined technology developed in the Intel Architecture Lab (IAL) with technology obtained in the acquisition of Digital Semiconductor. 3Com was Intel's primary competitor in this segment.

Network Adapters   Intel had become a major player in the market segment for network adapters, which had previously been dominated by 3Com. Intel continued its strategy in this segment of leveraging its strengths in silicon and OEM channels, which the company believed positioned it favorably vis-a-vis 3Com. In 1999, Intel expected to ship 25 million units and earn about $500 million in revenue. Intel's market segment share had grown from 8 percent in 1993 to 40 percent in 1999. 3Com had about a 40 percent share as well.

Network Systems for Small and Medium-Sized Businesses   The network systems business consisted of hubs, switches, and routers targeted primarily at small businesses. Intel did not consider this segment to be

their strongest area, but the business had grown from 0 to $300 million. Intel had made several acquisitions in this area. Intel competed primarily with 3Com and Cisco in this segment.

Communications Silicon   Intel viewed communications silicon as a major strategic growth area. The market for communication chips was growing about twice as fast as the microprocessor market segment.[19] Intel believed that the communications and networking industries would undergo a similar transformation to that undergone previously by the PC industry in transforming from a vertical to a horizontal industry structure. Intel hoped that its chips would become successful in this industry just like they had with PCs. This would not be an easy task. Networking companies understood well the history of the PC industry. In addition, the Intel brand was associated with the computer products, not networking products per se.

Networking chips came from dozens of players, including Lucent Technology, IBM, and Broadcom. In March 1999, Intel acquired Level One Technologies, the premier supplier of network interface chips, in a transaction valued at $2.2 billion. Level One's products were used by network equipment makers such as Cisco, Lucent, 3Com, and Hewlett Packard. Broadcom, a Level One rival, said it expected to gain market share as a result of the Intel acquisition. Broadcom believed that network equipment companies, such as Bay Networks, 3Com, and Cisco, would prefer to buy chips for their hubs, switches, and routers from a noncompetitor.

Relationship with Cisco   Intel's advances in the networking market had in some ways complicated the company's relationship with Cisco. Intel's approach was to leverage its own strengths in silicon, OEM channels, and consumer brand awareness, and to avoid competing directly in the enterprise market, where Cisco's strengths in direct sales to large accounts and servicing of end users were advantages.

Acquisitions   Acquisitions had become a central aspect of Intel's strategy in the networking business. This was a departure for Intel. According to Mark Christensen,

> Around 1996, we said that we needed to do acquisitions, but this was very painful since the internal view was that any acquisition would fail due to the strong culture of

---

[19]Source: Dataquest, as quoted by CNET, 3/4/1999.

Intel. But, we convinced the board of directors, Andy, and Craig that we could do them successfully. Since then, we have continued to get a lot of support from Craig and Andy and we have now done seven or eight acquisitions with very good results thus far. It remains a critical element of our growth strategy.

After the Level One acquisition, Craig Barrett said, We're continuing to look for other acquisition candidates. We are deadly serious about our networking communications group.[20]

The New Business Group

Under Craig Barrett's leadership, Intel had significantly expanded its emphasis on building new businesses inside the company. In 1997, Barrett had commissioned a course on "Growing the Business." Each of the top 100 managers in the company attended a week of classes that focused on developing new business models and a common vocabulary to discuss them. Intel's executive staff also was exposed to a condensed version of ideas on how to manage new ventures, as well as how to capitalize on disruptive technologies. As a result of this course, Intel managers began to refer to its core microprocessor business as the "blue" business, and new business ventures as "green" businesses.[21] According to Barrett, "If Intel wants to continue to occupy a central position [in high tech], it's just not enough to build the hearts and brains of computers."[22]

Barrett organized many of Intel's "green" businesses into a single organization, called the New Business Group (NBG), and he asked Gerry Parker, one of two executive vice presidents at Intel, to lead the group. According to one of Parker's direct reports,

> Gerry is very process oriented, he's very senior, and he's one of the few people that can effectively manage Craig and Andy. He's working on a process to develop a portfolio of new businesses. He's combining a formula of getting great people, training them, practicing, etc., and he ends up being a lot like the coach on the sidelines.

Parker recruited senior Intel people from throughout the organization. Enthusiasm to join the new effort was very high, especially from managers who had completed the "Growing the Business" training. Said Parker, "Intel is moving on Internet time. And we don't think it is much different from chip time."[23]

Intel Data Service (IDS) In early 1999, Intel announced plans to develop a major Internet hosting service. As part of the plan, Intel would host Web applications and data in huge "bit factories" around the world with thousands of servers. Mike Aymar, a 25-year Intel veteran, was chosen to lead IDS, reporting to Gerry Parker. According to Parker, "Our ideal dream is to host a significant percentage of the world's digital content on our servers, and to be number one or number two in this market."

Renee James, the group's marketing manager, had been instrumental in developing the unit's business plan. As the former technical assistant to Andy Grove, she had been asked to research new business opportunities around the Internet and to present her findings to the executive team at SLRP.[24] James discussed three different opportunities. Internet hosting was one of them, and it got the go-ahead. Explained James,

> We knew we were never going to be a portal, a content company, or a phone company. But we wanted [the opportunity] to be big enough to capture interest. Some people in IT [at Intel] had similar ideas, and we've retained some of what they had been thinking. They were looking at outsourced IT, but were not necessarily Internet focused.

According to *The Wall Street Journal*, Intel planned to invest more than $1 billion in IDS,[25] and although Intel senior management was enthusiastic in its support, Intel's control structure created challenges for IDS. For example, while building the first data center, which would cost approximately $250 million, the finance group stopped the purchase orders for the equipment. According to Executive VP Gerry Parker,

> Three levels down finance stopped the PO. They said "you don't have Andy [Grove]'s approval." I said, "who gives a [damn]." We need to be able to balance moving fast with the discipline of the company. The real issue in an internal bureaucracy is that if it thinks upper management doesn't like it, they will stop it at every level just to ask more questions and look at more alternatives, whereas if Grove says

---

[20]"Intel Inks $2.2 Billion Chip Deal," *CNET*, 3/4/1999.

[21]Note: "Blue" business development continued to be driven by top management through an induced strategy process; "green" business development was expected to be driven more through managers lower in the organization through an autonomous strategy process.

[22]"Reinventing Intel," *Forbes*, May 3, 1999.

[23]"Internet Ho! Intel Launches Charge Into Cyberspace," *The Wall Street Journal*, 5/18/1999.

[24]Note: SLRP refers to strategic long-range planning.

[25]Source: *The Wall Street Journal*, 5/18/1999.

"do it," no one in the bureaucracy dares slow it down. In my case Craig acted hesitant at the wrong moment and it was a license for every level of finance to slow it down for more justification. We are working our way through this but I'm constantly amazed at how difficult it is to do something different in an area where none of us have a good experiential base or good intuition.

Parker continued,

The finance guys are the hardest, because they think it's their money. I've been given a fair amount of rope on this thing. . . . I'm trying to be fiscally responsible. But with the data center for example, I try to avoid pitching a real detailed plan that locks you in. [I say], "don't get too enamored with any part of the plan."

Intel believed that its competencies in streamlining complex processes, running tight operations, and managing large investments would give it an advantage in this business. Intel planned to refine one data center, and then replicate the data center following Intel's "Copy Exact" process for building chip factories. According to Ellen Hancock, CEO of potential rival Exodus Communications, "I think it's a stretch for them to say they have some expertise here. We've taken years to set up our operations. I'm befuddled that they think this is like building chip factories."[26]

Digital Imaging   The Digital Imaging division, led by Don Whiteside, combined two previously separate organizations. The first group, based in Oregon, was more consumer marketing and software oriented, whereas the second group, based in Phoenix, was more engineering and hardware oriented. Don Whiteside discussed some of the challenges he had encountered since taking over the group:

We have a tendency to take a technology driven view rather than a market driven perspective to things. . . . The basic thinking is that we're a technology company, this is technology, so we should be doing it. What we should be asking is what value does Intel provide to the market opportunity.

Much of the funding for the Digital Imaging group came out of discretionary funding, which had a less rigorous allocation process than the formal POR[27] process.

[26]"Internet Ho! Intel Launches Charge Into Cyberspace," *The Wall Street Journal,* 5/18/1999.

[27]Note: POR, or plan of record, is the process for determining head count and budget allocation for each department in the company.

Nonetheless, the group had encountered some challenges with funding. According to Lorie Wigle, marketing manager of the group,

New things kept getting added to Digital Imaging . . . but we never got more resources, which meant that we needed to cut existing projects. . . . We were one of the first green businesses and there was a lack of clear understanding: do we get new incremental resources or do we have to carve it out of existing budget.

Intel Play   Intel® Play™ toys were the result of a collaborative partnership with Mattel to develop and produce "smart toys" that could be used with the PC. The toys would be manufactured, distributed, and marketed by Mattel under the "Intel Play" brand, and developed in a joint lab in Oregon staffed by both Intel and Mattel engineers and product designers. The underlying technology for the products came from the Intel Architecture Lab. According to Michael Bruck, who co-managed the partnership for Intel, "The idea behind the project is to take advantage of Intel's strengths in technology and Mattel's strengths in toy design."

The effort came about as a result of joint work being done between Intel's Content Group and Mattel on CD-ROMs. Michael Bruck explained,

[Mattel] approached us with the idea to apply the Intel brand to electronic learning toys. . . . Jill Barad, Mattel's CEO, met with Andy Grove and pitched Mattel and their capabilities. . . . Intel did a lot of research on the opportunity. We did market research to identify how the Intel brand was perceived by parents and their kids. . . . We found that parents recognized the Intel brand, but that there needed to be a connection to the PC to support the brand extension.

Business Communications Product Division (BCPD) BCPD's charter was to design and build PC-based videoconferencing systems for desktops and conference rooms. BCPD was the successor to ProShare, and by early 1999, the group had become profitable, but revenues remained relatively low. The group was leveraging PC technology to increase the accessibility and decrease the costs of video conferencing.

New Business Investments (NBI)   NBI was established in late 1998 with the charter of creating new businesses within Intel. NBI played a role similar to that of a venture capitalist and focused on capitalizing on ideas that were emerging within Intel. NBI worked closely with CBD, but had different goals and objectives. While CBD emphasized external investments and acquisitions, NBI was more internally focused. NBI invested relatively small amounts of money in a venture's early stages of development (as in a seed or first round), whereas CBD invested relatively larger amounts in later stages of development. This also implied that NBI would take a relatively active management and advisory role with its investments compared to CBD.

Intel Service Operation (ISO)   Intel Service Operation was run by Jim Johnson, an executive with a long history of entrepreneurial initiatives at Intel. ISO provided PC help services to small businesses and consumers. Callers were serviced by live technicians who offered technical support for both hardware and software, including all of the most popular desktop applications. ISO reported a 96 percent customer satisfaction rating. However, very few of the customers who had subscribed to the service actually used it. The value of the service seemed to be viewed by the consumer as more of an insurance policy. Johnson believed that the service would not be successful without significant investments to promote the service and increase customer awareness.

Intel Architecture Lab (IAL)   For most of the 1990s, IAL's primary role was to support Intel's microprocessor business, and many important developments came out of the lab, including chipsets, motherboards, software, and many of the company's networking products. In 1998, the charter of the group expanded to include the goal of generating new businesses for Intel. For example, IAL engineers contributed to the development of the electronic toys made in partnership with Mattel.

Pandesic[28]   Established in August 1997, Pandesic was a 50/50 joint venture between Intel and SAP, based in Sunnyvale, California. Pandesic had developed an electronic commerce software and service package that allowed companies to outsource the development and hosting of their e-commerce systems. The Pandesic product was based on SAP's enterprise resource planning software and ran on Intel systems. Pandesic was led by Harold Hughes, former CFO of Intel, and many of Pandesic's senior executives were former Intel employees. Pandesic software was being used by a

number of Internet start-ups, including DVDExpress.com and ALLHerb.com, as the backbone of their e-commerce infrastructures.

Challenges in New Businesses

In discussions with Intel managers across the company who were involved with new ventures, several themes came through. There were certainly many advantages to these ventures of being associated with Intel. However, there were also many challenges and disadvantages.

The Creosote Bush—The Gravity of the Core Business   The enormous success of Intel's core business created challenges for the new ventures. Being inside a $26 billion company that made over $6 billion in profits caused even the most promising new ventures to struggle to become relevant. Reflecting the view of many Intel managers, Jim Johnson said, "Building new businesses within Intel can be very hard. The microprocessor business is so large that it wipes out anything that gets close to it." Claude Leglise continued, "Everyone's thinking PC around here. The review systems and management processes, while they're the right process for the existing business, they're a pain in the butt for what I'm doing. . . . The gravity of the organization is strong." According to Patty Murray, Intel's head of human resources, "Intel is the world's largest single cell organism."

Craig Barrett and the Executive Staff, however, had made changes to make the environment more supportive of the new businesses. According to Claude Leglise, "The CEO has said 'do this.' Everyone else, leave them alone. It's become socially acceptable to do what I'm doing—not PCs."

Don Whiteside described how these changes had influenced the Digital Imaging group:

> We entered both of these initiatives as Job 1 businesses. They both supported our desire to sell more and faster PCs . . . Now we're looking at both of these businesses in the following way: if they happen to support Job 1, that's nice, but that's not one iota of justification for doing these businesses. We're looking at them as stand-alone, money-making businesses.

Claude Leglise added,

> The core business is 95 percent of what Intel's doing, and it's not broken, so let's not fix it. The chaos that I'm fostering (in my new business focus) would be disastrous in

---

[28]Note: Pandesic does not report to NBG; it is included here for completeness.

the PC business. We need to adapt the management approach to the demands on the organization.

Marketing and Brand Strategy   The consensus view was that the Intel brand created many advantages for new ventures, but that there were significant challenges to using it effectively. The Intel name inspired trust and confidence, and it helped open doors with potential customers, partners, and suppliers, giving Intel new ventures a significant advantage relative to typical start-ups. Jim Johnson explained:

> The Intel brand was very useful. When we launched our service, the corporate marketing group did a phenomenal job. We received almost as much activity from our launch as a microprocessor launch typically receives. They put together press kits, radio spots, and TV spots, and we ended up getting phenomenal press. . . . Also, the Intel Web site put a pointer on our home page, and this generated 10,000 hits per day of visitors coming to our section of the Web site. From a marketing point of view, we did a wonderful job of using the Intel name.

There were also major challenges related to marketing and branding. According to Jim Johnson (ISO), "Although the brand name is a huge asset, it's hard to use the asset unless you're a part of the microprocessor business." For example, Mark Christensen (NCG) noted,

> Intel's brand stands for a lot of things . . . [but] we're probably not known as a networking company. It's probably easier for us to extend the brand to "the Internet building block company" than it is to extend it to "the networking company."

Dennis Carter, VP Marketing, discussed how the role of marketing had evolved across the three epochs:

> During the first epoch, marketing allowed us to differentiate our products from others. We made a number of innovations in sales and marketing techniques that allowed us to sell high value semiconductors. We were virtually unknown outside of the engineering community, but were innovators in business to business marketing. During the second epoch, we were again able to differentiate our product from a marketing perspective, but this time via Intel Inside®. We successfully took our brand to the end user. Marketing was a key element in the success of our microprocessor business. During the third epoch marketing must again play a key role, we will need to move our brand to include a broader set of products, and we need to make the Intel brand relevant in the Internet space.

Sales and Marketing Channels   For the most part, the new ventures relied on Intel's existing sales forces to sell and market their products in the field. This created challenges in terms of mind share, and conflicts in funding occasionally arose. According to Jim Yasso, a veteran of Intel's sales force before his tenure as GM of RPD,

> The sales force is part of the blue process. For anything that's green, it's very hard to get resources, unless they are explicitly included as part of the original plan and budget allocations. You also need to have marketing people in place in the geographies. . . . We have quarterly POR processes where we get funding approved or adjusted. Within a division or geography, we can be subject to headcount or spending cuts, and in some cases these budget decisions can conflict [with funding for the new ventures]. This can be a real killer for green businesses. . . . With NBG, we've kept the [green] businesses separate and shielded them from the ongoing [blue] business.

Lorie Wigle mentioned another issue: "Getting mind share of the sales force is difficult."

The new emphasis at Intel on noncore businesses created challenges for the sales force. According to Tom Lacey, a vice president in Intel's sales and marketing group,

> A lot of the sales reps at Intel have been here for a long time. Most of them grew up on the IA bandwagon. We're now trying to sell more Intel products through the same channels. This is requiring people to learn more about some of our other products. . . . This has been a bit of a transformation for the sales force. . . . We're in the process right now of reorganizing the sales force. We're creating a separate sales force that is focused on non-CPU businesses.

Finance and Resource Allocation   Intel's financial resources created a tremendous advantage for the company. At the same time, Intel faced challenges in terms of allocating resources to new businesses. Speaking of the funding challenge that new ventures faced at Intel, Tom Lacey explained:

> We apply the POR process to establish budgets for all of our projects. . . . Virtually every single quarter, the requests outweigh the willingness to spend. We would end up "ZBB-ing"[29] the lower ROI projects. The larger ROI projects were almost always related to the mainstream CPU business. Therefore, if you were not part of

---

[29]Note: ZBB: zero-based-budgeting.

the mainstream business, you needed to be very spirited and very perseverant to drive your projects through that POR process every quarter. In many cases they were great businesses by any other metric, just not compared to the microprocessor business. Three or four years ago I asked Craig [Barrett], "shouldn't we be diversifying more?" His answer was "Absolutely not. It takes every bit of our energy to execute on the microprocessor business." If you were in a non-CPU business, it was tough.

Les Vadasz summarized part of the challenge that Intel faced in this area:

> One of the biggest dangers for big companies is not being able to manage small amounts of money. For some top managers, these new ventures are trivial stuff. But these ventures are necessary to stay on the bleeding edge. On the other hand, you can easily overspend too early. I have done this various times in my life!

A pronounced tension existed between Intel's strong control structure and the patience that many Intel managers believed was necessary for new ventures to thrive. Subjecting new ventures to the POR process created difficulties. During Epoch II, the highest ROI projects were typically connected to the microprocessor business. Hence, few opportunities outside the core business survived the funding process. In Epoch III, being subject to the quarterly POR process still created challenges. According to Jim Johnson,

> When ISO was established, I tried to get a fixed amount upfront. Then if we run out of money, it's our problem. It turned out that we were funded out of the quarterly POR, which means that our budget is reviewed every quarter. This creates major challenges. I had taken over 1 year to negotiate an advertising arrangement with AOL that included key pages on AOL sponsoring our service. [The deal] required us to make a $2 million commitment over a 12-month period. At the end of the negotiation, [my boss at the time] said he wasn't going to sign it. . . . The $2 million investment was key. If we had been given our funding upfront, rather than quarterly, we could have saved money in other areas and found enough to do this deal.

Though most managers gave their finance counterpart high ratings, one senior executive said,

> My controller runs my business. He spends very little time on it, and he doesn't understand my strategy, my customers, etc. Yet, he controls my purse strings, and gives me very little flexibility. With the POR process, you go in with your request by department. He says which

department gets funded and which one does not. This happens every quarter. We spend the last 30 days of the quarter preparing for the budget review, then the first 30 days of the next quarter appealing the budget cuts. So we end up spending 60 out of 90 days negotiating our budget.

Intel's hard-nosed culture and financial discipline served it well in the core business, but could be a liability to the new businesses. For example, there seemed to be a common perception that Intel lacked patience with new ventures. According to Scott Darling,

> We tend to want to go from zero to a multibillion dollar business very rapidly. . . . We've been too mechanistic. We are an engineering company, and we've approached new businesses like you'd solve an engineering problem. But there is serendipity in new ventures. We're often wrong about new markets. . . . And we have tended to micromanage, although Gerry [Parker] has avoided this.

Renee James discussed the objectives of Intel Data Services, "The edict from Craig [Barrett] is to make this a $1B business in 3 years." Dennis Carter added,

> A key challenge that we face in new businesses is patience—the popular conception is that we don't have any. Craig says that these green businesses will be successful within 2 years. People respond, "But the networking business took 8–10 years to build up." Craig correctly counters, "Yes, but if it was managed better, we could have grown it more quickly."

Craig Barrett addressed the patience issue head-on:

> For the people involved with the new ventures, I'm sure they see us as being impatient. What I tell them is, show me how you're going to be number 1 or number 2, and how you're going to build a viable business. If they can't do this, then we're not going to be patient. There are examples, such as chipsets and networking, where we've been very patient. My philosophy is to deal out patience in small doses. But I believe we've demonstrated to the company that we have a degree of patience. The damn environment changes so fast, that we have to adjust priorities and resource requirements as the environment dictates.

Another common theme that emerged was that having executive sponsorship for an opportunity was an important criterion for getting funded. According to Jim Johnson, "At Intel, if you have an idea, there are 20,000 people who can say no, but just a few that can say yes."

Speaking about the funding for the project with Mattel, Michael Bruck said,

> If the idea was not so compelling, it probably would not have worked. . . . I've seen good ideas get shot down at Intel. This project has involved high-level involvement at Intel, and we've received buy-in from the people at the top. At Intel, lots of people have veto power, but few have full approval power. . . . I've been surprised at how easy the funding has come about.

A popular view within the organization was that Intel's top executives did not always apply the same level of financial discipline to their own projects. Representing a common theme, one senior manager said, "One weakness within Intel is that new business activities get decided by executive prerogative." According to another manager, speaking of the Digital Imaging group,

> When they broke up the ProShare division (which had been strongly endorsed by Andy Grove) and moved it to the Create & Share division, they had to establish a culture of fiscal discipline because they had had an entitlement mentality. They had to do a similar thing with the silicon people because this had been Craig Barrett's pet project.

Compensation and Incentive Systems At Intel, the evaluation system worked as follows: goals and objectives for the coming year were established in December. Performance was evaluated the following December based on the achievement of these objectives. Employee bonuses, which were typically a very significant portion of overall compensation, were based on these evaluations. This created a major challenge for new ventures, where reasonable objectives were difficult to anticipate. According to Jim Johnson, "In these new ventures, things change about every 30 days. Yet the targets are frozen 12 months in advance. Our group has been reorganized since then!" Dennis Carter elaborated,

> Unfortunately, [objectives] are often hopelessly outdated after 12 months. Things just change too much. In the case of a start-up effort, it's even more difficult. . . . The system penalizes you for the downside, but does not reward you for the upside associated with these changes. A mechanism for relief might be useful.

Another challenge was how to provide appropriate incentives to the new venture groups. Compared to typical start-ups, new corporate ventures had relatively low upsides. According to Gerry Parker, "The EB payouts

were bad for my groups . . . Right now, it's all downside. This makes things not terribly easy."

According to Jim Johnson,

> Having done several of these new ventures. . . . Being part of Intel is a huge advantage when dealing with external organizations, but it can also be a huge disadvantage internally. . . . Within Intel, there's no way to have real equity, autonomy, or ownership.

Addressing the compensation issues, CFO Andy Bryant said,

> (The new businesses) say, we want the benefit like a start-up would have. Fine, then I'm going to take away the Intel stock options. I see it as a risk–reward issue. If you want to be rewarded like a start-up then you need to have the same motivation as another start-up. . . . The problems that we're having are often related to the expectations of the people who do it. They say we want to go off and be independent and have the upside of a start-up. OK, so we take away your Intel stock options. The translation when they go back to their groups is that "they're not working with us. I had a great idea, but they wouldn't fund it." But VCs only fund 20 percent of the plans. So if we do the same, the 80 percent that don't get funded complain and say we're not being supportive. Meanwhile we've funded the other 20 percent and they're busy getting implemented.

One of Intel's six core cultural values was risk taking. The philosophy was that with a leading edge technology strategy, Intel would always compete in an environment of constant change. Attempting to maintain the status quo in an environment of change was viewed by Intel as a recipe for failure. Therefore, risk taking was encouraged. However, as Epoch III began to unfold, a common view was developing in the organization that Intel did not particularly support risk taking any more. According to Dennis Carter,

> It is a commonly held belief among middle managers at Intel that it is difficult to take risks, . . . that Intel doesn't reward risk takers who fail, only those who have succeeded. This is certainly the perception, and possibly also the reality.

Building General Management Competencies During the first epoch, Intel's technical sales and field engineering teams played an essential role in applying the company's products and finding new applications for them. During the second epoch, the application—the PC—was clear, unchanging, and relatively homogeneous. This reduced the importance of inbound marketing, as well as Intel's capabilities in this area. Dennis Carter explained,

> During the 70s, there was a very good process for inbound marketing. Our sales force was in excellent touch with our OEM customers. During the second epoch, our sales force stayed in tune with the OEMs, but our marketing expanded to the much larger audience of PC consumers. We have limited marketplace feedback for things outside of processors and many of our internal processes withered. For the third epoch, it will be critical to redevelop these internal processes. . . . Product planning is often done too quickly by people too removed from the market. . . . Intel is very good at execution, and Intel management processes lead to the development of excellent intuition in familiar areas, but in new product areas we are bad at judging what will play in the market. . . . Today the link with the market is missing. . . . We need a closed loop into the product planning process.

Claude Leglise added, "The technology is the easy part. We know how to get that. It's not so hard and we know how to do it. The part that is frightening is what's the application." Gerry Parker said:

> At Intel, we have a propensity to focus on one thing, build it big, and then say "here it is." We have the mentality of "build it and they will come." . . . We're now making some real progress on being more customer responsive and my green teams are spending time at every staff meeting on customer status and finding customers.

One challenge facing Intel was developing corporate entrepreneurs who could turn good ideas into good businesses. According to Claude Leglise,

> We have labs in Oregon that are concocting ideas all day long. We have a resource pool for ideas. We've made equity investments in a couple hundred small companies. It's a matter of sifting through and seeing what makes sense, and taking the products to customers.

Dennis Carter added,

> There are lots of ideas and new projects sprouting up everywhere within Intel, but the real question is how we can turn them into a business. We have the capacity to do so, but is the infrastructure there to support it? . . . We have clever ideas coming from places like IAL and the Content Group, but little experience in making a business out of any of them. We need to develop the intuition for doing this. And we need to develop people with the entrepreneurial intuition.

Another important issue was developing general managers who could lead and manage these ventures. According to Craig Barrett:

> [During the second epoch] we became much more verticalized behind IA and related businesses. Now we're much more broad, with networking, Parker's businesses, and so forth. This requires less top-down management and more P&L and line management.

Andy Grove added, in a discussion with Intel's top management, "There's a lack of a merchant mentality inside Intel. We're not good at it. We need to get experience, and then build on that experience."

Looking Ahead

In spite of Intel's efforts to create new businesses, Chairman Andy Grove was not satisfied. Asked about the new businesses at Intel, Grove said in early 1999,

> We've been very consistent and uniform. All of the new efforts, like all of the other efforts before them, have all been failures. . . . Nobody can fault us for not trying. We've learned a lot, but we've not yet put those learnings into the creation of a third business.

Grove then brought Sean Maloney, senior vice president of sales, into the discussion:

> GROVE (to Maloney): "How have the new businesses gone?"
>
> MALONEY: "We've succeeded at changing the attitudes in the company from unrealistic expectations and an unsupportive management structure to more realistic expectations and a more supportive management structure. But at this point we have no results."
>
> GROVE: "I rest my case."

Then referring to Intel's vision of a billion connected computers:

> GROVE (to Maloney): "What percentage of ESM (executive staff management) would you say gets it?"
>
> MALONEY: "I would say a majority of ESM now gets it."
>
> GROVE, shaking his head no: "If by a majority you mean 51 percent, then I agree with you."

Grove himself felt compelled to become more educated in this area, and he had begun meeting with a wide range of successful Internet companies to better understand their businesses and financial models.

Speaking to his senior management team in mid-1999, Grove encouraged them to expand their expertise as well, telling them:

> There is lots of expertise and knowledge here. Most of us are engineers by training and one thing we know is how to learn. You need to go out in your own space and learn everything you can about this new environment.

At the same time, CEO Craig Barrett was spending a significant percentage of his time traveling internationally as part of his efforts to further stimulate international growth.

In leading Intel into the new millennium, Barrett seemed to relish the challenges facing him and his company. Barrett said,

> I've tried to spread a couple of messages around here. First is that there's a different vision. We have more business opportunities than just the microprocessor. Microprocessors by themselves will not be the growth engine that they've been in the past. . . . I try to challenge the new ventures to grow their businesses so that they're relevant, and I challenge the people in the microprocessor business to be successful enough so that the new ventures won't matter. . . . The creosote bush is still here. It hasn't gone away, and I hope it doesn't! We need to grow some other bases, but it would be inappropriate to say we have changed 100 percent.

Chairman Emeritus Gordon Moore described some of the challenges facing Barrett:

> Craig is a strong hands-on guy, like Andy, but even more so. He keeps himself in the loop a lot more. It's pretty amazing that he can do this, and it's because he has so damn much energy. . . . Eventually Craig will need to find someone to complement himself. . . . He has done a tremendous job, moving our focus from the microprocessor to the Internet building blocks. The key issue here is getting critical mass in an area. . . . Jack Welch at GE says that you have to be number one or number two in an industry, and this is especially true in technology. Hangers-on tend to not be very good. At the same time, we can't neglect the microprocessor business.

Case 1.3

Inside Microsoft: The Untold Story of How the Internet Forced Bill Gates to Reverse Course

. . . Until six months ago, it looked as if Microsoft might, in fact, be lost in cyberspace. It was so far behind Internet upstarts that industry analysts wondered if the company whose software dominated the PC era might be sidelined in a new age of Internet computing. . . .

BusinessWeek, July 15, 1996

Driving Everything

Even if Gates and his executives had had an inkling of the Web's trajectory, they had more pressing concerns. Government regulators were in the midst of a huge probe into Microsoft's alleged anticompetitive practices. A hush-hush group was creating a service to rival America Online Inc. Another was building Superhighway goodies—video servers for interactive TV, programs for set-top boxes, and so on. Most importantly, legions of programmers were jamming to finish what would become Windows 95.

Microsoft's public reaction to the Web remained muted until last fall, when the Web's momentum was too great to ignore—as was the threat to Microsoft. Some 20 million people were surfing the Net without using Microsoft software. Worse, the Web—with a boost from Sun Microsystems' Java programming language—was emerging as a new "platform" to challenge Windows' hegemony on the PC.

Gates had had enough. On Dec. 7, he staged an all-day program for analysts, journalists, and customers to show that Microsoft had every intention of playing—and winning—in the new software game. It would make Web browsers, Web servers, and "Web-ize" existing Microsoft programs. It would even license Sun's Java—whatever it took. . . .

The impact of those products has yet to be felt, but the speed and intensity of Microsoft's offensive has already changed the calculus of competitors and analysts. "People aren't asking anymore if Microsoft will be killed by the Internet but whether Microsoft will dominate the

---

Internet," says Scott Winkler, vice president at market researcher Gartner Group Inc.

Indeed, in just six months, Gates had done what few executives have dared. He has taken a thriving, $8 billion, 20,000-employee company and done a massive about-face. "I can't think of one corporation that has had this kind of success and after 20 years just stopped and decided to reinvent itself from the ground up," says Jeffrey Katzenberg, a principal of DreamWorks SKG, which has a joint venture with Microsoft. "What they're doing is decisive, quick, and breathtaking."

Gates, a keen student of business history, has been intensely aware of how other market-leading companies—from General Motors Corp. to IBM—have stumbled when their top executives failed to read the signs of fundamental change in their industries. Tackling that problem was a prominent theme in his best-seller, *The Road Ahead,* published last fall. "I don't know of any examples where a leader was totally energized and focused on the new opportunities where they totally missed it," he says.

Here, for the first time, is the inside story of Microsoft's dramatic turnabout. It's a tale full of twists, turns, miscues, and even a fatefully timed illness. And it's a story of how three young programmers became Net preachers, spreading the gospel and peppering management with e-mail that eventually helped get Gates and his team to act.

The Web-izing of Microsoft begins in February 1994, when Steven Sinofsky, Gates's technical assistant, returned to his alma mater, Cornell University, on a recruiting trip. Snowed in at the Ithaca (NY) airport, he headed back to the Cornell campus. That's when he saw it: students dashing between classes, tapping into terminals, and getting their e-mail and course lists off the Net.

The Internet had spread like wildfire. It was no longer the network for the technically savvy—as it had been seven years earlier when Sinofsky was studying there—but a tool used by students and faculty to communicate with colleagues on campus and around the world. He dashed off a breathless e-mail message called "Cornell is WIRED!" to Gates and his technical staff.

The response from one of Gates's staff: Someone in networking has been "bugging us about this same stuff. Maybe you should get together." The other guy was J. Allard. While being recruited in 1991, the cherub-faced programmer had worried whether Microsoft "had a clue about the Internet." He signed on anyway, figuring he could help make the company hip to the Net. In 1992, Allard was the only Microsoft programmer who had it on his business card: Program Manager, Internet Technologies. "I was a lonely voice," he recalls.

Fixing Bugs

Allard's job was building TCP/IP, the Net communications format, into Microsoft LAN Manager and Windows for Workgroups. TCP/IP had long been standard on Unix computers made by companies such as Sun Microsystems. But for Microsoft, says Allard, it was just a "checkbox item"—ordered by Executive Vice President Steven A. Ballmer. "I don't know what it is. I don't want to know what it is. My customers are screaming about it. Make the pain go away," Allard recalls Ballmer saying.

In an unsanctioned project in early 1993, Allard oversaw the development of Microsoft's first Internet server—a computer that could link Microsoft to other Net sites. It was programmed to distribute test copies of the TCP/IP code to customers. Soon, they were posting other bug fixes, and it became one of the 10 most-used servers on the Net.

Little of this was registering with top management, though. Gates, then 37, and his lieutenants had never seen the Net in use the way the incoming legions of twenty-somethings had. And with so much riding on the Windows rewrite, they had little time for new projects.

Allard was increasingly frustrated. The Net was abuzz over Mosaic, a browser program created by a precocious computer-science undergraduate at the University of Illinois and posted on the Net for anyone to download. Suddenly, the Web had an easy, point-and-click format—for the masses. On Jan. 25, 1994, he penned a call-to-arms memo titled "Windows: The Next Killer Application for the Internet."

Allard recommended building a Mosaic-like browser and including TCP/IP in Chicago, the code name for what became Win95. This memo also introduced the language that would become Microsoft's battle cry nearly two years later: "Embrace" Internet standards, and "extend" Windows to the Net. Says Allard: "I finally just couldn't take it anymore. I felt the company just didn't get it."

Once Sinofsky weighed in, things started happening. The two began talking, and Sinofsky soon got a Net connection. "I dragged people into my office kicking and screaming," says Sinofsky. "I got people excited about this stuff." Among the infected was Gates. "When

Sinofsky started talking about the phenomenon he'd seen at Cornell and [showing] me Gopher and the early Web stuff . . . it caught my attention," says Gates. "I thought, 'That's a good thing.'"

The boss gave the go-ahead for an executive retreat to discuss the Net. That was a key breakthrough: At Microsoft, such gatherings convene when Gates feels execs need to focus on a critical issue. On Apr. 5, 1994, two months after Sinofsky's Cornell visit, top brass holed up at the Shumway Mansion in nearby Kirkland, Wash., a 1909 estate used for conferences. Gates and his chiefs pored over a 300-page Internet briefing compiled by Sinofsky. At issue: How important was the Internet? And how much should Microsoft invest in it?

Baby Steps

In one breakout group, Allard tangled with Russell Siegelman, who was heading Marvel, the code name for what's now the Microsoft Network online service. Allard argued that instead of being proprietary, Marvel should be based on Web standards. Seigelman held his ground—and won. It was a decision that would later cost millions to reverse.

Still, Net progress was made: TCP/IP would be integrated into Win95 and Windows NT, the version of Windows that runs network-server computers. The sales team was told to use the Web to dispense marketing information. The applications group agreed to give Word, the word-processing program, the ability to create Web pages.

Next, Gates jumped deeper into the process by devoting much of his April Think Week—a semiannual retreat—to the Internet. His Apr. 16 memo, "Internet Strategy and Technical Goals," contained the first signs of a growing corporate commitment. "We want to and will invest resources to be a leader in Internet support," wrote Gates.

It was a first step, albeit a measured one. "I don't think he knew how much to bet yet," says Allard. But board member David F. Marquardt did: he recalls that he was "amazed" that Microsoft was putting so little into the Net. "They weren't in Silicon Valley. When you're here, you feel it all around you," says Marquardt, a general partner at Technology Venture Investors in Menlo Park, Calif. He broached the subject at the April board meeting that year. Gates's response? "His view was that the Internet was free," says Marquardt. "There's no money to be made there. Why is that an interesting business?"

To an increasingly important group of competitors, it was clear there was a huge opportunity—and if Microsoft didn't pursue it, they might be able to undo the behemoth's software dominance. Sun, Netscape, Oracle Corp., IBM, and others saw their chance to reset the rules on the Net.

So did the Net start-ups that were multiplying like cells. Yahoo!, Lycos, InfoSeek, PointCast—dozens were rushing into the vacuum where Microsoft wasn't. The most high-profile of these was headed by James H. Clark, who resigned as chairman of the company he founded, Silicon Graphics Inc., and latched on to the Internet opportunity. He had the goose that laid the golden egg: Marc Andreessen, that 23-year-old University of Illinois programmer. Netscape Communications (originally Mosaic Communications) was founded on Apr. 4, 1994, the eve of the Shumway retreat. By October, it was downloading its Navigator browser across the Internet.

In the spring of 1994, the Net was exploding. Millions of PC users were logging on. There were some 21,700 commercial Web sites, up from 9,000 in 1991. Even IBM had a home page, complete with a greeting from Chairman Louis V. Gerstner Jr. So did General Electric, Tupperware, Volvo, and Hyatt Hotels. Time Warner had Pathfinder, which featured electronic versions of its magazines. Increasingly, the Net, not interactive TV, looked like the route to the Info Highway. Grasping that, Sun Microsystems began adapting a software language for interactive TV into what would become Java.

That April, at the Spring Comdex trade show, Sinofsky saw Booklink, a browser owned by CMG Information Services. He showed it to Brad A. Silverberg, then head of Microsoft's Win95 business. Execs began negotiating to license the technology. But as the talks dragged on, AOL swooped in and bought BookLink for $30 million in November. Says Silverberg: "That woke us up. We had to be a lot more aggressive, a lot more lively. Time was ticking faster in this new world."

During this period, Gates was crafting a strategy for Microsoft in the emerging wired world. But as outlined in his October 1994, memo, "Sea Change," the approach was to use existing Microsoft products. Other Microsoftians were becoming convinced that the Internet was the way.

One was Benjamin W. Slivka, now 35 and project leader for Internet Explorer, Microsoft's browser. In mid-1994, he and three other programmers were looking into what features to plan for the successor to Win95. He got his Internet hookup and soon knew the answer: On Aug. 15, he sent e-mail to his small band, saying they needed a browser and might even get one ready for Win95. When Netscape's Navigator hit the Net that fall, Slivka checked it out, then grabbed six people and mapped out the browser features for Win95.

To get the work done faster, one of his programmers took a shopping trip—to Spyglass Inc. in Naperville, Ill., a Netscape rival. It was an ironic moment for Spyglass CEO Douglas P. Colbeth. Six months earlier, he had come calling on Microsoft—only to be rebuffed. "Typically, they said, 'We'll build it ourselves,'" says Colbeth. But by late 1994, Netscape was beginning its ascent and Microsoft was eager to deal. It signed a Spyglass license on Dec. 16.

Network News

Still, going into 1995, Microsoft management was focused on Chicago. Originally scheduled for December, 1994, it had been pushed back to mid-1995 and would emerge, finally, as Win95 that August. The company was scrambling to complete Windows NT for the corporate market, too. "Those were the focus," says Gates, "and the Internet was like an underlying rumble."

Gates had also ordered that Microsoft Network should make its debut in Chicago. The MSN story is loaded with might-have-beens. In December 1992, when Siegelman started the planning, the Net was hardly a showstopper. The real star was AOL, a Windows-based online service that was gaining members at a rapid clip. So in May 1993, Gates approved Siegelman's plan for a rival service that would have a big advantage—the software needed to use it would be included in Win95.

In fall of 1993, the MSN team ramped up to get done in time to come out with Chicago. But, heeding the Net rumblings, Gates agreed to let Rob Glaser, a longtime Microsoft exec who had pioneered the push into multimedia, do an analysis of how the Net affected MSN. His conclusion: Microsoft should "radically change" the strategy and make the online service part of the Net.

Then, fate stepped in. In November 1993, Siegelman, age 34, suffered a brain hemorrhage. He would recover, but his absence prompted the normally relentless Glaser to ease up. He presented his plan to Siegelman's staff, but with the boss away and the team already stressed out, he didn't push hard. "We just couldn't afford to spend a lot of energy changing our plan," says Jeffrey Lill, a former MSN team member. Adds Glaser: "I felt the stars were not aligning for Microsoft to really understand the Net early."

Besides, MSN was a high-profile project. Gates unveiled the planned service in a keynote speech at Comdex in November 1994, and within weeks persuaded Tele-Communications Inc. to pony up $125 million for a 20 percent stake in MSN. TCI chief John C. Malone had been on the verge of investing that amount in rival AOL.

But, says AOL CEO Steven M. Case, "in the final hour, Gates persuaded him—implored him—not to invest in AOL." Three weeks later, Microsoft paid $16.4 million for 15 percent of UUNet Technologies, Inc., which now carries MSN traffic.

Despite MSN, by May 1995, Gates was sounding the Internet alarm. He issued "The Internet Tidal Wave," a memo that hit on the themes that had been reverberating throughout Silicon Valley. He declared that the Net was the "most important single development" since the IBM PC. "I have gone through several stages of increasing my views of its importance. Now, I assign the Internet the highest level," he wrote.

On May 27, Slivka issued his own alarm, titled "The Web Is the Next Platform." He warned that the Web had the potential to supersede Windows. Says Slivka: "I don't know if I actually believed it would happen. But I wanted to make a point."

There was a growing sense among Microsoft execs that the Internet opportunity had to be seized—before it slipped to others. On June 1, 40 of them gathered at the Red Lion Inn in Bellevue, Wash., to brainstorm Net strategy. Gates gave a 20-minute talk on the "Internet Tidal Wave." Slivka's scheduled 15-minute talk ended up lasting more than an hour. "I got some people riled up," he says. At one point, Slivka proposed that Microsoft give away some software on the Net, as Netscape was doing. Gates, he recalls, "called me a communist."

Executives also went through every Net project that Microsoft had in the works and got their first peek at Java. The reaction? "Like the early reaction to my memo, it was lukewarm," says Allard.

Only after Win95 was shipping in August did Microsoft put full force into the Net. "In the three or four months before, there were symptoms that this thing was really accelerating," Gates says. "I said, 'OK, once we get Windows 95 shipped, I'm really going to put a lot of thinking into how this affects our strategy. Can we have a strategy where we bet on the Internet and assume it's really going to drive demand for PCs and software? And how would that reshape our strategy?'"

Gates had no time to lose. On Aug. 8, 1995, Netscape seized the spotlight with a spectacular initial public offering—which soared from $28 to $58 the first day and launched a bull market in Internet stocks. Chairman Jim Clark became a paper billionaire 18 months after launching his company. Gates didn't hit that milestone until Microsoft was 12 years old.

Netscape was gaining more than a following on Wall Street. It had Microsoft-like dominance in the Web-browser business and was signing up blue-chip customers who were building Web sites with the Netscape server program. Meanwhile, all of computerdom was getting jazzed about Java, the Sun software that would make it possible to zap programs as well as Web pages over the Net. That scheme threatened to make the Web a place where Windows mattered not at all. On Nov. 16, Goldman, Sachs & Co. removed Microsoft's stock from it's "recommended for purchase" list because of Internet concerns.

The message was clear: If Microsoft didn't want to be eclipsed in the network-computing era, it was going to have to play on the Internet—and it would have to play by Net rules. It would have to accept the Internet standards—embrace them—and try to hold on to its kingpin position by extending them with Microsoft embellishments.

Microsoft shifted to Internet time, with the bombastic Ballmer beating the tempo. Recalls Gates: "Ballmer is saying, 'Well, where are we?' We're saying, 'Well, we have a lot of pieces, but it's not as comprehensive as it should be.' Ballmer is saying, 'Make it comprehensive, and have an event. In fact, pick a date, and you'll have it comprehensive by then.'"

The date was set: Paul A. Maritz, group vice president for platforms, would pull together an elaborate Internet summit for Dec. 7. Microsoft would announce plans for browsers, Web servers, and a new Web-based MSN—and other initiatives. Holed up in the boardroom, Maritz listened for two days as execs streamed through with their plans. Richard Tong, a Microsoft general manager, hit the road, picking the brains of Net consultants. Slivka's group wrote a 14-page memo on how Microsoft could get 30 percent of the browser market. It suggested getting AOL and CompuServe Inc. to license Microsoft's browser.

Trash Talk

At 8 p.m. on Dec. 6, Microsoft's top execs gathered at the Seattle Center auditorium for a dress rehearsal. They carefully went through each presentation. Gates even noodled with the language on the slides. (At the same time, executives from Microsoft and Sun were working through the night on a Java licensing agreement.) By midnight, the show was ready—until a PR exec told Gates the presentations were overwhelming. They needed a three-point summary for reporters. An exhausted Gates slumped to the floor, Ballmer next to him. Everyone waited, unsure if Gates was thinking or furious. Finally he blurted out: "I just want them to get that we're hard-core about the Internet!"

Since then, there has been no looking back. Microsoft employees tuned in to closed-circuit TV to hear the Internet briefing, got the speeches by e-mail, and later received videotape copies. Gates wanted it perfectly clear what the new marching orders were. He need not have worried, notes Chris Peters, vice-president of the Vermeer Product Unit. "If the chairman says success is defined as *that,* you will get a lot of *that!*"

Today, the Microsoft organization is pumped. "The thing that really motivates us is paranoia and competition," says Maritz. The day after Microsoft's Dec. 7 splash, Netscape CEO James L. Barksdale was asked about the threat Microsoft posed. His joking response: "God is on our side." That was like putting a match to dry kindling. "It's the kind of stuff that gets people up in a locker room," says Silverberg, who now heads Microsoft's Internet division. "I want to thank Netscape. All this trash talk helped get us motivated."

Microsoft is using more than school spirit. Within days of the summit, insiders say, it tried to buy Excite. The start-up's "search-engine" technology, like that of its better-known rival, Yahoo!, would help make MSN a useful gateway to the rest of the Web. Insiders say Microsoft offered $75 million, but Excite turned it down after investment bankers said they could get more by going public. On Apr. 4, Excite went public and is now valued at $84 million. Microsoft's next bid, an estimated $130 million offer for Vermeer Technologies Inc., a start-up with scant sales, succeeded. Vermeer's highly regarded FrontPage is used for creating Web pages.

On Feb. 12, Microsoft unveiled a key weapon in its contest with Netscape: the Internet Information Server. Some 90,000 free copies have been downloaded to date. March brought another major coup: From under the nose of Netscape, Microsoft snared a deal to have its Internet Explorer used as the primary Web browser on AOL. In exchange, Microsoft offered a big concession: putting AOL in Win95, ending an exclusive edge for MSN. Microsoft was on its way from Web wannabe to Web contender. Says Intel Corp. CEO Andrew S. Grove: "That was a masterpiece of pragmatic business attitude."

In June, Microsoft turned its attention to intranets—corporate networks built on Internet technology. On June 13, it outlined an initiative centered on Windows NT 4.0, due late this summer. It will be crammed with Web features, including FrontPage and a new search program. That's attractive to outfits such as Merrill Lynch & Co. that would prefer one supplier for conventional software and the newer Net applications. It's rolling out a trading system around 25,000 Windows PCs and 1,200 NT servers—with intranet and Internet connections.

Bill Gates is counting on customers such as Merrill Lynch to stand by as his company fills in the remaining holes in its Internet strategy. Microsoft still lags in programs for collaboration and electronic commerce, for instance.

The Net upstarts that goaded Microsoft say it's missing a lot more than a few pieces. They claim what's coming out of Redmond is mainly talk. "It doesn't take long to write an ad," sniffs Sun Microsystems CEO Scott McNealy. Gates concedes his work is not done. "We're not saying we're out of the woods on this one," he says. "We have more than a year of incredible execution that we have to do." That's Internet time, mind you.

PART 3

Compounding Confluence—Take I: The Internet and E-commerce

"Netscape Communications Corporation in 1997" discusses how the confluence of several independent technological developments led to the founding and initial growth of the company that produced the first popular browser. By August 1997, Netscape had become one of the fastest growing companies in history. By positioning the company against Microsoft, IBM/Lotus, and other players in the computer industry, Netscape faced daunting strategic challenges, leading the company to shift its strategy several times.

Important discussion topics for this case are (1) the role of "strategic recognition," (2) occupying, defending, and leveraging a strategic position, (3) competing with the 800-pound industry gorilla, and (4) knowing when to "fold" and preparing for it. In terms of our three key themes, this case is a classic example of *P*-controlled change morphing into runaway change; it shows how competitive forces may lead a company to take strategic actions that diverge from its original strategy; and it offers the opportunity to examine the limits of corporate transformation.

"AOL: The Emergence of an Internet Media Company" shows how the confluence of technological forces gave rise to America Online (AOL) and how the company evolved from providing a proprietary online consumer services network of branded content to also becoming an Internet services provider (ISP) and creating a vast new audience for entertainment services. The confluence of forces also drove the merger of Internet audience company AOL with traditional media giant Time Warner.

Important discussion topics for this case are (1) sustaining versus disruptive technological change, (2) threats and opportunities driven by industry convergence, (3) strategy versus opportunism, and (4) managing complex acquisition integration. In terms of our three themes, the case offers an example of *P*-independent change morphing into *P*-controlled change and then into runaway change as the external environment changes within a short period of time; it shows how strategic actions may sometimes get ahead of articulating a clear corporate strategy and the risks of such; and it offers the opportunity to examine the unpredictable path caused by transient industry change of corporate transformation pursued opportunistically.

"Amazon.com: Evolution of the e-Tailer" sketches the growth of the most famous online retailer and examines the business and technological challenges Amazon faced in 2001. The case reviews the evolution of the company's business model and how over five years of phenomenal growth it expanded into international markets and added many categories, partners, and physical infrastructure.

Important discussion topics for this case are (1) vision versus strategy, (2) the logic of the Internet "boom," (3) exploiting opportunity versus managing growth, and (4) new business versus new capability. In terms of our three key themes, the case offers an example of *P*-controlled change that threatened on various occasions to morph into runaway change but has not done so yet; it shows the difficulties of keeping strategy and action aligned in the face of rapidly changing external forces; and it offers the opportunity to examine the various ways in which the company could transform itself again and what the most advantageous transformation would likely be.●

Case 2.1

Netscape Communications Corporation in 1997

Stanford Graduate School of Business

In a period of only 2 years, we distributed over 62 million copies of Navigator, making it the most prolific computer application in history. This helped us become the fastest growing software company in the Internet market. One challenge that we face is how to continue this growth. Where is the market, and what products can we build to grow into that market? Our projections indicate that software for intranets and extranets will become a $10 billion market by the year 2000. If we can capture half of that, we'll be the fastest growing software company in history. The question is how do we do that? This is the most competitive business on the planet. And honey attracts flies. If we find something that looks attractive, our competitors will be after it as well.

— **Jim Barksdale,** CEO, Netscape

Netscape burst onto the scene in 1995 with Internet software that popularized the World Wide Web, pioneering technology that promised to revolutionize the computer industry. Netscape had helped to establish the emerging standards for Internet computing, and was a strong proponent of Sun Microsystem's *Java*[1] programming language, which some analysts believed could challenge Microsoft's dominance of computer operating systems. By 1997, Netscape had the leading market share for *Web server* and *browser* software, its revenue was growing rapidly, and Netscape had become established as a powerful brand that was closely identified with the Internet.

Netscape was focused on the corporate software market for Internet, *intranet, extranet,* and *groupware* products, which positioned them against Microsoft and IBM's Lotus Division. Microsoft was actively targeting the corporate market with their own intranet and groupware product suites. Lotus had pioneered the groupware market with their Notes product, and planned to transform Notes into an open, modular, network computing platform based on Web standards.

By August 1997, in two short years, Netscape had become one of the fastest growing companies in history. But by positioning his company against two of the most formidable competitors in the computer industry, CEO Jim Barksdale realized that his young company faced daunting strategic challenges.

Internet Computing

In 1997, a new computing paradigm—"Internet computing"—was rapidly taking shape. This new paradigm was the result of the confluence of several independent technological developments: the emergence of the Internet and the World Wide Web, client/server-based computing, Web browsers and Web servers, and a new computer language called Java.

The Internet began in the late 1960s as an experiment by the U.S. Department of Defense to build a highly robust, fault-tolerant communication system. The Advanced Research Projects Agency Network (ARPANet) was established in 1969 with four interconnected computers. By the early 1980s, Transmission Control Protocol/Internet Protocol (*TCP/IP*) had emerged as the ARPANet's standard networking protocol, and there were approximately 200 computers attached to the network. In the mid-1980s, the National Science Foundation established a high-speed communications backbone across the United States, called the NSFNet, which became known as the Internet.[2]

The Internet grew to become a worldwide network of networks based on the TCP/IP networking protocol. Above the TCP/IP networking protocol, a number of different application protocols had been implemented, including SMTP (for e-mail), *FTP* (for file transfers), and *Telnet* (for remote terminal service). The World Wide Web was established in 1989 at CERN (Conseil Europeen pour la Recherche Nucleaire) in Switzerland by a research scientist who developed *hypertext* and *HTTP* to reference other authors' documents. By early 1996, there were approximately 40 million computers connected to the Internet or with access to the World Wide Web, and this number was growing rapidly (see Exhibit 1).

---

[1]Italicized words are included in the glossary; see Appendix.

This case was prepared by Raymond S. Bamford, MBA '96, under the supervision of Professor Robert A. Burgelman as a basis for class discussion, rather than to illustrate either effective or ineffective handling of a management situation.

---

[2]Source: *The Internet Report,* Morgan Stanley, 1996.

EXHIBIT 1 | Forecast for Client Computers on the Internet, 1995–2000 (millions)

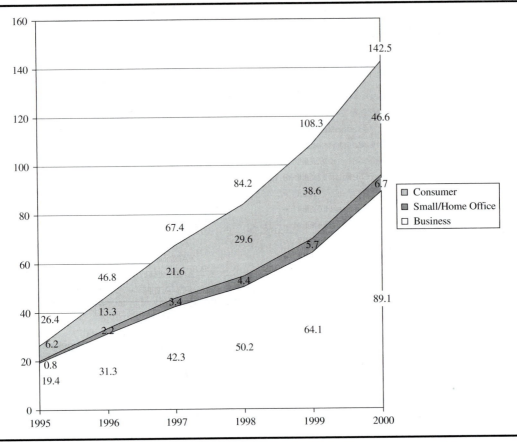

Source: International Data Corporation, September 1996.

Client/Server Computing

The growth of network computing led to the emergence of distributed applications that run and communicate across multiple computers. The vast majority of applications implemented on top of TCP/IP networks communicate using the client/server paradigm. Broadly speaking, a client program is one that initiates communication and sends requests, whereas a server program waits for communication and responds to requests.[3] In the late 1980s and early 1990s, client/server computing experienced rapid growth, as companies moved away from homogeneous computing systems based on mainframes and mini-computers and toward heterogeneous computing systems based on PCs and workstations. Internet computing is one specific example of client/server computing.

Groupware is a client/server application segment that was pioneered at Lotus and manifested in the Notes product. Groupware is a broad product category that includes a number of different collaborative functions, including e-mail, enterprise *directories,* discussion groups, *workflow* and group scheduling. In 1997, the four leading vendors of groupware products were Lotus, Novell, Microsoft, and Netscape.

Web Browsers and Web Servers

The Web browser is a client software application that allows a user to display Web content (*HTML*). Web servers are programs that wait for and respond to requests from browsers. Browsers typically request to view a particular Web page by submitting its *URL* (uniform resource locator, e.g. http://www.stanford.edu). Web pages can consist of static information stored in HTML files, or dynamic information that is generated

---
[3]*Internetworking with TCP/IP,* Douglas Comer, 1997.

by interactions between the Web server and other server applications and databases.

In late 1994, a number of firms were selling Web browsers. Mosaic had the dominant browser market share (40 percent), but a number of other firms were competing as well. Beginning in December 1994 with the introduction of Navigator, Netscape quickly captured a large share of the emerging browser market. By 1997, Netscape and Microsoft had become the leading players in both the browser and Web server software markets.

Java Computing

Sun Microsystems's Java had attracted considerable publicity, as well as support among Internet developers. As an object-oriented programming language, Java had several advantages.[4] *Objects* are self-contained, reusable fragments of software code that can be combined to form complete applications.[5] By using objects, application logic could be divided into smaller, task-specific components, which made them easier to write and update, and also made them well suited for distributed computing across networks. In addition, Java was easy for many programmers to learn. Java was first used to enhance Web pages with transportable *applets* that were downloaded from a server and executed on the client computer to provide features such as animated graphics and scrolling text. Increasingly in 1997, Java was also being used to write server applications and communicate with databases. Java played an integral part in Netscape's technology architecture, and Netscape and Sun were close partners in advancing and promoting Java.

Sun and Netscape positioned Java as a platform for Internet applications. The Java platform consisted of both a Java *virtual machine,* which provided the runtime environment[6] in which Java programs were executed, as well as Java APIs, which allowed Java programs to communicate outside the Java environment. The virtual machine provided an abstraction layer between the Java code and the underlying operating system. Thus, Java theoretically provided platform independence, although

incompatibilities between different vendors' virtual machines weakened Sun's marketing claims of "write once, run anywhere." In addition, Java was designed for networked environments and provided unique security features, such as the Java "sandbox" that limited what downloaded applets could do, thereby limiting the possibility of a security breach due to the execution of a malicious applet.

According to Marc Andreessen,

> Java enables a networked world where arbitrary applications are accessible on demand, to run anything you want anywhere you want. Java is still a new technology with a lot to prove. It's not at the level of maturity to replace everything else—yet. But we believe that it will result in profound changes for how software and services are developed and delivered both across the Internet and intranets. . . . When history looks back at the current era, it may judge the last 40 years of computing—where applications are bound to chips and OS's—as the exception. For the next 300 years, perhaps the norm will be for applications to be completely independent of silicon and operating systems. If you can use any chip, any OS, and any GUI, what is the spectrum of computing devices that will emerge? If our vision is right, the NC will happen and the applications will be there. Even my cell phone will have a GUI.

In spite of its wide support, Java did face several technical challenges. First, Java was an interpreted, rather than a compiled language. Thus, Java code must be distributed across the network and compiled before being executed, which negatively impacted performance. Java *"just-in-time" (JIT) compilers* promised to speed up Java execution, but had not yet achieved performance comparable to native, compiled applications.[7] Second, the Java sandbox provided necessary security for the Internet environment, but also constrained functionality that might limit its usefulness for intranet applications. Third, there was a trade-off between the goal of platform independence and the desire to optimize functionality by exploiting specific features of the different OSs.

Intranets and Extranets

Traditionally, most client/server applications required a separate, specialized program to run on the client machine. Developing and supporting these client programs can be expensive and difficult. With Web technology, a single

---

[4]As a programming language, Java is like a simplified version of C++.

[5]The term "object" is used with varying degrees of strictness. Typically, an object carries both its processing logic and data.

[6]The runtime environment refers to the environment where software code is actually executed; it is distinguished from the development environment, where programs are written, and the compile and test environments, where programs are converted to executable binary code (compiled) and then tested.

---

[7]Such as traditional desktop applications.

client program can be used—the Web browser—for a wide variety of applications. Intranets are private, intra-company networks and applications that are based on Internet and Web technologies. In 1997, companies were increasingly deploying intranets to facilitate internal communication, collaboration, and business process reengineering.[8] According to one analyst, 51 percent of major corporations had built or planned to build an intranet in the next 12 months, and the total market for intranet software[9] from 1996 to 2000 would be greater than $9 billion. Extranets extend Web technologies to carry private Web traffic between a company and its suppliers, partners, and customers. Extranets were being adopted to enhance communications, to reduce costs, and to implement electronic commerce.

Spawned by Internet Computing: Netscape Communications

Company Founding to IPO

Netscape was founded in April 1994 by Jim Clark and Marc Andreessen. Clark had previously founded Silicon Graphics and had worked as an associate professor at Stanford University. Andreessen had co-authored the original Mosaic Web browser while studying as an undergraduate at the University of Illinois. Mosaic, the first Web client with a graphical user interface, helped to popularize the Web. In early 1994, Andreessen and most of the Mosaic design team joined Netscape. Jim Barksdale became Netscape's CEO at the start of 1995, and immediately began building his management team (see Exhibit 2).

Navigator, Netscape's first client product, was developed with several key features that differentiated it from the original Mosaic browser. Navigator displayed text from a Web page before displaying graphics, so users could read the Web page while graphics were loading, (rather than having to wait until the graphics were loaded) thus giving the appearance of higher performance. Users could also click on a new Web page before the previous page had been fully downloaded. In addition, Navigator

cached Web pages in memory, which allowed users to instantly view Web pages that had been previously downloaded. Navigator also incorporated encryption capabilities for secure data transmission based on the Secure Sockets Layer (SSL) standard that Netscape helped establish. According to Marc Andreessen,

> Our goal with Navigator was to build off of Mosaic, to improve its deficiencies, and to be first to market with a commercial product. We achieved these goals, but it helped that the other major software companies were asleep at the switch.

Netscape's original strategy was to make their browser pervasive, and earn revenue from the sale of Netscape Commerce Server, the company's first Web server. The server was sold to companies wishing to offer Web applications and content to the large installed base of Netscape browsers. Netscape used the Internet as their primary distribution channel, allowing users to download free copies of Navigator. Navigator was made available on a number of operating system platforms, including Windows, Macintosh, and Unix. This strategy helped Netscape capture 80 percent of the browser market in 1995. According to Barksdale, "We were able to distribute millions of copies of Navigator at minimal cost, which helped us to become profitable almost immediately."

One of Netscape's early objectives was to establish a strong market presence for their brand. According to Barksdale,

> Our approach at Netscape was very different from my experience at Federal Express, where we could spend hundreds of millions of dollars to build our brand. At Netscape, we pursued almost every free medium we could. For the deployment of Navigator, we used the press and other free promotions to increase our visibility. The goal was to have Netscape everywhere, including on all platforms and operating systems. We even did our IPO earlier than we normally would have, at least in part to get more publicity and attention. The IPO allowed us to target a whole new audience with our brand. We used this brand recognition to help get into the business market.

In August 1995, Netscape went public with one of the most successful IPOs in history. The stock was expected to sell for $28 per share, but after rising to $71 per share, it finally ended the day at just over $58 per share.[10] Exhibit 3, on page 90, shows Netscape's stock price over time.

---

[8]Intranets were increasingly used to perform groupware functions such as collaboration and e-mail. Intranets also included more general information-sharing applications. For example, a corporate department could use an intranet Web server to share-information widely throughout the company.

[9]Intranet software defined as browsers, Web servers, firewall, and Web development tools.

---

[10]Datapro Information Services.

EXHIBIT 2 | Netscape Executive Team

James Clark, Chairman of the Board, 52

Dr. Clark cofounded the company in April 1994. From inception of Netscape to January 1995, Clark served as president and CEO. From 1981 to 1994, Clark was chairman of the board of Silicon Graphics, which he had founded in 1981. Prior to founding SGI, Clark was an associate professor at Stanford University. Clark holds a Ph.D. from the University of Utah and MS and BS degrees from the University of New Orleans.

James Barksdale, President and CEO, 54

Mr. Barksdale joined Netscape in January 1995 as president and CEO. From January 1992 to January 1995, Barksdale served as president and COO, and as of September 1994, CEO of AT&T Wireless. From April 1983 to January 1992, Barksdale served as executive vice president and COO of Federal Express. From 1979 to 1983, Barksdale served as CIO of Federal Express. Barksdale held various management positions, including CIO, with Cook Industries in the mid-1970s and was employed by IBM from 1965 to 1972. He serves as a director of 3Com Corporation, Hannah's Entertainment, Robert Mondavi Corporation, and @ Home Corporation. Barksdale holds a BA from the University of Mississippi.

Marc Andreessen, Senior Vice President, Technology, 25

Mr. Andreessen cofounded Netscape in April 1994. He received a BS from the University of Illinois in December 1993, where he coauthored the original NCSA Mosaic Web browser.

Eric Hahn, Senior Vice President and GM of the Server Product Division, 36

Mr. Hahn joined Netscape in November 1995 as VP, Enterprise Technology. He served as president and CEO of Collabra Software from February 1993 to November 1995. From September 1992 to February 1993 he worked for a venture capital firm. From June 1990 to August 1992, he served as VP, General Manager of the cc:Mail division of Lotus. Mr. Hahn holds a BS from the Worcester Polytechnic Institute.

Mike Homer, Senior Vice President, Sales and Marketing, 39

Mr. Homer joined the company in October 1994 as VP, Marketing. From April 1994 to October 1994, Mr. Homer was a consultant. From August 1993 to April 1994, he served as VP, Engineering at EO Corporation. From July 1991 to July 1993, he was VP, Marketing at GO Corporation. He had previously been Director of Product Marketing at Apple, where he served from 1982 through 1991. He holds a BS from the University of California, Berkeley.

Richard Schell, Senior Vice President and GM of the Client Product Division, 47

Dr. Schell joined Netscape in October 1994 as VP, Engineering. From January 1993 to October 1994, Schell was employed by Symantec Corporation, most recently as VP/GM of the Central Point Division. From March 1989 to December 1992, he served as VP, Languages and dBase, at Borland International. Prior to that, he held various positions at Sun Microsystems and Intel Corporation. Dr. Schell holds a Ph.D., an MS, and a BA from the University of Illinois.

James Sha, Senior Vice President and GM, Integrated Applications, 46

Mr. Sha joined Netscape in August 1994 as VP/GM, Integrated Applications. From June 1990 to August 1994, he served as VP, Unix Division, at Oracle. From June 1986 to June 1990, he served as VP/GM, Advanced Systems Division at Wyse Technology. Mr. Sha holds the MSEE from the University of California, Berkeley, an MBA from Santa Clara University, and a BSEE from National Taiwan University.

Browser Wars: Late 1995 to Late 1996

In August 1995, Microsoft released the beta version of its own browser, Internet Explorer, which was based on a license of the Mosaic browser.[11] This was followed by a December announcement from Bill Gates that Microsoft would "embrace and extend" Internet standards with Microsoft products and technologies.

In 1995, the online service providers (OLSPs), such as Prodigy and AOL, were one of the primary access channels to the Web for consumers. The OLSPs had either developed their own browsers, as Prodigy had, or they had acquired browser companies hoping that a superior browser would differentiate their service.[12] In late 1995 and early 1996, the OLSPs began supporting the browsers from Netscape and Microsoft, resulting in considerable consolidation of market share (see Exhibit 11). IBM announced that it had licensed Netscape Navigator for use in its own products, as well as for its Prodigy online service. On March 11, 1996, CompuServe announced that it would support Navigator and AOL announced that its customers would be able to download and use Navigator through their service. On March 12, 1996, Microsoft countered with an announcement with

---

[11]The Mosaic master license is held by Spyglass Technologies, which licenses the technology to several companies including Microsoft.

[12]Examples include CompuServe (which bought Spry) and AOL (which bought Booklinks/Interworks).

EXHIBIT 3 | Netscape Stock Price over Time Normalized to 100 on 8/15/95 (U.S. $)

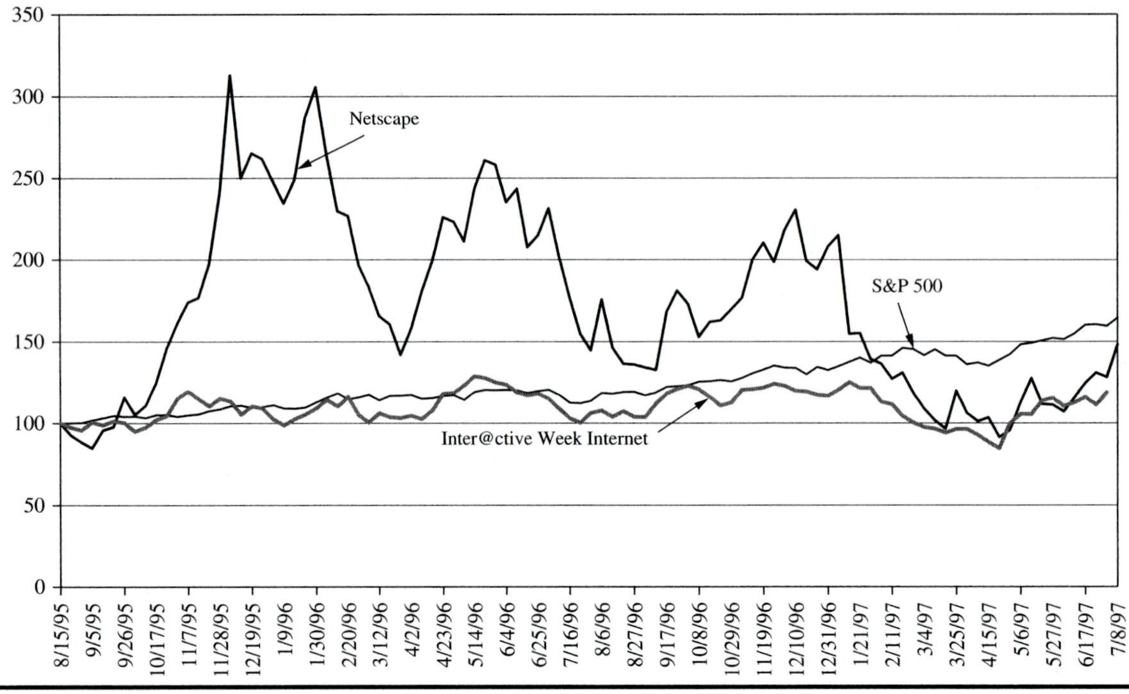

AOL that Explorer would be the "preferred" browser for AOL customers, a deal that they secured by agreeing to bundle AOL software with Windows 95. Microsoft also won a major deal with AT&T, where Explorer would be distributed through AT&T's WorldNet service in return for AT&T's software being included with Windows 95.[13]

In early 1996, Microsoft created a greater challenge for Netscape by announcing that Explorer would be bundled with Windows 95 and NT, thereby obviating the need for separate browser software. Microsoft's intent was to completely integrate the Web with a user's local PC. By offering the browser for free, Microsoft threatened a major source of revenue for Netscape, as well as their dominant market share.

In early 1996, Netscape hoped to maintain a six-month technology lead in the development of Navigator.[14] In August 1996, Microsoft announced Internet Explorer 3.0 with substantially enhanced product functionality. A week later, Netscape introduced Navigator 3.0 with its

own improvements. Referring to the browser battle, one analyst said, "Six months ago, it looked like Microsoft was 18 months behind Netscape. Now it is roughly equal in functionality and coming up quickly on all other measures."[15]

According to Jim Barksdale,

> One of the things that is really striking about our business is the rate of commoditization. At first, we offered just a browser on the client side. . . . But our strategy has always been focused on more than just a browser. We have to have a strategy that is harder to duplicate, and focused on providing more valuable services.

Targeting the Corporate Market with Product Suites

Netscape's strategy for 1997 called for a focus on corporate intranets as the target market, as well as plans for new client and server software, which would be available in mid-1997. This strategy marked a significant transition for the company. On the client side, Netscape announced that its browser would be bundled into an integrated

---

[13]Netscape lobbied the Justice Department's antitrust division, charging that Microsoft was using unfair sales practices through its dominance of the operating system market, to distribute its Internet Explorer browser.

[14]"The War of the Web," *International Data Corporation,* May 1996.

[15]"Browser Wars: Round Three," *International Data Corporation,* September 1996.

EXHIBIT 4 | Netscape Communicator

Netscape Communicator: An integrated suite of client software products, including a browser, an e-mail client, groupware, and scheduling. Communicator comes in both a Standard Edition and a Professional Edition. Communicator includes the following components:

>   **Navigator:** Web browser that provides users with access to information and applications on an intranet or over the Internet.
>
>   **Messenger:** Internet e-mail client that provides rich text messaging (including special fonts, italics, bullets, etc.), encryption, directory access, and support for mobile users.
>
>   **Collabra:** Group discussion software for sharing information among multiple users.
>
>   **Conference:** Real time conferencing over the Internet and intranets; allows users to share documents and converse in real time.
>
>   **Composer:** User-friendly authoring tool for creating Web, intranet, e-mail, and discussion documents.
>
>   **Netcaster:** Enables "push" delivery of information and offline browsing.

Professional Edition:

>   **Calendar:** Group scheduling solution, which was primarily targeted at enterprises.
>
>   **IBM Host on Demand:** Terminal emulator that provides a user-friendly way to access IBM mainframe information.
>
>   **AutoAdmin:** Tools for centralized management and control of Communicator settings across the enterprise.

Netscape Communicator Platform and System Requirements

Vendor	Architecture	Operating System	Recommended Memory Requirements
Intel	486 or later	Windows 3.×, 95, Windows NT 3.51, 4.0	16 MB
Apple	68030 or PowerPC	Macintosh System 7.5 or later	16 MB
Digital	Alpha	Digital Unix 3.2, 4.0	64 MB
Hewlett-Packard	700 series	HP-UX 9.05, 10.×	64 MB
IBM	RS/6000	AIX 4.×	64 MB
Caldera	Intel	Linux 2.0×	64 MB
Silicon Graphics	MIPS	IRIX 5.3, 6.2, 6.3	64 MB
Sun	SPARC	Solaris 2.4, 2.5, SunOS 4.1.3	64 MB

product family, called Communicator, that would include e-mail, groupware, scheduling, and other enterprise applications.[16] Netscape's goal with Communicator was to enable customers to "send anything, to anyone, anywhere."[17] On the server side, Netscape announced SuiteSpot, an integrated suite of 10 server products, which would include content publishing and management capabilities, as well as e-mail and groupware capabilities (see Exhibit 4 and Exhibit 5, which describe Communicator and SuiteSpot in detail).

With this strategy, Netscape was forced to enter several mature markets, including those for e-mail and groupware, that were dominated by vendors with fully functional products and established customer bases. Netscape believed that the integration of Web content with "everyday applications, especially e-mail and groupware,"[18] would become the killer application for 1997. According to Barksdale,

> The commitment to target the groupware and e-mail markets was a major decision for Netscape. At the

---

[16]Much of Communicator would be developed in-house, but key components were obtained through the November '95 acquisition of Collabra Software.

[17]"Netscape's Strategy and Products for 1997," http://www.netscape.com/comprod/announce/overview.html.

[18]"Netscape's Strategy and Products for 1997," http://www.netscape.com/comprod/announce/overview.html.

EXHIBIT 5 | Netscape SuiteSpot and Commercial Applications

Netscape SuiteSpot: An integrated suite of 10 server products that scale from the work group to the enterprise. SuiteSpot included content publishing and management capabilities, as well as e-mail and groupware capabilities. SuiteSpot would also support Netscape's Open Network Environment (ONE) platform.

Enterprise Server: Allows advanced Web services for content management and network-based applications.

Messaging Server: Sends, receives, and manages Internet e-mail.

Collabra Server: Manages secure newsgroups across the intranet or the Internet.

Media Server: Provides streaming audio for Web sites.

Calendar Server: Schedules people, groups, and resources.

Catalog Server: Creates, manages, and keeps current an online catalog of documents on a company's intranet.

Certificate Server: Enables an organization to issue, sign, and manage public key digital certificates.

Directory Server: Manages "white pages" information, including names, e-mail addresses, and digital certificates.

Proxy Server: Provides Content replication, traffic logging, and message filtering for Web publishing.

LiveWire Pro: Offers tools for developing and managing sophisticated Web sites and network-centered applications. Includes an Informix database and native connectivity to other leading databases.

Commercial Applications: Building blocks for handling Internet based electronic commerce, including billing, security, credit card transactions, etc. Examples include:

Publishing System: Tools for building free of fee-based publications on the Web; includes customizable billing options.

Merchant System: Tools for building a Web based shopping site, including automatic calculation of shipping and sales tax, product searches for customers, and easy updating of product information.

Netscape Enterprise Server 3.0 Supported Platforms and System Requirements

Vendor	Architecture	Operating System	Recommended Memory Requirements
Intel	486 or later	Windows NT	64 MB
Digital	Alpha	Windows NT, Digital Unix	64 MB
Hewlett-Packard	PA-RISC (HP 9000)	HP-UX	64 MB
IBM	RS/6000	AIX	64 MB
Silicon Graphics	MIPS	IRIX	64 MB
Sun	SPARC	Solaris	64 MB

time, it wasn't obvious that we should target the e-mail market where there were already a dozen or so established competitors.

After the release of Communicator in the spring of 1997, Navigator was no longer sold or licensed separately. In contrast, Microsoft offered Explorer separately and for no charge. Communicator was targeted primarily at the corporate market. But some analysts[19] questioned whether the companies that used Netscape's browsers would be willing to convert their e-mail and groupware applications to Netscape from their current supplier. According to Eric Byunn, senior product manager of Netscape Communicator,

Navigator was bundled with Communicator for both technical and marketing reasons. The mail client was

designed to be tightly integrated with the browser, so it was difficult to break them apart. In addition, it was important for us to be seen as a messaging and groupware solution provider, not just a browser company. The product bundle, combined with the name change, helped us to evangelize our total messaging solution.

Lotus had been bundling Netscape Navigator as part of Notes since late 1995. The release of Communicator put this agreement in jeopardy. Communicator contained groupware and messaging capabilities that competed directly with Notes. Lotus president Jeff Papows had said that if Netscape would separate Navigator from Communicator, they would likely continue to bundle the Netscape browser.[20] On August 4, 1997, Lotus made the highly publicized decision to drop Navigator for its

---

[19]For example, Forrester Research.

[20]"Groupware Cease-Fire," *PC Week*, June 1997.

Notes and SmartSuite products, and to bundle Internet Explorer instead. Perhaps even more significant, Lotus announced their intention to support the Microsoft development environment.[21]

The Lotus announcement closely followed a similar announcement by Intuit, which had been bundling Navigator since their merger deal with Microsoft collapsed in 1995, indicating that they would drop Navigator in favor of Internet Explorer. Also in August, Apple agreed to bundle Internet Explorer with their OS, instead of Navigator. As part of this deal, Microsoft invested $130 million in Apple. Similarly, after an equity investment from Microsoft for 10 percent of the company, Progressive Networks[22] agreed to collaborate closely with Microsoft on technology and products for streaming audio and video media over the Internet.

On August 18, 1997, Netscape announced the reversal of its policy of not selling the browser separately, and introduced Navigator 4.0. Navigator 4.0 includes Netcaster, which allowed news and information to be "pushed" to the browser in broadcast style; it included Messenger Express, a simplified version of Netscape's e-mail product; and it included Calendar Express, a scheduling program. Navigator 4.0 was priced at $39, while Communicator was priced at $59. As part of the announcement, IBM agreed to include Navigator 4.0 with its PCs and software, including Lotus Notes, but they would continue to honor their previous agreement with Microsoft as well. Other supporters included Sun Microsystems, Hewlett-Packard, Digital, Silicon Graphics, and Novell.

Content: A New Business Opportunity

In 1997, Netscape's Web site had become one of the most popular on the Internet. According to Jim Barksdale,

> We get 140 million hits per day on our Web site. This suggests that the Web is a great channel for the distribution of content. The traffic to our Web site gives us new marketing opportunities to sell products and to offer new services. And we can earn revenue from these services from either upstream or downstream sources.

Netscape had teamed with several major search-engine providers and content developers. For example,

Netscape and Yahoo! partnered to create Netscape Guide by Yahoo!, an Internet navigation service available from Netscape's Web site. Netscape had also formed a partnership with ABC News, whereby ABC news headlines would be accessible from Netscape's home page. In return, ABC's Internet site would utilize the unique features of Netscape Communicator.[23] Both Microsoft and Netscape had offered promotions with content providers that allowed users to receive free access to premium content if the user was using a particular browser. For example, Microsoft had teamed with Disney and Time Warner, and Netscape had teamed with ABC News and CNNfn. According to Marc Andreessen, "We have the most popular Web site on the Net. Last quarter [2Q97], our Web site generated over $25 million and this business is growing like a rocket."

Netscape Performance History

Netscape was unusual as a start-up in that it had become profitable soon after its inception, not counting merger related charges. Exhibit 6 shows Netscape's financial history over time. In the second quarter of 1997, Netscape had a net loss of $43.8 million on total revenue of $35.2 million (net income for the quarter would have been $8.8 million without the $52.6 million nonrecurring charge related to mergers and acquisitions). Total revenue increased 12 percent between the second and first quarters of '97, and 80 percent between the second quarter of '97 and the second quarter of '96. In the second quarter, Netscape revenue was divided roughly evenly among client product revenue (39.3 percent), server product revenue (33.9 percent), and service revenue[24] (26.7 percent) (see Exhibit 7). Netscape expected that the revenue composition between client and server products would increasingly favor server products. Netscape attributed its increases in service revenue primarily to increased Web advertising, content co-marketing, and trademark licensing, and to a lesser extent consulting, training, and support.

Netscape's Competitive Advantage

Netscape believed that its competitive advantage stemmed from its technology leadership, its adherence to open Internet standards, and its multiplatform support. One important factor in maintaining technology

---

[21]Including the Active Server Pages (ASP) in Internet Information Server (IIS), Active Directory services, the Channel Definition Format (CDF), and the entire Component Object Model (COM) framework for ActiveX objects.

[22]Progressive Networks is a private company based in Seattle, WA.

[23]Unique features were those not supported by Microsoft's Internet Explorer.

[24]Service revenues are derived from consulting, training, and support, as well as Web advertising, content co-marketing agreements, and trademark licensing.

EXHIBIT 6 | Summary of Netscape's Financial Results ($ millions)

	Q2 1997	Q1 1997	Year Ended December 31			
			1996	1995	1994	1993*
Revenues:						
Product revenues	99.1	89.8	291.1	77.5	3.3	1.0
Service revenues	36.2	30.5	55.1	7.9	0.8	.1
Total revenues	135.2	120.2	346.2	85.4	4.1	1.1
Cost of Revenues:						
Cost of product revenues	11.1	9.8	36.9	9.2	.2	.03
Cost of service revenues	6.2	6.1	13.0	2.5	.2	.04
Total cost of revenues	17.3	15.8	50.0	11.7	.4	.07
Gross Profit	117.9	104.4	296.2	73.7	3.7	1.0
Operating Expenses:						
Research & development	31.8	29.0	82.3	26.8	4.1	.9
Sales and marketing	61.7	54.0	153.6	43.7	7.8	1.5
General and administrative	10.8	9.7	30.6	11.3	3.4	.5
Property rights agreement and related charges	——	——	.2	.5	2.5	——
Merger related charges	52.6	——	6.1	2.0	——	——
Total operating expenses	157.0	92.7	273.5	84.4	17.8	2.9
Income:						
Operating income (loss)	(39.1)	11.7	22.7	(10.7)	(14.1)	(1.8)
Interest income, net	2.4	2.4	8.7	4.6	.2	0.0
Equity in net losses of joint ventures	(1.9)	(1.5)	(1.9)	——	——	——
Other income, net	.5	0.9	6.7	4.6	.2	0.0
Income (loss) before taxes	(38.6)	12.6	29.5	(6.1)	(13.8)	(1.8)
Provision for income taxes	5.2	4.7	8.5	0.5	——	——
Net income (loss)	$ (43.8)	$ 7.9	$ 20.9	$ (6.6)	$ (13.8)	$ (1.8)
Net income (loss) per share	$ (0.49)	$ 0.09	$ 0.24	$ (0.09)	$ (0.21)	$ (0.03)

Source: Netscape Financial Reports.

*Figures represent consolidated financial results; 1993 figures result from acquisitions.

EXHIBIT 7 | Netscape Revenue Breakdown, by Quarter* ($ millions)

	1997 2Q	1997 1Q	1996			
			4Q	3Q	2Q	1Q
Revenues:						
Client products	53.1	43.1	58.5	58.9	45.1	35.0
Server products**	45.9	46.6	37.5	24.9	17.2	14.1
Product revenues	99.1	89.8	96.0	83.8	62.3	49.1
Service revenues	36.1	30.5	19.1	16.3	12.7	7.1
Total revenues	135.2	120.2	115.1	100.0	75.0	56.1

*Netscape's fiscal year ends on 12/31.

**Includes server, commercial applications, and other.

Note: A significant percentage of Netscape's income in most quarters can be attributed to several large licensing transactions with enterprise customers. Thus, the company's quarterly revenue is subject to potentially significant fluctuations.

leadership is recruiting talented employees. According to Jim Barksdale,

> When it comes to the creation and use of the Net, we have the best minds in the world. We've got wizards that build this stuff like anyone on the planet. We have the Mosaic team that invented the Web browser at the University of Illinois. We have the team that created the *LDAP* technology at the University of Michigan. And we've used acquisitions to get experts in an emerging field. For example, the Collabra acquisition gave us some great expertise in the groupware market.

Netscape is a strong advocate of supporting open Internet standards. Netscape had helped establish HTTP, LDAP, and SMTP as industry standards, and was working to establish *IIOP* and other protocols as industry standards as well. Unlike its competitors, Netscape's products and services all related to the Internet. Netscape advocated deploying the same protocols and technologies inside and outside the enterprise, which simplified implementation (corporate developers only needed to learn one technology) and improved performance (by eliminating *gateways* that translated from one protocol to the other). One Netscape marketing manager commented that, "You wouldn't use a phone system that only worked inside your company."

Netscape's multiplatform support was a major differentiator, especially vis-à-vis Microsoft. Netscape client products were available on all of the major desktop operating systems, and Netscape server products were available on all of the major network operating systems (see Exhibits 4 and 5). Exhibit 8 shows the market share distribution of both client and server operating systems. According to Rick Schell, Netscape senior vice president and GM of Netscape's client product division,

> The networked computing environment is more complex than the desktop computing environment, and inherently heterogeneous. We support multiple platforms and open standards because this is the best way to solve fundamental customer problems in these heterogeneous environments.

The Competition for Internet, Intranet, and Extranet Computing

In 1997, the market for Internet software was developing very rapidly, and the competition for Internet computing was being waged on multiple fronts. The most important product categories were groupware, browsers, Web servers, directories, and electronic mail. In addition, the

battle to define the technology architecture for distributed computing would have a major impact on each of these product categories, and would profoundly influence the entire computer industry.

Groupware

Groupware includes a number of different collaborative functions, including e-mail, enterprise directories, discussion groups, workflow, and group scheduling. The four leading vendors in the groupware category were Netscape with Communicator and SuiteSpot, Microsoft with Outlook and Exchange, Lotus with Notes and Domino, and Novell with Groupwise. In 1997, a major trend in the groupware market was the integration of Internet technologies with these products for corporate intranets and extranets.

Netscape began shipping Communicator and SuiteSpot, its first products with groupware capabilities, in early 1997. Netscape's groupware products were distinguished by their adherence to open standards and their support for heterogeneous computing environments. In addition, Netscape's directory services and application development framework (both discussed below) were key advantages in this segment. Netscape's groupware products were relatively immature compared to Microsoft Exchange and Lotus Notes, and they lacked several important features, including workflow and *replication*. Netscape's calendar services were not initially well integrated with other groupware services.[25] For example, users could not yet receive meeting or scheduling notifications via Internet mail. In 1997, Netscape's installed base of groupware products was small, but they were widely viewed as a leading intranet provider (see Exhibit 9, which shows intranet server and groupware market share).

Microsoft began shipping its Exchange server in March 1996. Although the Exchange server and the Outlook client were primarily messaging products, they also provided groupware features in addition to e-mail, such as group scheduling, workflow, and document routing. Exchange offered advantages in price/performance relative to SuiteSpot and Notes.[26] Microsoft had tightened the integration of its Outlook e-mail client with the Exchange servers, improving what had been a major

---

[25]Netscape licensed its calendar client and server from a third party. The second release of these products would address the integration shortcoming.

[26]Source: Forrester Research, July 1997.

EXHIBIT 8 | Operating System Market Share, Client & Server, 1996

Server Operating System License Shipments, 1996*

	New Software Licenses (000s)	Market share (% by units)	CAGR 1996–2001
Novell Netware	993	33.3%	3.8%
Windows NT Server	732	24.5	29.7
Combined Unix Servers*	616	20.6	11.1
IBM OS/2	345	11.6	−2.5
Other Server NOSs	300	10.0	−4.4
Total	**2,986**	**100%**	**12.9%**

*Combined Unix Servers (100%) consists of SCO OpenServer (31%), IBM AIX (16%), HP-UX (11%), Sun Solaris (10%), SCO UnixWare (6%), Sun Interactive Unix (4%), Sun Solaris X 86 (3%), Digital Unix (3%), SGI Irix (1%), and Other Unix servers (15%).

Client Operating System License Shipments, 1996**

	New Software Licenses (000s)	Market share (% by units)
Windows 95	47,068	62.9
Windows 3.X/DOS	13,000	17.4
Mac OS	4,207	5.6
Windows NT Workstation	2,280	3.0
DOS alone	2,952	3.9
OS/2 client	2,125	2.8
Unix	801	1.1
Other	2,453	3.3
Total	**74,887**	**100%**

*"Server Operating Environments: Review and Forecast, 1996–2001," *International Data Corporation,* August 1997.

**"Client Operating Environments: Review and Forecast, 1996–2001," *International Data* Corporation, July 1997.

weakness.[27] Exchange was available only on Microsoft NT platforms and was based on a proprietary architecture. The most recent version, Exchange 5.0, supported Internet protocols such as HTTP, SMTP, and LDAP; however, it required a gateway to translate from one architecture to the other. Microsoft's distribution channels had less experience with groupware applications and enterprise customers than did those of IBM and Lotus.

Notes was the first groupware product, and Lotus still maintained the largest installed base in this segment. According to one analyst, "Most companies making enterprise decisions for groupware are rolling out Lotus Notes. Of the 20 percent of companies that are spending 80 percent of the money, most are locked into Lotus Notes."[28] The Notes product line was mature, and it provided a comprehensive set of groupware services, although according to one analyst, "it does none of these [functions] particularly well."[29] Lotus benefited from its

[27]Note: Before the release of Outlook 97 and Exchange 5.0, Outlook did not support all the Exchange features (only the Exchange client did). In 1997, Outlook was Microsoft's strategic client product (the Exchange client was still supported). Outlook Express (different from Outlook), another mail client, was targeted at consumers.

[28]Source: Aberdeen Group, as quoted in *LAN Times,* February 3, 1997.

[29]"Software Strategies," *Forrester Research,* June 1997.

EXHIBIT 9 |

Market Share for
Groupware and
Intranet Applications

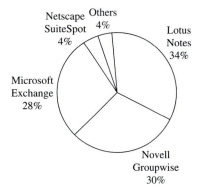

**Groupware Products Mentioned, 1997
Percentage of IT Managers Responding**

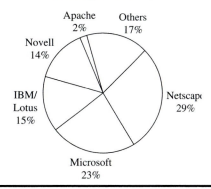

**Vendor Server Products Used for Intranets
Percentage of Users**

Source: Dataquest, April 1997.

large network of Notes resellers and system integrators. Notes had the most sophisticated and full-featured platform for groupware application development. However, the Notes development environment was complex and proprietary. In late 1996, Lotus introduced the Domino Server, which acted both as a typical Web server and as a gateway between the Web and the proprietary Notes environment, but this resulted in some loss of functionality and degraded performance. Nonetheless, Notes had approximately 10 million users in 1997, five times more than they had when IBM purchased Lotus in 1995.[30] In 1997, Lotus was moving aggressively to make Notes' proprietary architecture more fully interoperable with Web technologies, including Java.

Novell's Groupwise had a significant market presence in 1997, due largely to Novell's NetWare network operating system, which still had the largest installed base among network servers. Groupwise required at least one NetWare server, and most Groupwise sales were made to existing NetWare customers. Groupwise was noted for its messaging and document management functions. In 1997, NetWare was losing market share to NT and Unix.

Browsers beyond 1997

The market for browsers was expected to grow from $66 million in 1996 to $912 million by 2000.[31] By 1997, the browser market had come to be dominated by Netscape and Microsoft. For 1996 sales, Netscape had market share of 71 percent in terms of units (Microsoft had 25 percent) and 94 percent in terms of revenue

---

[30]Source: *The New York Times,* October 1, 1997.

[31]Source: *International Data Corporation,* May 1996.

EXHIBIT 10 | Browser Market Share, 1996

Company	Active New User Licenses	Market share (% by units)	Software Revenue ($M)	Market share (% by $)
Netscape	28,586,211	71.1%	197.5	94.3%
Microsoft	10,272,901	25.6	0	0
Lynx	400,000	1.0	0	0
AOL	250,000	0.6	0	0
NCSA Mosaic	180,018	0.4	0	0
NetManage	173,370	0.4	1.2	0.6
CompuServe	119,996	0.1	0	0
Others	201,599	0.5	10.7	5.1
Total	40,184,095	100%	209.4	100%

Source: Dataquest, 6/9/97.

(Microsoft had 0 percent, see Exhibit 10). Despite numerous predictions in 1996 that Microsoft would soon eclipse Netscape in browser market share,[32] Netscape still had

60–70 percent of the installed base in September 1997 (see Exhibit 11). Browser market share was important for a variety of reasons. According to Jim Barksdale,

> Market share helps you develop a brand and a market presence, which gives you viability. Rather than just talking about the features of our products and comparing

[32]Due to the improved functionality of Internet Explorer, the fact that Microsoft was giving away the browser for free, and was expected to bundle the browser with their operating systems.

EXHIBIT 11 | Browser Installed Base, Worldwide, 1994–1996

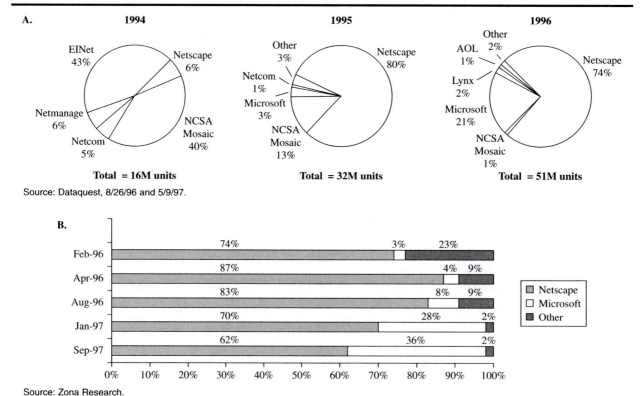

them to those of our competitors, we can refer to the 62 million customers that are already using our products. That's a pretty strong datum. Developers know that if they develop with our tools and architectures, they will have 62 million sets of eyeballs looking at their content or using their applications.

Several factors helped to explain Netscape's resilience. Navigator ran on many more computer platforms than Internet Explorer, including most Unix flavors, and even more Microsoft platforms.[33] The fact that Microsoft was giving away its browser meant relatively little to most corporate customers who also considered the costs of installing and supporting new software. In addition, Microsoft's success with online service providers, who primarily target consumers, had little impact in the corporate market. *The Economist* also cited a "pronounced anti-Gates movement: many geeks would not use Microsoft's browser on principle, no matter how cheap it was."[34] In August 1997, Netscape launched the "Netscape Everywhere" program that included free home licenses to those people licensed to use Navigator at work or school, as well as renewed efforts to push Navigator through each distribution channel.

Complementors   In addition to displaying Web content, browsers in 1997 increasingly interacted with e-mail clients and other desktop applications (see Exhibit 12). Microsoft had approximately an 85 percent market share of both desktop operating systems and desktop office suites.[35] As a result, Netscape would tightly integrate their browser products with Microsoft operating systems and desktop applications, and as a result would support some Microsoft technologies. According to Jim Barksdale,

> We strive to be an implementor of those things that are open and cross platform. Therefore, we support certain parts of *ActiveX*, but not others. Our products must work well and easily with our customers' environments, but we don't want to be a vehicle for Microsoft's strategy. Thus, we support Microsoft's *OLE* technology to facilitate interoperability with Office '97, but we do not support *DCOM*.

Netscape's dominant browser market share had allowed them to define industry standards and develop the server tools and software that would operate most effectively with those browsers. As part of their browser architecture, Netscape offered a set of application programming interfaces (APIs) that allowed developers to create browser *plug-ins*, applications that were invoked by the Navigator browser.[36]

APIs are a potential source of power and leverage in software. As developers and independent software vendors (ISVs) write programs to these APIs, this creates switching costs for them. As more developers adopt the APIs, the "platform" becomes more valuable and more likely to be adopted by consumers, which in turn makes them more attractive to developers. For example, Microsoft had exploited these dynamics with their OLE and *COM* technologies in the Windows environment. Web applications had emerged as "killer applications" that were attracting tremendous interest among ISVs. Many analysts[37] predicted that if Netscape succeeded in defining the APIs for client software, the browser could become an alternative platform for desktop application developers, threatening Microsoft's dominance of desktop operating systems.

Content developers were also important to Netscape. Browsers were used to view Web content and the latest versions from Netscape and Microsoft contained *channels* that automatically delivered personalized content to the user's desktop.[38] Netscape and Microsoft were competing to attract content developers and to offer their content as channels through their browser.

Distribution   In September 1997, Netscape sold its browser both as a product bundle in Netscape Communicator, and separately as Netscape Navigator. Browsers could be distributed through numerous channels. Netscape browsers were distributed by original equipment manufacturers (OEMs) such as PC makers, independent software vendors' (ISVs) who bundled them with applications, ISPs who sold to their own customers, a direct sales force that targeted corporate clients, and

---

[33]Note: Microsoft released its browser on the latest releases of Windows 95 and NT only, presumably to encourage customers to upgrade to those OSs.

[34]"Why Netscape Isn't Dead," *The Economist*, July 5, 1997.

[35]"Just How Serious a Threat Is Netscape to Microsoft?" *International Data Corporation*, June 1996.

[36]Note: Examples of prominent plug-ins included Adobe's Acrobat program for viewing documents created in Postscript format, Progressive Networks' RealAudio for streaming real-time audio across the Internet, and Macromedia's Shockwave for displaying digital video.

[37]For example, the GartnerGroup.

[38]In mid-1997, Netscape introduced Netcaster, a component of Communicator, that supported channels. Microsoft offered Webcaster as a feature of Internet Explorer.

EXHIBIT 12 | Internet Application Environment

Client Software

Suites
- Microsoft Office
- Lotus SmartSuite
- Corel Office

Word Processing
- Microsoft Word
- Corel WordPerfect
- Lotus AmiPro

Objects
- OLE ActiveX
- CORBA
- JavaBeans
- OpenDoc

Spreadsheets
- Microsoft Excel
- Lotus 1-2-3
- Corel Quattro Pro

Graphics
- Corel Draw
- Illustrator
- Photoshop

Presentation
- Microsoft P-point
- Lotus Freelance
- Harvard Graphics

Multimedia
- Macromedia Director
- Apple HyperCard

Desktop Publishing
- Adobe PageMaker
- Microsoft Publish
- Corel Ventura

Web Browser
- Navigator
- Internet Explorer
- Oracle PowerBrowser

Browser Plug-Ins
- Adobe Acrobat
- RealAudio
- ShockWave
- CoolTalk

Web Authoring
- Adobe PageMill
- Microsoft FrontPage
- HoTMetaL Pro

E-mail Client
- Netscape Messenger
- Microsoft Outlook
- Lotus cc:Mail/Notes

Document Publishing
- Adobe Acrobat
- Folio Views

Client and Server OS

PC OS
- Windows 3.1
- Windows 95
- Windows NT
- OS/2
- Macintosh

Unix OS
- AIX
- Digital Unix
- HP-UX
- Linux
- SGI's IRIX
- Solaris

Client and Server Hardware

CISC
- Intel iX86
- Intel Pentium
- Motorola 68xxx

RISC
- PowerPC
- Sun SPARC
- HP PA-RISC
- Digital Alpha
- MIIPS

Server Software

Web Server
- Netscape ONE
- Microsoft IIS
- IBM Internet Connection
- Lotus Domino
- Oracle WebServer

Directory Server
- Netscape Directory Server
- IBM Directory & Security Server
- Microsoft NT
- Novell NDS, NetWare

Enterprise Applications
- SAP
- Oracle
- Baan
- PeopleSoft
- Lawson

Data Warehousing
- Arbor
- Business Objects
- Information Advantage
- Oracle OLAP
- Red Brick

E-Mail Server
- Lotus Notes
- Microsoft Exchange
- Netscape Messaging Server
- Novell GroupWise
- HP OpenMail
- SunSoft Solstice Internet Mail
- Oracle Office
- DEC MailBus

Enterprise Connectivity
- Apertus
- BEA Systems
- Kiva Software
- OpenConnect Simware

RDBMS
- Oracle7, Rdb, Universal Server
- Informix OnLine, Dynamic Server, Universal Server
- Microsoft SQL Server
- Sybase System 11, SQL Anywhere
- IBM DB2
- Red Brick
- Warehouse

ODBMS
- Informix Illustra
- ObjectStore
- Versant
- CA-Jasmine

Customer Care
- Clarify
- Remedy
- Scopus
- Vantive

Multidimensional Database
- Oracle Express
- Arbor Essbase
- Gentia

Groupware Suites
- Netscape
- SuiteSpot
- Microsoft Exchange
- Lotus Notes

Document Mgmt.
- Documentum
- FileNet
- Interleaf

Sales Force Automation
- Aurum
- Clarify
- Scopus
- Siebel
- Vantive

Transaction Processing Monitors
- IBM CICS, Transaction Server
- Transarc Encina
- Microsoft DTC, Viper

Workflow
- Lotus Notes
- Microsoft Exchange
- Lotus Notes

their Web site from which the browser could be downloaded electronically. Microsoft distributed through these same channels, and planned to bundle the browser with their OSs as well. It was possible that browsers could also be bundled into a variety of consumer electronic devices, including televisions, telephones, and network computers. Netscape had embarked on an aggressive sales campaign (modeled after Intel's CRUSH program) that earned them over 200 design wins for their products from companies such as Audi, Eastman Kodak, Knight Ridder, and Shell, whereby each company would deploy a minimum of 500 units of Netscape software. According to Marc Andreessen, these design wins had resulted in "an average of 10,000 seats being deployed, not just 500, corresponding to over 2 million new users in less than 6 months."

Web Servers beyond 1997

Netscape received a major percentage of its revenue from the sale of server products, and this percentage was increasing in 1997. Servers were bought almost exclusively by corporations and other institutions, rather than consumers. Companies used servers both as external Internet Web servers and as internal intranet Web servers. The market for Web servers was growing rapidly, with intranet growth accounting for the majority of the growth. Exhibit 13 shows the projected growth of the Internet and intranet Web server software markets through 2000. By 2000, Web servers were expected to be a $1.4 billion market. In 1996, Dataquest estimated that Netscape's Enterprise Server had the leading installed base for Web servers with a 34.5 percent share, up from 13.4 percent in 1995. Microsoft's Internet Information Server (IIS) had a 22.7 percent share of the installed base, up from 0 percent in 1995 (see Exhibit 14). In 1996, Netscape had the leading market share in terms of both new server licenses and new server software revenue with 37 percent and 56 percent, respectively. Microsoft had a 26.4 percent share by units, and a 6.1 percent share by revenue (see Exhibit 15).

In late 1996, Microsoft shipped Internet Information Server (IIS) 3.0, offering functionality comparable to that of Netscape's Enterprise Server. As with browsers, Netscape offered its server products on many more OS platforms than Microsoft, including Unix, Windows NT, and Macintosh. IIS 3.0 was available for download from Microsoft's Web site for no charge and would be bundled with the next version of NT. This was putting price pressure on Netscape's server products. Lotus introduced the

Domino Server in late 1996. Domino included a proprietary database, which simplified the development of dynamic Web sites (assuming the developer is familiar with the Notes environment). When used as a Notes gateway, Domino's performance suffered because of the need to convert Notes documents into HTML. Oracle offered a Web server as well, called the Web Application Server, which was designed to work with Oracle's large installed base of database software. In 1997, Oracle's Web server was not considered to be a major threat to Netscape.

Complementors   Initially, the Web was used primarily for the distribution and display of static information, such as company or product information, that was stored in static HTML files on Web servers. More sophisticated applications, such as those for Internet banking and electronic commerce, require the ability for the Web server to receive information from the browser (such as usernames and passwords) and generate dynamic information from application servers and databases based on this input. The initial protocol for creating dynamic Web pages, the Common Gateway Interface (*CGI*), is a simple protocol for interfacing between Web servers and applications and databases (see Exhibit 16). CGI quickly became pervasive among Web developers and was supported by virtually every Web server. However, CGI was intended to handle low-volume server requests and suffers from poor scalability and performance.

To achieve higher performing dynamic Web sites, companies such as Netscape and Microsoft introduced proprietary server-based application programming interfaces (APIs) that allowed Web servers to directly access application and database servers. The proprietary nature of these APIs effectively locked developers into supporting a particular server platform. Netscape and Microsoft were also evangelizing competitive technology infrastructures for developing networked software applications (discussed in detail below).

Web server software was part of a larger infrastructure of complementary server applications (see Exhibit 10). Thus, application developers and independent software vendors (ISVs) were important constituencies for Netscape. According to Shazia Makhdumi, New Business Manager in Netscape's partner relations organization,

> We target the leading players in strategic vertical markets, such as data warehousing, enterprise connectivity, and sales force automation. We partner with companies such as SAP and Oracle, as well as start-ups with great technologies.

EXHIBIT 13 | Web Server Software Market, 1995–2000

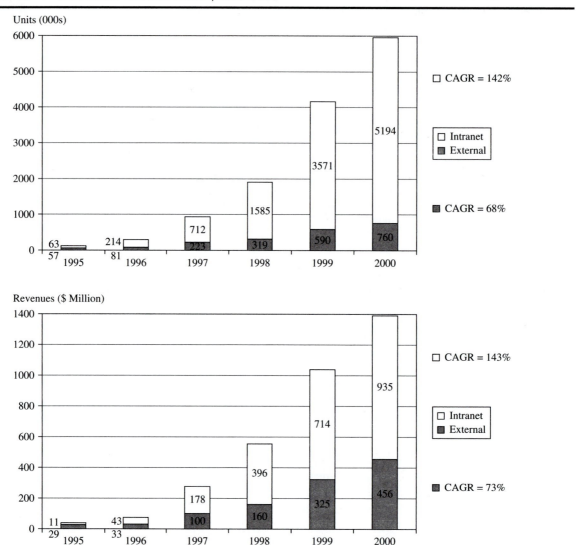

Source: International Data Corporation, May 1996.

EXHIBIT 14 | Web Server Installed Base, Worldwide, 1994–1996

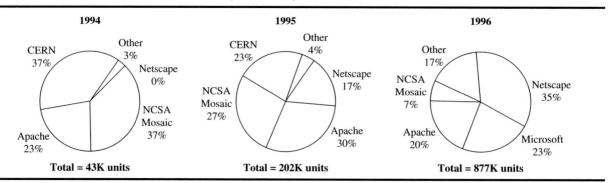

Source: Dataquest, 8/26/97 and 6/9/97.

EXHIBIT 15 | Server Market Share, 1996

Company	Active New User Licenses	Market share (% by units)	Software Revenue ($ M)	Market share (% by $)
Netscape	277,948	36.9%	75.6	56.2%
Microsoft	199,152	26.4	8.2	6.1
Apache	140,784	18.7	0.1	0.1
NCSA Mosaic	35,476	4.7	0.2	0.1
O'Reilly & Associates	30,276	4.0	9.5	7.1
Oracle	4,667	0.6	7.0	5.2
Others	64,457	8.6	33.9	25.2
Total	752,760	100	134.5	100%

In September 1996, Hambrecht & Quist released a study that indicated that more than 90 percent of the Fortune 200 was deploying intranets, and that of those companies, more than 59 percent were deploying Netscape solutions, 20 percent were deploying Microsoft solutions, and 7 percent were deploying Lotus Notes.

Source: Dataquest, 6/9/97

Distribution Netscape distributed its Web servers through a direct sales force, through system integrators (SIs), through value added resellers (VARs), through original equipment manufacturers (OEMs)[39] who bundle Web servers with their hardware boxes, and through independent software vendors (ISVs) who integrated

servers into their own applications. The corporate customers targeted by Netscape had high standards for product quality and integrity, much more so than their original customers on the Internet. In addition, these customers required a different selling model than Netscape's original customers, expecting much greater presale and postsale service and support. Netscape was expanding their professional services to assist in product implementations. In September 1997 Netscape's

---

[39]For example, HP, Sun, IBM, and Compaq.

EXHIBIT 16 | Architecture for Dynamic Web Applications

Architecture for HTTP/CGI

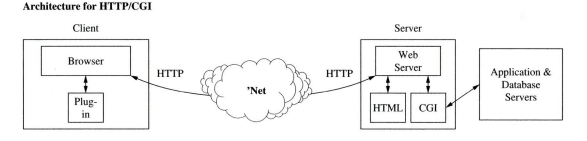

Architecture for CORBA/IIOP

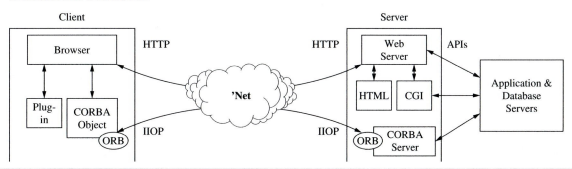

Professional Services Division employed 185 professionals, up from 70 at the end of 1996. Compared to its major competitors, Netscape had fewer deployment resources internally, and less mature distribution capabilities externally.

Directory Servers

Directories are information repositories that contain all of the information required to locate resources on a network, including software applications, files, printers, and other devices, as well as information about users, such as names, e-mail addresses, phone numbers, mailing addresses, passwords, and digital *certificates*.[40] Directories serve as the nerve center of the enterprise, controlling which users can access which functions, and facilitating services such as e-mail, security, and information management.

In 1997, there were two primary standards for directories, the ×.500 standard and the Lightweight Directory Access Protocol (LDAP), which was a simplified derivative of the ×.500 standard. In addition, many vendors built proprietary directories. The lack of support among application developers for a single standard forced most organizations to use multiple, non-interoperable directories (for example, Windows NT and Unix systems had traditionally required separate directories). This caused significant administrative difficulties. LDAP promised to simplify, standardize, and centralize the use of directories within organizations, and had been supported by all of the leading directory providers and many application developers. In 1997, the LDAP protocol was still relatively immature and some important features had yet to be defined by LDAP. The market for directory servers was potentially worth $580 million over the next several years.[41]

Netscape had been an early advocate of LDAP, and had succeeded in establishing LDAP's widespread industry support and its acceptance as an open Internet standard. Netscape began shipping its LDAP-enabled Directory Server in the spring of 1997, and each of its server and client products would support LDAP. Directory services were a key component of Netscape's strategy, which gave Netscape, "a significant competitive

advantage over Microsoft [and Lotus]."[42] Netscape's Directory server ran on multiple platforms, including NT and Unix. According to Rick Schell,

> Fighting the feature war on Microsoft's turf is hard to win. Our goal is not to have a war with Microsoft. Our goal is to solve customer problems, which often has nothing to do with features. We're solving fundamental problems, like how to find information, how to find people, and how to communicate with them easily once we've found them. Products like our Directory Server help to solve these fundamental problems.

Microsoft, Lotus, and Novell had all committed to support LDAP as well. However, Microsoft lacked a general purpose directory and would only offer full LDAP support with the release of Windows NT 5.0, scheduled for the second quarter of 1998. Lotus had integrated Notes with NT's domain-based administration system and had announced LDAP support only for its public address book. Lotus and Microsoft both lacked an enterprise directory service, and this was considered a major weakness by many analysts.[43] Novell had the largest installed base of directory services with its Novell Directory Services (NDS). However, Novell had not succeeded in raising the visibility of its market position, or in establishing NDS as a de facto standard. NDS ran only on Novell's network operating systems.

Electronic Mail

Electronic mail was used by companies to improve interpersonal communications and to distribute information more efficiently. The market for e-mail software could be divided into several segments, including Internet mail, LAN e-mail, Unix mail, and midrange/mainframe mail. In 1996, the overall number of new e-mail users grew by 46.5 percent to 31.6 million, while the Internet mail segment grew 726.6 percent to 11 million users.[44] (Exhibit 17 shows definitions, examples, segment size, and growth rates for each segment.) The number of servers grew 23.5 percent in 1996, which included 405,000 LAN

---

[40]Digital certificates contain the private encryption keys that are used for electronic signatures.

[41]Dataquest, April 1997.

[42]"Netscape Communicator and SuiteSpot 3.0," The Burton Group, December 1996.

[43]Including International Data Corporation, The Burton Group, and Dataquest.

[44]"A Preliminary Look at the 1996 E-mail Software Market," February 1997.

EXHIBIT 17 |

Electronic Mail Market
Segments, 1997

# Users	Definitions
11 million	**Internet E-Mail:** Internet based e-mail software based solely on Internet messaging standards, including SMTP, MIME, POP, and IMAP; examples include Netscape Mail, Qualcomm's Eudora Pro.
16.7 million	**LAN E-Mail:** E-mail software designed to run on local area networks of personal computers; examples include Lotus Notes, Lotus cc:Mail, Novell Groupwise, and Microsoft Mail.
2.2 million	**Unix E-Mail:** E-mail software designed to run on systems that have a high reliance on Unix servers; examples include HP OpenMail and Oracle Office.
1.6 million combined	**Midrange E-Mail:** E-mail software designed to run on small-scale to medium scale systems and minicomputers, including IBM AS/400, Digital VAX, Wang VS, etc.; examples include IBM OfficeVision and Digital MailWorks.
	Mainframe E-Mail: E-mail software designed to run on mainframes and other large scale multi-user systems; examples include Verimation Memo and Fischer TAO.

Electronic Mail Growth Rates, 1996

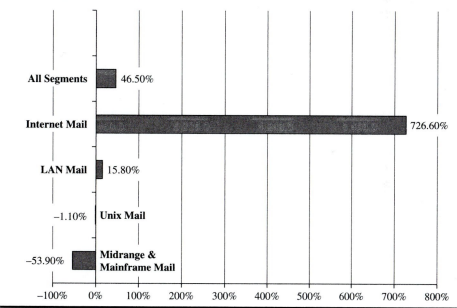

Source: International Data Corporation, February 1997.

servers and 69,000 Internet mail servers.[45] In a 1997 survey of IT managers, Lotus had the largest installed base with approximately 36 percent overall (19 percent and 17 percent for cc:Mail and Notes, respectively). This was followed by Microsoft Mail with 25 percent and Novell Groupwise with 23 percent. Netscape was named by less than 2 percent of organizations as their e-mail vendor. This was surprising,[46] given that Netscape had the leading market share for new e-mail client licenses with

---

[45]"A Preliminary Look at the 1996 E-mail Software Market," February 1997.

[46]One explanation was that the IT managers surveyed were considering which mail server they used. In 1996, Netscape's mail server penetration was small, but their mail client penetration was much higher.

EXHIBIT 18 |

Electronic Mail Market
Share, 1996/7

A. E-Mail Installed Base, 1997*
Percentage of IT Managers Responding

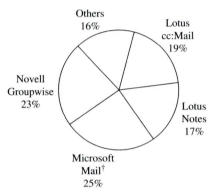

*Source: Dataquest April 1997.
†Microsoft share likely includes both Exchange
and MS Mail; not clear from source.

B. Worldwide E-Mail Software New Users, 1996**
(Client Licenses by Product)
100% = 31,558,000 new client licenses

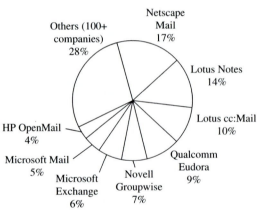

**Source: International Data Corporation, February 1997.

5 million new licenses (17 percent of the total market) in 1996 (see Exhibit 18). According to Chris Saito, senior product manager of Client Messaging at Netscape,

> Netscape believes that Internet standards are the way to go, and that there is a huge opportunity to move quickly and capture a significant share of the Internet mail market. . . . Bundling our mail client with our browser helped us to quickly grow our installed base of mail clients.

Netscape offered the Messenger client as part of Communicator, and the Messenger Server as part of

SuiteSpot. Netscape's mail client offered rich text (fonts, bullets, and other formatting features), and tight integration with the browser, which allowed Web pages to be e-mailed and viewed in a single client. Netscape's advantages in messaging included its support for Internet standards, its multiplatform support, and its integration with directory services. Netscape also offered the "Netscape In-Box" program for no charge to its e-mail users. Through this program, Web content from providers like *The New York Times* and *SportsLine* could be e-mailed directly to Netscape e-mail users. In

July 1997, Netscape claimed to have over 6.5 million subscriptions to Netscape In-Box Direct.[47]

With the release of Exchange 5.0 in early 1997, Microsoft improved support for Internet protocols. Their Outlook mail client tightly integrated messaging and scheduling, and supported rich text as well. Exchange and Outlook were Microsoft's strategic messaging products, but not its only ones. Microsoft also sold its Commercial Internet System Mail Server on the server side, and the Exchange client and Outlook Express (in addition to Outlook) on the client side. These products supported different standards and were not fully interoperable, creating confusing messages for customers. Microsoft planned to integrate its client and server messaging products, but this would create migration issues for customers.

Lotus was a leading player in every e-mail segment except Internet mail, and had the largest installed base overall. In 1997, Lotus had added to Notes support for some Internet mail protocols and planned to offer full Internet support before the end of 1997. Netscape, Microsoft, and Lotus each offered migration tools that allowed existing users of legacy mail systems to more easily transition to their own messaging products.

The Software Infrastructure Battle

In 1996, Netscape and Microsoft announced competing visions for developing Internet applications using object technologies. Netscape introduced the Netscape Open Network Environment (ONE), which outlined Netscape's vision for developers to build Internet applications and corporate intranets using Java. IBM, Oracle, and Sun announced similar frameworks that had much in common with Netscape ONE. Microsoft was advancing its own object technologies based on ActiveX and DCOM. Despite the enthusiasm around object technologies, the uncertainties in object standards could delay adoption of the technology among customers and developers.

Netscape Open Network Environment (ONE) As part of Netscape ONE, Netscape endorsed *CORBA*, the Common-Object-Request-Broker-Architecture, and IIOP, the Internet-Inter-ORB-Protocol. IIOP was a distributed communication protocol (like HTTP) that allowed CORBA objects, applications, and *ORBs* (Object Request Brokers), to interoperate across TCP/IP networks (see

Exhibit 14). For example, a CORBA-compliant Java applet running in Netscape Communicator could communicate via IIOP across the Internet to a bill payment server at a bank's Web site. Netscape differentiated IIOP/CORBA by emphasizing its openness, its multiplatform support, its security features, and its scalability. The CORBA standards are controlled by the Open Management Group, an industry standards body. A number of companies had endorsed IIOP/CORBA, including Apple, Digital, HP, IBM, Novell, Oracle, and Sun. When written in Java, CORBA objects became portable and could run on any platform with a Java virtual machine. IIOP/CORBA was a critical technology for Netscape, and with the release of SuiteSpot 3.0[48] and Communicator 3.0 in early 1997, Netscape began shipping its products with embedded IIOP/CORBA support.

One important component to Netscape's strategy was to define the software infrastructure that corporate developers and ISVs would use to build networked applications. According to Marc Andreessen,

> Microsoft has a large base of devoted developers, and many of them are unlikely to change their loyalty any time soon. To a large degree, we're targeting a completely different set of people—new developers building new applications. For example, there are hundreds of start-ups that are completely committed to Java. They won't all survive, but some of them could become the next SAP or Oracle.

One key advantage for Netscape ONE was the integration between Netscape's Directory Server and its other client and server products. An open, general-purpose directory service is of particular value in object oriented computing environments, because the directory service can be used by objects to locate other software components. Rather than hard-coding the physical locations of components in programs, the directory can handle these functions for them. Netscape was the first company to deliver an application framework that included a general purpose directory.

One challenge facing Netscape was achieving interoperability between the IIOP/CORBA implementations of different companies.[49] Netscape, IBM, Sun, and Oracle

---

[47]Netscape press release, 7/22/97.

[48]Specifically, Netscape Enterprise Server 3.0, a component of SuiteSpot 3.0.

[49]For example, a CORBA client such as Netscape Communicator, should be able to work with any CORBA server, such as Oracle's Web Application Server.

had agreed to work together to ensure IIOP/CORBA interoperability. According to Scott Johnston, senior product manager for Netscape Enterprise Server,

> It is essential that IIOP and CORBA are implemented consistently. To achieve this, marketing and technical representatives from Netscape, IBM, Sun, and Oracle, meet every week to discuss interoperability issues. This has helped us to coordinate our efforts.

In the past, different vendors (including Digital, HP, IBM, and Sun) had created their own ORB implementations, which had fragmented the CORBA market, much like different implementations of Unix had fragmented the Unix community. More recently, Netscape, Novell, and Oracle had each licensed their ORB from the same third party,[50] suggesting that interoperability was more likely. However, all of these companies were competitive in some ways. Thus, it was possible that different implementations of IIOP/CORBA could emerge.

In April 1997, IBM and Lotus announced the Network Computing Framework (NCF), a vision for electronic business that included support for Java and IIOP/CORBA. With NCF, IBM was attempting to unify its many different software efforts into one cohesive framework. Lotus was positioning Domino as an Internet/intranet server application platform, and Notes as a client application platform. Domino and Notes would support Java, IIOP, and CORBA. However, Lotus planned to continue to develop and support its proprietary application development model as well.

Sun was positioning Java as the preferred platform for Internet applications, both on the client and the server. Sun had announced its support for IIOP/CORBA. However, Sun's JavaSoft division had its own ORB, called JOE, and its own object model based on *JavaBeans*. Netscape had endorsed JavaBeans as part of Netscape ONE. It was not certain, however, that Sun would adopt Netscape ONE as *the* Java development standard.

Oracle, with strengths in databases and *transaction processing*, and Netscape, with strengths in collaborative applications and Web technologies, had complementary capabilities and market positions. Oracle had developed its own application development framework, called the Oracle Network Computing Architecture (NCA), that had much in common with Netscape ONE.

Oracle had announced its intention to support CORBA and IIOP. However, in 1997, NCA supported a non-CORBA compliant ORB called the Web Request Broker. Oracle also had its own non-IIOP compliant communications protocol called the Inter Cartridge eXchange (ICX). In addition, Oracles' Web Request Broker API competed with the server APIs from Netscape and Microsoft. According to one analyst, "[Oracle's] NCA and Netscape ONE are competitive application frameworks."[51]

Microsoft's Internet Application Framework Microsoft's strategy was to embrace Internet technologies, to extend them with Microsoft technologies, and to optimize them for Windows platforms. Microsoft sought to establish ActiveX and DCOM as the application development standard for the Internet and the intranet. DCOM was the protocol used by Microsoft objects to communicate across networks. ActiveX and DCOM were based on COM, the Component Object Model. Since COM had been the object protocol supported by and included as part of Windows desktops, it was the most widely deployed object model with a large installed base of competent programmers. Although DCOM's market position was not as strong as COM's, Microsoft had begun shipping Windows 95 and NT with ActiveX and DCOM support to guarantee their wide availability.

One key advantage of Microsoft's ActiveX technologies was their tight integration with other Microsoft products, including Windows 95 and NT operating systems, the Office '97 client applications, and the BackOffice server applications. A major weakness of the Microsoft application framework was its lack of a general purpose directory. Microsoft planned to offer a directory as part of Windows NT 5.0, scheduled for release in the second quarter of 1998.

ActiveX, and COM before it, had been perceived as vendor-specific, proprietary protocols, despite Microsoft's attempts to convince the industry otherwise. In late 1996, Microsoft turned partial control of ActiveX to the Open Group, an industry standards body. However, many analysts[52] believed that Microsoft still retained ultimate control over the technology. By 1997, a new generation of programmers had emerged that was focused on developing applications in Java. With

---

[50]They have each licensed their ORB technology from Visigenic, a San Mateo, CA–based software company that was founded in 1993 and went public in August 1996.

[51]"Novell Partnerships Bolster IntranetWare," The Burton Group, April 1997.

[52]For example, the Burton Group.

ActiveX, Microsoft offered support for Java as a programming language, but not as a platform. By supporting Java only as a programming language, Microsoft sought to neutralize Java's impact as a separate application development platform.

In addition, Microsoft was actively promoting its own database product, SQL Server, and its own transaction processing monitor, Microsoft Transaction Server, that would compete directly with Oracle and IBM products in the enterprise transaction and database markets.

Browser and Server Interoperability   The interoperability (or lack thereof) between the browsers and servers from different vendors was a major issue. Although the basic Internet technologies, like HTTP, were implemented consistently across vendors, extensions to these technologies often were not. As Internet applications and content became more sophisticated, it was increasingly likely that they would become vendor or browser specific. This created difficulties for developers, who must either write to the least common denominator of the different technologies or select a particular vendor's technology, and thereby dictate to their consumers which browser they should use. On private intranets, it was possible for companies to dictate the browser environment. But on the public Internet, this was usually not realistic. Netscape and Microsoft had both announced their intentions to make their server and browser products interoperable, but given the competitive nature of their relationship and the differences in their technology architectures, this seemed unlikely.

According to Rick Schell,

We don't need to eliminate DCOM, but we do want to pressure Microsoft to support IIOP and CORBA. Microsoft didn't support Java because they wanted to, but because the market demanded them to. We would like to see the same thing happen with IIOP and CORBA. To do that, we're making IIOP/CORBA widely available, we're working closely with our partners, and we're generating support throughout the industry to make it pervasive.

Key Strategic Challenges

In early 1997, the software market for Internet, intranet, and extranet applications was characterized by increased competition and rapid technological change. Netscape had become one of the fastest growing companies in history, yet faced serious strategic challenges that could affect its future growth. Netscape was introducing new products at a breakneck pace, which created major development challenges. Netscape had teamed with other prominent companies, including Sun, IBM, and Oracle, in part to combat the threat posed by Microsoft. But these partners were also competitors, which exacerbated the strategic challenges. The competition for Internet computing had clearly begun. Netscape had already succeeded in revolutionizing the computer industry. The question facing Jim Barksdale and his executive team in September 1997 was how Netscape could win the competition that had ensued.

Appendix: Glossary of Internet Terms and Acronyms

ActiveX   Microsoft's Internet application framework; an extension of COM for distributed applications.

Applet   Small software applications written in Java that can be distributed across a network to be executed.

Browser   Client software used for viewing and exchanging information with Web servers.

Certificate   Digital documents that are provided by a Certificate Authority to authenticate an individual's identity using public key encryption technologies.

CGI   Common Gateway Interface: an interface, or a gateway, between a Web server and other application and database servers. CGI lets those programs receive data from clients, and then sends a response back to the client based on the input.

Channel   Web content that users can subscribe to and have automatically delivered to their desktop.

COM   Component Object Module: a set of object-oriented "interfaces and services" developed by Microsoft; COM provides the underlying object model that all ActiveX components use.

CORBA   Common Object Request Broker Architecture: the specification, defined by the Open Management Group, for how objects are defined, constructed, and distributed over a network.

DCOM   Distributed Component Object Module: the distributed form of COM; DCOM adds extensions to COM that make it suitable for networked environments.

Directory   Information repositories that contain all of the information required to locate resources on a network, including software applications, files, printers and other devices, as well as information about users, such as names, e-mail addresses, phone numbers, mailing addresses, passwords, and digital *certificates.*

Extranet   Used to connect a company with its customers, partners, and suppliers using Web or Internet technologies.

FTP   File Transfer Protocol: an important information exchange protocol on the Internet, FTP is used to transfer data between computers. All Web browsers support FTP, and use it automatically when the URL begins with ftp://.

Gateway   Applications or systems that translate from one protocol to another. Thus, a gateway can be used to allow communication between Internet protocols and mainframe protocols.

Groupware   Refers to a broad category of collaborative applications designed to enable groups to share information by electronic mail, information sharing, workflow, discussion groups, and document management.

Hypertext   Text or images on a Web page that when clicked on enable a user to navigate to another Web site. Hypertext can point to other Web sites, other Web pages at the same site, or to different parts of the same Web page.

HTML   Hyper Text Mark-up Language: the language that most Web sites use for Web pages. HTML is a scripting language for developing hypertext documents. It runs on a number of hardware and operating system platforms.

HTTP   Hyper Text Transfer Protocol: an application layer protocol for distributing HTML programs across the Web. Any URL that begins with http:// will use the HTTP protocol to transfer the information.

IIOP   Internet Inter-ORB Protocol: an application layer protocol (analogous to HTTP) that allowed distributed objects to communicate across networks.

Intranet   Refers to the use of Internet or Web technology within a company or other private organization. Intranets may or may not be connected to the public Internet.

ISAPI   Information Server API: Microsoft's server-side API for applications to interface with Microsoft's Internet Information Server.

Java   Sun Microsystem's object oriented programming language and runtime execution environment that has become popular among Internet developers.

Java Beans   Sun's object model, written in Java, that used to create traditional applications or applets. Netscape has announced comprehensive support for the JavaBeans model. JavaBeans can communicate with each other using IIOP/CORBA.

JIT Compilers   Intended to speed up the execution of Java programs. They compile the entire Java application before execution by the virtual machine.

LDAP   Lightweight Directory Access Protocol: an Internet standard, controlled by the Internet Engineering Task Force, for storing and retrieving information from directories.

NSAPI   Netscape Server API: Netscape's server side API for interfacing between server applications and Netscape Enterprise Server.

Objects   Objects are self contained software modules that contain both data and its associated processing logic. Because objects encapsulate all of the data and processing details, their complexity is hidden from developers and they are relatively easy to use.

OLE   Object Linking and Embedding: based on COM and developed by Microsoft, OLE defines the interface standards that allow software components to interface with each other and share functionality.

ORB   Object Request Broker: ORBs connect objects to other object or applications; the ORB takes care of the details of locating the objects, routing the request (often under IIOP), and returning the result.

Plug-in   Software applications that extend the functionality of the Web browser or the Web server.

Replicate   To duplicate or copy files, applications, or components and to make them available from multiple locations across the network.

SMTP   Simple Mail Transfer Protocol: An Internet standard for transfering e-mail messages between servers.

TCP/IP   Transmission Control Protocol/Internet Protocol: the standard networking protocol used by the Internet, intranets, and extranets, as well as the World Wide Web; invented in the early 1970s by Vint Cerf.

Telnet   The standard protocol for remote terminal service. TELNET allows a user at one site to interact remotely with a computer at another site.

Transaction Processing   Network based transactions typically require multiple steps; transaction processing systems monitor the progress of these steps, ensure that each step is completed properly, and if each step is not completed properly, returns settings, variables, and database entries back to their original values (as if the transaction had not began).

URL   Uniform Resource Locator: refers to an Internet address; for example http://www.stanford.edu is one example of a URL.

Virtual Machine   Provides the interface between Java applications and the operating system. The Java VM executes Java programs and handles functions such as memory allocation and memory management.

Web Server   Server application that delivers Web content using the HTTP protocol. Web servers may be used on intranets or the Internet. They also include security and management features.

Workflow   Sofware applications with the primary function of automating and managing the flow of information.

Case 2.2

AOL: The Emergence of an Internet Media Company

Introduction

On January 10, 2000, AOL Chairman and CEO Steve Case and Time Warner Chairman and CEO Gerald Levin announced the $165 billion merger of their two companies—the largest corporate takeover to date. Internet service provider AOL owned valuable Internet real estate frequented by 23 million subscribers visiting 59.8 million times a month, and boasted a market capitalization of $125 billion (see Exhibits 1 and 2a, 2b). Time Warner owned a host of venerable media brands and the second largest cable system in the United States with 13 million subscribers[1] (see Exhibit 3). At the press conference announcing the deal Case said, "This merger will launch the next phase of the Internet revolution." Still, within

five weeks of the announcement, even before the NASDAQ slide in March, the two companies had lost almost $50 billion of market capitalization.[2] Some thought the attempt to combine Internet assets with media brands was reminiscent of Barry Diller's failed $22 billion attempt to merge his USA Networks with the Internet portal Lycos and Disney's struggle to convince investors of the value of its $1.6 billion acquisition of Internet portal Infoseek. Others believed that the AOL/Time Warner merger would mark the beginning of an inevitable convergence of old and new media, a combination of hitherto separate Internet Service Providers (ISPs), portals, and content providers, and that AOL was uniquely suited to lead this convergence (see Exhibit 4).

---

[1]"How Can Tim Koogle Stay So Cool in the Face of AOL's Assault?," *BusinessWeek*, Steve Rosenbush, May 15, 2000. Note: Yahoo is the second most visited site, receiving 48.3 million visits per month.

Professor Robert A. Burgelman and Philip E. Meza prepared this case as the basis for class discussion rather than to illustrate either effective or ineffective handling of an administrative situation.

---

[2]"Will Markets Ever Accept an Internet/Content Marriage?" *The Investment Dealers' Digest*, Jeffrey Keegan, February 28, 2000.

EXHIBIT 1 | Overview of Key Data

	America Online	**Time Warner**
CEO	Steve Case	Gerald Levin
Market capitalization Jan 7, 2000, $bn	163.2	83.5
Sales,* $bn	5.2	26.6[†]
Net income,* $bn	0.53[‡]	1.19[†]
Employees, 000	12.1	67.5
Paying customers	23.4m members	13m U.S. cable subscribers; 120m magazine readers

*12 months to Sept 99

[†]Consolidated, restated

[‡]Fully taxed

Compiled from company reports; Reuters, Primark Datastream; *The Economist*.

NB: Market capitalizations prior to slide in share prices.

EXHIBIT 2a | Overview of AOL Subscriber Data (millions)

AOL's North American Combined Subscriber Growth 1999–2009

	1999	2000E	2001E	2002E	2003E
Slow speed	16.010	19.435	23.793	26.324	27.002
Cable	0.000	0.043	1.024	1.865	6.467
DSL	0.000	0.200	0.990	1.665	2.945
Other	0.579	0.478	0.573	0.613	0.616
Total	19.465	23.339	29.819	34.239	41.258
Brand growth	33.3%	19.9%	27.8%	14.8%	20.5%

Compiled from: Sanford C. Bernstein & Co., Table Base.

Conduit versus Content

While Time Warner brought AOL a number of proven and valuable assets, none was more important to AOL than Time Warner's cable assets: the company owned 3,300 cable franchises that served 12.6 million customers and passed 21.3 million homes.[3] In 2000, some analysts believed the growth outlook for the cable network industry was very good. In 1999, total cable network revenues for advertising and subscription fees were about $24 compared to the $16 for broadcast network advertising. By comparison, in 1992 broadcast TV networks generated $10 billion in advertising revenue versus $6 billion in total revenues for the cable network business.[4] Still, the paramount reason for the merger may have been plumbing rather than programming. Time Warner's cable properties would give AOL control of valuable broadband distribution assets.

AOL had grown nervous about its lack of broadband distribution capability. It feared being relegated to a backwater of some other company's broadband distribution network, or worse, being excluded completely. Since 1998, AOL earned substantial revenue from the fees it charged companies for the privilege of carrying their content and accepted shares and options in exchange for attractive placement in AOL's real estate. Companies that failed to pay risked getting lost in the "noise" of the Internet—getting overlooked by AOL's millions of users who instead noticed the companies that occupied the superior anchor positions on AOL screens. The specter of broadband Internet access controlled by others threatened to change the balance of power AOL had enjoyed.

For over a year, AOL led the effort to force cable companies to provide "open access" (nondiscriminatory access) for content providers to America's cable lines. AOL needed fast, inexpensive connections to its customers to remain competitive as broadband delivery increased in popularity. AOL invested $1.6 billion in Hughes Electronics Corporation, which offered the possibility of high-speed wireless connections. It also struck deals with regional Bell operating companies (RBOCs) for digital subscriber lines (DSL) packages. But in 1998, when AT&T announced mergers that would give it 60 percent of the U.S. cable capacity, AOL felt threatened, and began lobbying to ensure open access.[5] Thus, AOL joined and helped fund a group of consumer advocates lobbying state and national legislatures to ensure that whoever controlled the broadband distribution channel (e.g., cable companies) could not exclude programming and Internet services from cables, phone lines, or satellites. However, following the announced merger with Time Warner, AOL seemed to change its position about the importance of open access. Risking corporate whiplash, Case was quoted as saying, "we need to take [open access] off the table."[6] AOL has since publicly reaffirmed its support of open access.

One of the most vocal opponents to the AOL/Time Warner merger was The Walt Disney Company. Disney feared that the new AOL Time Warner would have ample motivation and power to steer customers to its own sites. Indeed, in September 1999, CNN abruptly blocked scheduled advertising from online magazine *Salon*, citing a CNN policy of not running advertising from competitors. *Salon* claimed fewer than 2 million unique

---

[3]"Disney Campaigns against AOL-Time Warner," *The Wall Street Journal*, Kathy Chen, May 18, 2000.

[4]"Viacom," Viacom Research Report by E. Hatch, S. G. Cowen, April 26, 2000.

[5]"AOL's Access Saga," *Chief Executive*, Sally C. Pipes, March 2000.

[6]"A Media Monopoly in the Making?," *BusinessWeek*, Ronal Grover, May 15, 2000.

EXHIBIT 2b | Overview of AOL Subscriber Data

America Online's forecast number of North America subscribers for each of six ancillary Internet services in 2002 to 2009, with AOL's forecast revenues in dollars ($ millions) from each of those online services.

Ancillary Subscriber Revenue Components 2002–09

	2002E	2003E	2004E	2005E	2006E	2007E	2008E	2009E
Picture Albums								
Pct of AOL HHLDS Taking	3.0%	5.0%	7.0%	9.0%	11.0%	13.0%	15.0%	17.0%
Album Subscribers	0.85	1.69	2.72	3.77	4.82	5.95	7.17	8.50
Monthly Revenue	$1.00	$1.15	$1.32	$1.52	$1.75	$2.01	$2.31	$2.66
Picture Album Revenue to AOL	10	23	43	69	101	144	199	271
Voice Mail Conversion								
Pct of AOL HHLDS Taking	3.0%	5.0%	7.0%	9.0%	11.0%	13.0%	15.0%	17.0%
Subscribers	0.85	1.69	2.72	3.77	4.82	5.95	7.17	8.50
Monthly Revenue	$1.00	$1.00	$1.00	$1.00	$1.00	$1.00	$1.00	$1.00
Voice Mail Conversion Revenue to AOL	10	20	33	45	58	71	86	102
Ancillary Devices								
Pct of AOL HHLDS Taking	2.0%	3.0%	7.0%	11.0%	15.0%	19.0%	23.0%	27.0%
Subscribers	.57	1.01	2.72	4.60	6.57	8.69	11.00	13.51
Monthly Revenue	$2.30	$2.65	$3.04	$3.50	$4.02	$4.63	$5.32	$6.12
Picture Album Revenue to AOL	16	32	99	193	317	483	702	992
Simultaneous Usage								
Pct of AOL HHLDS Taking	1.0%	3.0%	6.0%	8.0%	10.0%	12.0%	14.0%	16.0%
Subscribers	0.28	1.01	2.33	3.35	4.38	5.49	6.69	8.00
Monthly Revenue	$10.00	$10.00	$10.00	$10.00	$10.00	$10.00	$10.00	$10.00
Simultaneous Usage Revenues to AOL	34	121	280	402	526	659	803	961
Software Services								
Pct of AOL HHLDS Taking	—	2.0%	4.0%	6.0%	8.0%	10.0%	12.0%	14.0%
Subscribers	—	0.67	1.56	2.51	3.51	4.58	5.74	7.00
Monthly Revenue	—	$3.00	$3.30	3.63	$3.99	$4.39	$4.83	$5.31
Software Services Revenues to AOL	—	24	62	109	168	241	333	447
Television Services								
Pct of AOL HHLDS Taking	—	—	5.0%	10.0%	17.0%	24.0%	31.0%	38.0%
Subscribers	—	—	1.95	4.18	7.45	10.98	14.82	19.01
Monthly Revenue	—	—	$10.00	$11.00	$12.10	$13.31	$14.64	$16.11
Television Services Revenues	—	—	233	552	1,082	1,754	2,604	3,674

Source: Sanford C. Bernstein & Co., Inc. Reproduced with permission.

visitors per month while CNN consisted of six cable and satellite networks that reached 800 million homes worldwide and ran nine Web sites.[7] Without its own broadband distribution assets, Disney feared that AOL, acting as a broadband gatekeeper, could choke off access to Disney's crown jewels—its content. During

the all-important "sweeps weeks" in May 2000, when ratings were determined for prime time broadcasts, a spat between Disney's ABC and Time Warner over an ABC price hike resulted in Time Warner blocking ABC programming on Time Warner cable stations in critical markets such as Los Angeles and New York for two days. Two months later, broadcaster NBC, owned by conglomerate General Electric, joined Disney in filing its merger concerns with the U.S. Federal Communications

[7]"CNN Rejects Dot-Com Ads," *The Standard*, James Ledbetter, October 6, 1999.

EXHIBIT 3 | Time Warner Selected Businesses, Brands, and Products

Time Warner Cable Assets

Clusters of more than 100,000 subscribers:

Divisions/Clusters

Subscribers (thousands)

Region	Subscribers (000)	Region	Subscribers (000)
New York City	1,177	Columbus	305
Tampa Bay	903	Rochester	304
Florida	669	Albany	296
Houston	665	Austin	285
Raleigh/Fayetteville	441	Suburban New York	256
Milwaukee	426	Memphis	230
Western Ohio	415	San Diego	205
Northeast Ohio	393	Binghamton	166
Charlotte	374	Green Bay	146
Los Angeles	360	Wilmington	141
Greensboro	343	Palm Springs	124
Hawaii	340	Indianapolis	121
Syracuse	332	El Paso	120
Cincinnati	328	Jackson/Monroe, MS	113
San Antonio	327	Waco	110
Kansas City, MO	313	Portland, ME	102
Columbia, SC	305		

Local News Channels

- Bay News 9, Tampa, FL
- Central Florida News 13, Orlando, FL
- NY1 News, New York, NY
- R/News, Rochester, NY
- Austin 8 News, Austin TX

Joint Ventures

- Road Runner
- Time Warner Telecom, LLC

Warner Music Group Incorporated

- Atlantic Recording Corporation
- Elektra Entertainment Group Inc.
- Rhino Entertainment Company
- Sire Records Group
- Warner Bros. Records Inc.
- Warner Music International
- Warner/Chappell Music
- Warner Bros. Publications
- WEA Inc.
- WEA Corp.
- WEA Manufacturing
- Ivy Hill Corp.

Warner Special Products

Joint Ventures

- Columbia House
- 143 Records
- Alternative Distribution Alliance
- Giant (Revolution) Records
- Maverick Recording Company
- Qwest Records
- RuffNation Records LLC
- Tommy Boy Music

EXHIBIT 3 | Time Warner Selected Businesses, Brands, and Products (cont.)

Warner Bros. Assets

- Warner Bros. Pictures
- Warner Bros. Television
- Warner Bros. Animation
- Looney Tunes
- Hanna-Barbera
- Castle Rock Entertainment
- Telepictures Productions
- The WB Television Network
- Kids' WB! Warner Home Video

- Warner Bros. Consumer Products
- Warner Bros. Studio Stores
- Warner Bros. International Theatres
- Warner Bros. Online
- DC Comics
- MADMagazine

New Line Cinema Assets

- New Line Cinema
- Fine Line Features
- New Line Home Video
- New Line International
- New Line New Media
- New Line Television
- New Line Cinema Studio Store

Time Inc. Assets

- Time
- People
- Sports Illustrated
- Fortune
- Life
- Money
- Parenting
- In Style
- Entertainment Weekly
- Cooking Light
- Baby Talk
- Bébé
- Fortune Small Business
- Coastal Living
- Health
- People en Español
- Progressive Farmer
- Southern Accents
- Southern Living

- Sports Illustrated For Kids
- Sports Illustrated for Women
- Sunset
- Teen People
- This Old House
- Time Digital
- Time for Kids Mutual Funds
- AsiaWeek
- Dancyu
- President
- Wallpaper
- Who Weekly
- Family Life
- Real Simple (March 2000)
- eCompany Now (April 2000)

- Time Life Inc.
- Book-of-the-Month Club
- Time Warner Trade Publishing Little, Brown and Company, Warner Books
- Oxmoor House
- Leisure Arts
- Sunset Books
- Media Networks Inc.
- Time Inc. Custom Publishing
- Targeted Media Inc.
- Time Inc. Interactive
- Time Distribution Services
- Warner Publisher Services
- First Moments

Turner Entertainment Group Assets

- TBS Superstation
- Turner Network Television
- Cartoon Network
- Turner Classic Movies
- Turner South
- TNT Europe
- Cartoon Network Europe

- TNT Latin America
- Cartoon Network Latin America
- TNT & Cartoon Network/Asia Pacific
- Atlanta Braves
- Atlanta Hawks
- Atlanta Thrashers
- World Championship Wrestling

- The Goodwill Games
- Boomerang (Spring 2000)
- Joint Ventures
- Cartoon Network Japan
- Court TV (TWE-owned)

(continued)

EXHIBIT 3 | Time Warner Selected Businesses, Brands, and Products (cont.)

Cable News Network Assets

- CNN
- CNN Headline News
- CNN International
- CNNfn
- CNN/Sports Illustrated
- CNN en Español
- CNN Airport Network

- CNNRadio
- CNNRadio Noticias
- CNN Interactive
- CNN Newsource
- CNN+
- CNN Turk

Home Box Office Assets

- HBO
- HBO Plus
- HBO Signature
- HBO Family
- HBO Comedy
- HBO Zone
- Cinemax
- MoreMAX
- ActionMAX
- ThillerMAX
- HBO en Español

Joint Ventures

- Comedy Central
- HBO Ole
- HBO Brasil
- HBO Asia
- HBO Hungary
- HBO Czech
- HBO Poland
- HBO Romania

Source: Time Warner.com

EXHIBIT 4 | Ownership Structure of Selected AOL and Time Warner Media assets as of January 2000

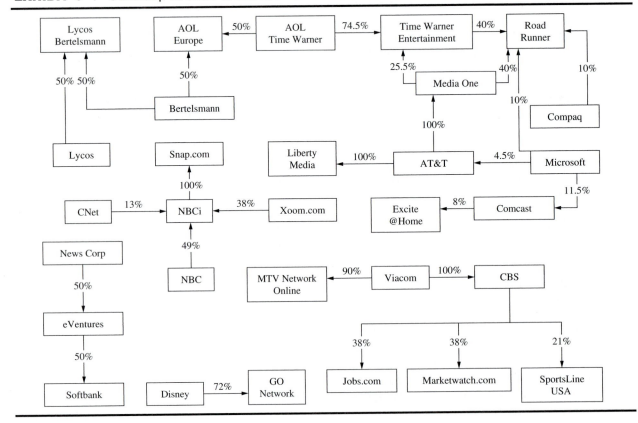

Source: Reprinted with permission of ARC chart.

Commission (FCC). NBC sought "meaningful, enforceable commitment by AOL Time Warner to provide nondiscriminatory access" to Time Warner's cable networks by other providers of programming.[8]

Now a Word from Our Sponsor

Advertising and e-commerce would be the lifeblood of the merged AOL Time Warner. Revenue from advertising and e-commerce increased by 23 percent at Time Warner in the second quarter of 2000. During AOL's fiscal fourth quarter 2000 ending June 30, advertising and e-commerce revenues increased more than 80 percent from the previous year. Speaking about the revenue generating prospects of a combined AOL and Time Warner, Gerald Levin said:

> If you combine that [Time Warner's advertising and e-commerce revenue] with where AOL is going, you have the predicate for a new model. . . . We're not just talking about measured media advertising that's brand promotion. We're talking about information that leads to transactions where you are really partnering with advertisers, where there is event marketing and where you are in effect renting your third-party facilities. . . . When you see it in that sense, you're not just talking about the $165 billion measured media universe. You are talking about the $256 billion universe of how companies market themselves, and suddenly you are in the $6 trillion transactional dome. The old ad model was based on the eyeballs television guaranteed at any given moment during a particular program to deliver an advertiser's one-way message. The new ad model is based on the consumers reached and then transformed into interactive buyers in a two-way learning and communication process that is punctuated by a transaction. It's not just the pitch; it's the sale.[9] (See Exhibits 5 and 6.)

Some new technologies, such as interactive TV, in which viewers using personal video recorders and other devices can skip over advertisements, threatened the traditional advertising model. To combat this, AOL Time Warner could develop new forms of ad-based revenue generated through e-commerce and ad-supported content featured in a closed AOL Time Warner universe.

Calling AOL

AOL undertook a series of acquisitions in order to make it easy to access the service via any medium. AOL enabled access to its service via digital subscriber lines (DSL) announcing alliances with GTE, Ameritech Communications, and Bell Atlantic, where AOL offered asymmetric DSL (ADSL) service to subscribers. The same fiber and coax cable that delivered Time Warner's cable service could also be used to deliver voice service (VoIP). AOL owned a 5.4 percent stake in Internet telephony company Net2Phone and a 10 percent stake in Palm.com, which sold AOL-branded long distance to AOL subscribers.[10]

Several of AOL's key businesses (such as AIM, ICQ, and Buddy Lists) are essentially telecommunications assets. Operations such as AIM, ICQ and Buddy Lists made the company a telecommunications player. ICQ had 62.4 million registered users who used the service an average of 75 minutes per day (see Appendix 1)—the potential for advertising revenue was substantial.[11] Together, AOL's AIM and ICQ software claimed to have 130 million users, while Microsoft reported 18 million users. Yahoo, another leader in the field, does not reveal its total instant-messaging user base.[12]

Until 1999, most users could send messages only to users of the same software. Competitors then added interoperability features that enabled their users to send messages to AOL's users. AOL repeatedly blocked those attempts. AOL claimed that allowing competitors to create clients that access its IM servers and customers jeopardized the security and privacy of its system.

AOL's policy of not allowing other ISPs to link to its ICQ system brought charges of anticompetitive behavior from ISPs and attention from the Federal Trade Commission (FTC). Competitors ranging from big players like Microsoft and AT&T to smaller players like iCast and Tribal Voice criticized AOL for its refusal to allow people using other products to trade instant messages with its users. They charged that AOL tried to block competition. The issue took on renewed urgency for AOL as its rivals' complaints of alleged anticompetitive practices received the attention of regulators at the

---

[8]"NBC Warns on Merger Plans," *Financial Times*, July 26, 2000.

[9]"AOL-Time Warner Creates New Rules for Advertising," *Electronic Media*, Diane Mermigas, July 24, 2000.

[10]"Why AOL is on the Case," *America's Network*, Shira Levine, May 15, 2000.

[11]"AOL Research Report," Scott Reamer, S. G. Cowen, April 19, 2000.

[12]"Point-Counterpoint on Instant Messaging," *The Standard*, Aaron Pressman, July 21, 2000.

EXHIBIT 5 | Selected Time Warner Advertising Expenditures

United States advertising spending by Time Warner by media and by brand
(operation) and global and United States sales and earnings for both years in dollars.

United States Ad Spending ($000)

By Media	1997	1996	% Chg
Magazine	$ 180,057	$ 157,313	14.5
Sunday magazine	3,379	4,857	−30.4
Newspaper	134,519	124,030	8.5
National newspaper	9,159	9,320	−1.7
Outdoor	3,656	2,109	73.4
Network TV	192,774	208,592	−7.6
Spot TV	86,345	90,947	−5.1
Syndicated TV	41,536	36,090	15.1
Cable TV networks	105,682	100,917	4.7
Network radio	6,576	7,906	−16.8
National spot radio	15,424	15,538	−0.7
Internet	2,054	938	119.0
Measured media	781,162	758,558	3.0
Unmeasured media	232,018	279,141	−16.9
Total	1,013,181	1,037,699	−2.4

By Brand	1997	1996	% Chg
Warner Bros studios	$ 243,900	$ 241,500	1.0
New Line Cinema	118,400	97,700	21.1
HBO cable TV	112,062	111,240	0.7
Time-Life multimedia	52,766	77,880	−32.2
Sports Illustrated	36,694	47,081	−22.1
Warner Bros. Entertainment	21,624	17,534	23.3
Pay Per View cable TV	19,461	15,873	22.6
TNT cable TV	16,582	9,042	83.4
Warner Bros TV network	13,386	18,211	-26.5
CNN cable TV	13,206	18,018	−26.7
Time Warner Cable	12,946	5,917	118.8
TBS cable network	11,335	11,752	−3.5

Federal Trade Commission (FTC) and the FCC, who were reviewing the Time Warner deal.[13]

Regulatory Uncertainty

In addition to the regulatory issues surrounding open access that Disney and NBC raised, the FCC also had to wrestle with a potential reclassification of Internet over cable lines as a telecommunications service, with concomitant regulation implications. In June 2000, the Ninth U.S. Circuit Court of Appeals ruled that Internet service over cable should be classified—and potentially regulated by the FCC—as a form of telecommunications service, which would give the FCC jurisdiction over broadband cable services. The appeals court ruled that the service is no different from high-speed Internet traffic traveling over phone lines. The ruling struck down a lower court decision concerning open access in Portland, Oregon, in which Internet over cable was classified as a

[13]"AOL Offers IM Sharing Plan," *The Standard*, Aaron Pressman, June 14, 2000.

EXHIBIT 5 | Selected Time Warner Advertising Expenditures (cont.)

Sales and Earnings ($ in millions)			
Worldwide	**1997**	**1996**	**% chg**
Sales	$24,622	$23,660	4.1
Earnings	246	−317	NA
U.S. **1997**		**1996**	**% chg**
Sales	19,255	15,989	20.4
Operating income	NA	732	NA
Division sales	1997	1996	% chg
Publishing	4,290	4,117	4.2
Music	3,691	3,949	-6.5
Cable TV	997	909	9.7
Cable TV networks—TBS	2,900	680	326.5
Filmed entertainment—TBS	1,531	455	236.5
Filmed entertainment	5,472	5,648	−3.1
Broadcasting—WB	136	87	56.3
Cable networks—HBO	1,923	1,763	9.1
Cable	4,243	3,851	10.2

Compiled from Crain Communications, Inc., Table Base.

form of cable TV service and thus subject to less stringent control based on cable franchising rules.[14]

[14]Discussion of regulatory implications of the appeals court ruling and FCC action is from "FCC to Examine Cable Broadband," *The Standard*, Aaron Pressman, June 30, 2000.

The service classification was important because providers of telecommunications services were regulated as "common carriers," forbidden from discrimination, while cable providers operated under a looser regime that allowed companies to select which channels their customer receive. Cable companies limited access

EXHIBIT 6 | World Wide Advertising Spending

Worldwide Internet Advertising Spending, by Region ($M)			
	1999	**2000**	**2001**
North America	2,831.0	5,410.0	8,773.0
Europe	286.0	621.0	1,217.0
Asia/Pacific	166.0	346.0	691.0
Latin America	51.0	121.0	259.0
Rest of World	2.0	4.0	8.0
Total	3,336.0	6,502.0	10,948.0
	2002	**2003**	**2004**
North America	12,740.0	17,482.0	22,589.0
Europe	2,169.0	3,589.0	5,480.0
Asia/Pacific	1,235.0	2,070.0	3,322.0
Latin America	517.0	949.0	1,647.0
Rest of World	14.0	23.0	37.0
Total	16,675.0	24,113.0	33,075.0

Compiled from Forrester Research, Table Base.

to their broadband pipes to only Internet service providers they own. Telecommunications rules requiring interconnection and prohibiting discrimination of ISPs could compel cable companies to share lines even beyond voluntary agreements struck by AT&T and Time Warner allowing limited open access in a few years.

Legal battles between ISPs and cable operators could drag on for years, creating substantial uncertainty for investors and consumers. FCC Chairman William Kennard said the FCC might decide to conduct its own proceeding to reclassify Internet service over cable as something other than a telecommunications service or the agency might adopt the court's classification but exempt such service from telecom rules. Cable companies welcomed Kennard's remarks because they expected that the FCC would follow Kennard's lead and continue to avoid regulating cable-broadband services. "In light of the way some are trying to spin the decision, clarification from the FCC would be expected and welcome," an AT&T spokesman said.

America Online

Company Vision[15]

Walking the halls of AOL's corporate headquarters in Dulles, Virginia, employees and visitors were constantly reminded of the company's vision, which was prominently displayed in glossy frames in almost every hallway: To build a global medium as central to people's lives as the telephone or television . . . and even more valuable.

From the outset, Steve Case envisioned AOL as a consumer services company, not a technology company. Unlike many Silicon Valley companies that set out to bring the latest technology to the market, AOL had focused on the customer experience. The relentless focus on customer experience led to a graphical user interface (GUI) for the service that was so easy to use that many observers derided it as the "Internet on training wheels." AOL realized early that the overwhelming majority of U.S. consumers wanted their online service to be easy to use above all else.

Chip Bayers, Internet analyst for *Wired* magazine, commented on AOL's consumer focus:

AOL's mass-market style and its unsophisticated look may not be sexy, but they're keys to its success. Over the years, the company has masterfully created a likeable, homey interface for its customers. When you look at AOL today, you're looking at the future of the Internet: where technology companies riding cool new hacks succumb to relentless marketing machines that are endlessly patient about building brand loyalty.[16]

AOL's company vision was to provide online users with a service that was fundamental to their lives. For millions of Americans who spent time online, AOL had already become a fact of life—a medium as central to their daily lives as the telephone or television. The average AOL user in 1999 spent 54 minutes on the service per day.[17] Indeed, surveys showed that for millions of Americans, AOL was far more than a company that connected people to the Internet—for millions of people, AOL was the Internet.

Company History

Steve Case was designing new types of pizzas for Pizza Hut in the early 1980s when he began using an online service called the Source. At the time, dial-up computer bulletin board services (BBSs) such as the Source featured text-based interfaces, enabling users to share information via message boards. The service was used almost exclusively by early tech-savvy adopters interested more in the ability to connect with others online than with the ease with which they accessed the service. Case believed that user-friendly technology had the potential to attract mass consumer usage.

In 1983, Case took a marketing job with Control Video, which ran an online service similar to the Source for users of Atari computers and games. Control Video soon ran into trouble and Case helped the new CEO, Jim Kimsey, raise money to resurrect the company. In 1985, Control Video was renamed Quantum Computer Services, and it launched the Q-Link online service (see Exhibit 7). Four years later, with Case as the top visionary, the company unveiled a nationwide service called America Online. First available only for users of Commodore computers, in 1989 the company debuted America Online for the Macintosh. Much like the Macintosh computer, the AOL service featured an easy-to-use graphical interface with large buttons that directed users to categories such as news, sports,

---

[15]The sections discussing AOL's history were excerpted from "America Online: The Online Giant in 1999," by Jason Goldberg, EC-4, Stanford Graduate School of Business.

[16]Quoted in "Over 17 Million Served," *Wired*, Chip Bayers, October 1999, p. 134.

[17]Source: AOL Annual Report, 1999.

EXHIBIT 7 | Important Historical Dates for AOL

06/29/00	AOL completes acquisition of MapQuest.Com
06/22/00	Winamp surpasses 25 million registrants
06/16/00	AOL service surpasses 23 million members
05/11/00	ICQ tops 65 million registered users
03/21/00	AOL surpasses 22 million members
02/15/00	Netscape Netcenter passes 25 million registrant Milestone
02/02/00	AOL surpasses 21 million members
01/20/00	AOL Latin America files registration statement for IPO
01/10/00	America Online & Time Warner announce plans to merge
12/17/99	AOL surpasses 20 million members
12/01/99	ICQ surpasses 50 million registered users
11/22/99	Splits stock two-for-one
11/16/99	AOL Brazil launches
10/25/99	AOL surpasses 19 million members
10/20/99	AOL and Gateway announce strategic partnership
10/19/99	Netscape breaks 20 million registrant milestone
10/14/99	AOL Germany surpasses 1 million members
10/13/99	Motorola and AOL plan to develop wireless application for AOL instant messenger
09/28/99	Launch of AOL Hong Kong
09/22/99	Netscape search ranked #1 by Search Engine Watch publication
08/24/99	AOL Instant Messenger (AIM) surpasses 45 million users; launches next generation AIM Version 3.0
08/17/99	AOL surpasses 18 million members
08/09/99	ICQ exceeds 40 million registered users, 14 months following its acquisition by AOL, more than tripling the number of registered users
07/27/99	AOL and GTE partner to provide ADSL service
06/22/99	AOL and 3Com Corporation announce a strategic relationship to give AOL members access to their e-mail for the first time via a handheld computer
06/21/99	AOL and Hughes Electronics form a strategic alliance to market unparalleled digital entertainment and Internet Services
06/21/99	AOL signs pacts with DIRECTV, Inc., Hughes Network Systems, Philips Electronics, and Network Computer, Inc. to help bring connected interactivity to TV experience
06/15/99	AOL acquires Digital Marketing Services, Inc., the leader in online incentive marketing programs and online custom market research
06/01/99	AOL acquires leading Internet music brands—Spinner.com, Winamp, and SHOUTcast
05/21/99	AOL completes its acquisition of MovieFone, Inc.
04/14/99	AOL surpasses 17 million members
04/05/99	AOL acquires When Inc.
03/24/99	AOL announces a new organization to integrate Netscape's operations and build on the strengths of the Netscape brand
03/17/99	AOL completes its acquisition of Netscape Communications Corporation
03/11/99	AOL and SBC Communication announce partnership to deliver high-speed DSL access
02/22/99	Splits stock two-for-one
02/17/99	AOL announces that Marc Andreessen of Netscape Communications Corporation will become Chief Technology Officer
02/09/99	AOL surpasses 16 million members
02/03/99	AOL and First USA announce agreement that represents the Internet's largest advertising and marketing partnership to date, valued at up to $500M
02/01/99	AOL announces intention to acquire MovieFone, Inc. the nation's #1 movie listing and ticketing service
01/26/99	AOL Inc. surpasses 3 million AOL and CompuServe members outside of the U.S.

(continued)

EXHIBIT 7 | Important Historical Dates for AOL (cont.)

01/12/99	AOL and Bell Atlantic announce partnership to deliver high-speed DSL access
12/30/98	AOL surpasses 15 million members
12/22/98	Standard and Poor's announces that America Online will be added to the S&P 500 Index
12/15/98	AOL and The Cisneros Group announce Latin America joint venture
11/24/98	AOL announces acquisition of Netscape; strategic partnership with Sun Microsystems
11/17/98	Splits stock two-for-one
11/12/98	AOL exceeds 14 million members
10/07/98	AOL and Bertelsmann launch AOL Australia
08/27/98	AOL surpasses 13 million members
06/08/98	AOL announces intention to acquire Mirabilis LTD and its ICQ Technology
04/16/98	AOL passes 12 million members
03/16/98	Splits stock two-for-one
02/10/98	AOL and CIC announce plans to launch online service in Hong Kong
02/02/98	AOL completes acquisition of CompuServe
01/20/98	AOL passes 11 million members
12/16/97	Passes 1-million member mark outside of U.S.
11/17/97	AOL passes 10 million members
10/27/97	AOL Studios launches Entertainment Asylum
10/07/97	AOL and Bertelsmann, AG announce plans to launch an online service in Australia
09/08/97	AOL announces intention to acquire CompuServe Online Services
09/02/97	AOL passes 9 million members
06/16/97	Passes 750,000 member mark internationally
04/15/97	Launches AOL Japan
03/10/97	Acquires Lightspeed Media to create original content for Greenhouse Entertainment Network
03/04/97	Opens Chat rooms to advertisers
02/25/97	Multiyear, $100 million marketing deal announced with Tel-Save Holdings
01/16/97	Passes 8 million members
12/01/96	Introduces unlimited use pricing plan of $19.95 per month
11/25/96	Excite becomes AOL's exclusive Internet search and directory service
11/13/96	Reaches 7 million members
09/16/96	Moves from Nasdaq to the New York Stock Exchange, where it is listed under symbol "AOL"
08/06/96	Acquires ImagiNation Network (INN) to expand multiplayer games offering
07/01/96	Launches version 3.0 for Windows
05/30/96	Exceeds 6 million members
05/08/96	Announces joint venture with Mitsui and Nikkei to launch service in Japan
03/18/96	Launches AOL France
03/12/96	Marketing distribution alliances announced with Apple and AT&T. Browser partnerships announced with Microsoft and Netscape Communications. Licensing and developing agreement announced with Sun Microsystems.
02/06/96	Passes 5 million members
01/31/96	Launches AOL UK and AOL Canada
12/28/95	Exceeds 4.5 million members
11/28/95	Third two-for-one stock split in just over one year (closing price, postsplit: $39 7/8)
11/28/95	Bertelsmann, AG and America Online launch AOL Germany
11/08/95	The Developers Studio launched to provide AOL software tools to third-party developers
11/08/95	*PC Magazine, Family PC Magazine, Online Access Magazine* and the Information Industry Association rate AOL "Best Consumer Online Service"
10/19/95	Completes sale of previously registered shares at $58.38
10/30/95	Launches GNN, AOL's direct Internet service

EXHIBIT 7 | Important Historical Dates for AOL (cont.)

09/22/95	Acquires Ubique, Ltd., creator of Virtual Places
09/19/95	Files registration for secondary offering of 3,500,000 shares
07/06/95	Passes 3,000,000 members
06/01/95	Acquires Global Network Navigator (GNN) as platform for direct Internet service; acquires WebCrawler search tool
05/22/95	Acquires WAIS, an Internet publisher, and Medior, a developer of interactive media
05/03/95	Exceeds 2,500,000 members
04/27/95	Splits stock two-for-one
04/03/95	First participants of the Greenhouse announced: The eGG, Health ResponseAbility Systems, InterZine Productions, The Motley Fool, NetNoir, and Health Zone
03/01/95	Joint venture with Bertelsmann, AG announced to create European online services
02/21/95	Passes 2,000,000 members
02/17/95	Acquires ANS, a commercial Internet access provider
12/29/94	Acquires BookLink Technologies, developer of Internet applications
11/30/94	Acquires NaviSoft, developer of Internet publishing tools
11/28/94	Splits stock two-for-one
11/17/94	Launches the Greenhouse to develop original content online
08/19/94	Acquires Redgate Communications, a multimedia publishing company
08/16/94	Reaches 1million members
12/07/93	Secondary offering for 1,000,000 shares
12/93	Exceeds 500,000 members
01/93	Launches Windows version of America Online
03/19/92	America Online goes public on the NASDAQ market at original price of $11.50, under symbol AMER
10/91	Quantum Computer Services changes name to America Online, Inc.
02/91	Launches DOS version of America Online
06/90	Launches Quantum's "Promenade" service for the IBM PS/1
10/89	Launches "America Online" service for Macintosh and Apple II
08/88	Launches Quantum's "PC-Link" through a joint venture with Tandy Corporation
11/85	Launches Quantum's first online service, "Q-Link," on Commodore Business Machines
05/24/85	Date of incorporation under original founding name, Quantum Computer Services, registered in Delaware

Source: AOL.

entertainment, and chat rooms—which quickly became the service's most popular feature.

In 1991, the company formally changed its name to America Online. From the beginning, America Online was a dial-up online service that utilized a proprietary technology platform, which the company called Rainman. Rainman was a software package used to create the GUI that allowed images and text to be seen by users connected to America Online. Rainman did not operate on or link to the World Wide Web, which had not yet been adopted for wide consumer use.

Users dialed into the America Online service by using modems attached to their personal computers. Once connected to America Online, users were able to read news, sports, and entertainment content, or chat with other users online—all presented in the Rainman format. Like most all other online services at the time,

America Online could only be accessed by members supplying a registered username and a password, and the company charged a monthly subscription fee as well as a fee for usage time.

AOL went public in 1992, and Case became the company's CEO. AOL spent heavily on marketing in an effort to pass rival online services Prodigy and CompuServe, while it also worked to expand its content lineup. Prodigy and CompuServe focused on technology enthusiasts and business users by accentuating features such as message boards for computer service help, online bill payment, and forums for discovering the latest technologies. AOL targeted mainstream users by making the service easy and fun to use and by heavily promoting its user chat rooms. At the end of fiscal year 1992, AOL had 181,000 paid subscribers—less than half the number of Prodigy. In January 1993, AOL began distributing a Windows-based version of its online software, which, with AOL's own easy-to-use interface, attracted even more subscribers.

Silver Coasters

In 1994 and 1995, AOL launched a major direct marketing blitz. While Prodigy and CompuServe ran television ads promoting their services and sold their software in retail stores, AOL went directly to consumers and gave away AOL software disks and CD-ROMs just about everywhere imaginable. AOL disks were found in the seat pockets of airplanes, inside the covers of almost every major computer magazine, at thousands of retail stores, and in the mailboxes of millions of American households. Each disk included a copy of the AOL software that enabled the user to log on to AOL, as well as a trial three months of AOL service. In all, AOL distributed more than 300 million disks. In January 1994 alone, the company gained 70,000 new members. By August 1994, AOL had more than 1 million subscribers, twice that of its closest rival, Prodigy.

Steve Case declared that the first 1 million subscribers were just the beginning. "The challenge now for America Online is to move this medium into the mainstream by reaching out to the 97 million households not online," Case wrote in a letter to AOL's customers, "It's 1 million down, 97 [million] to go."[18]

In 1994 and 1995, AOL faced increasing threats to its business model from the growing number of ISPs offering direct dial-up access to content on the Internet using either the Netscape browser or Microsoft's Internet Explorer. Unlike AOL's proprietary service, which served up specific content to AOL users, ISPs afforded their users the freedom to browse the World Wide Web to find any content they chose. As the number of ISPs grew from 1,800 in 1994 to 3,200 in 1995, many analysts predicted that the reigning kings of the online world, CompuServe, America Online, and Prodigy, with their closed proprietary services, were bound to be put out of business by the ISPs.

In addition to competition from ISPs, AOL recognized the threat posed by Internet browsers. After talks broke off to purchase startup Netscape Communications in 1994, AOL took action to stave off this burgeoning threat by purchasing multimedia developer Redgate Communications and Internet browser software maker Booklink Technologies, which made a browser rivaling

the increasingly popular Netscape Navigator Web.[19] The Booklink browser was quickly integrated into the America Online service, enabling AOL members to surf the Web. While AOL members had easy access to the Internet, however, America Online's proprietary Rainman content and chat rooms remained closed to nonservice members.

Case stated emphatically at the time that most consumers would prefer to use AOL as their gateway to the Internet because the America Online service was more user-friendly and trustworthy than ISPs that just connected users directly to the Internet. "I think the conventional wisdom is dead wrong, because we deliver what consumers care about—community and information; and what they don't care about is the underlying system they get it on."[20] Case also realized that AOL's Rainman technology was better suited for the slower consumer modems used at the time; Rainman pages loaded on the consumer's computers in a matter of seconds, while Internet HTML pages often took several minutes to load.

While ISPs focused on providing Internet access at a fixed price of $19.95 a month, AOL focused on making the online experience more than just a connection to the World Wide Web. AOL made the online experience fun through such simple things as a friendly voice greeting members each time they logged on to the service, with the message "Welcome." Moreover, when users received an e-mail, the same friendly voice told them, "You've got mail." Another popular user-friendly feature was the "buddy list" that enabled members to know when their friends were on the service. The service promoted a new type of simple communication, the "Instant Message," which enabled users to send quick messages to other users in real time. AOL also addressed growing consumer concerns about Internet safety and child usage by creating parental controls for its service, which had not yet been widely developed or used by ISPs.

By February 1995, AOL's mass-market, user-friendly strategy paid off. The AOL Service had registered 2 million paid subscribers and was averaging 250,000 new subscribers per month. An Internet user survey by FIND/SVP in late 1995 found that AOL was responsible for more than 30 percent of all Internet access—by far the market leader.[21]

---

[18]Quoted by Kara Swisher in *AOL.Com,* p. 103.

[19]NB: AOL won a bidding war with Microsoft for the Booklink Web browser. Microsoft intended to use Booklink as the browser for its MSN online service.

[20]Quoted by Kara Swisher in *AOL.Com,* p. 103.

[21]As reported by Kara Swisher in *AOL.Com,* p. 131.

All You Can Eat

A year later, in February 1996, AOL, with 5 million members, had more than doubled its membership over the course of one year. However, the company faced a new threat: price pressure. At the time, AOL based its subscription fee on a combination of a monthly fee as well as a per hour charge: $9.95 per month for five hours of service, with a $2.95 hourly fee for usage in excess of five hours per month. For moderate AOL users, monthly fees amounted to about $30. Heavy users often received bills in excess of $100 or $200. The ISPs, however, charged a flat-fee of $19.95 a month for unlimited access. On October 10, 1996, the Microsoft Network (MSN), which had surpassed Prodigy and CompuServe to be AOL's number one competitor in online services, announced a switch to $19.99 unlimited service.

To face the growing price pressure, on December 1, 1996, AOL started charging its members a flat rate of $19.99 for unlimited access. The effect was dramatic. Membership instantly shot up—more than 1 million new members joined in the first month of the change. At the same time, however, users vastly increased the amount of time they spent online. Whereas under the old pricing scheme AOL members constantly watched the clock, under the new pricing scheme members could stay on the AOL Service for days at a time without paying extra charges. On December 1 alone, the first day of the pricing change, more than 2.5 million hours of member sessions were logged, an enormous increase over the 1.6 million member session hours on an average day. E-mail doubled from 12 million to 24 million pieces per day. AOL service levels plummeted. Hundreds of thousands of users were unable to log on because the AOL network could not handle the increased traffic. In the press, America Online became known as "America On Hold," as hundreds of thousands of users got nothing but busy signals as they tried in vain to access the America Online network.[22] Case saw positives even in this time of crisis.

> What was happening for really the first time, was that we impacted people's daily lives in a significant way. Suddenly, almost overnight, we became part of everyday life. That's why there was this national outrage and tremendous passion and frustration, because people needed us, and many of them loved us, and we had disappointed them. It was a coming of age for the medium.[23]

[22]Ibid., p. 102.

[23]*Fortune*, March 30, 1998.

By 1996, AOL's business model started to include significant new streams of revenue (see Exhibit 8). Ten percent of AOL's first quarter 1996 revenue came from new revenue streams including advertising, transaction royalties, and merchandising.[24] Advertising emerged as a large potential revenue source as both the Web and online services enabled targeted advertising, something highly coveted by marketers. By 2000, 60 to 70 percent of AOL's revenue came from members.[25] Most observers expected that percentage to decrease as access increasingly became a commodity.

Evolution of Strategy

On the cost side, the industry had three primary expense categories: (1) telecommunications, (2) customer acquisition, and (3) content royalties. Telecommunications expenses were substantial in the industry because the online service paid telcos for a variety of access fees, including connecting local calls from users to their locations and connecting their servers to the Internet backbone. In an effort to control these expenses, AOL bought ANS, a company that provided AOL with a proprietary backbone through which it could connect its customers to the Internet.[26] Customer acquisition became increasingly more expensive due to competition, both among the online service providers and from other Internet-related companies. Content royalties had traditionally amounted to 15 to 30 percent of overall revenues in aggregate based on the usage patterns of each content site. Microsoft and other Internet content aggregators put a crimp in this part of the business model when they began paying their content partners 60 to 80 percent of subscriber revenues, relying much more on advertising as a source of revenues.[27]

As a way to both avoid content charges and keep users in the company's cyber neighborhoods, AOL flirted with content development. AOL launched the "Greenhouse Program" in which the company took equity stakes in over fifty start-up studios. AOL invested $200,000 to $1 million to select studios in exchange for 19 to 50 percent of the equity. AOL also provided the

[24]*Digital Media*, March 12, 1996.

[25]"The View From AOL," *The Wall Street Journal*, Nick Wingfield, April 17, 2000.

[26]A backbone consists of a number of high-speed lines and a series of connections that form a major pathway within a network.

[27]Excerpted from and informed by "Note on the Consumer Online Services Industry in 1996," Matthew Murphy, Stanford Graduate School of Business, SM-33, July 1997.

EXHIBIT 8 | AOL Financial Data

America Online, Inc.

Supplemental Consolidated Statements of Operations Fully Taxed

	Year ended June 30,		
	1999	1998	1997
	(Amounts in millions, except per share data)		
Revenues:			
Subscription services	$3,321	$2,183	$1,478
Advertising, commerce and other	1,000	543	308
Enterprise solutions	456	365	411
Total Revenues	4,777	3,091	2,197
Costs and expenses:			
Cost of revenues	2,657	1,811	1,162
Sales and marketing			
Sales and marketing	808	623	608
Write-off of deferred subscriber acquisition costs	—	—	385
Product development	286	239	195
General and administrative	408	328	220
Amortization of goodwill and other intangible assets	65	24	6
Acquired in-process research and development	—	94	9
Merger, restructuring and contract termination charges	95	75	73
Settlement charges	—	17	24
Total costs and expenses	4,319	3,211	2,682
Income (loss) from operations	458	(120)	(485)
Other income, net	638	30	10
Income (loss) before provision for income taxes	$1,096	$ (90)	$ (475)
Reconciling items:			
Gain on sale of Excite	(567)	—	—
Special charges	95	186	491
Transition costs	25	—	—
Adjusted net income before taxes	649	96	16
Assumed tax provision at 39%	(253)	(37)	(6)
Adjusted net income—fully taxed	$ 396	$ 59	$ 10
Fully-taxed earnings per share:			
Earnings per share—diluted	$ 0.34	$ 0.06	$ 0.01
Weighted average shares outstanding—diluted	1,182	1,070	1,004
Earnings Before Interest, Taxes, Depreciation and Amortization (EBITDA)	968	302	111

Source: Company reports.

EXHIBIT 8 | AOL
Revenue Breakdown
(cont.)

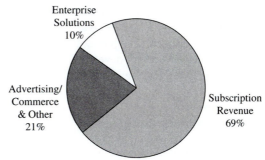

1999 Revenue Breakdown

NB: The Netscape Enterprise Group is the primary product group in the Enterprise Solutions business of AOL. The company formed Netscape Business Solutions to sell AOL and Netscape products and services. The Netscape Enterprise Group develops, markets, sells, and supports a broad suite of enterprise software, which consists of electronic commerce infrastructure and electronic commerce applications targeted primarily at corporate intranets and extranets, as well as the Internet. The Netscape Enterprise Group also provides a variety of services to support its software products, including technical support, professional services, and training. Following the merger with Netscape in March 1999, the Netscape Enterprise Group began contributing to the Company's strategic alliance with Sun Microsystems, Inc.

Compiled from InfoTech Trends, AOL.

studios with marketing, ad sales, engineering and production support, and a platform to access over 5 million customers. In early 1996, AOL had twenty-three greenhouse services running and planned to have over 100 by June 1996. Motley Fool was one Greenhouse studio success. Started by two brothers in their mid-twenties who had an idea for a new financial advice service, within ninety days it had become one of the top three finance sections on the service.[28] This success encouraged AOL to aggressively pursue other Greenhouse programs.

Ted Leonsis, then president of AOL Services, directed the greenhouse services. Leonsis was an extremely successful executive at AOL. When he was in charge of sales, marketing, and business development, AOL's membership increased tenfold and revenues jumped from less than $100 million to more than $1.5 billion.[29] While AOL had agreements with some major media players, such as its 50–50 joint venture for The Hub with New Line Cinemas (a Time Warner subsidiary), it downplayed the importance of its relationships with traditional media companies. When AOL lost NBC content to Microsoft, which was developing its own entertainment division, and also lost some Time Warner content to CompuServe, Leonsis said, "We don't

think established brands are that important because we're the brand. We're MTV or HBO. People tune into HBO or tune into MTV. They don't tune into the CBS music video on MTV."[30] By 1996 Leonsis gave up his job as president of Services to focus exclusively on content creation as president of a new division called AOL Studios.

The benefit to content partners was clear. AOL provided an audience that many of AOL's content partners could not have attracted themselves. Less clear was AOL's ability to consistently pick content hits.

In 1996, AOL board brought in Bob Pittman, founder of MTV, to run AOL's day-to-day operations as the company's president, while Case stayed on as company CEO, focusing on corporate strategy and product development. Pittman declared two goals for AOL: to make the company profitable and to make AOL one of the leading brands in the world.

Under Pittman, the company scaled back its direct marketing campaign, reducing customer acquisition costs from $375 to $90.[31] In addition, Pittman focused on solving AOL's network traffic problems. Facing possible lawsuits from states' Attorneys General, AOL agreed to pay refunds to customers who had experienced

[28]*Digital Media*, March 12, 1996.

[29]The Standard.com.

[30]*Digital Media*, March 12, 1996.

[31]"The Internet Is Mr. Case's Neighborhood," Marc Gunther, *Fortune*. March 30, 1998.

difficulty getting online. In 1997, the company spent over $1 billion to improve its network.

By February 1998, Pittman oversaw all of AOL's major divisions. It was then that AOL's new strategy was enacted. With almost 14 million subscribers, but not many content hits or obvious talent for content development, AOL scaled back its efforts at developing and producing entertainment. Instead of buying or developing its own content, AOL used its massive audience to force content providers to pay for the privilege of carriage.

AOL Partnership Deals

The partnership deals that Pittman forged with providers and advertisers generally involved a combination of cash payments and cross-marketing provided to AOL by the partner in exchange for carriage on the AOL Service and a guaranteed number of impressions by AOL users (see Appendix 2).

The price tag associated with a particular deal was determined by a number of factors, including:

- The level of exclusivity on AOL (e.g., First USA paid AOL a premium in order to be the exclusive credit card marketer on AOL).

- The areas in which placement was guaranteed on AOL (e.g., the Personal Finance Channel carried a high CPM because of the demographics and habits of channel users, whereas chat rooms carried a low CPM because audiences were less targeted and usage history showed that chatters rarely left chat rooms in order to visit promotional content or commerce seen in their chat rooms).

- The AOL brands on which a content partner gained carriage (e.g., CompuServe carried a high CPM because its 2 million users were generally much more educated and older than typical online users, Digital Cities also carried a high CPM because its content was locally targeted to specific cities and therefore more relevant to its users).

There were generally four types of partnership deals with AOL: Anchor Tenancy, Exclusive Provider, Primary Provider, and Premier Provider.

Anchor Tenancy   Each of AOL's eighteen channels typically had up to four anchor tenants. As opposed to rotational ad banners or promotional links, anchor tenants had fixed placements on their respective pages. For example, AOL's Personal Finance Channel featured anchor tenant buttons for four separate online brokerage houses—each of them paying AOL over $25 million for their fixed placements. Anchor tenancy spots either linked to a special AOL area for that anchor tenant or to the anchor tenant's own Web site.

Exclusive Provider   Exclusivity on AOL came at a steep price. First USA paid $500 million for that honor. Barnes & Noble paid over $100 million for its exclusive relationship with AOL.

Primary Provider   An AOL primary provider was the featured provider in a particular space, but without the guarantee of being the only provider. For instance, eToys paid AOL $18 million over three years to be the primary commerce provider of toys on AOL. Even though AOL has since struck a deal with Toys R Us, eToys will retain greater levels of promotion because of its prior "premier" status deal.

As another example, Preview Travel agreed in 1997 to pay AOL a minimum of $32 million over five years to become the primary provider of travel services on America Online's Travel Channel. As part of that deal, Preview Travel achieved exclusivity in the "reservations service" space across AOL's properties but was not given exclusive rights to all travel information and promotions on AOL's brands. It received only a guarantee of continued premier placement. As part of that deal, AOL and Preview Travel shared advertising and transaction revenues upon the achievement of thresholds specified in the agreement.

Premier Provider   Being a Premier AOL Provider generally included a combination of Anchor Tenancy, some exclusive content, and multifaceted placement and promotion. For instance, by paying AOL $21 million in 1999, CBS MarketWatch became the premier provider of business and financial news across several of the largest AOL brands (the America Online Service, Netscape, CompuServe, and AOL.Com). Under the three-year agreement, CBS MarketWatch provided business and financial news and analysis on the AOL properties. In addition, CBS MarketWatch became an anchor tenant in AOL's Business News Center, Investment Research, and Active Trader areas of AOL's Personal Finance channel. Links across several AOL brands provided instant and direct access to a CBS MarketWatch/AOL co-branded site. CBS MarketWatch headlines were provided through AOL, AOL.COM, Netscape Netcenter, and CompuServe, linked back to stories on the co-branded site. As part of the deal,

MarketWatch.com produced daily multimedia correspondent packages, executed in a "slide show" format for AOL's users, as well as provided business and financial radio news. As was typical with such AOL deals, both companies involved shared advertising revenue generated through designated areas on the AOL brands that incorporated CBS MarketWatch programming.

In another deal announced in November 1999, computer game maker Electronic Arts (EA) paid AOL $81 million to program AOL's games channel with EA content. In order to execute this large transaction, EA created a separate division, EA.com, and issued a tracking stock for EA's online gaming businesses.[32] At the time of the deal, 42 percent of AOL's audience played online games on a regular basis.[33]

Partnerships/Acquisitions   Through the 1990s, AOL had established strategic alliances with dozens of companies including Time Warner, ABC, Knight-Ridder, Tribune, Hachette, IBM, American Express, AT&T, Netscape, and Microsoft to provide content, distribution, and the latest technology to its users. AOL's most notable alliances had occurred in early 1996 with Microsoft and AT&T. AOL made Microsoft's Explorer their featured Internet browser in exchange for an AOL icon in every copy of Windows 95. In an alliance with AOL, AT&T agreed to offer a link to AOL from its WorldNet Internet access service providing AOL with potential access to AT&T's 80 million customers.

AOL pursued a strategy to boost its market share on its own and through deals with distributors like AT&T. AOL bet that people would flock to a few known brands in cyberspace and struggled to make sure AOL was one of them. The company also believed that most consumers would stick with AOL branded and organized content rather than roam through the "digital clutter." At the same time, AOL believed the market was becoming increasingly segmented between two primary groups.

One segment was comprised of "the masses," either new or non—Web-savvy users who wanted a condensed and organized way to view online content. The second segment was made up of more Web-savvy users who had diverse needs and liked the variety offered on the Web. AOL felt that many basic users would stay loyal due to the ease of use of its proprietary service while hoping that the more sophisticated users would graduate to its Global Network Navigator (GNN) Internet access service. AOL planned to offer services that catered to both segments. AOL had differentiated itself through its aggressive marketing, its user-friendly, attractive interface and its breadth of content. Finally, AOL littered the country with millions of computer disks offering ten free trial hours of its service. AOL simplified its interface and developed popular proprietary content.

In 1998, AOL sold the ANS Communications transmission network to telecommunications provider WorldCom (later MCI WorldCom) in exchange for rival CompuServe's content operations, 2 million subscribers, and $175 million in cash. With a top competitor out of the way, AOL announced a rate increase to $21.99—$2 more than typical ISPs. AOL saw little to no effect from the rate increase; AOL users were willing to pay more to stay with AOL.

In November 1998, AOL announced an agreement to purchase Netscape Communications at a price of about $4 billion in stock. By the time the deal closed in April 1999, AOL paid $10 billion.

International

In fiscal year 1999, AOL International (including AOL and CompuServe) had topped 3 million members outside the United States—just two and a half years after the first AOL International service was founded in Germany in partnership with Bertelsmann AG, one of the world's largest media conglomerates, with over $14 billion in revenue in 1999. In addition, in fiscal year 1999, AOL partnered with Mexico's Cisneros group to launch AOL Latin America services in Brazil, Mexico, and Argentina in 2000. According to the information technology research firm IDC, the number of Internet subscribers in Latin America will grow by an average of 41 percent per year from 1998 to 2003, and e-commerce in the region will grow by an annual 122 percent.[34]

---

[32]A tracking stock is a special type of stock issued by a publicly held company to track the value of one segment of that company. By issuing a tracking stock, the different segments of the company can be valued differently by investors. Companies choose to issue tracking stocks for several reasons. The issuer can retain operating control over the subsidiary company. The subsidiary might also be able to reduce its cost of capital by using the parent's credit rating. Further, if the value of the tracking stock increases, the parent company can make acquisitions with its new currency. Source: invest-faq.com.

[33]"Big Week for Games Deals, But Online Games Not Yet Big Business," Anya Sacharow, Jupiter Communications.

---

[34]"AOL's Perilous Journey South," *Financial Times*, Tim Jackson, July 25, 2000.

Indeed, AOL estimated that average user time is thirty-five to forty-five minutes per day in Brazil and Mexico, respectively, which exceeded usage in Europe where the average was only twenty-three minutes per day.[35] The company also launched AOL Japan and AOL Australia, and made a strategic investment in China.com to strengthen AOL's role in that region and to set the stage for the launch of AOL Hong Kong in 2000. By August 2000, AOL operated in seventeen countries worldwide.[36]

Despite an attempt to be local in the markets where it operated—something "Yahoo!" has done with great success—AOL ran into problems in Europe.[37] AOL's partnership in Germany with Bertelsmann was devalued by the AOL/Time Warner merger. The media conglomerate, which owns significant media assets in publishing (Random House), music (BMG Entertainment), and the Internet (41 percent of barnesandnoble.com and several other Web properties), felt jilted by AOL's proposed takeover of Time Warner. Following the AOL merger announcement, Bertelsmann became a "strategic partner" with Terra Networks, which had spent $12.5 billion to purchase Lycos. Bertelsmann committed to purchase $1 billion worth of advertising and services from Terra Lycos over the next five years. In return, Terra Lycos would get access to Bertelsmann content on preferential terms.[38] While plans for a listing of America Online Latin America progressed on schedule in 2000, the prospectus warned of potential management problems stemming from the minority ownership stakes controlled by AOL and Cisneros, creating two sets of bosses, as well as difficult operating conditions in Latin America. Still, the company's bankers estimated the per share price from $15 to $18, which would give the listing a valuation ranging between $3.9 billion and $4.4 billion.[39] By August 2000, the IPO launched at $8 per share, raising $200 million, roughly half of the amount initially expected. One analyst was quoted as saying, "the business plan has not been well accepted by the market. . . . Having the AOL brand name is not enough. They do not have strong local content and without the content it is difficult to get heavy traffic."[40]

---

[35]"AOL Stands by Latin American Strategy," *Financial Times*, Raymond Colitt, August 9, 2000.

[36]Ibid.

[37]"AOL's Perilous Journey South."

[38]"The Internet—Portal Plays," *The Economist*, May 20, 2000.

[39]"AOL's Perilous Journey South."

[40]"AOL Latin Arm Price Cut," *Financial Times*, Geoff Dyer and Christopher Grimes, August 2, 2000.

Time Warner

In 2000, Time Warner was the world's largest media company (see Exhibit 9a).[41] It published and distributed books and magazines; produced and distributed recorded music, movie, and television programming; owned and operated retail stores; owned and administered music copyrights, and operated cable TV systems. The company owned 75 percent of Time Warner Entertainment (Media One Group owned 25 percent),[42] which was comprised of Warner Bros., Time Warner Cable, and several other entertainment holdings.

Time Warner's Businesses

At the time that the merger was announced, Time Warner Inc. operated five businesses. These were Cable Networks, Publishing, Music, Filmed Entertainment, and Cable Systems.[43]

Cable Networks   Time Warner's Cable Networks group, including Turner Entertainment's basic cable networks (TBS Entertainment), CNN News Group, and Home Box Office:

- *TBS Entertainment*   The Turner entertainment networks housing TBS Superstation, TNT, Cartoon Network, Turner Classic Movies, and the new Turner South.
- *CNN News Group*   CNN featured more than 77 million U.S. subscribers and over 600 news affiliates in the United States and Canada.
- *Home Box Office*   This division featured both HBO and Cinemax, with 35.7 million subscribers in the United States and 10 branded channels.

Publishing   Time Inc., featured thirty-six magazines with a total of 130 million readers. The company published thirty-six *New York Times* bestsellers in 1999.

---

[41]Hoover's online.

[42]NB: On June 15, 2000, AT&T closed its purchase of Media One for $44 billion. The acquisition gave AT&T 16 million cable subscribers, potentially reaching 28 million homes. The purchase was made with the blessing of Time Warner. Due to regulatory and tax reasons, AT&T may be forced to divest its newly acquired interests in Time Warner Entertainment. "AT&T Closes Its $44 Billion Purchase of Media One," *The Wall Street Journal*, Rebecca Blumenstein, June 16, 2000.

[43]Source of company information is www.timewarner.com.

EXHIBIT 9a | Time Warner Financial Data

Annual Income Statement
(millions of U.S. dollars)

	December 31				
	1999	**1998**	**1997**	**1996**	**1995**
Sales—Core business	27,333.0	14,582.0	13,294.0	10,064.0	8,067.0
Total sales	27,333.0	14,582.0	13,294.0	10,064.0	8,067.0
Cost of goods sold	14,940.0	8,210.0	7,542.0	5,922.0	4,682.0
SG&A Expense	7,513.0	3,698.0	3,187.0	2,188.0	2,129.0
Depreciation	1,298.0	1,178.0	1,294.0	988.0	559.0
Other operating expense	−2,344.0	0.0	0.0	0.0	0.0
Unusual income/expenses	−109.0	0.0	0.0	0.0	0.0
Total expenses	21,298.0	13,086.0	12,023.0	9,098.0	7,370.0
Interest expense, nonoperating	−1,897.0	−1,180.0	−1,044.0	−1,174.0	−877.0
Other—Net	−638.0	270.0	605.0	212.0	182.0
Pretax income	3,500.0	586.0	832.0	4.0	2.0
Income taxes	1,540.0	418.0	531.0	160.0	126.0
Income after taxes	1,960.0	168.0	301.0	−156.0	−124.0
Preferred dividends	−52.0	−540.0	−319.0	−257.0	−52.0
Net Income (excluding E&D)	1,908.0	−372.0	−18.0	−413.0	−176.0
Discontinued operations	0.0	0.0	0.0	0.0	0.0
Extraordinary items	−12.0	0.0	−55.0	−35.0	−42.0
Net Income (including E&D)	1,896.0	−372.0	−73.0	−448.0	−218.0
Primary EPS excluding E&D	1.51	−0.31	−0.02	−0.48	−0.23
Primary EPS including E&D	1.50	−0.31	−0.06	−0.52	−0.28
Dividends per common share	0.18	0.18	0.18	0.18	0.18
Shares to calculate primary EPS (millions of shares)	1,267.0	1,194.7	1,135.4	862.4	767.6

Source: Company reports.

Music   Time Warner's Warner Music Group labels comprised Warner Music International, Atlantic, Elektra, Rhino, Sire, Warner Bros. Records, and their affiliate labels. Warner Music International had a roster of more than 1,000 artists and was expanding its efforts to sign local artists and devoting greater resources to marketing U.S. artists oversees. The Group had thirty-eight of the top 200 U.S. albums in 1999 and owned 1 million music copyrights.

Filmed Entertainment   Time Warner's filmed entertainment group consisted of Warner Bros. and New Line Cinema. Warner Bros. owned 5,700 feature films, 32,000 television titles, and 13,500 animated titles, including 1,500 classic cartoons. New Line Cinema produced four of 1998's top twenty-five box-office hits.

Cable Systems   Time Warner Cable featured the Road Runner high-speed online service. Time Warner cable had more than 12.6 million customers and passed 21.3 million homes.

Cross-promotion

When Time Inc. and Warner Bros. merged in 1989, it was with the idea of bringing together different media platforms so that the same piece of content could be used in different ways, and so that different products could promote each other.[44] The Time and Warner merger, which tried to combine the different cultures of publishing and movie production, was thought to have been

___
[44]"One House, Many Windows," *The Economist*, August 19, 2000.

EXHIBIT 9b |
Time Warner
Financial Data

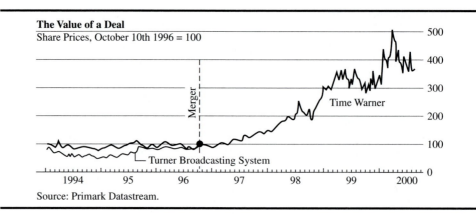

The Value of a Deal
Share Prices, October 10th 1996 = 100

Source: Primark Datastream.

troubled. In addition to integration problems, Time Warner failed to exploit its central strategy of leveraging its media assets until the 1996 acquisition of Turner Broadcasting System (see Exhibit 9b).

Richard Parsons, President of Time Warner, described Turner assets as the third side of the [Time Warner] triangle. For example, Turner cable networks buy content from Warner Bros., and co-brand cable television shows with *Time* Magazine and *Sports Illustrated*. Similarly, Turner could finally structure deals to show movies before they appeared on broadcast television, changing the old order whereby cable television was at the bottom of the entertainment food chain, after United States, Foreign, pay-per-view, and video exhibition, and thus increased cable viewership and advertising rates.[45]

Time Warner's Earlier Efforts on the Internet

While Time Warner owned valuable media brands generating predictable free cash flow, the company failed to leverage these brands over the Internet.

In 1994, Time Warner launched Pathfinder, a portal to its various media properties. Pathfinder helped evolve the concept of the Web portal as an organized gateway that sites like Yahoo! and search engines like Excite and Infoseek later exploited far more successfully. Initially popular, Pathfinder was soon plagued with problems, including management changes and a graphically rich interface that took too long to download. By May 1999, Time Warner dropped the site. "The problem was that

they buried their many great brand names under Pathfinder, a nameplate that no one had ever heard of," said Mark Mooradian, a senior analyst at Internet market-research firm Jupiter Communications.[46] The company was estimated to have spent $15 million on the portal.

In the wake of Pathfinder, Time Warner changed its Internet strategy to emphasize five vertical "hub" Web sites featuring news, sports, entertainment, lifestyle, and money. By the time the AOL Time Warner merger was announced, only the entertainment hub, called "Entertaindom," which had been the original Warner Bros. online site, had launched. While Levin singled out that hub as one Time Warner Internet offering that would carry over postmerger, the company was tight-lipped on the status of the other hubs. Some employees suggest they had been abandoned altogether.[47]

According to February data from Nielsen NetRatings, Entertaindom ranked 664 overall and 66 in the entertainment category—just ahead of Backstreetboys.com.[48] Perhaps disappointed by a lackluster launch, Time Warner soon announced top management shake-ups at the hub when its president and another key executive were forced out.[49]

[45]Ibid.

[46]"Pathfinder, Rest in Peace," *U.S. News and World Report*, Jack Egan, May 10, 1999.

[47]"A New World Order," *The Standard*, James Ledbetter, January 14, 2000.

[48]"What's Next for Entertaindom?" *The Standard*, Laura Rich, March 20, 2000.

[49]"Entertaindom's Cliff-Hanger Episode," *The Standard*, Laura Rich, April 24, 2000.

Other Players in an Internet Media Ecosystem

Six months after the announcement of the merger, few details were known. The press debated the merits of the deal. Some pointed out that Time and Warner had not made much of their earlier merger a decade ago.[50] Others pointed to Disney's failure to make much of its November 1999 takeover of Infoseek as an indication of how difficult it was to successfully merge content and Internet assets into an Internet media entity. "From any standpoint, this kind of marriage has not been a success to date," said Jeff Mallett, Yahoo's President and COO. "Controlling access and packaging content is more of a cable model than an Internet model."[51] Yahoo!, second in traffic only to America Online, had committed to remaining independent. However, analysts pointed out that Yahoo! was a strong narrowband player without an obvious broadband strategy. Industry watchers speculated about the possibility of other significant mergers in the space, with a Yahoo! takeover of Disney often proposed, in spite of the fact that Disney already owned the Go network, Disney's Internet portal.

Once AOL's main competitor was the MSN Network. Microsoft had since sent mixed signals in this space. The company bought into cable, investing $1 billion in Comcast and $5 billion in AT&T. However, Microsoft's motivation for the cable alliances may have been to help keep Windows, which generated most of Microsoft's $19.75 billion in sales in 1999, and was an integral part of next-generation media devices like digital cable set-top boxes and wireless Web gadgets.[52]

Rupert Murdoch's News Corp. had structured itself around a future in which consumers would demand wireless Web access and interactive TV. News Corp. owns a movie studio, network and cable TV stations in the United States, and vast overseas holdings, including satellite TV networks, and print assets. However, with nearly $19 billion in fiscal year 1999 revenue, News Corp.'s market capitalization is less than a quarter of Yahoo's!. The company is tightly controlled by Murdoch, who is considered unlikely to relinquish control.

Consumer electronics giant Sony, with fiscal year 1999 revenue of $56.6 billion, had been building an online empire. But its many autonomous divisions meant Sony was more fractured than focused. Video games, which in 1999 accounted for more than 10 percent of revenue, could unify many of Sony's assets. Its new Play Station 2 could serve as a hub for games, music, and other digital entertainment via broadband.

Viacom, which already stood as one of the world's largest entertainment companies, extended its leading global media position with its merger with CBS. Operations included MTV Networks, Blockbuster, Paramount Pictures, Paramount Television, Paramount Parks, Showtime Networks, Spelling Entertainment, nineteen television stations, United Paramount Networks (UPN), and movie theatres located in twelve countries. Viacom also owned 50 percent of Comedy Central. With the CBS acquisition, Viacom added the CBS Television Network and television stations; Infinity radio stations and outdoor systems; CBS Productions and King World Productions.[53]

General Electric: With MSNBC, CNBC, and NBC, General Electric, which earned $100 billion in 1998 revenue, owned leading network and cable brands and their mildly successful Internet counterparts. General Electric purchased NBCi, a conglomerate of NBC's Internet interests with Xoom.com and Snap.com, in 2000. CEO Jack Welch consistently denied speculation that the network properties were on the block.

AT&T was the largest telecom company in the United States, with more than 80 million customers. AT&T provided long distance, wireless, and local telephone service, along with Internet access (AT&T WorldNet), and a full range of telecom services for businesses. The company sold a stake in its wireless unit to the public, in the form of a tracking stock. Driving toward domination of the cable TV market, AT&T became the largest cable operator in the United States with its purchase of MediaOne. The company intended to use cable to offer local phone service. Concert, AT&T's joint venture with British Telecommunications, targeted multinational corporations.[54]

The cost to AT&T of putting together its cable empire had been enormous, with an estimated $9 billion in upgrades to fix the aging cable plant that it inherited from TCI—costing as much as $200 million in key

[50]"Don't Overestimate AOL Time Warner's Clout or Business Model," Jupiter Communications, David Card, January 17, 2000, and "AOL Time Warner: What's the Big Deal?" *Upside*, Loren Fox, March 2000.

[51]"AOL Time Warner: What's the Big Deal?."

[52]The following evaluation of post merger competitors is informed by "And Now for the Competition," *The Standard*, Kenneth Li and Bernhard Warner, January 14, 2000.

[53]"Viacom," by F. W. Moran, Jefferies & Company, Inc., April 5, 2000.

[54]http://www.thestandard.com.

EXHIBIT 10 | Share Price Data for Selected Companies

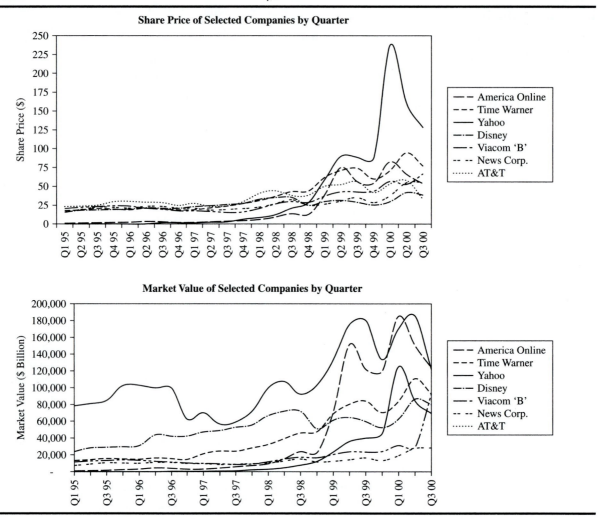

markets like Denver alone. But the company was still confident the big cable bet would pay off. Internet access, video, local telephone service, and other services were to be piped into homes on cable lines, while competitors tried to do the same thing with their DSL and wireless offerings. (See Exhibits 10 and 11 for financial overview of selected ecosystem companies.)

Conclusion

Soon after the merger was announced, the key roles were already determined. Case, in effect the acquirer, declined the role of CEO in favor of the chairmanship of AOL

Time Warner. Case said he planned to concentrate on long-term strategy, leaving the day-to-day operation of the company to Levin, who would keep his current position as CEO.[55] Bob Pittman, AOL's President and COO would share a co-COO role with Time Warner's President, Dick Parsons. Pittman was assigned subscription, advertising, and commerce businesses, while Parsons was to run content from film, television production, music, and books. Ted Turner, Time Warner's vice chairman, was to retain that role in the merged company,

---

[55]Steve Case quoted on "The Charlie Rose Show," May 17, 2000.

EXHIBIT 11 | Financial Data for Selected Companies

AT&T Corporation
Annual Income Statement
(millions of U.S. dollars)

	31 December				
	1999	**1998**	**1997**	**1996**	**1995**
Sales—Core business	62,391.0	53,223.0	51,577.0	50,688.0	48,445.0
Total sales	62,391.0	53,223.0	51,577.0	50,688.0	48,445.0
Cost of goods sold	29,071.0	25,823.0	26,388.0	24,625.0	25,375.0
SG&A expense	13,516.0	12,770.0	14,371.0	14,535.0	14,366.0
Depreciation	7,439.0	4,629.0	3,982.0	2,819.0	3,520.0
Research & development	0.0	0.0	0.0	0.0	0.0
Other operating expense	0.0	0.0	0.0	0.0	0.0
Unusual income/expenses	1,506.0	2,514.0	0.0	0.0	0.0
Total expenses	51,532.0	45,736.0	44,741.0	41,979.0	43,261.0
Interest expense, nonoperations	−1,651.0	−427.0	−307.0	−417.0	−490.0
Other—Net	−2,523.0	1,247.0	443.0	405.0	284.0
Pretax income	6,685.0	8,307.0	6,972.0	8,697.0	4,978.0
Income taxes	3,257.0	3.072.0	2,723.0	3,239.0	1,943.0
Income after taxes	3,428.0	5,235.0	4,249.0	5,458.0	3,035.0
Preferred dividends	0.0	0.0	0.0	0.0	0.0
Miscellaneous earnings adjustment	2,022.0	0.0	0.0	0.0	0.0
Net income (excluding E&D)	5,450.0	5,235.0	4,249.0	5,458.0	3,035.0
Discontinued operations	0.0	1,300.0	166.0	355.0	−2,896.0
Extraordinary items	0.0	−17.0	0.0	0.0	0.0
Accounting change	0.0	0.0	0.0	0.0	0.0
Net income (including E&D)	5,450.0	6,398.0	4,415.0	5,793.0	139.0
Primary EPS excluding E&D	1.77	1.96	1.59	2.07	1.28
Primary EPS including E&D	1.77	2.39	1.65	2.19	0.06
Dividends per common stock	0.88	0.88	0.88	0.88	0.88
Shares to calculate primary EPS (millions of shares)	3,082.0	2,676.0	2,671.5	2,640.0	2,376.0

Source: Company reports.

(continued)

acting as a senior advisor across all of the new company's operations, but with no operational duties.[56]

---

[56]"Management Team and Organization Announced for AOL Time Warner," Time Warner Press Release, May 4, 2000.

The merger tested the ability of AOL (an Internet pure play with 12,000 employees) to make something greater than AOL and Time Warner (a 67,000-employee traditional media conglomerate), would otherwise produce independently.

EXHIBIT 11 | Financial Data for Selected Companies (cont.)

Sony Corporation
Annual Income Statement
(millions of Japanese yen)

	31 March				
	2000	**1999**	**1998**	**1997**	**1996**
Sales—Core business	6,618,718.0	6,754,786.0	6,715,866.0	5,611,831.0	4,547,102.0
Sales—Other	67,943.0	49,396.0	45,138.0	51,303.0	45,463.0
Total sales	6,686,661.0	6,804,182.0	6,761,004.0	5,663,134.0	4,592,565.0
Cost of goods sold	4,954,474.0	4,955,107.0	4,889,696.0	4,138,928.0	3,419,331.0
SG&A expense	1,491,560.0	1,500,863.0	1,345,584.0	1,153,876.0	937,910.0
Unusual income/expenses	0.0	0.0	0.0	0.0	0.0
Total expenses	6,446,034.0	6,455,970.0	6,235,280.0	5,292,804.0	4,357,241.0
Interest expense, nonoperations	−42,030.0	−48,275.0	−62,524.0	−70,892.0	0.0
Other—Net	65,713.0	77,554.0	−3,937.0	12,991.0	−97,165.0
Pretax income	264,310.0	377,691.0	459,263.0	312,419.0	138,159.0
Income taxes	94,644.0	176,973.0	214,868.0	163,570.0	77,158.0
Income after taxes	169,666.0	200,718.0	244,395.0	148,859.0	61,001.0
Minority interests	−10,001.0	−12,151.0	−16,813.0	0.0	0.0
Miscellaneous earnings adjustment	−37,830.0	−9,563.0	−5,514.0	−9,399.0	−6,749.0
Net income (excluding E&D)	121,835.0	179,004.0	222,068.0	139,460.0	54,252.0
Primary EPS including E&D	144.58	218.43	278.85	183.87	72.53
Dividends per common share	25.00	25.00	30.00	27.50	25.00
Shares to calculate primary EPS (millions of shares)	842.7	819.5	796.4	758.5	748.0

Source: Company reports.

EXHIBIT 11 | Financial Data for Selected Companies (cont.)

Viacom, Inc.
Annual Income Statement
(millions of U.S. dollars)

	31 December				
	1999	**1998**	**1997**	**1996**	**1995**
Sales—Core business	12,858.8	12,096.1	10,684.9	9,683.9	10,915.9
Total sales	12,858.8	12,096.1	10,684.9	9,683.9	10,915.9
Cost of goods sold	8,337.9	8,506.3	7,476.3	6,340.2	6,689.5
SG&A expense	2,358.6	2,060.9	1,750.6	1,442.0	2,111.0
Depreciation	844.7	777.3	772.6	654.3	716.7
Unusual income/expenses	70.3	0.0	0.0	50.2	0.0
Total expenses	11,611.5	11,344.5	9,999.5	8,486.7	9,517.2
Interest expense, nonoperations	−448.9	−622.4	−772.9	0.0	0.0
Other—Net	45.5	8.1	1,266.0	−787.1	−818.9
Pretax income	843.9	137.3	1,178.5	410.1	579.8
Income taxes	411.4	138.7	646.4	243.3	367.1
Income after taxes	432.5	−1.4	532.1	166.8	212.7
Preferred dividends	−12.4	−27.2	−60.0	−60.0	−60.0
Miscellaneous earnings adjustment	−60.8	−42.1	−158.6	−14.6	−62.2
Net income (Excluding E&D)	359.3	−70.7	313.5	92.2	90.5
Discontinued operations	0.0	−4.2	420.1	1,095.7	72.0
Extraordinary items	−37.7	−74.7	0.0	0.0	0.0
Accounting change	0.0	0.0	0.0	0.0	0.0
Net Income (including E&D)	321.6	−149.6	733.6	1,187.9	162.5
Primary EPS excluding E&D	0.52	−0.10	0.44	0.13	0.13
Primary EPS including E&D	0.46	−0.21	1.04	1.63	0.22
Dividends per common share	0.00	0.00	0.00	0.00	0.00
Shares to calculate primary EPS (millions of shares)	695.2	708.7	705.8	728.0	725.0

Source: Company reports.

(*continued*)

EXHIBIT 11 | Financial Data for Selected Companies (cont.)

Walt Disney Company
Annual Income Statement
(millions of U.S. dollars)

	30 September				
	1999	1998	1997	1996	1995
Sales—Core business	23,402.0	22,976.0	22,473.0	18,739.0	12,151.0
Total sales	23,402.0	22,976.0	22,473.0	18,739.0	12,151.0
Cost of goods sold	19,715.0	18,466.0	17,722.0	15,406.0	9,685.0
SG&A expense	196.0	236.0	367.0	309.0	239.0
Depreciation	456.0	431.0	439.0	0.0	0.0
Other operating expense	−345.0	0.0	−135.0	0.0	0.0
Unusual income/expenses	132.0	64.0	0.0	525.0	0.0
Total expenses	20,154.0	19,197.0	18,393.0	16,240.0	9,924.0
Interest expense, nonoperations	−612.0	−622.0	−693.0	−438.0	−110.0
Other—Net	−322.0	0.0	0.0	0.0	0.0
Pretax income	2,314.0	3,157.0	3,387.0	2,061.0	2,117.0
Income taxes	1,014.0	1,307.0	1,421.0	847.0	737.0
Income after taxes	1,300.0	1,850.0	1,966.0	1,214.0	1,380.0
Net income (excluding E&D)	1,300.0	1,850.0	1,966.0	1,214.0	1,380.0
Discontinued operations	0.0	0.0	0.0	0.0	0.0
Accounting change	0.0	0.0	0.0	0.0	0.0
Net income (including E&D)	1,300.0	1,850.0	1,966.0	1,214.0	1,380.0
Primary EPS excluding E&D	0.63	0.91	0.97	0.67	0.87
Primary EPS including E&D	0.63	0.91	0.97	0.67	0.87
Dividends per common share	0.00	0.20	0.17	0.14	0.12
Shares to calculate primary EPS (millions of shares)	2,056.0	2,037.0	2,021.0	1,827.0	1,590.0

Source: Company reports.

EXHIBIT 11 | Financial Data for Selected Companies (cont.)

Yahoo! Inc.
Annual Income Statement
(millions of U.S. dollars)

	31 December				
	1999	**1998**	**1997**	**1996**	**1995**
Sales—Core business	588.6	245.1	84.1	21.5	1.4
Total sales	588.6	245.1	84.1	21.5	1.4
Cost of goods sold	101.8	52.2	19.9	4.7	0.2
SG&A	251.2	148.9	71.3	22.0	1.8
Depreciation	13.8	2.6	0.0	0.0	0.0
Research & development	67.5	33.9	16.7	5.7	0.3
Unusual income/expenses	87.5	21.2	25.1	0.0	0.0
Total expenses	521.9	258.8	133.0	32.4	2.3
Interest net, nonoperations	37.7	18.8	4.8	4.0	0.1
Other—Net	−2.5	0.1	0.7	0.5	0.0
Pretax income	101.9	5.2	−43.4	−6.4	−0.8
Income taxes	40.8	17.8	0.0	0.0	0.0
Income after taxes	61.1	−12.7	−43.4	−6.4	−0.8
Preferred dividends	0.0	−1.4	0.0	0.0	0.0
Net income (including E&D)	61.1	−14.1	−43.4	−6.4	−0.8
Primary EPS excluding E&D	0.12	−0.03	−0.11	−0.02	−0.00
Primary EPS including E&D	0.12	−0.03	−0.11	−0.02	−0.00
Dividends per common share	0.00	0.00	0.00	0.00	0.00
Shares to calculate primary EPS (millions of shares)	515.9	440.0	391.5	314.6	218.5

Source: Company reports.

Appendix 1

AOL's Features in 2000[57]

AOL's array of communications, content, commerce, search and access features included:

E-mail America Online's e-mail feature remained the world's most popular online application among home users, with members sending 70 million e-mails every day.

AOL Instant Messenger (AIM) A pioneering innovation that was faster and more direct than e-mail, America Online's instant message feature generated more than 474 million real-time, one-on-one conversations a day. AIM enabled AOL members to send "instant messages" to other AOL members on the American Online Service, as well as to non-AOL members who downloaded AIM free from the AOL.COM Web site and on the company's other brands and services, including CompuServe and Netscape Netcenter. AIM was packaged into the Netscape Navigator Web Browser as well as the popular Real Player and Real Jukebox from RealNetworks.

ICQ AOL gained ICQ (a play on the words "I-Seek-You") when it purchased the Israeli company Mirabelis in 1998 for $400 million. At the time, ICQ—which provided free instant messaging over the Internet to anyone who downloaded the ICQ software—had 25 million registered users worldwide. As of September 1999, nearly two-thirds of ICQ's 45 million registrants were based outside the United States. ICQ's members were extremely active Web users: over 7 million ICQ registrants in 1999 averaged more than one hour of daily use.

Keywords America Online's service was designed so that members could type "keywords" into the America Online browser window instead of having to memorize URL addresses.

Content The America Online service featured several content areas known as "channels." The America Online channel lineup included the following:

Commerce Relevant commerce opportunities were presented on each of America Online's content channels. For example, fantasy sports games and sports memorabilia were sold on the Sports Channel and on the Shop@AOL Shopping Channel.

Parental controls America Online was widely known for creating a family-friendly service where parents could limit access to the Web, e-mail, and the America Online Instant Message™ feature.

Additional security features "Notify America Online" provided members with quick help from a trained America Online professional; the Download Sentry Alert let members know when downloadable files were coming from non-AOL members; and AOL's Integrated Web Security Browser guaranteed that online shopping via AOL was 100 percent secure.

You've got pictures In 1999, America Online joined with Eastman Kodak to offer a service that made sharing pictures with family members and friends as easy as sending e-mail.

"My calendar" The service included an interactive calendar that allowed members to plan and manage important parts of their life by tracking appointments, key dates, and other personal events online.

AOL search AOL search enabled AOL members to search America Online's content and the entire Internet at the same time.

Broadband connectivity America Online version 5.0, released in September 1999, was AOL's first software that supported DSL, T1, cable, and satellite broadband connectivity.

---

[57]Review of AOL's brands in 2000 was excerpted from "America Online: The Online Giant in 1999," by Jason Goldberg, EC-4, Stanford Graduate School of Business.

The software automatically detected whether a member was accessing the service with broadband or narrowband connectivity, providing those with high-speed access rich interactive content and features including enriched video and games, and online catalog shopping.

AOL.com   The company's AOL.COM Web site functioned as a portal for America Online members when they ventured from the proprietary service onto the Internet, as well as a general portal for nonmembers. AOL.COM offered content, features, and tools, including AOL NetFind, an Internet search and rating tool, and added functionality for the AOL Instant Messenger service. AOL.COM also offered AOL members the opportunity to access and exchange e-mail on the Internet, without signing onto the service, through AOL NetMail.

CompuServe   The company's CompuServe online brand, which targeted businesses and tech-savvy users, drew 2.5 million worldwide subscribers. In mid-1999, through an agreement with eMachines, AOL offered CompuServe subscribers $400 rebates on selected eMachine computers—including one model priced at $399—which made the computer free to consumers as long as they committed to paying for the CompuServe online service. Over 300,000 new members were added to CompuServe in the first four months of the eMachines deal.

Netscape/iPlanet   AOL's 1999 acquisition of Netscape Communications for about $10 billion in stock significantly expanded the company's profile. Through the acquisition, AOL gained control of the number two Web browser, Netscape Communicator (second to Microsoft's Internet Explorer); Netscape's Netcenter Web-portal, which claimed 18 million members and was consistently one of the top five most frequented Web sites per month; as well as Netscape's burgeoning Web server systems business.

AOL believed that Netscape's brand complimented and extended its own mass-market audience appeal among Netscape's Netcenter portal users.[58] The Netscape acquisition also paved the way for AOL's joint venture with Sun Microsystems through which the two companies began developing enterprise software and business-to-business e-commerce solutions under the iPlanet name. In the fall of 1999, over 50 percent of the Fortune 100 companies were Sun-Netscape Alliance customers.

MovieFone   In 1999, AOL purchased MovieFone, the leading provider of online movie times and ticket purchases. MovieFone was the premier United States movie information and ticketing brand. It was available in more than sixty markets nationwide, covering more than 19,000 movie theaters. In 1999, AOL-Moviefone boasted 12 million weekly users and served one out of every five moviegoers in the United States.

Digital City   The Company's subsidiary, Digital City, Inc., owned in part by the Tribune Company, was a local online content network that offered a network of local content and community guides in over sixty American cities. Local content provided by DCI included original and third party news, sports, weather, a local guide service with directory and classified listings, and an interactive forum. As of June 1999, DCI had more than 5 million unique visitors monthly. In the first half of 1999, 85 percent of DCI users shopped online.

Spinner.com, Winamp, and SHOUTcast   The company acquired several Internet music brands in May 1999 through the acquisition of Spinner Networks Incorporated and Nullsoft, Inc. The Spinner.com Web site offered over 100 channels of programmed music in various formats. Content included over 175,000 songs and related material. The music players provided links that enabled real-time listener feedback and instant purchasing of the music being played. Nullsoft, Inc. was the developer of both Winamp, a branded MP3

---

[58]Source: Customer Cast: Web Site Visitor Survey (WSVS-6/99), Cyber Dialogue: American Internet User Study (AIUS-6/99).

player for Windows, and SHOUTcast, an MP3 streaming audio system. The SHOUTcast streaming audio system enabled individuals to broadcast their own content over the Internet. The company planned to make these music features available to consumers across its brands, as well as to customize them for the audience and partners of the company's brands. Nullsoft also developed Gnutella, a software application that enables peer-to-peer exchange of MP3 files. AOL discontinued work on Gnutella; however, the software was leaked onto the Web and has been widely distributed and improved by rogue groups of programmers.[59]

AOLTV   AOLTV aimed to advance America Online's "AOL Anywhere" strategy of making its brands and features available to online consumers anywhere, anytime, through a range of devices. In 2000, the service was available via a set-top from Philips Electronics for a suggested retail price of $249.95. The service cost AOL members $14.95 per month in addition to the unlimited use AOL subscription price of $21.95 per month. Non-AOL members could subscribe to AOLTV for $24.95 per month.

---

[59]"Nightmare for the Music Industry," *Financial Times,* Tom Foremski, June 7, 2000.

Appendix 2[60]

The CPM and Advertising on AOL

The CPM, a standard media measure used in both offline and online advertising, equals the cost per thousand sets of eyeballs that have an opportunity to see an advertiser's ad. In online advertising, the opportunity equals an impression, which is the standard term for what happens when a Web page containing a banner ad is served as a result of a user's request. Serving, or displaying, the ad counts as an impression whether or not the user looks at or clicks on the advertisement. Banner advertisers (advertisements on the top or sides of Web pages) were priced according to a CPM rate for a particular Web site. The CPM rate was an advertising rate for the page based on a combination of factors such as the number of unique visitors per month, the demographics of the visitors, and usage behaviors of the visitors.

As Web advertising developed, the CPM became a crucial element in evaluating a site's possible success or failure. Those sites with the most traffic demanded the highest CPM, since they could deliver viewers. While revenue models could effect E-Commerce measures like transaction fees, ad revenue and the value of a site's CPM remained a significant source of income for Web sites. In fact, ad spending is expected to increase to $22 billion in 2004 from $2.9 billion in 1999,[61] a sign that the CPM continued to be an important measure of Internet value.

Internet advertising is a small but growing proportion of total United States advertising spent.

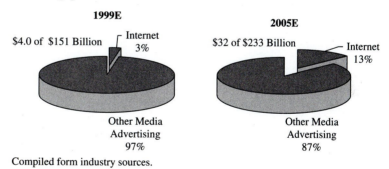

Compiled form industry sources.

Internet Advertising, measured by effective CPM, is comparatively inexpensive.

Media	CPM
Daily Newspapers	$19
Prime Time Broadcast TV	$16
Radio	$6
Magazine	$6
Day Time Broadcast TV	$5
Internet-Effective CPM	$4

Compiled from industry sources.

---

[60]Aspects of this section are from "America Online: The Online Giant in 1999," by Jason Goldberg, EC-4, Stanford Graduate School of Business.

[61]Forrester Research.

Because 75 percent of online ad revenues flowed to the top ten Web publishers,[62] it was critical that these sites delivered the value expected by their advertisers. Not surprisingly, as the number of sites available to advertising increased, the average CPM decreased from $37.78 in June 1998 to $34.23 in June 1999.[63] While the list price of CPM was expected to decrease, some analysts expected the effective CPM to rise.[64]

While AOL sold some banner advertisements (on a CPM basis) that rotated throughout portions of the America Online Service and on AOL's other brands, the majority of the advertisements on AOL's properties were negotiated as part of much larger content or commerce partnership deals. For instance, in exchange for paying AOL millions of dollars to be the exclusive online greeting cards provider on the America Online service, American Greetings also received a guaranteed number of monthly ad impressions on the service. FirstUSA, eBay, eToys, and other major AOL partners had similar promotional deals that included banner advertising. Impressions were the number of times an advertisement, promotion, or link either to content or commerce was seen by AOL users, as opposed to click-through percentage, which is the ratio of clicks per impressions. AOL rarely did deals based on click-throughs.

---

[62]Internet Advertising Board.

[63]Ad Knowledge.

[64]Effective CPM is the rate if all space is sold. Thus list CPM of $20–$40 with a 20% sellout yields an effective CPM of $4. Source: "Internet Advertising and Direct Marketing," Michael J. Russell, Morgan Stanley Dean Wittter.

Case 2.3

Amazon.com: Evolution of the e-Tailer

We are not a retailer and we are not a technology company. We are a customer company.

—Jeff Bezos, Founder, CEO, Amazon.com, February 2001[1]

Introduction

Since going online in July 1995, Amazon.com grew from a tiny warehouse containing the "Earth's Biggest Bookstore,"[2] to the leading Internet retailer in the world. The company's growth was phenomenal: it expanded from books to offering 28 million items across numerous categories and acquired 29 million global customers along the way. In 1999, Amazon's founder and chief executive officer Jeff Bezos was named *Time* Magazine's Man of the Year. By 2000, according to Interbrand, Amazon.com became the forty-eighth most valuable brand in the world, embodying the principle of electronic commerce for people worldwide.[3]

However, that global growth came at a price. By late 2000, Amazon's U.S. books/music/movies segment had lost $2.3 billion and Amazon had borrowed $2.1 billion for the sake of its international investments. Its share price, which had ascended to vertiginous heights in 1999, had plummeted. (See Exhibit 1.) By late 2000 and early 2001, a few analysts were beginning to question

Amazon's ability to survive until it reached profitability, although such dire forecasts were hotly contested by the company and other analysts. Still, on the heels of a technology and Internet stock shakeout that stripped billions of dollars from the valuations of Internet-related stocks and saw many once high-flying Web companies close their doors, 2001 was a watershed year for the company.

Asked in early 2001 what were the key bridges that Amazon must cross over the next three years, Bezos did not hesitate:

First is profitability by fourth quarter 2001. We want to make the company as a whole profitable so that the U.S. businesses subsidize international business. This past quarter, the U.S. books, music and video business had a profitability of 2 percent of sales with an operating loss, and business as a whole had a 6 percent operating loss. The majority of investment is in International.

Second is to take advantage of the opportunity to be the first truly global retailer.

Third is to expand product selection.

Fourth is to institutionalize at Amazon the ability to continually innovate. This is still the "Kitty Hawk" era of e-commerce. We want to innovate on a large scale. The very DNA we have [must code for] inventiveness. This has to be owned by all employees.

Amazon's DNA may code for inventiveness: The company had evolved over the past five years from selling other distributors' book inventories to owning a national and then global fulfillment system for a wide range of categories. The potential market size was enormous. Jupiter research estimated that U.S. online sales reached almost $12 billion in 2000, up 66 percent from 1999. However, that was still a small drop in the bucket compared to the $2.7 trillion spent on U.S. retail sales in 2000. If estimates were correct, and between 4 and 8 percent of all U.S. retail sales would take place online by mid-decade, then Amazon would be in a good position to capture a piece of that $125 to $250 billion market.[4]

---

[1]All quotes from Jeff Bezos are from the authors' interview on February 5, 2001, unless otherwise cited. Subsequent quotes from this interview will not be cited.

[2]Amazon.com prospectus (S-1) March 24, 1997, p. 2.

[3]Daniel Bögler, Andrew Edgecliffe-Johnson, "Jeff Bezos: The Man of Last Year, Revisited," *Financial Times,* Philip E. Meza December 27, 2000.

Professor Robert A. Burgelman and Philip E. Meza prepared this case as the basis for class discussion rather than to illustrate either effective or ineffective handling of an administrative situation.

---

[4]Jeff Fisher, "Clicks for Bricks," *Newsweek,* February 12, 2001.

EXHIBIT 1 I Share Prices of Selected Companies and the NASDAQ Composite Index from January 1996–February 2001

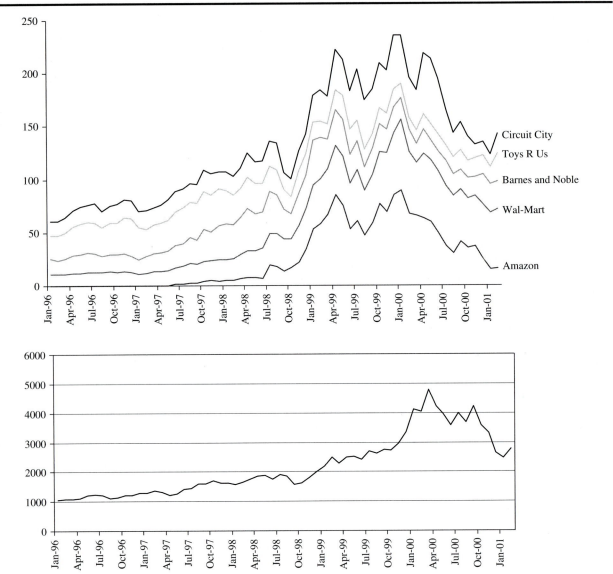

In the Beginning

Jeff Bezos founded Amazon in 1994 with the intention of riding the Internet wave he perceived as inevitable. The then thirty-two-year-old vice president at D. E. Shaw, a New York City–based brokerage firm, noticed the incredible current and projected growth of Web sites and Internet access. Bezos was particularly optimistic about online retail opportunities and set out to develop a business model to leverage growth in Internet access in the United States. After researching a variety of retail categories, Bezos selected bookselling, believing that an online business model offered superior economics to established competitors in the physical world.

In the prospectus to Amazon.com's initial public offering ("IPO"), the company drew a comparison between an online book retailer and traditional competitors:

> Amazon.com was founded to capitalize on the opportunity for online book retailing. The Company believes that the retail book industry is particularly suited to online retailing for many compelling reasons. An online bookseller has virtually unlimited online shelf space and can offer customers a vast selection through an efficient search and retrieval interface. This is particularly valuable in the book market because the extraordinary number of different items precludes even the largest physical bookstore from economically stocking more than a small minority of available titles. In addition, by serving a large and global market through centralized distribution and operations, online booksellers can realize significant structural cost advantages relative to traditional booksellers.[5]

In particular, Amazon.com's management cited important key advantages of its online business model to the traditional book retailing industry:

> Several characteristics of the traditional book industry have created inefficiencies for all participants. Physical store–based book retailers must make significant investments in inventory, real estate, and personnel for each retail location. This capital and real estate intensive business model, among other things, limits the amount of inventory that can be economically carried in any location. The average superstore stocks less than 10 percent of the estimated 1.5 million English-language books believed to be in print, which limits customer selection and available retail shelf space for the majority of published titles. In addition, publishers typically offer generous rights of return to their customers and, as a result, effectively bear the risk of their customers' demand forecasting which encourages over ordering. As a result, returns in the book industry are high, creating substantial additional costs. Finally, publishers and traditional book retailers cannot easily obtain demographic and behavioral data about customers, limiting opportunities for direct marketing and personalized services.[6]

The company boasted that its online business model was superior to those of brick and mortar competitors. Amazon.com's IPO was hugely successful, selling over 3 million shares at $18 per share.

---

[5]Amazon.com Prospectus (S-1) March 24, 1997, p. 4.
[6]Ibid., p. 23.

Get Big Fast

Since its IPO, Amazon grew as if it had a hyperactive corporate pituitary gland—even by Internet standards. (See Exhibit 2.) Bezos told *Fortune* Magazine, "Our initial strategy was very focused and very uni-dimensional. . . . It was GBF: Get Big Fast."[7] Indeed, Bezos still regards the company's audacious start—offering 1 million titles—as one of his best corporate decisions.

> What once looked foolish can seem smart now. When we started the company on July 16, 1995 we offered one million titles. We were advised by very knowledgeable people to offer only three hundred thousand titles. That was twice the size of the inventory carried by the largest physical bookstores. The catalog was hard for us, but doable. Obtaining the books was really hard. But the success generated word of mouth.

In 1998, Amazon started selling music, videos, and DVDs and expanded overseas facilities in England and Germany to sell books (see Exhibit 3 on page 157). Bezos described Amazon's expansion into new categories as a customer-led evolution. He recalled:

> Our evolution [beyond books] came as the result of customer requests. We got a constant stream of e-mails from customers asking for other products. As a result, we launched music, selling only popular music titles. Surprisingly, most of the e-mails that followed were requests for classical music.

In 1999, Amazon continued to expand its category offerings, adding products such as electronics, toys, and software to its U.S. operations and music to its European operations. That year the company also added entirely new businesses; it introduced both co-branded auctions and zShops Marketplaces. The revenue models for these types of businesses were fundamentally different from Amazon's initial model. Amazon's storefront model, while more efficient than brick and mortar competitors, still had a significant capital component, since the company had to make investments in inventory and fulfillment. In Amazon's new businesses, the company acted as an agent by facilitating transactions and taking a fee. For example, Amazon's zShops were a virtual shopping mall, where sellers could quickly set up an electronic storefront. Amazon charged sellers $39.99 a month to list up to

---

[7]Katrina Brooker, "Beautiful Dreamer," *Fortune,* December 18, 2000.

EXHIBIT 2 | Amazon Financial Data

Amazon Quarterly Income Statement ($ millions, except per share data)

	30-Jun-01	31-Mar-01	31-Dec-00	30-Sep-00	30-Jun-00
Sales—Core business	667.6	700.4	972.4	637.9	577.9
Total sales	**667.6**	**700.4**	**972.4**	**637.9**	**577.9**
Cost of goods sold	487.9	517.8	748.1	470.6	441.8
SG&A expense	143.0	160.9	214.5	164.6	158.3
Depreciation	53.2	53.7	78.1	83.3	88.6
Research & development	64.7	70.3	69.8	71.2	67.1
Unusual income/expenses	58.7	114.3	184.1	11.8	2.4
Total expenses	**807.5**	**917.0**	**1,294.5**	**801.4**	**758.3**
Interest Expense, nonoperations	−35.1	−33.7	−36.1	−33.8	−33.4
Other—Net	16.9	39.9	−149.4	25.1	7.0
Pretax income	**−158.0**	**−210.4**	**−507.6**	**−172.2**	**−206.7**
Income taxes	0.0	0.0	0.0	0.0	0.0
Income after taxes	**−158.0**	**−210.4**	**−507.6**	**−172.2**	**−206.7**
Equity in affiliates	−10.3	−13.2	−37.6	−68.3	−110.5
Net income (excluding E&D)	**−168.4**	**−223.6**	**−545.1**	**−240.5**	**−317.2**
Accounting change	0.0	−10.5	0.0	0.0	0.0
Net income (including E&D)	**−168.4**	**−234.1**	**−545.1**	**−240.5**	**−317.2**
Primary EPS excluding E&D	−0.47	−0.63	−1.53	−0.68	−0.91
Primary EPS including E&D	−0.47	−0.66	−1.53	−0.68	−0.91
Dividends per common share	0.00	0.00	0.00	0.00	0.00
Shares to calculate primary EPS (millions of shares)	359.8	357.4	355.7	354.0	349.9

NB: E&D stands for Extraordinary Items and Depreciation.

Source: Company Reports; OneSource.

5,000 items, $0.10 for every additional item listed, and a completion fee of 1.25 to 5 percent of the final price. Amazon Payments, the company's credit card processing system, allowed it to monitor zShop transactions and allowed sellers to avoid the bother of transaction payment processing. By the first quarter of 2001, the partnerships started to pay off. Amazon's alliances, including high profile agreements with Toys R Us and drugstore.com, generated gross profit margins of 67 percent, compared to 23 percent gross margins across the rest of the company.[8]

By the end of 1999, Amazon began to leverage its impressive traffic numbers by creating the Amazon Commerce Network ("ACN"), acting as a portal for other retailers, taking fees and equity in addition to direct investments. From 1998 to the end of 2000, Amazon opened thirty-one stores selling 28 million items—everything from books to barbeques.

On December 28, 2000, Amazon opened an online bargain outlet store. The company reduced prices up to 70 percent on a variety of items. While the company offered discounted items in all of its categories, it thought the outlet would be particularly successful with consumer electronics and toys. Analysts thought the outlet would serve as a vehicle to liquidate excess inventory from Amazon's stores and zShops. Amazon.com expected to soon see its inventory balance drop to less than $175 million, down 20 percent from the fourth quarter 2000. Analysts estimated the inventory-carrying cost of excess merchandise was approximately 20 to

---

[8]Andrew Edgecliffe-Johnson, "Amazon Links Start to Pay Off," *Financial Times*, April 25, 2001.

EXHIBIT 2 | Amazon Financial Data (cont.)

Historical Income Statement 1997–2000

	Year ended December 31,				Quarters Ended Fiscal Year 2001,		Quarters Ended Fiscal Year 2000,			
	2000	1999	1998	1997	31-Mar-01	30-Jun-01	31-Dec	30-Sep	30-Jun	31-Mar
Net sales	$2,761,983	$1,639,839	$609,819	$147,787	$700,356	$667,625	$972,360	$637,858	$577,876	$573,889
Cost of sales	2,106,206	1,349,194	476,155	118,969	517,759	487,905	748,060	470,579	441,812	445,755
Gross profit	655,777	290,645	133,664	28,818	182,597	179,720	224,300	167,279	136,064	128,134
	23.7%	17.7%	21.9%	19.5%	26.1%	26.9%	23.1%	26.2%	23.5%	22.3%
Operating expenses:										
Fulfillment	414,509	237,312	65,227	15,944	98,248	85,583	131,027	96,421	87,597	99,463
Marketing	179,980	175,838	67,427	24,133	36,638	34,658	55,196	41,921	42,216	40,648
Technology and content	269,326	159,722	46,424	13,384	70,284	64,710	69,791	71,159	67,132	61,244
General and administrative	108,962	70,144	15,618	6,741	26,028	22,778	28,232	26,217	28,468	26,045
Stock-based compensation[1]	24,797	30,618	1,889	1,211	2,916	2,351	(1,112)	4,091	8,166	13,652
Amortization of good will and other intangibles[1]	321,772	214,694	42,599	—	50,831	50,830	79,210	79,194	80,413	82,955
Impairment-related and other[1]	200,311	8,072	3,535	—	114,260	58,650	184,052	11,791	2,449	2,019
Total operating expenses	1,519,657	896,400	242,719	61,413	399,205	319,560	546,396	330,794	316,441	326,026
Loss from operations	(863,880)	(605,755)	(109,055)	(32,595)	(216,608)	(139,840)	(322,096)	(163,515)	(180,377)	(197,892)
Interest income	40,821	45,451	14,053	1,901	9,950	6,807	10,979	9,402	10,314	10,126
Interest expense	(130,921)	(84,566)	(26,639)	(326)	(33,748)	(35,148)	(36,094)	(33,809)	(33,397)	(27,621)
Other income (expense)	(10,058)	1,671	—	—	(3,884)	(1,178)	(5,365)	3,353	(3,272)	(4,774)
Noncash investment gains and losses[1]	(142,639)	—	—	—	33,857	11,315	(155,005)	12,366	—	—
Net interest income (expense) and other	(242,797)	(37,444)	(12,586)	1,575	6,175	(18,204)	(185,485)	(8,688)	(26,355)	(22,269)
Loss before equity in losses of equity-method investees	(1,106,677)	(643,199)	(121,641)	(31,020)	(210,433)	(158,044)	(507,581)	(172,203)	(206,732)	(220,161)
Equity in losses of equity-method investees net[1]	(304,596)	(76,769)	(2,905)	—	(13,175)	(10,315)	(37,559)	(68,321)	(110,452)	(88,264)
Cumulative effect of change in accounting	—	—	—	—	(10,523)	—	—	—	—	—
Net loss	$(1,411,273)	$(719,968)	$(124,546)	$(31,020)	$(234,131)	$(168,359)	$(545,140)	$(240,524)	$(317,184)	$(308,425)
Basic and diluted loss per share	$(4.02)	$(2.20)	$(0.42)	$(0.12)	$(0.66)	$(0.47)	$(1.53)	$(0.68)	$(0.91)	$(0.90)
Basic and diluted loss per share—pro forma	$(1.19)	$(1.19)	$(0.25)	$(0.11)	$(0.21)	$(0.16)	$(0.25)	$(0.25)	$(0.33)	$(0.35)
Shares used in computation of basic and diluted loss per share	350,873	326,753	296,344	260,682	357,424	359,752	355,681	353,954	349,886	343,884

(1) Amounts excluded from pro forma calculations.

Source: Company reports

(*continued*)

EXHIBIT 2 | Amazon Financial Data (cont.)

Historical Income Statement 1997–2000

	Quarters Ended for Fiscal Year 1999,				Quarters Ended for Fiscal Year 1998,				Quarters Ended for Fiscal Year 1997,			
	31-Dec	30-Sep	30-Jun	31-Mar	31-Dec	30-Sep	30-Jun	31-Mar	31-Dec	30-Sep	30-Jun	31-Mar
Net sales	$676,042	$355,777	$314,377	$293,643	$252,828	$153,648	$115,982	$87,361	$66,040	$37,887	$27,855	$16,005
Cost of sales	588,196	285,300	246,846	228,852	199,475	118,823	89,794	68,063	53,127	30,717	22,641	12,484
Gross profit	87,846	70,477	67,531	64,791	53,353	34,825	26,188	19,298	12,913	7,170	5,214	3,521
	13.0%	19.8%	21.5%	22.1%	21.1%	22.7%	22.6%	22.1%	19.6%	18.9%	18.7%	22%
Operating expenses:												
Fulfillment	107,070	53,707	42,374	34,161	26,797	16,906	12,612	8,912	6,837	3,996	3,335	1,777
Marketing	72,354	33,135	43,793	26,556	21,581	20,497	14,356	10,993	9,943	7,409	4,636	2,146
Technology and content	57,720	44,451	34,149	23,402	17,194	13,288	8,745	7,197	5,118	3,845	2,856	1,565
General and administrative	26,051	18,382	14,468	11,243	5,413	4,936	3,273	1,996	2,007	1,898	1,718	1,118
Stock-based compensation[1]	14,049	11,789	4,669	111	298	1,214	192	185	333	339	340	199
Amortization of good will and other intangibles[1]	82,301	74,343	37,150	20,900	20,452	16,737	5,410	—	—	—	—	—
Impairment-related and other[1]	2,085	1,779	3,809	399	1,281	2,254	—	—	—	—	—	—
Total operating expenses	361,630	237,586	180,412	116,772	93,016	75,832	44,588	29,283	24,237	17,486	12,885	6,805
Loss from operations	(273,784)	(167,109)	(112,881)	(51,981)	(39,663)	(41,007)	(18,400)	(9,985)	(11,324)	(10,316)	(7,671)	(3,284)
Interest income	8,972	12,699	12,860	10,920	4,263	4,755	3,390	1,645	783	688	366	64
Interest expense	(18,142)	(21,470)	(28,320)	(16,634)	(8,622)	(8,419)	(7,569)	(2,029)	(267)	(19)	(40)	—
Other income (expense)	(366)	2,159	(73)	(49)	—	—	—	—	—	—	—	—
Non-cash investment gains and losses (1)	—	—	—	—	—	—	—	—	—	—	—	—
Net interest income (expense) and other	(9,536)	(6,612)	(15,533)	(5,763)	(4,359)	(3,664)	(4,179)	(384)	516	669	326	64
Loss before equity in losses of equity-method investees	(283,320)	(173,721)	(128,414)	(57,744)	(44,022)	(44,671)	(22,579)	(10,369)	(10,808)	(9,647)	(7,345)	(3,220)
Equity in losses of equity-method investees net[1]	(39,893)	(23,359)	(9,594)	(3,923)	(2,405)	(500)	—	—	—	—	—	—
Cumulative effect of change in accounting	—	—	—	—	—	—	—	—	—	—	—	—
Net loss	$(323,213)	$(197,080)	$(138,008)	$(61,667)	$(46,427)	$(45,171)	$(22,579)	$(10,369)	$(10,808)	$(9,647)	$(7,345)	$(3,220)
Basic and diluted loss per share	$(0.69)	$(0.59)	$(0.43)	$(0.20)	$(0.15)	$(0.15)	$(0.08)	$(0.04)	$(0.04)	$(0.04)	$(0.03)	$(0.01)
Basic and diluted loss per share – pro forma	$(9,55)	$(0.26)	$(0.26)	$(0.12)	$(0.07)	$(0.08)	$(0.06)	$(0.04)	$(0.04)	$(0.03)	$(0.03)	$(0.01)
Shares used in computation of basic and diluted loss per share	338,389	332,488	322,340	313,794	308,778	301,405	292,554	282,636	278,826	275,190	255,840	232,860

(1) Amounts excluded from pro forma calculations.

Source: Company Reports

EXHIBIT 2 | Amazon Financial Data (cont.)

Amazon.com, Inc.
Historical Balance Sheets

	30-Jun 2001	31-Mar 2001	31-Dec 2000	30-Sep 2000	30-Jun 2000	31-Mar 2000	31-Dec 1999	30-Sep 1999 (Unaudited)	30-Jun 1999 (Unaudited)	31-Mar 1999 (Unaudited)
ASSETS										
Current assets:										
Cash and cash equivalents	$462,949	$446,944	$822,435	$647,048	$720,377	$755,132	$133,309	$73,542	$105,757	$72,881
Marketable securities	146,020	196,029	278,087	252,976	187,244	253,749	572,879	832,143	1,038,480	1,370,084
Inventories	129,035	155,562	174,563	163,880	172,360	172,257	220,646	118,793	59,387	45,236
Prepaid expenses and other current assets	71,353	57,175	86,044	88,061	76,864	82,004	79,643	55,590	53,334	37,077
Total current assets	809,357	855,710	1,361,129	1,151,965	1,156,845	1,263,142	1,006,477	1,080,068	1,256,958	1,525,278
Fixed assets, net	292,422	304,179	366,416	352,290	344,042	334,396	317,613	221,243	156,333	60,600
Goodwill, net	89,002	123,996	158,990	383,996	441,240	471,748	534,699	514,098	563,884	153,763
Other intangibles, net	63,893	80,424	96,335	136,474	155,538	175,444	195,445	189,370	172,245	3,978
Investments in equity-method investees	12,223	22,539	52,073	91,131	211,715	271,542	226,727	156,157	102,361	23,817
Other equity investments	24,729	28,503	40,177	73,345	88,261	150,782	144,735	40,113	3,659	3,849
Other assets	53,410	54,804	60,049	54,306	53,294	54,882	40,154	38,750	42,774	41,699
Total assets	$1,345,036	$1,470,155	$2,135,169	$2,243,507	$2,450,935	$2,721,936	$2,465,850	$2,239,799	$2,298,214	$1,812,984
LIABILITIES AND STOCKHOLDERS' EQUITY (DEFICIT)										
Current liabilities:										
Accounts payable	$257,976	$257,411	$485,383	$304,709	$286,239	$255,797	$463,026	$236,711	$165,983	$133,018
Accrued expenses and other current liabilities	241,149	217,613	272,683	148,953	137,079	137,008	176,208	95,728	72,603	47,728
Unearned revenue	86,945	93,661	131,117	142,046	115,566	134,758	54,790	2,411	5,525	4,546
Interest payable	43,833	16,720	69,196	35,056	41,213	15,812	24,888	10,045	23,960	9,107
Current portion of long-term debt and other	18,337	19,305	16,577	17,213	17,731	15,983	14,322	12,776	9,873	7,186
Total current liabilities	648,240	604,710	974,956	647,977	597,828	559,358	733,234	357,671	277,944	201,585
Long-term debt and other	2,126,727	2,118,856	2,127,464	2,082,697	2,131,531	2,136,961	1,466,338	1,462,203	1,449,224	1,533,862
Commitments and contingencies										
Stockholders' equity (deficit):										
Preferred stock, $0.01 per value:										
Authorized shares—500,000										
Issued and outstanding shares—none										

(continued)

EXHIBIT 2 | Amazon Financial Data (cont.)

Historical Balance Sheets (Mar 31, 1999–June 30, 2001) (cont'd)

	30-Jun 2001	31-Mar 2001	31-Dec 2000	30-Sep 2000	30-Jun 2000	31-Mar 2000	31-Dec 2000	30-Sep 1999 (Unaudited)	30-Jun 1999 (Unaudited)	31-Mar 1999 (Unaudited)
Common stock, $0.01 par value:										
Authorized shares—5,000,000										
Issued and outstanding shares	3,622	3,588	3,571	3,561	3,554	3,500	3,452	3,393	3,364	3,228
Additional paid-in capital	1,356,216	1,344,083	1,388,303	1,342,574	1,335,733	1,293,761	1,194,369	1,026,484	976,571	303,701
Stock-based compensation	(10,132)	(10,532)	(13,448)	(19,504)	(25,410)	(34,889)	(47,806)	(32,180)	(37,743)	(1,275)
Accumulated other comprehensive income (loss)	(83,846)	(63,118)	(2,376)	(65,637)	(84,664)	(46,302)	(1,709)	(18,957)	(9,411)	(4,390)
Accumulated deficit	(2,695,791)	(2,527,432)	(2,293,301)	(1,748,161)	(1,507,637)	(1,190,453)	(882,028)	(558,815)	(361,735)	(223,727)
Total stockholders' equity (deficit)	(1,429,931)	(1,253,411)	(967,251)	(487,167)	(278,424)	25,617	266,278	419,925	571,046	77,537
Total liabilities and stockholders' equity	$1,345,036	$1,470,155	$2,135,169	$2,243,507	$2,450,935	$2,721,936	$2,465,850	$2,239,799	$2,298,214	$1,812,984
	30-Jun 2001	31-Mar 2001	31-Dec 2000	30-Sep 2000	30-Jun 2000	31-Mar 2000	31-Dec 2000	30-Sep 1999	30-Jun 1999	31-Mar 1999
Key Metrics—quarterly										
Inventory turns—annualized	13.71	12.55	17.68	11.20	10.26	9.08	13.86	12.81	18.88	24.50
A/P days	48.12	44.74	59.69	59.57	58.96	51.65	72.42	76.33	61.19	52.89
Inventory days	24.07	27.04	21.47	32.04	35.50	34.78	34.51	38.31	21.89	17.99
A/R days	2.63	1.54	0.73	3.86	4.77	4.62	1.54	2.83	3.91	3.08
Operating cycle	(21.42)	(16.17)	(41.28)	(44.52)	(43.93)	(37.95)	(57.02)	(60.69)	(38.40)	(25.32)
Days in period	91	90	92	92	91	90	92	92	91	91

EXHIBIT 2 | Amazon Financial Data (cont.)

Historical Balance Sheet (31 Mar, 1997–Dec. 31, 1998)

	31-Dec 1998	30-Sep 1998 (Unaudited)	30-Jun 1998 (Unaudited)	31-Mar 1998 (Unaudited)	31-Dec 1997	30-Sep 1997 (Unaudited)	30-Jun 1997 (Unaudited)	31-Mar 1997 (Unaudited)
ASSETS								
Current assets:								
Cash and cash equivalents	$71,583	$76,320	$328,351	$98,662	$110,119	$45,177	$6,847	$2,799
Marketable securities	301,862	260,940	8,261	18,659	15,258	3,494	50,220	4,346
Inventories	29,501	19,772	17,035	11,674	8,971	2,732	1,652	939
Prepaid expenses and other current assets	21,308	17,625	12,679	4,486	3,363	1,824	1,189	942
Total current assets	424,254	374,657	366,326	133,481	137,709	53,227	59,908	9,026
Fixed assets, net	29,791	23,821	15,587	10,276	9,726	4,801	3,832	2,605
Goodwill, net	174,052	207,070	52,398	—	—	—	—	—
Other intangibles, net	4,586	5,994	2	—	—	—	—	—
Investments in equity-method investees	7,740	—	—	—	—	—	—	—
Other equity investments	—	—	8,246	—	—	—	—	—
Other assets	8,037	8,172	7,907	2,343	2,409	350	331	196
Total assets	$648,460	$619,714	$450,466	$46,100	$149,844	$58,378	$64,071	$11,827
LIABILITIES AND STOCKHOLDERS' EQUITY (DEFICIT)								
Current liabilities:								
Accounts payable	$113,273	$60,046	$47,780	$34,610	$33,027	$15,659	$10,395	$5,685
Accrued expenses and other current liabilities	47,484	37,545	23,110	11,782	8,871	4,415	6,857	3,353
Unearned revenue	—	1,064	909	627	816	—	—	—
Interest payable	10	116	85	1,260	177	—	—	—
Current portion of long-term debt and other	808	684	751	1,297	1,660	228	156	653
Total current liabilities	$161,575	$99,455	$72,635	$49,576	$44,551	$20,302	$17,408	$9,691
Long-term debt and other	348,140	340,495	332,406	76,702	76,702	181	181	—
Commitments and contingencies								
Stockholders' equity (deficit)²:								
Preferred stock, $0.01 per value:								
Authorized shares—500,000								
Issued and outstanding shares—none	—	—	—	—	—	—	—	—

6

(continued)

EXHIBIT 2 | Amazon Financial Data (cont.)

Amazon.com, Inc.
Historical Balance Sheets (Sept 30, 1999–June 30, 2001) (cont'd.)

	30-Jun 2001	31-Mar 2001	31-Dec 2000	30-Sep 2000	30-Jun 2000	31-Mar 2000	31-Dec 1999	30-Sep 1999 (Unaudited)
Common stock, $0.01 par value:								
Authorized shares—5,000,000								
Issued and outstanding shares	3,186	3,114	2,982	2,904	2,898	2,868	2,868	2,088
Additional paid-in capital	297,438	294,636	114,247	66,294	65,137	64,009	63,332	12,833
Stock-based compensation	(1,625)	(2,943)	(1,301)	(1,493)	(1,930)	(2,291)	(2,659)	(3,090)
Accumulated other comprehensive income (loss)	1,806	590	(41)	-	-	-	-	-
Accumulated deficit	(162,060)	(115,633)	(70,462)	(47,883)	(37,514)	(26,691)	(17,059)	(9,701)
Total stockholders' equity (deficit)	138,745	179,764	45,425	19,822	28,591	37,895	46,482	2,136
Total liabilities and stockholders' equity	$648,460	$619,714	$450,466	$146,100	$149,844	$58,378	$64,071	$11,827

Key Metrics—quarterly	31-Dec 1998	30-Sep 1998	30-Jun 1998	31-Mar 1998	31-Dec 1997	30-Sep 1997	30-Jun 1997	31-Mar 1997
Inventory turns—annualized	32	26	25	26	36	56	70	
A/P days	52	46	48	46	57	47	42	
Inventory days	14	15	17	16	16	8	7	
A/R days	3	3	3	1	1	1	1	
Operating cycle	(36)	(28)	(28)	(30)	(40)	(38)	(34)	
Days in period	92	92	91	91	92	92	91	

EXHIBIT 2 | Amazon Financial Data (cont.)

Formulas Used in Computations

Inventory Turns

3 months COGS*4/

Average (Inventory – current quarter, inventory – prior quarter)

AP Days

Accounts Payable*Number of days in quarter/

Current quarter COGS

Inventory Days

Inventory*days in quarter/

Current Quarter COGS

AR Days

[(average (AR – ending, AR – beginning)]*365/

[quarter revenue*4]

Operating Cycle

Inventory days + accounts receivable days – accounts payable days

30 percent of the cost of inventory. (See Exhibit 4.) Thus, margins started taking a hit when clearance markdowns reached over 50 percent.[9]

---

[9]"Amazon.com's New Outlet Store Confirms 'Deal' Mentality on Web," *DSN Retailing Today,* January 22, 2001, p. 6.

The Joy of a Negative Operating Cycle

A key advantage of Amazon's business model, particularly with respect to brick and mortar competitors, was the company's negative operating cycle. Amazon received credit card payment from customers within a few days of purchase, but it did not pay its vendors for

EXHIBIT 3 | Selected Data For Books and Music in the U.S.

Estimated Revenue, Printing Expenses and Inventories for Book Publishers: 1998 and 1999

	($ 000)		
	1999	**1998**	**% Change**
Revenue total	$24,129	$22,480	7.3
Sources of revenue			
Revenue from the sale of printed material	19,840	18,622	6.5
Total Revenue from the sale of electronic or nonprinted material (except audio)	2,434	2,168	12.2
Multimedia	811	748	8.4
Online	1,623	1,420	14.3
Revenue from the sale of audio books	198	191	3.8
Revenue from the sale of publication rights	247	235	5.2
Contract printing	361	428	−15.7
Other revenues	1,048	836	25.5
Expenses			
Purchased printing	1,104	3,908	5.0
Total Inventories at end of year	2,984	2,737	9.0
Finished goods and work-in-process	2,723	2,510	8.5
Materials, supplies, fuel, etc.	261	227	14.6

Source: U.S. Census Bureau.

EXHIBIT 4 |

Amazon Annualized
Inventory Turns

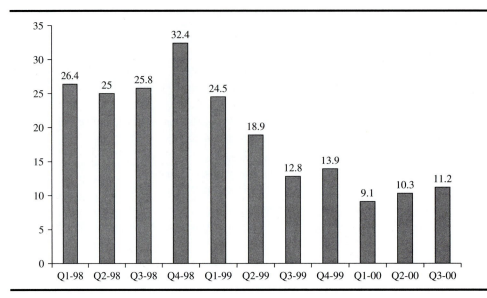

Source: Amazon company reports.

thirty to sixty days of sale. In addition, Amazon did not actually carry in inventory many of the products it sold, relying instead on suppliers to provide fast fulfillment and shifting inventory risk to its vendors in the process. According to Amazon, its typical operating cycle was around (−) forty-one days. Amazon estimated that the typical book retailing operating cycle was around (+) seventy-eight days. Thus Amazon generated interest on the full sale price (cost of goods and gross margin) for over a month.

Getting Physical

While negative operating cycles offered one important source of advantage over brick and mortar competitors, Amazon sought to reap even larger efficiencies from its comparative lack of physical infrastructure. The business model, as described in Amazon's prospectus, called for a minimum of bricks.

> The Company sources product from a network of book distributors and publishers. The Company carries minimal inventory and relies to a large extent on rapid fulfillment from major distributors and wholesalers which carry a broad selection of titles. The Company purchases a substantial majority of its products from Ingram and B&T. Ingram is the single largest supplier and accounted for 59 percent of the Company's inventory purchases in 1996. Of the more than 2.5 million titles offered by the Company, up to 400,000 are currently supplied by book

distributors and wholesalers, including Ingram and B&T. . . . The Company utilizes automated interfaces for sorting and organizing its orders to enable it to achieve the most rapid and economic purchase and delivery terms possible. The Company's proprietary software selects the orders that can be filled quickly via electronic interfaces with vendors, and forwards remaining orders to its special order group. Under the Company's arrangements with its distributors, electronically ordered books often are shipped by the distributor within hours of receipt of an order from Amazon.com. The Company has developed customized information systems and dedicated ordering personnel that specialize in sourcing hard-to-find books. The Company currently processes all sales through its warehouse in Seattle.[10]

This worked when Amazon offered only books. However, as the company expanded its offerings, it necessarily expanded its infrastructure. In 1999, Amazon built twelve distribution centers in the United States, adding over 3 million square feet, at a cost of $200 million.

What Do You Own?

By 1999, Bezos had pinned his hopes on synergy developing from Amazon's e-commerce technology platform, brand power, and fulfillment infrastructure that he had

---

[10]Amazon SEC Form 424B1, June 15, 1997.

quickly built in the United States and overseas. In the company's 1999 Annual Report, Letter to Shareholders, Bezos wrote:

> At a recent event at the Stanford University campus, a young woman came to the microphone and asked me a great question: "I have one hundred shares of Amazon.com. What do I own?"
>
> I was surprised that I had not heard the question before, at least not so simply put. What do you own? You own a piece of the leading e-commerce platform. The Amazon.com platform is comprised of brand, customers, technology, distribution capability, deep e-commerce expertise, and a great team with a passion for innovation and a passion for serving customers well. . . . We believed we have reached a "tipping point,"[11] where this platform allows us to launch a new e-commerce business faster, with higher quality of customers' experience, a lower incremental cost, a higher chance of success, and a clear path to scale and profitability than perhaps any company.[12]

Competitors

Amazon did not fit comfortably into existing industry categories. When asked whether Amazon was really a software company—its key asset being its information systems—Bezos replied, "I always think of that as a semantic issue. We are not a retailer and we are not a technology company. We are a customer company." Still, discussion of likely competitors usually included companies such as Wal-Mart, Barnes & Noble, and Kmart. (See Exhibit 5.)

Not surprisingly, competition from Wal-Mart loomed large in Bezo's mind. Wal-Mart had more than 3,600 stores across the globe, boasted state-of-the-art inventory management skills, and owned one of the best brands in mass retailing. The retailer had also moved onto the Web. Customers could order a wide range of goods from walmart.com, which were delivered a few days later. Or customers could order products through the Web site and pick them up from their local Wal-Mart store.

Similarly, Kmart's Bluelight.com, a partnership with Softbank and Martha Stewart Living Omnimedia,

leveraged Kmart's vast physical presence. As with Wal-Mart, Bluelight placed Web kiosks in each of Kmart's 1,100 stores in the United States. In May 2000, Bluelight launched a free ISP service, gaining four million subscribers in four months.

The number two-ranked online bookseller behind Amazon, B&N.com, was also integrating into the physical network of 550 superstores owned by Barnes & Noble, which controlled 40 percent of the online bookstore. New service counters were installed to enable customers to log on to B&N.com to order any book or other product through the Web site. Customers could pick up their orders at the store or have them delivered. (At the time of this writing, delivery was limited to the New York area.) In addition, customers who bought books or music CDs through B&N.com were able to return items to Barnes & Noble stores for credit or exchange.

After the Fall

The year 2000 marked the end of a steady increase in the NASDAQ. From its all-time high of 5,049 on March 10, 2000, the exchange lost 59 percent of its value; in the following twelve months. A long list of famous Internet companies lost the majority of their value, many closed their doors. By many measures, 2000 was a good year for Amazon. Revenues totaled $2.8 billion, an increase of 68 percent over 1999. Not surprisingly, the best growth was in new domestic categories, e.g., tools and hardware and consumer electronics, with sequential revenue increases of 317 percent in fiscal 2000 to $683 million. Amazon's international segment also experienced significant growth, up 127 percent year over year to $381 million in 2000. The international growth reduced the impact of Amazon's traditional U.S. books/music/movie segment, which accounted for just over 60 percent of consolidated sales in 2000, down from 80 percent in 1999. Amazon increased its cumulative customer base 16 percent to 29 million through the addition of 4.1 million customers during the fourth quarter of 2000. Of the 4.1 million new customers added, about 1.1 million were international customers, which increased Amazon's total international client base to 5 million customers, a boost of 72 percent.

Also by the fourth quarter 2000, twelve-month sales per active customer reached $134, up from $130 in the previous quarter, and customer acquisition costs

---

[11]"Tipping Point" is the concept that small changes will have little or no effect on a system until a critical mass is reached. Then further small changes "tip" the system and a large effect is observed.

[12]Amazon.com *1999 Annual Report,* Letter to Shareholders, p. 2.

EXHIBIT 5 | Selected Financial Information $000

	12/31/2000	9/30/2000	6/30/2000	3/31/2000
Net Sales				
U.S. books, music, and DVD/video	$ 511,671	$ 399,905	$ 385,275	$ 401,415
U.S. electronics, tools, and kitchen	220,203	97,597	91,755	74,596
Total U.S. retail	731,874	497,502	477,030	476,011
U.S. services	95,601	52,691	27,453	22,746
Total U.S.	827,475	550,193	504,483	498,757
International	144,885	87,665	73,393	75,132
Consolidated totals	972,360	637,858	577,876	573,889
Gross Profit				
U.S. books, music, and DVD/video	138,989	108,746	86,862	82,855
U.S. electronics, tools, and kitchen	22,407	8,940	6,249	7,059
Total U.S. retail	161,396	117,686	93,111	89,914
U.S. services	36,672	30,711	26,667	22,184
Total U.S.	198,068	148,397	119,778	112,098
International	26,232	18,882	16,286	16,036
Consolidated totals	224,300	167,279	136,064	128,134
Pro forma income (loss) from operations				
U.S. books, music, and DVD/video	39,122	24,688	10,056	(2,425)
U.S. electronics, tools, and kitchen	(72,725)	(60,839)	(69,077)	(67,249)
Total U.S. retail	(33,603)	(36,151)	(59,021)	(69,674)
U.S. services	17,207	7,281	4,175	(2,144)
Total U.S.	(16,396)	(28,870)	(54,846)	(71,818)
International	(43,550)	(39,569)	(34,503)	(27,448)
Consolidated totals	$ (59,946)	$ (68,439)	$ (89,349)	$ (99,266)

Source: Amazon.com.

declined from $15 in the third quarter to $13 by the end of the year. Repeat customers comprised 75 percent of total orders for the fourth quarter, up from 73 percent from the previous year.[13]

Despite the relatively robust performance in 2000, Amazon expected sales growth in 2001 to slow to 20–30 percent, or around $3.4 billion, far below the 43 percent growth previously expected. In an effort to drive toward profitability, the company laid off 1,300 employees comprising 15 percent of its workforce. Amazon also closed one of its twelve distribution centers and one of its nine customer service centers.[14]

---

[13]S. Rashtchy, " Amazon.com," U.S. Bancorp Piper Jaffray Inc., January 31, 2001.

[14]*BusinessWeek,* February 12, 2000, p. 39.

Amazon Today

Speaking about Amazon.com today, Bezos said:

> Our mission is to be the earth's most customer-centric company. We intend to do this through actions in three categories:
>
> - Listen: the traditional definition applies;
>
> - Invent: because you can listen to customers, but they don't always know what they want or what is possible;
>
> - Personalize: we are investing heavily in personalization technology.
>
> We want to set a new worldwide standard for customer centricity. Our vision is to build a place where people can come to find and buy whatever they want online. The first and foremost step is to build the discovery

EXHIBIT 5 | Selected Financial Information (cont.)

**Income Statements for Barnesandnoble.com, Barnes and Noble, Inc.,
Wal-Mart Stores, Inc., Kmart, and Circuit City for financial year 2000**

	Barnesand noble.com 31-Dec-2000	Barnes and Noble, Inc. 29-Jan-2000	Wal-Mart 31-Jan-2000	Kmart 31-Jan-2001	Circuit City 29-Feb-2000
($000, except EPS)					
Sales—Core business	320.1	3,486.0	165,013.0	37,028.0	12,614.4
Sales—Other			1,796.0		
Total sales	**320.1**	**3,486.0**	**166,809.0**	**37,028.0**	**12,614.4**
Cost of goods sold	261.8	2,483.7	129,664.0	29,658.0	9,751.8
SG&A expense	194.5	651.1	27,040.0	7,415.0	2,309.6
Interest expense			1,022.0		24.2
Depreciation	47.8	112.3			
Research & development	40.4	6.8			
Unusual income/expenses	75.1				
Total expenses	**619.6**	**3,253.9**	**157,726.0**	**37,073.0**	**12,085.6**
Interest net	23.7	−23.8		−287.0	
		10.3			
Pretax income	**−275.7**	**218.6**	**9,083.0**	**−332.0**	**528.8**
Income taxes	0.0	89.6	3,338.0	−134.0	200.9
Income after taxes	**−275.7**	**129.0**	**5,745.0**	**−198.0**	**327.8**
Preferred dividends				−36.0	
Interest adjusted for primary EPS					
Minority interests			−170.0		
Net income before E&D	***−275.7***	***129.0***	***5,575.0***	***−198.0***	***327.8***
Accounting change		−4.5	−198.0		
Discontinued operations					−130.2
Extraordinary items					
Net income after E&D	***−275.7***	***124.5***	***5,377.0***	***−198.0***	***197.6***
Preferred dividends				−36.0	
Income Av. to common shareholders				−234.0	
Dividends per common share			0.20		0.07
Shares to calculate primary EPS (millions of shares)	147.4	69.0	4,451.0	482.0	201.3
Primary EPS excluding E&D	−1.87	1.87	1.21	−0.49	1.63
Primary EPS including E&D	−1.87	1.80	1.25	−0.49	0.98

Source: Company reports.

NB: E = extraordinary items, D = discontinued operations.

(*continued*)

EXHIBIT 5 | Selected Financial Information (cont.)

Sales per Employee of Barnesandnoble.com, Barnes and Noble, Inc., Wal-Mart Stores, Inc., and Kmart in fiscal year 2000 ($M)

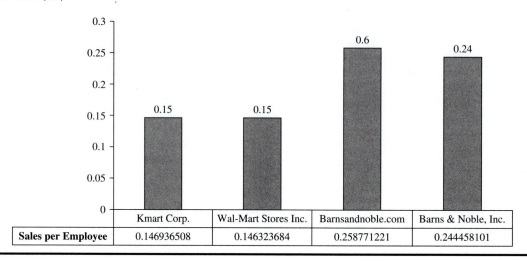

	Kmart Corp.	Wal-Mart Stores Inc.	Barnsandnoble.com	Barns & Noble, Inc.
Sales per Employee	0.146936508	0.146323684	0.258771221	0.244458101

mechanisms [that customers can use to find] products. We want to build a place where people can find anything with a capital "A."

Summing up his vision for the company, Bezos said: "We don't see it as our job to sell people things as much as it is to help people make purchase decisions. It's a subtle but important difference."

Amazon created one way of making that "help" pay. The company announced that it planned to start charging publishers for recommending selected titles in e-mail promotions to Amazon customers. Publishers would be charged as much as $10,000 per title to be spotlighted in the e-mail. Amazon would also require publishers to purchase advertising spots on its Web pages, pushing the total cost up to $17,000. In the past, the online retailer had recommended books for free in those e-mails. The titles were selected by Amazon editors solely according to content. Amazon still planned to recommend books it considered worthwhile for free via e-mails. Amazon said it would disclose which e-mails were paid advertisements.[15]

Touching Atoms versus Streaming Bits

For many investors, part of Amazon's financial charm stemmed from its fundamental business model, the negative operating cycle it allowed, and the other efficiencies associated with and expected of Web-based businesses.

But there always had been a fulfillment component to Amazon's primary business model, whereby employees actually had to "touch" items (often referred to as picking and packing, whereby items are picked from inventory shelves and packed into a box for shipping). Amazon expanded its categories of offerings and its geographic presence, and it also expanded its infrastructure. Bezos said:

> The first day, $5\frac{1}{2}$ years ago, we touched every book the customer bought. There are few ways to reliably get products to customers without touching the products. It's part of the path to maturation. I have heard a story, maybe it's apocryphal, that Henry Ford had to go into iron ore mining because there wasn't enough iron ore available in the country at the time.

Asked if Amazon's fundamental business model would continue to span Web vision and fulfillment skills, Bezos said:

> There will always be products that require [our touching]. We will have a competence [in distribution] that will be hard to compete with . . . real competence from our distribution network.

> Most businesses have two things in the physical world in which they are excellent. Look at Wal-Mart. Its physical attributes are excellent: greeters, clean stores, right locations, and it has the lowest cost structures. It is a rare business that has only a single competency.

[15]*The Wall Street Journal,* February 7, 2001, p. B1.

There are many cases where we do not touch the products, for example, Drugstore.com. The physical distribution of pharmaceuticals is very different from the physical distribution of the products we got good at distributing.

Bezos described the type of product that Amazon wanted to offer.

The items we touch should have two attributes:

- Conveyable, i.e., on a conveyer belt and smaller than a bread box.

- Nonperishable.

We have millions of SKUs (stock keeping units) in our distribution center network. It's difficult to ship singles, from a selection of millions, to individuals.

Bezos viewed Amazon's distribution facility a key competitive advantage. Yet, Amazon enjoyed a much higher valuation than even best of breed retailers with state-of-the-art distribution skills. For example, while companies in the Standard & Poor's 500 had an average PE multiple of eighteen, most retailers generate only single digit PE ratios.

Getting Personal

What then separates Amazon from other retailers? For many observers it is the potential power of the data generated by millions of transactions. Bezos said:

We use collaborative filtering, a statistical method that looks at your purchase history, compares it to other customers, builds a statistical aggregate electronic "soul mate" that tells you what your soul mate has purchased that you have not.

But it's still early. The algorithms themselves are hard and they are constrained by processing power.

For Bezos, personalization would be a hallmark of the Amazon brand and experience. He observed, "The business reason to do personalization is so that we build a deep relationship with customers that they would miss if they went away." Bezos saw Amazon as a mix of Web skills (including e-commerce platform and payment mechanisms) and fulfillment expertise. Bezos summed up: "These come together at software."

But For *You* the Price Is . . .

That software was increasingly sophisticated. For example, by drawing on known demographics and purchase history, algorithms could estimate a buyer's price elasticity for a given item and raise or lower a price to meet the maximum that an individual was likely to pay. This practice was known as dynamic pricing. Broadly speaking, prices were free to move in response to demand, supply, aggregate buying, reverse auctions, or haggling. Jupiter research projected that revenue from these online dynamic pricing formats would reach $1 billion in 2000 and grow to $7 billion by 2004.[16] While dynamic pricing was not a new concept, shops in high-income areas often charged more for items than shops in lower income areas. When wedded to Web technology and customer-specific databases, the practice could become a powerful tool for maximizing pricing and margins. For brick and mortar sellers, tests of price elasticities could be expensive and time consuming. Therefore, most sellers confined tests to a narrow range of prices on a limited number of items. By contrast, Web-based sellers could easily perform continuous, real-time price testing that produced immediate customer responses. For example, if a seller wanted to know the sales impact of a 5 percent price increase, he or she could conduct a test by charging every fiftieth visitor this increased price. By studying responses, researchers could gain important insights into the role price plays in customers' buying decisions.[17]

One high-profile example of Web-based dynamic pricing in practice occurred with Amazon in September 2000. Users in a chat room on the DVDtalk.com Web site noticed that some Amazon customers paid more for given DVDs than others. The visitors noticed that Amazon's prices seemed higher for regular customers. One chat room visitor said, "They [Amazon] must figure that with repeat customers they have 'won' them over and they can charge them slightly higher prices since they are loyal and don't mind and/or won't notice that they are being charged three to five percent more for some items." When the chat room visitors complained about the pricing variation to Amazon, the company's spokesman Bill Curry replied, "It was done to determine consumer responses to different discount levels . . . this was a pure and simple price test. This was not dynamic pricing. We don't do that and have no plans to ever do that." However, in an e-mail response to an individual DVDTalk.com member, another Amazon representative wrote, "I would first like to send along my most sincere

---

[16]Jupiter Research, Forecasts and Projections, Commerce Infrastructure, August 2000.

[17]Michael V. Marin, "Virtual Pricing," *The McKinsey Quarterly*, no. 4, 2000.

apology for any confusion or frustration caused by our dynamic price test. Dynamic testing of a customer base is a common practice among both brick and mortar and Internet companies." Indeed, Curry later observed, "Dynamic pricing is stupid, because people will find out. Fortunately, it only took us two instances to see this."[18]

Still, Jupiter Research believed dynamic pricing practices would increase in the online retail industry. Jupiter expected customers to receive offers to which they were more likely to respond based on a variety of factors including "purchase history, including lifetime customer value and demonstrated price sensitivity; clickstream history (site versioning based on affiliate and advertising linkage); preferences and interests reported by customers; and products purchased by other individuals with similar purchase patterns, demographic, or psychographic profiles."[19]

The Amazon Effect

In the e-tailing world, Amazon had quickly become the proverbial 800-pound gorilla. Bezos and others credited the company's innovativeness for its success. Indeed, Amazon originated or quickly adopted a host of innovations that set it apart from the prevailing competition.

Amazon's "one-click" checkout process offered one contentious example. In September 1997, Amazon launched a system that allowed shoppers to buy items without completing long registration and shipping forms—a chore shoppers found tedious and that inhibited buying. Instead, Amazon designed software and redesigned its processes to allow repeat buyers to purchase items by clicking one button. Two years later Amazon was awarded a patent on its one-click process.

In 1998, B&N.com introduced a similar one-click service. Amazon sued and in December 1999 was awarded an injunction in U.S. District court in Seattle. In February 2001, the U.S. Court of Appeals in Washington D.C. issued a unanimous decision to overturn the injunction awarded in 1999. Both sides were scheduled to go to trial over the issue in September 2001.

Meanwhile, independent booksellers looked to join forces to compete with Amazon. According to the Book Industry Study Group, a market research firm, independent booksellers owned a 15.2 percent share of the nearly 1.1 billion adult consumer books sold in the United States

in 1999, down from their 19.5 percent share in 1995. Similarly, national chains also saw their market share slip, falling to 24.6 percent in 1999 from 25.5 percent in 1995. Book e-tailers, led by Amazon, garnered 5.4 percent of the overall market in 1999, up from 0.4 percent in 1997, the first year for which data is available.[20]

To combat the market share loss, independent booksellers set up their own Web site and some joined forces with companies such as BookSite.com, an online clearinghouse and database-management firm that let independent booksellers set up their own Web pages, backed up by BookSite's online title list and delivery system. BookSite had two hundred independent bookstores as members, each with annual revenue of $250,000 or more. Members maintain their own individual storefronts on the Web, but pay a fee of about $2,500 a year for access to BookSite's book-title database, search-engine software, and access to warehouses of book distributors, such as Ingram Book Group, the distributor featured prominently in Amazon's prospectus.

BookSite's founder said, "I think there's an image that independent booksellers are kind of shy little fellows sitting in the corner crying . . . That's not the case. There's a whole cadre of booksellers out there carrying on the battle."[21]

BookSite, however, would soon have some competition. The American Booksellers Association, a trade group representing small bookstores, was in March 2001 testing Booksense.com. Part of a larger marketing plan to raise the profile of independent booksellers nationwide, Booksense would offer the same kind of back-office e-commerce services as BookSite, including fulfillment and distribution and a database of titles. Booksense would charge its members $100 a month and 4.25 percent of the store's online sales.[22]

BookSite had 1.2 million titles, and Booksense planned to offer 2.4 million titles using a database it licensed from Baker & Taylor Corp., the distributor formerly used exclusively by Amazon before it deployed its own internal-fulfillment system.

BookSite and Booksense would each depend to some degree on their wholesaler partners to fulfill orders.

One analyst estimated the size of the online book sales market at $1.44 billion in 2000, or 7.5 percent of the estimated $19 billion in total consumer book sales for that year. But he estimated that by 2003, the online market

[18]David Streitfeld, "On the Web, Price Tags Blur; What You Pay Could Depend on Who You Are," *Washington Post,* September 27, 2000.

[19]Michele Rosenshein, "Dynamic Merchandising," Jupiter Research, Vol. 5, October 24, 2000.

[20]Scott Eden, "Independent Booksellers Hope to Find Strength in Numbers," *The Wall Street Journal,* July 17, 2000.

[21]Ibid.

[22]Ibid.

could increase 90 percent to $2.7 billion. Total book sales were projected to grow only 18 percent, to $22.5 billion.[23]

Conclusion

It was clear that Amazon had matured far beyond the initial online business concept described in its 1995 prospectus. What was less clear was what the company would become in the future, what kind of business model it should adopt, and how such a model should be valued. Like that woman from Stanford, shareholders would want to know what they had bought and where Amazon was going. Amazon innovated and created a new form of retail organization. The question was whether the new form was viable or whether existing firms could imitate and incorporate some the features of the new form to enhance their own survival chances in the quickly changing retail ecology.

---

[23]Ibid.

PART 4

Compounding Confluence—Take II: Saving or Sinking Software

"BEA Systems, Inc. in 2003: Reaching for the Next Level" is a very complex case that offers the opportunity to get some insight in the interrelated layers of enterprise software products. The case illustrates several strategic challenges that BEA faced as a focused "application server" ("middleware") company increasingly competing against larger rivals such as IBM, Oracle, and Microsoft. Seeking further growth opportunities, the company was broadening its product portfolio into the integration and portal software market segments, but had also been first in bringing all of these software pieces together in an integrated middleware "platform." Top management felt BEA had to become the preferred platform partner for the high-end enterprise computing market segment. At the same time, a new category of Internet-based Web services offered the opportunity to become a key player in the midsize and small company market segment. The company also faced strategic challenges in collaborating and competing with some the major application software companies. This was especially the case with SAP, which was moving downward into BEA's application server layer of the software stack.

Important discussion topics for this case are (1) horizontal strategy in the enterprise software market segment, (2) advantages and disadvantages of a "pure play" strategy, (3) the role of channel strategy in corporate growth, and (4) challenges of competing on the "intersecting ground" (Sun Tzu). In terms of our three key themes, the case offers an example of P-controlled change threatening to morph into P-independent change; it shows how clarity of strategy allows top management to align strategic action with strategy; but it also shows how industry change puts severe pressure on the alignment of strategy and action and forces top management to consider options for corporate transformation.

"The Open Source Software Challenge in 2001" deals with the "open source" phenomenon, which refers to any software program (such as an application or even an entire operating system) whose source code is made available for use or modification as users or other developers see fit. The note highlights the strategic challenges and opportunities that open source software (OSS) poses to traditional software companies (such as Microsoft), computer companies (such as IBM, Hewlettt-Packard, and Sun Microsystems), and hardware component suppliers (such as Intel).

Important discussion topics for this industry note are (1) the advantages and disadvantages of self-organizing versus planned software development, (2) the strength and weaknesses of "social movements" versus "for profit" hierarchical systems, (3) how to defend or attack pieces of the potential industry earnings (PIE), and (4) conjectures about the future of OSS. In terms of our three key themes, the note illustrates some of the "social" forces that can produce P-independent change; it shows how these forces may challenge the alignment between strategy and action of differentially positioned players in the industry; and it provides examples of how OSS has instigated at least partial corporate transformation of different players.

"MySQL" discusses the strategy of a small Scandinavian software company that has come into a position to challenge IBM, Microsoft and Oracle in the high-margin database market with a form of open source software (OSS). The case is an example of how OSS has opened opportunities for new entrants to gain a foothold in a low-cost segment of the market, which may eventually allow them to challenge well-established incumbents at the high end. As MySQL relied on a low cost business model with a global, virtual organization, the case also frames the question whether their innovative, Internet-based business model could be scaled into a large profitable growth company.

Important discussion topics for this case are (1) understanding the basis of competitive advantage and the reasons of success, (2) identifying the "minimum winning game," (3) identifying the key strategic options for growth and the inherent trade-offs that they imply, (4) allying yourself with an 800-pound gorilla but maintaining control of your destiny. In terms of our three key themes, this case provides another example of P-controlled change (but as yet on a small scale); it shows the difficulties of maintaining alignment between strategy and action in the face of fast growth and potentially conflicting further growth options; and it shows the importance of preparing for industry change and making sure that the corporate transformation that is involved is based on careful strategic analysis of the external and internal forces.●

Case 3.1

BEA Systems, Inc. in 2003: Reaching for the Next Level

Introduction

In 2003, BEA Systems, Inc., headquartered in San Jose, California, was a leading provider of application infrastructure software, with over 13,000 customers worldwide, including the majority of the Fortune Global 500. Application infrastructure software—often called "middleware"—was sandwiched between application users at their PCs and the databases and legacy systems that directly managed data. BEA's customers used its software products to integrate private client/server networks, the Internet, intranets and applications such as billing, provisioning, and customer service. BEA provided software that enabled development, implementation, and production of a new application or a new business process in an existing enterprise. For example, a financial services company implementing a new online process to handle trades needed to develop a user interface for brokers to input data, to make it feed into the application performing the trade, and to connect the application to existing legacy systems to update various databases. BEA's software brought all of these pieces together.

Early in 2003, BEA's top management team was contemplating the company's future. BEA had come a long way from its founding eight years ago to become a billion-dollar enterprise. It was performing well and demonstrating resilience during the downturn in the technology sector. BEA was taking advantage of the slow economy to focus on R&D and recruiting top talent. (Exhibits 1 and 2 show BEA's recent financial and stock market

performance.) During the past 12 months, the company had significantly enhanced top management bench strength by hiring key players from leading information technology companies. And now the new top management team was eager to reevaluate the corporate strategy. So far, BEA's strategy had been growth through acquisition, but it was unclear if this was sustainable and whether it would allow BEA to achieve the next level of growth necessary to become the predominant player in its industry. Some analysts were even raising the question whether BEA could stay independent.[1]

To become the predominant player in its industry, the company faced several strategic challenges. IBM, Oracle, and Microsoft posed an increased competitive threat in BEA's core application server market segment. Seeking further growth opportunities, the company was broadening its product portfolio into the integration and portal market segments where it faced strong competition from pure plays such as SeeBeyond, Vitria, Web Methods and others. At the same time, there were increasingly strong pressures to bring all of these pieces together in an integrated "platform" that could be effectively used by corporate software developers seeking to write additional applications or better integrate existing ones, as well as by independent software developers writing major new applications. Top management felt BEA had to win the major battle for becoming the "preferred platform partner" for the high-end enterprise computing market segment. At the same time, a new category of Internet-based "Web services"[2] offered the opportunity to also become a key player in the mainstream—midsize and small company—market segment. In order to be able to effectively compete with its much larger rivals and to successfully pursue its preferred platform ambitions, top management felt that it needed to carefully formulate and implement a radically innovative product strategy combined with an equally innovative comprehensive distribution channel strategy.

Professor Robert A. Burgelman prepared this case with the assistance of Sweta Sarnot, MBA Class of 2003, as the basis for class discussion rather than to illustrate either effective or ineffective handling of an administrative situation.

[1]On December 20, 2002, for instance, there had been rumors of an acquisition by Oracle and BEA's share price had jumped from $11.12 to $12.15. Jason Maynard and Bryan McGrath, "Will Oracle Acquire BEA?" Wachovia Securities, December 20, 2002.

[2]This was possible because standards had developed that allowed applications to communicate with each other. Web service products could connect to and communicate with different applications and systems such as SAP, Siebel, Mainframe and WebLogic. In the past, these applications could not easily interconnect. BEA, IBM and Microsoft drove progress toward interconnection standards.

EXHIBIT 1 | BEA Systems' Financial Performance Consolidated Statements of Income

In Thousands $ Except Per Share Amounts for Period Ended Jan 31, 2003

	1/31/2003	1/31/2002	1/31/2001
Revenues:			
License fees	515,883	597,909	476,573
Services	418,175	377,984	343,187
Total revenues	$934,058	$975,893	$819,760
Cost of revenues:			
Cost of license fees	18,797	21,087	19,724
Cost of services	178,105	182,678	197,567
Amortization of acquired intangible assets	25,388	26,324	38,466
Impairment of certain acquired intangible assets	—	7,082	—
Severance charges	—	2,461	—
Total cost of revenues	$222,290	$239,632	$255,757
Gross profit	711,768	736,261	564,003
Operating expenses:			
Sales and marketing	368,874	400,860	335,501
Research and development	132,771	120,875	89,247
General and administrative	76,390	75,671	57,611
Amortization of goodwill	—	46,384	59,192
Facilities consolidation and severance charges	—	37,992	—
Impairment of goodwill	—	73,068	—
Acquisition-related charges	—	—	2,200
Total operating expenses	$578,035	$754,850	$543,751
Income (loss) from operations	133,733	(18,589)	20,252
Interest and other, net:			
Interest expense	(22,086)	(22,259)	(22,910)
Write-down of equity investments	(24,174)	(22,922)	(16,211)
Net gains on sale of equity investments	3,659	19,623	18,595
Interest income and other, net	28,691	39,879	47,736
Total interest and other, net	(13,910)	14,321	27,210
Income (loss) before provision for income taxes	$119,823	$(4,268)	$47,462
Provision for income taxes	35,947	31,410	30,380
Net income (loss)	$83,876	$(35,678)	$17,082
Other comprehensive income (loss):			
Foreign currency translation adjustments	5,477	(5,427)	(213)
Unrealized gain (loss) on available-for-sale investments, net of income taxes of $834, $203 and $(12), respectively	1,943	474	(29)
Comprehensive income (loss)	91,296	(40,631)	16,840
Net income (loss) per share:			
Basic	0.21	(0.09)	0.05
Diluted	0.20	(0.09)	0.04
Shares used in computing net income (loss) per share:			
Basic	405,515	396,498	377,070
Diluted	418,540	396,498	412,700

Source: Disclosure.

EXHIBIT 1 | BEA Systems' Financial Performance Consolidated Balance Sheet (cont.)

In Thousands $ for Period Ended Jan 31, 2003

	01/31/03	01/31/02
ASSETS		
Current Assets:		
Cash and cash equivalents	578,717	821,802
Restricted cash	4,369	6,903
Short-term investments	688,753	205,395
Accounts receivable, net of allowance for doubtful accounts of $11,210 and $10,700 at January 31, 2003 and 2002, respectively	208,189	193,099
Deferred tax assets	—	1,983
Other current assets (see Note 17—Related Party Transaction)	43,869	34,247
Total current assets	$1,523,897	$1,263,429
Property and equipment, net	63,938	79,204
Goodwill, net of accumulated amortization of $133,348 at both January 31, 2003 and 2002	53,565	46,545
Acquired intangible assets, net	16,159	26,497
Long-term restricted cash	131,727	122,839
Other long-term assets (see Note 7—Related Party transaction)	20,673	121,437
Total assets	$1,809,959	$1,659,951
LIABILITIES AND STOCKHOLDERS' EQUITY		
Current liabilities:		
Accounts payable	10,807	23,111
Accrued liabilities	89,348	95,001
Accrued facilities consolidation and severance charges	17,617	26,552
Accrued payroll and related liabilities	54,295	52,948
Accrued income taxes	38,992	34,719
Deferred revenues	233,758	194,846
Deferred tax liabilities	600	—
Current portion of notes payable and other obligations	164	1,340
Total current liabilities	$445,581	$428,517
Deferred tax liabilities	4,214	4,383
Notes payable and other long-term obligations	4,215	3,135
Convertible subordinated notes	550,000	550,000
Commitments and contingencies Stockholders' equity:		
Preferred stock—$0.001 par value; 5,000 shares authorized; none issued and outstanding	—	—
Common stock—$0.001 par value; 1,035,000 shares authorized; 405,751 and 403,860 shares issued and outstanding at January 31, 2003 and 2002, respectively	406	404
Additional paid-in capital	1,002,846	913,574
Treasury stock, at cost	(42,095)	—
Accumulated deficit	(137,675)	(221,551)
Deferred compensation	(18,479)	(12,037)
Accumulated other comprehensive income (loss)	946	(6,474)
Total stockholders' equity	$805,949	$673,916
Total liabilities and stockholders' equity	1,809,959	1,659,951

Source: Disclosure.

EXHIBIT 2 |

BEA Systems' Stock
Market Performance

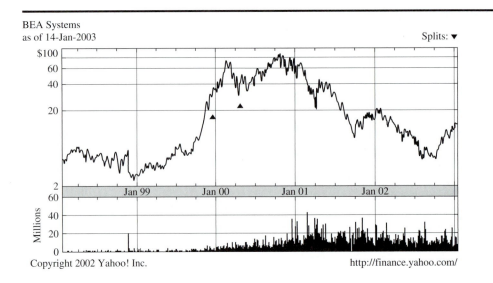

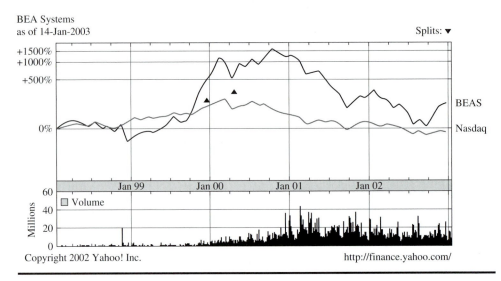

Source: Reproduced with permission of Yahoo! Inc. © 2005 by Yahoo! Inc. YAHOO! And the YAHOO! logo are trademarks of Yahoo! Inc.

Company History[3]

The Vision

In 1993, William ("Bill") Coleman had been running the software development at Sun Microsystems for three years. While skiing in Aspen, Colorado during a six-month unpaid leave of absence, he came to the conclusion that he wanted to continue working in the computer industry but do something different. He said he wanted ". . . to do in a small way what Dave Packard did in a big way—create a company that was 'built-to-last,' and also give something back to society while staying in the computer industry."[4]

---

[3]The structure and content of this section have benefited from reading the Harvard Business School case: "BEA Systems, Inc.: Constant Reinvention to Cope with Market Waves," N9-803-118, January 28, 2003, pages 5–10. We thank Professor Donald N. Sull, one of its coauthors, for giving us access to this case while its use was still restricted.

[4]All quotes from Bill Coleman are from the author's interview on February 17, 2003. Subsequent quotes from this interview will not be cited.

Coleman's vision was inspired by several insights. First, during the early 1990s, distributed computing—so-called "client-server" systems—seemed to be on the way to replacing mainframe computing. While client-server systems had several advantages, mainframes provided high scalability, reliability, and manageability which the client-server systems did not, thereby making the latter unfit for running mission-critical applications. The claim that "mainframes were dead, PCs were kings" was therefore premature.[5] Yet, the drive toward outsourcing of noncore functions had gained force in the corporate world and for the efficiencies of outsourcing to be realized, the "virtual corporation," for instance, needed to be linked to its suppliers. This increased the role of distributed computing. Large enterprises now needed to extend their mission-critical applications beyond the legacy mainframe systems to the distributed computing environment. But Coleman realized that "people will not give away their data, hence applications must go to the data," along with providing reliability and scalability. Earlier applications, however, used to run on different operating systems and were not scalable as there was a need to reprogram the application on each machine. The evolution of computer systems during the early 1990s thus had created tremendous heterogeneity in corporate hardware, software, and databases with attendant high costs of ownership. Around the same time, Sun Microsystems had announced its vision for the future that "the network is the computer." Coleman realized that this created the opportunity for building "an operating system for the network": a software layer that would allow effective and efficient interoperability of all these information technology components and processes. These insights formed the seed for the idea of what would eventually become an "application server."[6] Appendix A provides some further details of the technological aspects of the application infrastructure industry.

Returning from Colorado, Coleman was able to interest two other veteran Sun Microsystems executives, Edward Scott and Alfred Chuang, and during 1994 the three of them began to give more concrete shape to the initial vision. They developed an idea for a distributed transaction processing software product that could perform some of the functions envisaged in Coleman's initial vision, but their experience made them realize that developing and commercializing such a product from scratch would be a multiyear endeavor. Their alternative approach was, as Coleman put it, "to use a market-focused rather than a product-focused strategy for building a company," and "to use distribution channels, not products, as the basis for scaling the company." While this was not the traditional strategy well understood by Silicon Valley venture capitalists, they were able to get introduced to Bill Janeway, a venture capitalist at Warburg Pincus, who was interested in investing around the client-server market opportunity, in areas such as distributed management and distributed transaction systems. According to Bill Coleman, "Janeway was interested in investing in large opportunities that were not owned by IBM at the time. Middleware for distributed computing fit the bill." Warburg Pincus provided $750,000 in funding for a research project in return for the right of first refusal to fund the business plan that would result from it. In January 1995, BEA was founded (named after the first initials of the founders' names).

Strategic Evolution

Phase I (1995–1997)   Using the $750,000 seed funding, the founding team studied the products that were already available and tried to get a handle on customer needs. Rather than developing a new product from scratch, they were keen to buy the most promising existing product and to only build the missing complementary products. They identified two promising existing products. TopEnd was owned by NCR but management changes in that company interfered with BEA's plans to acquire the product. The second product was Tuxedo—a transaction processing monitor[7]—owned by networking giant Novell, Inc. Novell had originally obtained Tuxedo

---

[5]IBM's CEO Lou Gerstner made reference to "Mainframes are dead, PCs are king" in a speech on December 11, 1996, http://www.ibm.com/lvg/iw96.phtml.

[6]An application server is a category of system software that layers between an operating system (OS) below it and an application above it, isolating the application from the OS. Typically, an application server also wraps the application code to the extent that the application code does not interact directly with the DBMS, the communications software and other external environments. An application server acts essentially as an isolating container that permits the application code to be relatively simple by managing many of the complexities of the modern computing environment on behalf of the application. Source: "Application Server Basics: Where Sun and Microsoft Agree," Gartner, Inc., October 16, 2002.

---

[7]Transaction processing monitors are located between front-end clients and back-end databases and are designed to manage transactional integrity in high-transaction environments. They ensure that master files, such as database, are updated as soon as the data is verified and the transaction is executed.

through its acquisition of UNIX Systems Laboratories from AT&T, which originally developed the product in its Bell Labs division in 1994. Novell was strongly oriented toward the retail channel and Tuxedo did not fit with its strategy; yet Novell initially declined to sell. Not willing to give up, BEA management was able to obtain $50 million funding from Warburg Pincus to buy two leading resellers of Tuxedo, Information Management Company and Independence Technologies, in 1995. This gave BEA ownership of about 50 percent of Tuxedo's worldwide distribution channels and access to existing customers. After BEA guaranteed Novell $90 million in revenues for the next three years, the company was able to acquire the rights to the Tuxedo product and its development and sales groups with all attendant exclusive development and distribution rights in 1996. Reflecting on the Tuxedo acquisition, Coleman recalled: "We had been using Tuxedo for Sun Professional Services, which in a way served as a workshop for BEA because we learned to sell to CIOs." (Exhibit 3 shows BEA's acquisition history.)

As a result of its telecommunications roots, Tuxedo was capable of processing millions of on-line transactions and provided BEA immediate credibility within transaction-intensive industries such as financial services, telecommunications, retail and transportation. Tuxedo, however, had been sold as source code licenses in the past, which had created more than 40 different versions in the market. During 1996, BEA faced the task of rolling up all these licenses and consolidating the product into a worldwide standard. As part of its strategy to rapidly build an international sales and support organization, BEA also further acquired a number of sales and support organizations located in France, South Africa, Finland and Australia in 1996. Sales were organized along geographical lines, with the Americas, Europe, South Africa, and Asia Pacific broken down by country and each country being responsible for its own profits and losses. The acquisition of integration tools, called ObjectBroker and MessageQ, from Digital Equipment Corporation (DEC) gave BEA the opportunity to become the first full-service, cross-platform provider to address complete enterprise customer needs. DEC also became a worldwide reseller of BEA products. In April 1997 the company went public to raise funds to pay back debt incurred from the acquisition of Tuxedo distributors and to support further growth. By the end of 1997, BEA had captured 36 percent share of the transaction processing software market. This marked the first phase in the company's

evolution, which focused on building a scalable direct channel model.

Phase II (1998–1999)   By 1998, it had become clear that the Internet was going to transform the computer industry and that Java was going to be important in this emerging environment. The second phase in the evolution of the company therefore involved the transition of BEA products based on CORBA,[8] an older technology, to building a Java[9]-based platform. Java offered several advantages over CORBA. It was a much simpler environment for developers to develop applications. Also, it was portable in that it could run on different operating systems without modification. After unsuccessfully trying to develop a Java initiative in-house, Alfred Chuang, who was one of the cofounders and head of product development at the time, identified a company called WebLogic in San Francisco that was developing an application server to support the emerging Java standards. In spite of initial board opposition, Chuang persisted and got BEA to buy WebLogic, which had less than $10 million in sales, in September 1998 in a stock deal valued at the time at $160 million. Bill Coleman appointed Chuang as general manager of the newly formed WebLogic division formed around the WebLogic acquisition. The new division used the Netscape model of free Internet trials and only made products available that could be downloaded, installed, and brought up in 15 minutes. Within a short period of time, WebLogic reached about half a million downloads per quarter. WebLogic was expected to generate $40 million in revenue during the first year, but instead generated $135 million. WebLogic

---

[8]CORBA is the acronym for common object request broker architecture, an open, vendor-independent architecture and infrastructure that computer applications use to work together over networks. Because of the easy way that CORBA integrates machines from so many vendors, with sizes ranging from mainframes through minis and desktops to hand-helds and embedded systems, it is the middleware of choice for large (and even not-so-large) enterprises. CORBA is defined by an organization called the Object Management Group.

[9]A programming language introduced by Sun Microsystems. Java is a platform-independent, object-oriented programming language. Java programs are not compiled, but rather interpreted as run. In most computer languages, such as C++, you must write a different version of your program for each hardware platform you want it to run on. A Java program only has to be written once, because instead of being compiled into machine language, it is compiled into an intermediary language called Java bytecode. Java bytecode can be run by any hardware that has access to a Java Virtual Machine.

EXHIBIT 3 | BEA Systems' Acquisition History

Date	Company/Product	Price	Description
September 1995	Information Management Company	N/A	Leading reseller of Tuxedo in U.S.
September 1995	TP Blue product (from VI Systems, Inc.)	N/A	Integration of legacy mainframe applications into distributed computing environments
November 1995	Independence Technologies, Inc.	N/A	Leading reseller of Tuxedo in U.S.
February 1996	Tuxedo (from Novell)	$90 m	Transaction processing monitor
May 1996	USL Finance	$3.3 m	Distributor in France
June 1996	Client Server Technologies	$2.2 m	Distributor in Finland
September 1996	South African Tuxedo Solutions supplier	N/A	Systems integration firm
January 1997	Bay Technologies	$1 m	Distributor in Australia
February 1997	ObjectBroker object request broker (from Digital Equipment Corporation)	$22 m	DECmessageQ message-oriented middleware product
March 1998	Penta Systems Technology, Inc.	$5.7 m	Distributor of BEA Tuxedo in Korea
May 1998	Leader Group	$14.5 m	Professional services in Object Technology
May 1998	TOP END (from NCR)	$92.4 m	Transaction processing monitor
July 1998	Entersoft	$3 m	Independent distributor of TOP END products
September 1998	WebLogic	$90 m	Java-based application server
June 1999	Component Systems		Consulting firm specializing in Java, Enterprise JavaBeans (EJB), and CORBA technologies
July 1999	Technology Resource Group, Inc.		Java educational force
August 1999	Avitek, Inc.		Software development based on Java and EJB technology
November 1999	The Theory Center	$154.9 m	Software development firm focused on EJB component solutions
March 2000	The Workflow Automation Corporation	$28.6 m	Java-based business process engine
April 2000	The Object People	$20.5 m	Consulting and education services
June 2000	Softport Systems, Inc.	N/A	Systems integration solutions
October 2000	Bauhus Technologies, Inc.	$19.8 m	E-business consulting
October 2000	Liam	N/A	Distributor in Israel
July 2001	Crossgain Corporation	N/A	Software engineering skills
February 2002	Appeal Virtual Machines AB	N/A	Java Virtual Machine (JVM) software

Source: Company Web site, Bear Stearns, "BEA Systems. Inc.: Shifting Sands," October 11, 2001. NB: BEA acquired an additional five single-digit, or near single-digit acquisitions between November 2001 and July 2003.

rapidly grew to represent 60 percent of the company's license revenues and the majority of its growth. But WebLogic's success had begun to conflict with the Tuxedo business. BEA now had two sales forces competing for the same customers. To solve the problem, Coleman brought Chuang back as head of worldwide sales with the mandate to integrate the two sales forces. The company also integrated Tuxedo's transaction processing capabilities into WebLogic and created the first application server to give Java programmers an enterprise-class application deployment platform that was easy to implement, scalable, and reliable.

BEA continued to grow through acquisitions. Commenting on BEA's approach, Coleman said: "Since 1996, we have extended our footprint through acquisitions. If we didn't have the required core competencies we looked to buy the best team of developers who had them. We always moved the head of the acquired team elsewhere in the company and we threw away all their

EXHIBIT 4 | BEA Systems' Products

Application Server

- *BEA WebLogic Server:* This application server enabled companies to deploy highly scalable and reliable applications.
- *BEA WebLogic Enterprise:* This combined BEA's application server with its transaction processing monitor, Tuxedo, to provide a scalable and reliable transaction platform.
- *BEA WebLogic Express:* A lighter version of WebLogic Server designed for the development and deployment of applications that did not require the transaction capabilities found in WebLogic Server.
- *BEA Tuxedo:* A transaction server designed for applications demanding the highest availability, scalability, and reliability.
- *BEA WebLogic JRockit:* A high-performance Java Virtual Machine (JVM) developed uniquely for server-side applications and optimized for Intel architectures designed to ensure reliability, scalability, manageability, and flexibility for Java applications.

Integration

- *BEA WebLogic Integration:* This provided application server, integration server, business process management, and B2B integration features in one solution for a complete e-business application development and deployment platform, with WebLogic Server as its platform.
- *BEA eLink:* This was a family of enterprise application integration (EAI) products that leveraged the BEA WebLogic Enterprise Platform to integrate existing legacy applications with customer-focused e-commerce and business-to-business initiatives.

Portal

- *BEA WebLogic Portal:* Built on the WebLogic Server, BEA WebLogic Portal provided a platform with portal service, personalization and interaction management, intelligent administration, and integration services. WebLogic Portal provided access to information, applications, and business processes for employees, partners, and customers. WebLogic Portal also included the Personalization Server, which enabled the personalization of the visitor experience.
- *BEA Liquid Data for WebLogic:* This simplified access and aggregation of distributed information, providing real-time visibility for front-office applications such as portals, customer service and support. It provided integrated views of enterprise information from different data sources: databases, XML files, Web applications, integration adapters, and the like.

Other Products

- *BEA WebLogic Workshop:* This was an integrated development framework targeted at system and application developers. With the introduction of this product, the addressable developer market for BEA's products grew from around 2 million developers to around 11 million developers.*

*BEA 10-K SEC filings.

---

code and replaced it with Java. That's a key reason why we are fast! We have only one source code base."

By the end of 1998, some estimated that BEA was the market leader in distributed transaction processing with 51 percent market segment share against IBM's estimated 20 percent. During 1999, BEA expanded its customer base by helping businesses of all sizes create e-business applications and began a branding campaign to reintroduce itself as the e-commerce transaction processing company. The company continued to acquire complementary technology assets and was able to enter into major partnerships with Hewlett-Packard and Unisys. The deal with HP involved a three-year alliance valued in the tens of millions of dollars for joint development and staffing of support centers around the world to help customers build and deploy e-commerce solutions. HP also agreed to resell and promote all of BEA's products as its premier cross-platform middleware solution. Unisys used

the partnership with BEA to help its customers with transitioning their legacy information infrastructure to BEA WebLogic products running on Unisys platforms.

Phase III (2000 and Beyond)   Mid-2000 marked the end of the dot-com boom and the start of a rapid decline in corporations' information technology investments. Until then, BEA had focused on selling an increasingly diverse range of products directly to developers in the high-end enterprise computing market segment, who clearly understood the capabilities of these products. Corporate decision makers such as CFOs and CEOs, who were increasingly involved in authorizing information technology investment decisions based on ROI and customer value considerations, however, had a hard time understanding the plethora of products. (Exhibit 4 shows BEA's product offering.) Also, the evolution of computing over the previous three decades had left corporations with a heterogeneous mix of hardware, operating system, and applications. As a result, interoperability between various systems was a key challenge and corporations were now increasingly looking to integrate applications, data and processes within and beyond the enterprise. The emergence of Web services, a set of technologies that enabled companies to use the Internet to integrate their internal and external information systems, seemed to promise a solution to this problem. By 2001, several major information technology vendors were developing products to help companies develop Web services. Finally, potential customers in the mainstream and low-end enterprise software market segments, which offered BEA potential new growth avenues, were relatively unfamiliar with its product offerings.

The third stage in the evolution of the company was therefore focused on several key strategic actions. Realizing the need for developing an indirect sales channel, BEA hired an experienced executive from IBM. By the end of 2000, this executive had built the indirect channel by partnering with system integrators and service companies. The company also strengthened its consulting, training, and development capabilities. On the product side, BEA expanded its core product offering from application server to integration and portal products. It also acquired Crossgain in July 2001 to gain a foothold in the emerging Web services market segment. At the time of the acquisition, one industry publication wrote, "BEA got 80 of the world's best engineers that are gurus in Web services, in addition to Tod Nielsen and Adam Bosworth, both former Microsoft executives."[10]

Perhaps most important, the company wanted to consolidate its expanded core product offerings (portal, application server, integration, and Web services) into an integrated new software infrastructure platform that would provide a solid foundation for its strategic growth initiatives in both the high-end and mainstream enterprise software market segments. Not surprisingly, these strategic changes were accompanied by changes in strategic leadership. In October 2001, Bill Coleman asked Alfred Chuang to take over as CEO. Coleman stepped down as CEO to take on a new job as chief strategy officer and continue as chairman. While Chuang would be running the day-to-day operations, Coleman took on a two-part role. The first, he said, would be to look at where the company will be in two to five years, what the challenges are, and how to lead the market. The second job was to work with key partners and customers to set the strategy to keep BEA on top of the application server market.[11] In August 2002, Chuang also became chairman of the board. In the midst of cost cutting at BEA as the computer industry meltdown continued, Chuang nevertheless simultaneously began to build a new top management team. Bill Klein, Tod Nielsen, Tom Ashburn, Olivier Helleboid, and Charlie Ill were executives with strong track records recruited from major established information technology companies.

By 2002, the total number of customers and end users of BEA's products and solutions was greater than 12,500 worldwide. BEA's target end-user customers were organizations with sophisticated, high-end information systems with numerous, often geographically dispersed users and diverse, heterogeneous computing environments. Typical customers were mainframe-reliant, had large-scale client/server implementations that handled very high volumes of business transactions, or had Web-based applications with large and unpredictable usage volumes. No customer accounted for more than 10 percent of total revenues in any of the fiscal years 2002, 2001 or 2000. (A representative list of BEA customers is shown in Exhibit 5.) In fiscal year 2002, around 57 percent of BEA's revenues came from the Americas while around 30 percent of revenues came from the European, Middle-Eastern, and African regions and the remainder from the Asia-Pacific region.

BEA's Strategic Position and Industry Dynamics in 2003

As noted earlier, despite the benefits of client-server computer architectures' mission-critical applications that enabled and supported fundamental business processes, such as airline reservations, credit card processing, and customer billing and support systems, largely remained in mainframe environments. For several decades, the high levels of reliability, scalability, security,

---

[10]Tom Sullivan and Laura Rohde, "BEA Buys Crossgain for WebLogic Server Help," *Infoworld,* July 10, 2001. Cited in Jeannette Dale, Ramiro Montealegre, Donald N. Sull, "BEA Systems, Inc.: Constant Reinvention to Cope with Market Waves," Harvard Business School, January 28, 2003, N9-803-118, p. 10.

[11]Tom Sullivan, "BEA's Coleman Turns over the Reins," *Infoworld,* October 3, 2001, http://archive.infoworld.com/articles/hn/xml/01/10/03/011003hnbeaceo.xml.

EXHIBIT 5 | BEA Systems' Customers

Financial Services

Axa, BACS, Bank of New York, Bear Stearns, Bombay Stock Exchange, Charles Schwab, China Construction Bank, Citicorp, Credit Suisse Group, Depository Trust Company, Deutsche Bank, E*Trade, Fannie Mae, Ford Motor Credit, Franklin Templeton, GE Capital, JP Morgan Chase, Lehman Brothers, Marsh & McLennan, Merrill Lynch, Mizuho Securities, Morgan Stanley Online, Nasdaq, Nordea, Prudential Group, Societe Generale, SWIFT, The Hartford, TIAA-CREF, United Overseas Bank (Singapore), and Wells Fargo

Telecommunications

AT&T, BellSouth, British Telecomm, China Telecom, Cingular Wireless, DirecTV, Nextel, NTT DoCoMo, Sprint, Sprint PCS, Telecom Italia, Telia Mobile, Verizon, Virgin Mobile, and Vodafone

Manufacturing

BMW, BP Amoco, DuPont, GE Power Systems, Honeywell International, Kuwait Petroleum, Lockheed Martin, Motorola, Network Appliances, Pentax, Pepsico, Texas Instruments, Toshiba American Business Solutions, Toyota Motor Sales, and Vattenfall

Services and Retail

Amazon.com, American Airlines, American President Lines, AOL/TimeWarner, Bertelsmann, China Post, Cox Interactive Media, Delta Airlines, DHL, Electronic Arts, FedEx, Financial Times, Knight Ridder, NCS Pearson, Northwest Airlines, Sony, United Airlines, United Parcel Service, Universal Music Group, and Vivendi

Government

EUCARIS, Italian Ministry of Finance, Republic of Ireland, UK Companies House, UK Employment Service, UK HM Customs and Excise, UK Inland Revenue, U.S. Bureau of Labor and Statistics, U.S. Central Intelligence Agency, U.S. Defense Information Systems Agency, U.S. Defense Logistics Agency, U.S. Federal Bureau of Investigation, U.S. General Services Administration, and U.S. National Security Agency

Healthcare/Medicine

3M Health Information Systems, AstraZeneca, Blue Cross/Blue Shield, Incyte Genomics, McKesson, Medtronic, Ortho-McNeil Pharmaceutical, Pfizer, PSS World Medical, and Sapient Health Network

Source: Company SEC filings.

manageability and control required for such complex, transaction-intensive systems had been provided by application server functionality included in the mainframe operating system. Mainframe environments, however, were inflexible, required lengthy development and maintenance cycles, and supported only limited, character-based user interfaces. Typically, when a company wanted to add a new application or upgrade one, it had to hire a system integrator (SI) to perform the programming tasks. The shortcomings of both the mainframe and client-server architectures had created the opportunity for a multitier infrastructure, with a central role for a separate layer of application servers that BEA had capitalized on in the mid-1990s (Appendix A).

By the end of the 1990s, many large companies were also using the Internet as an element of their infrastructure for many of the business processes involved in selling products to customers and buying from suppliers. In addition, many used intranets for functions such as inventory control, decision support, logistics, reservations, customer care, and provisioning. But this created additional integration issues and the opportunity for a new category of Web services to help solve the overall integration problem faced by just about all established companies.

Having made very large investments in information technology during the Internet boom, many corporate information technology (IT) departments were coming under increased pressure to more effectively manage their infrastructures in order to ensure better reliability, availability, and performance. Given the severe pressure on IT spending since 2001, this made the selling environment very challenging. By early 2003, BEA was also facing intensifying competition from some of the biggest players in the information technology industry. (Exhibit 6 provides high-level competitive data.) In the past, BEA had been able to obtain the highest prices on the market

EXHIBIT 6 | BEA Revenue Mix and Comparison with Competitors

BEA Revenue Mix FY2000–FY2003

$000	FY2002	FY2001	FY2000
License revenues	$ 597,909	$ 476,573	$ 292,855
Service revenues*	$ 377,984	$ 343,187	$ 171,555
Total revenues	$ 975,893	$ 819,760	$ 464,410

*Service revenues comprise consulting and education and customer support revenues.

Revenue Mix of Selected Companies

$ m	BEA	IBM	Microsoft	Sun
Software license revenues $ m	516	13,074	NA	NA
Total revenues $ m	934	81,186	28,365	12,496
Gross profit	76%	37%	82%	39%
R&D	39	6	15	15
SG&A	48	24	25	31
Income before taxes	13	14	41	−8
Net income	9	4	28	−5
Market cap (5/16/03) $ m	$4,550	$153,775	$274,526	$13,884
Long-term debt $ m	$554	$19,986	$0	$1,449
Cash + marketable securities $ m	$1,272	$5,975	$38,652	$2,885
Enterprise value $ m	$3,832	$167,786	$235,874	$12,448
App server customers	12,500	35,000	NA	NA
App server revenues	496	221	NA	NA
App server revenues %	51%	0.3%	NA	NA

All data (except app server data) for fiscal year end: BEA (1/31/03), IBM (12/31/02), Microsoft and Sun (6/30/02)

Source: OneSource's Business Browser, Thomson Research, Pezzini, M., "Will IBM Be the E-Business Middleware 800-pound Gorilla?," Gartner Group, 2/20/01; Williams, Brent C., "BEA Systems, Inc.," McDonald Equity Research, 1/15/02.

and the lowest discounts but this pricing strategy was increasingly coming under pressure.[12] BEA now needed to differentiate its products from its larger, diversified competitors. According to Bill Coleman: "Infrastructure is sold to the CIO based on total cost of ownership as key differentiator, and companies don't buy infrastructure till they need it, whereas applications are bought by the business user and based on an ROI sell." Coleman also saw a threat of commoditization, which was, however, different from the commoditization that had happened in the PC industry. He said: "The [application server] market is commoditizing in the sense that it brings together different

elements and is becoming ubiquitous but not in the sense of giving product away for free!"

BEA's Product-Market Position

In 2003, the application infrastructure industry comprised three major market segments: application server, integration, and portal market. Also included in the application infrastructure industry were products related to security, development and deployment, and operations, administration, and management. (Exhibit 7 shows BEA's product offering.) BEA's primary product category was application servers, and it had leveraged its success in the application server market segment by expanding into complementary product categories to meet a broader set of customers' application infrastructure

---

[12]Yefim Natis, "BEA Systems: A Billion-Dollar Vendor Ponders Its Future," Gartner Group, 07 February 2002.

EXHIBIT 7 |
BEA System's
Product Offering

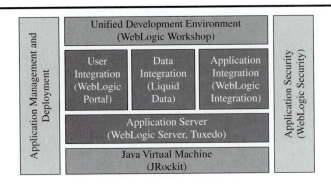

Source: Company interviews.

Applications consisted of software for automating core back-office functions such as accounting, manufacturing, distribution, and human resources as well as front-end processes such as sales force automation, customer relationship management, etc. The *application server* was the platform that helped to manage the complexity and heterogeneity inherent in distributed systems. *Application integration* software focused on tying heterogeneous systems (hardware, operating systems, and applications) to make them work together in a seamless way. The application server freed developers from a need to create much of the low-level infrastructure plumbing so developers could focus engineering efforts on the value-enhancing elements of development and allowed for faster development and deployment of applications.* *Data integration* was a new space that BEA had entered and comprised real-time data integration. *Portals* integrated access to information and applications and presented it to the user in a useful format. *WebLogic Workshop* provided an integrated development environment that spanned the entire software development lifecycle from designing to development to testing to deployment to management. *Java Virtual Machine* was not visible to outside customers but it provided performance advantage to BEA. *Application management* was offered through BEA's partnership with HP.

* Robertson Stephens, "BEA Systems, Inc," June 15, 2001.

needs. In 2001, BEA led the application server market with 25 percent share, closely followed by IBM at 23 percent, Oracle at 12 percent, Sun at 8 percent and the remaining from other vendors.[13] In early 2003, Bill Klein estimated BEA's share in the application server segment at about 30 percent. He noted, however, that there was variation in reported market shares depending on whether standalone application servers or embedded ones were considered. In the integration market, Klein estimated that BEA had 1 to 2 percent market share while its share in the portal market was about 9 percent.[14]

Application Server Market Segment   The application server market was projected to grow from $2.2 billion in 2001 to $4.4 billion in 2006, representing a CAGR of

14.7 percent.[15] This market forecast was highly dependent upon a rebound in overall IT spending. The application server market segment distinguished between products in terms of their functionality. Higher-end application servers were used in complex logic and transactions requiring high availability/scalability (e.g., completing online purchasing transactions). Low-end application servers were used in developing "informational" Web sites (e.g., providing product information). At the lower end of server functionality, pricing was dramatically impacted by open-source software such as Tomcat[16] as well as freeware from hardware vendors such as Sun Microsystems, IBM, and Hewlett-Packard.

---

[13]Michele Rosen, "Worldwide Application Server Software Platform Forecast and Analysis, 2001–2006," IDC Report, June 2002.

[14]All quotes from Bill Klein, CFO, are from the authors' interview on February 10, 2003. Subsequent quotes from this interview will not be cited.

[15]Michele Rosen, "Worldwide Application Server Software Platform Forecast and Analysis, 2001–2006," IDC Report, June 2002.

[16]Tomcat is an application server from the Apache Software Foundation that executes Java servlets and renders Web pages that include Java Server Page coding. Described as a "reference implementation" of the Java Servlet and the Java Server Page specifications, Tomcat is the result of an open collaboration of developers and is available from the Apache Web site in both binary and source versions.

BEA's WebLogic Server constituted the majority of the company's product revenue, representing 67 percent of the total in 2Q03, followed by Tuxedo with 13 percent.[17] The remaining 20 percent came from the company's other products. BEA was one of the few vendors offering a combined transaction-processing monitor combined with a high-end application server. For industries such as financial services and transportation where high transaction loads and transaction integrity were requisites of applications (e.g., for online banking), BEA provided one of the few comprehensive development platforms.

BEA's WebLogic Workshop was a new product that provided simplicity for the independent software vendors and developers. Previously, developers had to code applications in the application server. With WebLogic Workshop, they could work at a higher level and not have to worry about the infrastructure plumbing. BEA gave away WebLogic Workshop for free to encourage development of applications, which would in turn drive demand for BEA's platform. IBM had begun offering a similar product and Microsoft was trying to get its .NET platform adopted by developers by distributing test copies and posting test versions on the Internet for downloading. However, according to Olivier Helleboid,[18] BEA's head of product development: "BEA's WebLogic Workshop brings together reliability and ease of use. The latter gives us advantage with respect to IBM who focuses on enterprise-class reliability only. The former gives us advantage with respect to Microsoft. Another advantage over Microsoft is that they focus on Windows and have a homogenous view of the world while BEA supports heterogeneity."

Integration Market Segment   Application integration addressed the need to combine key elements of several disparate applications that were independently developed but were required to interoperate. This market segment consisted of software needed to integrate applications that were internal or external to an organization. Internal application integration leveraged the legacy system to improve operational efficiency, reduce costs, and provide users with improved IT systems access. External application integration increased interoperability of a company's IT system with its suppliers, customers, or partners, thereby increasing efficiency in the supply chain. This market segment was projected to grow from $1.9 billion in 2001 to $4.9 billion in 2006 representing a CAGR of 21.5 percent.[19]

Within the integration marketplace, BEA addressed the business process management and data integration segments. Business process management was the process of establishing instructions for a computer system to follow when predetermined events occurred. Data integration utilized data translation and transformation to distribute information across a company's network and between heterogeneous computing systems. In order to streamline and coordinate interoperating resources within complex e-Business processes, organizations faced many challenges.[20] First, there is need for internal application integration. For example, front-end Web applications must access inventory data to ensure that customer orders can be fulfilled on a timely basis. Second, there is a need for integrating business processes. For example, placing an order for a computer on a Web site may lead to an inventory check, credit-card validation, a confirmation e-mail, building an order, and shipping the order. Third, there is need to integrate with partner companies. For example, a financial services company that sells its products through a network of agent companies or brokers, needs to distribute new policy or pricing information on a real-time basis. Here, BEA competed with independent integration vendors including webMethods, Inc., SeeBeyond, Vitria, and TIBCO, as well as larger enterprise vendors including IBM (which had purchased CrossWorlds Software[21]). There were several key drivers of demand for integration software. These included reducing the cost of common business operations by linking applications and processes, increasing customer loyalty by presenting a consistent view of the enterprise regardless of the customer touch point (e.g., a call center or a company Web site), and enabling participation in e-marketplaces.

---

[17]Robert C. Stimson, Kirk Materne, and Hung Hoang, "BEA Systems, Inc.," Bank of America Securities, September 4, 2002.

[18]All quotes from Olivier Helleboid are from the authors' interview on April 16, 2003. Subsequent quotes from this interview will not be cited.

[19]"Worldwide Integration Server Software Platforms Forecast, 2002–2006," IDC Report, March 2002.

[20]"Building a Fully Integrated, Extended Enterprise: A Closer Look at WebLogic Integration," BEA Systems White Paper, November 12, 2001.

[21]IBM acquired CrossWorlds Software in October 2001 for $129 million in cash to bolster its e-business infrastructure offerings. CrossWorlds made integration software that was very specific to certain industries—complex industrial manufacturing, process manufacturing, financial services and telecommunications. IBM intended to absorb CrossWorld into its software group, then market and sell CrossWorld products with a joint sales force under the WebSphere brand.

Portal Market Segment   Enterprise information portals provided a front-end interface that integrated access to information and applications and presented it to the business user in a useful format. As corporations rolled out new applications to employees, partners, and customers, portals offered a single aggregation point for accessing information. The portal software market was projected to grow at a CAGR of 41 percent, from $550 million in 2001 to over $3.1 billion by 2006.[22] However, this market could be less than anticipated as some vendors were giving away the portal product as a bonus.

The portal market segment offered opportunities to infrastructure vendors (IBM, Microsoft, BEA Systems, and Sun Microsystems), portal pure-plays (such as Plumtree Software and Epicentric), as well as application software vendors (SAP and PeopleSoft). Over 50 vendors including IBM, Microsoft, BEA, Yahoo!, Citrix Systems, SAP, PeopleSoft, Siebel Systems, BroadVision, Art Technology Group, and Epicentric were targeting this segment. Portals were a compelling opportunity, in part because they represented a significant investment on the part of customers and, once locked in, created switching costs with end users. In addition, they potentially drove additional revenue by selling more seats or licenses for the applications beneath the portal layer (e.g. SAP R/3). BEA addressed the portal market with its WebLogic Portal product, which like the integration product, shared the common infrastructure of the WebLogic application server.

Toward a "Preferred Platform"   In early 2003, it seemed clear that the application server, integration server, and portal technologies were collapsing to form a single entity as companies increasingly used the new e-business infrastructures and related applications to streamline internal business operations and collaboration with business partners and customers. It was predicted that by 2006, more than 60 percent of enterprises deploying enterprise application servers would also use the other component parts of the same vendor's application platform suite as a "platform."[23] Several forces drove this platform strategy. First, most IT organizations believed that they had too many different systems and therefore needed a foundation that was provided by an application infrastructure standard. Such standardization would also result in reduced investment in training, saving time and cost. Customers thus were pushing for a platform approach as they cared about solutions but did not necessarily care about the details of the infrastructure. This increased desire for simplicity drove vendors to consolidate their offerings. Further, the economic environment was also a driving force as there was emphasis on cost cutting and companies were looking to reduce the number of products and vendors. Finally, the standards on the technology side such as J2EE, XML and Web services were established.[24] This offered BEA the opportunity to bring to market a platform that was based on standards. Customers wanted the simplicity of the platform but did not want to get locked in. Thus the emergence of standards allowed BEA to develop its platform strategy.

In June 2002, BEA announced the first unified application infrastructure product that combined application server, integration server, and portal product functionality.[25] This had taken a fair amount of coordination and team effort. According to Tod Nielsen, BEA's chief marketing officer: "For a long time BEA was running the company in a 'GE-model' as separate business units (application server, integration, portal) with separate sales and marketing for different product offerings. However, the customers viewed these products as one and this created an opportunity for BEA to exploit synergies and drive the platform strategy."[26] Soon, however, all major application server vendors followed suit. In particular, IBM was pursuing this strategy through its WebSphere platform. As the application server vendors pursued a platform strategy and began offering integration and portal products, pure play vendors in those areas were affected. In the enterprise application integration space, pure play vendors such as webmethods, TIBCO, Vitria,

---

[22]Brian McDonough, "Worldwide Enterprise Information Portal Software Forecast and Analysis," *IDC Report,* 2001–2006, June 2002.

[23]"Application Server or Application Platform Suite?" Gartner, October 29, 2002.

---

[24]J2EE (Java 2 Platform, Enterprise Edition) is a Java platform designed for the mainframe-scale computing typical of large enterprises. XML (extensible markup language) offers a flexible way to create common information formats and share both the format and the data on the World Wide Web, intranets, and elsewhere.

[25]"BEA WebLogic Platform 7.0 to Ship, Delivering the Industry's First Unified Application Infrastructure Platform," *BEA Press Release,* http://www.bea.com/press/releases/2002/0625_platform_ship.shtml.

[26]All quotes from Tod Nielsen are from the authors' interview on February 26, 2003. Subsequent quotes from this interview will not be cited.

and SeeBeyond also began moving towards this platform strategy and were adding the portal and application server to their offering. On the other hand, the portal pure plays such as Plumtree and Epicentric were in danger of being marginalized. According to Tod Nielsen industry forces were driving toward a clear winner.

BEA top management believed that it had both competence and strategic position advantages in the race to become the "preferred platform." As noted earlier, Bill Coleman was convinced that BEA's unified source code provided BEA with a significant competence-based speed advantage. Olivier Helleboid echoed this view: "We have an advantage over IBM as we have been doing this for a while. For IBM, providing a platform is difficult as it literally has ≈300 products in this space. For example, it has five to six flavors of application servers that don't work together. Therefore it is a big challenge technically for IBM to provide a unified platform to customers." And Bill Klein underscored BEA's strategic positioning advantage: "BEA has a distinct advantage as a pure-play application infrastructure provider which means that we can move very fast and maintain a two-year lead on our closest competitor. We are highly focused, unlike our competitors— IBM, Sun, etc.—who have competing priorities." For instance, Klein believed that BEA's WebLogic was two years ahead of IBM's WebSphere on a functionality/ features basis. He also believed that the total cost of ownership of BEA's software was lower than that of its major competitors. He said:

> For every dollar spent in licensing fees, IBM generated $10–14 of service revenue while BEA products require less than half as much consulting. BEA's products are easy to install and a customer could get up and running within a day while some of the competitors' products could take up to months. Furthermore, BEA's products were platform agnostic in that they were not tied to any hardware, database or operating system and offered good interoperability.

BEA, however, seemed potentially competitively exposed in the lower-end of product functionality that was in demand in the small business area. The company had recently launched WebLogic Express, which it claimed had better capability than the open source software to meet demand for low-end functionality with price point of around $4,000. Although developers of high-end projects continued to be very selective in their choice of platform software, the mainstream users could choose from many application servers that met their moderate requirements in comparable ways. For these less-demanding projects,

selection of an application server was based on business viability of the vendor, price and availability of tools—not attributes of the application server technology. This had forced most vendors to reduce prices on their low-end application servers and look elsewhere for significant profit opportunities.[27]

BEA'S Marketing Strategy in 2003

The continued slowdown in the economy created a challenging selling environment as IT spending had declined drastically and buying decisions were being pushed up in the organization, resulting in enterprise sales decisions being increasingly based on relationships and partnerships. According to Tod Nielsen, chief marketing officer: "In the days of the technology boom, BEA's approach had been one of 'drive-by selling' that relied on answering the phone and taking the order. This worked well during the technology bubble when demand for BEA's products was exploding but now BEA had to go to customers, understand their needs, and offer them BEA's products. As a result, the entire customer sales model had to be reinvented." As a first step, BEA started developing industry focus with initial emphasis on financial services and telecommunications verticals because of their transaction-intensive nature and the fact that IT is an advantage in these verticals and companies invest in IT. BEA was not strong in laggard industries such as manufacturing and their goal was to do a better job in financial services and telecommunications and gain presence in manufacturing, retail, pharmaceuticals, and transportation. More recently, BEA had been focusing on the government—it did 90 deals in 90 days and grew revenues by 300 percent in the last fiscal year. In early 2003, Tod Nielsen cast BEA's marketing strategy in terms of two vectors: growing the number of dollars per account and growing the number of accounts.

BEA focused on account expansion. BEA kept track of customer accounts in which it had a strong hold and aimed to increase the number of CPUs in those companies. A large portion of BEA's marketing spend was targeted on these companies. Over the previous 18 months, the goal had been to get significant multimillion-dollar deals, a shift upwards from the previous goal of milliondollar deals. There had been a change in the decision maker as a result of the economic conditions and these

[27]Gartner, "Application Server Scenario: From Stovepipes to Services", October 26, 2001.

buying decisions were now increasingly being made at the executive level. The focus was also on providing a complete offering to these customers and using services to increase customer loyalty. According to Tom Ashburn, President of Worldwide Services:[28] "One of the goals of the services business is to build strong ongoing customer relationships. Our aim is to use all touch points within services to solve customer problems and to build loyalty and lasting relationships. Customers should view BEA as an enterprise solution provider that provides more than just a technology. We need to position ourselves as a company that a customer can trust and that is here to stay."

BEA also focused on establishing additional beachheads by growing the number of accounts. This part of the strategy was aimed toward companies that had historically not purchased from BEA. In these cases, BEA looked at their propensity to buy based on factors such as when they were due to upgrade or renew license agreements. Nielsen saw a great opportunity due to the dot-com meltdown. In 1997 there were 57 application server companies (e.g., ATG, Blue Stone) but by 2003 there were only two major players left: IBM and BEA. So BEA attempted to identify companies that bet on the wrong horse earlier and sell them BEA products. Here the approach was not to sell the entire suite, but rather to be tactical and sell one product based on the customer's needs and get a foot in the door. These were companies that often had long-term relationships with IBM, Siebel, and other software companies. The goal was to have a sales cycle of no longer than 90 days as these were small deals and often BEA gave away product for free to get a foot in the door.

Nielsen said that in 2003, 75 percent of marketing dollars were spent on "farming" while 25 percent were spent on "hunting." The goal was to show revenue growth through account expansion and demonstrating viability to customers. But once the economy picked up, Nielsen planned to focus again on hunting for more market share by targeting major new accounts.

Competitive Dynamics

The market for application server, integration software, and portal software was becoming increasingly competitive and the race for preferred platform predominance would be tight. BEA's competitors were diverse and offered a variety of solutions directed at various segments of this marketplace. (Exhibit 8 shows product portfolio of various players.) They included hardware vendors such as IBM and Sun Microsystems, who bundled their own application server and integration software products, or similar products, with their computer systems. PC and server software giant Microsoft had released products that included some application server functionality and had announced that it intended to include application server and integration functionality in future versions of its operating systems.[29] In addition, database giant Oracle advocated an application server product software tightly integrated with the database server, and heavily advertised its integrated platform in general interest business magazines. These competitors had considerable pricing leverage for their application server solutions as a result of their broad product offering.[30] They could cross-subsidize their application server by bundling it with their core product offering and gain an installed customer base. For example, IBM and Sun could integrate their application servers with their hardware products, Microsoft with the operating system, and Oracle with its database products. In addition to these major competitors, BEA also competed with pure-play vendors in the integration market segment (such as webMethods, Vitria, and Tibco) and portal market segment (such as Plumtree Software and Epicentric). Also, internal development groups within prospective customers' organizations could develop software and hardware systems that would substitute for BEA's products.

IBM   IBM's sale of application server and integration functionality along with its proprietary hardware systems required BEA to compete with IBM in its installed base. But here IBM had inherent potential advantages due to its significant customer relationships based on greater financial, technical, marketing, and other resources; greater name recognition; and the integration of its enterprise application server and integration functionality with its proprietary hardware

---

[28] All quotes from Tom Ashburn are from the author's interview on February 26, 2003. Subsequent quotes from this interview will not be cited.

[29] Microsoft had announced that it intended to include certain application server and integration functionality in its .NET initiative. Microsoft's .NET initiative was a proprietary programming environment that competed with the Java-based environment of BEA's products. A widespread acceptance of Microsoft's .NET initiative, particularly among the large and midsized enterprises who were the major source of BEA's revenues, could curtail the use of Java and adversely impact the sales of BEA's products.

[30] Robert C. Stimson, Kirk Materne, and Hung Hoang, "BEA Systems, Inc.," Bank of America Securities, September 4, 2002.

EXHIBIT 8 | Product Portfolio of Various Players

	bea®	IBM®	Sun	ORACLE	Microsoft
Development Environment/Tools	WebLogic Workshop	VosialAge. WebSphere Studio	Sun ONE Studio	Oracle9*i* JDeveloper	Visual Studio, .NET
Content Management & Presentation	WebLogic Portal Server	WS Portal Server, WS Personalization	Sun ONE Portal Server	Portal & Personalization	SharePoint Portal Server
Security		Tivoli Secure Way			Internet Security & Application Server
Application Server	WebLogic Workshop	WebSphere	Sun ONE Application Server	Oracle9*i* AS	Application Center
Integration Server	WebLogic Integration Server	MQSSenes WS Business Integrator	Sun ONE Integration Server		BizTalk
Database		DB2, Informix		Oracle9*i*	SQL Server
Operating System		OS/400, OS/360 AIX	Solaris		Windows 2000
Hardware		Mainframes, Servers	Servers		

Competitive

◼ Leadership Position   ☐ Competitive Offering   ◼ Emerging Capabilities

Source: Banc of America Securities, Basic Report on BEA Systems, Inc., September 4, 2002.

and database systems. IBM typically had very large, sometimes multi–hundred-million-dollar contracts with its large enterprise customers and provided them with dedicated support personnel ready to help them leverage these large technology investments. During the 1990s, IBM had deliberately adopted a software and services-oriented corporate strategy to replace its traditional hardware-oriented strategy. Almost all of IBM's roughly $20 billion of revenue growth during Lou Gerstner's tenure as CEO (1993–2002) had come from services.[31] By the beginning of 2002, IBM's services and software businesses represented 35 percent and 13 percent, respectively, of the company's $85.9 billion of annual revenue. IBM's new software strategy seemed to focus on layers above the operating system, while helping along the process of commoditizing operating system software

through its support of the Open Source movement. To that end, IBM was reportedly planning to spend $1 billion in 2001 on Linux development.[32] IBM's Vice President of Technology and Strategy Irving Wladawsky-Berger wrote in the IBM 2000 Annual Report:

> It (Linux) alters the way our industry delivers value to its customers (which is very good news for IBM). A lot of people who have played by one set of rules in this industry are going to find out they're now playing a different game. The widespread adoption of Linux is going to neutralize any vendor's ability to exercise control—over customers or software developers—based on that vendor's proprietary operating system. When applications are no longer lashed to a specific operating platform, control and choice shift away from the technology company, and into the hands of customers. This makes

---

[31]Steve Lohr, "He Loves to Win. At I.B.M., He Did," *The New York Times,* March 10, 2002.

[32]Joe Wilcox, "I.B.M. to Spend $1 Billion on Linux in 2001," Cnet News.com, December 12, 2000.

possible an equally seismic shift in the way value is delivered—through services, through middleware, through servers.

IBM reportedly wanted to "crush" BEA, and its new CEO, Sam Palmisano, who had led most of the growth of IBM's Global Services group was deeply involved in the effort.[33] In early 2003, BEA and IBM were involved in a heated public relations battle over which company was taking share in the current marketplace. BEA indicated that it won 325 deals from IBM in the quarter ending October 2003 while IBM claimed that its WebSphere product recorded 500 wins against WebLogic during IBM's September quarter.[34] Not surprisingly, Bill Klein said: "IBM is likely our toughest competitor. It has done a lot to validate the market. IBM has reconfigured itself by de-emphasizing hardware, growing services, and building software through acquisitions. However, IBM lacks a focused product capability in the application server market and lags behind BEA's technology. Due to its acquisition strategy, WebSphere has 300 product versions that require a lot of services." According to Charlie Ill, Head of Sales:

> IBM has some advantages over BEA. Its size gives an advantage of deep pockets. IBM can afford to make mistakes and still be in business. Size and age also brings process and maturity. IBM has a lot of good processes in place to help drive consistent performance in business. BEA has grown very rapidly and this is a challenge for us. Further, IBM is recognized as a leader in the IT industry across the board and has strong established customer relationships. It sells the lion's share of its business (70–80 percent) to top 3,000 accounts. However, it is not present in small accounts and this holds back IBM in terms of growth. IBM does not know how to get down to smaller accounts and therefore cannot generate real growth. In contrast, BEA's business is built mostly around accounts outside the 3,000 accounts. It has 14,000 customers. There are a lot of $50,000 to $70,000 transactions per quarter.[35]

Sun Microsystems   Traditionally, Sun had bundled for free a version of BEA's application server software. According to Tod Nielsen: "About 18 months ago,

more than 75 percent of deployments were on Sun platform while last quarter 58 percent deployments were on Sun platform with Intel/HP picking up the rest." However, Sun had rolled out the latest upgrade to its Solaris operating system in May 2002, announcing a plan to add key middleware and management components that broaden the capabilities of its Unix platform.[36] Sun recently entered the application server market with a free offering to its Solaris customers. Sun's main software stack continued to be run on the reduced instruction set computing (RISC) SPARC microprocessor architecture which, lacking the benefit of economies of scale in manufacturing, was much more expensive than Intel-based architectures. According to Alfred Chuang, "Just before I left Sun in 1994, the most expensive machine, the Sun SPARC 2000, was sold for $1.6 million; today the most expensive one costs $10 million. That's going in the wrong direction!" Tod Nielsen said: "A Sun box may sell for $3 million and for that price you can get ten Intel-based boxes."

Oracle   Oracle Corporation was the world's second largest software developer, after Microsoft, with almost $9.7 billion in revenue in 2002. The company developed and distributed two categories of software products: database technology software and applications software. Its database technology software enabled users to develop and execute applications on Internet or corporate intranet platforms. Its applications software was accessible through standard Web browsers and could be used to automate business processes and to provide corporate data to functions such as marketing, sales, order management, procurement, supply chain management, and others. Oracle also offered a range of consulting and outsourcing services. An estimated 80 percent of Oracle's annual revenue came from its core database business. However, the company was spending time and money further developing its applications products, and some thought that the company could use these products to spur its database business.[37]

Oracle was somewhat of an enigma in the application infrastructure market, given its predominant position in the database market but only a fledgling presence

[33]Vogelstein, Fred, "Can BEA Outrace IBM?," *Fortune,* March 17, 2003.

[34]Salomon Smith Barney, BEA Systems, Inc., November 19, 2002.

[35]All quotes from Charlie Ill are from the authors' interview on April 16, 2003. Subsequent quotes from this interview will not be cited.

[36]Paul Krill, Ed Scannell, Joris Evers, "Sun Renews BEA App Server Tension," *InfoWorld,* May 22, 2002, http://www.infoworld.com/article/02/05/22/020522hnsunbeaapps_1.html.

[37]Brian Skiba, et al., "Oracle Corporation," Deutsche Bank Securities, April 22, 2003.

in the application server space. By introducing a J2EE-compliant version of its application server and focusing more directly on its existing installed base of database and applications users, Oracle had grown its application server revenues by 56 percent and overtaken Sun to become the number three vendor in the market. However, Oracle's 12 percent market share still lagged behind that of BEA and IBM. Oracle's challenge in the application server space stemmed from its strong cultural and market orientation around the database. Although Oracle had started marketing its 9iAS application server as a separate, standalone infrastructure product, there was a lack of follow-through in the field organization where the belief was still that the database was an all-encompassing product with value-added services such as application server and integration. Another deterrent for Oracle in the application infrastructure space was its difficulty in attracting independent software vendors to develop applications on its platform. Since the early 1990s when Oracle launched its applications business, it had a love–hate relationship with the very application vendors that were customers of its database platform. Despite all these challenges, Oracle posed a considerable challenge to BEA, as more than 80 percent of BEA's customers ran Oracle databases under their WebLogic server.[38]

As there had been rumors of an acquisition of BEA by Oracle, that company actually launched a hostile bid (i.e., unsolicited by the target) for PeopleSoft, an enterprise software company, in June 2003. PeopleSoft's board rejected Oracle's first offer. Oracle raised its bid by about a billion dollars, to approximately $6 billion. The matter was unresolved by July 2003.

Microsoft   In early 2003, Microsoft led in worldwide shipments of operating systems for servers, with 60 percent market segment share against 15 percent for Unix and 14 percent for Linux.[39] Microsoft seemed poised to capitalize on a decade of efforts to leverage its predominant position in personal computing operating software into a strong one in the corporate data center. Announcing the third generation of its corporate data center software called Windows Server 2003, Bill Gates was quoted as saying: "This is about scaling up . . ." and "We can now compete

with the most expensive machines in the world."[40] One part of Microsoft's strategy was to bundle its other products, such as its SQL database and Exchange e-mail, with the new server product and to also provide easy links to its desktop application programs. Another key part involved efforts to replace competitors' products running on expensive proprietary microprocessor architecture with its own server products running on the much less expensive Intel microprocessor architecture. According to Steve Ballmer, Microsoft's CEO: "It's key to us to winning the battle to take essentially servers that would have gone to Sun, IBM, and others and move them onto Intel hardware."[41]

In the application server market segment, Microsoft competed with its .NET[42] platform. With .NET and its associated development tools, called Visual Studio, Microsoft hoped to win over many independent software developers currently writing Java-based applications for its rivals, including BEA. While similar in functionality to the J2EE platform,[43] .NET could only be deployed on proprietary Microsoft-based systems. It supported several languages but not Java. It was also not quite clear how Microsoft's platform would deal with the challenge posed by Linux, even though a version of .NET that would run on Linux was in the works.[44]

Microsoft's strategic thrust in middle ware would have to overcome several potential weaknesses associated with its formidable strategic position in the PC market segment. In particular, Microsoft did not yet have much experience in the extended, consultative sales process involved in enterprise software sales and lacked a strong direct sales force to mount an aggressive attack on the enterprise customer base. The company also had relatively little experience in managing the sorts of channel conflict that tend to unavoidably emerge between various types of resellers and direct sales representatives. Independent software vendors, on the other hand, were all too aware of Microsoft's ability and tendency to bring winning new applications in-house

---

[38]Robert Stimson et al, "Oracle Corporation," Banc of America Securities, March 24, 2003.

[39]Robert A. Guth, "Microsoft's New Server Software Taps into an Old Strategy," *The Wall Street Journal*, April 21, 2003.

[40]John Markoff, "Microsoft Tries to Conquer the Corporate Data Center," *The New York Times*, April 24, 2003.

[41]Robert A. Guth, "Microsoft's New Server Software Taps into an Old Strategy," *The Wall Street Journal*, April 21, 2003.

[42]Broadly speaking, .NET was an extension of Microsoft's Windows platform to the Internet. With .NET, Microsoft aimed to leverage its strength in personal computing into the emerging market for Web Services.

[43]Java evolved into a platform with the release of Java 2 Enterprise Edition (J2EE).

[44]http://news.zdnet.co.uk/story/0,,t269-s2090149,00.html.

and integrate them directly with the platform. The low-cost, silicon-based economics of Intel combined with the mass-volume software economics pursued by Microsoft was naturally driving prices of enterprise solutions downward, which created new challenges for system integrators used to working under the high-price umbrella of traditional solutions. Nevertheless, analysts predicted that Microsoft would be a formidable force in the looming battle for platform supremacy.

Application Vendors: Complementors or Competitors?

In 2003, another important competitive dynamic was emerging between the application server platform providers and the major application vendors, such as Siebel, SAP, JD Edwards, PeopleSoft, and others. Siebel was the leading provider of front-end customer relationship management (CRM) and distribution management (DRM) systems. (See Exhibit 9 for financial data on Siebel, SAP, and PeopleSoft.) SAP was the leading provider of back-end enterprise resource planning (ERP) systems. PeopleSoft was a "best-of-breed provider" of human resource management systems. Other application areas had emerged in supply chain management (e.g., i2 and Magnustics), and procurement and b2b exchanges (e.g., Ariba, CommerceOne). To varying degrees, these applications vendors had to concern themselves not only with developing their applications but also with making sure that they would run effectively on the existing, highly heterogeneous information technology infrastructure of their customers. Hence, they had to spend significant resources on integrating their software with the corporate "IT plumbing."

The challenge for BEA was to make the application vendors realize that they would be better off outsourcing the application infrastructure or plumbing business to BEA. According to Tod Nielsen, "Application vendors believe that customers' top priority was applications and that they would change their infrastructure for them. This is not true. In reality IT departments want the applications to fit their infrastructure." He further added, "BEA's value proposition is that it brings world-class engineers who are focused on application infrastructure so there is no need for application vendors to dilute their resources and they can focus on applications." Nielsen continued: "If SAP is spending $400m per year in application infrastructure development then it can pay a portion to BEA to outsource this and it will be a win-win proposition for both." BEA had some initial success with PeopleSoft. The two companies formed a partnership

wherein they planned their product road maps together. According to Craig Conway, president and CEO of PeopleSoft: "The high performance and flexibility of the BEA Weblogic platform, coupled with our pure Internet architecture, provides our customers with a lower cost of ownership, rapid implementation, and faster return on investment."[45]

Alfred Chuang provided a strategic perspective: "[The major application vendors] think that they are 'the platform.' But you are only a platform if you have many people standing on it. SAP, for instance, wants to be the 'only thing' and a platform. That creates a conflict. Applications companies can only scale through providing functionality. The closer you get to the users, the higher the margins you can get. So they must try to go up in the value stack, but they cannot expect to proliferate. They must choose!" Chuang also said that BEA would never get into vertical spaces because otherwise it could not be a platform. He noted that this was very controversial because newcomers within BEA often wanted to try to do this. He also noted, however, that the definition of platform changes over time and some routinized applications, e.g., receivables, could become blended into the platform. Nevertheless, this required careful consideration: "[Otherwise] you become the worst enemy of people that should be supporting you. We always say that SAP is as responsible for Oracle's success as Oracle. Never forget how you got somewhere!"

BEA's Sales and Distribution Channel Strategy in 2003

In 2003, BEA's sales strategy relied on its direct sales, services, and technical support organizations, complemented by indirect sales channels such as hardware original equipment manufacturers (OEMs), independent software vendors (ISVs), ASPs, and systems integrators (SIs). The direct sales force provided 69 percent of the company's revenue while the indirect sales channel accounted for 31 percent.[46] Web sales were used to target the lower end of the market. BEA offered downloads with a free 30-day trial version of its software, enabling BEA to make the cost of sale comparable to the size of sale and close thousands of deals per quarter.

[45]"Peoplesoft Embeds BEA Weblogic in Industry Leading Peoplesoft 8 Enterprise Applications—Peoplesoft and BEA Strengthen Long-Standing Alliance," *PR Newswire,* September 24, 2001.

[46]Source: BEA 10-K SEC filing for FY ending Jan 31, 2002.

EXHIBIT 9 | Selected Financial Data Siebel Systems, SAP, AG., and PeopleSoft

Siebel Systems

Key indicators ($ millions)	Annual Year End 31-Dec-2002	1-Year Growth Rate	3-Year Growth Rate	Quarter Ending 31-Mar-2003	Quarter Ending 31-Mar-2002
Sales	$1,635.3	−21.6%	26.2%	$332.8	−30.4%
Operating income	−$94.3	N/A	N/A	−$3.3	N/A
Net income	−$35.7	N/A	N/A	$4.6	−92.9%
Earnings per share ($)	−$0.08	N/A	N/A	$0.0	−92.7%
R&D expense	$366.2	9.8%	65.3%	$79.3	−5.3%
Capital expenditures	$70.8	−71.2%	15.8%		
Cash flow from operations	$433.2	−26.4%	69.0%		
Total assets	$3,033.0	10.5%	33.5%	$3,022.4	3.4%
Long-term debt	$315.6	4.1%	1.7%	$316.3	−1.2%
Employees	5,909				

	31-Dec-2002	1-Dec-2001	31-Dec-2000	31-Dec-1999	31-Dec-1998
Margins					
Gross margin	65.6%	69.2%	73.6%	77.1%	82.7%
Operating margin	−5.8%	17.2%	17.7%	19.8%	15.4%
Pretax margin	−2.2%	12.2%	12.2%	13.5%	10.1%
Net profit margin	−2.2%	12.2%	12.2%	13.5%	10.1%
Ratios					
Long-term debt/equity	0.16	0.17	0.23	0.41	0.00
Interest coverage	−1.8	23.0	22.5	N/A	N/A
Return on equity	−1.9%	16.3%	23.1%	23.5%	16.9%

SAP, AG

Key ind.icators (millions of Euro)	Annual Year End 31-Dec-2002	1-Year Growth Rate	3-Year Growth Rate	Quarter Ending 31-Mar-2003	Quarter Ending 31-Mar-2002
Sales	€7,412.8	1.0%	13.2%	€1,520.0	−8.3%
Operating income	€1,625.7	23.9%	26.9%	€298.0	60.2%
Net income	$502.8	−13.5%	−5.8%	€186.0	186.2%
Earnings per share	$1.61	−13.1%	−5.7%	$0.6	188.9%
R&D expense	$909.4	1.2%	6.9%	€218.0	−1.8
Capital expenditures	$308.7	−18.3%	−4.5%	N/A	N/A
Cash flow from operations	€1,686.7	70.6%	47.2%	N/A	N/A
Total assets	€5,609.8	−9.5%	5.1%	€6,050.0	−4.8%
Long-term debt	$9.7	32.5%	97.1%	$0.0	N/A
Employees	28,654				

	31-Dec-2002	1-Dec-2001	31-Dec-2000	31-Dec-1999	31-Dec-1998
Margins					
Gross margin	62.0%	61.1%	60.5%	57.9%	86.4%
Operating margin	21.9%	17.9%	12.8%	15.6%	21.9%
Pretax margin	6.9%	7.9%	9.8%	11.8%	11.9%
Net profit margin	6.9%	8.1%	9.9%	11.8%	12.2%

Source: OneSource.

(continued)

EXHIBIT 9 | Selected Financial Data Siebel Systems, SAP, AG., and PeopleSoft (cont.)

People Soft

Key indicators ($ millions)	Annual Year End 31-Dec-2002	1-Year Growth Rate	3-Year Growth Rate	Quarter Ending 31-Mar-2003	Quarter Ending 31-Mar-2002
Sales	$1,948.9	−8.0%	10.9%	$460.3	−4.8%
Operating income	$252.6	0.3%	N/A	$51.8	−14.5%
Net income	$182.6	−4.7%	N/A	$38.5	−13.6%
Earnings per share ($)	$0.59	−8.6%	N/A	$0.1	−15.9%
R&D expense	$341.2	14.1%	4.7%	$83.7	1.7%
Capital expenditures	$93.3	1.4%	17.7%	N/A	N/A
Cash flow from operations	$389.1	−16.7%	N/A	N/A	N/A
Total assets	$2,848.6	10.0%	19.2%	$2,884.0	8.1%
Long-term debt	$0.0	N/A	−100.0%	$0.0	N/A
Employees	8,180				

Margins	31-Dec-2002	1-Dec-2001	31-Dec-2000	31-Dec-1999	31-Dec-1998
Gross margin	63.4%	57.6%	55.3%	55.8%	65.4%
Operating margin	13.0%	11.9%	4.0%	−16.7%	15.0%
Pretax margin	9.4%	9.0%	8.2%	−12.4%	9.5%
Net profit margin	9.4%	9.0%	8.2%	−12.4%	9.5%

Source: OneSource.

Direct Sales Force, Support, Consulting, and Training

The direct sales force (DSF) focused on large accounts (Fortune 1000 companies). BEA had traditionally sold to the IT organization and this continued to be the case, although senior executives and business managers were increasingly getting involved because of the dollar value of the deal. The channel partners, especially the big systems integrators, had more account control with high-level executive (CEO, CIO, etc.) access. BEA's sales force was divided almost exclusively by geography, with limited vertical specialization. In U.K. and Europe, the DSF was organized into three industry groups—finance, government, and telecom. In the United States, there were size-specific accounts and there was no strict industry orientation. However, there were some areas that had an industry focus; for example, DSF in New York City had a financial focus. Deal sizes varied but on average were not very large. The direct sales force in the Americas and Europe was large and handled all deal sizes. At the time, the sales cycle was around three to six months.

As of January 31, 2003, BEA had approximately 2,100 employees in consulting, training, sales, support, and marketing, including over 530 quota-bearing sales representatives, located in 81 offices in 34 countries. BEA typically used a consultative, solution-oriented sales model that entailed the collaboration of technical and sales personnel to formulate proposals to address specific customer requirements, often in conjunction with hardware, software, and services providers. Since BEA's solutions were typically used as a platform or integration tool for initiatives and applications that were critical to a customer's business, BEA focused its initial sales efforts on senior executives and information technology department personnel responsible for such initiatives and applications.

According to Tom Ashburn, the goal of the services organization was threefold: "To grow the license business, to build customer relationships and to add to the financial success of the company." This approach was very different from that of competitors, which were primarily focused on creating standalone services businesses. On the other hand, at BEA, the success of the consulting business was measured by the ability to transfer knowledge to customers, to get them up and running and provide value-added technical and architecture advice. Thus, the focus was not on building a big services organization for its own sake. As mentioned previously, at BEA, the goal was to use all touch points within services to solve customer problems quickly and to build loyalty and long-term relationships. To measure success for the services organization, the most important questions were: "Is BEA taking care of customers? Is it adding value?"—not how fast growing or how profitable the services business was. Ashburn used revenue growth as a proxy for market and customer acceptance of BEA, while profitability was used as a proxy for improving operational efficiency.

Indirect Channels

The fact that scaling the direct sales force was not possible to keep up with sales growth projections, especially during the technology boom of the late 1990s, had been a primary driver of BEA's indirect channel strategy. In August 2000, BEA had announced a major planned investment in expansion of its indirect distribution network through stronger relationships with systems integrators, independent software vendors, application service providers, original equipment manufacturers, and distributors. In the words of Bill Coleman, "Our success going forward will heavily leverage partners to expand our sales and service capacity as we continue to extend our market-leading position in the industry."[47] Further, Coleman believed that it was possible to have quantitative metrics to gage the success of the indirect channel. He said that in order to develop the indirect channel and convince partners to sign up, BEA needed to address three issues: (1) Was there a market big enough to be attractive for channel partners? (2) Could BEA add value for channel partners such as systems integrators? and (3) Was there a potential for channel conflict, real or perceived, with the direct sales force? According to Coleman: "You can't build an indirect channel from the existing direct sales force. Setting up the right organization is critical." As a result, BEA had hired the head of IBM worldwide indirect sales who was tasked with building a 200-person organization.

In 2000, the goals of the program were twofold. Indirect channels were to increase their revenue contribution from approximately 20 percent prior to the program to approximately 40 percent in fiscal 2005. They also were expected to increase the number of projects that could be addressed by increasing the pool of consultants available to assist customers with application development and deployment. In fiscal 2002, approximately 31 percent of BEA's revenue was influenced by indirect sources. At inception of the program, approximately 2,000 independent consultants had been trained on BEA software. By 2002, the number had grown to approximately 11,000 consultants.

Even though BEA had made significant progress towards its goal of driving sales through indirect channels, there was little channel leverage present at the time, with only Accenture and PeopleSoft generating meaningful revenue.[48] Hence, BEA needed to continue to expand its indirect channel relationships. A recent IDC report showed that the two biggest influencers in the IT spending decision are software vendors and IT services firms.[49] According to Charlie Ill, BEA possessed certain inherent advantages in being able to form partnerships:

> IBM partners and competes with everyone in the IT industry. Therefore, it never gets itself settled around whether they want to beat you or to help you. It is very difficult for them to completely eliminate a competitor. In contrast, BEA has a clear picture. It is a software vendor and has a clear value proposition to the customer. It is not playing in hardware, services, or chip businesses. It only competes with others in the application infrastructure software space. Therefore, it can partner with systems integrators, hardware vendors, and chip vendors. This gives BEA an edge.

The indirect channels enabled BEA to broaden its product offering and to provide a total solution as shown in Exhibit 10. Indirect channel partners also provided an ecosystem influence. They generated and qualified sales leads, made initial customer contacts, assessed needs, recommended use of BEA solutions prior to their introduction to the customer, and introduced BEA at high levels within the customer organization. The actual involvement of BEA in indirect channel initiated deals varied depending on the deal size. In small deals (less than $100,000), BEA often did not get involved and let the channel partners handle them. This provided BEA with a leverage model whereby it could do large number of deals (2,600 to 2,700 per quarter). In deals above $100,000, the channel partners typically involved BEA.

[47]BEA Web site, http://www.bea.com/press/releases/2000/ 0815_partnerstrategy.shtml.

[48]Steven M. Ashley and Timothy P. Bryne, "BEA Systems, Inc.," Robert W. Baird & Co., January 15, 2003.

[49]"Capturing Market Share with Influence Relationships," IDC Global Software Partnering and Alliances Group, January, 2003.

EXHIBIT 10 |

BEA's Product
Offering with Indirect
Channels

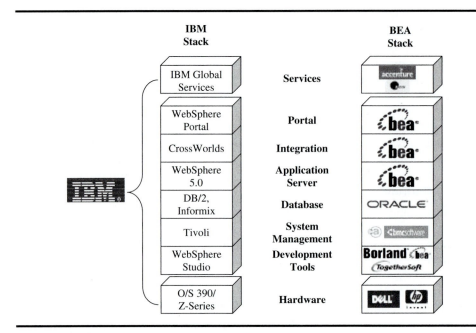

Source: Banc of America Securities, Basic Report on BEA Systems, Inc., September 4, 2002

According to Charlie Ill, indirect channels also provided geographical reach, especially in the Asia-Pacific region where the culture was very relationship driven and sales were done through distributors and BEA provided support. In Asia, SIs were critical for success and BEA operated a partner-driven model with a small DSF. On the other hand, in Europe and the United States, the SIs were important in a more supportive role. Here the goal was to drive the relationships with the key SIs—Accenture and HP—and ISVs. For Ill, one measure of the success of the indirect channel was whether the partners were generating incremental business or not. Ill explained: "Partnerships are a give and take of [customer] prospects. This is often difficult because companies are wary of sharing their customer lists and usually give information on only those customers where they don't care if you mess up. BEA has developed partnerships where both parties can be more open and share opportunities in the pipeline." Commenting further on the key to success in working with partners, Ill said: "Successful partnerships in the IT industry are few and far between because they never go down to the sales rep level. Most companies do partnerships at management level but never at process implementation level. For BEA, driving partnership at the account level is important in order to generate sales through these partnerships." For

example, in the U.K., Accenture is an important partner for BEA and BEA has identified people involved at different levels (from the industry level to the account level) and has developed relationships at all these levels in order to drive sales together.

In early 2003, BEA's indirect channel included several types of partners, each one of which posed different management challenges.

Systems Integrators and Independent Consultants
Systems integrators (SIs) acted as resellers for BEA's products. They often referred their customers to BEA and built custom solutions on BEA's products. BEA's main SI partners were Accenture, HP, and EDS but it had also established partnerships with other leading SIs such as Cap Gemini Ernst & Young, CSC, Deloitte Consulting, KPMG Consulting, PricewaterhouseCoopers, and Schlumberger Sema.

System Platform Companies These often acted as resellers of BEA solutions, either under the BEA product name or integrated with the platform vendor's own software products or products BEA recommended to their customers and prospects. Historically, BEA's most important partnership was with Sun Microsystems. However, this was showing signs of strains as Sun began pushing its own application server (iPlanet).

BEA had established partnerships with hardware OEMs including PC OEMs such as Compaq, Dell, and Hewlett-Packard. In June 2002, BEA and HP announced a strategic partnership to jointly market and sell integrated solutions across all of HP's multioperating systems, and multiplatform enterprise solutions. Partnerships with wireless OEMs such as Ericsson and Nokia were aimed towards establishing standards in the enterprise wireless space.

In July 2001, BEA announced a significant relationship with Intel, initiating collaborative engineering efforts to optimize BEA's software to run on Intel architecture. For Intel, the deal with BEA was another way to penetrate the profitable high-end server market with its faster Itanium processors. For BEA this deal brought with it the massive marketing and sales power of Intel, giving the company the chance to be the de facto solution for Itanium-based servers. According to Coleman: "With this relationship with Intel, our goal is to extend customer demand for BEA WebLogic on Intel-based platforms for development and deployment."[50] Alfred Chuang pointed out: "Our partnership with Intel is helping us change the environment. It used to be that 80 percent of enterprise software was run on proprietary hardware; now that's closer to 60 percent."

Application Service Providers ASPs such as System SpA, Digex, eBreviate, and the like bought and maintained the hardware, infrastructure software, and application software necessary for Web sites and e-businesses, and rented access to these systems to their customers, primarily small and medium-sized businesses, who did not have the resources or the desire to buy and maintain these systems themselves. BEA licensed its software to ASPs who used it as an exclusive or optional feature in their systems.

Distributors To supplement the efforts of its direct sales force, BEA used software distributors to sell its products in Europe, Asia, Latin America and, to a lesser degree, North America.

To date, BEA had signed up more than 2,100 partners and alliances. BEA's Star Partner Program was focused on expanding opportunities, accelerating time-to-market, and improving profitability.

Reflecting on BEA's sales and distribution channel strategy in April 2003, Alfred Chuang identified a strategic dichotomy:

> On the one hand, we must scale by volume, but that requires a lower-touch sales effort—reduced sales cycles and less customization. So, we must train the customer to accept shrink-wrapped software. On the other hand, we must ask the hard questions about which parts of the value stack can be commoditized—and ratchet them down the stack. This can be painful if you have to give up margins. It's like braces on your teeth: When you start feeling comfortable, it's time to tighten them. I'm the dentist in this place.

Chuang said it was important to develop a model for doing this in order to force themselves to keep doing it. Microsoft, for instance, had stopped doing that in the desktop market segment because it was difficult to develop new layers in the value stack with high margins. BEA needed to make sure it continued to tighten the braces.

The Battle for Independent Software Vendors' Mind Share

Some analysts predicted that by 2006, 70 percent of application server technology would be acquired bundled and embedded in other categories of software provided by independent software vendors (ISV); the remaining 30 percent would be bought directly as an application server platform.[51] ISVs included solution providers in several categories such as packaged applications, integration, development and deployment, operations, administrations and management, portal, security, and ASPs. BEA licensed its software to ISVs such as PeopleSoft, Hyperion, Documentum, Manugistics, and Verisign, among others, who built applications on BEA's infrastructure or provided solutions that complemented and completed its product. They embedded BEA's software in their product, thereby giving ubiquity to BEA's application server. There was, however, a need to prioritize the ISVs and actively formulate a value proposition for them. Over the last two years, ISVs were increasingly concerned about top-line growth. BEA also had to decide whether to use an OEM strategy or a co-sale arrangement with the ISVs. In an OEM strategy, the ISVs would develop applications on WebLogic platform and sell BEA's products as part of their application sale.

---

[50]"BEA, Intel Forge Alliance to Target High-End Server Market," *Dow Jones Business News,* July 23, 2001, http://www.cfo.com/article/1,5309,4259%7C%7CA%7C274%7C6,00.html.

[51]"Application Server Scenario: From Stovepipes to Services," Gartner, October 26, 2001.

In a co-sale arrangement, BEA would work with the ISV in order to make a joint sale for the application and BEA's underlying platform, thereby providing a complete solution to the end customer.

In April 2003, Alfred Chuang saw the battle for the ISV's mind share as crucial to BEA's success in proliferating its platform: "Proliferation requires that you gain the support of developers. We think of this as established compatibility, rather than as developing a standard. So we don't think of ourselves as chasing the low end, but rather as chasing developers to make sure proliferation happens. [But] to grow the community of developers, a company has to do some unnatural acts, such as be willing to give up developer license revenue, and spend more on training and support rather than on advertising." Chuang saw this as a strategic imperative: "If we don't do this, we cannot reach the strategic inflection point." Chuang anticipated that it would be difficult for companies with expensive proprietary architectures, such as IBM and Sun, to change the game. He viewed BEA's partnership with Intel and the growth of the Linux operating system as key drivers in BEA's efforts to change the game. The relationship with Microsoft was more complicated: "Microsoft could be an ally because they need a homogenizing world. But we must compete with Microsoft for the hearts and minds of the developers. As we gain mind share among developers, this will become a key concern to them."

BEA Beyond 2003: A Vision for Growth

In April 2003, CEO Alfred Chuang reflected on the strategic challenges facing BEA:

> The most important issue I think about is growth. We are trying to make people more productive. The question is how much impact can we have and how can we get growth in return—not linear growth, but step-function growth. There is no fixed formula for this. Growth, in turn, depends on two things. First, there is our product, which is really "productivity." BEA has two faces. BEA looks like a high-touch software company, like IBM and Oracle. But BEA also looks like Microsoft, focusing on adoption and the developer community. We are a mutating animal. We must do radical things to get the step function in growth. Second, there is the channel: What is the delivery vehicle to get the order? We must constantly reengineer this, reinvent it.

Chuang felt that BEA's current $1 billion size indicated that the strategic inflection point (SIP) had not yet been

reached. He compzared the situation to the desktop market segment, where Microsoft had "arrived" because they were able to change how people work and process information and had created a balanced "value stack" (layers of technology) to deliver on this change. He said:

> Microsoft has been able to convince people that, in order of importance, their data is the most important thing they have; that they need tools to accumulate information; that they need a software platform for processing it; and that hardware is secondary to all of this. As a result, their value stack has proliferated: Volume is the justification of having arrived! In the enterprise market segment, on the other hand, the value stack has not yet arrived. There is not yet a consistent way of doing things. It's as if you were looking at a highway and see horse-and-buggy, steam engine, and car all traveling down the same road. People use the Internet to buy something, but they would be shocked to find out that their order is often printed out, three guys pass it along, put it in a box and type it back into a confirmation system. We are in a race to try to fix this!

Chuang was convinced that the SIP would be reached soon and that BEA was in a good position to capitalize on the new opportunities that it brought: "It is not natural for companies that make large sales to groom a community of people that create the inflection point. We can do it because we have nothing to protect. We don't have mainframes, armies of service people, etc. But we must get proliferation. Software developers must be willing to do it." Chuang viewed IBM as a "transient" competitor and said, "When we face Microsoft head-on, we will know that we have arrived." But for this to come about, Chuang felt that BEA would have to get to revenues of $3 to $5 billion first. He said "We need a mass adoption event." But he saw reasons why this could happen in a depressed economy ("People want to increase productivity and are ready to throw some old things away"), as well as in a resurging one ("People will want to have the infrastructure in place to catch the new opportunities").

Conclusion

By mid-2003, BEA faced a number of strategic challenges. The paramount challenge for BEA was how to achieve the next level of growth. A healthy rate of growth for a nearly $1 billion company required major expansion of its market—a difficult proposition for a specialist middleware vendor. The adjacent markets, natural for BEA to attack for new growth opportunities (integration, development frameworks, business applications, operating systems, professional services, portal products, database management systems), were mostly mature markets with well-established leaders, while BEA lacked a record or expertise in most.

So far BEA had exclusively focused on the enterprise application infrastructure market. However, this was increasingly becoming too narrow and a limiting factor to its competitive positioning, given the diversified nature of BEA's now-primary competitors, IBM, Sun, Oracle, and Microsoft. Further, BEA had successfully grown through acquisition. However, as BEA faced increasingly bigger competitors, it was questionable whether it could continue to rely on its acquisition strategy.

Perhaps the most acute strategic challenge facing BEA in 2003 was the increasing competitive threat in its core application server market segment. BEA believed in the "market share" model and realized that a clear leader would emerge to dominate. BEA, however, was no longer the "only game in town." IBM had come from behind and threatened to overtake BEA's No. 1 position. Another area of concern was the declining cooperation with Sun Microsystems and the growing commitment of Sun to its iPlanet platform at the expense of BEA.

BEA had made significant progress towards its goal of driving sales through indirect channels, but there was room for increased channel leverage. In particular, it needed to leverage its relationships with some of the major system integrators and develop relationships with the remaining ones. Developing relationships with independent software vendors (ISVs) seemed crucial in winning the market share battle. Moreover, to effectively target the small and midsize business (SMB) market, BEA would have to develop new sales models and new sales channels to make this low-margin market profitable. Finally, BEA was still nearly absent from the emerging mobile and wireless middleware market. While this market was still small, it was likely to be of long-term strategic importance.

To address these challenges, BEA had undertaken significant changes to increase top management bench strength in the past 18 months. In addition to a new CEO, BEA had broadly reorganized and hired a number of outside executives for key leadership positions. BEA continued to maintain its technology leadership, still had a strong position in its core application server market segment, and was clearly focused on becoming the "preferred platform" in the enterprise software industry. It seemed to have the advantage of focus and speed compared with its larger, more diversified competitors. Its significant indirect sales channel was a key asset, enabling BEA to compete against larger, more integrated solutions vendors such as IBM and Oracle. But the key question in 2003 was whether BEA's strategic actions so far were sufficient to double or triple its sales revenues in the next three years.

Appendix A: Note on Application Infrastructure Market

The application infrastructure market comprised technologies that provided the infrastructure necessary to build and run an enterprise application. Often called "middleware," it included not only run-time environments, but also integration technologies that allowed an application to communicate and exchange information with back-end systems. To define middleware in layman's terms, it was any software component that was sandwiched between application users at their PCs and the databases or legacy system that directly managed underlying data—thus enabling applications and end users to exchange information across networks. (See Exhibit A-1 below.) The requirement for middleware stemmed from the need to integrate the different applications running on different computers, which in turn ran varied operating systems and software tools.

More specifically, the application infrastructure or middleware market comprised application server products, mainly J2EE-based application servers, as well as Microsoft NT-based application servers. Simple integration technologies such as adapter tool kits and queuing systems were included in this market segment, as were more complex enterprise

EXHIBIT A.1 | Core Infrastructure Stack

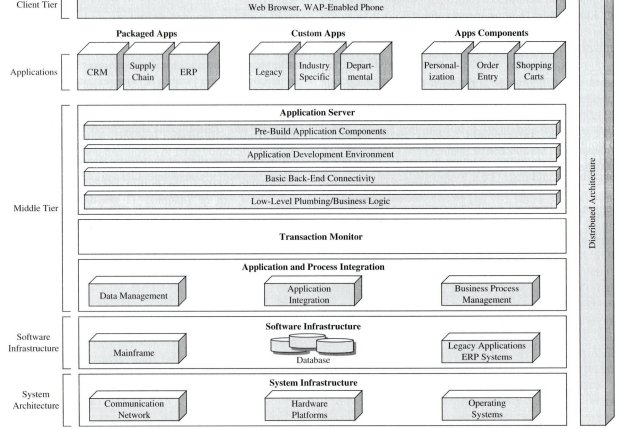

Source: Robertson Stephens.

EXHIBIT A.2 |

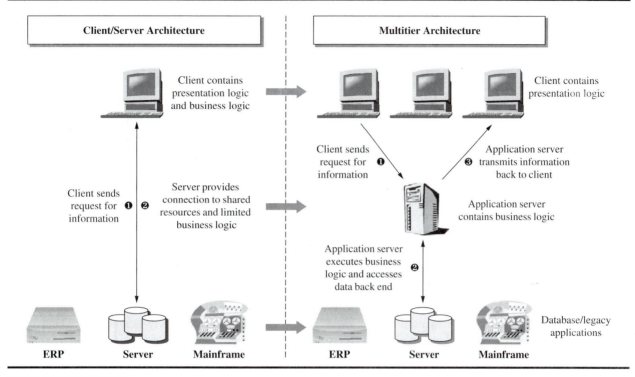

Source: Robertson Stephens.

application integration (EAI) tools. Other infrastructure tools such as business process management (BPM) and B2B integration software were also included. Web services, a technique for data integration and access, permeated all aspects of this segment.

In the late 1980s, client/server computing became popular. Prior to that mainframes were prevalent that were especially strong for specialized computing tasks, capable of handling massive transaction volumes, and easy to update due to their centralized nature. They suffered from the drawbacks of stark user experience, inability to customize and slow system response time. The client was the computer platform that requested the information or processing help from the server that was a computer platform or software module. The user's desktop contained the application logic and user interface while the server handled the data management. Client/server architecture had a number of strengths: rich audiovisual user capabilities, more responsive user interaction and more user independence. At the same time, this client/server architecture suffered from a number of deficiencies: (1) these systems were complex and expensive, (2) there were significant software distribution and version control problems as every time the application was updated, new copies had to be installed on every computer, and (3) this architecture had limited scalability: as the number of client computers needing access to an application increased, the server's processing power slowed and performed poorly.

To overcome the scalability and performance issues in the client/server environment (two-tier architecture), software developers shifted to the three-tier model,[52] with a separate application server between the server-database and the client. (See Exhibit A.2).

---

[52]Three-tier architecture later morphed into n-tier architectures with the application server tier expanding.

As a result the application logic was centralized on the application server and the processing was offloaded from the database server. This allowed for recentralizing processing and data to reduce software deployment time and improved hardware and software scalability.

Exhibit A.2: The Shift from Client/Server to Multitier Architecture

An application server was a software platform that acted as a communication switch between the user, the application, and the database. By separating the processing (business) logic from the application to the application server, and providing advanced functionality (clustering, distributed transaction processing, application integration, system management, messaging, etc.), application servers created a standardized environment that led to high levels of scalability, performance, increased availability and improved reliability. Application servers made it easier for commercial and internal Web sites to deliver dynamic information like stock quotes, personalized information, secure transaction verification, or shopping carts.

More recently, the multitier architecture was giving way to a new trend—Web services architecture. Web services enabled firms to integrate their internal and external systems, even if they did not have their own networks, by using the Internet. Web services are software components that interact with one another dynamically and use standard Internet technologies, making it possible to build bridges between systems that otherwise would require extensive development efforts.[53] Web services architecture provides the benefits of easier, faster and less costly software development. The drawbacks are that application-to-application communication utilize XML and Internet connections, which could hinder performance and create new security issues.

---

[53]Whit Andrews, Daryl Plummer and David Smith, "How Web Services Mean Business," Gartner, May 9, 2001.

Case 3.2

The Open Source Software Challenge in 2001

I think you have to rate competitors that threaten your core higher than you rate competitors where you're trying to take from them. It puts the Linux phenomenon and the Unix phenomenon at the top of the list. . . . I'd put the Linux phenomenon really as threat No. 1.

—Steve Ballmer, President and CEO, Microsoft Corporation[1]

Introduction

The source code for software programs, especially operating systems like Windows and UNIX, were extraordinarily valuable, on a par with the world's most valuable proprietary recipes, such as the secret formula for Coca-Cola.[2] In the case of operating systems, lucrative business models and extensive ecosystems have been built around secret, proprietary source codes that drive over 70 percent of enterprise systems and over 90 percent of home personal computers. (See Exhibit 1.)

Source code has not always been kept secret. In the early days of computing, software programs included their source code and were bundled with hardware. Early users had to tweak their programs, and they often shared the improvements they made. In the 1970s software companies such as Microsoft started to withhold source codes to protect their proprietary software.[3] (See Exhibit 2.) Although the existence of organized, nonproprietary open source software program development reaches back over twenty years, in 2001 operating systems leaders such as Microsoft and others depended upon business models based on closed source or highly individualized operating systems driving proprietary hardware. These companies, though extraordinarily valuable, faced a serious challenge from a fast-growing open source operating system called Linux, whose development had been led by a Finnish undergraduate named Linus Torvalds, who started developing his homegrown operating system project "just for fun."[4] By early 2001, Linux had grown beyond its cult origins and was installed on 27 percent of network servers worldwide. Microsoft's Windows NT drove 41 percent of the world's network servers, but Linux grew at an annual rate of 24 percent compared to Windows NT, which managed 20 percent annual growth in this market in 2000. (See Exhibit 3.)

Commenting on the forces behind the Linux phenomenon, Patrick P. Gelsinger, vice president and chief technology officer of Intel said:

> The Linux phenomenon today is a culmination of three forces: culture, technology, and personality. The culture that created GNU[5] and the GPL[6] sowed the seeds of open source development in the developer community for the past twenty years. The technology needed (i.e., the Internet) became ubiquitous enough to give people all over the world ready access to each other's work. Finally, Linus was good. He provided the right spark on the ingredients. Without Linus, the necessary ingredients might still be bubbling today.[7]

---

[1]Steve Ballmer quoted at the Morgan Stanley Internet Conference, 8 January 2001. Ballmer identified Oracle and Sun as second-tier rivals: "I think [server sales are] our biggest potential short-term return." In statements made last summer, Ballmer identified America Online as the top threat to Microsoft. But in January 2001 he said, "I'd put AOL probably at that level or a half-step down [from Oracle and Sun]." Paula Rooney, "Ballmer Calls Linux Top Threat to Windows, Microsoft's Concern Grows," *CRN,* January 10, 2001.

[2]Interbrand Group estimated the brand value of Coca-Cola in 2000 at $72.5 billion, down 13 percent from 1999. It estimated that the brand value of Microsoft Windows increased by 24 percent in 2000 to $70.2 billion.

[3]"Out in the Open," *The Economist,* April 14, 2001.

[4]Linus Torvalds and David Diamond, *Just for Fun: The Story of an Accidental Revolutionary,* 2001. NB: Linux is often pronounced LIH-huhks with a short "i."

[5]GNU (pronounced gah-NEW) is an open source UNIX-like operating system developed by programmer Richard Stallman and others in 1984. See Richard Stallman's, "The GNU Project," www.gnu.org.

[6]GPL stands for general public license. The GPL license stipulates that all released improved versions of software originally developed under GPL in turn be free software.

[7]All quotes from Patrick Gelsinger are from the author's interview.

Professor Robert A. Burgelman and Philip E. Meza prepared this case as the basis for class discussion rather than to illustrate either effective or ineffective handling of an administrative situation. The case was edited by Mary Petrusewicz.

EXHIBIT 1 | PC and Server Operating System Market Share by Platform

Market Share of Server Operating Environments, by Platform

	1999	2000
Windows	37.5%	40.5%
Linux	24.0%	27.0%
Unix	14.5%	14.0%
NetWare	19.5%	13.0%
Other	4.5%	4.5%

Source: IDC.

PC Client Operating System Shipments 1988 and 1999

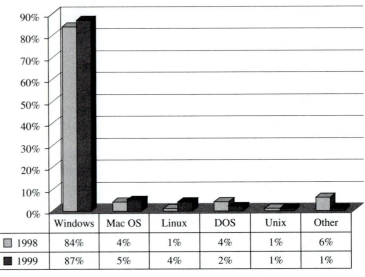

	Windows	Mac OS	Linux	DOS	Unix	Other
1998	84%	4%	1%	4%	1%	6%
1999	87%	5%	4%	2%	1%	1%

Source: IDC.

While Microsoft's president and CEO identified Linux as "threat number one," it was unclear what exactly was driving Linux and the open source movement that made Microsoft feel so threatened. Nor was it clear what Microsoft or others such as IBM, HP, Intel, or Sun Microsystems could do to combat or co-opt the forces driving the open source movement. Each of these companies grew very successful by competing in a closed source, proprietary environment. As the open source paradigm, with its emphasis and legal stipulations on unfettered collaboration grew, how should these companies change their strategies to compete in this new open world?

The Origins of Open Source Software

Open source describes any software program distributed under a license agreement that stipulated the source code be made available for use or modification, either free or for a fee. Open source software was usually developed through public collaboration and was made freely available, though not necessarily for free.

Free Software Foundation's General Public License (GPL)

A landmark open source development initiative was GNU, a UNIX-like operating system driven by source code that could be copied, modified, and redistributed.[8] The GNU project was started in 1984 by the renowned former MIT programmer Richard Stallman and others, who went on to form the Free Software Foundation (FSF). Stallman believed that users should be free to do

---

[8]UNIX was developed at Bell Labs in 1969 as a proprietary software operating system for AT&T. Because UNIX was developed for time-sharing capability and was written in the well-known C language, it became the first proprietary operating system that could be improved or enhanced by independent developers. Stallman chose to make his new open source operating system compatible with Unix so that it would be portable, and so that Unix users could easily switch to it. The name GNU (pronounced gah-NEW) was chosen for the new UNIX-like operating system following a hacker tradition, as a recursive acronym for "GNU's Not Unix." See Richard Stallman, "The GNU Project," www.gnu.org.

EXHIBIT 2 |
Revenue Data by
Platform

Revenues for Server Operating System Software, Worldwide in 1999 ($ Mil)

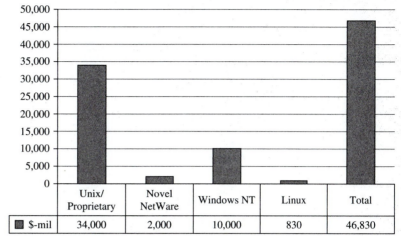

	Unix/ Proprietary	Novel NetWare	Windows NT	Linux	Total
■ $-mil	34,000	2,000	10,000	830	46,830

Source: Computer Reseller News.

Server Hardware Growth by Operating System 1996–2005E ($ Million)

	1996	2000	2005E
NetWare	4,053	3,091	1,825
Linux	NA	1,737	6,440
NT	3,739	13,863	34,496
Subtotal IA-based	7,793	18,691	42,761
UNIX	20,439	29,051	42,686
Other Proprietary	18,257	9,712	3,826
Total	46,032	57,454	93,098

	CAGR 1996–2000	CAGR 2000–2005E
NetWare	–7%	–10%
Linux	NA	30%
NT	39%	20%
Subtotal IA-based	24%	18%

NB: Other Proprietary consists of Open VMS, OS390, OS400 and others.

Source: Enterprise Hardware, Sanford C. Bernstein & Co., Inc., March 30, 2001.

(continued)

whatever they want with software they acquire, including copying and modifying the source code and even repackaging it with a distribution charge.[9] The FSF developed its source code under a set of copyright provisions it called "copyleft," also known as the General Public License (GPL). Copyleft stipulated that users could copy the program, modify it and sell the original or modified versions. However, users could not modify the rights granted under the copyleft. Thus the new source code that was based on the copied software program under GPL had to be freely available. Additionally, under these provisions, modifications made to a program under GPL had to be freely available under the conditions of copyleft. Finally, if software released under the GPL was combined with other, proprietary software, the resulting combination had to be released under the GPL. This last feature had been

---

[9]Since "free" refers to freedom, not to price, there was no contradiction between selling copies and free software. Stallman believed that the freedom to sell copies is crucial: Collections of free software are important for the community, and selling them is an important way to raise funds for free software development. See Richard Stallman, "Free as in Freedom" section of "The GNU Project," www.gnu.org.

EXHIBIT 2 | Revenue Data by Platform (cont.)

Software Industry by Computing Platform ($ b)

	Host*	Desktop	Client/Server	Internet	Total
1998					
Infrastructure	13.7	8.5	15.3	3.0	40.5
Tools	9.3	4.5	15.6	2.0	31.4
Applications	13.5	27.1	22.0	0.5	63.1
Total	36.5	40.1	52.9	5.5	135.0
2003					
Infrastructure	18.0	12.0	23.0	25.0	78.0
Tools	12.0	7.0	23.0	15.0	57.0
Applications	13.0	42.0	48.0	27.0	130.0
Total	43.0	61.0	94.0	67.0	265.0
5-Year CAGR					
Infrastructure	6%	7%	8%	53%	14%
Tools	5%	9%	8%	50%	13%
Applications	−1%	9%	17%	122%	16%
Total	3%	9%	12%	65%	14%

Source: IDC, SG Cowen.

*In this context, Host refers to a mainframe computer.

likened to a virus, spreading open source provisions to formerly closed source software.

EXHIBIT 3 | Linux Sales and Share Data

Forecast Revenues for Linux Server Operating System Software

Year	$ (millions)
1999	67
2004	85
AGR	4.9%

Source: IDC.

Market Share of Linux Server Sales, by Vendor, in 2000

	% Share
Compaq	30.5
Dell	13.7
IBM	13.5
VA Linux Systems	8.6
HP	6.9
Others	26.8

Source: IDC.

An example of a widely used application released under GPL was PERL (Practical Extraction and Reporting Language). Released under GPL in 1989, PERL was used to communicate between Web servers and clients. Companies such as Yahoo and Amazon used PERL to drive e-commerce applications.

Berkeley Software Distribution License (BSD)

A slightly different license agreement was devised and used by the Computer System Research Group at the University of California, Berkeley, when they released their popular version of UNIX, which had been so extensively rewritten that it no longer fell under the original AT&T license agreement. The software programs they wrote came to be known as the Berkeley Software Distribution, and the governing distribution agreement came to be known under the shorthand BSD.

The BSD agreement was similar to the GPL in many respects. For example, anyone could modify and redistribute the software alone or with other software as long as the copyright notice was included unchanged. Similarly, source code had to be made available and programmers could modify the source code to create a new piece of software as long as they included the original copyright notice and made it clear that the original program had been changed. The main difference between GPL and BSD, however, was that under BSD, the new or modified software did not have to be freely distributed.

Thus the BSD was not considered a "viral" license agreement. Different camps formed among the enthusiasts for the two license agreements. Companies tended to favor the looser constraints allowed under the BSD agreements while individuals who weren't striving for an exclusive marketing advantage in their work often preferred using the GPL. The GPL provided for the distribution of multiple generations of source code. The BSD license encouraged more people and companies in wider ranging situations to try out, and maybe release, source code, but still allowed for new variants to become closed in the future.[10]

Perhaps the most popular application released under BSD was Sendmail, a mail transfer agent (MTA) used to direct e-mail over the Internet to recipients. Sendmail's author Eric Allman built the first Internet MTA at the University of California at Berkeley in 1981. Bundled with all of the leading UNIX operating systems and distributed freely as open source code on the Internet, Sendmail grew exponentially with the explosion of the Internet. With ubiquity driven by open source distribution, Sendmail became one of the de facto standards of the Internet's infrastructure. By 2001, the majority of worldwide Internet Mail servers were powered by Sendmail. In addition, 9 of the Fortune 10 and 84 of the Fortune 100 as well as 29 of the world's 36 largest Internet service providers rely upon Sendmail technology.[11]

Allman, Sendmail's creator, went on to co-found Sendmail, Inc. a for-profit company that sells e-mail–related products and services such as simplified administration and management tools, encryption and authentication, and spam and virus filtering support. Sendmail, Inc. is privately held and its investors include Intel among others.

The Open Source Initiative

In addition to the FSF, another body, the Open Source Initiative (OSI), formed in 1998, emerged to develop and guide a branded model for software that was intended to be freely shared, improved, and redistributed by others. By 1998, software developed under the auspices of OSI certified that its distribution terms conformed to the

OSI's Open Source Definition, which included freely available source code, unrestricted distribution of modified software, and a stipulation that improved versions of the software could carry a different name or version from the original. In addition, software released under OSI could be bundled with closed-source software without "contaminating" or requiring that the closed-source software turn open source. This and other stipulations were thought to make the OSI licensing agreement less "viral" compared to GPL.

Open Source Movement Gains Momentum with Linux and Apache

Many parts of the later UNIX-based operating systems (such as Linux and the various other flavors of UNIX) were developed by modifying the GNU open source operating system. Linux was a UNIX-like operating system designed to provide personal computer users a free or inexpensive operating system comparable to the various UNIX systems.[12]

Linux

The Linux kernel was developed by Linus Torvalds while he was an undergraduate at the University of Helsinki in Finland.[13] To complete the operating system, Torvalds and other team members used system components developed by members of the Free Software Foundation for the GNU project. Linux was a remarkably complete operating system, offering features usually found in a comprehensive UNIX system. Linux was distributed using the Free Software Foundation's GPL stipulations, thus all modifications that were redistributed in turn had to be freely available. By the late 1990s, Linux enjoyed a reputation as a very efficient and fast-performing system.

---

[10]Morris McGee, June 10, 2000, Librenix.com.

[11]Source: www.sendmail.com

[12]The popularity of UNIX blossomed with the growth in the computer industry. The UNIX environment and the client/server program model were important elements in the development of the Internet and the reshaping of computing as centered in networks rather than in individual computers.

[13]The kernel is the nucleus of an operating system. It provides basic services for all other parts of the operating system. For example, the kernel schedules and supervises all processing requests that programs make of the operating system. A kernel can be contrasted with a shell, the outermost part of an operating system that interacts with user commands. Some kernels have been developed independently for use in any operating system that can employ it. A well-known example is the Mach kernel, developed at Carnegie-Mellon University, and currently used in a version of the Linux operating system for Apple's PowerMac computers.

EXHIBIT 4 | Forrester Research Survey of Corporate MIS Departments

Do you use any open source software today?

	No. of companies	% of companies
Yes	28	56%
Not now, but will within two years	3	6%
Not now, and will not in the future	19	38%
Number of responding companies	50	

If yes, how many installations do you now have of . . . ?

	No. of installations	Avg. no. of installations
Client OS	601,820	19,414
Server OS	121,104	3,907
Web servers	11,301	365
Programming tools	2,115	68
Database servers	737	24
Mail systems	108	3
Number of responding companies	31	

Which products have been affected the most by open source software? (multiple responses accepted)

	No. of companies	% of companies
Windows products	20	40%
Web servers	10	20%
Unix	5	10%
Anything proprietary	3	6%
Sun Solaris	2	4%
IBM AIX	1	2%
Microsoft Outlook	1	2%
Programming tools	1	2%
Other	1	2%
No effect	14	28%
Don't know	6	12%
N/A	0	0%
Total number of responses	76	
Number of responding companies	50	

By the late 1990s, the open source movement gained momentum as commercial enterprises began to view Linux as a credible, open alternative to closed source, proprietary operating systems such as Windows. (See Exhibit 4.) Unlike Windows and other proprietary systems, Linux was available publicly and was extendible by contributors. Linux programs could also be ported to other operating systems. Linux came in versions for all the major microprocessor platforms including Intel, PowerPC, Sparc, and Alpha. In addition to being available on the Internet, Linux was distributed commercially by a number of companies such as Red Hat and VA Linux,

public companies that sold and serviced the Linux for corporate users. (See Exhibit 5 for financial results.)

While Linux was gaining popularity among corporate users, its usefulness with mainstream consumers was far more limited. Linux could not run the thousands of programs that were written for Windows. Developers could create Linux versions of these programs, but few had done so because Linux was not popular enough with their customers. Some substitute Linux programs were available, but these often were not as complete, or easy to use, or compatible with the files of popular Windows programs such as Quicken. Alternatively, PC owners

EXHIBIT 4 |

Forrester Research
Survey of Corporate
MIS Departments
(cont.)

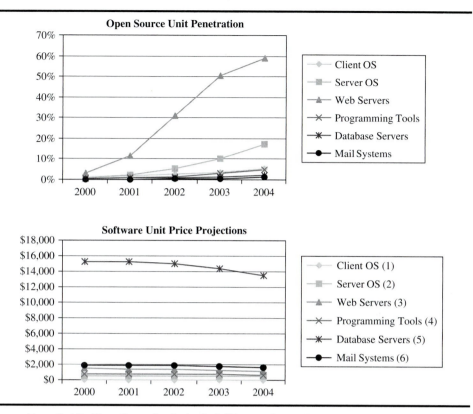

Source: Howe, Carl D., "Open Source Cracks the Code," Forrester Research, August 2000.

could use a Linux Windows emulator program called Wine that was able to emulate some of the underlying characteristics of Windows and trick some Windows programs into running on Linux.[14]

Apache

The Apache HTTP server was based on software developed by Rob McCool at the National Center for Supercomputing Applications at the University of Illinois. McCool's software was widely used on the Web, but the development stalled when McCool left the NCSA in 1994. A small group of users decided to coordinate their development work on the server software and formed the Apache Group. Their first release came in April 1995; however, a thorough overhaul of the code and documentation was needed. The result was Apache 1.0 released in December 1995.[15]

In June 1998, IBM announced it would begin bundling the freeware Apache Web server with its newly released WebSphere line of application servers and software. In so doing, IBM gave the open source Web server and by extension the open source movement a large corporate seal of approval. Websphere, and by extension Apache, gained a large measure of corporate credibility in September 2001 when online auctioneer eBay selected WebSphere as its platform for managing high-volume transactions.

Apache was a freely available Web server that was distributed by the Apache Software Foundation. under an open source license.[16] Version 2.0 runs on most UNIX-based operating systems (such as Linux, Sun Microsystems' Solaris, Digital UNIX, and IBM's own AIX), on other UNIX/POSIX-derived systems, Windows 2000, and other operating systems. According to the Netcraft Web server survey in February, 2001, 60 percent of all Web sites on the Internet were using Apache,

[14]Walter S. Mossberg, "Mossberg's Mailbox," *The Wall Street Journal,* October 4, 2001.

[15]Dorte Toft, "Open Source Group Forms Nonprofit," *The Standard,* July 1, 1999.

[16]Specific to the Web, a Web server is the computer program that serves requested HTML pages or files.

EXHIBIT 5 | Hewlett-Packard Company Annual Income Statement (millions of U.S. Dollars, except EPS)

	31-Oct-2000	31-Oct-1999	31-Oct-1998	31-Oct-1997	31-Oct-1996
Sales—Core business	48,782.0	42,370.0	39,419.0	35,465.0	38,420.0
Total sales	**48,782.0**	**42,370.0**	**39,419.0**	**35,465.0**	**38,420.0**
Cost of goods sold	34,864.0	29,720.0	27,790.0	24,524.0	25,499.0
SG&A expense	7,383.0	6,522.0	5,850.0	5,345.0	6,477.0
Research & development	2,646.0	2,440.0	2,380.0	2,191.0	2,718.0
Total expenses	**44,893.0**	**38,682.0**	**36,020.0**	**32,060.0**	**34,694.0**
Interest expense	−257.0	−202.0	−235.0	−215.0	−327.0
Other—Net	993.0	708.0	530.0	378.0	295.0
Pretax income	**4,625.0**	**4,194.0**	**3,694.0**	**3,568.0**	**3,694.0**
Income taxes	1,064.0	1,090.0	1,016.0	1,053.0	1,108.0
Income after taxes	**3,561.0**	**3,104.0**	**2,678.0**	**2,515.0**	**2,586.0**
Net income *(Excluding extraordinary items and depreciation)*	**3,561.0**	**3,104.0**	**2,678.0**	**2,515.0**	**2,586.0**
Discontinued operations	136.0	387.0	267.0	604.0	0.0
Accounting change	0.0	0.0	0.0	0.0	0.0
Net income *(Including extraordinary items and depreciation)*	**3,697.0**	**3,491.0**	**2,945.0**	**3,119.0**	**2,586.0**
Primary EPS *(Excluding extraordinary items and depreciation)*	1.80	1.54	1.30	1.23	1.27
Primary EPS *(Including extraordinary items and depreciation)*	1.87	1.73	1.42	1.52	1.27
Dividends per common share	0.32	0.32	0.30	0.26	0.22
Shares to calculate primary EPS (millions of shares)	1,979.0	2,018.0	2,068.0	2,052.0	2,038.0

Source: Company reports.

making Apache more widely used than all other Web servers combined. Microsoft's Internet Information Server followed with 19 percent, and Netscape's iPlanet server had a 6 percent market share.

The Fragmentation of Open Source Operating Systems

UNIX, an early, proprietary operating system, was developed at Bell Labs in 1969 by Ken Thompson and Dennis Richie. The program started as an interactive time-sharing system. The popularity of UNIX blossomed with the growth in the computer industry. The UNIX environment and the client/server program model were important elements in the development of the Internet and the reshaping of computing as centered in networks rather than in individual computers.

Fork in the Road and Inefficiencies

Many companies developed their own, sometimes proprietary, versions of the UNIX operating system. This process, whereby developers take a software program's source code and start a new development branch, is called "forking." By the late 1990s, several UNIX-based

EXHIBIT 5 | Intel Corporation Annual Income Statement (millions of U.S. Dollars, except EPS) (cont.)

	30-Dec-2000	25-Dec-1999	26-Dec-1998	27-Dec-1997	28-Dec-1996
Sales—Core business	33,726.0	29,389.0	26,273.0	25,070.0	20,847.0
Total sales	**33,726.0**	**29,389.0**	**26,273.0**	**25,070.0**	**20,847.0**
Cost of goods sold	12,650.0	11,836.0	12,088.0	9,945.0	9,164.0
SG&A expense	5,089.0	3,872.0	3,076.0	2,891.0	2,322.0
Depreciation	1,586.0	411.0	56.0	0.0	0.0
Research & development	3,897.0	3,111.0	2,509.0	2,347.0	1,808.0
Unusual income/expenses	109.0	392.0	165.0	0.0	0.0
Total expenses	**23,331.0**	**19,622.0**	**17,894.0**	**15,183.0**	**13,294.0**
Interest expense	0.0	−36.0	−34.0	−27.0	−25.0
Other—Net	4,746.0	1,497.0	792.0	799.0	406.0
Pretax income	**15,141.0**	**11,228.0**	**9,137.0**	**10,659.0**	**7,934.0**
Income taxes	4,606.0	3,914.0	3,069.0	3,714.0	2,777.0
Income after taxes	**10,535.0**	**7,314.0**	**6,068.0**	**6,945.0**	**5,157.0**
Net income *(Excluding extraordinary items and depreciation)*	**10,535.0**	**7,314.0**	**6,068.0**	**6,945.0**	**5,157.0**
Extraordinary items	N/A	N/A	N/A	N/A	N/A
Accounting change	0.0	0.0	0.0	0.0	0.0
Net income *(Including extraordinary items and depreciation)*	**10,535.0**	**7,314.0**	**6,068.0**	**6,945.0**	**5,157.0**
Primary EPS *(Excluding extraordinary items and depreciation)*	1.57	1.10	0.91	1.06	0.78
Primary EPS *(Including extraordinary items and depreciation)*	1.57	1.10	0.91	1.06	0.78
Dividends per common share	0.07	0.06	0.03	0.03	0.02
Shares to calculate primary EPS (millions of shares)	6,709.0	6,648.0	6,672.0	6,542.0	6,580.0

Source: Company reports.

(continued)

operating systems were used to drive computers from Sun Microsystems, Silicon Graphics, IBM, and a number of other companies.

Forking led to UNIX-like systems being used across the industry; it also led to considerable inefficiencies. By 1993, Sun Microsystems, which used its own flavor of UNIX, SunOS 4, was close to abandoning it to adopt AT&T's version called UNIXWare. At the time, a Sun engineer named Larry McVoy aptly described the state into which all UNIX had evolved. "UNIX needs our [Sun's] help because UNIX is dying. UNIX is no longer even close to competitive." McVoy estimated that collectively UNIX vendors were spending around a billion dollars a year on development, much of which was redundant. The fragmentation that had occurred with the various flavors of UNIX led to decreased direct competition among vendors, which in turn led to increased user cost. McVoy observed that Microsoft, with its competing Windows NT corporate operating system, was able to spend far less on development than the collective UNIX

EXHIBIT 5 | International Business Machines Annual Income Statement (millions of U.S. Dollars, except EPS) (cont.)

	31-Dec-2000	31-Dec-1999	31-Dec-1998	31-Dec-1997	31-Dec-1996
Sales—Core business	88,396.0	87,548.0	81,667.0	78,508.0	75,947.0
Total sales	**88,396.0**	**87,548.0**	**81,667.0**	**78,508.0**	**75,947.0**
Cost of goods sold	55,972.0	55,619.0	50,795.0	47,899.0	45,408.0
SG&A expense	15,639.0	14,729.0	16,662.0	16,634.0	16,854.0
Research & development	5,151.0	5,273.0	5,046.0	4,877.0	5,089.0
Unusual income/expenses	0.0	0.0	0.0	0.0	0.0
Total expenses	**76,762.0**	**75,621.0**	**72,503.0**	**69,410.0**	**67,351.0**
Interest expense	−717.0	−727.0	−713.0	−728.0	−716.0
Other—Net	617.0	557.0	589.0	657.0	707.0
Pretax income	**11,534.0**	**11,757.0**	**9,040.0**	**9,027.0**	**8,587.0**
Income taxes	3,441.0	4,045.0	2,712.0	2,934.0	3,158.0
Income after taxes	**8,093.0**	**7,712.0**	**6,328.0**	**6,093.0**	**5,429.0**
Preferred dividends	−20.0	−20.0	−20.0	−20.0	−20.0
Net income (Excluding extraordinary items & depreciation)	**8,093.0**	**7,712.0**	**6,328.0**	**6,093.0**	**5,429.0**
Accounting change	0.0	0.0	0.0	0.0	0.0
Net income (Including extraordinary items & depreciation)	**8,093.0**	**7,712.0**	**6,328.0**	**6,093.0**	**5,429.0**
Primary EPS (Excluding extraordinary items & depreciation)	4.58	4.25	3.38	3.09	2.56
Primary EPS (Including extraordinary items & depreciation)	4.58	4.25	3.38	3.09	2.56
Dividends per common share	0.51	0.47	0.43	0.39	0.33
Shares to calculate primary EPS (millions of shares)	1,763.0	1,808.5	1,869.0	1,966.6	2,113.4

Source: Company reports.

vendors, and in turn charged around $150 per seat, compared to the customer seat costs of $600–$3,000 charged by the various UNIX vendors.[17]

A composite of the C language and shell (user command) interfaces from different versions of UNIX were standardized only under the auspices of the Institute of Electrical and Electronics Engineers as the Portable Operating System Interface (POSIX). The official

trademarked UNIX is now owned by the Open Group, an industry standards organization, which certifies and brands UNIX implementations.

Windows NT: Competition for the Fragmented UNIX Market

While Microsoft was battling to win in the desktop operating system market, the company was also developing an operating system for the enterprise-level market. Microsoft's Windows NT effort was headed by Dave Cutler, who had built the operating system VMS for one-time computer giant Digital.

[17]Glyn Moody, *Rebel Code, Inside Linux and the Open Source Revolution*, Persus Publishing, 2001.

EXHIBIT 5 | Microsoft Corporation Annual Income Statement (millions of U.S. Dollars, except EPS) (cont.)

	30-Jun-2000	30-Jun-1999	30-Jun-1998	30-Jun-1997	30-Jun-1996
Sales—Core business	22,956.0	19,747.0	15,262.0	11,936.0	9,050.0
Total sales	**22,956.0**	**19,747.0**	**15,262.0**	**11,936.0**	**9,050.0**
Cost of goods sold	3,002.0	2,814.0	2,460.0	2,170.0	2,145.0
SG&A expense	5,150.0	3,920.0	3,261.0	2,773.0	2,501.0
Research & development	3,775.0	2,970.0	2,601.0	1,863.0	1,326.0
Other operating expense	92.0	115.0	230.0	259.0	19.0
Unusual income/expenses	0.0	0.0	296.0	0.0	0.0
Total expenses	**12,019.0**	**9,819.0**	**8,848.0**	**7,065.0**	**5,991.0**
Interest net	0.0	1,803.0	703.0	443.0	320.0
Other—Net	3,338.0	160.0	0.0	0.0	0.0
Pretax income	**14,275.0**	**11,891.0**	**7,117.0**	**5,314.0**	**3,379.0**
Income taxes	4,854.0	4,106.0	2,627.0	1,860.0	1,184.0
Income after taxes	**9,421.0**	**7,785.0**	**4,490.0**	**3,454.0**	**2,195.0**
Preferred dividends	−13.0	−28.0	−28.0	−15.0	0.0
Net income (Excluding extraordinary items and depreciation)	**9,421.0**	**7,785.0**	**4,490.0**	**3,454.0**	**2,195.0**
Net income (Including extraordinary items and depreciation)	**9,421.0**	**7,785.0**	**4,490.0**	**3,454.0**	**2,195.0**
Primary EPS (Excluding extraordinary items and depreciation)	1.81	1.54	0.92	0.72	0.46
Primary EPS (Including extraordinary items and depreciation)	1.81	1.54	0.92	0.72	0.46
Dividends per common share	0.00	0.00	0.00	0.00	0.00
Shares to Calculate Primary EPS (millions of shares)	5,189.0	5,028.0	4,864.0	4,782.0	4,737.0

Source: Company reports.

(continued)

Windows NT was aimed at the fragmented UNIX market—UNIX having already triumphed over Digital's VMS in the marketplace.[18]

Windows NT encompassed two products: the Microsoft NT Workstation operating system and Microsoft NT Server operating system. The Workstation operating system was designed for business users who needed faster performance and more reliability than that offered by Windows 95 and Windows 98. The Server operating system was designed for business machines to provide services for network-attached computers.

Shifting Platforms: Standardization of the Software Industry

Operating systems that were built on the instruction set for a processor or microprocessor—the hardware that performs logic operations and manages data movement

---

[18]Ibid. p. 6.

EXHIBIT 5 | Red Hat, Inc. Annual Income Statement (millions of U.S. Dollars, except EPS) (cont.)

	28-Feb-2001	29-Feb-2000	28-Feb-1999	28-Feb-1998	28-Feb-1997
Sales—Core business	103.4	64.8	63.4	22.6	2.6
Total Sales	**103.4**	**64.8**	**63.4**	**22.6**	**2.6**
Cost of goods sold	48.6	39.1	38.9	8.4	1.2
SG&A expense	79.6	51.7	20.9	12.7	1.0
Depreciation	66.9	9.7	1.0	0.0	0.0
Research & development	15.7	10.9	8.4	4.6	0.3
Other operating expense	0.0	0.0	0.0	0.0	0.0
Unusual income/expenses	0.0	0.0	0.0	0.0	0.0
Total expenses	**210.9**	**111.5**	**69.1**	**25.8**	**2.5**
Interest expense	−0.4	−0.7	−0.3	−0.1	0.0
Other—Net	21.4	5.1	0.4	0.5	0.0
Pretax income	**−86.4**	**−42.3**	**−5.6**	**−2.7**	**0.0**
Income taxes	0.3	0.2	0.8	0.2	0.0
Income after taxes	**−86.7**	**−42.4**	**−6.4**	**−3.0**	**0.0**
Preferred dividends	0.0	−0.1	0.0	0.0	0.0
Net Income (Excluding extraordinary items and depreciation)	**−86.7**	**−42.4**	**−6.4**	**−3.0**	**0.0**
Net Income (Including extraordinary items and depreciation)	**−86.7**	**−42.4**	**−6.4**	**−3.0**	**0.0**
Primary EPS (Excluding extraordinary items and depreciation)	−0.53	−0.42	−0.13	−0.06	0.00
Primary EPS (Including extraordinary items and depreciation)	−0.53	−0.42	−0.13	−0.06	0.00
Dividends per common share	0.00	0.00	0.00	0.00	0.00
Shares to Calculate Primary EPS (millions of shares)	164.7	102.5	49.6	47.0	47.0

Source: Company reports.

in the computer—were called platforms. Traditionally, a platform was an underlying computer system (software or hardware) on which application programs ran. On personal computers, Windows 2000 and the Macintosh are examples of two different platforms. On enterprise servers or mainframes, IBM's S/390 is an example of a platform. The operating system was designed to work with the particular processor's set of instructions. As an example, Microsoft's Windows 2000 was built to work with a series of microprocessors from Intel that shared the same or similar sets of instructions.[19] Since platforms were proprietary, they were defensible and thus offered an important source of rents.

---

[19]Richard Gabriel of Sun Microsystems uses a finer definition of platform: "platform is the set of facilities that applications need to execute on hardware. Usually a particular platform is so well-adapted to a particular piece of hardware that it is named after the hardware." Gabriel observes, "In general, the one with the greatest clout gets to name the platform."

EXHIBIT 5 | Sun Microsystems Annual Income Statement (millions of U.S. Dollars, except EPS) (cont.)

	30-Jun-00	30-Jun-99	30-Jun-98	30-Jun-97	30-Jun-96
Sales—Core business	15,721.00	11,806.00	9,862.00	8,598.30	7,094.80
Total sales	**15,721.00**	**11,806.00**	**9,862.00**	**8,598.30**	**7,094.80**
Cost of goods sold	7,549.00	5,670.00	4,713.00	4,320.50	3,921.20
SG&A expense	4,137.00	3,215.00	2,830.00	2,402.40	1,787.60
Research & development	1,630.00	1,280.00	1,029.00	826	653
Unusual income/expenses	12	121	176	23	57.9
Total expenses	**13,328.00**	**10,286.00**	**8,748.00**	**7,571.80**	**6,419.70**
Interest expense	0	0	0	−7.5	0
Other—Net	378	85	48	102.1	33.9
Pretax income	**2,771.00**	**1,605.00**	**1,162.00**	**1,121.20**	**708.9**
Income taxes	917	575	407	358.8	232.5
Income after taxes	**1,854.00**	**1,030.00**	**755**	**762.4**	**476.4**
Net income (Excluding extraordinary items and depreciation)	**1,854.00**	**1,030.00**	**755**	**762.4**	**476.4**
Net income (Including extraordinary items and depreciation)	**1,854.00**	**1,030.00**	**755**	**762.4**	**476.4**
Primary EPS (Excluding extraordinary items and depreciation)	0.59	0.33	0.25	0.26	0.16
Primary EPS (Including extraordinary items and depreciation)	0.59	0.33	0.25	0.26	0.16
Dividends per common share	0	0	0	0	0
Shares to calculate primary EPS (millions of shares)	3,152.00	3,088.00	3,014.00	2,947.40	2,969.10

Source: Company reports.

(continued)

One longtime industry executive, Gideon Kim, Sybase's senior strategic alliance manager/enterprise portal architect, and formerly an advisory programmer for IBM, thought the open source movement was driving a fundamental change in the platform-related software industry. Kim observed:

> Just as the components of PC hardware became standardized, and commoditized, we are seeing the similar phenomenon in software industry. In 1987 the "box" was called the platform for application developers. In 1990/1991 the operating system was the platform. By 1993/1994 the database server became the platform. By

1997/1998 the Web-level interface was the platform. Now, in 2001 the e-Business application server is the platform.

While acknowledging the significance of the open source movement, Kim pointed to what he perceived as a key impediment to open source software development: lack of centralized corporate responsibility for development. Kim said:

> Customers like the idea of open source in terms of lower cost and standardization but worry about the reliability and maintenance (e.g., bug-fixing and rolling back the fixes) of the code. The biggest problem with open source

EXHIBIT 5 | VA Linux Systems, Inc. Annual Income Statement (millions of U.S. Dollars, except EPS)

	28-Jul-2000	31-Jul-1999	31-Jul-1998	31-Jul-1997	31-Jul-1996
Sales—Core business	120.3	17.7	5.6	2.7	2.3
Total sales	**120.3**	**17.7**	**5.6**	**2.7**	**2.3**
Cost of goods sold	98.2	17.8	4.5	2.6	2.0
SG&A expense	38.5	9.0	0.8	0.5	0.3
Depreciation	57.7	2.3	0.0	0.0	0.0
Research & development	12.4	3.2	0.2	0.1	0.1
Unusual income/expenses	9.0	0.0	0.0	0.0	0.0
Total expenses	**215.7**	**32.2**	**5.5**	**3.2**	**2.4**
Other—Net	5.6	0.0	0.0	0.0	0.0
Pretax income	**−89.8**	**−14.5**	**0.1**	**−0.5**	**−0.2**
Income taxes	0.0	0.0	0.0	0.0	0.0
Income after taxes	**−89.8**	**−14.5**	**0.1**	**−0.5**	**−0.2**
Preferred dividends	−4.9	0.0	0.0	0.0	0.0
Net income (Excluding extraordinary items and depreciation)	**−89.8**	**−14.5**	**0.1**	**−0.5**	**−0.2**
Net income (Including extraordinary items and depreciation)	**−89.8**	**−14.5**	**0.1**	**−0.5**	**−0.2**
Primary EPS (Excluding extraordinary items and depreciation)	−3.52	−2.62	0.02	−0.05	−0.01
Primary EPS (Including extraordinary items and depreciation)	−3.52	−2.62	0.02	−0.05	−0.01
Dividends per common share	0.00	0.00	0.00	0.00	0.00
Shares to Calculate Primary EPS (millions of shares)	26.9	5.5	5.1	9.5	15.0

Source: Company reports.

is that no one owns it, thus no responsibility for liability and maintenance. Once reliable and responsible "OEM-manufacturers" of the open source become available [the concern will lessen]. Red Hat and VA Linux are good candidates but need to prove their viability to be established as a dependable source.

Corporate Seal of Approval for Open Source Software

By 2000, big server vendors supported Linux. IBM, Compaq, Dell, and Hewlett-Packard all sold Linux preinstalled on Intel-based boxes and offered techni-cal support for the platform. Major enterprise software vendors created Linux versions of their applications. Oracle ported their premier database and enterprise resource planning (ERP) applications to the platform and SAP, an early investor in Linux service company Red Hat, produced Linux versions of its applications.

A support industry led by service provider companies such as Red Hat and VA Linux emerged in the mid 1990s to buttress this corporate use of open source software by helping companies develop IT solutions. IDC estimated that the Linux support market, $56 million in 2001, would grow to $285 million in 2004.[20]

The Competitive Landscape for Open Source in 2001

(See Exhibit 5 for financial data concerning selected companies.)

Hewlett-Packard

Company Overview Hewlett-Packard is a global provider of computing and imaging solutions and services. The company develops operating systems utilities software; manufactures standard desktop computers and a full range of servers; and provides computer research and development and recovery services. HP provides a broad range of computing systems for the enterprise, commercial and consumer markets. Information Technology Services provides consulting, education, design and installation services, ongoing support and maintenance, proactive services like mission-critical support, outsourcing, and utility-computing capabilities.

How Open Source Affects HP The open source movement was likely to have a significant impact on Hewlett-Packard. In 2001, the company saw itself at the nexus where the computer and the Internet met. Martin Fink, general manager of the Linux System Operations (LSO) in Fort Collins, Colorado, was only two steps away from Duane Zitzner, HP's president of computing systems.

Fink described the challenge that open source posed to HP. Fink said, "Are you looking to build value for which you want to be able to charge? This is a challenge in the open source world. How HP does this depends upon our strategic objectives."

Reduced R&D Cost and Increased Functionality Fink pointed to economies offered by open source technologies in building and maintaining HP's common desktop environment for HP/UX. Fink said, "As your business decides where it wants to lead versus where it is okay to do parity or even lag, open source can be a great vehicle for investment choices." Fink added:

> By moving our strategic desktop to an open source desktop we are able to do a couple of things: we

substantially reduce our costs by not having to maintain the proprietary product and we have improved our functionality. Because the desktop was not strategic to HP, moving to the open source desktop actually is getting us to the point where we will have an increase in functionality for the customer base. While not an initial objective, we find that we have better compatibility between Linux and HP/UX.

Strange Bedfellows: Competitor Collaboration Perhaps a more critical issue for HP was how would it face open source challenges in areas it perceived as critical to the company's strategy. Fink drew an important distinction with development in strategic areas for HP:

> We believe that Linux (over many years) will make its way through the enterprise back-end infrastructure. For Linux to succeed in that space, it will have to scale better than it can today. In order to make this happen, investments must occur at the kernel level, which by definition implies open source. This is an internal struggle. If HP invests millions of dollars to make that happen, then all of our competitors, e.g., IBM, gain all of the benefits of that investment as much as HP does. The way for HP to mitigate this, given that we can't do zero investments, and it's critical to our long-term future, is to say we are forced into partnerships with the community and our competitors. IBM has the same problem. We are seeing HP and IBM working together in places you would not have expected them to work together.

Reduced Time to Market and Improved Products Fink discussed how HP hoped to earn money from open source–related development.

> There is a portion that is open source, and a portion that is closed. The portion that is open is seen as an enabler to the closed source portion for which we can charge money.

> A hardware example is with print appliance server that we did where we wanted to deliver a strong print server appliance capability. But in order to do that we needed to enhance the SAMBA[21] environment . . . the Linux version of the Microsoft Server message block protocol.

---

[21]Samba was a popular freeware program that allowed end users to access and use files, printers, and other commonly shared resources on a company's intranet or on the Internet. It could be installed on a variety of operating system platforms, including Linux, most common UNIX platforms, OpenVMS, and OS/2. See Whatis.com.

We had many engineers participate directly with the broader open source developer community and make many enhancements to Samba in order to bring it up to snuff. All of this was given away because our objective was to sell a print server appliance. In that example what really drives you is time to market.

HP dedicated six engineers to the Samba project. We typically see a 6:1 ratio of engineers. For every HP engineer deployed, we see as many as six engineers in the open source community working on the project.[22]

With Samba there was strong community interest so it got a better ratio. If we were talking something narrow, like an HP proprietary networking card then the interest level in the community would be low and we would be lucky to get one person.

Key Strategic Decisions for HP   Fink spent a good deal of time promoting open source development within the company. "I spend a lot of time talking to people within HP, telling them about open source. Some people think open source is hype and will go away. For others, open source represents a challenge to the status quo and these people are reluctant to change." Fink believed that open source development impacts technology companies like HP at their core.

> Open source reduces the value of IP over time. Take the example of network design and layout. This has been a high value field for HP for the past ten years. HP's product in this area, called OpenView, has been great and has generated good profits for us.
>
> But there is a competitive open source product called Open NMS. This could erode OpenView's business if we don't do something. I point to the value proposition facing customers: I need network and systems management, why would I pay $20,000 for a license when I can get an open source solution for free, and there is a huge support community furthering development. If you resist this change for too long, you can find that your market has evaporated underneath you and you weren't ready for it.

Asked what Fink would relate about open source technology to the HP executive council, he said:

> We need to worry about the erosion of technology in which we invest in infrastructure today. Low level infrastructure (e.g., OpenView) is going to be commoditized over time and the best thing we can do is

embrace that and stop investing there so we can invest higher up the value stack, into things we can charge more money.

The challenge with that comes from a subculture in which we have engineers who have been working for thirteen to fourteen years on something [that open source development could marginalize]. The possibility of this product being commoditized does not compute in their brains. Yet every year when we go through budgeting cycles we have heartache over deciding what to de-invest in so we can direct more resources to higher-end things. We should embrace open source as a mechanism for HP to be able to focus our investment on higher value items. There are many areas where we invest in infrastructure (e.g., OpenView, Blue Stone, Print Server) where we really don't need to.

All of the senior executives at HP are always told that every thing is the next greatest thing that is going to change the universe . . . and maybe only one in twenty delivers on that. I think open source is that one in twenty. Not everybody here believes this yet.

Competing with IBM   Asked which competitor, Sun or IBM, he worried about more, Fink did not hesitate:

> Three years ago, I [worried more about] Sun. Now it's IBM. IBM has internalized the magnitude of the paradigm shift that open source represents. Their approach is not what I think is quite right (see IBM below) but I think they get it in terms of the significance of open source and how it affects their business. But I don't know if IBM's DNA has the ability to follow someone else.

Sun Microsystems

Company Overview   Sun Microsystems is a worldwide provider of products, services and support solutions for building and maintaining network-computing environments. The company manufactures UNIX-based professional workstations and compatible software, as well as microcomputer chips, disk arrays, SPARC^{tm} high-end minicomputers, and network servers. The company also develops software products including operating systems and software for communications linking/network interconnect, Internet access and browsing, business graphics, programming utilities, application development tools, emulation/simulation, and JAVA code editing.

---

[22]Measured in engineer years.

How Open Source Affects Sun   In July of 2000, Sun Microsystems announced it would release the source code for its StarOffice productivity-application suite under the GNU GPL open source license. The StarOffice announcement was significant for the open-source community because developers have so far seen numerous large vendors port their software to Linux, but few companies have opened up their code like Sun. Previously, Sun made some of its software available under more restrictive "community source" licenses, including one that required developers to pay royalties to distribute their own work.[23]

By releasing the StarOffice source code under the GPL, Sun executives hoped outside developers would improve it and spread it to other platforms. While the software was free, Sun also hoped that continued development by the open source community would enable Sun to sell more servers and related software.

The person responsible for thinking about open source development at Sun is Dr. Richard Gabriel. Gabriel is a Sun Distinguished Engineer and a Consulting Professor of Computer Science at Stanford University. Gabriel runs a small laboratory at Sun whose charter includes studying open source and moving forward Sun's thinking about open source business models. Gabriel and his team also advise project leaders at Sun concerning the strategic and practical issues surrounding open source development. Gabriel works with the various Sun project groups to develop open source business models and design the mechanisms that will govern each project's open source initiative. Gabriel's lab acts as an open source epicenter at Sun; while project leaders do not have to take his advice, Gabriel exerted influence over the people who control their funding.

Sun Seeds the Clouds   Gabriel pointed to distinct advantages that open source offered Sun.[24] The company uses the open source arena to introduce ideas and projects that Sun wants to develop.

> Open source allows Sun to establish some ubiquity in the marketplace, particularly when we try to establish new market places. We did this with Jini (in community

source) and we are trying to do that now with JXTA.[25] By doing these projects in open source, we get to learn about what the market might be like as it evolves. This saves us from taking a guess and putting a product out there.

> Open source also helps with marketing . . . putting out the message. You can get information to the user community and customer base by allowing developers who are working in open source to talk about why they are making certain decisions. It gives Sun the opportunity to keep the world informed about new products without the annoying press releases.

Versioning   Gabriel pointed to another advantage that open source offered. The open source methodology opened up market opportunities for versioned products. Gabriel explained:

> We have projects that are proprietary, products for sale that were derived from open source work. NetBeans, which is a development environment for Java, is like that. There is an open source version and a proprietary version. The proprietary version is well tested and stable. Because NetBeans uses a plug-in architecture, the proprietary versions can vary according to which for-sale modules are included.[26] The open source version has all the modules that you need to do work, but if you are in a specialized area, like in an enterprise situation where you have database connections, etc., there are proprietary modules that Sun sells that help you. So open source establishes a marketplace, a plug-in market for things. And Sun sells the support for a well-tested version of the open source things. NetBeans is the open source program and Forte is Sun's proprietary, "premium" product.[27]

Open Source Strategy   Open source also served as a lance against the bulwark from Redmond. Gabriel observed:

> Companies like Sun, HP, and IBM make money by selling things that weigh something: servers, computers,

---

[23]"Sun to Shine Open-Source Light on StarOffice," Elinor Abreu, *The Industry Standard,* July 20, 2000.

[24]All quotes from Dr. Richard Gabriel are from the author's interview on 18 July 2001.

[25]Pronounced "juxta," this is a peer-to-peer project.

[26]Plug-in applications are programs that can easily be installed and used as part of a Web browser. Some popular plug-ins include Adobe's Acrobat document presentation and navigation program and RealNetworks' streaming video player.

[27]Forte is a suite of software tools for developing entry-level to enterprise-class applications for the Solaris Operating Environment, Linux, and Microsoft Windows.

printers, etc. Software is secondary to how they make money—but central in generating the pull for the hardware. They can use open source as a way of saying to the software world, 'we believe in the ideals embodied in the open source movement.' We also want to appeal to the community in hopes of getting to play a little in the Linux world. Anything that erodes a certain company's monopoly position is an opportunity for growth. We all use it, at least partially, for that reason.

There has been much speculation in the community about Sun open sourcing its popular Solaris operating system or Java programming language. Gabriel said:

One reason Sun hardware sells well is because the Solaris operating system is so good. It is better than what exists in NT or Linux. So a question is 'Do you open source Solaris?' A reason not to is because it is the family jewels and if you give it away, then other companies can use it to provide similar value to their hardware. On the other hand if you give it away and Linux picks it up, then you have opened up the field for operating systems quite a bit and reduced the 800-pound gorilla effect and made more opportunities for everyone.

The decision to open source can strike at the heart of a company's strategy.

Key Strategic Decisions for Sun   Gabriel said that most decisions at Sun concerning software, including decisions to open source, were made at the level of Patricia Sueltz, Sun's executive vice president, software systems group. However, decisions about open sourcing Solaris were kicked up to the highest levels of the company, to CEO Scott McNealy and the board of directors. Gabriel said, "The risk of open source is that you will make a strategic decision without realizing it."

Keeping in mind that Sun is a hardware company, it is difficult to quantify the revenue impact to Sun of open sourcing its key software products. Gabriel speculated about the revenue impact if Sun open sourced Java and Solaris.

The service organization will change from hand holding to professional services. So there is the opportunity for those revenues. You could better predict the revenues too. For Sun, there is no direct Solaris revenue *per se*. Solaris is looked upon as a tax, a necessary expense that contributes to hardware revenues. Direct revenue from Java licensing agreements is probably around $200 million a year. Of course, under open source, this would go to zero. On the other hand, by

opening Java and Solaris, we could free up large numbers of human resources, developers who could be redeployed to something else. In the end, Sun's bottom line is probably slightly better.

Still, there was the risk that a competitor could take Solaris and do it better than Sun, in effect beating the company with its own stick. Gabriel balances this risk against another key advantage of open source.

If you look at the lifecycle of computer languages, they die off after about ten years. By this reasoning, Java may start to die off in the middle of this decade. Well, by putting Java in open source, it could extend the currency of the language. While it is true that others could then adopt it, it will be a long time before any company other than Sun will be thought of as THE Java company.

Gabriel thinks open source has the potential to become the predominant software development strategy. He believes Sun will come to embrace it more, and is surprised that Microsoft has taken such a negative stance concerning open source. (See "Microsoft's Viewpoint" below.) Gabriel speculated that the revenue impact to Microsoft would not be negative.

If all Microsoft did was provide stable builds and iterations to Windows and backed them up, they would not have to charge the box makers one dime less than they do now. In addition, they would benefit from another open source advantage. There are always those users who want the latest release while others only want only well-tested, stable releases. Open source allows you to serve both customers.

If Microsoft said it was going to open source stuff, Sun, HP and IBM would be a little panicked, because that's one of the few leverage points we have left except for having hardware. That would be a devastating thing for Microsoft to do [to us].

Their objection to open source must stem from their culture. Love makes you stupid. I know Java makes us at Sun a little stupid. There is something they say or do at Microsoft that makes them stupid, that they are not seeing this. But I think eventually they will.

A Billion Reasons IBM Loves Linux

Company Overview   International Business Machines Corporation (IBM) manufactured a wide variety of computer hardware and peripherals and developed software. Computers include microcomputers, minicomputers, and mainframe computers as well as specialized terminals and servers. Software includes accounting, communications, database management, educational, office automation, manufacturing, utility, and engineering software.

How Open Source Affects IBM   "A lot of companies that embrace Linux view it as an operating system," said Irving Wladawsky-Berger, an IBM vice president who is responsible for all IBM-wide Linux strategy decisions. "We viewed it as a major game-changer in this whole world of technology."[28]

IBM's own Unix-based, proprietary AIX operating system was launched in February 1990 and represented about $257 million in revenue for IBM in 1999, according to IDC. Still, in December 2000, IBM's CEO Lou Gerstner announced plans to spend $1 billion in 2001 researching, developing, and marketing Linux-based products and services worldwide. Combined with IBM's dedication to Apache, the company seemed to fully back open source.

IBM was not taking any chances on missing out on Linux. The company established a Linux Strategy Team and Linux Technology Center. Daniel Frye, Director of IBM's Linux Technology center, described his group of 250 programmers as "IBM's development arm in Linux."[29] He said their mission was to "make Linux better by working as peers in the Linux development community." Frye reported to Helene Armitage, VP of UNIX development, and the person responsible for AIX, SP software, and the Linux Technology Center.

Frye, who co-authored IBM's early Linux strategy in 1998, supported the consolidation of Linux strategy under one person (Wladawsky-Berger). Frye said, "strategy for a technology that touches all parts of IBM—hardware, software, services, etc.—has to be done in a centralized fashion, otherwise we'd be all over the map. Think of distribution partners alone—every brand would be different." However, Frye said IBM is looser with development, "It is both centralized and distributed. Open source development to enhance Linux is centralized in my shop. All the brands do basic hardware or software enablement themselves—there is no centralized authority for that type of development."

Lou Gerstner has been quoted as saying that Sun, EMC, and Microsoft "are running the last big proprietary plays we'll see in this industry for a long time to come." Further, Irving Wladawsky-Berger wrote in the IBM 2000 Annual Report:

> It (Linux) alters the way our industry delivers value to its customers (which is very good news for IBM). A lot of people who have played by one set of rules in this industry are going to find out they're now playing a different game. The widespread adoption of Linux is going to neutralize any vendor's ability to exercise control—over customers or software developers—based on that vendor's proprietary operating system. When applications are no longer lashed to a specific operating platform, control and choice shift away from the technology company, and into the hands of customers. This makes possible an equally seismic shift in the way value is delivered—through services, through middleware, through servers.

Describing how IBM would make money out of a nonproprietary system, and the impact of Linux on IBM's business model, Frye said:

> Simple—we sell the hardware under Linux, the software on top of Linux, and the services all around it. The fact we don't sell Linux itself is irrelevant in the big picture. Our business model has been heterogeneous in operating systems and focused on open standards forever—Linux is not a change to our business model—with the very minor change of an open source OS.

According to Frye, most of IBM is on the Linux bandwagon. Frye said there is little opposition anymore to Linux in the company. "There is some valid debate about the rate and pace and specific strategy, but no debate about Linux's importance." Nor is Frye concerned about risks that Linux, and its amorphous open source community, may pose to IBM. Frye said, "Linux represents new markets and new ways to serve customer needs. We have become very comfortable in working with the community. So comfortable, we guarantee the same level of 24/7 worldwide service and support for Linux that we do for all our supported OS platforms."

Linux and Open Source at Intel

While Linux and the open source movement was a software phenomenon, it still attracted the attention of Intel Corporation. Intel was the world's leading semiconductor chipmaker; it supplied the computing and communications

---

[28]Elinor Abreu, "Behind the Big Blue Wall," *The Industry Standard,* January 22, 2001.

[29]All quotes from Daniel Frye, Director of IBM's Linux Technology Center, are from the author's interview dated July 22, 2001, unless otherwise indicated.

industries with chips, boards, and other systems building blocks that were integral to computers, servers, and networking and communications products. Linux and the open source movement represented important opportunities for the chip giant, but it was also fraught with risks. Pat Gelsinger, the chief technology officer for the Intel Architecture Group, which represented the core of Intel's nearly $34 billion in sales in 2000, spearheaded Intel's strategy making for Linux and open source. Gelsinger explained Intel's interest in Linux:

> Our interest in open source development in general and Linux in particular is consistent with our general strategic policy that we call "Port of Choice." For over twenty years, Intel has been committed to making sure that all important software runs on Intel architecture.
>
> While the majority of what we do is related to Microsoft, this Port of Choice strategy means that Intel must be consistently engaged in the software industry. Therefore, we work with all of the major players such as Oracle, BEA, and others. Our job is to make sure that Linux runs best on Intel. Right now, a high percentage of all Linux runs on Intel-based hardware.
>
> In addition, the growth of Linux has been phenomenal. So while working with Linux fits our general strategic policy, Linux and the open source movement just feels like its getting legs. It offers extraordinary growth and undeniable intellectual appeal.
>
> However, Linux is a different animal. Working with Linux has risks and benefits to Intel's business model.[30]

Linux Inside

As was the case with many companies, Intel was initially surprised by the stealthy introduction of Linux into its own organization. Gelsinger recalled:

> Two years ago, I was in charge of Intel's initial Linux strategy review. The IT manager, who was the CIO said, "there will not be any Linux at Intel." Well, it seemed like a good idea to find out how much Linux was out there already. We held an informal Linux user group meeting open to anyone at Intel. I expected maybe 100 to 150 people. Instead, 2,000 people showed up! Hundreds of machines at Intel were running Linux and the IT managers didn't know about it.

Entire design teams had moved over to Linux without telling the IT people. It was then that I realized how powerful the Linux intellectual phenomenon was. While I am certain Linux will not be used in all areas, e.g., the desktop environment or in high-end hardened data centers, it still is useful in many other applications.

"Intel Inbetween"

Intel saw opportunities for Linux outside of the desktop. The company carefully staked its territory. Gelsinger said:

> The desktop battle is over. Microsoft won. We think an area that we call "Bookends" is still open. This includes servers, data centers, embedded space, Palm OS, etc. Microsoft is playing here, but it is not dominant. In fact, some players such as Telcos don't want Microsoft. So if Intel did not have a Port of Choice strategy, it couldn't get into this space.

While Linux "had legs" and boasted a compelling growth trajectory, working with Linux in particular posed a touchy problem for Intel. Gelsinger said:

> Microsoft is our closest business partner. Microsoft has called Linux its "Enemy Number 1." We must be conscious of the engagements we do and don't do in the Linux space. Let's say there is a major effort to get Linux on the desktop. Assume that Linus and the open source community really get behind it and that there is a successful effort to overcome the issues like standardizing UIs, etc. Well, Intel wouldn't choose to work on those projects. But that wouldn't affect Intel's work on Linux in the server environment.
>
> There are also the licensing issues surrounding the GPL. We have to be careful about the intellectual property we expose to GPL. When we work with Novell, Oracle, or other [closed source] developers, Intel's roles and responsibilities are much clearer. When we work in open source, things get bizarre. There are no NDAs, no licenses other than the GPL or the BSD license. It's often not clear who makes what decisions. It's culturally dichotomous to how we are accustomed to working. Much of the work is very sensitive to Intel, especially advanced technology discussions and information concerning chip sets and processors.
>
> We were more random in how we dealt with these issues but now we are trying to develop more clear and consistent policies concerning how and where we will participate in open source projects.

---

[30]All quotes from Patrick Gelsinger are from the author's interview on 1 June 2001, unless otherwise noted.

Finally, open source development impacts our overall development cycle. Eventually, chip set information gets public. But we like to control that. Under open source, we face the challenge of working with the open source community with technologies that we are not yet prepared to expose to competitors and critics.

Beyond the inherent political and cultural drawbacks, open source did not always offer the best development methodology. Intel and others could count on some leverage from the open source community, but working in this loosely managed open source Linux development environment also posed drawbacks.

> It's not unreasonable to plan for a 5:1 developer ratio in the open source community. Of course, if the project isn't interesting to the community you might not attract anyone. Working in open source, you may be able to use this leverage to reduce your time to market and increase your R&D leverage. However, if I need to get something into the standard kernel release, this could slow me down because Linux kernel release cycles are slower than Microsoft's. I can always try to negotiate with Microsoft to incorporate an important change into its kernel; I can get it in quicker than I can with Linux. In this case, Linux gives me R&D leverage, but no time to market advantage over Microsoft.

Microsoft's Viewpoint

Microsoft believed that open source development offered an unsustainable business model. In May 2001, Microsoft's senior vice president for applied strategies, Craig Mundie, compared open source to the failed Internet business models that littered the ground. Mundie said:

> . . . it is also important that we learn from the lessons of the past year and apply them in order to make the most of the potential that lies ahead . . .
>
> But there is a broader lesson as well—companies and investors need to focus on business models that can be sustainable over the long term in the real world economy. A common trait of many of the companies that failed is that they gave away for free or at a loss the very thing they produced that was of greatest value—in the hope that somehow they'd make money selling something else.[31]

Mundie explained that he believed the Internet was in a third phase of its evolution. The first phase introduced delivery of static information over the Internet. The second phase witnessed the birth of online transactions and the promise of online business models. The third phase was about "connecting the currently separate complex systems of information and transactions and bringing that power to the individual in a readily accessible format on a variety of devices." This phase was the focus of Microsoft's .NET strategy to support the convergence of personal computing with the Web.[32]

Mundie envisioned a business model called the "Commercial Software Model" that would underpin the third phase of the Internet. According to Mundie, such a model was built around five key elements:

Community:	A strong support community of developers
Standards:	Promotes collaboration and interoperability while supporting innovation and healthy competition
Business Model:	Promotes the growth of profitable business
Investment:	Level of R&D investment drives resources for future innovation
Licensing Model:	Provides product and source access without jeopardizing the intellectual property rights of those who create or use the software

Mundie observed that in order to be ready for the Internet's third phase, Microsoft needed to improve its licensing model. To this end, Mundie described Microsoft's "Shared Source Philosophy" as an alternative to open source.

Free Love versus Discrete Dating

Microsoft proposed sharing with developers those parts of its source code that they needed to make their applications work with Windows and other Microsoft programs.

[31]All quotes from Craig Mundie are from his speech, "The Commercial Software Model," delivered on May 3, 2001, at New York University Stern School of Business. Prepared text is available at: www.microsoft.com/presspass/exec/craig/05-03sharedsource.asp.

[32].Net is the name Microsoft gave to its strategy converge personal computing with the Web. Microsoft's stated goal was to provide individual and business users with a seamlessly interoperable and Web-enabled interface for applications and computing devices and to make computing activities increasingly Web browser-oriented.

This was a far cry from the free-wheeling environment created by the GPL. Mundie said:

> The GPL mandates that any software that incorporates source code already licensed under the GPL will itself become subject to the GPL. When the resulting software product is distributed, its creator must make the entire source code base freely available to everyone, at no additional charge. This viral aspect of the GPL poses a threat to the intellectual property of any organization making use of it. It also fundamentally undermines the independent commercial software sector because it effectively makes it impossible to distribute software on a basis whereby recipients pay for the product rather than just the cost of distribution.

> [Open source] puts at risk the continued vitality of the independent software sector. The business model for [open source] may well be attractive for software as an adjunct to hardware—the model of the 60s and 70s—or for service businesses that do not generate the revenue needed for major investments in technology. But as history has shown, while this type of model may have a place, it isn't successful in building a mass market and making powerful, easy-to-use software broadly accessible to customers.

Beyond what he viewed as a bankrupt business model, Mundie pointed to the dangers that open source represented to software development. In addition to the inherent security risks posed by having source code in the public domain, Mundie said, "the [open source] development model leads to a strong possibility of unhealthy "forking" of a code base, resulting in the development of multiple incompatible versions of programs, weakened interoperability, product instability, and hindering businesses ability to strategically plan for the future."

Conclusion

Even if, as Intel's Gelsinger believed, Microsoft long ago won the battle for the desktop, it was easy to see why Microsoft's CEO viewed Linux as a threat. The success of open source operating systems, particularly Linux, presented a real challenge to the software giant. The notion of open source development, where the vital source code must be made public for any and all to copy and improve, and the thriving open source applications such as GNU, Apache, Sendmail, and Linux, threatened Microsoft's closed source business model. Less clear was the impact open source development would have on how companies such as HP, IBM, and Sun competed with each other. These companies built businesses supporting their own versions of operating systems. In an open source world, the basis of competition would shift, but to where? Companies would have to depend upon the achievements of an independent and amorphous open source "community" instead of solely driving their own software development. Where would companies find rents in what looked to some like a free-for-all commune?

Appendix

What Is an Operating System?

An operating system manages software applications that run on a computer. Applications use the operating system by making requests for services through a defined application program interface (API). An operating system performs three main tasks within a computer:

- Determines which applications should run in what order and how much time should be allowed for each application before giving another application a turn.

- Manages the sharing of internal memory among multiple applications.

- Handles input and output to and from attached hardware devices, such as hard disks, printers, and dial-up ports.

Case 3.3

MySQL Open Source Database in 2004

We feel that open source is a smarter way to produce and distribute software. It's not a religion. It's not a political inclination; it's only a smarter way to produce software. It's inexpensive and it produces good quality. Combined with the Internet we have a smarter way of distributing the software. This is similar to what Dell did to PCs. The cornerstone of their business model is the ability to produce at a lower cost and to sell at a lower cost, and that's also what open source is about.

—Mårten Mickos, CEO MySQL AB

Introduction

In February 2004, Mårten Mickos leaned back in his chair and let his eyes wander out of the window towards the soft hills of the Silicon Valley peninsula. He had just read the article in *Fortune* Magazine portraying open source as one of the 10 tech trends to bet on, and specifically MySQL as one of the key players behind that movement. Not even three years earlier MySQL founders had asked Mickos to be CEO and help turn their "chaos" into a real company. He first said "never" but later agreed. Now *Fortune* Magazine noted his success in steering the company by commenting that Mickos must be "Larry Ellison's worst nightmare."[1] MySQL had grown fast, had gained powerful allies, and had received venture funding from a premier venture capitalist on Sand Hill Road.

MySQL's success was also reason for concern. Mickos knew that eventually Oracle, Microsoft, and IBM would wake up and realize that MySQL could in fact be a threat to their $10 billion database business. With some 120 employees and $10 million in revenue in 2003, Mickos was David against Goliath.

Mickos was pondering some very important questions. Would MySQL's open source approach be able to reshape the database software category, as Linux had reshaped the server operating systems category? Would MySQL be able to drive down the high unit prices for database software by a factor of 10 or more? Would MySQL's low cost business model be scalable to $100 million in revenue? Mickos knew that it would take another two to three years before the big three would feel real pain through MySQL's competition. How would they react?

Company History

MySQL grew out of the contractual data mining work that the three Scandinavian founders, David Axmark, Allan Larsson, and Michael "Monty" Widenius, performed in the early 1990s. Though clients requested that they use standard tools for data analysis, Axmark, Larsson, and Widenius believed that self-developed tools were better suited to manage large data. As the World Wide Web emerged as a powerful business tool in 1994–95, they realized that a database management system specifically suited for the Web was needed. When they decided to formalize these efforts into a single product, MySQL was born.

In order to penetrate markets fast but still collect license revenue, the founders adopted a dual licensing concept as the basis of their business model. An open source software (OSS) version of the product was distributed freely and a commercial version was distributed under a low price license scheme. An important target market was unsophisticated day-to-day users who did not receive much benefit from the feature richness of established database management systems (DBMS) such as Oracle. Therefore, a key to product development was to make the product easy to install and use. The founders established a 15-minute design rule to help minimize the time a user spent on installation and evaluation, much less time than that of competitors (see Exhibit 1 and Exhibit 2 for an introduction to OSS and DBMS respectively).

---

[1] *Fortune* Magazine, February 23, 2004, page 97. Larry Ellison is CEO of Oracle Corporation.

Christof Wittig, Sloan '04, and Sami Inkinen, MBA '05, prepared this case under the supervision of Prof. Robert A. Burgelman as the basis for class discussion rather than to illustrate either effective or ineffective handling of an administrative situation.

EXHIBIT 1 | The Open Source Challenge[a]

Companies that develop software products make significant investments. The source code, which is the software program written by software developers, is proprietary material of any closed source software company. It contains the core for the company's business model, usually consisting of license fees (for a compiled, runtime version of the source code), complementary products, and services. Since the 1990s, software vendors were exposed to a new phenomenon called open source software (OSS) such as the operating system Linux, which a Finnish undergraduate named Linus Torvalds had written "just for fun." He distributed the software free and made the source code available to everybody over the Internet, inviting other programmers to add to Linux and make it better, though not offering any compensation for it. This movement was driven by a cult (with ideas ranging from software should always be free to a grassroots resistance against the monopoly power of Microsoft), technology (Linux is said to be an excellent system), and personality of the protagonists. While there has been a strong nonprofit community attribute to open source in its origins, for-profits have started to adopt and extend many concepts of OSS that seem commercially viable. These second-generation open source companies and initiatives are often regarded with repulsion by first-generation protagonists.

The License Agreements: GPL and BSD

Over time, tens of different standardized license agreements for OSS have evolved. The reciprocal GPL and the academic BSD became the most popular ones. In 1984, the Free Software Foundation (FSF) and a "copyleft," called General Public License (GPL), emerged out of a project to develop and freely distribute GNU, a UNIX-like operating system. The copyleft stipulated that users could copy the program, modify it, and sell the original or modified versions. Any program that used source code under the GPL had to become in its entirety freely available under the GPL itself, even if parts of the program consisted of proprietary software. The authors of the copyleft wanted to "spread" free software like a virus in the community. In 1989, the PERL communication language product was released under GPL.

In contrast BSD enabled software vendors to use sources released under BSD without disclosing their proprietary code, but with a mere mention of the originating source in a copyright disclaimer. The most popular application under BSD was Sendmail, a mail transfer agent that powered the vast majority of all Internet e-mail services. Its author, Eric Allman, incorporated Sendmail, Inc. to commercially exploit his product in 1998. The company was profitable since 2003 with some $15m of revenues.

Software companies liked to use BSD licenses for input components, but disliked using them for their output, as any other vendor could reap the benefits for free. Under GPL this was only possible if all of the derivative work became GPL itself, making a commercial exploitation difficult. This made GPL licensed software a very unattractive input component.

Linux and Apache

Linux was an operating system (OS) that ran on servers, desktops, and embedded systems. Its source code was freely distributed under the GPL. Unlike Microsoft's Windows it could be used on all major microprocessor platforms such as Intel, PowerPC, Sparc, and Alpha. It was known to be very robust and technologically very advanced. Though Linux was freely available on the Internet, commercial distributors such as SuSE and RedHat (see Exhibit 1A for financials) have been successful in selling Linux packages and complementary services. While the desktop and embedded version have been less pervasive, the server OS has captured a significant share of the market and poses a significant threat to Microsoft's proprietary core product, Windows. A survey by Goldman, Sachs & Co. in early 2003 showed that 39 percent of large corporations use Linux.[b] Other research suggested market share of around 50 percent and 30 percent for Windows NT and Linux, respectively, with Windows' share stagnating, and Linux' growing steadily.

The Apache HTTP Web server was another OSS product that has become very successful. According to the Netcraft Web server survey in February 2004, 67 percent of the worldwide 47 million Web sites were hosted on Apache[c], leaving Microsoft's proprietary Internet Information Server (IIS) with 21 percent far behind.

The Battle of Giants over OSS

While OSS started as a private initiative of individuals who would hardly be seen as suppliers to corporate customers, it gained the approval of many big players such as IBM and Hewlett-Packard. Oracle and IBM offered their database products and SAP, and Oracle their enterprise resource planning (ERP) products for Linux. Market research suggested an increasing penetration of OSS products in corporate MIS departments.

[a]In this exhibit we will only briefly summarize the open source software challenge which is more deeply explored in case SM-85 by Prof. Robert A. Burgelman and Philip E. Meza, Stanford Graduate School of Business, 2001.

[b]Ravi Madapati, "Microsoft and the Linux Threat," *Global CEO*, April 2003.

[c]http://news.netcraft.com/archives/2004/02/01/february_2004_web_server_survey.html.

(continued)

EXHIBIT 1 | The Open Source Challenge (cont.)

IBM. IBM was arguably the most important protagonist for OSS. While many companies just embraced Linux as an operating system, IBM viewed it as a "major game-changer in this whole world of technology."[d] IBM's strong commitment towards Linux and Apache changed the rules. Now "Big Blue" supported a once grass-root–based project and permitted any corporate CIO to choose Linux without risking his career. In its annual report of 2000 IBM wrote:

> It (Linux) alters the way our industry delivers value to its customers (which is very good news for IBM). A lot of people who have played by one set of rules in this industry are going to find out they're now playing a different game. The widespread adoption of Linux is going to neutralize any vendor's ability to exercise control—over customers and software developers—based on that vendor's proprietary operating system. When applications are no longer lashed to a specific operating platform, control and choice shift away from the technology company, and into the hands of the customers. This makes possible an equally seismic shift in the way value is delivered—through services, through middleware, through servers.
>
> We sell hardware under Linux, the software on top of Linux, and the services all around it. The fact we don't sell Linux itself is irrelevant in the big picture.

In 2000, IBM put 200 employees into its independent "Linux development center," to make Linux better, expand Linux's reach, and enable IBM products in 50 different projects.[e] By 2004, this number had grown to 600 people and 150 projects. Other OSS projects included Apache, XML, Jakarta, Eclipse (an OSS development tool to create cross-platform applications) and Globus (grid computing), all of these helping to commoditize their respective categories or to unlock them from a single vendor.

IBM's support for open source DBMS was much less embracing. While its own proprietary DB2 product ran well on Linux, it was very difficult to access DB2 on mainframes from a Linux server which could host another DBMS such as MySQL. The necessary OCL client was developed by IBM but strategically held back from release, which upset clients such as Coca-Cola, who wanted to switch to low cost databases for some less strategic applications.

Microsoft. Microsoft saw Linux and the open source software movement as threat number one and identified Oracle and Sun as only second-tier rivals. In his yearly memo to all Microsoft employees on June 4, 2003, Microsoft's CEO and president Steve Ballmer wrote:[f]

> Noncommercial software products in general, and Linux in particular, present a competitive challenge for us and for our entire industry, and they require our concentrated focus and attention. IBM's endorsement of Linux has added credibility and an illusion of support and accountability [. . .]. We will rise to this challenge, and we will compete in a fair and responsible manner that puts our customers first. We will show that our approach offers better value, better security, and better opportunity.

Microsoft was not only threatened by the OSS product substitution, but seemed to be at the heart of the noncommercial, political movement of OSS. In newsgroup communities, Microsoft was often written with a dollar sign (Micro$oft) in order to defame it as exploitative. Furthermore, the commoditization effect hit Microsoft's core customers more than other software vendors. Oracle's Ken Jacobs commented: "Microsoft is more challenged than Oracle because both the operating system and potentially the database have a proprietary platform from beginning to end. I do think that because of their focus on the low end of the market, which is the most cost sensitive, they're going to be the most vulnerable in the industry."

In response, Microsoft learned from open source and established the "Shared Source Initiative." Through this program, they provided the source code of 10 technologies to customers, partners, governments, and academics worldwide. For Windows, Microsoft allowed only a limited number of customers to obtain the source code, whereas for technologies such as .NET-related components there are hundreds of thousands of individual developers who have access and rights to modify and redistribute the source code. Jason Matusow, shared source manager of Microsoft, pointed at the convergence aspects of the second generation of open source businesses and Microsoft's Shared Source policy. Both were very concerned about owning and managing their intellectual assets and both were about business, not ideology.

[d]Irving Wladawsky-Berger, "IBM's VP Responsible for All IBM-wide LINUX Strategy Decisions," in Elinor Abreu, "Behind the Big Blue Wall," *The Industry Standard*, January 22, 2001.

[e]Scott Handy, VP Worldwide Linux Strategy, IBM, *Keynote*, OSBC San Francisco, March 16, 2004.

[f]Memo of Steve Ballmer, June 4, 2003, cited from: http://www.itmweb.com/f060903.htm.

EXHIBIT 1A | Red Hat Annual Income Statement

(in millions of U.S. Dollars)	Feb 28, 2003	Feb 28, 2002	Feb 28, 2001
Subscription and services revenue:			
Subscription:			
Enterprise technologies	30.438	17.734	16.260
Retail	14.833	19.054	20.604
Embedded	3.321	5.512	8.634
Total subscription revenue	48.592	42.300	45.498
Services:			
Enterprise technologies	38.522	24.354	16.002
Embedded development services	3.812	12.256	19.332
Total services revenue	42.334	36.610	35.334
Total revenue	**90.926**	**78.910**	**80.832**
Cost of subscription and services revenue:			
Subscription	9.121	9.887	14.660
Services	22.341	18.628	20.485
Total cost of revenue	**31.462**	**28.515**	**35.145**
Gross profit enterprise technologies and retail	56.573	40.082	30.192
Gross profit embedded	2.891	10.313	15.495
Gross profit on hardware resale revenue*	—	—	131
Total gross profit	**59.464**	**50.395**	**45.818**
Operating expense:			
Sales and marketing	32.969	33.442	38.355
Stock-based sales and marketing expense	505	2.080	6.816
Research and development	21.274	16.429	15.713
Stock-based research and development expense	1.165	4.106	3.069
General and administrative	15.239	13.491	18.910
General and administrative—mergers and acquisitions	522	4.735	9.220
Stock-based general and administrative expense	2.146	3.991	7.239
Lease buyout costs	285	1.501	—
Amortization of goodwill	—	48.397	40.586
Amortization of intangibles	1.062	1.150	1.088
Restructuring charges	1.461	56.122	—
Total operating expense	**76.628**	**185.444**	**140.996**
Loss from continuing operations	**−17.164**	**−135.049**	**−95.178**
Other income (expense), net	10.826	15.535	20.766
Loss from continuing operations before extraordinary item	**−6.338**	**−119.514**	**−74.412**
Discontinued operations:			
Loss from discontinued operations	—	−10.355	−12.303
Loss before extraordinary item	−6.338	−129.869	−86.715
Extraordinary item—loss on disposal of discontinued operations	**−261**	**−10.347**	**—**
Net loss	**−6.599**	**−140.216**	**−86.715**

*$0.747m revenue and $0.646m cost for hardware in 2000 excluded for simplicity.

Source: Company reports.

EXHIBIT 2 | Database Management Systems (DBMS)[a]

A system that enables end users or application programmers to share data. It provides a systematic method of creating, updating, retrieving and storing information in a database. DBMSs also typically perform data integrity, data access control, and automated rollback, restart and recovery functions.

Data was stored in binary information. In order to save a piece of data, such as a credit card number, the DBMS provided programmers with the opportunity to refer to this data with real world name reference such as "CREDIT_CARD" and access the data being stored and retrieved upon request. Many further functions made the system complete, such as transaction management (guaranteeing the integrity of the database if an application failed) and the possibility of querying data according to different search algorithms. While many people used databases, (i.e., when using an online bank account or entering procurement data into an ERP system), the DBMS itself was only visible to the programmer who linked the data formats with the program code that contained the functions and user interfaces.

The choice of a DBMS determined the format in which data was stored. Three fundamentally different DBMS categories were recognized. While prerelational (mainly on mainframes) and object-oriented databases held some market share, the lion's share (86 percent) belonged to relational database management systems (RDBMS). Most mainstream RDBMS supplied a standardized query language (SQL), but every product had slight proprietary features that made it expensive to switch from one product to another. While it was possible to recover data from most if not all systems, it was time- and cost-prohibitive to switch databases in the life cycle of an application.

The use of databases could be distinguished as follows:

Enterprisewide

Used databases mainly on dedicated servers. While DBMS, including MySQL, ran on all common server operating systems (UNIX, NT, or Linux), only Microsoft limited its SQL server to its own Windows NT/2000 platform. For enterprisewide use, DBMS was chosen by the enduser as a strategic platform. It was usually shared by many, if not all applications, so that a common set of data could be accessed, thus avoiding redundancies. Therefore, the life of a database could be longer than that of the application, making long-term availability, reliability, and future compatibility a key factor for enterprise DBMS selection. DBMS replacement cycles were long, making it difficult for new entrants to displace existing DBMS vendors.

Web Sites

Used databases on application servers to store and/or cache data. Similar rules as to enterprisewide use. Sometimes intermediary DBMS cached the data between the Web application and the enterprisewide database. Those intermediary DBMS were seen as a less strategic choice. An example would be cached data of flights and tariffs of an online travel agent while the accounting system ran on Oracle's DBMS.

[a]Definition and categorization from *Gartner Dataquest Guide,* "Infrastructure and Applications Worldwide Software Market Definitions," June 10, 2002 rev. October 1, 2002.

Launch, Growth, and Fame

In August 1996, the company released its first version of the MySQL database management system. Within four months, the company saw 1,000 downloads from its Web site. The first commercial licenses were sold in 1997. One year after its first product launch, the company boasted more mentions and links on the World Wide Web than Oracle (9,410,000 versus 7,610,000 and 23,600 versus. 10,700, respectively). By 1999, an infrastructure supporting the product emerged. Independent authors published the first MySQL book, which became a bestseller. Conferences picked up the topic and made the product well known throughout the industry. Oracle introduced a MySQL migration kit in 2001 in response to customer demand to connect data from less critical applications running on MySQL with corporate repositories running on Oracle. MySQL received the Readers' Choice award of the *Linux Journal* every year beginning in 1998, as well as numerous other awards. The number of downloads soared to 35,000–40,000 per day (see

Exhibit 3 for Internet metrics on MySQL). Some industry experts estimated that MySQL held 4 million out of 12 million total RDBMS servers, yielding a 25 percent installed base market share. By 2004, MySQL had become "the poster child of open source business"[2] with considerable news coverage in both national and international business and technology press.

Incorporation in 2001

In 2001 the company consisted of 20 people focusing mainly on technology, leaving the rest of the business in a "chaotic" state.[3] The founders felt that they needed a real management structure to make the company prosper further. They recruited an experienced chairman of the board, John Wattin, and CEO Mårten Mickos (see

[2]Quote from an anonymous visitor to the OSBC conference, San Francisco, March 17, 2004.

[3]This and other quotes on company history from: David Axmark, Keynote, Kuala Lumpur, August 26, 2003.

EXHIBIT 2A |

Total DBMS Market Revenue Split by the Size of the User Base and DBMS Market Niches by Size in 2003

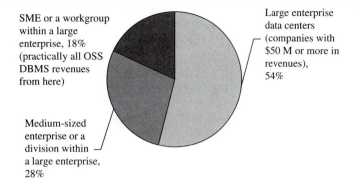

SME or a workgroup within a large enterprise, 18% (practically all OSS DBMS revenues from here)

Large enterprise data centers (companies with $50 M or more in revenues), 54%

Medium-sized enterprise or a division within a large enterprise, 28%

DBMS market niche	Estimated size of the DBMS niche
Embedded databases (e.g., in a hardware device)	~$400 Million
Content management databases and other specialty DB	~$400 Million
Small footprint application databases (workgroup/desktop/mobile)	~$150 Million
2nd tier databases, e.g., cache database in web architecture having another database behind	~$100 Million

Exhibit 4 for biographies) and incorporated the company as MySQL AB in Uppsala, Sweden.

Standalone Software   Stored data in standalone databases, which were usually not transparent to the user when installed on a local PC together with the application software package. An example would be a personal tax manager package where personal financial data was stored on a local disk. The decision for a DBMS was generally made by the application software producer who looked for longevity, low license fees, and robustness to avoid service costs.

Embedded and Integrated Systems   Used databases to store data such as microwave oven settings or to buffer data of railway signals for system failure recovery. The decision was made under similar criteria as standalone software. As there was less standardization in embedded operating systems, a larger variety of choices was available.

　　The majority of the annual $10.5 billion DBMS business resulted from the enterprisewide use, leaving an estimated 10 percent of the business to the other uses (see Exhibit 2A) for market segmentation).

Main RDBMS Competitors

Three companies dominated the RDBMS market: Oracle, IBM, and Microsoft. The former fourth player, Sybase, did not play a significant role any more (see Exhibit 2B) for market shares).

Oracle   Oracle was a very successful software company (see Exhibit 2C) for financials) that employed 40,000 people globally. The company's products consisted of its flagship RDBMS 10g (complemented by many platform technologies) and applications like the E-Business Suite, contributing 74 percent and 26 percent, respectively, to the company's total revenue of almost $9.5 billion in fiscal year 2003. With 39.7 percent market share in 2001, Oracle was the leading provider of RDBMS. Its main strength was its 63.3 percent market share on the UNIX platform (IBM had 24.7 percent and Microsoft had no DBMS offering for UNIX).[4] From 2001–2003, however, Oracle's license revenue from DBMS declined

---

[4]Gartner, 2001 Database Management Systems Software Market Share, July 2002.

EXHIBIT 2B

Worldwide Total
RDBMS Market Share
in 2001 and 2002
Based on New
License Sales

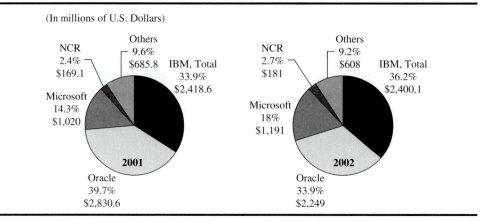

(In millions of U.S. Dollars)

2001

NCR 2.4% $169.1
Others 9.6% $685.8
IBM, Total 33.9% $2,418.6
Microsoft 14.3% $1,020
Oracle 39.7% $2,830.6

2002

NCR 2.7% $181
Others 9.2% $608
IBM, Total 36.2% $2,400.1
Microsoft 18% $1,191
Oracle 33.9% $2,249

4–5 percent, strongly correlating with the rise of NT versus the decline of UNIX as server OS. One of Oracle's most significant distributors was SAP.

IBM   IBM claimed the largest total share of market for DBMS with 34.6 percent (versus Oracle 32.0 percent). IBM's product offerings included prerelational DBMS running on mainframe computers. Their RDBMS were DB2 and the acquired Informix product line with a market share of 30.7 percent and 3.3 percent, respectively. From 2001 to 2003, IBM's DBMS license revenues increased 5 percent due to mergers, favorable bundling, and price discounts. IBM was famous for its direct sales force, selling to top executives of large corporations.

With revenues of $81 billion and 320,000 employees, IBM was the largest IT company in the world (see Exhibit 2D for financials). Total software revenues accounted for $13.4 billion (16.5 percent of total revenues) with around $8.2 billion (around 10 percent of total revenues in 2001) estimated to represent DBMS revenues (new licenses, updates and services).[5]

Microsoft   Software giant Microsoft was a latecomer to the DBMS market. While it originally sold Sybase's DBMS, branded as Microsoft SQL Server, it started its own development in the mid-1990s, receiving significant

help from SAP to make it an enterprise class DBMS. In the last decade, it grew its DBMS revenues at rates of 15–25 percent, especially due to favorable bundling and compatibility with Microsoft's successful server operating system NT. Its license fees were much lower than those of Oracle and IBM as well. As of 2001, Microsoft held 16.3 percent total DBMS and 14.4 percent RDBMS market share. On the Windows NT/2000 platform, Microsoft was in the lead with 39.9 percent against Oracle and IBM with 34.0 percent and 20.7 percent, respectively. Microsoft sold through distributors and direct marketing, targeting mainly small and medium enterprises. Out of $32 billion (2002: 28,365/2001: 25,296) in total revenues, DBMS were estimated to represent 10–15 percent. Microsoft had well over 50,000 employees.

Open Source and DBMS

From the outset, DBMS have been a target of OSS initiatives. Among the most important were MySQL, Sleepycat (Berkeley DB), and PostgreSQL. While the motivation differed, the driving force behind their growth was the low cost of their freely available version, as well as the spillover effect from the momentum of Linux.

PostgreSQL   PostgreSQL emerged from a project started at the University of California, Berkeley, in 1986 to a self-governed, nonprofit OSS community of individuals and companies, distributing its product under the BSD license. While the main initiator for this project was obtaining control over the product design,

---

[5]IBM and Microsoft do not disclose data on a product level. This number is estimated by the relation of total DBMS revenues compared to new license sales disclosed by Oracle (×2.7), applied to IBM's and Microsoft's new license sales in 2001 as of $3,064 m and $1,442m, respectively.

EXHIBIT 2C | Oracle Annual Income Statement

(in millions of U.S. Dollars)	May 31, 2003	May 31, 2002	May 31, 2001
Revenues:			
New software licenses and other	$ 3,270	$ 3,513	$ 4,707
Software license updates and product support	3,929	3,540	3,301
Services	2,276	2,620	2,953
Total revenues	**9,475**	**9,673**	**10,961**
Operating expenses:			
Sales and marketing	2,072	2,209	2,691
Software license updates and product support	474	462	551
Cost of services	1,868	1,944	2,346
Research and development	1,180	1,076	1,139
General and administrative	441	411	457
Total operating expenses	**6,035**	**6,102**	**7,184**
Operating Income	**3,440**	**3,571**	**3,777**
Net investment losses related to equity securities	(111)	(244)	(17)
Other income, net	**96**	**81**	**211**
Income before provision for income taxes	3,425	3,408	3,971
Provision for income taxes	**1,118**	**1,184**	**1,410**
Net income	**$ 2,307**	**$ 2,224**	**$ 2,561**

Product revenue analysis	2003	2002	
Database technology business:			
New software licenses and other	$ 2,618	$ 2,739	
Software license updates and product support	3,086	2,794	
Services	1,282	1,433	
Total revenues	**6,986**	**6,966**	
Applications business:			
New software licenses and other	$ 605	$ 703	
Software license updates and product support	843	746	
Services	1,041	1,258	
Total revenues	**2,489**	**2,707**	

Margins*	2003	2002	2001
New software licenses and other:	51%	52%	55%
Software license updates and product support	89%	88%	85%
Consulting, services and other	22%	30%	25%
Totals	**60%**	**59%**	**56%**

Source: Company Reports

*The margins reported reflect only the direct controllable expenses of each line of business and do not represent the actual margins for each operating segment because they do not contain an allocation of product.

EXHIBIT 2D | IBM Annual Income Statement

(in millions of U.S. Dollars)	Dec 31, 2002	Dec 31, 2001	Dec 31, 2000
Revenues:			
Global Services	$ 36,360	$ 34,956	$ 33,152
Hardware	27,456	30,593	34,470
Software	13,074	12,939	12,598
Global Financing	3,232	3,426	3,465
Enterprise Investments/Other	1,064	1,153	1,404
Total revenues	**81,186**	**83,067**	**85,089**
Cost:			
Global Services	26,812	25,355	24,309
Hardware	20,020	21,231	24,207
Software	2,043	2,265	2,283
Global Financing	1,416	1,693	1,965
Enterprise Investments/Other	611	634	747
Total cost	**50,902**	**51,178**	**53,511**
Gross Profit	**30,284**	**31,889**	**31,578**
Expense and other income:			
Selling, general and administrative	18,738	17,048	17,393
Research, development and engineering	4,750	4,986	5,084
Intellectual property and custom development income	(1,100)	(1,476)	(1,664)
Other (income) and expense	227	(353)	(990)
Interest expense	145	234	344
Total expense and other income	**22,760**	**20,439**	**20,167**
Income from continuing operations before income taxes	7,524	11,450	11,411
Provision for income taxes	**2,190**	**3,304**	**3,537**
Income from continuing operations	5,334	8,146	7,874
Discontinued operations:			
(Loss)/income from discontinued operations	**(1,755)**	**(423)**	**219**
Net Income	**$ 3,579**	**$ 7,723**	**$ 8,093**
Pretax income margins	**2002**	**2001**	**2000**
Software	25%	23%	21%

Source: Company reports.

its main advantage in the market was its free-for-any-purpose unit price. Josh Berkus, member of the five-person steering committee, explained that the project had started from academia to implement advanced theories. The order of importance of product characteristics was: reliability, specification compliance, features, performance, and ease-of-use. Contributors made money by building applications on top of it. Berkus admitted the great marketing of MySQL, but pointed out that MySQL was focused on speed and ease-of-use rather than reliability. This was a diametrically opposed design concept to what he calls the superior architecture of PostgreSQL. Berkus insisted that MySQL was not really open source but shareware.[6]

Michael Olson, CEO of Sleepycat, noted: "PostgreSQL did a good job of becoming ubiquitous but never succeeded in the way that MySQL has. I believe that the reason for that is that PostgreSQL was inappropriately licensed. It was BSD-licensed, and you

---

[6]Interview with Josh Berkus, March 18, 2004.

EXHIBIT 3 | Key Internet Metrics Related to MySQL

[3 mos. Avg.]	oracle.com	mysql.com
Traffic Rank	1,778	1,891
Rank among the Web's most frequently visited Web sites		
Change	−312	+73
Reach	**426**	**557**
Users per million Web users who visit a given site		
Change	−5%	+7%

Source: www.alexa.com, February 7, 2004.

Number of Downloads at MySQL's Web Site (per month)

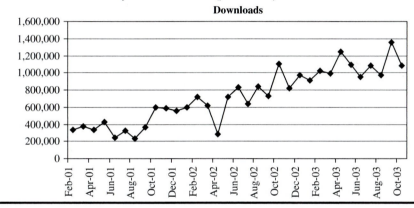

Source: Company.

couldn't build a profitable business in any reasonable way." Olson hinted at the personality aspect of open source: "[Linus and Monty] built a community around themselves that's excited and motivated in their success. You know, who's that guy in PostgreSQL? I don't know; it's like the Politburo. There's like 20 guys but none of them are attractive."

Sleepycat's Berkeley DB Sleepycat offered a prerelational DBMS mainly used in embedded systems and thus targeted a different market than MySQL's RDBMS. Its product was used widely because it was bundled with most OSS products such as Linux and Apache. While the company estimated to have some 200 million installations, its paying customers numbered only in the hundreds. The company moved from its original BSD free licensing to a dual licensing with a GPL-derivative for the open source version. Products were sold through a direct sales force at

prices well above $100,000. The founders bootstrapped in 1996 and passed a million dollars in revenues in 1999. CEO Michael Olson commented, "We don't disclose how much we make annually, but I can tell you that we earned millions of dollars of profit on millions of dollars of income in calendar year 2003. It was a record year for us in many respects, but every single year has been a record in number of new customers, average deal size, total income, total profits, and number of returning customers." In 2004, the company had 20 employees in Emeryville, California, and Boston, Massachusetts, and was still privately held without venture funding.

While in many respects the business model of Sleepycat was similar to that of MySQL, there were some significant differences. Sleepycat's deal sizes were much larger (between $100,000 and $250,000) because embedded databases were never purchased in single units like MySQL but always licensed to be redistributed in large numbers embedded in their customers' products.

EXHIBIT 4 | MySQL's Key Management Team Members

Mårten Mickos, CEO

Mårten Mickos brings a strong track record of leadership in global high-tech companies to MySQL AB. Prior to joining MySQL in 2001, Mårten was CEO at MatchON Sports, which he grew to become the 24th "hottest e-business" in Europe within nine months of its inception. Mårten was also previously the CEO at Intellitel Communications, where he was instrumental in transitioning the company from a development lab to a commercial software vendor. He has also directed worldwide sales efforts at several technology companies.

Hans von Bell, CFO

Hans von Bell is a seasoned financial executive with extensive experience of building up operations in new countries. Hans is well versed in the telecom and software businesses. Most recently, he served as CFO of Incirco AB in Sweden, where he had overall responsibility for finance, administration, and human resources of the Incirco group of companies.

Michael "Monty" Widenius, CTO and Co-founder

Monty Widenius is the designer and lead programmer for the MySQL database. His database software programming dates back to 1978 and his work with TCX DataKonsult AB, to 1981. Since 1995, Monty has been the primary force behind MySQL, devoting his time to product strategies, software design, and the development and reviewing of MySQL source code.

David Axmark, Vice President of Open Source Relations and Co-founder

David Axmark was involved with the MySQL database well before it had a name. David's primary focus now at MySQL is open source licensing and strategy, as well as community relations. He also actively promotes open source software and MySQL at conferences and other venues around the world. Interested in free software since the early '80s, David is committed to developing a successful business model through open source software.

Larry Stefonic, Executive Vice President, Sales

Larry Stefonic brings years of successful database business experience to MySQL AB. Prior to MySQL, Larry was in charge of Worldwide Embedded Sales at Mbrane in Seattle, Washington. He has also led international sales and business development teams at Centura Software, Raima Corporation, and Micro Database Systems.

Kaj Arnö, Vice President, Training

Kaj Arnö is the creator of the MySQL training program. In his career, Kaj has trained more than 2,000 IT users and developers at about 200 training classes across Europe, the United States, and Asia. With successful track record in consulting assignments, often serving customers in their respective native languages, Kaj leads the localization efforts of MySQL AB. Prior to joining MySQL AB in June 2001, Kaj was founder and CEO of the Finnish solution provider Polycon AB.

Zack Urlocker, Vice President, Marketing

As vice president of marketing, Zack Urlocker oversees MySQL global corporate and product marketing. Zack is a veteran marketer, with more than 15 years' enterprise software marketing experience. Prior to joining MySQL, Zack held executive marketing and product management positions at M7, Active Software, webMethods, and Borland International.

John Wattin, Chairman

John Wattin has been actively involved in the IT industry for 30 years. He founded or has successfully managed companies such as Enator AB, Sigma AB, Mandator AB, Astral AB, Scandiaconsult AB, and Indevo AB. Today, John works as an independent investor. He is the author of an award-winning book on running and developing service companies.

Source: www.mysql.com, January 25, 2004.

The Berkeley DB is also a new, innovative product, rather than one that commoditized an established, well-understood category.

Later in 2001 they received their first round of financing from Scandinavian venture capitalists. Investors were impressed by the rise of Linux and Apache and saw open source software (OSS) as a truly disruptive innovation, targeting the established software companies at their very heart—high margin software licensing fees. Analysts and the press noticed MySQL as well. In August, 2002, Bloomberg raised the question of whether Oracle, IBM, and Microsoft would lose business to the free database software MySQL due to its commoditizing effect.[7]

---

[7]Bloomberg.com, August 17, 2002.

EXHIBIT 5 | MySQL Annual Income Statement

(in millions of U.S. Dollars)	Dec 31, 2003	Dec 31, 2002	Dec 31, 2001
Revenues:			
Total revenues	Ca. $ 10.0	$ 6.2	$ .7
Net income	N/A	($ 1.9)	($ 1.0)

Source: *KreditFakta Kreditupplysningar i Norden AB,* 2003; exchange rate US$/SEK = 7.69.

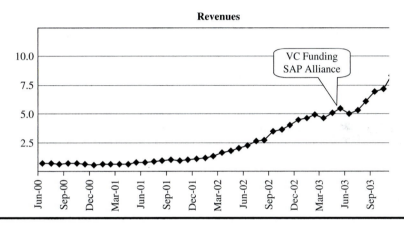

Source: Company.

Benchmark Capital and other investors such as the board of trustees of Stanford University, invested $19.5 million in 2003. Kevin Harvey, a partner with Benchmark Capital, explained: "The database itself is getting commoditized. What MySQL has is an innovation in the business model that I think is a barrier for any of the big competitors to replicate. If MySQL had some different feature of technology, Oracle and Microsoft could easily add that. That's not that interesting. It's about sales and marketing."[8]

By the end of 2003, the company employed approximately 120 people. While the company did not disclose financials, Mickos revealed in February 2004: "We did about 10 million euros last year, with the last months being profitable. We're going to run this year around break-even, although we're going to double the revenues and we're investing in many things."[9] The company had

approximately 5,000 paying customers, having added more than 2,000 in 2003 (see Exhibit 5 for other available financial information).

MySQL in the Marketplace

MySQL used its open source status as a viral marketing vehicle to penetrate markets. In the wake of the OSS flagships Linux and Apache, MySQL gained a tremendous amount of visibility in the developer community by appearing in newsgroups, blogs,[10] and other virtual information exchanges. MySQL was often used together with PHP, a language to create Web sites, so that eventually LAMP (standing for: Linux, Apache, MySQL, PHP) became an acronym for coherent OSS building blocks.

MySQL's products were available in their entirety under a dual licensing policy. Any user could download the product under the GPL and use it without fees or purchase it for a much lower fee than that of other commercial DBMS. While the product features of both licenses

[8]These and the following quotes from an interview with Kevin Harvey, Partner, Benchmark Capital, February 25, 2004.

[9]These and the following quotes from interviews with Mårten Mickos, February and March 2004, and from the Top Management Speaker series of the Stanford Sloan Program, February 10, 2004.

[10]A blog is a Web-based public diary of individuals that want to share their ideas and gather feedback.

were identical, three differences applied. Commercial MySQL software:

- Could be distributed with nonopen source software.
- Included a warranty from MySQL AB.
- Came with development support.

Mårten Mickos explained the dual licensing model:

> You can use MySQL free of charge, provided you follow the GPL license. Any derivative work must follow the same license. So then [customers] come back and say, 'Yes. We like your product, but we'd like to avoid the GPL license.' So we say, 'Fine. Give us some money and you will be freed from whatever burdens of the GPL.' This is a profitable business for us.

MySQL's marketing strategy was to provide a basic good-enough product at a low price, penetrating the market fast to achieve positive network effects through a large installed base. Mickos explained the appeal of a basic database:

> By one of our so-called competitors, I've seen a four-page listing of features that MySQL lacks and they have. They say, 'This is why you shouldn't buy MySQL. This is our argument.' I take that same list and say, 'This is *our* argument.' They have to have feature, feature, feature. But the customers don't need any more features. We say, 'If you need all the features, feel free to pay and use them. If you don't need all the features, see what savings you can make.'

Commoditization

As DBMS products became more difficult to differentiate, price became an ever more important criterion in the product selection process. Many industry observers described the falling prices as an effect of commoditization. Kevin Harvey, a former entrepreneur in the DBMS space, stated:

> The database itself is getting commoditized. There's no doubt. What are the aspects of other things like Linux or Apache to be a driver of commoditization? It was things like a standard API [application program interface], a product that's been around for 15 years, that's well entrenched and no longer really evolving. And the database has all those aspects. Talk to customers—the Oracle license is probably one of their most painful [investments], other than maybe their Windows license. For what they have to pay they're getting some of the least value from it.

Ken Jacobs, VP of product strategy at Oracle, disagreed with Harvey about commoditization and felt that it did not apply to the database business:

> A commodity is a product that is undifferentiated, where all the products are the same, suppliers come and go at ease and customers can switch easily from one to another. None of the above is true about software in general, and in particular, is not true about the database market.[11]

Customers and Market Segments

MySQL initially appealed to the rapidly growing number of Web application developers during the Internet boom era. Customers were often small start-ups or individuals developing components or products to enable Web sites and services. Decisions to select a database were often less focused on long-term strategy but rather driven by rapid prototyping needs with low upfront costs and a short-term horizon. As it quickly became a part of the LAMP software stack, MySQL seemed a natural choice for users who wanted standard, open software components at a low cost. Many Internet-enabled companies like Google, Yahoo!, Amazon, and Travelocity were very familiar with LAMP open source software. They had become large corporations, exploiting open source not only through low component cost, but also by modifying the sources to meet specific needs and enhancing the customer experience on their Web sites.

Paul Meyers, CEO of CanyonBridge (a 12-employee software company) in Orem, Utah, outlined his reasons for selecting MySQL. According to Meyers, MySQL had a great reputation that included excellent marketing, big customer names like Google, and a large installed base. He liked their flexible dual licensing model and felt that MySQL offered a large and advantageous performance-to-price ratio that made his company more competitive in the marketplace.[12]

Traditional large corporations, however, embraced MySQL to a much lesser extent than Linux. MySQL was used in less strategic subsystems, if at all. A key reason for this might have been lack of functionality for large enterprise business computing needs. SAP's ERP application, for instance, did not run on MySQL. Other reasons included lack of support and an intense vendor relationship.

---

[11]These and the following quotes from an interview with Ken Jacobs, VP of product strategy, Oracle, March 8, 2004.

[12]These and the following quotes from an interview with Paul Meyers, CEO, CanyonBridge, March 17, 2004.

In a panel at the Open Source Business Conference,[13] CIOs from various large organizations supported the idea that vendor support and relationships were important. They explained their criteria for selecting system software (e.g., server OS, DBMS). Marc West, CIO of Electronic Arts commented, "We buy from Red Hat[14] so that someone picks up the phone. We don't care about discount but we want service. We are the internal salespeople for the external vendors. It's very much a relationship business." William Rachmiel, IT manager at McKesson, added a slightly more skeptical viewpoint to the discussion: "We're conservative. We want to buy from people who are around next year. MySQL? Does anybody support this?"

All CIOs on the panel pointed out that, if service and long-term relationships were provided, open source products were not much different from what they were used to. Before closed software became more widespread, large corporations used to write their own legacy software and hence were also able to view the sources of a software program. But they would "sleep better at night" if they had some of the authors on staff. When asked, Marc West said that open source software would be in the "memory stack" of Electronic Art's CEO—labeled as "commodity computing."

Many observers felt that MySQL wanted to move upmarket, selling to large corporations where more money could be earned. Customer Paul Meyer explained, "I think it's inevitable that MySQL will target large corporations. The question is whether this is compatible with serving small and medium enterprises. Can a company focus on both segments? I doubt it. My worry is that they will focus on extracting profits rather than remaining a fair team-player." Investor Kevin Harvey had a different view. "I can't imagine that it would make sense for the company to ever abandon its low-end commodity roots. That should always be a good market."

MySQL's Competitors

Zack Urlocker, MySQL's VP of marketing, explained the company's official position on competition:

> We compete against nonconsumption; there are 4 million active installations and 10 million downloads [of MySQL.] These are people who wouldn't have a database otherwise. We're selling to the commoditized market. We don't have all the bells and whistles, but it's

also 1 percent of the total cost of ownership. We're JetBlue against American Airlines.[15]

Jason Matusow, shared source manager at Microsoft, saw MySQL as a competitor to Microsoft's SQL Server business, targeting both small and medium enterprises as well as going upmarket.[16]

Ken Jacobs, Oracle's VP of product strategy, saw MySQL as a complement to Oracle's DBMS and believed it would take many years before MySQL would be a true competitor. He formulated Oracle's official position:

> Technically, in terms of capabilities, MySQL is a decade or more behind Oracle. For example, MySQL lacks many of the most basic relational database features . . . such as stored procedures, triggers, and views. MySQL has been useful for Web sites where the task involves serving up mostly static content, not for the more transaction processing and business intelligence applications that constitute the majority of enterprise database deployments. As a company, MySQL is doing a fantastic job of marketing itself, but as a practical matter, they are a complement, not a competitor, to Oracle's Database.

When MySQL launched a cluster solution[17] in April 2004, Oracle was again very keen to point out the technical inferiority of MySQL. Analysts, however, believed that Microsoft SQL Server's low price points and MySQL's free offerings gave Oracle's and IBM's corporate customers leverage to negotiate higher price discounts than in the past (despite lack of functionality).

At the same time, MySQL created a huge barrier to entry by using the dual licensing model. Michael Olson, CEO of open source company Sleepycat, explained the mechanism which applied to his company as well as to MySQL:

> Who else can compete with it [an OSS product] once you have that amount of penetration in the marketplace? And the fact that it has this dual license characteristic essentially prevents people from duplicating what we have. Why would they? So there are two classes of people that

---

[13]OSBC Open Source Business Conference 2004, San Francisco, March 16–17, 2004.

[14]Red Hat sells LINUX though it is freely available elsewhere.

[15]SD Times, "Free, as in for Profit," New York, February 15, 2004.

[16]These and the following quotes from an interview with Jason Matusow, March 17, 2004.

[17]A cluster solution helps to run DBMS on several, distributed server processors at a time. The benefit is to scale modularly without creating the need to purchase faster processors if demand for computation capacity rises. This complex feature is targeted at large-scale enterprise data warehouses of large corporations and would be of little to no use to small enterprises.

might want to compete with this. One is open source developers, and they can't possibly release something under better open source terms than we do, so why should they waste their time? Anyone who wants to compete commercially has to match up or beat us for price, and in a lot of circumstances our price is zero. So the only way to beat us on price is to pay people to use the software, and that's . . .[18]

In product evaluations, customers defined performance, stability/reliability, functionality/ease of use, and cost as the main evaluation criteria for DBMS. The license price was of minor importance because implementing and switching costs drove total cost of ownership far beyond the license price. Furthermore, different customers ranked these criteria in different orders. In Exhibit 6 we describe typical DBMS product evaluations.

Complements Drive the Success of Open Source Products

A driving force behind open source was the support that it received from companies that saw it as a good business opportunity for their existing business. The success of Linux did not arise from its direct competition to Windows NT in terms of product features, price, channel availability or others. Linux's success originated in support from companies that saw it as an important complement to their products. By bundling with free Linux they captured more value in their layer of the IT value stack (see Exhibit 7) and drove out value from the server OS category, especially at the expense of Microsoft. From a product standpoint, these companies were happy to support Windows NT instead of Linux. From a business standpoint, the fact that Linux was free, open source and was not owned by any single company provided great advantages. This set-up was a built-in mechanism to prevent any server OS vendor from becoming the predominant force in the industry. IBM's Scott Handy listed Linux's advantages: bigger than any single vendor—hardware and vendor independent—great momentum.[19]

Aside from SAP, important MySQL partners included Veritas, Novell, and Sun—all of which did not offer their own DBMS products. Robert Soderbery, VP

of business development, explained Veritas's support for diversity in the database segment:

> Veritas believes that competition and choice are important in the database marketplace. MySQL provides the customer with solutions for applications which have commodity database requirements. In those areas, it succeeds by a focus on low cost, basic features and flexibility due to the open source development model. Veritas benefits by seeing greater diversity in the database layer. That greater diversity drives higher value for Veritas's value proposition of simplifying the management of heterogeneous IT infrastructures and improves Veritas's strategic position vis-à-vis the vendors that incorporate database offerings.[20]

A driving force was the structure of the IT value stack as a whole. One view, supported by MySQL, was that the Internet facilitated the emergence of distributed architectures with smaller, more lean, and heterogeneous components that resulted in large networks and clusters. Another view, supported by Oracle, pointed to the difficulties posed by a lack of consolidation and seamless integration. Ken Jacobs, VP of product strategy at Oracle, explained that "point solutions drive incredibly high costs, decreasing maintenance efficiency and increasing total cost of ownership. As a result, companies find true value in integration between the database and the application server, for instance."

In effect, this question touched the fundamentals of the IT industry, which had been organized in horizontal layers since the triumph of the modular PC architecture. With a strategy dubbed "embrace and extend," Microsoft has started to leverage its dominance in the OS and office categories into other software categories. It did so by introducing strategic incompatibilities and bundling products. Support for open source products by software vendors is often understood as a reaction to this policy.

SAP and MySQL Join Forces

In June 2003, MySQL announced an alliance with SAP AG, the world's largest vendor of ERP software with €7,025m ($8,781m) in revenues in 2003. This was MySQL's most important alliance. The companies cooperated on developing and marketing enterprise class open source DBMS, merging MySQL and SAP's own SAP

[18]These and the following quotes from an interview with Michael Olson, CEO of Sleepycat, March 1, 2004.

[19]Scott Handy, Keynote OSBC conference, March 16, 2004.

[20]Interview with Robert Soderbery on February 10, 2004.

EXHIBIT 6 | DBMS Product Evaluation

The main evaluation criteria for DBMS were performance, stability/reliability, functionality/ease of use, and cost. The license price was of minor importance because implementing and switching costs drove total cost of ownership far beyond the license price. Different customers ranked criteria in different order.

Dwight B. Clark, from a NASA procurement office, revealed his order of importance when evaluating for the future strategic DBMS platform by testing different products in-house: "Initial cost, implementation cost, conversion cost, maintenance cost, conversion time frame, retrieval speed, hardware resources required, security, industry acceptance, standard adherence, maintainability, robustness, and ease of use."[a]

Another evaluation study for a large Swiss insurance company, conducted by external consultants who relied on third-party information rather than their own tests listed: "Performance, adaptability to existing infrastructure, market share, functionality, complexity of administration, interoperability, ability to migrate data from SQL Server 7, and education."[b]

Performance

In an independent benchmark conducted by eWEEK publication in 2002, five RDBMS products were tested with the fictional bookstore application NILE simulating up to 2,000 concurrent users requesting access simultaneously to the database. The database contained 20 million book records and 5 million customer records, roughly equivalent to the data volume of Amazon.com. Though Oracle outperformed all other databases, MySQL could secure a close second, leaving products from IBM, Sybase, and Microsoft in a JSP (Java) Environment far behind.[c] While the insurer's evaluation also quoted the eWEEK benchmark, Ken Jacobs, VP of product strategy at Oracle, discounted the relevance of this benchmark claiming that an apples-to-apples comparison would have greatly increased Oracle's performance advantage. In NASA's own "benchmark environment, MySQL exceeded the performance of Oracle by an average of 40 percent," said Clark.

Stability and Reliability

NASA's Clark commented: "Research indicated that [MySQL's] stability and reliability was at worse equal to the other commercial off-the-shelf products, and that finding has been proven in the [. . .] application experience." The consultants authoring the insurer's evaluation looked at market share to measure reliability, and referred to Gartner's research (Exhibit 8), which did not display MySQL's unit share of market due to its insignificant revenues.

Functionality and Ease of Use

NASA's decision was to employ only standardized SQL statements. Therefore, "in our application environment there is no difference in ease of use. However from a Sys Admin and implementation perspective, MySQL requires far less resources and time to configure and maintain," said Clark. The insurer's study claimed that there were many fewer functionality and administration tools available for MySQL than for Oracle, but pointed to the availability of third-part products to overcome this weakness (i.e., SQL Porter or Chyfo Pro for migration needs).

Price

While the former criteria did not reveal greater than 10 times the difference in benefits between the products, the price criteria certainly did: MySQL, distributed under the GNU General Public License (GPL) was free, while Oracle charged between $195 and $1,099 per named user. If MySQL was used commercially, the per-user license fee was around $5 to $10. Server licenses (as used in the NILE benchmark) from Oracle were $40,000 compared to MySQL at $495 (see Exhibit 9 for license fee price points). While NASA was under heavy cost pressure due to budget constraints, the insurer's study did not consider cost at all in its evaluation.

Final Evaluation

Due to the lock-in and high switching costs of a DBMS, it was very important that the chosen platform be available and supported for a long period of time. Besides demonstrated product value, vendors who had a long history, a strong brand, and a large installed base had a key positional advantage over new entrants. Much perception arises also from the presence of the vendor's name in media and at conferences, as well as having cross-references from peers. While Oracle, IBM, and Microsoft all represent top brands, MySQL seemed to have a good standing with younger, Web-oriented programmers, who grew up with MySQL's ubiquity in the Web. Clark saw "a generational difference" in the customer base.

Decision

Due to lowest total cost of ownership, NASA's MSFC decided to migrate from Oracle to MySQL.

Due to Oracle's high market share and completeness of the product, the insurance company decided to migrate from SQL Server to Oracle. Microsoft was disqualified due to its attempt to lock the customer into their ASP (i.e. not Java-compatible) platform. MySQL was disqualified for its "open source limitations, especially for mission critical and enterprise applications," without specifying what these limitations were.

---

[a]These and the following quotes from interview with Dwight B. Clark, IT manager, procurement office, NASA Marshall Space Flight Center, March 16, 2004.

[b]The source of this study is anonymous.

[c]eWEEK, Timothy Dick/Sahil Gambhir, Server Databases Clash, March 26, 2002. While Microsoft's SQL Server performed rather poorly in a Java environment, an ASP test netted much better results. It is clear that SQL Server is optimized for Microsoft's own .NET environment.

EXHIBIT 6A | RDBMS License Fees

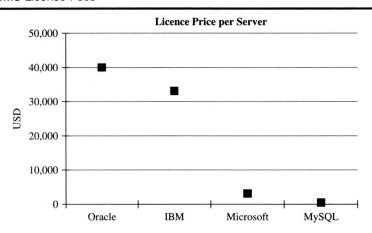

Licence Price per Server

Oracle	Distributor Website	Unit Price	Price per User
Oracle Standard Edition One 1 Processor 5 User	Oracle.com	$5,995	$1,199
Oracle Standard Edition One 1 Named User[a]	Oracle.com	$195	$195
Oracle Enterprise Edition One 1 Processor 25 User	Oracle.com	$40,000	$1,600
Oracle Enterprise Edition One 1 Named User	Oracle.com	$800	$800

IBM			
DB2 Personal 1 User	ibm.com	$461	$461
DB2 Workgroup Server Edition 1 User	ibm.com	$311	$311
DB2 Enterprise Server Edition 1 Processor*	ibm.com	$33,125	$663

Microsoft

Microsoft			
SQL Server 2000 Standard—5 User	Electronic Universe	$855	$171
SQL Server 2000 Standard—10 User	nextag.com	$1,065	$107
SQL Server 2000 Standard—25 User	thebestpricing.net	$1,999	$80
SQL Server 2000 Enterprise—1 Processor*	nextag.com	$3,150	$63

MySQL			
GNU General Public License (GPL)	mysql.com	$0	$0
Classic—1 Server*	mysql.com	$250	$5
Pro—1 Server*	mysql.com	$495	$10

*Estimated User/Server Processor: 50

Source: Websites of companies and distributors as of January 25, 2004.

[a]Named User licensing means that any potential user for a database application needs to hold a license. All other products are licensed by concurrent users, i.e., only the number of any users working at the same time is decisive for the numbers of licenses. The concurrent factor can be between 2 to 10, depending on the nature of the application, driving the per-user license cost of Oracle by factor 2 to 10 to obtain comparable results to all other products.

EXHIBIT 7 |

The IT Value Stack

Andy Grove's IT Value Stack[*]**—Revisited in Early 2004**

		Microsoft		IBM		Open Source	
Service	e-Commerce	Etc.	Etc.	eBay	Amazon	Google	Yahoo!
	Professional Services	Accenture		BearingPoint	IBM (PWC)	HP	etc.
	Network Services	MSN/Hotmail		ComCast	AOL	etc.	Yahoo!
Software	Web Server	IIS		Apache			
	Applications ERP	Great Plains	SAP		Oracle	PeopleSoft	etc.
	Office	MS Office				Open Office	
	Languages	C++/C#		Eclipse	etc.	Java	Perl
	Application Server	.NET	Websphere	Oracle	SAP	BEA	jBoss
	Database	SQL Server	DB2		Oracle		MySQL
	Operating Sys Server	Windows 2000/NT		UNIX		Linux	
	Desktop	Windows 2000/XP				Mac	Linux
Hardware	Peripherals	Epson	IBM	Etc.	Etc.	HP	
	Assembled Hardware	Dell		IBM	Sun	HP (Compaq)	
	Microprocessors	Intel			Moto	AMD	Etc.

Zoom – Strategic Enterprise Software Stack

		Microsoft	IBM	Oracle	SAP
	Sales & Services	Channel	Own	Own/Partner	Own/Partner
Software	ERP	Proprietary	Proprietary	Proprietary	Proprietary
	Application Server	Proprietary	Proprietary	Proprietary	Proprietary
	Database	Proprietary	Proprietary	Proprietary	Open Source
	Operating System	Proprietary	Open Source	Open Source	Open Source
	Hardware	Intel	Own/Intel	Agnostic	Agnostic

Source: Compiled by case authors from a variety of different sources.

[*]From Saloner, Shepard, Podolny, *Strategic Management*, New York, 2001, quoting from: Andrew S. Grove, *Only the Paranoid Survive*, New York, 1996 et. al.

DB into one distribution channel. SAP's stated intention was to pull out of the DBMS business altogether.

Observers believed SAP's motivation was to build leverage against Oracle. The two companies had an ambiguous relationship: On one side, SAP was a fierce competitor to number two Oracle in the ERP space. On the other side, it was a large distributor of Oracle's DBMS with 20 percent of Oracle's DBMS sold for SAP installations. Insiders familiar with the industry estimated that two-thirds of SAP's 70,000 installations ran on Oracle.[21] As Oracle cross-subsidized its weak ERP business with its high DBMS margins, SAP was looking for several leverage points. One was to support Microsoft in developing SQL Server to an enterprise class DBMS in the 1990s. Another opportunity came up,

when Software AG intended to discontinue its database product ADABAS-D.

In 1994, SAP licensed ADABAS-D broadly to continue providing their customers a high-end DBMS choice, then called SAP DB, putting 50+ developers behind the product. While management had initially hoped to grow the DBMS business and to expand SAP DB beyond Germany, it consequently saw its already small share of only 5 percent of SAP's users relying on SAP DB decline continuously. The decision in 2000 to go open source and distribute SAP DB for free did not stop the decline, as the product lacked a community. Eventually management decided to pull out of the DBMS business and entered into an agreement with MySQL.

SAP and MySQL started to work jointly on building the next-generation open source enterprise-class DBMS. A long-term product road map determined the development of MySQL's software according to SAP's customers' needs, phasing out SAP DB eventually. Bill Claybrook,

---

[21]20 percent run on Microsoft's SQL server, less than 10 percent on IBM's DB2.

research director, Linux and open source, Aberdeen Group, commented:

> The partnership between SAP and MySQL will put one of the largest open source communities and one of the world's largest software companies firmly behind the development of a free open source database for large commercial applications. This validates the potential for open source software to extend beyond the operating system level to power business-critical database applications.[22]

Zia Yusuf, SVP of SAP's Corporate Consulting Team, noted that the partnership with SAP would enable MySQL to become a player in the enterprise class database market. MySQL could immediately start creating a community around the enterprise-class, high-performance SAP DB (now MaxDB by MySQL), and increase market penetration. To serve large corporations, MySQL needed to build—with SAP's help—its own support and service infrastructure, suited for global corporations with around-the-clock service requirements in different languages.[23]

Oracle's Ken Jacobs commented: "That's certainly an interesting move on their part. It's not at all clear that this changes the game. MySQL may in fact find itself a little bit distracted with having two products. It's not a winning strategy, typically, to have two products in the same space."

Both MySQL revenues and SAP DB's percentage share in SAP installations increased sharply since the start of the alliance in June 2003 (see Exhibit 5). Estimates of observers familiar with the products indicated that MySQL would need another three to four years to become an enterprise-class player with its own products. Some insiders saw a "clash of cultures" between SAP's staff developers and MySQL's distributed home office workers. At first, one SAP developer described MySQL's developers as "lunatics." Both parties, however, noticed that great progress had since been made to bring the two cultures together into a productive alliance.

MySQL's Business Model

Open source helped MySQL lower its production and distribution costs and enabled a culture that allowed for a virtual organization, where some 120 employees,

scattered around 17 countries, were held together mainly by e-mail and Internet communication. This gave the company a global presence at a low cost.

The Development Cycle

Unlike first-generation, nonprofit OSS projects such as Linux, Apache, or PostgreSQL, all lines of code of MySQL were exclusively written by employees of MySQL. What started as an accidental fact, turned out to be beneficial, as the monolithic structure of a DBMS made uncoordinated work of many people on a very small and compact kernel very difficult. Furthermore the customers liked MySQL to take ownership in the software they produce. Last but not least it enabled the dual licensing model, as the company owned all of the intellectual property of MySQL. Writing and owning all code through one company made MySQL (like all second-generation OSS products) a *proprietary* software, while Linux (and all first-generation OSS products) are effectively *nonproprietary,* that is, they are not owned by a single vendor.

MySQL did not have significant cost advantages of being OSS until it released its new product version in a preliminary alpha release. Once this was available (along with the last fully released version), the community tested the product in its applications and generated bug lists and change requests. MySQL reacted to these requests in a timely fashion and obtained a heavily tested product by the time the version was fully released. While it was difficult to generalize the cost savings compared to a closed software company's in-house testing, MySQL estimated that development costs were arguably lower by 60 to 80 percent. This was significant as a product such as a DBMS relied on being very stable in a multitude of environments. This model also increased the number of potential releases making MySQL able to react faster to changes in the marketplace than closed source vendors (see Exhibit 10). Mickos elaborated:

> People think that open source means that everybody is contributing code. Code is just 10 or 5 or 1 percent of the total production cost of the product. So at MySQL, we produce the code ourselves. When we release a new version, within 24 hours 35,000 people have downloaded and tested it. That's fantastic. Not even Microsoft has 35,000 QA engineers. Even if Microsoft had, they would need another 3,500 managers to manage them. Just based on statistics, we know that there are enough

---

[22]Press release, "MySQL AB and SAP AG Partner to Bring New Open Source Database Technologies to the Enterprise," MySQL AB, May 27, 2003.

[23]Interview with Zia Yusuf, March 17, 2004.

EXHIBIT 10 |
MySQL's Virtuous
Development Cycle

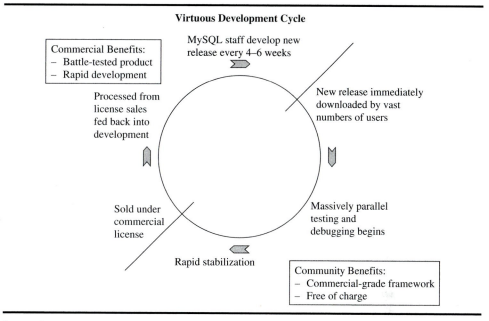

Source: Company's Web site as of March 5, 2004.

people out there who certainly test all relevant features, without our specific instruction.

Microsoft's Jason Matusow, shared source manager, explained the problems that he saw with MySQL's testing process and why Microsoft's process was superior:

> Microsoft has two testers for every developer, systematically testing the code. This is not only in the core, but also in the periphery of the product where community testing often lags because it is not "cool" to work in these areas. Community testers have no systematic approach to quality assurance which becomes more important in highly integrated advanced application development environments.

> When it comes to binary testing, i.e., to get the product out and tested in many different environments by users rather than developers, Microsoft's products similarly profit from the law of large numbers. For any software provider, it is extremely helpful when users of the software are finding and reporting flaws. Additionally, we work closely with our Shared Source customers, who have source-level access, as well. We receive detailed bug reports, which improve our response times for our customers and represent cost-savings for us. Open source software is certainly a way to defray R&D cost. Microsoft takes advantage of it through its Shared Source initiative.

Members of the open source community were usually software professionals, working either on their own during their free time or paid by their employers (i.e., IBM's 600 Linux technology center employees). Free contribution was motivated by at least two factors—indirect tangible benefits and intangible benefits. The tangible benefits included receiving a patch or fix within a few days by identifying and reporting bugs to MySQL. Instead, a closed code vendor might release a new version of their software every year or so. The more intangible benefits included exposure to the latest technological trends, access to social networks, or the sense of being part of an underdog (taking on Microsoft).

Sales and Marketing

MySQL's strength was great brand awareness among customers. This had been achieved through viral Web marketing within the developer community and extensive press coverage of open source products during the rise of Linux—both at a very low cost. By allowing customers to download products from its Web site, MySQL also had a very low-cost sales and distribution channel. Members of the developer community appreciated the free opportunity to download and evaluate MySQL products before they purchased a commercial version. MySQL added telesales capability and also hired account managers for large accounts. Account managers resold MySQL in volume to such customers as Novell and Veritas. While 53 percent of the units sold in 2003 had price points below $1,000 (yielding only 4 percent of the company's revenue), 69 percent of the company's revenue came from deals larger than $10,000. As of April 2004, the company had nine job openings on its Web site, all of them in sales functions around the globe, indicating that MySQL was active in building a distributed, direct sales force.

Kevin Harvey, a partner at Benchmark Capital, saw MySQL's customer acquisition model as a key competitive advantage that could be scaled upmarket:

> At the very least we should have an advantaged means of acquiring customers. Customer acquisition is a big cost, one of the biggest for any software company. We should have a much larger inside sales force than Oracle. We don't have to come and convince the customer, introduce them to a product, and convince them to buy it. People are already using the product. It's free. They already like the product. We should only spend time on the ones that have used the free software, decided they like it, and would like to order it.

Michael Olson, CEO of open source DBMS Sleepycat, whose company only sold at price points above $100,000, confirmed how an open source strategy could indeed minimize the cost-of-sales: "At Sleepycat, open source is a distribution strategy. It's not a development model. It's really our sales and marketing model, to get us visible and in the market in a way that we never could do if we spent huge sums of marketing dollars. So our cost-of-sales is actually quite low."

Service and Support

The developer community also provided a dynamic support resource and a source of add-ons for all other users of MySQL. E-mail lists, Web sites, newsgroups, conferences, and published books provided up-to-date information about the product and its features. Plug-ins or add-ons, developed under the GPL, enhanced the product without consuming resources from MySQL. MySQL also did not need to provide printed manuals. This created an ecosystem around the product without straining MySQL's resources.

MySQL's Virtual Organization

From the outset, the founders worked from their home offices and communicated mainly by e-mail and Internet communication. This virtual organization

gave MySQL an advantage in acquiring the best-suited developers from the OSS community since their physical location was unimportant. The company had low screening and selection costs by hiring developers that had already proven their skills in the OSS community. Having established a global presence from day one, MySQL developers represented many backgrounds and perspectives, promoting a high level of innovation and sensitivity towards new trends around the globe.

In 2004, the company had seven office locations in Scandinavia, the United States. Germany, and Russia. Three-quarters of MySQL's 120 employees worked from their home offices in 17 different countries. The management team was spread out over four countries. Only in Menlo Park, California, did two management team members (CEO and VP of marketing) share the same location.

Mårten Mickos understood that not everybody could work in this type of organization:

> We naturally have to hire people with robust personalities because we are not there sitting with them all the time. We have no joint coffee breaks and we can't be physically present encouraging our employees every day. Maybe here our Scandinavian heritage plays in because we must have people who can just go out in the forest and ski around there for three weeks, and hunt bears and wolves and get back home, but manage on their own. It's a somewhat brutal way of organizing a team, but it works extremely well for those who are ready for it.

However, the virtual approach changed over time. Mickos explained:

> When I started with the company, Monty, the founder, said, 'We have no offices now and we will never have an office because that would destroy the company culture.' But we did set up offices. I think that was some sort of a change. We have physical offices now, and scaling from here to 500 and 1,000 [employees] might just ease the pain, because we'll have hubs [and need to travel less].

Although management traveled extensively, other members of the organization met in person only once a year in annual meetings. E-mail and Internet Relay Chat (IRC) were the most important means of communication. The company committed resources and time to enhancing e-mail communication skills and teaching employees how to efficiently communicate with a medium that was often seen as less than optimal for communication. In an effort to keep costs low, MySQL tested IP phones and desktop video conferencing only in 2003 among a selected group of employees.

Setting strategy in such a virtual organization was a challenge. Mickos admitted that this could not be done through MySQL's typical communication modes:

> If you need to change the strategy of the company, how do you do that? [Can] you send an e-mail saying, 'This is the CEO, and we're now changing from databases to operating systems,' and then trying to get that message across? So we end up having clear strategies that we set up at the meetings where we physically meet. Then we don't change much in terms of direction because it can be so difficult to get the message across.

Mickos was also faced with the challenge of overseeing and managing employees across the company's vast virtual network:

> Because of our distributed organization structure, we have to coordinate work in a different way. First, we do little micromanagement and instead focus on fostering a culture of mutual trust and high discipline. Roles and job descriptions have to be defined clearly as the person will not receive day-to-day guidance except over e-mail and phone.

Conclusion: The Challenges Ahead

Mickos was aware of the challenges he faced in growing MySQL to a $100 million company. While difficult for any company, Mickos had to deal with the added complexity of having employees scattered around the globe. Investors were closely scrutinizing MySQL's challenge of growing sales. The current strategy constrained Mickos to keep costs low, as this was key to MySQL's competitive advantage.

Mickos also wondered whether the MySQL brand could be stretched from an easy-to-use, low-cost DBMS to an enterprise-class DBMS enabled to run SAP's sophisticated products. Would the product road map that MySQL had committed towards SAP cause conflict with the interests of other customers? Would the grass-root OSS community learn to live with terms like "total cost of ownership (TCO)" on their Web site? By aligning with SAP, Mickos had gained the attention of giants such as Oracle and IBM. While there were huge benefits to the alliance with SAP, Mickos pondered the potential downsides.

Mickos was confident that a large market for commodity databases existed. He recognized, however, that the power balance between competitors and complementary players in the industry would change enormously if his strategy worked. That shift would trigger seismic forces that could easily overwhelm a company as small as MySQL was.

PART 5

Convergence or Collision—Take I: Computing Meets Cellular Phone and Consumer Electronics

"Intel Beyond 2003: Looking for Its Third Act" examines Intel's efforts to redefine itself as an "Internet building block company" since Craig Barrett took over from Andy Grove as CEO in 1998, and the company's strategic actions during the Internet "boom" followed by the "bust" of the early 2000s. In 1998, Intel's top management believed that the company was well positioned to capitalize on the convergence between computing, communications, and consumer electronics and spent over $10 billion to acquire companies with technologies needed to become a world leader in telecommunications infrastructure and wireless communications. During 1998 and 2003, Intel was also trying to reposition itself as a "platform" rather than a "component" company in its various businesses, and to develop new performance vectors beyond processor speed to accommodate more varied "usage models." While in 2003 the company was struggling to cope with a severe recession in both its core computing and new communications market segments, top management nevertheless decided to keep up its multibillion-dollar investments in new manufacturing technology and capacity to be ready for the upturn.

Important discussion topics for this case are (1) maintaining execution discipline during executive succession (2) learning from new business development efforts, (3) reassessing positioning and distinctive competence in the face of industry conversion and changing customer needs, and (4) examining the implications of "capacity equals strategy." In terms of our three key themes, this case offers an example of how *P*-controlled change may morph into limited change and *P*-independent change; it shows the difficulties of aligning strategy and action when the company attempts to diversify into new product-market segments; and it shows how industry dynamics may require a company to once again seek to transform itself.

"Nokia Beyond 2003: A Mobile Gatekeeper?" discusses the strategic challenges facing a company that was the dominant maker of cell phones around the world. While still in a position of strength in 2003, the company faced the slow arrival and uncertain consumer reception of the so-called third generation (3G) of mobile technology. In addition, there was uncertainty about which type of 3G technology would dominate. As mobile communication devices become more intelligent, such as Web-enabled phones with PDA capability, video games, and the like, the importance of handset operating systems greatly increased. By 2003, Microsoft entered the mobile phone market segment with its own handset operating system. This posed a major challenge to Nokia's dominance in mobile phone handset operating systems and, more broadly, to its highly successful vertically integrated strategy. In addition, it could be expected that the major service operators would begin to assert their power derived from owning the end-customer relationship more strongly in the battle of providing an increasingly rich menu of services.

Important discussion topics for this case are (1) analyzing industry conversion or collision, (2) understanding the evolving basis of competitive advantage when industries converge, (3) being clear about the company's evolving value proposition, and (4) adapting a winning strategy, organization, and culture. In terms of our three key themes, this case offers another example of *P*-controlled change morphing into limited change and even *P*-independent change; it shows the pressure of environmental change on the alignment of strategy and action; and it shows how uncertainty associated with industry convergence makes it difficult to clearly see the path for optimal corporate transformation.

"Samsung Electronics in 2004: Conquering the Wireless Digital World" looks at the strategic choices facing Samsung as it tried to secure a winning position in the new consumer electronics (CE) market segment, especially the "digital home" of the future. Digital CE products were expected to proliferate based on new interoperability standards that would allow any content to be played on any device. The digital home was at the intersection of three industries: computers, mobile communications, and CE. In each of these intersecting industries giant companies were solidly entrenched. A battle had started between a vertical industry model promoted by traditional CE companies (such as Sony and Philips) and cellular manufacturers eager to defend their market shares (such as Nokia), and a horizontal model advocated by information technology (IT) companies such as Intel and Microsoft, eager to reproduce the situation that had made their fortune in the PC world. While already a world leader in semiconductor memory businesses, Samsung had also set its sights on surpassing Intel to become the leading semiconductor company in the world.

Important discussion topics for this case are (1) managing corporate transformation, (2) managing the scope of corporate strategy, (3) relating culture and corporate strategy, and (4) competing and collaborating in the new consumer electronics industry. In terms of our three key themes, this case offers an example of both *P*-controlled change and the potential for runaway change; it shows how top management can align strategic action with strategy to achieve great success fairly rapidly; and it offers the opportunity to examine corporate transformation in advance of major industry change.

"The New, New HP in 2004 (A): Leading Strategic Integration" examines the challenges and opportunities facing HP subsequent to completing and integrating its merger with Compaq, and the new ways in which HP intends to utilize its postmerger asset base to better compete in the converging computing, communications, and consumer electronics industries. The case describes HP's new leadership framework and operating model to help the company capitalize on its scale and scope to improve its marketing strengths, achieve focused innovation, and develop a high level of strategic integration among the core businesses.

Important discussion topics for this case are (1) examining strategic leadership issues in corporate transformation, (2) identifying growth vectors for a multibusiness corporation, (3) achieving strategic integration, (4) managing strategy content and strategy process, and (5) identifying key elements of a corporate (multibusiness) strategy. In terms of our three key themes, this case provides an example of efforts to achieve *P*-controlled change; it shows the importance of formulating a clear corporate strategy to align strategic action throughout the organization; and it raises additional issues about leading corporate transformation in the face of major industry changes, especially about how to pursue the vertical and horizontal dimensions of the corporate strategy simultaneously and effectively.

The companion case, "The New, New HP in 2004 (B): Winning in the Core Business" discusses the competitive challenges and opportunities HP faces in each of its core businesses: imaging and printing, computers (consumer and enterprise), and IT services. It can be taught independently of the (A) case, and even in reverse order if both cases are used. Important discussion topics for this case that help deepen the discussion of the (B) case are (1) business-level strategic logic, (2) generic strategies and disciplines of market leaders, and (3) strategic collaboration between businesses with different strategic logics. Each of the three key themes could also be discussed at the level of each of the businesses. ●

Case 4.1

Intel Beyond 2003: Looking for Its Third Act

There are no second acts in American lives.
—F. Scott Fitzgerald, *The Last Tycoon*

Introduction

There had been a second act for Intel. The company first came to prominence under the leadership of Robert Noyce, co-inventor of the integrated circuit,[1] and Gordon E. Moore, who first described the phenomenon, later called "Moore's Law,"[2] that has governed integrated circuit development since 1965. Intel had been the pioneering maker of computer memory chips in the 1970s.[3] When this market became commoditized in the mid-1980s, and pressures from Japanese memory chip manufacturers marginalized the company, Intel had been forced to look for its next big idea. The company found it in what had started as a small side project for Intel early in its history: microprocessors. In 1985, Intel bet the company on developing and selling leading-edge microprocessors that powered the rapid rise of personal computers (PCs).

Under the direction of Andrew S. Grove, who succeeded Gordon Moore as CEO in 1987, Intel became a major driver of the development of the PC market segment. Intel dominated the market segment for microprocessors, winning up to a 90 percent share of the PC segment of that market. Operating systems produced by Microsoft attained similar market share in the PC segment. Together, Intel and Microsoft created the so-called "Wintel" standard that made both companies extraordinarily valuable.[4] For most of the 1990s, microprocessors for PCs represented more than 80 percent of Intel's annual revenue and all of its profits. Intel and its investors became accustomed to extraordinary success as the company rode a 15-year wave of exploding growth in demand for its microprocessors. Through most of the 1990s, Intel's annual revenue grew at a compound annual growth rate (CAGR) of 25 percent, reaching a peak CAGR of 36 percent in 1996. By 1998, however, sales of PCs and the microprocessors that powered them began to slow. In 2000, revenue grew by only 15 percent, and dropped by 21 percent in 2001. Intel's operations, apart from its core PC microprocessor activities, were losing money (Exhibit 1).

As of 1997, Craig Barrett, Intel's COO at the time, became concerned about the company's growth depending entirely on microprocessors for the PC market segment. He also worried that the microprocessor business had become, for Intel, like a "creosote bush": a desert

---

[1]Robert Noyce, then of Fairchild Semiconductor, and Jack S. Kilby, of Texas Instruments (TI), both independently created designs and prototypes for an integrated circuit (IC) within a few months of each other in 1958/1959. After an extended and complicated legal wrangling over the patent, an appeals court found for Noyce. However, both inventors agreed that the other was a genuine co-inventor and Fairchild and TI agreed to cross license the IC. Robert Noyce died in 1990. Jack Kilby was awarded one-half of the 2000 Nobel Prize in Physics in recognition for his "part in inventing the integrated circuit." Nobel Prizes are not awarded posthumously.

[2]Gordon E. Moore, "Cramming More Components onto Integrated Circuits," *Electronics*, April 19, 1965. Moore's Law describes the exponential growth in the number of transistors that could occur on an integrated circuit every year or two, and predicts its continuation—which has held true for over 35 years. The impact of Moore's Law was predicted (presciently) in a cartoon in that 1965 article which depicted "Handy Home Computers" being sold next to notions and cosmetics in a department store.

[3]Intel's first products, a static random access memory (SRAM) chips and later a dynamic random access memory (DRAM) chips, were designed to replace the magnetic core memory then standard on mainframe computers.

---

[4]For an in-depth review and analysis of key strategic events at Intel including its exit from the memory business and entrance into the PC microprocessor business, see R. A. Burgelman, *Strategy Is Destiny*, (New York: Free Press, 2002).

EXHIBIT 1 | Intel Selected Summary Financial Information

Operating Segment Information

($ millions)	Q3 2002	Q2 2002	Q1 2002	Q4 2001	Q3 2001	Q2 2001	Q1 2001	Q4 2000	Q3 2000	Full Year 2001	Full Year 2000
Intel Architecture Group											
Revenues	5,407	5,213	5,768	5,793	5,393	5,127	5,133	6,851	7,039	21,446	27,301
Operating profit	1,405	1,362	1,802	1,813	1,329	1,444	1,666	3,211	3,347	6,252	12,511
Intel Communications Group											
Revenues	482	536	518	590	580	635	775	924	948	2,580	3,483
Operating loss	(177)	(127)	(150)	(129)	(218)	(235)	(153)	67	102	(735)	(319)
Wireless Communications and Computing Group											
Revenues	586	532	459	518	509	510	695	819	667	2,232	2,669
Operating loss	(30)	(98)	(68)	(20)	(59)	(158)	(19)	161	149	(256)	(608)
All other											
Revenues	29	38	36	82	63	62	74	108	77	281	273
Operating loss	(234)	(498)	(269)	(656)	(663)	(834)	(852)	(863)	(741)	(3,005)	(3,043)
Total											
Revenues	6,504	6,319	6,781	6,983	6,545	6,334	6,677	8,702	8,731	26,539	33,726
Operating profit	964	639	1,315	1,008	389	217	642	2,576	2,857	2,256	10,395

Intel Architecture Group products include microprocessors, motherboards and other related board-level products, including chipsets.

Intel Communications Group products include Ethernet connectivity products, network processing components, embedded control chips and optical components.

Wireless Communications and Computing Group products include flash memory, application processors and cellular chipsets for cellular handsets and handheld devices.

The "all other" category includes acquisition-related costs, including amortization of identified intangibles, in-process research and development, and write-offs of acquisition-related intangibles. The "all other" category also includes the results of the Web hosting business. In addition, the "all other" category includes certain corporate-level operating expenses, including a portion pf profit-dependent bonus and other expenses that are not allocated to the operating segments. In Q2 2002, "all other" included the charge for impairment of identified intangibles, primarily related to the previous acquisition of Xircom, as well as the charge related to winding down the Web hosting business. For quarters in 2001, "all other" includes goodwill amortization, whereas goodwill is no longer amortized beginning in 2002.

Source: Company reports.

(continued)

EXHIBIT 1 | Intel Selected Summary Financial Information (cont.)

Intel Percent of Revenue by Group 2001

Group	% Total Revenue 2001
Intel Architecture Group (IAG)	81
Intel Communications Group (ICG)	10
Wireless Communications and Computing Group (WCCG)	8.5
New Business Group (NBG)	0.5

Selected Financial Data 2001–1995

(in millions)

Year	Net Revenues	Cost of Sales	Research and Development	Operating Income	Net Income	Employees at Year End
2001	$26,539	$13,487	$3,796	$2,256	$1,291	83.4
2000	33,726	12,650	3,897	10,395	10,535	86.1
1999	29,389	11,836	3,111	9,767	7,314	70.2
1998	26,273	12,088	2,509	8,379	6,068	64.5
1997	25,070	9,945	2,347	9,887	6,945	63.7
1996	20,847	9,164	1,808	7,553	5,157	48.5
1995	16,202	7,811	1,296	5,252	3,566	41.6

Source: Company reports.

plant that poisons the ground around it so that no other plants can grow nearby. Barrett succeeded Andy Grove as Intel's CEO in 1998. Under his direction Intel began to search for growth in areas beyond its core PC microprocessor market segment, redefining itself as an Internet building block company. He also initiated executive development programs to augment Intel's leadership capability for new business development.

Over the next several years, Intel spent more than $10 billion in acquisitions, buying companies in the communications and networking industries, and also invested heavily in Internet-related services. Several billions of dollars of those investments came to nothing, as Intel bought its way into markets it soon exited. Nevertheless, by 2002 Intel's corporate strategy had broadened to encompass three strategic business areas: Intel Architecture Group (IAG), which created building blocks for desktop, mobile and server businesses; Intel Communications Group (ICG), which sold building blocks to the telecommunications industry; and Wireless Computing and Communications Group (WCCG), which sold building blocks to the wireless communications industry. General managers who were long-term Intel employees ran each of these businesses. Parallel to these business groups remained pow-

erful functional organizations: Intel Capital, Technology and Manufacturing Group (TMG), Sales and Marketing Group (SMG), Finance, and Human Resources, among others.

By late 2002, amid the most prolonged technology recession in the memories of Intel's long-serving senior executives, the company had refocused and was directing its financial and engineering muscle toward its new concept of the convergence of communications and computing at the chip level. Intel's new mission was now captured in six key words: Silicon Leadership, Architectural Innovation, and Worldwide Opportunity. Intel also decided to maintain its traditionally high levels of capital expenditure and R&D investments in order to be in a strong strategic position when the recession ended (Exhibit 2). Some financial analysts, however, had begun to question Intel's heavy capital investments. In November 2002, Intel's stock was trading at $18.80, down from $72.84 at its peak in July 2000, and the price/earnings (P/E) ratio was at a low of 47.96 in the trailing 12 months, compared to a 5-year high of 162.62 (Exhibit 3).[5]

---

[5]Intel stock price at market close on 15 November 2002. PE ratio comparisons as of 8 November, 2002.

EXHIBIT 1 | Intel Income Statement Data—Most Recent Seven Quarters

(In millions, except per share amounts)

	Q3 2002	Q2 2002	Q1 2002	Q4 2001	Q3 2001	Q2 2001	Q1 2001
INCOME:							
Net revenues	**$6,504**	**$6,319**	**$6,781**	**$6,983**	**$6,545**	**$6,334**	**$6,677**
Cost of sales	$3,331	$3,350	$3,301	$3,402	$3,553	$3,307	$3,225
Research and development	$1,006	$1,024	$982	$952	$930	$919	$995
Marketing, general and administrative	$1,095	$1,063	$1,072	$1,071	$1,064	$1,174	$1,155
Amortization of goodwill	$0	$0	$0	$405	$447	$417	$441
Amortization of acquisition-related intangibles and costs	$102	$229	$111	$145	$162	$177	$144
Purchased in-process research and development	$6	$14	$0	$0	$0	$123	$75
Operating costs and expenses	$5,540	$5,680	$5,466	$5,975	$6,156	$6,117	$6,035
Operating income	**$964**	**$639**	**$1,315**	**$1,008**	**$389**	**$217**	**$642**
Gains (losses) on equity securities, net	($96)	($59)	($46)	($287)	($182)	$3	$0
Interest and other	$49	$43	$48	$73	($70)	$126	$264
Income before taxes	**$917**	**$623**	**$1,317**	**$794**	**$137**	**$346**	**$906**
Income taxes	$231	$177	$381	$290	$31	$150	$421
Net income	**$686**	**$446**	**$936**	**$504**	**$106**	**$196**	**$485**
Basic earnings per share	**$0.10**	**$0.07**	**$0.14**	**$0.08**	**$0.02**	**$0.03**	**$0.07**
Diluted earnings per share	**$0.10**	**$0.07**	**$0.14**	**$0.07**	**$0.02**	**$0.03**	**$0.07**
Common shares outstanding	**6,646**	**6,677**	**6,684**	**6,698**	**6,718**	**6,725**	**6,721**
Common shares assuming dilution	**6,712**	**6,803**	**6,861**	**6,851**	**6,876**	**6,889**	**6,899**
Gross margin % of revenues	49%	47%	51%	51%	46%	48%	52%
Research & development % of revenues	15%	16%	14%	14%	14%	15%	15%
Marketing, general and administration % of revenues	17%	17%	16%	15%	16%	19%	17%
Income before taxes % of revenues	14%	10%	19%	11%	2%	5%	14%
Net income % of revenues	11%	7%	14%	7%	2%	3%	7%
Pro forma information excluding acquisition-related costs:							
Pro forma operating costs and expenses	$5,432	$5,437	$5,355	$5,425	$5,547	$5,400	$5,375
Pro forma operating Income	$1,072	$882	$1,426	$1,558	$998	$934	$1,302
Pro forma net income	**$768**	**$620**	**$1,022**	**$998**	**$655**	**$854**	**$1,099**
Basic EPS excluding acquisition-related costs	**$0.12**	**$0.09**	**$0.15**	**$0.15**	**$0.10**	**$0.13**	**$0.16**
Diluted EPS excluding acquisition-related costs	**$0.11**	**$0.09**	**$0.15**	**$0.15**	**$0.10**	**$0.12**	**$0.16**

Source: Company reports.

(continued)

EXHIBIT 1 | Intel Balance Sheet Data—Most Recent Seven Quarters (cont.)

	Q3 2002	Q2 2002	Q1 2002	Q4 2001	Q3 2001	Q2 2001	Q1 2001
BALANCE SHEET:							
Current assets:							
Cash and short-term investments	$9,615	$8,957	$9,231	$10,326	$9,158	$9,340	$10,058
Trading assets—fixed income	$1,313	$1,185	$1,047	$836	$726	$813	$1,123
Trading assets—equities	$89	$187	$256	$74	$67	$77	$107
Trading assets—SERP+	$225	$278	$314	$314	$266	$335	$315
Total trading assets	$1,627	$1,650	$1,617	$1,224	$1,059	$1,225	$1,545
Accounts receivable	$3,089	$2,907	$2,883	$2,607	$3,043	$2,904	$3,432
Inventories:							
Raw materials	$286	$242	$265	$237	$297	$379	$406
Work in process	$1,520	$1,393	$1,301	$1,316	$1,308	$1,431	$1,367
Finished goods	$675	$870	$914	$700	$746	$1,016	$879
Subtotal inventories	$2,481	$2,505	$2,480	$2,253	$2,351	$2,826	$2,652
Deferred tax assets and other	$1,233	$1,182	$1,278	$1,223	$1,256	$1,010	$1,052
Total current assets	**$18,045**	**$17,201**	**$17,489**	**$17,633**	**$16,867**	**$17,305**	**$18,739**
Property, plant and equipment, net	$17,970	$18,176	$18,314	$18,121	$18,138	$17,828	$16,774
Marketable strategic equity securities	$56	$96	$129	$155	$165	$649	$1,159
Other long-term investments	$1,182	$1,438	$1,605	$1,319	$1,249	$1,094	$1,141
Good will, net	$4,334	$4,338	$4,338	$4,330	$4,714	$5,300	$5,037
Other assets	$2,049	$2,249	$2,514	$2,837	$3,098	$3,448	$3,399
Total assets	**$43,636**	**$43,498**	**$44,389**	**$44,395**	**$44,231**	**$45,624**	**$46,249**
Current liabilities:							
Short-term debt	$317	$383	$412	$409	$302	$411	$479
Accounts payable and accrued liabilities	$4,492	$4,195	$4,604	$4,755	$4,616	$4,984	$5,398
Deferred income on shipments to distributors	$512	$498	$572	$418	$507	$549	$648
Income taxes payable	$960	$672	$1,017	$988	$768	$869	$862
Total current liabilities	**$6,281**	**$5,748**	**$6,605**	**$6,570**	**$6,193**	**$6,813**	**$7,387**
Long-term debt	$1,000	$1,081	$1,064	$1,050	$972	$928	$704
Deferred tax liabilities	$1,048	$1,089	$860	$945	$1,164	$1,145	$1,240
Total stockholders' equity	$35,307	$35,580	$35,860	$35,830	$35,902	$36,738	$36,918
Total liabilities and stockholders' equity	**$43,636**	**$43,498**	**$44,389**	**$44,395**	**$44,231**	**$45,624**	**$46,249**

Source: Company reports.

Looking beyond 2003, Intel's top management faced some big strategic questions: Would the envisaged convergence materialize and give Intel the opportunity to extend the company's position and competencies into lucrative new markets? How likely was it for Intel to get a return on the enormous investments in manufacturing and technology it was making in the face of major market uncertainties? Was Intel's executive leadership bench strong and deep enough to address the various challenges associated with the widened corporate strategic scope? Was Intel's organization optimally structured to implement the new corporate strategy? Would Intel find a successful third act?

EXHIBIT 1 | Intel Supplemental Financial and Other Information—Most Recent Seven Quarters (cont.)

SUPPLEMENTAL FINANCIAL AND OTHER INFORMATION:	Q3 2002	Q2 2002	Q1 2002	Q4 2001	Q3 2001	Q2 2001	Q1 2001
GEOGRAPHIC REVENUES:							
Americas	32%	35%	33%	33%	37%	37%	35%
Asia-Pacific	38	38	36	35	31	31	28
Europe	23	20	23	25	25	22	25
Japan	7	7	8	7	7	10	12
CASH INVESTMENTS:							
Cash and short-term investments	$9,615	$8,957	$9,231	$10,326	$9,158	$9,340	$10,058
Trading assets—fixed income	$1,313	$1,185	$1,047	$836	$726	$813	$1,123
Total cash investments	$10,928	$10,142	$10,278	$11,162	$9,884	$10,153	$11,181
INTEL CAPITAL PORTFOLIO:							
Trading assets—equity securities	$89	$187	$256	$74	$67	$77	$107
Marketable strategic equity securities	$56	$96	$129	$155	$165	$649	$1,159
Other strategic investments	$1,169	$1,177	$1,241	$1,499	$1,772	$1,985	$2,032
Total Intel capital portfolio	$1,314	$1,460	$1,626	$1,728	$2,004	$2,711	$3,298
SELECTED CASH FLOW INFORMATION:							
Depreciation	$1,136	$1,135	$1,161	$1,093	$1,054	$1,050	$934
Amortization of goodwill	$0	$0	$0	$405	$447	$417	$441
Amortization of acquisition-related intangibles and costs	$102	$229	$111	$145	$162	$177	$144
Purchased in-process research and development	$6	$14	$0	$0	$0	$123	$75
Capital spending	($955)	($1,115)	($1,430)	($1,136)	($1,365)	($2,144)	($2,664)
Stock repurchase program	($1,001)	($1,002)	($1,005)	($1,003)	($1,002)	($1,002)	($1,001)
Proceeds from sales of shares to employees, tax benefit & other	$279	$239	$360	$298	$314	$224	$356
Dividends paid	($133)	($134)	($134)	($134)	($135)	($135)	($134)
Net cash used for acquisitions	($7)	($50)	$0	($4)	$0	($381)	($498)
SHARE INFORMATION (adjusted for stock splits):							
Average common shares outstanding	6,646	6,677	6,684	6,698	6,718	6,725	6,721
Dilutive effect of:							
Stock options	66	126	177	153	158	164	178
Convertible notes	0	0	0	0	0	0	0
Common shares assuming dilution	6,712	6,803	6,861	6,851	6,876	6,889	6,899
STOCK BUYBACK:							
BUYBACK ACTIVITY:							
Shares repurchased	56.6	37.2	30.9	35.0	34.9	34.1	29.4
Cumulative shares repurchased	1,651.4	1,594.8	1,557.6	1,526.7	1,491.7	1,456.8	1,422.7
OTHER INFORMATION:							
Employees (in thousands)	81.7	83.2	82.9	83.4	86.2	88.2	90.2
Days sales outstanding	36	37	37	37	38	39	40

Source: Company reports.

(continued)

EXHIBIT 1 | Intel Consolidated Statements of Income 2001–1995 (cont.)

THREE YEARS ENDED DECEMBER 29

(in millions—except per share amounts)	2001	2000	1999	1998	1997	1996	1995
NET REVENUES	$26,539	$33,726	$29,389	$26,273	$25,070	$20,847	$16,202
Cost of sales	13,487	12,650	11,836	12,088	9,945	9,164	7,811
Research and development	3,796	3,897	3,111	2,509	2,347	1,808	1,296
Marketing, general and administrative	4,464	5,089	3,872	3,076	2,891	2,322	1,843
Amortization of goodwill and other acquisition-related intangibles and costs	2,338	1,586	411	56	–		
Purchased in-process research and development	198	109	392	165	–	–	–
Operating costs and expenses	24,283	23,331	19,622	17,894	15,183	13,294	10,950
Operating income	**2,256**	**10,395**	**9,767**	**8,379**	**9,887**	**7,553**	**5,252**
Interest expenses				(34)	(27)	(25)	(29)
Gains (losses) on equity securities, net	(466)	3,759	883	–	–	–	
Interest and other, net	393	987	578	792	799	406	415
Income before taxes	**2,183**	**15,141**	**11,228**	**9,137**	**10,659**	**7,934**	**5,638**
Provision for taxes	892	4,606	3,914	3,069	3,714	2,777	2,072
Net income	**$1,291**	**;10,535**	**$7,314**	**$6,068**	**$6,945**	**$5,157**	**$3,566**
Basic earnings per common share	**$0.19**	**$1.57**	**$1.10**	**$1.82**	**$2.12**	**$1.57**	**$4.03**
Diluted earnings per common share	**$0.19**	**$1.51**	**$1.05**	**$1.73**	**$1.93**	**$1.45**	
Weighted average common shares outstanding	**6,716**	**6,709**	**6,648**	**3,336**	**3,271**	**3,290**	
Dilutive effect of:							
Employee stock options				159	204	187	
1998 Step-up warrants				22	115	74	
Weighted average common shares outstanding, assuming dilution	**6,879**	**6,986**	**6,940**	**3,517**	**3,590**	**3,551**	**884**

Source: Company reports.

Let Chaos Reign, Then Rein in Chaos[6]

Internet Euphoria

During 1998–2001, Intel invested heavily in industries outside its traditional areas of expertise, buying its way into communications, information appliances and Internet services. Barrett decentralized the company and restructured business groups three times in three years.[7] Within two years, Intel shuttered many of its operations in these new areas. Barrett described events at Intel over the past few years: "There was a little road-kill along the way. We diverged into other elements of the Internet. Our actions since 1999 were partially driven by environmental factors, in particular the dotcom meltdown, the telecom meltdown and the internationalization of business."[8]

The roadkill that Barrett mentioned included Intel's forays into services, organized under a new group called Intel Online Services (IOS) and system products organized under another new group called Communications Products Group (CPG). In a little over two years the company spent $4 billion acquiring server farms, manufacturing servers,

[6]See Andrew S. Grove, *Only the Paranoid Survive* (New York: Doubleday, 1996), p.123. Grove writes, "Getting through a strategic inflection point involves confusion, uncertainty and disorder, both on a personal level and if you are in management on a strategic level for the enterprise as a whole.

[7]Cliff Edwards and Ira Sager, "Can Craig Barrett Reverse Intel's Slide?" *BusinessWeek*, October 4, 2001.

[8]All quotes from Craig Barrett are from the author's interview on 30 October 2002. Subsequent quotes from this interview will not be cited.

EXHIBIT 1 | Intel Consolidated Balance Sheets 2001–1995 (cont)

(In millions—except par value)	2001	2000	1999	1998	1997	1996	1995
Assets							
Current assets:							
Cash and cash equivalents	$ 7,970	$ 2,976	$ 3,695	$ 2,038	$ 4,102	$ 4,165	$ 1,463
Short-term investments	2,356	10,497	7,705	5,272	5,630	3,742	995
Trading assets	1,224	350	388	316	195	87	–
Accounts receivable, net of allowance for doubtful accounts of $68 ($84 in 2000.)	2,607	4,129	3,700	3,527	3,438	3,723	3,116
Inventories	2,253	2,241	1,478	1,582	1,697	1,293	2,004
Deferred tax assets	958	721	673	618	676	570	408
Other current assets	265	236	180	122	129	104	111
Total current assets	**17,633**	**21,150**	**17,819**	**13,475**	**15,867**	**13,684**	**8,097**
Property, plant and equipment:							
Land and buildings	10,709	7,416	7,246	6,297	5,113	4,372	3,145
Machinery and equipment	21,605	15,994	14,851	13,149	10,577	8,729	7,099
Construction in progress	2,042	4,843	1,460	1,622	2,437	1,161	1,548
	34,356	28,253	23,557	21,068	18,127	14,262	11,792
Less accumulated depreciation	16,235	13,240	11,842	9,459	7,461	5,775	4,321
Property, plant and equipment, net	18,121	15,013	11,715	11,609	10,666	8,487	7,471
Marketable strategic equity securities	155	1,915	7,121				
Other long-term investments	1,319	1,797	790	5,365	1,839	1,353	1,653
Goodwill, net	4,330	4,977					
Acquisition-related intangibles, net	797	964	4,934				
Other assets	2,040	2,129	1,470	1,022	508	211	283
TOTAL ASSETS	**$ 44,395**	**$ 47,945**	**$ 43,849**	**$ 31,471**	**$ 28,880**	**$ 23,735**	**$ 17,504**
Liabilities and stockholders' equity							
Current liabilities:							
Short-term debt	$ 409	$ 378	$ 230	$ 159	$ 212	$ 389	$ 346
Long-term debt redeemable within one year				–	110		
Accounts payable	1,769	2,387	1,370	1,244	1,407	969	864
Accrued compensation and benefits	1,179	1,696	1,454	1,285	1,268	1,128	758
Deferred income on shipments to distributors	418	674	609	606	516	474	304
Accrued advertising	560	782	582	458	500	410	218
Other accrued liabilities	1,247	1,440	1,159	1,094	842	507	328
Income taxes payable	988	1,293	1,695	958	1,165	986	801
Total current liabilities	6,570	8,650	7,099	5,804	6,020	4,863	3,619
Long-term debt	1,050	707	955	702	448	728	400
Deferred tax liabilities	945	1,266	3,130	1,387	1,076	997	620
Put warrants			130	201	2,041	275	725

Source: Company reports.

(*continued*)

EXHIBIT 1 | Intel Consolidated Balance Sheets 2001–1995 (cont.)

(In millions—except par value)	2001	2000	1999	1998	1997	1996	1995
Commitments and contingencies							
Stockholders' equity:							
Preferred stock, $0.001 par value,							
50 shares authorized; none issued	−	−			−		
Common stock, $0.001 par value,	8,833	8,486	7,316	4,822	3,311	2,897	2,583
Acquisition-related unearned stock compensation	(178)	(97)					
Accumulated other comprehensive income	25	195					
Retained earnings	27,150	28,738	21,428	17,952	15,926	13,975	9,557
Accumulated other comprehensive income			3,791	603	58		
Total stockholders' equity	**35,830**	**37,322**	**32,535**	**23,377**	**19,295**	**16,872**	**12,140**
Total liabilities and stockholders' equity	**$44,395**	**$47,945**	**$43,849**	**$31,471**	**$28,880**	**$23,735**	**$17,504**

Source: Company reports.

acquiring Web casting services, and even producing MP3 players and toy digital microscopes. In 2001, Intel dissolved CPG and stopped making network servers and routers after some of its biggest customers, including Dell Computer, Compaq, and Cisco Systems, complained about Intel's competition in their markets. In 2002, Intel also dropped most of its Internet services operations and dissolved IOS. Barrett said, "I do regret our forays into services businesses like streaming media and Intel Online. These were our contributions to the dot-com euphoria."

Remembering the Importance of Execution

For much of the 1990s, under Barrett's tenure as COO, Intel earned a reputation for flawless execution. The company's technological prowess, manufacturing excellence, and financial power kept at bay most competitors in its core PC microprocessor market segment. Over the past few years, however, Intel suffered hiccups in its core markets.

Reflecting on these events since he assumed the CEO job, Barrett said:

Two things happened: We stumbled and took our eye off the ball.

We did not execute well because we didn't follow our own methodology. For example, we had to recall some motherboards. With the management changes and because we were growing too fast, we did not follow our own best-known methods.

We used to use leapfrog teams to speed up innovation. These teams worked on technologies that were a generation ahead of the technologies just being introduced. We purposely abandoned the leapfrog strategy, which was put in place to facilitate product development during the four years between major microprocessor architecture innovations. With Itanium [see below], we cut back on parallel design teams for the desktop. This left a gap in technology. The gap made it easier for our competitors to compete with us. This was a conscious decision to make a structural change in the development cycle. But without perfect execution, the hole got bigger.

Some observers noted that Barrett, when he became CEO, needed as good a COO as he had been under Grove. For a time, Barrett tried to play both roles, but found it difficult to juggle the demands. Barrett said, "The problems were further exacerbated by the internationalization of business. Do you spend time in factories or in new, emerging markets?" In January 2002, Barrett named Paul Otellini to the position of president and COO. Barrett described Otellini as, "Mr. Inside," with his hands on all of the levers at the company, much as Barrett's had worked the switches when he had been COO. Meanwhile, Barrett continued his role as "Mr. Outside," orbiting the company that now spanned the globe to a degree that it never had before, setting strategies and direction.

Barrett's "Mr. Inside," President and COO Paul Otellini, offered his assessment on Intel over the past few years: "Craig took over at a time that coincided with industry, technology and with hindsight, company change. The specter of the Internet and dot-com became catalysts to take action. Before Craig's changes, we did

EXHIBIT 1 | Intel Consolidated Statements of Cash Flows 2001–1995 (cont.)

(In millions)	2001	2000	1999	1998	1997	1996	1995
Cash and cash equivalents, beginning of year	**$ 2,976**	**$ 3,695**	**$ 2,038**	**$ 4,102**	**$ 4,165**	**$ 1,463**	**$ 1,180**
Cash flows provided by (used for) operating activities:							
Net income	1,291	10,535	7,314	6,068	6,945	5,157	3,566
Adjustments to reconcile net income to net cash provided by (used for) operating activities:							
Depreciation	4,131	3,249	3,186	2,807	2,192	1,888	1,371
Net loss on retirement of property, plant and equipment	119	139	193	282	130	120	75
Amortization of goodwill and other acquisition-related intangibles and costs	2,338	1,586	411				8
Purchased in-process research and development	198	109	392	165	—	—	
Gains (losses) on equity investments, net	466	(3,759)	(883)				
Gain (loss) on investment in Convera	196	(117)	—				
Deferred taxes	(519)	(130)	(219)	77	6	179	346
Tax benefits from employee stock plans	435	887	506	415	224	196	116
Changes in assets and liabilities:							
Trading assets	898	38	(72)				
Accounts receivable	1,561	(384)	153	(38)	285	(607)	(1,138)
Inventories	24	(731)	169	167	(404)	711	(835)
Accounts payable	(673)	978	79	(180)	438	105	289
Accrued compensation and benefits	(524)	231	127	17	140	370	170
Income taxes payable	(270)	(362)	726	(211)	179	185	372
Other assets and liabilities	(1,017)	558	(819)	249	(21)	439	(324)
Total adjustments	7,363	2,292	4,021	3,123	3,063	3,586	450
Net cash provided by operating activities	**8,654**	**12,827**	**11,435**	**9,191**	**10,008**	**8,743**	**4,016**
Cash flows provided by (used for) investing activities:							
Additions to property, plant and equipment	(7,309)	(6,674)	(3,403)	(3,557)	(4,501)	(3,024)	(3,550)
Purchase of Chips & Technologies, Inc., net of cash acquired				(321)	—	—	—
Purchase of Digital Equipment Corporation semiconductor operations				(585)	—	—	—
Acquisitions, net of cash acquired	(883)	(2,317)	(2,979)	(906)			

Source: Company reports.

(continued)

EXHIBIT 1 | Intel Consolidated Statements of Cash Flows 2001–1995 (cont.)

(In millions)	2001	2000	1999	1998	1997	1996	1995
Purchases of available-for-sale investments	(7,141)	(17,188)	(7,055)	(10,925)	(9,224)	(4,683)	(685)
Sales of available-for-sale investments				201	153	225	114
Maturities and sales of available-for-sale investments	15,398	17,124	7,987	8,681	6,713	2,214	1,444
Other investing activities	(260)	(980)	(799)				
Net cash used for investing activities	**(195)**	**(10,035)**	**(6,249)**	**(6,506)**	**(6,859)**	**(5,268)**	**(2,677)**
Cash flows provided by (used for) financing activities:							
Increase (decrease) in short-term debt, net	23	138	69	(83)	(177)	43	(179)
Additions to long-term debt	306	77	118	169	172	317	—
Repayment and retirement of long-term debt	(10)	(46)	—	—	(300)	—	(4)
Proceeds from sales of shares through employee stock plans and other	762	797	543	507	317	257	192
Proceeds from sales of put warrants	—	—	20		288	56	85
Repurchase and retirement of common stock	(4,008)	(4,007)	(4,612)		(3,372)	(1,302)	(1,034)
Payment of dividends to stockholders	(538)	(470)	(366)		(180)	(148)	(116)
Proceeds from exercises of 1998 Step-up warrants				1,620	40	4	
Net cash used for financing activities	(3,465)	(3,511)	(4,228)	(4,749)	(3,212)	(773)	(1,056)
Net increase (decrease) in cash and cash equivalents	4,994	(719)	1,657	(2,064)	(63)	2,702	283
Cash and cash equivalents, end of year	**$7,970**	**$2,976**	**$3,695**	**$2,038**	**$4,102**	**$4,165**	**$1,463**
Supplemental disclosures of cash flow information:							
Cash paid during the year for:							
Interest	$ 53	$ 43	$ 40	$ 40	$ 37	$ 51	$ 182
Income taxes	$1,208	$4,209	$2,899	$2,784	$3,305	$2,217	$1,209
					$3,305	$2,217	$1,209

Certain 1997 and 1996 amounts have been reclassified to conform to the 1998 presentation.

Source: Company reports.

EXHIBIT 2 | Intel Capital Expenditure (CapEx) 2002 and 2001

2001: $7.3 Billion	2002: $5.5 Billion
300 mm	300 mm
22% of total capital	56% of total capital
27% of fab capital	72% of fab capital
0.13 micron and smaller	0.13 micron and smaller
60% of total capital	73% of total capital
78% of fab capital	95% of fab capital

Source: Andy Bryant, "To Recovery and Beyond," Intel Spring Analysts' Meeting, April 25, 2002.

EXHIBIT 3 | Intel Selected Share Price, Volume and Price/Earnings (P/E) Data

Intel Share Price and Volume December 31, 1996 – September 9, 2002

Source: Thompson Financial.

Intel PE Ratio Data

Year	Intel Average P/E Ratio	Year	Intel Average P/E Ratio
1992	12.3	1997	20.6
1993	11.3	1998	24.3
1994	10.7	1999	29.5
1995	13.9	2000	36.1
1996	14.2	2001	55.0

(As of 8 Nov 2002)	Intel	Semiconductor Industry	Technology Sector	S&P 500
P/E Ratio (TTM)	47.96	47.73	34.76	24.74
P/E High (past 5 years)	162.62	91.96	67.14	49.33
P/E Low (past 5 years)	17.46	16.64	19.90	16.90

Source: ValueLine Investment Survey; OneSource.

NB: TTM = trailing 12 months.

not have expertise in communications, beyond copper Ethernets. We obtained important communications architectures from our acquisitions."[9]

The company learned lessons from its failures over the past few years. Otellini said, "IOS was an orthogonal departure for us. Just as Microma[10] was about fashion and not technology, Web hosting turned out to be about consulting and not technology."

According to Otellini, "Where we are today, we are better off than if we had not taken those excursions. We have hitched ourselves to communications as a means to capitalize on Internet growth. It focuses on what we are good at: architectures and silicon. Silicon is the engine that will make convergence between communications and computing happen. Silicon is the template upon which to embed architectures." Otellini explained further:

> We are incredibly strong in computing. We will lever that strength to become a first mover in communications. In five years, if communications and computing are separate activities at Intel, we've failed. Intel understands software tools and architectures that can be reproduced by the hundreds of millions. We understand:
>
> - Computer architectures
> - Microprocessors
> - Core logic
> - Memory
> - Communications architectures and silicon
>
> All of these things are central in a range of devices from servers to phones.

Intel's New Focus

By 2002, Intel had gained new focus. Barrett described Intel as a stool with four legs. The company would be supported by—R&D, capital expenditure, its branding program, and increasingly, its venture capital investments through Intel Capital. These would serve as the company's foundation as Intel sought opportunities in silicon and digital computing and communications architectures around the world.

Barrett said Intel's organizational structure was now straightforward: "We have five business units. Three are microprocessor-oriented: these are Mobile, Desktop and Server-Enterprise. In addition Intel is organized around handheld devices and network and communication infrastructure" (Exhibit 4).

For Barrett, the distractions of the past few years were now behind the company: "We are refocused on silicon, architectures, and worldwide business opportunities for the core business. This has led to the crystallization of our strategy. Our mission statement hasn't changed, but the definition of 'building blocks' of the Internet has become clearer."

The convergence of communications and computing architectures seemed a natural extension for the company to Barrett: "Silicon devices incorporating both logic and communications capability are important now. Our R&D budget goes into communications and the convergence of communication and computing. The branding program continues, plus Intel Capital has spent $150 million to fund communications investments, particularly in 802.11." [802.11 refers to a group of specifications governing wireless fidelity (Wi-Fi), a high-frequency wireless local area network protocol.] In 2001, Intel spent $3.8 billion on research and development, 31 percent of which went to communications investments. In 2002, Intel would spend $4.1 billion on R&D, with 30 percent going to communication. In both years, the largest portion of R&D spending was directed toward silicon products and processes.[11]

To Intel's mission of "Silicon Leadership, Architectural Innovation, and Worldwide Opportunity," Barrett added one further challenge: "Our goal is to be *one generation ahead* in each of these three areas."

Now that the company had refocused and redefined itself, President and COO Paul Otellini looked to the future.

> I have been chartered with growing the earnings of the company. Figuring out where the opportunities are over

---

[9]All quotes from Paul Otellini are from the authors' interview on 9 October 2002, unless otherwise indicated. Subsequent quotes from this interview will not be cited.

[10]In 1972, Intel acquired Microma, a solid-state watch company, with the hope that it would provide an outlet for EPROM chips. The foray into watches failed and Intel left the watch business in 1977. Gordon Moore referred to the Microma watch he wore as his "$15 million watch." He said in 1988, "If anybody comes to me with an idea for a consumer product, all I have to do is look at my watch to get the answer." Source: R. A. Burgelman, *Strategy Is Destiny*, (New York: Free Press, 2002) p. 115, and Intel Company Museum, Santa Clara, CA.

[11]Source: Andy Bryant, "To Recovery and Beyond," Intel Spring Analysts' Meeting, April 25, 2002. NB: According to Bryant, manufacturing accounted for more spending in 2002 due to costs associated with tooling fabs to produce on silicon wafers with wafer areas of 90 nm.

EXHIBIT 4 | Intel Organization Chart 2002

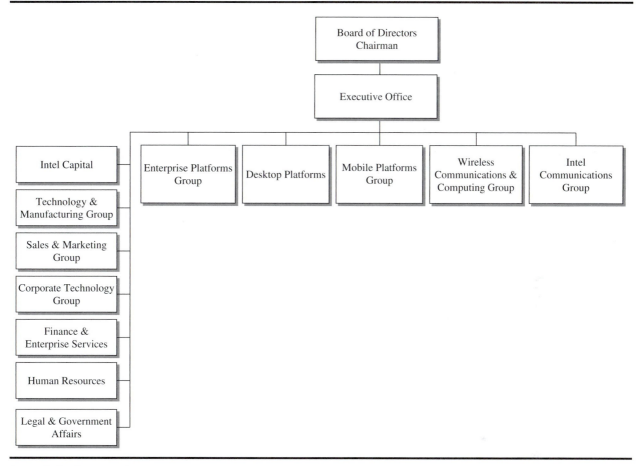

Source: Authors' reconstruction; company reports.

the next five years and refining our bets. We are also figuring out learning and culture. Half of our employees have been here five years or less and have never seen a recession in their working lives. We must spend time creating the institutional learning [needed to carry the company forward].

Otellini depended upon that classic Intel asset to propel the company to the future: "We will take advantage of the world's greatest manufacturing network. Our manufacturing capabilities are either our best asset or worst liability because of the sunk costs."[12]

---

[12]It cost around $2.5 billion to build a fab, and Intel estimated that a fab depreciated by $500 million per year, whether or not it was active.

Beyond 2002: Intel's Functional Organizations

Technology and Manufacturing: Feeding the Giant

Intel relied on its manufacturing arm, the Technology and Manufacturing Group (TMG), to help the company obtain scale economies and manufacturing leadership. About 25 percent of Intel's R&D budget was dedicated to supporting TMG. Intel's manufacturing infrastructure was like a giant: great to have on your side to wield against enemies, but hungry and expensive to feed.

For Intel's Chairman Andy Grove, "Capacity is strategy." "Henry Ford used [capacity] to revolutionize the automobile industry; the Japanese used it to push us out of the memory-chip business 25 years ago; we used it a decade ago to ignite the explosion of the PC industry. Now we're using it again so we can broaden our business beyond the PC,"[13] said Grove. Intel planned to spend $10 billion over the next two years on fabs. Bryant indicated that three 300 mm fabs equaled the capacity of seven 200 mm fabs.[14] In spite of the prolonged recession in technology, Intel continued to push the state-of-the-art in manufacturing technology.

Foundries: When You Look Fabless   Intel believed that the superior returns from its process technology advances would push the company further ahead of its competition, threatening their ability to maintain their current business models. Pat Gelsinger, Intel's chief technology officer (CTO) explained:

> Unless you are a certain size, you can't afford to manufacture. Simple return on investment (ROI) states you can't economically produce microprocessors using 300 mm wafers unless you sell $5–$6 billion in revenue. Less volume and you can't get the ROI. Further, with each factory costing at least $2.5 billion to build and with a two-year technology cycle, you can't stay current with less than $1.25 billion per year in capital investments.[15]

Gelsinger thought that the increasing costs of manufacturing would force some companies to abandon some or all of their fabs in favor of foundries. Foundries are fabs for hire, owned by companies that specialize in chip manufacturing, as opposed to integrated design manufacturers (IDMs), which design, manufacture and market their own semiconductors. The economic rationale behind the foundry model is that their focus on manufacturing allows them to make more efficient use of the large amounts of capital required to build fabs. The advent of foundries over the last decade has created a class of "fabless" chip design houses. But the real hope for future growth for foundries came from production outsourced by IDMs, electronics companies that had once relied on in-house chip manufacturing.

The leading foundry companies, Taiwan Semiconductor Manufacturing (TSMC) and its local rival United Microelectronics (UMC), together accounted for nearly two-thirds of the global market in made-to-order integrated circuits. Some analysts believed that the continued downturn in the semiconductor industry would boost this outsourcing model. Outsourcing to large foundries by IDMs actually declined from 13 per cent of their output at the end of 2000 to around 7–8 percent in late 2002, as the big electronics companies struggled to keep their own production lines employed. However, many observers expected more IDMs to give up production in favor of going fabless. The economics were compelling: some analysts estimated TSMC's breakeven capacity utilization rate at around 44 percent, while UMC's was estimated at around 50–55 percent. Most IDMs only managed to break even at higher rates of 60–70 percent utilization.[16]

Intel, and many of its most important competitors, owned their own fabs. Sunlin Chou, Intel senior vice president and general manager of TMG, described the virtues Intel perceived it derived from its position as an IDM.

> Intel has both the integration advantage of an IDM, and the high production volumes that give the multifactory scale advantage enjoyed by foundries. Integration enables us to develop technologies that are optimized for our products, and to ramp them smoothly and rapidly into volume production, while avoiding the yield and reliability problems that others (particularly foundries) have reportedly had with 130 nm technologies. Scale gives us economic benefits, keeps us cost competitive and generates revenue to pay for R&D and future capacity. This combination of integration and scale is becoming scarcer in the industry and increases our competitive advantage.[17]

Being a successful IDM involved more than just throwing funding at fabs. Chou worked hard to make sure TMG was closely integrated with the business units that developed and marketed Intel's products. Chou said, "We have to work with our business groups to do technology and capacity planning. We coordinate with product development teams to define technology features, and to make both the technologies and products ready for

---

[13]Brent Schlender, "Intel's $10 Billion Gamble," *Fortune*, November 11, 2002.

[14]Andy Bryant, "To Recovery and Beyond," Intel Spring Analysts' Meeting, Intel Corporation, April 25, 2002.

[15]All quotes from Pat Gelsinger are from the author's interview on 16 October 2002. Subsequent quotes will not be cited.

[16]Mure Dickie, "Foundry Model Holds up Despite Slump in Demand," *Financial Times*, October 1, 2002.

[17]All quotes from Sunlin Chou are from the authors' interview on 13 November 2002, unless otherwise indicated. Subsequent quotes from this interview will not be cited.

manufacturing at the same time. We work with business managers to forecast future production requirements. These take a tremendous amount of mindshare in TMG."

By 2002, many IDMs were reluctant to shoulder alone the burden of building new $2.5 billion 300 mm wafer fabs. Advanced Micro Devices (AMD) and Infineon both launched joint ventures with UMC. European chipmaker STMicroelectronics and Motorola increased their outsourced volume to TSMC.[18]

Fabs as a Weapon   Intel raised the bar for the entire industry when it launched its 300 mm fab in 2002. Few other semiconductor companies could afford investments of this size. Intel's CTO Gelsinger explained his outlook on the impact that the escalating cost of manufacturing was having on the semiconductor industry: "The capitalization issue is driving three business models. You have to make a $10 billion investment every two years or so. The dot-com madness funded Intel's 300 mm conversion. This technology cost about $2–3 billion, but gave us 2X chips per wafer, and gives a 30 percent reduction in cost per die." Gelsinger surmised, "Our 300 mm technology gives Intel a whole generation's lead over its competitors."

What effect would 300 mm manufacturing have on the industry? According to Gelsinger, three sustainable business models were emerging in semiconductors:

- Leaders: for example, Intel, AMD, IBM, Texas Instruments (TI), and Motorola. Companies that can afford to maintain leadership in logic and the integration of process and logic products

- Foundries: for example, TSMC and UMC. Companies that amortize investment over many products for different companies.

- Low-cost suppliers, for example, Samsung, Micron, Infineon. Companies that become high-volume suppliers of slightly differentiated chips for specific markets, such as mobile.

Gelsinger said, "We wonder if a company must be #1 or #2 in one of these business models or exit? As the costs of R&D and production continue to increase, one wonders whether a company like TI will become a fabless semiconductor company" (Exhibit 5).

It was far from clear that TI would go gently. The company had a long and distinguished history in semi-conductors in general and in communications in particular. They would likely prove a formidable competitor for even a refocused Intel. In September 2002, TI announced its plans to integrate several technologies, such as wireless networking and global positioning system locators, into one chip. Most observers agreed that TI already had the lead in integrating such technology. In 2002, TI accounted for about 50 percent of the cell phone semiconductor market. This was a sizeable market for chipmakers. Some estimated that silicon represented $40–$50 of the bill of materials for a mobile handset, resulting in a $20 billion market for silicon for mobile phones per year.[19] Some thought that the market for the next generation of cell phone semiconductors would be TI's to lose.[20] Chairman Andy Grove was cautious: "Intel's wireless strategy seems predicated on beating TI. But TI has honed its skills in this area; it has been a core competency of theirs for the past 15 years."[21]

Extending Moore's Law

Intel planned to compete against companies like TI by taking its proven skills into new areas. Intel's CTO Pat Gelsinger said, "Soon we'll be moving to the nano[22] region where we will encounter completely new physical challenges (Exhibit 6). We call this extending Moore's Law." Intel wanted to extend Moore's Law into the backyards of its competitors.

In a year or so, Intel would be manufacturing using 90 nm processes. The transistors manufactured in this process would be around 50 nm, roughly the size of a virus. Gelsinger noted, "Below 5 nm, entirely new processes will be needed." To paraphrase *Star Trek*'s William Shatner, who appeared at a recent Intel Developer Conference, Intel was planning to go where no company had gone before. To get there, Intel was reaching out beyond its own talent pool into universities. Intel was seeding the science with grants made directly to researchers at various colleges around the country. Some of these grants, for example, for projects that

---

[18]Ibid.

[19]Estimate from Intel senior executive.

[20]Crayton Harrison, "Texas Instruments to Integrate Technologies into Single Chip for Cell Phones," *Dallas Morning News*, September 04, 2002.

[21]All quotes from Andy Grove are from the author's interview on 25 October 2002, unless otherwise indicated. Subsequent quotes from this interview will not be cited.

[22]Nano refers to a one-billionth (10^{-9}) part, e.g., nanometer or nanosecond.

EXHIBIT 5 | Top 25 Semiconductor Companies by Sales and Market Share Worldwide, 2001 and 2000

2001	2000	Company	Worldwide Sales ($ millions) 2001	Market Share 2001	Worldwide Sales ($ millions) 2000	Market Share 2000
1	1	Intel	$23,850	17.6%	$30,400	15.5%
2	2	Toshiba	$6,781	5.0%	$11,388	5.8%
3	6	STMicroelectronics	$6,359	4.7%	$7,910	4.0%
4	5	Texas Instruments	$6,100	4.5%	$9,200	4.7%
5	4	Samsung	$5,814	4.3%	$10,592	5.4%
6	3	NEC	$5,309	3.9%	$10,900	5.6%
7	8	Hitachi	$5,037	3.7%	$7,286	3.7%
8	7	Motorola	$4,828	3.6%	$7,875	4.0%
9	9	Infineon	$4,558	3.4%	$6,853	3.5%
10	12	Philips	$4,235	3.1%	$5,837	3.0%
11	17	IBM	$3,898	2.9%	$4,329	2.2%
12	15	AMD	$3,892	2.9%	$4,644	2.4%
13	14	Mitsubishi	$3,473	2.9%	$4,740	2.4%
14	18	Matsushita	$3,176	2.6%	$4,150	2.4%
15	16	Fujitsu	$3,084	2.3%	$4,470	2.1%
16	13	Agere (Lucent Tech.)	$3,051	2.3%	$4,875	2.3%
17	19	Sanyo	$2,675	2.3%	$3,260	2.5%
18	10	Hynix	$2,450	2.0%	$6,400	1.7%
19	11	Micron	$2,411	1.8%	$6,314	3.3%
20	20	Sony	$2,100	1.8%	$2,817	3.2%
21	21	Analog Devices	$1,897	1.6%	$2,710	1.4%
22	22	Sharp	$1,858	1.4%	$2,550	1.4%
23	24	Agilent	$1,671	1.4%	$2,414	1.3%
24	25	National Serni.	$1,626	1.2%	$2,301	1.2%
25	23	LSI Logic	$1,597.00	1.2%	$2,448	1.2%
			$111,729	1.2%	$166,663	1.2%
Total				82.6%		85.1%

Global chip sales in July 2002 totaled $11.7 billion, only 8 percent more than in July 2001, according to the Semiconductor Industry Association. Chip sales fell by one-third in 2001 from the year before, the worst annual decline ever. The association predicted that the industry will grow 20 percent in both 2003 and 2004, propelled mainly by digital consumer and wireless products.

Source: IN-STAT/MDR www.instat.com.

might be as far away as 10 or more years from fruition, were for amounts as low as $50,000. For projects closer to realization, say 5 to 10 years out, Intel sponsored "lablets," funding laboratories at selected universities. For nearer-term strategic research projects (SRPs) that loomed about two to five years off, Intel used its own labs. Gelsinger said:

Intel's work here has two themes:

1. Recognition of the limits of traditional scaling in the way we think.

2. Necessity for Intel to start very advanced seeding.

Through this program, we are moving closer to the origins of science and technology. We engage with anybody who is of interest.

A metaphor describing our efforts at expanding Moore's Law is: For us, silicon is like a canvas. We have been using oil to paint on this canvas, but there are other mediums to use, such as watercolors and pastels. Our efforts in wireless, optical, etc., are like these different mediums. We are looking for domains of potential participation by Intel where silicon could become relevant.

EXHIBIT 5 | Advanced Micro Devices (AMD) Selected Financial Information 2001–1997 (in $ millions) (cont.)

	30-Dec-2001	31-Dec-2000	26-Dec-1999	27-Dec-1998	28-Dec-1997
Sales—Core business	3,891.8	4,644.2	2,857.6	2,542.1	2,356.4
Total sales	**3,891.8**	**4,644.2**	**2,857.6**	**2,542.1**	**2,356.4**
Cost of goods sold	2,589.7	2,514.6	1,964.4	1,718.7	1,578.4
SG&A expense	620.0	599.0	540.1	419.7	400.7
Research & development	650.9	641.8	635.8	567.4	467.9
Unusual income/expenditures	89.3	0.0	38.2	0.0	0.0
Total expenses	**3,950.0**	**3,755.5**	**3,178.5**	**2,705.8**	**2,447.0**
Interest expense, nonoperations	−61.4	−60.0	−69.3	−66.5	−45.3
Other—Net	25.7	423.2	463.8	22.7	35.1
Pretax income	**−93.9**	**1,251.9**	**73.6**	**−207.4**	**−100.8**
Income taxes	−14.5	256.9	167.4	−91.9	−55.2
Income after taxes	**−79.5**	**995.0**	**−93.7**	**−115.6**	**−45.7**
Equity in affiliates	18.9	11.0	4.8	11.6	24.6
Preferred dividends	0.0	0.0	0.0	0.0	0.0
Net Income (excluding extraordinary items and depreciation)	**−60.6**	**1,006.1**	**−88.9**	**−104.0**	**−21.1**
Net income (including extraordinary items and depreciation)	**−60.6**	**983.0**	**−88.9**	**−104.0**	**−21.1**

International Business Machines (IBM) Selected Financial Information 2001–1997 (in $ millions)

	31-Dec-2001	31-Dec-2000	31-Dec-1999	31-Dec-1998	31-Dec-1997
Sales—Core Business	85,866.0	88,396.0	87,548.0	81,667.0	78,508.0
Total sales	**85,866.0**	**88,396.0**	**87,548.0**	**81,667.0**	**78,508.0**
Cost of goods sold	54,084.0	56,342.0	55,994.0	50,795.0	47,899.0
SG&A expense	17,197.0	17,535.0	16,294.0	16,662.0	16,634.0
Research & development	5,290.0	5,374.0	5,505.0	5,046.0	4,877.0
Unusual income/expenditures	0.0	0.0	0.0	0.0	0.0
Total expenses	**76,571.0**	**79,251.0**	**77,793.0**	**72,503.0**	**69,410.0**
Interest expense, nonoperations	−238.0	−347.0	−352.0	−713.0	−728.0
Other—Net	1,896.0	2,736.0	2,354.0	589.0	657.0
Pretax income	**10,953.0**	**11,534.0**	**11,757.0**	**9,040.0**	**9,027.0**
Income taxes	3,230.0	3,441.0	4,045.0	2,712.0	2,934.0
Income after taxes	**7,723.0**	**8,093.0**	**7,712.0**	**6,328.0**	**6,093.0**
Preferred dividends	−10.0	−20.0	−20.0	−20.0	−20.0
Net income (excluding extraordinary items and depreciation)	**7,723.0**	**8,093.0**	**7,712.0**	**6,328.0**	**6,093.0**
Accounting change	0.0	0.0	0.0	0.0	0.0
Net income (including extraordinary items and depreciation)	**7,723.0**	**8,093.0**	**7,712.0**	**6,328.0**	**6,093.0**

Source: OneSource.

(continued)

EXHIBIT 5 | Texas Instruments (TI) Selected Financial Information 2001–1997 (in $ millions) (cont.)

	31-Dec-2001	31-Dec-2000	31-Dec-1999	31-Dec-1998	31-Dec-1997
Sales—Core business	8,201.0	11,875.0	9,759.0	8,875.0	9,972.0
Total sales	**8,201.0**	**11,875.0**	**9,759.0**	**8,875.0**	**9,972.0**
Cost of goods sold	5,824.0	6,120.0	5,069.0	5,605.0	6,179.0
SG&A expense	1,361.0	1,669.0	1,556.0	1,549.0	1,571.0
Research & development	1,598.0	1,747.0	1,379.0	1,265.0	1,556.0
Total expenses	**8,783.0**	**9,536.0**	**8,004.0**	**8,419.0**	**9,306.0**
Interest expense, nonoperations	−61.0	−75.0	−76.0	−76.0	−94.0
Other—Net	217.0	2,314.0	403.0	301.0	199.0
Pretax income	**−426.0**	**4,578.0**	**2,082.0**	**681.0**	**771.0**
Income taxes	−225.0	1,491.0	631.0	229.0	432.0
Income after taxes	**−201.0**	**3,087.0**	**1,451.0**	**452.0**	**339.0**
Preferred dividends	0.0	0.0	0.0	0.0	0.0
Interest adjustment for primary EPS	0.0	0.0	0.0	0.0	0.0
Net income (excluding extraordinary items and depreciation)	**−201.0**	**3,087.0**	**1,451.0**	**452.0**	**339.0**
Discontinued operations	0.0	0.0	0.0	0.0	1,525.0
Extraordinary items	0.0	0.0	0.0	0.0	1,525.0
Accounting change	0.0	−29.0	0.0	0.0	0.0
Net income (including extraordinary items and depreciation)	**−201.0**	**3,058.0**	**1,451.0**	**452.0**	**1,842.0**

Sun Microsystems Selected Financial Information 2002–1998 (in $ millions)

	30-Jun-2002	30-Jun-2001	30-Jun-2000	30-Jun-1999	30-Jun-1998
Sales—Core business	12,496.0	18,250.0	15,721.0	11,806.0	9,862.0
Total sales	**12,496.0**	**18,250.0**	**15,721.0**	**11,806.0**	**9,862.0**
Cost of goods sold	7,580.0	10,041.0	7,549.0	5,670.0	4,713.0
SG&A expense	3,812.0	4,445.0	4,065.0	3,196.0	2,830.0
Depreciation	0.0	285.0	72.0	19.0	0.0
Research & development	1,832.0	2,016.0	1,630.0	1,280.0	1,029.0
Unusual income/expenditures	520.0	152.0	12.0	121.0	176.0
Total expenses	**13,744.0**	**16,939.0**	**13,328.0**	**10,286.0**	**8,748.0**
Interest expense, nonoperations	−58.0	−100.0	−84.0	0.0	0.0
Other—Net	258.0	373.0	462.0	85.0	48.0
Pretax income	**−1,048.0**	**1,584.0**	**2,771.0**	**1,605.0**	**1,162.0**
Income taxes	−461.0	603.0	917.0	575.0	407.0
Income after taxes	**−587.0**	**981.0**	**1,854.0**	**1,030.0**	**755.0**
Net income (excluding extraordinary items and depreciation)	**−587.0**	**981.0**	**1,854.0**	**1,030.0**	**755.0**
Accounting change	0.0	-54.0	0.0	0.0	0.0
Net income (including extraordinary items and depreciation)	**−587.0**	**927.0**	**1,854.0**	**1,030.0**	**755.0**

Source: OneSource.

EXHIBIT 6 | Extending Moore's Law

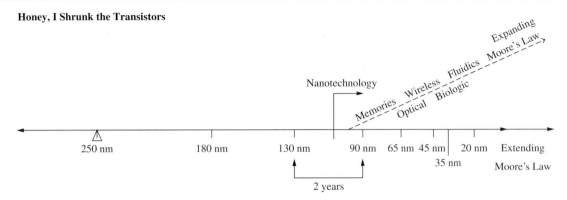

Honey, I Shrunk the Transistors

By following Moore's Law, Intel hopes to reduce the size of transistors to the point where they are smaller than viruses (< 100 nm). Intel hopes that silicon devices this small will exhibit a host of benefits including: allowing new materials and device structures to be used, incrementally changing the silicon technology base; manipulating materials on an atomic scale in one or more dimensions; and increasing use of self-assembly using chemical properties to form structures.

Source: Pat Gelsinger, Intel Corporation.

Sales and Marketing: Reigniting Growth

In 2002, Intel's products were sold by a central sales organization, the Intel Sales and Marketing Group (SMG). Intel moved to a centralized sales group in its reorganizations in 2001 and 2002. The group was led by Michael Splinter, executive vice president and director of SMG. As Intel expanded into new areas beyond the microprocessors for PCs, its sales force faced new challenges. Splinter said:

> Because we are trying to create products for the data center, we had to establish a reputation with IT managers who run data centers. A few years ago, the view was that Intel makes microprocessors for the PC. They were concerned that we weren't reliable enough. We needed to establish credibility with end users . . . the CIOs (chief information officers) and IT decision makers. Most OEMs were conflicted and slow to drive Intel architecture in the data center. For example, HP had its own HPUX on their own Performance Architecture, IBM had its own version of AIX on their P series hardware . . .[23]

Despite the success of its global brand, the company had to work to establish its credentials in new marketplaces

(Exhibit 7). Splinter pointed out that Intel's thrust into the telecommunications industry required a different kind of "sell" than in the computer industry:

> The network design win is more complicated and takes longer to achieve revenue than the computer design win. We sell to TEMs [telecommunications equipment manufacturers], which in turn must sell to the telcos. Some products never get into production or at least not high-volume production in the current environment. Because of the competitive nature of the telecommunications industry, the telecom part of the [Intel's] sales force works under very strict cost targets.

Splinter also observed that the microprocessor development cycle was quite long (up to four years), which makes it difficult to incorporate short-term marketing input. Other products, such as telecom, chipsets, and graphic chips are developed on shorter cycles. One solution, he said, was to "use the end user market information in the peripheral chips, and then integrate it later into the microprocessor."

Intel thought its matrix organization was working well to meet the challenges associated with the convergence of computing and communications, Splinter said: "The beauty of the Intel matrix is that you can manage through this kind of change. You must be able to matrix the communications specialists with the computing specialists, have computing people working on account teams for communications customers."

---

[23]All quotes from Michael Splinter are from the author's interview on 14 November 2002. Subsequent quotes will not be cited.

EXHIBIT 7 | Top 10 Global Brands and Estimated Brand Value 2002 and 2001
(Brand Value in $ billion)

Rank	Company	2002 Estimated Brand Value	2001 Estimated Brand Value
1	Coca-Cola	$69.64	$68.95
2	Microsoft	$64.09	$65.07
3	IBM	$51.19	$52.75
4	GE	$41.31	$42.40
5	**Intel**	**$30.86**	**$34.67**
6	Nokia	$29.97	$35.04
7	Disney	$29.26	$32.59
8	McDonald's	$26.38	$22.05
9	Marlboro	$24.15	$22.05
10	Mercedes	$21.01	$21.73

NB: Interbrand attempts to estimate how much of a boost each brand delivers, how stable that boost is likely to be, and how much those future earnings are worth today. Interbrand uses analysis of cash flows rather than consumer perceptions to calculate brand values.

Sources: Interbrand Corp., J.P. Morgan Chase & Co; "The Best Global Brands," *BusinessWeek,* August 5, 2002.

Some of the ever-present challenges Splinter faced nevertheless included creating the right balance between centralization and decentralization in the company's sales and marketing activities. "This tension is especially acute during acquisitions, because the companies always want to keep their own models and sales forces," Splinter said. Acquisitions notwithstanding, Intel had a history of evolving decentralized sales forces. "A renegade division would create its own sales force and one group's salespeople would come across another's at a client. We work hard on eliminating that because of the ultimate inefficiencies and the confusion that it creates with the customers. They ask, 'Who is the account manager?' Fortunately, all of the senior managers (e.g., Sean Maloney, Ron Smith, et al.) have a long history of working together. It is easy for us to get together to hammer out these issues."

In addition to competing in new product categories, Splinter also highlighted the importance of emerging markets to the company: "Emerging markets have become far more important to Intel. Our revenues would have shrunk more if not for our sales from the emerging markets (Exhibit 8). To be successful in these markets, we have to make sure our efforts are more than just sales. We have to take our brand there first; but also consider the right investments (e.g., R&D, design and manufacturing), invest in education in the country, and work with governments on technology policies." Splinter also mentioned that he saw SMG's role, in part, as educating people at Intel on what was going on in the world. Splinter wanted Intel's executives and engineers to travel. He also has set up Corporate Strategic Discussion (CSD) meetings to focus on one major emerging market country at a time (e.g., China. India, Russia, etc.). "The CSD involves at least 70 percent of top management at any given time."

Asked what the top priorities were for SMG beyond 2002, Splinter said: "Number one is to reignite the corporate refresh cycle for computers; number two is to establish the mobile wireless computing experience. If we achieve these then we can grow again. My number three priority is to keep the emergent markets going."

Intel's Finance Group: Playing Devil's Advocate

A critically important asset for Intel was its financial strength. This resource was managed by Intel's CFO, Andy Bryant. For all of the reorganization and strategic refocusing Intel underwent during the past few years, the role of the finance group remained largely unchanged. Bryant said:

> The finance group at the corporate level is much the same, even after the addition of the network group and wireless group (see sections on ICG and WCCG below). We have always had a variety of businesses around microprocessors; some had lower margins [and thus similar financial challenges to those our new groups face today].

> The biggest change to the finance group, given the $10 billion in acquisitions, is that the level of focus in the new

EXHIBIT 8 | Selected Global Data for the Semiconductor Market

Total Semiconductor Market Data by Region in 2001

Region	Total Semiconductor Industry Market Share for Region	Value ($ US) of Semiconductor Market for Region in 2001
Asia-Pacific	28%	$39.8 billion
Americas	26	35.8 billion
Japan	24	33.1 billion
Europe	22	30.2 billion

Source: Tom Foremski, "Hopes Dashed as Income Falls," *Financial Times,* September 23, 2002.

Intel Top Ten Country Markets

Rank in 2000	Country	Rank in 2005 (Intel est.)	Country
1	USA	1	USA
2	Japan	2	China
3	PRC/Hong Kong	3	Japan
4	Germany	4	Germany
5	UK	5	UK
6	France	6	India
7	India	7	Brazil
8	Canada	8	France
9	Brazil	9	Russia
10	Korea	10	Korea

Source: "Intel Executive Webcast," October 22, 2002.

areas has increased—as would be expected when the investment levels increase this much. We have created more tools to communicate with both management and the board of directors. The general management of our acquisitions has increased the level of financial scrutiny. They have to present and defend their data. The finance group still plays devil's advocate with management, making sure they have really thought about the businesses and their strategies, instead of just writing it down on paper.[24]

Intel's financial resources gave the company many options. Intel's bank account and free cash flow gave it several options for growth. Bryant said:

There are three ways to broaden the company:

1. Acquire a business (this will usually be a company renewing its product cycle).

2. Develop our own technologies.

3. Develop technology plus acquire complementary technologies.

We favor the third option. This gets the technologies just as they are becoming meaningful and getting ready to go to market. This has the best chance of success: Combining emerging technologies with Intel strategies. For example, we acquired an optical company in Fremont, California. They were ahead of us in their specific technology. After we acquired them, we were able to combine Intel's manufacturing process and technologies into the optical space.

Still, there was a limit to the depth of Intel's pockets and the downturn in the technology market had hit hard at Intel and other technology companies. Bryant considered some of the ways it would affect Intel:

How do you manage the company in a flat environment? If you think the recession will last for 12–18 months, you invest to take advantage. But if you think it will last for 18–36 months, that is a more difficult question.

An important question for Intel during a recession is: Will increased performance offer commensurate

---

[24]All quotes from Andy D. Bryant are from the author's interview on 1 October 2002, unless otherwise noted. Subsequent quotes from this interview will not be cited.

increased returns? Do you continue to widen performance gaps in an economic downturn? If you get too far ahead, you may not get a return on your investment.

Bryant offered the following illustration:

We have to ask, what does it cost to maintain products and capabilities one to two years ahead of your competitor? And do you earn enough to still get a reasonable return on investment?

Perhaps the Athlon architecture won't allow AMD to catch up to Intel, but perhaps if the Opteron architecture comes into the mainstream they can become a more credible threat [to Itanium in 64-bit processing].[25] Or perhaps a merger between AMD and any number of other companies in the business would help them catch up. Our job it to anticipate and be prepared for various competitive strategies.

The same sets of questions are relevant for networking. Can Intel overinvest for the lift off?

Chairman Andy Grove also considered the fundamental strategic question facing the company. While Grove observed that "capacity is strategy," it was unclear whether the strategy of continuing investments in manufacturing was correct. Grove said, "Aggregate semiconductor sales volume has been flat since 1995, with the exception of 2000 when there was a blip upward. For every new fab we add, it gives us around five times the capacity of an individual old fab. Do we have too much fab capacity? Too little? What choice do we have?"

Intel Capital: Investing for the Future

Intel Capital was the investment arm of the company. It charter was to "make and manage financially attractive investments in support of Intel's strategic objectives."

The program began in the early 1990s, and initially invested externally in PC and chip-related technologies that Intel needed to pursue its own business strategies. Les Vadasz, Intel Executive Vice President and President of Intel Capital, explained: "Working with leading-edge technologies often involves dependencies on the success of other, smaller companies. Intel needed to make investments and provide other support to assure timely delivery of these technologies for our needs."[26] Eventually the investment scope expanded to include investments into companies that complemented Intel's product lines. Vadasz said:

We are an OEM supplier, and our customers need the availability of a number of other products and capabilities in addition to ours, to create new generations of products. By investing in companies that deliver these additional capabilities and aligning our mutual strategies, we are able to accelerate the development of market ecosystems. In a market segment like ours, where product cycles are relatively short, this can have huge financial benefits to all participants.

Intel Capital Investments The primary purpose for Intel Capital's investing was strategic. An investment opportunity needed to satisfy the requirement that its success would help Intel achieve its strategic goals. The investments were also evaluated for their potential for financial return. Vadasz said: "A company that has interesting technology, but fails to develop any commercial presence is not likely to help our strategies." This dual-test approach characterized Intel Capital's investment discipline. Intel Capital had not disclosed specific financial results from its strategic investments, but the program was said to have contributed billions in cash to Intel in its 10-year history.

The program typically made small investments for minority stakes, generally less than $10 million each, in private and some public companies. Additionally, Intel Capital had responsibility to oversee the acquisition of companies that helped Intel enter new business areas or that strengthened Intel's businesses.

In the late 1990s, Intel established a New Business Group to incubate various businesses. This activity was merged with Intel Capital in Q3 of 2002, and subsequent to this, Les Vadasz and John Miner (VP and GM of NBG, see below) were jointly managing Intel Capital. From this point on, Intel Capital's charter included not only external but also internal investments in areas that were potentially important for Intel's future businesses. These internal investments were done with similar investment philosophy as venture funded companies.

---

[25]Athlon is AMD's microprocessor that competes with Intel's Pentium line. Opteron is AMD's microprocessor that competes with Intel's Itanium line. Opteron can run both 32-bit and 64-bit applications.

[26]All quotes from Les Vadasz are from the author's interview on 9 October 2002. Subsequent quotes from this interview will not be cited.

Intel Capital made different types of investments:

- *Building ecosystems:* A number of Intel Capital investments were made in technologies and supported the final products in which Intel's products were used. These companies' products complemented and helped drive demand for Intel products. For example, investments in enterprise software companies accelerated deployment of solutions optimized for the Intel Itanium processor family.

- *Developing international business:* Intel Capital invested in companies that helped accelerate the adoption of technology in emerging markets. For example, investments were often made in companies that provided local language content or services via the Internet or that helped improve or optimize the Internet infrastructure in a given region.

- *Working with the supply chain:* Investments were made in companies that sold products and technologies Intel needed to help market or produce its products. For example, Intel Capital invested in semiconductor equipment companies and process technology companies to fund next-generation technology development and/or accelerate product development. Those investments facilitated Intel's move to new manufacturing process generations every two to three years. Intel also invested in other suppliers, such as DRAM manufacturers Micron, Samsung, and Infineon, to help improve the availability of critical PC components to the PC market segment as a whole.

- *Fostering new silicon technologies:* Access to new companies and technologies provided a competitive advantage to Intel's Technology and Manufacturing Group. Intel made investments to ensure availability of advanced materials, next-generation lithography tools, as well as new etching and deposition techniques. To address manufacturing quality issues, various investments were made in innovative defect diagnosis and location technologies, that helped speed Intel's progress by accelerating equipment availability.

- *Scouting new technologies* (being the "eyes and ears" for the corporation): Intel Capital made small investments in emerging technologies that prove useful in the future, but were not necessarily related to a current Intel business. For example,

Intel Capital had personnel looking at investments in MEMS,[27] nanotechnology, and robotics. Vadasz said: "We can often sniff out trends earlier than greater Intel can act on them. We get the company's technologists involved, and that creates a more open mind about important technologies."

Intel Capital portfolio companies enjoyed benefits beyond Intel's financial contribution. An investment by Intel Capital offered credibility to co-investors in the technology sector. Intel Capital also brought significant technological expertise from Intel Corporation and had the ability to work with other industry participants to help foster technology standards. Occasionally, Intel Capital facilitated the diffusion of Intel-developed technology to a portfolio company.

Intel Corporation had a worldwide marketing presence, and there was the opportunity for portfolio companies to network with a diverse range of companies whose technologies or business models may have been complementary. Intel Capital itself had a worldwide presence and had dramatically expanded its non-U.S. investing over the past few years. Vadasz said: "Developing international markets in emerging countries is important for Intel's continued growth. If the future of Intel's business is in the continued convergence of computing and communications, then the question arises what is the future of the Internet in China, India, Poland, and Brazil? Forty percent of our deals (by number) are outside the United States."

Intel Capital has physical presence in some 28 countries, and had investments in companies headquartered in more than 30 different countries, on five continents. Investments were often made in companies that provide local language content or services via the Internet or that help improve or optimize the Internet infrastructure in a given region. Through these investments, Intel was able to support evolving computer and communications usage requirements and technology trends across many cultures and languages.

To provide investment focus on specific technologies critical to Intel's efforts, two specialized funds were developed within Intel Capital in 1999.

- The Intel 64 Fund was a $253 million equity fund created by Intel and other corporate investors to

---

[27]Micro-electromechanical systems (MEMS) is a technology that combines computers with tiny mechanical devices such as sensors, valves, gears, etc., embedded in semiconductor chips.

accelerate the development of solutions for the Intel Itanium processor family. The Intel 64 Fund included participation from computer makers and information technology companies.

- The $500 million Intel Communications Fund, which was funded solely by Intel, focused on accelerating Intel's voice and data communications and wireless networking initiatives. The Intel Communications Fund made more than 80 investments in 17 countries on five continents. In Q4 of 2002, Intel Capital committed $150M of this Fund to be invested to accelerate the deployment of WiFi technologies and services around the world.

WiFi—An Illustrative Example   For Vadasz and Intel, there were few adjacencies more compelling than wireless connectivity based on 802.11 protocols, commonly known as "WiFi" (wireless fidelity). WiFi was an emerging technology used to provide high-speed, wireless Internet access in many locations around the world, including airports, retail establishments, corporate offices, universities, factories, and homes.

According to Vadasz: "WiFi started as a wireless Ethernet technology for the home market, but now we find many enterprises are deploying it. It currently has warts; it is ugly in that in many cases it requires some new technical understanding to use. But, WiFi enables ad hoc networks, and its adoption has been rapid when compared to other wireless data technologies such as 2.5G and 3G.[28] In fact, WiFi is happening in spite of the carriers: It's not elegant, but it's revolutionizing telecom."

Intel had high hopes for WiFi. Vadasz believed "eventually WiFi could lead to a restructuring of the wireless telecom industry." In October 2002, Intel Capital announced that it planned to spend $150 million in companies developing WiFi technologies. Intel Capital had invested in many companies to round out a more robust WiFi ecosystem, including component suppliers; application development tools and management utilities; system level hardware and software; and even service providers

In December 2002, Intel Capital, Apax Partners, and 3i announced the creation of a new company designed to meet the growing demand for wireless network access services. The company, Cometa Networks, will provide high-speed, nationwide wholesale wireless network access that will enable carriers, service providers, and national retail chains to offer WiFi services to their customers.

Cometa Networks will allow users to access the Internet wirelessly using 802.11a or 802.11b technology from thousands of hot spots, using the same sign-on procedure, e-mail address, ID, password, and payment method that they now use from their current ISP providers and corporate VPN, DSL, or cable operators. IBM and AT&T were recruited to provide Cometa's network operating center and data center capabilities.

The idea for Cometa Networks was generated in Intel Capital based on a perceived need for such services.

In March 2003, Intel introduced its Centrino™ mobile technology. This technology promises connectivity for notebook uses, which should become more and more ubiquitous over time. By the time of this introduction, Intel Capital made 15 investments in companies that can help make that happen.

New Business Incubation: Growing the Future

Companies and technologies that were too new to be easily placed within Intel were cared for in a corporate greenhouse where they could be nurtured and protected from the demands of the established groups. This was itself a new group called New Business Group (NBG) and run by John Miner, former general manager of CPG and now general manager of NBG. Miner said:

> After reorganizing the New Business Group, we completely refocused on activities that benefit from being part of Intel. All our ventures build products that can be done on a wafer. We have activities in handheld wireless, display and pixel processing technologies, wireless and nonwireless broadband, and photonic components. We focus on the early technology capture process to develop new business applications, and look for commercialization opportunities.[29]

Miner emphasized, "We always look for two-way linkages with other parts of Intel. Two business opportunities came directly from WCCG; they will go back there. On the other hand, we also have two for which it is not yet clear where they will go."

Miner also addressed some of the management issues associated with NBG activities:

> A key challenge is how to maintain corporate level interest. We continuously try to develop strategic value for

---

[28]2.5G and 3G refer to advanced ("third-generation") mobile communications technologies.

[29]All quotes from John Miner are from the author's interview on 9 October 2002. Subsequent quotes from this interview will not be cited.

the company and we want to pay our own way doing it. The biggest challenge is lateral, how to work with peers in other parts of the company and look farther out for strategic gaps they may need to fill without necessarily having agreement on the strategy. We think that doing new businesses internally and organically makes them easier to assimilate, and less costly. But sometimes we do it in parallel, both through incubation and through small acquisitions.

Miner said that Intel uses milestones as proxies for assessing the strategic value of new ventures. He concluded: "We need some successes. We already have some small successes. We need to prepare a fourth business for Intel."

Human Resource Management: Building Organizational Capability

Intel's new focus brought challenges to its organizational structure. The company needed to develop personnel capable of managing in this new, more interdependent environment. Barrett explained:

> We have to grow and develop general managers to be more encompassing in their abilities. We do this by burdening them with making decisions, giving them accountability and responsibility for product lines. We want to take the executive office out of every product decision. This is a work in progress. We are not doing enough to develop overseas talent. Of the 16 members of the executive staff, only one lives outside of the United States [in Israel]. We will also place development facilities in overseas locations, particularly emerging markets with good educational systems, such as Russia, China, and India.

> We used to say that Intel is the largest single cell organism in the world. Well, we were a $20 billion company with great market share and terrific margins [from its core business]. But that's not where we'll be 10 years from now.

That organism has changed its size, up and down, in the past. Patricia Murray, vice president and director of Human Resources said, "Intel has a very effective system of redeployment that operated well to exit businesses and reduce teams, e.g., from one microprocessor to another, from one factory to another."[30] While the company faced layoffs in the past, including letting go

3,000 people in 1998, Murray said the recent retrenchment "has been an emotionally wrenching experience. We had to close down segments of businesses. We had to make sure we treated redundant people well in a declining environment."

Intel struggled with finding the right number of employees. Recently, Intel reduced headcount from 92,000 to 80,000 employees through a combination of business closures, attrition, and layoffs. Still, with 80,000 employees and declining sales, Wall Street suspiciously eyed the company's costs. Murray said:

> At 80,000 employees, we are still above our historical run rates for revenue per employee. But that is a gross measure that does not take into consideration a company's efforts to grow into new businesses. One could take a simple financial point of view and say that we have too much headcount for our revenue when compared to the past. In order to reduce our headcount further than we have already done, one has to balance the cost of the reduction against the possibility of future growth. Reducing headcount to meet some revenue per employee metric may have a short-term upside in Wall Street's eyes, but if you balance this against the cost in dollars, perhaps a charge of around $500 million, and the cost of being unprepared for the future, it is not as clear as it may have initially appeared. If you are unprepared for the future and you have to spend more money to rehire people six months later in a recovery, you made the wrong bet and you have lost great people at the same time. At our present level of headcount, we are making a bet on keeping our people.

A few years earlier, Intel was faced with a very different human resources challenge. Murray recalled, "We had to balance keeping compensation fair while dealing with the upward pressure on starting salaries. Sometimes the market had increased salaries by 300 percent, particularly in Intel Capital, and for senior management people. During the boom, our overall turnover never hit double digits. Some segments were higher, e.g., Intel Capital hit about 48 percent. But over 50 percent of our employees have been here less than five years. This is a function of the hiring we did in 1999 and 2000."

Intel believed that changes in technology, particularly the convergence between communications and computing, would force organizational and human resource changes at the company. Murray said, "We are still the world's biggest single cell organism." That single cell was governed from a nucleus located in Intel Architecture Group (IAG), which earned about 80 percent of the

---

[30]All quotes from Patricia Murray are from the author's interview on 30 October 2002. Subsequent quotes will not be cited.

company's annual revenue. To be successful in new technologies, this would have to change. Murray said:

> What is the right structure for the future? There is a lot of overlap with three of our businesses. They are closely aligned. But the skill sets that we have to attract and develop are different.
>
> We need general management skills. It is not true—at least not at Intel—that you have to run a P&L to be a good general manager. We have to develop virtual team skills, cross-organizational skills, and the ability to get results without direct line authority. If you are in the microprocessor group and you want to stay there and not interact with other groups, you won't be successful. Now, you have to work closely with WCCG, etc. Moreover, as a follow-on to our hiring, we are learning that we have too narrow a span of control and too many levels. Decision making has become too difficult. At the moment, we are flattening the organization posthiring spree.
>
> We also have to learn the language of our newer businesses to ensure effective communications across the company. For development, the challenge will be to manage cross-organizational opportunities. We have a few things working for us . . . we have a pretty honest culture. We are measurement based and analytical.

Murray believed that the culture of honesty and analytical rigor would help employees make the organizational adjustments that would be required to operate in a more interdependent company.

Beyond 2002: Intel's Business Groups

Intel Architecture Group

The Intel Architecture Group (IAG) designed and produced microprocessors for PCs and servers, and other devices such as PC tablets. The group also designed and produced chipsets, which perform the essential logic functions surrounding the CPU, and motherboards, which combine Intel microprocessors and chipsets to form the key subsystem of a PC or server. This was the engine for Intel's cash machine, responsible for 81 percent of the company's revenue in 2001.

IAG had turned out to be an intermediate step. Intel combined its Intel Architecture Business Group and Microprocessor Products Group into a single organization to deliver platforms and solutions for the Internet economy. The group had been jointly run by senior vice president Albert Yu, a veteran Intel executive who retired in June 2002, and Paul Otellini. Under this reorganization, development of microprocessors, chipsets, motherboards, systems and related software at the platform level was combined into platform-focused business operations targeted at the enterprise (servers and workstations), desktop, and mobile market segments. In addition, the research and technology laboratory activities of the groups were combined.

Until recently, IAG had been run by Paul Otellini, who was promoted to president and COO. Under Otellini, the general manager of IAG oversaw all of Intel's computing business units, including the Enterprise Platforms Group, the Desktop Platforms Group, the Mobile Platforms Group, the Technology and Research Labs, Microprocessor Marketing, and Business Planning. When Otellini vacated the general manager position, IAG was split into three subgroups. These were the newly formed Enterprise Platform Group run by Mike Fister; the Desktop Platform Group run by Louis Burns; and the Mobile Platform Group run by David Perlmutter. Each of these general managers reported to CEO Barrett and President and COO Otellini. This restructuring also created two new business groups: Intel Communications Group (ICG) and Wireless Communications and Computing Group (WCCG).

Desktop Platform Group: The New Millennium Opens with a Thud   Intel's core market—desktop microprocessors—was suffering from a recession that began around 2000 and lasted two years and counting. This slowdown had serious implications for Intel, since around 80 percent of IAG's revenue, and most of the company's profits, were derived from the sale of microprocessors for desktop PCs (Exhibit 9). In 2001, microprocessor unit demand fell and Intel earned lower average selling prices for microprocessors as competitors increased pricing pressure and raised their quality. Prices for Pentium 4 chips dropped between 50 percent and 60 percent in 2001. Prices for Intel's 1.7-gigahertz Pentium 4 dropped from $700 on its April 23, 2001, release date to $350 six days later. Intel wanted its 1.7-gHz chip to be at a mainstream price point before the company introduced its 2-gHz Pentium 4 later in 2001. Intel hoped to see computers with its Pentium 4 processors priced as low as $999 for a PC and monitor. Intel's moves may also have been designed to force AMD to reduce prices for its 1.2-gHz Athlon chip, which had outperformed Intel's 1.5-gHz Pentium 4 chip at equal clock speeds. AMD priced its chips according to their megahertz rating. Megahertz was one of the most important determinants to pricing,

EXHIBIT 9 |

PC Industry Profit Pool 1990–2001 Vendors and Suppliers

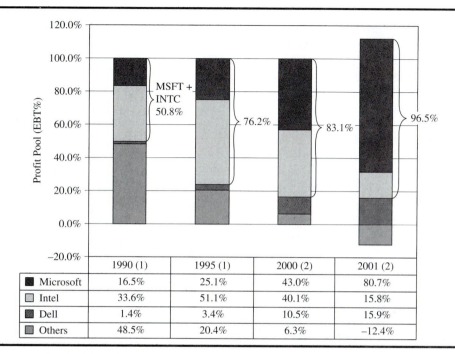

	1990 (1)	1995 (1)	2000 (2)	2001 (2)
■ Microsoft	16.5%	25.1%	43.0%	80.7%
▢ Intel	33.6%	51.1%	40.1%	15.8%
▨ Dell	1.4%	3.4%	10.5%	15.9%
▧ Others	48.5%	20.4%	6.3%	−12.4%

Source: "Computer Hardware," Bear Stearns, July 2002

(1) Data for Others category in 1990 and 1995 include total results for Apple Computer. Compaq Computer, and Gateway; Hewlett-Packard and IBM did not disclose data for PC operations.

(2) Data for others category in 2000 and 2001 include total results for Apple Computer and Gateway, as well as the PC operations of Compaq Computer, Hewlett-Packard, and IBM.

despite its being only one aspect of a chip's overall performance.[31]

In some desktop microprocessor categories, Intel dueled with AMD over performance specifications such as processor speed and processing power. Meanwhile, the recession in technology sectors forced the consolidation of the original equipment manufacturer (OEM) market for PCs. To a degree, moves like the merger of Hewlett-Packard (HP) and Compaq increased OEM buyer power while PC industry leader Dell extended its domination of the market. In the middle of a recession, that build-to-order PC maker predicted it would increase its PC share of market in the United States from 15 percent to 40 percent over the coming few years.[32]

Mobile Platforms Group Intel's work in mobile computing technologies was led by its Mobile Platforms Group (MPG). This organization was based in both Haifa, Israel, and Santa Clara, California, and Portland, Oregon,

in the United States. The group was run under the direction of Vice President and General Manager of MPG David Perlmutter and Vice President and General Manager of MPG Anand Chandrasekher.[33] In late 2002, this group was preparing to launch a project code named "Banias";[34] a new mobile PC platform featuring an entirely new processor microarchitecture. The Banias project was designed to provide PC makers with ingredients to build mobile PCs with extended battery life, improved performance, reduced/varied form factors, and easier-to-use wireless connectivity. The Banias platforms would include single band (802.11b) or dual band (802.11a and 802.11b) Wi-Fi capability through an mPCI communication device, code named "Calexico," which would contain the first 802.11 chips made by Intel. The company also planned to provide Calexico with its desktop processors and chipsets as well as a series of new "digital hubs" that would let consumers wire their TVs or other consumer electronics products to the Web via their

---

[31]Robyn Weisman, "Intel to Slash Pentium 4 Prices," NewsFactor Network, April 16, 2001.

[32]Caroline Daniel, "Inside Dell," *Financial Times*, April 2, 2002.

[33]Several key positions at Intel were shared by two senior executives. In Intel parlance, Perlmutter and Chandrasekher were "two-in-a-box."

[34]Pronounced "Ban-yes."

PCs. In January 2003, Intel publicly launched Banias under the new brand name, "Centrino," the first time Intel branded a combination of technologies under one name.[35]

Intel's efforts to provide Calexico with its Centrino notebook microprocessor recalled the company's earlier strategies in chipsets. Intel designed its chipsets to complement the latest processor features and brought them to market in time to support the new processors. For PC makers, Centrino and Calexico could reduce the amount of independent validation work they have to perform and make it easier for them to design mobile PCs with easier-to-use wireless capabilities and bring them to market more quickly. Perlmutter described the Mobile Platforms Group's strategy: "We want to expand what we do today to drive into what we are calling 'mobility.' We want to excel in all vectors of mobility: These are performance, form function, wireless communication, and extended battery life. We want to use these vectors to expand the market and grow revenues."[36]

The vectors of mobility that the Mobile Platforms Group sought were in conflict with the performance measures that had driven Intel's success in the past, particularly in desktop microprocessors. Perlmutter said:

> There are some areas of divergence between us and the desktop group. The desktop microprocessor and chipset gives higher performance, but in the past this always led to increased power dissipation.
>
> From a mobility perspective, these features require increased power consumption, expensive cooling systems, and a thicker box [increased form factor]. These contrast with mobility needs.
>
> As recently as three years ago, we were reusing desktop microprocessors, and scaled voltages and frequencies to reduce power consumption, which reduced performance, until it fit into a reasonable form factor, with additional features to extend battery life. However, it started becoming clear back then that we would not be able to retrofit our desktop microprocessors into form factors much smaller than 1.2 inches of thickness.

To succeed in the mobile market, Perlmutter's group had to promote features that amounted to apostasy for Intel. However, the toxins of the Intel "creosote bush"

did not extend to the Middle East. Perlmutter explained:

> The development group in Israel, even before it was tasked as the mobility group, pushed ideas for mobility that went against the common wisdom at Intel.
>
> Being located in Israel both helped and hurt the effort to convince the company to pursue mobility. The Israeli team has a "renegade" culture, so we were very open to the idea of mobility in the first place. However, being in Israel, far apart from Intel's HQ, made it difficult to convince the company to move toward mobility. It took blood, sweat, and tears.
>
> We did this by creating alliances with the people who were influential and had a need for some of the mobility vectors that we were pushing. For example, at the time, I was heading a development team in Israel. We created alliances with a mobile team in the U.S. that was already finding that continuing on the path of using slightly modified desktop PC microprocessors for mobile PC segment would create some issues discussed above. The effort was greatly helped by the fact that Craig [Barrett] and other Intel executives were on a vengeance that the microprocessor was starting to draw too much power, particularly in power-sensitive environments like mobile PCs. Craig found the idea of a low power microprocessor very appealing, although nobody had a clear idea of where it would lead.

The vectors of mobility seemed to apply equally to other devices in addition to computers. Perlmutter discussed the implications of the convergence of PCs and devices such as personal digital assistants (PDAs) and mobile phones.

> PDAs and mobiles phones are converging into what I like to call "smart phones." These will be devices that you can carry in your pocket. However, real computing requires a human interface: a keyboard or screen. Smart phones and mobile computers will have some similar capabilities; you will want both to be always "best connected." The user interface will decide which you use for what tasks.
>
> Intel is pursuing the smart phone market with its XScale technologies. We will sell our silicon into smart phones with XScale. But since we want to have the capabilities of a notebook, e.g., user interface, computing power, etc., we are in the course of considering selectively adding some of the PDA and smart phone-like functions into notebook PCs to improve synergies among these devices.

---

[35]"Intel Announces Centrino™ Mobile Technology Brand Name," Intel Press Release, 8 January 2003.

[36]All quotes from David Perlmutter are from the author's interview on 12 December 2002.

Intel's success with this strategy relied upon certain dependencies. Perlmutter said:

> We have dependencies on big manufacturers like Dell and IBM selling more; and on their and our abilities to promote new usage models using types of notebook PCs that excel in all four vectors of mobility. Also, Intel must help create the infrastructure for wireless (e.g., promote hot spot deployment) to help motivate consumers to use wireless connected notebooks. In addition, there are technological dependencies, such as making sure we improve our performance along the vectors of mobility.

Enterprise Platform Group: Itanium Finally Inside

Before, during, and after the dot-com euphoria, indeed for most of the 1990s, Intel, in cooperation with Hewlett-Packard, worked to develop a new processor that would compete in the highest ends of the server market. In 2001, Intel released Itanium, a 64-bit microprocessor aimed at the server market. The Itanium processor family would likely compete with 64-bit architectures designed by Sun Microsystems and IBM. Itanium had a troubled history. Its development was slower than planned, four years late by some estimates. The project took a decade to complete. News reports speculated that Itanium cost around $5 billion to complete.[37] Intel did not release the figure, but said it was less than $5 billion. Itanium was also subject to litigation; Intel lost a court case in October 2002 when a United States Federal Judge ruled that the design of Intel's Itanium violated two patents held by Intergraph Corporation. Intel could be liable for up to $250 million in damages.

Mike Fister, senior vice president and general manager of Intel's Enterprise Platform Group, discussed some of the bumps Itanium experienced along the way.

> The problems were directly related to its complexity. The technological leap was probably underestimated on our part. Examples include defining the 64-bit instruction set, working in collaboration with HP, and engaging the software industry. We under-scoped in the beginning. The Itanium instruction set, VLIW [very long instruction words], was complex. Itanium involved creating a new overall architecture (think of this as "what the outside of the building looks like") and a new microarchitecture (analogous to optimizing the building for its intended use).[38]

Much of Itanium's early development had been shrouded in secrecy. Missed milestones led to rumors that Intel and HP were not working well together. When asked if having to collaborate outside of Intel presented problems, Fister said, "Working with HP made things a bit more complicated, but the stories in the press were a bit overdone. Frankly we drove the process and we are used to collaborating on instruction set architectures. We do that all of the time, working with companies."

When the microprocessor did hit the market, customers had already slashed their IT budgets and Intel seemed to take an arms-length approach to its commercialization. Intel made the decision to leave it to original equipment manufacturers (OEMs) to work with solution providers to prime the channel for its 64-bit platform, at least at the outset. Paul Otellini, then executive vice president at Intel and general manager of the IAG said, "From Intel's perspective, this is not a channel-enabled product the way we do with boxed processors and motherboards. At this point in its life, [Itanium] is strictly an OEM product, and the channel will get trained and served from the OEM customers."[39]

In July 2002, Intel began shipping its second-generation Itanium microprocessor, Itanium 2, and seemed to more heartily embrace this version. Twenty major computer systems makers, including HP, IBM, and NEC, planned to use the Itanium 2 chip. Several leading software makers, including Oracle, SAP, IBM, and Microsoft, were making commitments to tailor their programs to run on Itanium 2. Analysts thought that the Itanium 2 could gain 10 percent of the high-end market through 2007.[40]

Intel's domination of the lower-end server microprocessor market segment, with 85 percent share of segment,[41] resembled its position in the PC microprocessor market. However Intel's server market share resulted from sales of chips for less-expensive server computers, which handle tasks such as managing shared printers and distributing Web pages to desktop users. Half the revenue in the $49 billion-a-year computer server market was generated by more expensive higher-end server computers, selling for more than $50,000, that used non-Intel technology to perform crucial tasks such as automating the manufacturing, procurement, marketing, and financial operations of large companies. Intel aimed Itanium at

[37]John Markoff and Steve Lohr, "Intel's Bet Turns Iffy," *The New York Times,* September 29, 2002.

[38]All quotes from Mike Fister are from the author's interview on 31 October 2002. Subsequent quotes from this interview will not be cited.

[39]Edward F. Moltzen, "HP Plans Exit From PA-RISC Technology," *Computer Reseller News,* June 25, 2001, p. 36.

[40]Markoff and Lohr.

[41]Intel's share of segment revenue was estimated by the company at approximately 40 percent.

that market, which used microprocessors with reduced instruction set computing (RISC) architectures and ran the UNIX operating system. In the fourth quarter of 2002, Advanced Micro Devices (AMD) planned to introduce its Opteron chip, which would offer both 32-bit and 64-bit processing, a capability that helps run large databases and solve scientific problems.[42] Opteron was part of a new AMD line, code-named "Hammer," that was due out in 2003.

In a high-profile endorsement for AMD's Opteron, reports emerged in October 2002 that Sandia National Laboratories, which does research for the United States Department of Energy, and Cray Inc. planned to build a massive supercomputer using the chip. AMD said Hammer-based computers could run both 32-bit and 64-bit software at high speed. AMD released preliminary test results for Opteron that claimed to show the chip exceeded Intel's latest Itanium 2 model on one of two widely used speed measures. Meanwhile, Itanium 2 had enjoyed several important design wins since its release in the summer of 2002, including at least a half-dozen high-performance computing project installations.[43]

More worrying to Intel was the possibility that the market Itanium was designed to address, high-performance corporate computing, was fundamentally changing. At a conference at Stanford University in August 2002, Eric Schmidt, a computer scientist and CEO of the popular Internet search engine Google, discussed his vision for the industry. Schmidt spoke of small and inexpensive processors acting as Lego-style building blocks to execute powerful processing applications, displacing expensive server processors and the market that Itanium aimed to serve. Google cared less about raw processing power—the product of Moore's Law—and more about lower power consumption. Data centers, such as those used by Google, consumed as much electricity as cities. Google currently used servers with Intel's Xeon processors, which suited its requirements. Itanium was not aimed at search engines, which executed large volumes of processing power to execute fairly simple tasks, but the bigger and more complex problems of data warehousing and high-performance technical computing. If Itanium failed to find success with companies in these markets, the ability of Itanium 2,

or subsequent iterations to pay back Intel's heavy investment with expected margins, was less certain.

AMD also snapped at Intel's heels in other markets. Early in 2002, AMD expanded its Athlon processor family by introducing three high-end chips: the Athlon XP processor 2100+ for desktop PCs, the Athlon MP processor 2000+ for servers and workstations, and the mobile Athlon 4 processor 1600+ for notebook PCs, priced at $420, $415, and $380, respectively. At about this time Intel introduced the multiprocessor Xeon microprocessor at 1.4, 1.5, and 1.6GHz, priced from $1,177 to $3,692.[44] AMD also targeted its lower priced K7 line of microprocessors to compete against Intel's Xeon. AMD's Athlon chip line, mainly used in personal computers, had been falling behind the performance of comparable Intel chips.

Intel Communications Group

The Intel Communications Group (ICG) was formed in April 2001. Led by Sean Maloney, executive vice president and general manager, the group was involved in a variety of activities including designing and manufacturing microchips used in systems that transmit and direct traffic across the Internet and corporate networks; designing and manufacturing networking devices and equipment that provide access to the Internet, as well as local area networks and home networks; and designing and manufacturing hardware components for high-speed, high-capacity optical networks. Maloney said, "We will use Moore's Law to drive down the costs of chips, without threatening the business models of our customers. Internet traffic is approximately doubling every 12 to 18 months and I believe it will continue to do so through 2010."[45] To exploit this growth, ICG would look to double-down [bet heavily] on Ethernet and pull away as the world's largest supplier. In addition, ICG would provide three things:

1. Break through cost/performance optical components.

2. Low-cost, high-performance processors to handle IP packets.

3. World-leading Wi-Fi technology.

When the ICG was formed, Intel was extricating itself from its failed attempts in selling system products through

[42]Steve Lohr, "Intel to Begin Shipping a 64-Bit Microprocessor," *The New York Times*, July 8, 2002.

[43]Don Clark, "AMD Stages Supercomputer Coup—Hammer Chips Are Selected for U.S. Red Storm Project over Intel's Itanium Line," *The Wall Street Journal*, October 21, 2002.

[44]Robert Ristelhueber, "AMD, Intel Unveil Rival Processors at CeBIT Show," *EBN*, March 18, 2002. NB: prices are for 1,000-unit purchases.

[45]All quotes from Sean Maloney are from the author's interview on 24 October 2002. Subsequent quotes from this interview will not be cited.

CPG (see earlier). Maloney said: "There was fairly serious dissonance between Network Communications Group (NCG) and Communications Products Group (CPG). We needed to be either a components company or a systems company, but not both. We decided to aim to be the world's largest communications components supplier."

John Miner, who had been general manager of CPG, recalled the reason for the group's founding and disbanding:

> We met with Dell, Compaq, and IBM to convince them to go where Sun was. They were reluctant to join us in this space, except Compaq, who wanted to go it alone. We decided if they [the OEMs] didn't want to do it with us, we should go it alone. So we created CPG as a separate group because we didn't want to be perceived as competing with our customers. . . . We started in the middle of 1999. We wound down in 2001. We had over $1 billion in server sales in nine months. In the market place, the unbranded white box became equivalent to Intel. . . . Looking back, it was bad strategy to enter the market, but there had been some positive consequences. The OEMs did step in and participate when Intel showed them the way. However, it was not sustainable. Core microprocessor customers would eventually see that it was a good business, get into it themselves, and scream about competition from us. We have to listen to big microprocessor customers.

Sean Maloney also observed:

> We manufactured around 80 percent of our communications chips in outside foundries. Our designers felt we couldn't (economically) make communications chips. I felt that Intel was essentially a building block company and the best manufacturer in the world. We know how to approach complex problems at the chip level and solve them. We should look to expand into adjacencies of approach or thought. After spending multiple hundreds of millions of dollars, we are now on track to make 90 percent of our communications chips in-house, with the world's best manufacturing technology.

In the reorganization that produced ICG, and the hard times the communications industry faced in the prolonged economic downturn, ICG reduced its headcount from 10,700 employees to 6,700. Maloney recalled, "It was a painful process getting here. We shut 15 manufacturing and design sites. It was time consuming and expensive to do it right, to do it with dignity for the people." But now, Maloney was confident that Intel had

right tools, correctly aligned to compete in the telecommunications market. "We have been accumulating communication chip skills for some time. We now have more communication chip skills than any other company in the industry. In Wi-Fi, Optical, etc. we have no excuses; we have the skills to be number one. We have our fate in our hands."

With the skills collected at ICG, Intel hoped to develop standardized chip-level products, or "building blocks" that would serve the telecommunications industry. Currently, telecommunications suppliers such as Lucent and Cisco use specially designed, proprietary microprocessors and software in their products. In the absence of standard architectures for such systems, suppliers gained some advantage as customers tended to remain with their suppliers once such systems had been installed. Maloney hoped to use Moore's Law as a wedge to open—and perhaps standardize at the chip architecture level—the telecommunications supplier market. Maloney said, "The telecommunications industry had not benefited from Moore's Law because most of the processors used in their networks were not manufactured in volumes large enough to support leading-edge research or manufacturing technology. A standard 'building block' made with cutting-edge manufacturing technology, along with standard programming tools, could allow Intel to bring Moore's Law to the telecom industry."

Intel looked to key customers to help provide the volume necessary to get the benefits of Moore's Law to apply to this jurisdiction. Cisco, for example, would make a particularly valuable customer. Cisco was not immune to the technology downturn that affected the telecommunications and technology industries, but it fared better than most in those sectors. Its annual revenue in fiscal year 2002 exceeded $18 billion, with a gross profit margin of 68 percent. By the end of its fiscal year in July 2002, the company was sitting on a cash pile totaling $21 billion. Indeed, for the latter half of the 1990s, Cisco's revenues grew fivefold. But this growth decelerated by FY2001 and turned negative by FY2002. Some analysts estimated that the company's future annual growth rates would range between 7 and 8 percent, resembling those associated with more mature companies.

To boost its margins and protect against declines in its core router business, Cisco was likely to move into new markets such as storage, security, and voice over Internet Protocol (VOIP) technologies. With a mountain of cash and a profitable but declining core market, Cisco resembled its would-be supplier, Intel.

Why would Cisco, mindful of how most of the margins from the PC market migrated to Microsoft and Intel, choose to work with Intel rather than going it alone in these new areas? "Because many communications customers feared another potential Wintel architecture, we had to overcome an attitude of 'ABI' (Anything but Intel)," Maloney explained, continuing:

> A large problem we had to overcome with our customers was convincing them that we are not trying to commoditize their business. They suspected that we were trying to establish another "Wintel" standard. It took up to 10 visits to convince them otherwise. It was a very complicated conversation.
>
> Why do they not need to worry? Because there is no standard software and the rate of technology change is far higher than in the PC industry. It is a long way from commoditization with endless changes to differentiate in software and services.
>
> We tell potential customers that the economics governing components at the chip level forces the industry into mass manufacturing and integration. You must embrace this trend and transformation. Intel helps you with this transformation. Our advice is: 'Your intellectual property is above ASICs.[46] Customized components increase your inventory problem. Your value-add is in understanding and designing traffic networks, a far bigger challenge.'

If entering the telecommunication supplier industry in the teeth of an extended telecom downturn did not seem like auspicious timing, according to Maloney, Intel had no alternative. He observed, "Our industry is already migrating to the communication space. PCs have been primarily about communications for almost 10 years (e.g., the popularity of e-mail, etc.). We woke up to this fact. We want to lead it rather than be led by it." For Maloney, ICG's goal was to "supply the underlying technologies that allow others to be creative." He held high hopes for WiFi and considered 802.11 directly analogous to the browser 10 years ago. Still, Maloney did not expect ICG to be profitable in the foreseeable future. He felt that in the meantime, appropriate performance measures would be the ability to get design wins in the right product-market spaces and to bring down the break-even level.

The communications market was both competitive and contracting. The market for communications systems (wired and wireless) semiconductors and optical components shrank by 38 percent in 2001. Analysts said a combination of demand-side issues, such as the worldwide economic slowdown, decreased spending for IT products, and decreased capital spending by telecommunications carriers, and an oversupply of components in the market at the beginning of 2001 led to the market decline. Looking at the broader telecommunications market, including optical components 2001, Intel ranked second, behind Agere Systems Inc., largely thanks to revenues Intel derived from sales of flash memory and because it gained share in the LAN adapter market. Agere Systems was an integrated design manufacturer specializing in optoelectronic components for communications networks. Agere had been spun out from Lucent Technologies in March 2001. In June 2002, Lucent sold its remaining shares of Agere, which then became a fully separate company. Although Intel's communications revenue fell 22 percent to $2.7 billion, the decrease was relatively small enough to push it from fourth in 2000 to second place in 2001. Industry leader Agere earned sales of $2.8 billion. TI ranked third with communications revenues of $2.4 billion, a 33.1 percent decrease from 2000. Agere's captured 5.8 percent share of the communications market, compared to Intel's 5.7 percent and TI's 5.1 percent.[47]

Wireless Communications and Computing Group

Another group at Intel was interested in creating helpful and profitable building blocks. Intel's Wireless Communications and Computing Group (WCCG) designs and produces processors for data functions such as calendar and e-mail programs, chipsets that enable voice communication functions for wireless handheld devices, and cellular phones and flash memories that retain data when a device's power is turned off.

This group is operated under the direction of Ron Smith, senior vice president and general manager. Smith described Intel's interest in wireless technologies:

> WCCG's goal is not to make the final product, but rather to provide the building blocks that make up the final product. These blocks must be standard, open, and allow ease of programming. For example, they must allow for ease of migration of applications from PC to handheld devices.
>
> We want to be the building block supplier to the wireless data industry. We aim to construct an architecture that

---

[46]ASIC is an acronym for application-specific integrated circuit.

[47]"Intel Nears Top of Shrinking Comms Market," *Electronic News,* May 27, 2002, p. 24.

we call Personal Internet Client Architecture. This involves us in application processors, communications processors, and memory subsystems. We also provide core, low-level enabling software. We are evangelizing for increased performance, less power [energy consumption] and smaller size.[48]

For Smith, this did not entail a radical departure from Intel's core interests, at least as they have been aligned for the past few years.

Intel was moving toward communications and computing convergence. For us, this convergence is embodied at the chip level. In 1996, Andy [Grove] told me we are a bit industry . . . moving bits, processing bits. If you consider a cell phone, a huge fraction of the bill of materials value is concerned with semiconductors. We thought there were opportunities to add value to integration. Now we are moving digital binary information units . . . done in silicon. Our currency is silicon, not our product. Our product is architecture, software support, etc.

Smith summed up his goals for WCCG and Intel in a formula that he described as a "figure of merit."

We have created a new figure of merit: 2M/2m. That is MIPS $\times$ Mb/mW $\times$ mm^3.

- We want to increase MIPS, by keeping up with Moore's Law.

- We want to increase Mb (storage). We are already the world's leader in flash technology.

Their business models work more like ours. More like what Apple does; developing software and hardware in harmony. This gives you vertical integration because of aligned set of business priorities.

This interdependence goes across devices. We are aligned 80 percent of the time with Microsoft in what we do. Take telcos for example. Microsoft does less well in this space. We want to create reprogrammable silicon architectures based on Intel standards that people add value on top of. Sometimes with Microsoft, sometimes not. In this case, we use Linux and UNIX.

There has not been much internal resistance to the change in focus. The biggest problem is getting people over the "brand barrier." It takes longer to create a brand than a product. We need to reevaluate our brand. This will change the meaning of Intel Inside™. The brand change takes as much management encouragement as the planning issues.

Barrett compared this to where Intel has been. "In the past, we called Andy Grove the 'chief marketing officer.' In the 1990s, we were very vertical around desktop microprocessors. Every decision was make-or-break because we were a single-product company. Now we are migrating to a more horizontal structure."

Looking Ahead

Otellini was specific about where he wanted Intel to go in the future. He said:

We put stakes in the ground five years out. We have decided to focus on:

- Digital home

- Digital office/enterprise

- Mobile Internet clients

- Telco infrastructure

That's how people use computers. Our goal is to get Intel chips inside every one of those devices. Look at what we are doing for the next-generation notebook. We are not just branding the chip, but branding the entire silicon platform. We will advertise the platform's usefulness, not its gigahertz. There may be a significant benefit to the consumer from an increase from 2.3 to 2.4 gHz, but it is increasingly difficult to make that case to consumers.

Barrett was confident about Intel's future and its bet on the convergence of communication and computing. Barrett said:

It is happening at an interesting time. The convergence has been touted for a long time, but now we have the technical capability to create interesting mixed architecture solutions for communications and computing.

Historically, microprocessors are cool, unique devices. The faster, the better. More recently, it's not about the microprocessor, but about the architecture of the device (e.g., PCs). Now the architecture of the platform is important. The lack of investment by PC OEMs forced us to pick up the slack (e.g., chipsets).

More recently, it's about solution. We work with ISVs and operation system vendors. Processors are part of the solution. It's about much more than clock speed.

I am spending more time working with Adobe, for example, making Photoshop run best on a Pentium 4.

---

[48]All quotes from Ron Smith are from the author's interview on 24 October 2002. Subsequent quotes from this interview will not be cited.

Intel used to live by the performance of its microprocessors for PCs. Moore's Law governed the company, and its engineers devised sophisticated solutions to keep Intel pushing against the Moore's Law curve. Now, Intel worried about new and different performance features, some of which had little to do with cramming more transistors onto integrated circuits. Barrett said, "We are looking at four aspects of performance: battery life, form function, wireless, and clock speed."

Barrett discussed the implications of these new performance measures.

> Now we have to do joint marketing with companies; our hardware and software engineers have to interact with their counterparts at other companies. There are also architecture implications: What's important in the next product? In the past we let desktop functionalities cascade to laptops. Now we design from the ground up, with segmentation and use in mind at the beginning.

Usage Models

The company now thinks about development in terms of usage models, evaluating at the outset how the architecture or platform will be used. Barrett said, "All customer expectations require individual design. We had to segment our products because the end users' segmentation was growing. There are growing differences between desktops, mobiles, etc. The market segmentation drives our segmentation of development processes."

Paul Otellini explained:

> The usage model gets us away from diminishing returns on processor speeds. It gets away from the 'who cares?' question. This changes the value proposition of what we offer.
>
> We want to start driving markets. We can do this because of the platforms. There are huge interdependencies, e.g., Microsoft, but our business models are more aligned. It used to be that Microsoft focused on installed base, while Intel focused on incremental units. Now, both care most about incremental units.
>
> - We want to decrease power usage (mW). We are using low-power architectures based on ARM[49] and Intel technologies. Intel acquired strong ARM from the Digital acquisition.

- We want to decrease size (mm3). We have developed products such as "stacking package" and Intel StrataFlash™ to achieve this.[50]

Smith said, "Each component in this figure of merit is now a competency at Intel. We are leading in all the 'Ms' [each component of the figure of merit]."

In February 2003, some of these figures of merit translated into a new microprocessor, code-named Manitoba, for the cell phone market. Manitoba offered cell phone manufacturers a low power consuming processor combined with flash and SRAM memories that will allow manufacturers to produce smaller phones with additional features. Intel looked to products like Manitoba, combining microprocessors and memories, to give the company—and a potential Intel platform—entrée into the growing cell phone market. Unlike its position in the PC microprocessor market, Intel was a relative newcomer to the wireless market, behind its well-established competitor TI. While some analysts estimated worldwide PC sales to increase from 136 million units in 2002 to 192 million units by 2006; more rapid growth was expected from the cell phone market, with increases expected from 400 million units sold worldwide in 2002 to 600 million units sold by 2006.[51]

Beyond 2002: The Corporate Perspective

The Challenge of Making It Work Together

Much of the work that will govern the future of Intel involved formerly disparate groups working together. Barrett said, "If we have different architectures and want to simplify the software, we must set targets and reward employees on their ability to work across groups."

Asked how he gets employees to change long-standing habits, Barrett said:

> Communicate, communicate, communicate + organize, organize, organize + reward, reward, reward. That's how you turn the Queen Mary.

---

[49]ARM (originally advanced RISC machines) technologies offer high performance with low power consumption, an important attribute for battery-powered devices.

[50]Stacking is a process whereby components that were formerly housed in separate chips are combined or stacked onto a single chip. For example, Intel integrates flash memory and RAM functionality into a single package for wireless OEMs. This stacking saves board space, an important attribute as devices become smaller.

[51]Cliff Edwards, Andy Reinhardt, Roger O. Crockett, "The Hulk Haunting Cell Phones," *BusinessWeek*, March 3, 2003, p. 44.

We communicate directly to employees. For example we do a Webcast to all employees at the same time we do our presentations to analysts. Andy Bryant and Paul Otellini speak to Wall Street and I speak to employees. I don't want our employees to have to get their information from the street.

Barrett had to communicate closely with more than just his employees:

> The telecom world is imploding from its historical structure. The same changes the PC industry underwent in a decade have happened to telecoms in 12 months. For example, Lucent, Nortel, Motorola, Ericsson, etc., are all laying-off large fractions of their development staffs. That means they'll have to add value by getting out of proprietary architectures and use standardized building blocks.

For the boldness of these bets, Intel was not betting the company on any of them, like it did with its decision to abandon memories in favor of microprocessors. Barrett continued:

> I used to say that we're heading at 120 mph toward a brick wall . . . but it is worse to invest too late.

> Our strategy of maintaining cash has never wavered. We want a big bank account because the environment will be difficult, but we'll want to continue to invest. Our revenue is down 20 percent from 2000, but we're still profitable, generating cash and we have $10 billion in the bank. We are doing a $4 billion stock buyback. Use it or lose it? We chose to use it and replenish it. It's a prudent bet.

Conclusion

Due to the success of the company's "second act," dominating the market segment for PC microprocessors, Intel owned a cash-generating machine, a large bank account and a valuable global brand. The company would need these assets as it faced the simultaneous challenges of competitive pressure in its core and new market segments; a prolonged global technology recession, and the risk that its huge investments in manufacturing would not pay off as handsomely or strategically as it hoped. By late 2002, Intel had moved from letting chaos reign for a few years in order to explore new growth opportunities, to reining in chaos to focus on exploiting the opportunities it had found in the convergence of communications and computing at the building block level. Yet, it was not proven that this convergence would be as profitable to Intel as the company hoped. Top management needed to address several key strategic questions. Is communications worth winning? What forms of communications? Does Intel have a clear strategic vision? How aggressively should the company pursue these market segments? Many interested outsiders as well as insiders were trying to determine what would have to happen for the company to replicate its past success—and whether Intel would be able to find a comparable "third act."

Case 4.2

Nokia Beyond 2003: A Mobile Gatekeeper?

Introduction

For over a billion people around the world, mobile phones have become an increasingly important device. For consumers they have been part phone, part personal computer, and part fashion statement. For mobile phone makers and service operators, they represented gateways to new services and, perhaps, new sources of cash flow and profits. Nokia alone sold over $23 billion in handsets in 2002. With the advent of advanced mobile services such as wireless Internet access, photos and video clips and games, made possible with new third-generation (3G)[1] mobile networks, mobile phones could represent an important new nexus of consumer applications—a gateway to the Internet and a wealth of services.

By 2003, the telecom industry in the United States and much of the world was in the third year of economic downturn. The number of new mobile subscribers declined globally in 2001. Service operators, particularly mobile providers, were suffering from the effects of overinvestment in the late 1990s. For example, European mobile operators spent over $100 billion on 3G licenses,[2] purchased from their governments' regulators, in the late 1990s and had little to show for the investments by 2003. Many handset makers and network equipment manufacturers were also hurting. With the

roll-out of new 3G network technologies proceeding slowly, the promise of new revenue streams from new 3G applications seemed like a mirage that was tantalizingly close, but still just out of reach.

The experience of the PC industry—where Microsoft and Intel were able to command the greatest rents in the industry with their "Wintel" platform—was fresh in the minds of handset makers, network equipment companies, and service operators. By 2003, the software driving mobile telephony took on increased importance with industry participants and investors. Indeed, Microsoft offered an operating system for the mobile telephony industry, which made handset makers—especially Nokia—very wary; and Intel was entering the market for increasingly sophisticated mobile chipsets. Nokia, Motorola, Sony Ericsson, Samsung, and others did not want to be marginalized in the same way as some PC makers. Mobile telephony operators, with their direct relationships with consumers, and themselves the largest customers of the handset makers, wanted to make sure they too remained a valuable part of the 3G mobile value chain. With the global telecommunications industry in recession, most handset and mobile operators hurting, and Microsoft sitting on $40 billion in cash, what could Nokia do to make sure it continued to capture a good share of industry profits from mobile telephony?

Mobile Phone Standards

The first generation (1G) of cell phone technology, initially called "cellular mobile radio telephone" was launched in the late 1970s and lasted through the 1980s. These networks used analog voice signaling technology. The 1G technology was highly fragmented, with various incompatible standards, such as AMPS, NMT, TACS, and others competing for share. Since the late 1980s, two different and incompatible cell phone standards were used around the world. The split occurred when carriers moved from analog mobile phone standards to second-generation (2G) digital mobile technologies.

By the early 1990s, one mobile phone standard, Global System for Mobile (GSM),[3] dominated the

---

[1] Third-generation (3G) mobile networks support high data exchange rates, measured in megabits per second (Mbps), intended for bandwidth-hungry mobile applications such as full-motion video, video-conferencing, and full Internet access.

[2] "Computing's New Shape," *The Economist*, November 21, 2002.

Professor Robert A. Burgelman and Philip E. Meza prepared this case as the basis for class discussion rather than to illustrate either effective or ineffective handling of an administrative situation.

[3] Historically known as Groupe System Mobile, named for the advisory body of European Union's Conférence des Administrations Européenes des Postes et Télécommunications charged with developing a pan-European mobile communications network.

industry around the world. By 2003, around three-quarters of the world's mobile phone subscribers used GSM systems. The GSM standard was created in the mid-1980s with the intention of developing a mobile digital standard to replace spectrum-hungry analog systems. A digital standard offered more efficient use of finite frequency spectrum and additional services that were not possible with analog technology. In Europe, where regulators promulgated the GSM standard, operators (which were then often government-owned companies) could offer customers continent-wide roaming and digital services such as short messaging services (SMS) and overall improved call quality. GSM proliferated in Europe and elsewhere around the world, but not in the United States.

In 1985, at the time that the GSM standard was being developed, a competing standard, called code division multiple access (CDMA), was developed by a San Diego, California, start-up called Quality Communications, later known as Qualcomm. Qualcomm succeeded in getting its standard used in several important markets including the United States and South Korea. As of December 2002, there were 127 million CDMA users worldwide, with 55 million of these in the United States.

Each of these two systems used a different method to transmit voice and data. GSM used a variation of time division multiple access (TDMA), a technology that uses a common channel for communications among multiple users by allocating unique time slots to different users. GSM digitizes and compresses data, then sends it down a channel with two other streams of user data, each in its own time slot. Code division multiple access (CDMA) digitizes the call and spreads it out over the entire bandwidth available to it. Multiple calls are overlapped on top of each other (instead of being placed side by side in slots, as with TDMA and GSM), and each is assigned a unique sequencing code to unlock the information only when and where it should be unlocked.

Qualcomm owned a large number of CDMA patents, including many essential patents that were necessary for the deployment of any proposed 3G CDMA system, such as TD-SCDMA and CDMA 2000-1x. The company granted royalty-earning licenses to more than 75 manufacturers for CDMA and, as part of these licenses, transferred technology and know-how in helping these companies develop and deploy CDMA products.

As the market for telecom services, including mobile, declined, operators looked to 3G technologies to spur growth. Two incompatible 3G standards emerged:

W-CDMA[4] and CDMA2000. European regulators promulgated W-CDMA with the hopes that a single technology standard would help 3G gain the rapid dominance enjoyed by the GSM technology. Of 112 network operators around the world who had been granted 3G licenses, over 100 selected (or were forced by standards bodies to select) W-CDMA technology.[5] European operators paid €100 billion (around $107 billion) for 3G licenses that specified using W-CDMA technology, and in some cases these fees would be forfeit without refund if a different standard was used by the operator. As they tried to roll out W-CDMA services in late 2002 and early 2003, many operators ran into problems with handset operability; handsets made by one firm did not always work properly with network equipment made by another firm. While this and other problems were worked out, many expected that 3G services would meet lukewarm acceptance by users in Europe. In the face of these troubles, some European operators such as Orange (in Sweden) and Germany's Mobilcom, among others, backed out of their 3G commitments or tried to extract renegotiated license terms from regulators.[6]

Meanwhile, a rival 3G technology, called CDMA2000, seemed to be working well in various markets. Whereas an industry consortium controlled W-CDMA, CDMA2000 was controlled by Qualcomm. In its rollout, operators did not experience the interoperability problems faced by many in Europe. By the middle of 2002, over 17 million people in South Korea, Japan, and the United States used a version of the standard called CDMA2000-1x. In Japan, CDMA2000-1x and W-CDMA competed head to head. Japanese operator NTT DoCoMo launched the world's first commercial W-CDMA network in October 2001. It met with lackluster results, signing up fewer than 200,000 subscribers within a year of operation, largely due to high handset prices and lack of demand for the applications offered. Meanwhile, rival operator KDDI launched a CDMA2000-1x service in April 2002, and quickly signed up 2.3 million subscribers.[7]

The Role of Network Operators

In 2002, network operators (purchasers of handsets and the networking equipment to operate 3G systems) spent 20 percent less on network equipment than in 2001.

[4]Wideband CDMA (W-CDMA) is also known as UMTS in Europe.

[5]W-CDMA selection data from Nokia SEC Form 20-F, 2002, p. 23.

[6]William Clark, et.al., "European Vendors Face Challenges for W-CDMA Adoption," Gartner Commentary, COM-19-2551, February 20, 2003.

[7]"Time for plan B," The Economist, September 26, 2002.

In 2003, some analysts forecast that operators would cut spending on equipment by an additional 20 percent.[8] All network equipment makers were hurting in the three-year worldwide recession in telecommunications. Equipment and handset makers, such as Nokia, and network operators, such as Hutchison in the United Kingdom, faced great uncertainty over the roll-out of 3G services. For many consumers, the services offered by enhanced second-generation systems (2.5G) currently in operation were good enough. Operators, hungry for the revenue-enhancing new services that could be offered via 3G networks, were interested in rolling out a 3G network, but fearful of slow customer adoption. Consumer uptake of 3G was inhibited by the fact that 3G handsets were often larger than current 2.5G models and featured shorter battery life than models already in use. In addition, 3G handsets were expensive. In the United Kingdom, Hutchison launched its 3G service in March 2003, selling 3G handsets (supplied by Motorola and Japan's NEC) at £400 ($627). In the face of slow sales, the operator initiated a series of special offers that reduced handset prices to under $200, even though the company had earlier stated that it would not subsidize 3G handsets.[9]

Nokia in 2003

Nokia was founded in 1865 as a paper manufacturer and took its name from Finland's Nokia river. As the company grew, it added Finnish Rubber Works Ltd., a maker of tires, rubber boots, and other consumer and industrial rubber products, and Finnish Cable Works, a manufacturer of cable for power generation and telecommunications.[10] The company continued to grow as a conglomerate throughout the 1960s through the 1980s, buying and developing a diversified body of unrelated businesses. In the early 1990s, Nokia decided to focus on telecommunications, one of its core operations at the time, and divested its nontelecommunications businesses. At the same time, the company greatly benefited from deregulation in telecommunications within Europe that occurred in the early 1990s as well as from the European Union's decision to support the GSM platform for mobile communications.[11] The first GSM mobile call was made using a Nokia phone over a Nokia-built network in Finland in 1991.

In 2003, Nokia Corporation was organized into two primary business segments: Nokia Mobile Phones and Nokia Networks (Exhibit 1). In addition, the company operated the separate Nokia Ventures Organization as well as a corporate research unit called Nokia Research Center. The company was headquartered in Finland, but maintained research centers and factories around the world. Nokia employed 58,000 people in 2003.

Handsets

As recently as 1999 there was rough parity in the handset market. Since then Nokia had eclipsed the competition. By 2002, Nokia Mobile Phones was the world's largest mobile phone producer and had over twice the market share of Motorola, its closest competitor (Exhibit 2). In 2002, Nokia's market share rose for the fifth consecutive year to an estimated 38 percent. Handsets were the lifeblood of the company, generating almost 80 percent of sales and 90 percent of earnings, with operating margins of 20 percent.[12] In the first quarter of 2003, the handset division reported sales of €5.47 billion ($5.95 billion) and an operating profit margin of 23.9 percent. However, average selling prices (ASPs) had slipped from €147 to €145. In the same period in 2001, handset ASP was €164.[13]

Nokia estimated that the mobile handset market returned to growth in 2002, with projected market volumes reaching about 405 million units; a 5 percent increase over volume sold in 2001. Nokia estimated that the global mobile phone subscriber base reached 1.125 billion users in 2002 and projected this number to exceed 1.5 billion users by 2005. Global penetration in 2002 reached 18 percent, with penetration exceeding 80 percent in Europe, 50 percent in the United States, and 16 percent in China.[14]

---

[8]Christopher Brown-Humes, "Nokia to Cut 1,800 Jobs in Networks Unit," *Financial Times*, April 11, 2003, p. 20.

[9]Robert Budden, "Customers Call the Shots in 3G Battle," *Financial Times*, April 15, 2003, p. 23.

[10]http://www.nokia.com/nokia/0,8764,1126,00.html.

[11]In 1987, the EC, then called EEU, issued a resolution to adopt GSM as the European digital standard by July 1, 1991. Source: Nokia SEC Form 20-F, 2002, p. 19.

[12]Ben Hunt and Paul Abrahams, "Microsoft's Battle with Symbian," *Financial Times*, February 25, 2003.

[13]Christopher Brown-Humes, "Nokia Upbeat as Handset Sales Grow," *Financial Times*, April 19/April 20, 2003, p. 10.

[14] Nokia SEC Form 20-F 2002, p. 22.

EXHIBIT 1 | Nokia Corp. Consolidated Profit and Loss Accounts

Financial year ended Dec. 31	2002 EURm	2001 EURm	2000 EURm
NET SALES	30,016	31,191	30,376
Cost of sales	−18,278	−19,787	−19,072
Research and development expenses	−3,052	−2,985	−2,584
Selling, general and administrative expenses	−3,239	−3,523	−2,804
Customer finance impairment charges, net	−279	−714	—
Impairment of goodwill	−182	−518	—
Amortization of goodwill	−206	−302	−140
OPERATING PROFIT	4,789	3,362	5,776
Share of results of associated companies	−19	−12	−16
Financial income and expenses	156	125	102
PROFIT BEFORE TAX AND MINORITY INTERESTS	4,917	3,475	5,862
Tax	−1,484	−1,192	−1,784
Minority interests	−52	−83	−140
NET PROFIT	3,381	2,200	3,938

Source: Nokia Annual Report 2002.

(continued)

Nokia manufactured most of its own handsets in 10 plants around the world. The company outsourced 15–20 percent of its manufacturing volume, with no plans to increase or decrease that percentage in the near future. Nokia assembled most of its own handsets, but relied on others to supply the raw materials, including semiconductors.[15]

Networks

Nokia Networks researched, manufactured and marketed a variety of infrastructure equipment for the GSM standard. This segment of the mobile communications industry was particularly hard hit in 2002. Nokia estimated that that overall network infrastructure market decreased by approximately 20 percent in 2002—a time when the market for handsets was estimated to have increased by 5 percent (see below).[16] Nokia Networks was a global leader in GSM technology, supplying 35 percent of the market for GSM network equipment.[17] In 2002, Nokia Networks represented approximately 22 percent of Nokia's net sales. Nokia Networks operated seven production facilities, four in Finland and three in China. Over 60 percent of its manufacturing volume was outsourced.[18]

Nokia Networks did not produce network equipment for TDMA or CDMA networks,[19] but it did produce W-CDMA equipment. Such networks were capable of handling wireless high-speed data transfer rates, which supported applications such as fast Internet access, music and video file viewing and swapping and games, all via mobile phones. 3G phones were expected to have roaming capability throughout Europe, Japan, and North America.

In 2002, Nokia had agreements to supply WCDMA networks to 37 customers. Deliveries to 25 operator customers had begun by the end of 2002. In December 2002, first commercial launch of a Nokia-delivered W-CDMA 3G network took place in Japan with Japan Telecom's J-Phone. Nokia estimated that at the end of 2002, it had a leading position in GSM networks with a market share of over 25 percent, and a 15–20 percent share of the total mobile network infrastructure market.[20]

[15]Ibid., p. 34.

[16]Ibid., p. 22.

[17]Christine Whitehouse, "Nokia Plans to Cut 1,800 Jobs in Network Equipment Unit," *The New York Times*, April 11, 2003, W1.

[18]Nokia SEC Form 20-F, 2002, p. 34.

[19]Nokia did produce handsets that operated using CDMA and TDMA technologies.

[20]http://www.nokia.com/cda2/0,4268,3627,00.html

EXHIBIT 1 | Nokia Corporation Consolidated Balance Sheet (cont.)

Dec. 31	2002 EURm	2001 EURm
ASSETS		
Fixed assets and other noncurrent assets		
Capitalized development costs	1,072	893
Goodwill	476	854
Other intangible assets	192	237
Property, plant and equipment	1,874	2,514
Investments in associated companies	49	49
Available-for-sale investments	238	399
Deferred tax assets	731	832
Long-term loans receivable	1,056	1,128
Other noncurrent assets	54	6
	5,742	6,912
Current assets		
Inventories	1,277	1,788
Accounts receivable	5,385	5,719
Prepaid expenses and accrued income	1,156	1,480
Other financial assets	416	403
Available-for-sale investments	7,855	4,271
Bank and cash	1,496	1,854
	17,585	15,515
	23,327	22,427

Dec. 31	2002 EURm	2001 EURm
SHAREHOLDERS' EQUITY AND LIABILITIES		
Shareholders' equity		
Share capital	287	284
Share issue premium	2,225	2,060
Treasury shares, at cost	−20	−21
Translation differences	135	326
Fair value and other reserves	−7	20
Retained earnings	11,661	9,536
	14,281	12,205
Minority interest	173	196
Long-term liabilities		
Long-term interest-bearing liabilities	187	207
Deferred tax liabilities	207	177
Other long-term liabilities	67	76
	461	460
Current liabilities		
Short-term borrowings	377	831
Accounts payable	2,954	3,074
Accrued expenses	2,611	3,477
Provisions	2,470	2,184
	8,412	9,566
Total shareholders' equity and liabilities	23,327	22,427

Source: Nokia Annual Report 2002.

(*continued*)

EXHIBIT 1 | Nokia Corporation Consolidated Cash Flow Statement (cont.)

Financial year ended Dec. 31	2002 EURm	2001 EURm	2000 EURm
Cash flow from operating activities			
Net profit	**3,381**	2,200	3,938
Adjustments, total	**3,151**	4,132	2,805
Net profit before change in net working capital	**6,532**	6,332	6,743
Change in net working capital	**955**	978	−1,377
Cash generated from operations	**7,487**	7,310	5,366
Interest received	**229**	226	255
Interest paid	**−94**	−155	−115
Other financial income and expenses	**139**	99	−454
Income taxes paid	**−1,947**	−933	−1,543
Net cash from operating activities	**5,814**	6,547	3,509
Cash flow from investing activities			
Acquisition of Group companies, net of acquired cash			
(2002: EUR 6 mil, 2001: EUR 12 mil, 2000: EUR 2 mil	**−10**	−131	-400
Purchase of non-current available-for-sale investments	**−99**	−323	−111
Additions to capitalized development costs	**−418**	−431	−393
Long-term loans made to customers	**−563**	−1,129	−776
Proceeds from repayment and transfers of long-term loans receivable	**314**	—	—
Proceeds from (+)/payment of (−) other long-term receivables	**−32**	84	—
Proceeds from (+)/payment of (−) short-term loans receivable	**−85**	−114	378
Capital expenditures	**−432**	−1,041	−1,580
Proceeds from disposal of shares in Group companies, net of disposed cash	**93**	—	4
Proceeds from sale of non-current available-for-sale investments	**162**	204	75
Proceeds from sale of fixed assets	**177**	175	221
Dividends received	**25**	27	51
Net cash used in investing activities	**−868**	−2,679	−2,531
Cash flow from financing activities			
Proceeds from stock option exercises	**163**	77	72
Purchase of treasury shares	**−17**	−21	−160
Capital investment by minority shareholders	**26**	4	7
Proceeds from long-term borrowings	**100**	102	—
Repayment of long-term borrowings	**−98**	−59	−82
Proceeds from (+)/repayment of (−) short-term borrowings	**−406**	−602	133
Dividends paid	**−1,348**	−1,396	−1,004
Net cash used in financing activities	**−1,580**	−1,895	−1,034
Foreign exchange adjustment	**−163**	−43	80
Net increase in cash and cash equivalents	**3,203**	1,930	24
Cash and cash equivalents at beginning of period	**6,125**	4,183	4,159
Cash and cash equivalents at end of period	**9,328**	6,113	4,183

Source: Nokia Annual Report 2002.

(continued)

EXHIBIT 1 | Nokia Corporation (cont.)

Key Data 2002

The key data is based on financial statements according to International Accounting Standards.

Nokia	2002 EURm	2001 EURm	Change %	2000 EURm
Net sales	30,016	31,191	−4	30,376
Operating profit	4,780	3,362	42	5,776
Profit before taxes	4,917	3,475	41	5,862
Net profit	3,381	2,200	54	3,938
Research and development	3,052	2,985	2	2,584
	2002,%	2001,%	2000, %	
Return on capital employed	35.3	27.9	58.0	
Net debt to equity (gearing)	−61	−41	−2.6	
	2002 EUR	2001 EUR	Change %	2000 EUR
Earnings per share, basic	0.71	0.47	51	0.84
Dividend per share	0.28*	0.27	4	0.28
Average number of shares (1,000 shares)	4,751,110	4,702,852		4,673,162

*Board's proposal

Business Groups	2002 EURm	2001 EURm	Change %	2000 EURm
Nokia Mobile Phones				
Net sales	23,211	23,158	0	21,887
Operating profit	5,201	4,521	15	4,879
Research and development	1,884	1,599	18	1,306
Nokia Networks				
Net sales	6,539	7,534	−13	7,714
Operating profit	−49	−73	33	1,358
Research and development	995	1,135	−12	1,013
Nokia Ventures Organization				
Net sales	459	585	−22	854
Operating profit	−141	−855	84	−387
Research and development	136	221	−38	235

Personnel, Dec. 31	2002	2001	Change, %	2000
Nokia Mobile Phones	26,080	26,453	−1	28,047
Nokia Networks	17,361	19,392	−10	23,965
Nokia Ventures Organization	1,506	1,886	−20	2,570
Common Group Functions	6,791	6,118	11	5,707
Nokia Group	51,748	53,849	−4	60,289

EXHIBIT 2 |
Handset Market
Share in 2002

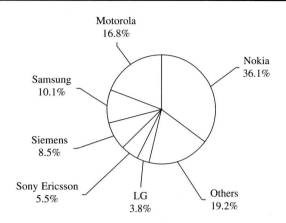

Source: "In 126 Years, Ericsson Has Never Experienced Anything Like This," *Financial Times,* April 3, 2003. NB: specific numbers vary by source. For example, in its Analysts' Briefing dated March 17, 2002, Motorola reports that it had 17.5% of the handset market in 2002.

Nokia Mobile Phone Percentage of Net Sales by Region

	2002	2001	2000
Europe	54%	48%	47%
Americas	22	30	32
Asia-Pacific	24	22	21

Source: Nokia SEC Form 20-F, 2002, p. 28.

Ventures

Nokia Ventures Organization identified and developed new business ideas outside Nokia's current business focus. The division included two established businesses: Nokia Internet Communications, which developed IP security and virtual private network (VPN) solutions for corporate enterprise and managed service provider networks, and Nokia Home Communications, which designed and manufactured digital communications solutions for the home environment. Nokia Ventures Organization also invested in Nokia Venture Partners, an independent venture capital firm investing in mobile and IP related start-up businesses. With $650 million under management in 2003, Nokia Venture Partners invested in mobile and IP-related start-up businesses at an early stage, with investments typically ranging between $2 million and $10 million. The object of Nokia Venture Partners was to gain high-risk returns as well as exposure to markets, technologies, and business models beyond the reach of Nokia's current business units. One of Nokia Venture Partners' portfolio companies, PayPal, successfully staged an IPO in February 2002, and in October 2002 it was acquired by eBay. In 2002, Nokia

Ventures Organization represented approximately 1 percent of Nokia's net sales.[21]

A Chipset off the Old Block

A key element of any handset was the chipset that drove its operation. In 2002, Texas Instruments accounted for about 50 percent of the cell phone semiconductor market. This was a sizeable market for chipmakers. Some estimated that silicon represented $40–$50 of the bill of materials for a mobile handset, resulting in a $20 billion market for silicon for mobile phones per year.[22] CDMA pioneer Qualcomm used to manufacture handsets and network equipment, but sold those businesses to Kyocera and Ericsson, respectively, to focus on chipset design and manufacture and technology licensing. In 2002, Qualcomm shipped 87 million chipsets and

---

[21]Ibid.

[22]Robert A. Burgelman and Philip E. Meza, "Intel beyond 2003: Looking for Its Third Act," Stanford Graduate School of Business case study, SM-106, March 2003, p. 9.

expected to sell 103–110 million units in 2003. For 3Q 2003, the company expected 96 percent of the chipsets sold in the quarter to be for the 3G CDMA200-1x technology. Korean handset maker Samsung, which had used Qualcomm chipsets exclusively, planned to introduce its own chipsets for CDMA 2000 handsets as well as sourcing from Qualcomm. Prior to Samsung's move, Nokia had been the only major handset maker to design its own CDMA 2000 chipsets. Nokia dedicated about 1,000 employees to work on the technology. Critics of Nokia's decision to make its own CDMA chipsets noted that Nokia lagged behind other handset makers in introducing new CDMA2000 handset models. Nokia was estimated to have less than 5 percent of the global market for CDMA 2000 phones, and CDMA 2000 accounted for about 9 percent of the global mobile phone market in 2002.[23]

Microprocessor giant Intel also eyed the mobile chipset market.[24] By early 2003, it had only about 1 percent of the market for mobile phone baseband chips, which controlled a handset's basic functions. It was a major supplier of memory chips to the mobile handset market.[25] As mobile phones became more robust, particularly with 3G systems, Intel aimed to penetrate that fast-growing market, as its traditional market for PC semiconductors slowed. Intel wanted to bring its deep experience in chipset design and manufacturing to mobile phone technologies and gain the advantages of scale it wielded so successfully in the market for PC semiconductors. Qualcomm, for one, claimed not to be worried. The company thought that Intel would take a few years to gain expertise in the CDMA technologies and that handset makers, aware of how PC makers were marginalized by the "Wintel" standard would balk at working with Intel. Don Schrock, president of Qualcomm's wireless chip business said, "I'm not saying everyone trusts Qualcomm, but at least we have a track record, which Intel doesn't."[26]

Nokia Restructures Its Handset Group

In May 2002, Nokia Mobile Phones restructured itself into nine new business units with separate P&Ls.[27] The groups consisted of:

Mobile Phones: to continue the development of voice-centric mobile phones. This group would focus on high-end GSM phones and their successors.

Mobile Entry Products: to produce low-end phones for developing regions such as China. The group would also work with local mobile operators to develop affordable ownership and service packages.

Imaging: to develop visual mobile products, such as camera phones.

Entertainment and Media: to develop mobile products to play and transmit games, music and other media. The N-Gage device (see below) was a key product.

Time Division Multiple Access Unit: to develop and market mobile phones using TDMA technology, mainly in the Americas. Nokia wanted to use this group to maintain its 50 percent share of the declining TDMA market.

Code Division Multiple Access Unit: to serve the CDMA market by expanding Nokia's product portfolio and working closely with mobile network operator customers. Nokia had only 9 percent share of CDMA phones worldwide.

Mobile Enhancements: to develop and sell handset accessories, such as nonstandard faceplates.

Mobile Services: to work with operators to sell branded features and services, such as Club Nokia (see below).

Other Handset Competitors

Motorola captured 17.5 percent of the global market for handsets in 2002. The company was number 1 in greater China and the Americas, but trailed Nokia in the Asia-Pacific region (#2), Europe (#3) and Latin America (#2). The company also made semiconductors and was the world's number-one producer of embedded processors.

Nokia's Nordic competitor, the Swedish telecommunications company Ericsson, suffered the largest reverses

[23]David Pringle, "Samsung Develops CDMA Chips," *The Wall Street Journal*, April 14, 2003.

[24]For a detailed description of Intel's efforts in this area, see Robert A. Burgelman and Philip E. Meza, "Intel Beyond 2003: Looking for Its Third Act," Stanford Graduate School of Business case study, SM-106, March 2003.

[25]David Pringle, Kevin Delaney, and Don Clark, "PC Industry Bets on Cellphones," *The Wall Street Journal*, February 17, 2003, p. A6.

[26]Jennifer Davis, "Microsoft, Intel Aiming for Big Chunk of the Wireless Market," *San Diego Union*, March 23, 2003.

[27]Nokia SEC Form 20-F, 2002, p. 27; Andy Reinhart, "Nokia's Next Act."

EXHIBIT 3 | Motorola, Inc. Annual Income Statement ($ millions)

	31-Dec-2002	31-Dec-2001	31-Dec-2000	31-Dec-1999	31-Dec-1998
Sales—core business	26,679.0	29,873.0	37,346.0	33,075.0	31,340.0
Total sales	**26,679.0**	**29,873.0**	**37,346.0**	**33,075.0**	**31,340.0**
Cost of goods sold	17,938.0	22,661.0	25,168.0	20,631.0	19,396.0
SG&A expense	4,147.0	4,723.0	5,733.0	5,220.0	5,807.0
Depreciation	0.0	0.0	0.0	2,243.0	2,255.0
Research & development	3,754.0	4,318.0	4,437.0	3,560.0	3,118.0
Interest expense	0.0	0.0	0.0	138.0	215.0
Other operating expense	833.0	2,116.0	517.0	1,406.0	109.0
Unusual income/expenditures	1,820.0	1,858.0	596.0	−1,406.0	1,720.0
Total expenses	**28,492.0**	**35,676.0**	**36,451.0**	**31,792.0**	**32,620.0**
Interest expense, nonoperations	−668.0	−786.0	−633.0	0.0	0.0
Other—net	−965.0	1,078.0	1,969.0	0.0	0.0
Pretax income	**−3,446.0**	**-5,511.0**	**2,231.0**	**1,283.0**	**−1,280.0**
Income taxes	−961.0	−1,574.0	913.0	392.0	−373.0
Income after taxes	**−2,485.0**	**−3,937.0**	**1,318.0**	**891.0**	**−907.0**
Interest adjustment for primary EPS	0.0	0.0	0.0	0.0	0.0
Net Income	**−2,485.0**	**−3,937.0**	**1,318.0**	**891.0**	**−907.0**
Accounting change	0.0	0.0	0.0	0.0	0.0
Net Income	**−2,485.0**	**−3,937.0**	**1,318.0**	**891.0**	**−907.0**

Source: Motorola Annual Report

(continued)

in the handset market. By March 2003, Ericsson had hired its fourth CEO (and first outsider) in five years. The company's stock lost 96 percent of its value between March 2000 and March 2003. When Ericsson suffered a loss of $2 billion in the handset business in 2000, it decided to join forces with Sony and combined its handset business into a joint venture called Sony Ericsson. The group still had not made a profit by early 2003. (See Exhibit 3 for Motorola and Ericsson financial data.)

Operating Systems

Since 2001, the number of new mobile subscribers declined globally. The mobile infrastructure market fell 20 percent in 2002 and many expected it to drop 10 percent by the end of 2003.[28] Still, around 408 million mobile phones were sold in 2002. Phone makers and service operators hoped that new 3G services would drive new subscribers and encourage current subscribers to upgrade. Nokia expected to sell around 50 million to 100 million color screen handsets in 2003. Some

industry analysts forecast that around 300 million Europeans would own handsets with color screens, cameras, music players, support for downloadable games, and other features by 2007. As of 2003, those features were already available in Japan and South Korea.[29]

Such features could offer new sources of revenue to mobile network operators and others. This would be particularly welcome by operators who, in Europe alone, spent over $107 billion on licenses for the radio spectrum that will allow them to operate 3G services. They would have to spend tens of billions more to build the infrastructure to support them. But it was not a sure bet. Under the current business models, hardware makers and service operators captured most of the industry profits from the mobile voice communications and (data) messaging. As mobile phones became more complex, companies providing e-mail, games, imaging software, and the sophisticated operating systems to handle these applications could be in a position to command a portion of the rents. For example, by bundling its Smartphone operating system together with applications such as Internet Explorer and Exchange e-mail,

---

[28]Christopher Brown-Humes, "In 126 Years, Ericsson Has Never Experienced Anything Like This," *Financial Times*, April 3, 2003.

[29]"The Fight for Digital Dominance," *The Economist*, November 23, 2003.

EXHIBIT 3 | Selected Ericsson Financial Information (cont.)

CONSOLIDATED INCOME STATEMENT

Years ended December 31,
SEK million

	2002	2001	2000	2001	2000
Net sales	145,773	210,837	221,586	231,839	273,569
Cost of sales	−98,635	−138,123	−120,617	−165,555	−172,892
Restructuring costs	−5,589	−4,858	—	−8,345	−7,500
Gross margin	**41,549**	**67,856**	**100,969**	**57,939**	**93,177**
R&D and other technical expenses	−29,331	−40,247	−34,949	−43,094	−41,421
Selling expenses	−20,422	−27,585	−26,563	−30,844	−35,197
Administrative expenses	−9,556	−11,175	−12,004	−12,409	−13,311
Capitalization of development expenses, net	3,200	—	—	—	—
Restructuring costs	−6,292	−6,242	—	−6,655	−500
Total operating expenses	−62,401	−85,249	−73,516	−93,002	−90,429
Other operating revenues	543	8,575	27,463	8,398	27,983
Share in earnings of joint ventures and associated companies	−1,220	−14,662	−16,088	−715	97
Restructuring costs net, phones	230	−3,900	−8,000	—	—
Operating income	**−21,299**	**−27,380**	**30,828**	**−27,380**	**30,828**
Financial income	**4,253**	**4,815**	**3,698**	4,815	3,698
Financial expenses	**−5,789**	**−6,589**	**−4,887**	−6,589	−4,887
Income after financial items	**−22,835**	**−29,154**	**29,639**	**−29,154**	**29,639**
Minority interest in income before taxes	−488	−1,155	−947	−1,155	−947
Income before taxes	**−23,323**	**−30,309**	**28,692**	**−30,309**	**28,692**
Taxes					
Income taxes for the year	4,165	8,813	−7,998	8,813	−7,998
Minority interest in taxes	145	232	324	232	324
Net income	−19,013	−21,264	21,018	−21,264	21,018

Source: Company reports.

as well as instant messaging and other software, Microsoft wanted to earn a royalty on each phone maker using the system sold. Some handset makers looked askance at Microsoft's involvement. San-Jing Park, vice president of Mobile Communications at Samsung was quoted as saying: "We have good reason to be concerned . . . [Microsoft and Intel] took all the value and left hardware makers as clone producers. We don't want a repeat of that situation."[30]

The potential market for operating systems looked large. Some estimated that of the 408 million handsets sold in 2002, only about 2 million to 2.5 million had an embedded operating system.[31] The market for, and

importance of, operating systems would grow as 3G systems offered more and more applications. However, operating systems were expensive to design. By 2003, a group of handset makers banded together to create an operating system for the industry.

Symbian

In 1998, Ericsson, Nokia, Motorola, and British personal digital assistant maker Psion established Symbian, a private, independent company in June 1998. The company is a software developer and licensing company that created the Symbian OS, an advanced, open standard operating system for data-enabled mobile phones. Symbian software provided the underlying software code that enabled handset support functions and applications such as graphics, security, and Internet

---

[30]Ben Hunt and Paul Abrahams, "Microsoft's Battle with Symbian," *Financial Times*, February 25, 2003.

[31]Caroline Daniel, "Wanted: a Mass Market System with Extra Pizzazz," *Financial Times*, February 25, 2003.

EXHIBIT 4 |

Symbian Ownership
As of April 2003

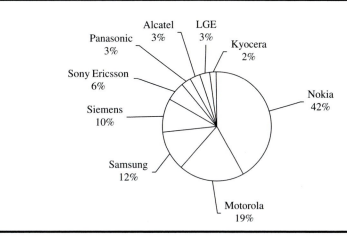

Source: Symbian

access. However, Symbian's licensees and software developers were given full access to the source code that drove the operating system, which enabled individual handset makers and applications providers the ability to modify the system to suit individual products. Thus handset makers could differentiate themselves by offering unique features built upon a common platform. For example, Symbian's licensees could change the software's on-screen menus and graphics ("user interface") to suit their needs. This was how Nokia was able to license its popular interface, called Series 60, to other handset makers such as Samsung and Panasonic. The group's mission was: "Symbian OS in every phone."[32] By 2003 Symbian's ownership had expanded to include its original founders and Siemens, Panasonic, Samsung (which paid £17 million for a 5 percent stake in 2003), and others (Exhibit 4).

Symbian licensees accounted for more than three-quarters of all mobile phones sold worldwide in 2002 As of 2003, few of these phones actually used Symbian software since most licensees were still developing their 3G handsets, but most were expected to use it in the future. Symbian's owners banded together to share the development costs to create a 3G operating system. Between them, Symbian licensees accounted for almost 80 percent of all handsets sold.[33] David Levin, Symbian's chief executive officer said, "$300 million has been spent on this [software] platform. There are few

manufacturers that can drop that sort of development. . . . This allows them to pool their resources and make sure they are abreast of technical developments."[34] One company that could afford the costs of developing an operating system by itself was Microsoft (Exhibit 5).

Microsoft

In October 2002, Microsoft introduced its Smartphone operating system in the United Kingdom, with plans to launch in the United States in mid-2003. The Smartphone operating system was a mobile phone platform that enabled users to communicate via voice, e-mail, instant messaging, or SMS over the same sleek handset. The software was designed to work well with other Microsoft applications such Outlook. Smartphone handsets featured high-resolution color screens and had the ability to play digital media and mobile games. The operating system offered a full range of personalization options, such as ring tones, color schemes and home screens, mobile access to the Internet, and new mobile services.

Microsoft planned to work with both handset makers and network operators to promote the Smartphone system. Juha Christensen, corporate vice president, Mobile Devices Marketing Group at Microsoft said:

We've been working very closely with all types of market participants—especially with the mobile operators and

[32] Symbian.

[33]"The Fight for Digital Dominance," *The Economist*, November 23, 2003.

[34]Hunt and Abrahams, "Microsoft Battles with Symbian."

EXHIBIT 5 | Selected Microsoft Income Statement Information

In $ millions, except earnings per share

Year Ended June 30	2000	2001	2002
Revenue	$22,956	$25,296	$28,365
Operating expenses:			
Cost of revenue	3,002	3,455	5,191
Research and development	3,772	4,379	4,307
Sales and marketing	4,126	4,885	5,407
General and administrative	1,050	857	1,550
Total operating expenses	11,950	13,576	16,455
Operating income	11,006	11,720	11,910
Losses on equity investees and other	(57)	(159)	(92)
Investment income/(loss)	3,326	(36)	(305)
Income before income taxes	14,275	11,525	11,513
Provision for income taxes	4,854	3,804	3,684
Income before accounting change	9,421	7,721	7,829
Cumulative effect of accounting change	—	(375)	—
Net income	$9,421	$7,346	$7,829

Source: Company reports.

handset makers who are essential to the market—both to ensure Smartphone's success, and to ensure their success with Smartphone. Mobile operators, for example, own the customer relationship. They're the experts at segmenting their customers, getting to those segments, bringing together the right devices, services, and distribution channels, and so on. They're at the hub of the ecosystem.[35]

Microsoft thought mobile operators would welcome the Smartphone platform as a way to move away from simply providing voice and SMS—their traditional sources of revenue—to include new potential revenue streams from applications such as games and e-mail among others. In addition, Microsoft thought the Smartphone platform would encourage other participants in the mobile ecosystem, such as systems integrators, distributors, and retailers to develop products and services for the platform. This group had reduced its spending by about 20 percent in 2002, and some analysts were looking for additional 20 percent reductions in spending by operators in 2003.[36]

Microsoft was also working with handset makers. Christensen said:

On the handset side, Samsung, one of the world's leading handset makers, will use Smartphone to power their next-generation handsets. Samsung's commitment is a wonderful endorsement for Smartphone right out of the gate, and virtually assures the product's worldwide availability. We're also working with Compaq, HTC (the hardware manufacturer of the Compaq iPAQ), Sendo [a U.K. handset manufacturer], and TCL.[37]

By the end of 2002, Smartphone users from the European service Orange browsed the Internet five times a day using the phone, three times more than previous phone users did, 88 percent of users synchronized their phones to their personal computers, and 73 percent used e-mail features on the phone.[38]

By April 2003, Microsoft was having difficulty with some if its Smartphone partners. Sendo abandoned the Microsoft partnership in favor of Symbian, citing its

[35]"Launching Smartphone: Microsoft's Christensen on the Marriage of 'Smart Software and Small, Stylish Mobile Handsets,'" Microsoft Press Release, October 22, 2002.

[36]Christopher Brown-Humes, "Nokia to Cut 1,800 Jobs in Networks Unit," *Financial Times*, April 11, 2003.

[37]"Launching Smartphone: Microsoft's Christensen on the Marriage of 'Smart Software and Small, Stylish Mobile Handsets,'" Microsoft Press Release, October 22, 2002.

[38]Hunt and Abrahams, "Microsoft's Battle with Symbian."

EXHIBIT 5 | Selected Microsoft Cash Flow Statement Information (cont.)

In $ millions

Year Ended June 30	2000	2001	2002
Operations			
Net income	$9,421	$7,346	$7,829
Cumulative effect of accounting change, net of tax	—	375	—
Depreciation, amortization, and other noncash items	1,250	1,536	1,084
Net recognized (gains)/losses on investments	(1,732)	2,221	2,424
Stock option income tax benefits	5,535	2,066	1,596
Deferred income taxes	(425)	(420)	(416)
Unearned revenue	6,177	6,970	11,152
Recognition of unearned revenue	(5,600)	(6,369)	(8,929)
Accounts receivable	(944)	(418)	(1,623)
Other current assets	(775)	(482)	(264)
Other long-term assets	(864)	(330)	(9)
Other current liabilities	(992)	774	1,449
Other long-term liabilities	375	153	216
Net cash from operations	11,426	13,422	14,509
Financing			
Common stock issued	2,245	1,620	1,497
Common stock repurchased	(4,896)	(6,074)	(6,069)
Sales/(repurchases) of put warrants	472	(1,367)	—
Preferred stock dividends	(13)	—	—
Other, net	—	235	—
Net cash used for financing	(2,192)	(5,586)	(4,572)
Investing			
Additions to property and equipment	(879)	(1,103)	(770)
Purchases of investments	(42,290)	(66,346)	(89,386)
Maturities of investments	4,025	5,867	8,654
Sales of investments	29,752	52,848	70,657
Net cash used for investing	(9,392)	(8,734)	(10,845)
Net change in cash and equivalents	(158)	(898)	(908)
Effect of exchange rates on cash and equivalents	29	(26)	2
Cash and equivalents, beginning of year	4,975	4,846	3,922
Cash and equivalents, end of year	$4,846	$3,922	$3,016

Source: Company reports.

inability to access Microsoft's source code.[39] Samsung also joined Symbian in February 2003. The defections left Microsoft with its partnerships with Taiwanese original device manufacturers (ODMs), such as TCL, and the mobile network operators. Microsoft concentrated its efforts on propagating its Smartphone operating systems through mobile carriers. The ODMs produced phones with the Smartphone OS that were sold bearing the network operators' brands. It was reported that Microsoft signed agreements with service providers including T-Mobile, Verizon, AT&T Wireless, and Sprint in the United States; T-Mobile, Vodafone, and others in Europe; and Japan's NTT DoCoMo and Singapore's SingTel in Asia.

A key selling point for Smartphone was its presumed seamless interoperability with Microsoft applications. Nokia, who had already sold its popular Series 60

---

[39]"Special Report: The Fight for Digital Dominance—Nokia v. Microsoft," The Economist, November 23, 2002.

interface software to rival handset makers made this a priority. Niklas Savander, senior vice president of Nokia Mobile Software said, "People who buy Series 60 are going to have excellent interoperability with Microsoft Office products, such as e-mail and calendar, and they will be able to synchronize with their PCs and corporate servers. What you will not see is Microsoft-powered applications on Series 60." [40]

At the prospect of Nokia's Series 60 becoming the standard user interface for 3G phones, as Windows had for PCs, Ed Suwanjindar, lead product manager in Microsoft's Mobility division was skeptical, saying: "Every one of Nokia's Series 60 licensees is a competitor in the hardware arena. If you're Siemens, does Nokia have your best interest at heart?"[41]

The Advantages of Size

Network operators, faced with customer churn and declining new subscriber rates, might have welcomed Microsoft's plan to offer operator-branded handsets. The market for ODM-produced handsets was well established. Some analysts estimated that up to 26 percent of mobile phone handsets were manufactured by ODMs in 2002.[42] Many brand name makers outsourced some or all of their manufacturing to ODMs.

Still, scale economics looked as if they were on the side of Nokia. Network operators offering Smartphone were likely to order handsets in quantities of hundreds of thousands. By contrast, market leading brand name makers, such as Nokia, Motorola, and others produced handsets in quantities in the millions. Such scale disadvantages were likely to make Smartphones more expensive to produce. In addition, Nokia had proven itself to be a very efficient manufacturer.

Matti Alahuhta, president of Nokia's handset division, said that Nokia sourced about 20 percent of its handsets from ODMs, which gave the company knowledge of the manufacturing competition.[43]

It was estimated that consumers around the world would buy 460 million cell phones in 2003 and spend $390 billion on their cell services, according to an esti-

mate from Yankee Group, a research firm in Boston. Yet competition among carriers has driven down the average per minute revenue they collect from their users. In the United States, wireless calls cost close to 10 cents a minute—about half what they were three years ago,

Playing Games with Nokia

By 2003, Nokia was moving deeper into the entertainment industry by launching the N-Gage game console, a portable game console with a built-in cellular connection that allowed users to play games with each other over the cellular network or make voice calls. Players would also be able to use a short-range Bluetooth[44] wireless connection to connect with players in the same room. Nokia planned to include a built-in digital music player and radio in the console. The company expected consumers to purchase N-Gage consoles in addition to regular mobile phones.[45]

Nokia planned to charge game makers a fee for every game published on its console. By February 2003, five game publishers agreed to develop games for the system. The games would be sold on wafer-sized cartridges for the console, which resembled Nintendo's Game Boy Advance. However, priced at around $550, Nokia's offering would be about five times more expensive than its Nintendo competitor.[46] Nokia planned to introduce its console around the world by the fourth quarter of 2003, in time for the holiday season. Fees from game producers would represent a new source of revenue for Nokia, which already sold simple games for its phones, as well as graphics and ring tones from its "Club Nokia" Web site.

Nokia also established separate partnerships with Sony and Matsushita to develop software that would allow video, pictures, and music files to be swapped between mobile phones and home-electronics devices. Nokia had not announced how the company would proceed in the games market, but company spokesman Pekka Isosomppi said phones "could be regarded as a remote control for the other equipment that surrounds

---

[40]Hunt and Abrahams, "Microsoft Battles with Symbian."

[41]"Special Report: The Fight for Digital Dominance—Nokia v. Microsoft."

[42]"Ibid.

[43]"Ibid.

[44]Bluetooth is a protocol used by devices such as mobile phones, computers, and personal digital assistants (PDAs) to interconnect with each other using a short-range wireless connection.

[45]David Pringle, "Nokia Plans Game Levy in Bid to Raise Revenue," *The Asian Wall Street Journal*, February 6, 2003.

[46]David Redhead, "Raising the Tone in a Pocket Battle," *Financial Times*, April 10, 2003.

you. The advantage of the phone is that you carry it with you."[47]

Conclusion

The bottom fell out of the mobile communications market just as substantial new investments were needed to introduce 3G services. Operators craved the cash flow that new services could bring, but had little money left to invest. Meanwhile, by 2003, handset makers found themselves at the beginning of the curve for economies of scale, producing small quantities of expensive 3G handsets that did not thrill consumers, who were happy with their 2.5G models. Nokia was the undeniable leader in 2.5G technology, and looked to extend its dominance into 3G. However, where it handily beat competitors in the past, it now faced the possibility of a new game. Would companies like Qualcomm, Microsoft, or Intel appropriate more of the industry's profits from 3G technologies? Would service providers? How would Nokia ensure that it continued to command rents from mobile telephony when 3G became a reality around the world?

---

[47]David Pringle, "CeBit Technology Fair: Nokia, Sony and Microsoft Vie to Be Gateway for Digital Media," *The Asian Wall Street Journal*, March 17, 2003.

Case 4.3

Samsung Electronics in 2004: Conquering the Wireless Digital World

We invite you to join us in a journey of connection, convergence, and communication.

—Jong-Yong Yun, Vice Chairman and CEO, Samsung.[1]

Introduction

Founded as a trading house in the late 1930s, Samsung had penetrated world markets through cheap products, first in heavy industry, then in low-end consumer electronics (CE), and eventually in semiconductors. During the second half of the 20th century, Samsung had gone from a second-tier follower to an extremely responsive competitor, with the capacity to catch even the most innovative Western companies within a few months. Still, Samsung's generic strategy had been cost leadership and the capacity to adjust to the strategies of companies such as Intel and Texas Instruments.

By early 2004 this had changed. U.S.-educated managers were engaging Samsung in one of the most promising future markets: the digital home. Digital products were expected to conquer homes, based on new interoperability standards that would allow any content to be played on any device. The digital home was at the intersection of three industries: computers, mobile communications, and CE; its first applications were Smartphones and online home theaters. In each of these industries giants were solidly entrenched. Questions of software interoperability and hardware component modularity were at the core of the struggle for industry control. Players in each of the industries were trying to make their products the center of the digital home. In particular, a battle raged between a vertical industry model promoted by traditional CE companies and cellular manufacturers eager to defend their market shares, and a horizontal model advocated by information technology (IT) companies such as Intel and Microsoft, eager to reproduce the situation that had made their fortune in the PC world.

Samsung, a telecommunication, semiconductor and consumer electronic giant, had a position to take and alliances to forge. Which of the industry models should Samsung endorse? What battles should they focus on? And, whatever strategic choices they made, did they have the resources to carry out their new, audacious strategy?

Samsung

History of the Samsung Group

The Samsung Group began as a small trade exports company on March 1, 1938, in Taegu, Korea, founded by Byung-Chull Lee. The original purpose of the company was to sell dried Korean fish, vegetables, and fruit to Manchuria and Beijing. In half a century, Samsung—meaning literally "three stars" in Korean—grew from a local trade small enterprise to a modern global corporation with large-scale plans.

One critical turning point, in the early 1980s, was a strategic change in corporate priorities. The main focus of the company switched from heavy industry to electronics. In 1980 Lee received important advice from a Japanese friend: Semiconductors would play a critical role in the future of manufacturing industry.[2] The company focus became high technology. In early 1983, Samsung made a massive investment in the construction of a memory chips and microprocessors plant, thus creating the foundations of future growth in home electronics.[3] Japanese and Western engineers

---

[2]Youngrak Choi, *Dynamic Techno-Management Capability* (Brookfield: Ashgate Publishing, Limited, 1996), p. 147.

[3]Ibid., p. 155.

Jean-Bernard Rolland (MBA 2004) prepared this case under the supervision of Professor Robert A. Burgelman as the basis for class discussion rather than to illustrate either effective or ineffective handling of an administrative situation.

---

[1]Samsung Electronics, "Company Annual Report 2002," December 31, 2002, p. 15, http://www.samsung.com/AboutSAMSUNG/ CompanyProfile/AnnualReport/pdf/2002/eng_all.pdf, (April 26, 2004).

were hired at salaries 10 times higher than that of their Korean counterparts. The whole Samsung Group put all its resources into becoming a technology company and Samsung Electronics became the flag bearer of the entire group. In the process, Samsung Electronics came several times to the verge of financial disaster, only surviving through the support of the other companies of the group (these diversified groups were called *chaebol*[4] in Korean).

Initial yields were low, and quality was disappointing. In this period, Byung-Chull Lee was personally responsible for the choice of high-risk strategies. Plant construction would start months before product design phases were completed. In 1984, Samsung decided to construct a line that produced six-inch-diameter wafers for DRAM memory chips, at a time when even the most advanced companies such as Intel were producing six-inch-diameter wafers on an experimental scale.[5] Byung-Chull Lee encouraged the management not to be sensitive to financial difficulties but to focus on developing technology and producing good products.[6]

A second important strategic change was the New Management program in 1993. More than mere reengineering, the New Management was an effort to change the way Samsung did business and was perceived. It was a step in moving from follower or challenger in the electronic industry to integrated designer of world-class products, providing total customer satisfaction. Marketing became an essential element of the group's strategy. Samsung started to sponsor sports events. Samsung's chairman, Kun-Hee Lee, son of the founder Byung-Chull Lee, was selected as a member of the International Olympic Committee (IOC) in July 1996, greatly enhancing the company's image as a key contributor in world athletics. The late 1990s saw Asia shaken by the financial crisis. The strategic turning points of the 80s and early 1990s had created a considerable burden of debt for the company. Samsung had to decrease personnel by almost 50,000 and to divest assets to deleverage the company's structure, lowering

1997's $97.5 billion liabilities (86 percent debt to asset ratio) to $88.8 billion in 2001 (71 percent debt to asset ratio).[7]

Samsung in 2004

By 2004, the company had evolved into an extraordinarily diversified and successful one, with 175,000 employees throughout the world and a portfolio of products and services in industries ranging from financial services to aircraft engines, consumer electronics, or amusement parks. Net sales for the group were close to 117 billion dollars. The group had 14 listed companies and around 50 companies in total (Exhibit 1).

Superior products and brand value had been the strategic shift to restart the company after the turmoil of the years 1998–1999. By the end of 2003, the results were significant. Samsung was ranked 25th in *BusinessWeek*'s Top 100 Global Brands and had the fastest growing brand value in the world, at $10.8 billion.[8] Financial results were showing great improvement (Exhibit 2). Samsung's products used to be mere copies, which customers would buy when they could not afford Toshiba or Sony. They were now among the most valued in the world, and the company was positioning itself as the reference point of digital society: "In 2000, Samsung started its management program with a new twist and aimed to stay ahead of the great waves of digital change now engulfing the world. We expect nothing less than to lead the digitalization of society with our advanced technologies."[9]

The company's core had become its high tech division: Samsung Electronics.[10] The group's resources were mobilized to ensure the success of Samsung Electronics. Top managers from Samsung Electronics were granted the privilege of choosing their candidates ahead of any other division in the group in the batch of new hires from

---

[4]Like *keiretsus* in Japan, *chaebols* were conglomerates of several companies, each company holding shares in the others. Whereas *keiretsus* were centered on one large financial institution or bank, such as Mitsubishi, *chaebols* did not have their own financial institutions. *Chaebols* were also more centralized than *keiretsus* in terms of structures and control and were much more family based.

[5]For further information, see "Samsung Electronics' Semiconductor Division," GSB No.IB24A, p. 6.

[6]Youngrak Choi, op. cit., p. 120.

[7]Samsung, "Samsung Group Annual Report 2002," December 31, 2002, http://www.samsung.com/AboutSAMSUNG/ SAMSUNGGroup/AnnualReport/index.htm (April 10, 2004).

[8]Gerry Khermouch and Diane Brady, "Brands in an Age of Anti-Americanism," *BusinessWeek*, August 4, 2003, p. 69.

[9]Samsung Group, "Timeline and History—2000 to Present," http://www.samsung.com/AboutSAMSUNG/SAMSUNGGroup/ TimelineHistory/ (April 10, 2004).

[10]Samsung Electronics had three branches: the telecommunication branch, which designed and manufactured mobile phones, the CE branch, which designed and manufactured televisions (TV) sets and other high-end home appliances, and the semiconductor branch, which was the largest memory manufacturer in the world and also supplied other parts of the group with components.

EXHIBIT 1 | Samsung Subsidiaries and Sales

	Year	Sales
Samsung Electronics	2003	37,572.04 million U.S. dollars
Semiconductor	2003	15,431.59 million U.S. dollars
Memory	2003	7,922.70 million U.S. dollars
LSI	2003	1,579.37 million U.S. dollars
LCD	2003	4,481.20 million U.S. dollars
Other	2003	1,448.33 million U.S. dollars
Telecom	2003	12,227.16 million U.S. dollars
Wireless	2003	11,070.23 million U.S. dollars
Handsets System	2003	1,156.94 million U.S. dollars
Consumer electronics	2003	9,913.29 million U.S. dollars
Electronics Industries		
SAMSUNG SDI	2001	34.85 million U.S. dollars
SAMSUNG Electro-Mechanics	2001	2,832.86 million U.S. dollars
SAMSUNG Corning	2002	882.00 million U.S. dollars
SAMSUNG Corning Precision Glass	2002	335.00 million U.S. dollars
SAMSUNG SDS	2001	11.38 million U.S. dollars
SAMSUNG Networks	2002	3.44 million U.S. dollars
Machinery & Heavy Industries		
SAMSUNG Heavy Industries	2001	3,100.00 million U.S. dollars
SAMSUNG Techwin	2001	1,195.00 million U.S. dollars
Chemical Industries		
SAMSUNG ATOFINA	2002	1,800.00 million U.S. dollars
SAMSUNG Petrochemicals	2001	650.89 million U.S. dollars
SAMSUNG Fine Chemicals	2002	530.00 million U.S. dollars
SAMSUNG BP Chemicals	2001	196.00 million U.S. dollars
Financial Services		
SAMSUNG Life Insurance	2001	17,199.00 million U.S. dollars
SAMSUNG Fire & Marine Insurance	2001	45.84 million U.S. dollars
SAMSUNG Card	2001	29.14 million U.S. dollars
SAMSUNG Securities	2001	937.96 million U.S. dollars
SAMSUNG Investment Trust Management	2001	32.40 million U.S. dollars
SAMSUNG Venture Investment		N/A
Other Affiliated Companies		
SAMSUNG Corporation	2001	35,000.00 million U.S. dollars
SAMSUNG Engineering	2001	1,038.00 million U.S. dollars
Cheil Industries	2002	1,741.00 million U.S. dollars
SAMSUNG Everland	2001	7.22 million U.S. dollars
The Shilla Hotels & Resorts	2002	346.00 million U.S. dollars
Cheil Communications	2002	2.74 million U.S. dollars
S1 Corporation	2001	243.00 million U.S. dollars
SAMSUNG Lions	2001	20.00 million U.S. dollars
SAMSUNG Medical Center		N/A
SAMSUNG Human Resources Development Institute		N/A
SAMSUNG Advanced Institute of Technology		N/A
SAMSUNG Economics Research Institute		N/A
SAMSUNG Foundation of Culture		N/A
SAMSUNG Welfare Foundation		N/A
The Ho-Am Foundation		N/A
SAMSUNG Press Foundation		N/A

Source: Compiled from Samsung, "Affiliated Companies," http://www.samsung.com/AboutSAMSUNG/SAMSUNGGroup/index.htm (April 21, 2004).

EXHIBIT 2 | Samsung Electronics Financial Statements

Balance Sheet (millions $)

	1996	1997	1998	1999	2000	2001	2002	2003
Assets	13,654	19,885	17,911	21,302	23,186	24,069	29,690	33,797
Cash & cash equivalent	830	1,178	1,023	1,013	2,242	2,434	4,898	4,754
Marketable securities	44	38	85	204	3	3	1,494	2,130
Accounts receivable	1,197	2,423	1,397	1,151	1,002	766	953	1,191
Inventory	1,911	2,018	1,612	1,949	2,416	1,694	1,959	2,138
Liabilities	9,266	14,859	11,902	9,809	9,226	7,281	8,018	8,439
Debt	6,751	11,189	8,810	4,953	3,501	2,332	1,402	999
Shareholders' equity	4,388	5,026	6,009	11,494	13,960	16,789	21,672	25,358
Debt ratio (debt/equity)	*154%*	*223%*	*147%*	*43%*	*25%*	*14%*	*6%*	*4%*
Income Statement (millions $)								
Sales	13,686	15,919	17,314	22,516	29,556	27,915	34,323	37,572
-COGS	10,279	10,950	12,049	15,226	18,960	21,134	22,674	25,448
Gross profit	3,407	4,969	5,266	7,291	10,595	6,781	11,649	12,124
(Margin)	*24.9%*	*31.2%*	*30.4%*	*32.4%*	*35.8%*	*24.3%*	*33.9%*	*32.3%*
-SG&A	2,815	3,177	3,595	3,427	4,183	4,802	5,202	5,923
Operating profit	592	1,792	1,671	3,864	6,410	1,979	6,447	6,201
(Margin)	*4.3%*	*11.3%*	*9.6%*	*17.2%*	*21.7%*	*7.1%*	*18.8%*	*16.5%*
-Non Operating Income (Expense)	(399)	(1,658)	(1,291)	(161)	441	679	1,200	(248)
-Extra gain (loss)	(13)	(2)	(26)	(229)	133	—	—	—
Income before tax	180	133	354	3,473	6,983	2,658	7,647	5,952
(Margin)	*1.3%*	*0.8%*	*2.0%*	*15.4%*	*23.6%*	*9.5%*	*22.3%*	*15.8%*
-Income tax expense	38	26	84	739	1,798	117	1,568	815
Net Income	142	107	270	2,733	5,186	2,541	6,079	5,137
(Margin)	*1.0%*	*0.7%*	*1.6%*	*12.1%*	*17.5%*	*9.1%*	*17.7%*	*13.7%*
Cashflow statement (millions $)								
Cash from operating	900	1,993	4,173	7,078	9,456	6,291	11,193	9,848
Cash from investing	(3,525)	(3,774)	(3,086)	(4,552)	(6,062)	(3,838)	(8,462)	(7,644)
Cash from financing	2,430	2,186	(1,268)	(2,538)	(2,637)	(2,231)	(2,312)	(2,345)
Increase (decrease) in cash	(195)	404	(180)	(12)	757	222	419	(141)

Source: Compiled from Samsung, "Financial Summary of SAMSUNG Electronics,"
http://www.samsung.com/AboutSAMSUNG/InvestorRelations/FinancialInformation/Financial_history.htm (April 21, 2004).

Korean and international universities. As a symbol, the Web site www.samsung.com was actually the Web site of Samsung Electronics, emphasizing what the Samsung name should primarily be used for.

The Wireless World

The Wireless Digital Home: A Simulation

On January 3, 2004, John and his wife Elisa were comfortably installed in the cozy living room of their upper-middle-class house in Menlo Park, California.

John was a successful engineer in a Silicon Valley high-tech company. His hobby was managing the content of his digital creations about his family and friends. For example, during the holiday season, John had shot many digital pictures of their parties with relatives and friends. Using his brand-new camcorder, John had also shot a few movies of their daughter Cleo and their dog Ubrix. John liked to edit those documents on his PC, then watch them on his home theater and possibly duplicate them and carry them on his personal digital assistant (PDA) to show to his colleagues.

EXHIBIT 3 |

Long Distance and
Local Wireless
Networks

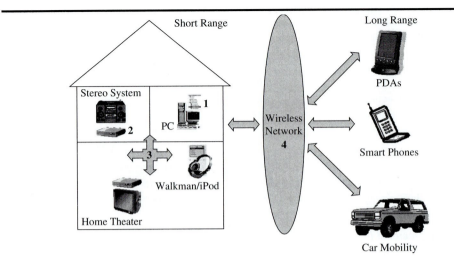

Legend

Item	Description
1	Media centers: PC, stereo or television.
2	Wireless plug-in to allow inbound and outbound communication from the media centers. These could be wireless cards in PCs or wireless media adapters such as Linksys from Cisco.
3	Wireless local network, as described in Exhibit 4.
4	Wireless long distance network, as described in Exhibit 4.

Source: Compiled from Digital Home Working Group, *Digital Home White Paper* (final version June 2003),
http://www.dhwg.org/resources/ (April 11, 2004).

On the other hand, Elisa was not really interested in pictures, but she had a passion for classical music. She had an extensive collection of opera CDs. As a journalist at a local newspaper, she often worked from home. She particularly enjoyed listening to her CDs when she was working in the living room, the garden, her office on the second floor, or anywhere else in the house (Exhibit 3).

Unfortunately for John and Elisa, in early 2004, CE, PCs, and mobile devices such as PDAs and cell phones were isolated islands in the digital house. Interoperability did not really exist outside of heterogeneous point-to-point links such as USB.[11] Thus, John would have to copy his movie creations from the PC hard disk to his camcorder using USB, take the camcorder and the USB cable to the living room and then connect the camcorder to the family television set. Wireless kits partially allowed "gluing"[12] all devices, sharing folders and accessing any content from any device. But the quality was choppy and unsatisfying.

Wireless connections, described in Exhibit 4, reduced the need to connect cables, but did not solve the heterogeneity problem. They were simply more convenient to use, although the different solutions were proprietary and often incompatible. Companies such as Apple, Cisco, Lucent, and 3Com would support the 802.11b (WiFi) standard that was also not working well with Bluetooth. Often too, the media formats were different and devices did not recognize their counterpart formats. Last but not least, wireless solutions were too slow to allow video broadcasting throughout the house.[13] In addition to the lack of

---

[11]Universal Serial Bus (USB) was a standard port that enabled the connection of external devices (such as digital cameras, scanners, and mice) to Windows and Macintosh computers. The USB standard supported data transfer rates of 12Mbps (million bits per second). USB was designed to connect devices on a one-to-one basis, as opposed to local networks that connected multiple computers. Similar links were PCI links or 1394 links.

[12]A "glue" in technical jargon was a middleware layer that created seamless connections between devices, thus giving the impression of uniformity from one device to another.

[13]Although 802.11a and g allowed broadcast of data at 54 Mbps, a speed that was sufficient to play videos. Practical applications were still unsatisfactory.

EXHIBIT 4 | Current Digital Wireless Solutions Products

Local Networks

Name	Speed	Range	Description
802.11b (WiFi)	11 Mb/s	100 meters	A wireless network protocol. It offered the same degree of network management as any comparable wired network (in particular Ethernet). WiFi worked at 11mbps, a speed still too slow to allow video. WiFi was designed to hook up an entire network; it could be used connect one computer directly to another, but that was not its real purpose.
802.11a	54 Mb/s	30 meters	A revision of 802.11 that operates in the unlicensed 5 GHz band and allowed transmission rates of 54Mbps.
802.11g	54 Mb/s	100 meters	Released during autumn 2001, 802.11g was an extension of the 802.11b standard, offering network speeds at up 26 and 54Mbps. It still used the 2.4GHz ISM band, which afforded it longer range than 802.11a (100m instead of 30m), but in a more congested band.
HomeRF	1 Mb/s	50 meters	A specification for wireless digital communication between PCs and consumer electronic devices used within the home environment. Based on frequency hopping for the transmission of voice and data. HomeRF had a range of up to 50 meters. In 2004, HomeRF had almost disappeared and was no match for WiFi.
Jini(Sun)	N/A	N/A	An open Java architecture network technology that enabled developers to create network-centric services that were highly adaptive to change. Jini was almost at the application level and could be used on top of Wifi or Bluetooth.
Bluetooth	720 Kb/s	10 meters	Bluetooth was a cable replacement, designed to connect devices point-to-point. Bluetooth could also bridge two networks. Bluetooth was too slow for video transfers or to move large images off a digital camera. A single device could be connected to up to seven other devices at the same time. This made it easy to find and connect to the desired device or to switch between devices, such as two printers. Bluetooth and WiFi shared the same band of frequencies and could, therefore, interfere with one another.
HiperLAN2	54 Mb/s	150 meters	A wireless LAN protocol developed by ETSI (European Telecommunications Standards Institute) akin to 802.11. There were two types of HiperLAN, both operating in the 5GHz band. HiperLAN/1 provided data-rates up to 20 Mbps, and HiperLAN/2 data-rates up to 54 Mbps.

Source: Compiled from Ksys, *Wireless LAN Glossary*, http://www.ksys.info/wlan_glossary.htm, 2002, (April 11, 2004).

(continued)

operability and bandwidth, consumers were complaining about uneasy setups of devices or connections, prices, and the limited user value of many products.

What Market for the Digital Home?

The digital home was only a part of a completely wireless "digital world." Smartphones[14] and high-end home theaters were the first tangible applications in this digital world (see Exhibit 5). But the potential for future applications was large.

---

[14]Smartphones were a combination of a mobile phone and a pocket computer. Smartphones could use 2.5G protocols (GPRS) or 3G protocols (W-CDMA). All 3G phones were Smartphones.

In the wireless world, wireless local networks in homes would be connected to long-distance wireless networks (as wired local networks were to land-phone networks), with a larger potential for innovation. In 1975, Bill Gates dreamed of bringing a computer into every house. The industry's new vision was to create a repository of information in everyone's house and make it available from everywhere via wireless networks. Bluetooth, for example, could be used not only to connect devices in a home, but also to pay for goods and services by connecting a cell phone to a vendor's point-of-sale terminal. The application would immediately update personal finance software. Via wireless Internet, customers would be able to listen to the music stored on their computer from any location such as their car or

EXHIBIT 4 | Current Digital Wireless Solutions Products (cont.)

Long Distance Networks

Name	Used In	Description
W-CDMA	Japan	Wideband Code Division Multiple Access, one of two 3G standards that made use of a wider spectrum than 2G standards and therefore could transmit and receive information faster and more efficiently. Co-developed by NTT DoCoMo, it was expected to compete with CDMA2000 to be the de facto 3G standard. It could offer data throughputs 384 kilobits per second.
CDMA2000	Korea, China, U.S.	A third-generation technology that was an upgrade to 3G features and services. CDMA2000 supported the second generation network aspect of 2G technologies (cdmaOne, IS-136 TDMA, or GSM). This standard was also known by its ITU name IMT-CDMA Multi-Carrier. It had been adopted by operators in the U.S., Japan and South Korea. It could offer data throughputs of 2 megabits per second.
PDC	Japan	Personal digital cellular. The digital wireless standard used in Japan. PDC used TDMA air interface.
GPRS	Europe, U.S.	General Packet Radio Service was a standard for wireless communications which ran at speeds up to 150 kilobits per second, compared with 2G GSM systems' 9.6 kilobits. GPRS, which supported a wide range of bandwidths, is an efficient use of limited bandwidth and is particularly suited for sending and receiving large volumes of data.

Source: Compiled from Ksys, *Wireless LAN Glossary,* http://www.ksys.info/wlan_glossary.htm, 2002, (April 11, 2004).

work;[15] they would be able to monitor the level of supplies in their refrigerator while shopping, or control the quantity of ice cream their children where consuming while they were away.[16]

As explained by industry analysts, the potential impact on consumers' lives was major (see Exhibit 6 for other examples).[17] Identifying which use would become a reality was however difficult. According to David Levin, CEO of Symbian: "Nobody can tell with certainty how Smartphones will be used. As they mature, they could become a gaming device, a payment device or a location device or any combination of those things. Nobody knows for sure."[18]

It was also difficult to assess the size of the demand for wireless digital products and whether or not the industry could be profitable. One of the only proxies of

future wireless markets was the market of third-generation (3G) Smartphones, in which penetration had proved elusive. During the Internet bubble, carriers paid 3G licenses in the hundreds of billions. Revenues for 3G services worldwide were expected to be about $321 billion in 2010.[19] However, they were only $1 billion in 2003, an amount that represented 10 million units shipped,[20] out of a total of around 500 million cell phones shipped worldwide.[21]

In terms of services, despite carriers' efforts, the demand had been low in Europe and in the United States. The only significant success was Japan, where NTT DoCoMo had launched a mobile Internet connection service in early 1999. In April 2004, DoCoMo had over 45 million subscribers,[22] out of which 3.6 million were using DoCoMo 3G network called FOMA.[23] In 2003,

---

[15]Graeme Wearden, "Mercedes Puts Mobile Office in High Gear," *ZDNet,* March 17, 2003, http://zdnet.com.com/2100-1103-992836.html (April 11, 2004).

[16]Samsung, "Refrigerators Have Acquired Intelligence," http://www.samsung.com/Products/Refrigerator/HomePADRefrigerator/Refrigerator_HomePADRefrigerator_RH2777AT.htm# (April 11, 2004).

[17]Gardner, "How Will Bluetooth and Jini Change People's Lifestyles?" http://www.gartner.com/1_researchanalysis/focus/2.1.5q a.html (April 11, 2004).

[18]All quotes from David Levin are from interview with the author on April 29, 2004.

[19]Dan Steinbock, *Wireless Horizon* (New York: Amacom, 2003), p. 359.

[20]Adrian Baschnonga, *Global Mobile Handset Trends—The Smartphone Sector,* World Market Research Center, April 8, 2004.

[21]Cliff Edwards, Moon Ihlwan and Andy Reinhardt, "Intel—What Is CEO Craig Barrett up to?" *BusinessWeek,* March 8, 2004, p. 58.

[22]Kyoko Hasegawa, "DoCoMo Falls to No. 3 in Japan in Terms of Number of Subscribers Added in Jan.," *AFX International Focus,* February 9, 2004.

[23]Jessica Ramakrishnan "NTT DoCoMo Launches Three New 3G Handsets," *WMRC Daily Analysis,* June 2, 2004.

EXHIBIT 5 | Percentages of Handsets Shipments by Technology and Market, in 2003 and 2008(e)

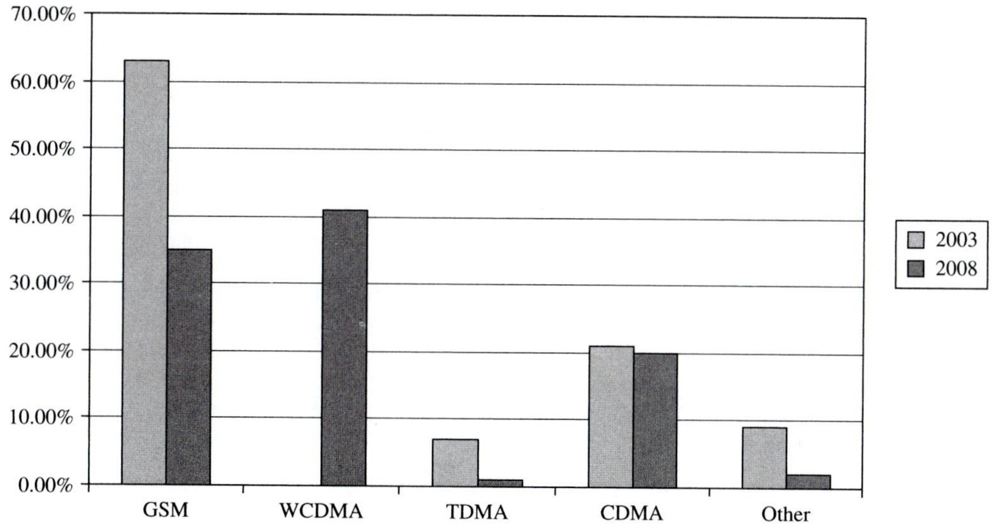

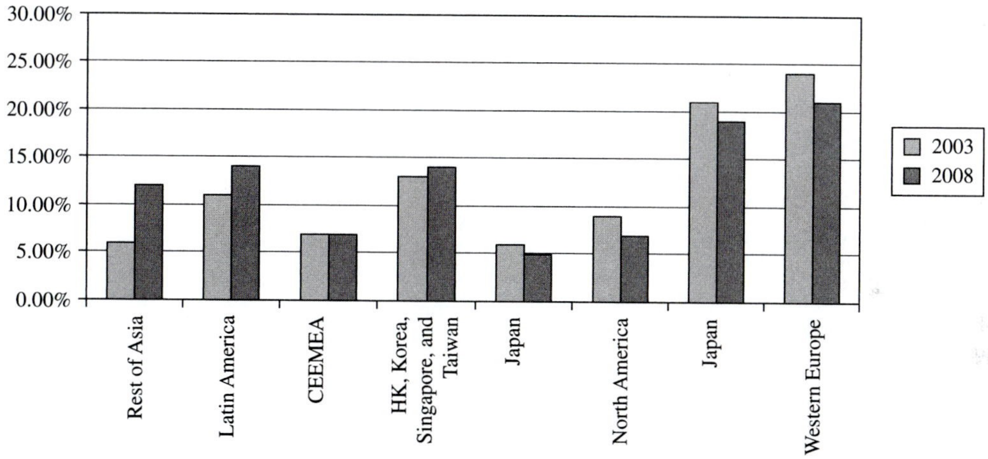

Source: Compiled from Angela Dean, Nokia—*Structurally Challenged in a Changing Industry,* (London: Morgan Stanley May 2004), p. 18.

Japan now has nearly 14 million 3G users.[24] By comparison, in 2003, Japan had a total of 79 million mobile subscribers. Extrapolated to the U.S., with 159 million subscribers,[25] the number of 3G service subscribers would reach 28 million if the service was available.

If 3G cell phone digital services had been slow to generate demand, the need for an integrated digital home was even more uncertain. David Levin explained: "Is

there a need for computing power in devices such as refrigerators or televisions? To answer this question, one needs to understand what creates utility for a device. In consumer electronics, ease of use makes the utility. There is no need for complexity."

Two Worlds Invaded by a Third

Digital appliances were putting together the processing power of computers, the communication power of cell phones, and the enjoyment of large-screen home TVs. The risks, however, were different for players in each of the three worlds. Computer companies were solidly

---

[24]Total Telecom, "Japan's DoCoMo Posts Profit, Reaffirms Outlook," February 4, 2004.

[25]The World Market Research Center, "Global Data," http://www.worldmarketsanalysis.com (April 11, 2004).

EXHIBIT 6 | Examples of 3G Wireless Services

- *Tracking children and pets.* In 1999 DoCoMo introduced *P-Doco* that wirelessly transmits the location of a badge to a designated phone number. This is used for tracking a small child, pet, vehicle, cargo container, or any other moving objects.

- *Traffic route advising.* A motorist is continuously updated on the traffic condition around the route she is taking and advised of alternative routes. The service may capture the historic pattern of the traffic situations and advise a better route in advance depending on time and the current location.

- *Map.* When a subscriber wants to reach a certain destination, the phone can display a map showing the current location and the destination. Soon the phone will be equipped with an electronic compass; as she turns her phone, the map will also turn, so the screen will truly reflect the geography she is facing.

- *Matchmaking service.* Suppose a teenager subscriber is at a shopping mall. He wants to find whether any of his friends listed on his directory are in the neighborhood. With a few clicks on the phone, he can find the names and locations of those friends. Even further, he may want to find some "new" friends at the mall that meet the criteria he presents. (Of course, he must also meet the criteria presented by the new friends.) The answer to the request may arrive *over time* as the mall's population changes.

- *Information depository.* Many retail Web sites (e.g., isize.co.jp/gourmet) carry the icon "iPick." If you click on it and enter your mobile phone number, it will send its phone number, address, business hours, and even a map to your phone number, which is then stored on your 104.com organizer's database. Depending on where you are, the nearest location will pop up upon your request.

Source: Compiled from interview with industry experts.

entrenched in a mature market that was not threatened. By contrast, CE and handset manufacturers were directly threatened. It was their products that PC giants were targeting, not the other way around. The scenario of Microsoft and Intel gaining the upper hand and forcing other companies to pay tribute was a serious concern for companies such as Nokia and Sony.

The global mobile phone market had reached a value of $65.4 billion in 2002 (for equipment only), representing 420.6 million shipments. Going forward, by 2007, the market was forecast to reach a value of $97.1 billion, an increase of 35 percent since 2002.[26]

In 2003, the global CE market had reached a value of $218.1 billion, with visual equipment accounting for 77.20 percent, audio equipment 15.60 percent, and games consoles 7.30 percent. The global CE market was forecast to have a value of $293.5 billion by 2008, an increase of 35 percent since 2003.[27]

By contrast, in 2002, the global PC market was worth $187.7 billion and was expected to be $227.1 billion by 2007, a 20 percent growth since 2002. PC manufacturers were eying large markets with higher growth potential than theirs and a need for new products that required some of their core competencies: storage and data processing.[28]

Horizontal Open Model versus Vertical Closed Model

A core question in the industry future was that of an industry model. By model, insiders meant the logic followed by manufacturers regarding the interoperability between different elements. Should the product's architecture be open, allowing similar products from different manufacturers to interact with them or, furthermore, for different components from different manufacturers to be assembled together by yet another? Or should it be closed, requiring components to come from one exclusive source? Correlatively, should players develop all elements of their products, thus controlling the complete product? Or should they focus on a specific part of the product in the hope that, as in the PC world, the benefits to the consumer would justify higher sales and therefore offset the loss of control of the entire architecture?

The Five-Layer Architecture Smart CE appliances were to be built on the same logic as microcomputers, following a five-layer architecture, as shown in Exhibit 7. The lower layer was a physical one whose major components were a data processing chip and a memory device. Next was the network layer that allowed appliances to exchange information with one or more networks. This layer required sophisticated components due to the complexity of network protocols and the need for the digital hardware to deal with the analog antennae. Most transmission problems came from inadequate interface between the analog world and the

[26]Datamonitor, *Global Mobile Phones—Industry Profile* (New York: Datamonitor, November 2003), pp. 8–9.

[27]Datamonitor, *Global Consumer Electronics—Industry Profile* (New York: Datamonitor, May 2004), p. 9.

[28]Datamonitor, *Global PCs—Industry Profile* (New York: Datamonitor, November 2003), p. 9.

EXHIBIT 7 | The Smart Device Layer Model

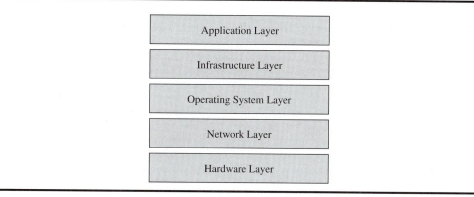

Source: Compiled from interview with industry experts.

digital world at the level of the network layer. The third layer was the operating system, which ensured the order and connection of components and provided the basic user interface. Because of space constraints, there was only room for one operating system on a given network appliance. Finally, at the top of the operating system came the infrastructure layer that provided foundation and components to the application layer, which in turn provided the specific service consumers wanted.

Software standards   Manufacturers such as Nokia, Motorola, Ericsson, Siemens, Samsung, Panasonic, NEC, Fujitsu, Sony, LGE, Casio, Kyocera, and Canon designed, manufactured, and marketed handsets. In second generation (2G) handsets, the software on each handset model had to be developed from scratch or by modifying an earlier version. Manufacturers generally outsourced this tedious task. There were more than a hundred different operating systems (OS), written in different languages and generally incompatible with each other. This approach was inconvenient because manufacturers had to rewrite or adapt the software for every new model. It was tolerable as long as handset operating systems were basic programs, as 90 percent of the treatments needed on a 2G-cell phone were dedicated to telecommunication functions.

In 3G handsets, however, handset processing power had increased to the point where specific functionalities (i.e., application software) of the handset had become as important as the communication functionalities and required a powerful operating system. Developers of a new handset would rewrite only the applications, while keeping the underlying OS somewhat steady over time. They might even use a third-party OS by Microsoft (Windows CE), Symbian, Palm, or Linux.

Symbian was a particularly interesting initiative, formed in 1998 by Ericsson, Nokia, and Motorola along with British Psion (see Exhibit 8 for Symbian equity structure). In February 2004, however, Psion, one of the leaders of digital technologies in the United Kingdom,[29] had walked away from Symbian. Other operating systems are described in Exhibit 9.

Hardware Modularity   Like interoperability, modularity was a key question in the battle for creating new products with both the processing power of computers and the communication capabilities of cell phones. Modularity was the capacity to assemble pieces of hardware from different vendors into one device. In the world of IT, modularity was almost total, at least for PCs. Components could be acquired from Intel (microprocessor), Samsung (memory), or 3COM (network) and assembled by Dell or Hewlett-Packard, or even by individual users with some computer science background. Similarly, software from

---

[29]Psion PLC, "Company Presentation," http://www.psion.com/ (April 11, 2004).

EXHIBIT 8 | Symbian Equity Structure in February 2004

Nokia	32.2%
Psion	31.1
Ericsson	17.5
Panasonic	7.9
Samsung	5.0
Siemens	4.8
Sony Ericsson	1.5

Source: Symbian

EXHIBIT 9 | Operating Systems for Smart Phones

Other than Symbian, the most important operating systems are presented below:

- **Palm OS (PalmSource)**—Developed by the software arm of Palm, Palm OS was licensed by industry leaders—including Aceeca, AlphaSmart, Fossil, Foundertech, Garmin, GSPDA, HuneTec, Kyocera, Lenovo, PalmOne, PerComm, Samsung, Sony, Symbol, and Tapwave—over 30 million hardware products worldwide had been shipped with the Palm OS and had given rise to a huge community of users, enterprises, developers, and manufacturers, who together made up the Palm Economy.

- **SmartPhone and PocketPC (Microsoft)**—For several years, Microsoft had seen this market as a great opportunity and put more and more resources in it. Microsoft's software, however, was considered of lesser quality. Microsoft had been struggling with right strategy moving between brands: Windows CE, Windows Mobile SmartPhone, Pocket PC.

- **Embedded Linux and Other Open Source Operating Systems**—In this environment and with the example of the PC industry some players had already opted to use an open source solution. Companies like Monta Vista offered a similar package to what Red Hat would offer in the PC world, combining the software with professional services, documentation, quality assurance, controlled and timed releases, and integrated and tested tools. Samsung, in particular, had been using a Linux–based operating system for some of its models. However, the big players had been reluctant to bet on an open source–based solution as the single operating system for their entire portfolio.

Of all the applications on the handset, perhaps the most important for wireless data was the microbrowser. The microbrowser was, like other Internet browsers, equipped with basic functionalities such as HTML or dynamic HTML[a] player, GIF[b] image display, reasonable security, and Java[c] layer, but was optimized for wireless communication. Most handset manufacturers used a browser developed by a third party. The most popular (70 percent market share) microbrowser on DoCoMo's i-mode phone was Compact NetFront provided by Access.[d] For the WAP browser, Phone.com (acquired by OpenWave) was the market leader.[e]

Source: Compiled from interview with industry experts.

[a]HTML (hypertext markup language) was the coded format language used for creating hypertext documents on the World Wide Web and controlling how Web pages appeared. Dynamic HTML (dHTML) was a set of features in Internet browsers that could be used to create HTML documents that dynamically changed their content and interacted with the user.

[b]GIP (graphic interchange format) was a common format for image files, especially suitable for images containing large areas of the same color. GIF format files of simple images were often smaller than the same file would be if stored in Joint Photographic Experts Group (JPEG), but GIF format did not store photographic images as well as JPEG.

[c]Java, a programming language introduced by Sun Microsystems, had been developed to be one of the most universal (multiplatform) programming languages. It was particularly suited to help diverse devices to communicate. The Java platform that targeted small, standalone, or connectable consumer and embedded devices was called Java Micro Edition (J2ME).

[d]Access Corporation, http://www.access-us-inc.com (April 11, 2004).

[e]OpenWave Inc., http://www.openwave.com/us/ (April 11, 2004).

---

different publishers, including operating systems, would operate perfectly whether the processor came from AMD or Intel. Assembling the PCs was a low added-value activity, and thus generated low margins. Operational excellence was the key value discipline for these companies.

In 2G handset manufacturing, a few manufacturers controlled the value chain from initial R&D to delivery to operators. This was already a change from the situation in the first-generation handsets (1G) where large carriers such as AT&T controlled the distribution as well as the manufacturing. It was, however, a situation far away from that of the PC world. The degree of complexity in manufacturing telecommunication and network equipment was so high that making phones remained far more difficult than assembling PCs. Yet, if standards of modularity and interoperability were to be adopted, Dell and

other low-cost assemblers would have an obvious diversification opportunity. They would be extremely well positioned if the industry's value discipline switched from product differentiation to low cost, where operational excellence became the key competitive advantage. In 2002, Dell's choice to start assembling PDAs seemed to be an indication of their willingness to penetrate the market of Smartphones as soon as commoditization advanced sufficiently to allow it.

As shown in Exhibit 10, a wide variety of chips and other components were used to build hand phones and network equipment. Chips were developed and manufactured by companies like Qualcomm. Qualcomm also sold IP licenses to various parties including CDMA-handset and chip manufacturers. The final quality and performance of a cell phone heavily depended on both the design and assembly.

EXHIBIT 10 | Smart Devices Value Chain

Content Providers
Amazon
Disney
AOL Time Warner

Service Providers
DoCoMo
KDDI
J-Tel, SKTel
KTF
LGT

Software Editors
Symbian
Pixo
Microsoft
Mira Vista
Sun
Cybird

Hardware Manufacturers	
Ericsson	Nokia
Motorola	Palm
Cisco	Siemens
Matsushita	Samsung
Ony	LEG

Component Manufacturers	
Arm	Tyco
INTEL	Qualcomm
RFMD	TI
STM	
BRCM	

Source: Compiled from interview with industry experts.

Home Appliances All audio or TV products could become "network CE" in the long term. In home networking, the challenge was to create and maintain short-range radio technologies that would ideally be compatible with wireless phone equipment. Thus, the objective was to enable a homeowner to set up a wireless home network to share voice and data between PCs, peripherals, and new devices such as portable, remote display pads. As shown in Exhibit 3 and Exhibit 4, Bluetooth and WiFi were the two most important potential standards. Around one hundred companies supported Bluetooth.[30] Although big names such as

Microsoft promoted both norms, Bluetooth promoters were predominantly North European telecommunication manufacturers.

Industry Evolution: Convergence or Collision?

Each group was trying to make its products the center of the digital home, and its industry model the standard in the emerging industry. Handset manufacturers were promoting a vertical model inherited from the end-to-end solution of the voice communication equipment; "Wintel" giants were promoting the horizontal model; and CE companies were trying to find a model to preserve their competitive position.

[30]Among those companies were Agere, Ericsson, IBM, Intel, Microsoft, Motorola, Nokia, and Toshiba.

The IT Vision

IT companies saw the opportunity of reviving the PC market. They were promoting an interoperable model in which the PC would be the central hub for the house. Microsoft and Intel had been trying for years to compete in CE. In the early 1990s, they had created TV set-boxes that were tested by cable TV companies but not widely deployed. In 2004, the situation appeared different. IT companies thought that PCs could become the center of the digital home, based on progress in wireless networks and increase in demand for media treatment software.

IT companies were already delivering the first products. Gateway's version was the "Gateway FMC-901X," released in 2004 and designed to be connected to a television set or a stereo, looking like an FM tuner but containing a powerful PC and allowing users to read e-mail or run programs such as Word and Excel on a television. On a giant TV screen, a user could simultaneously watch a football game and read his or her e-mails. Gateway had already been producing plasma TVs. Microsoft had released the New Windows "XP Media Center," a version of Windows focused on home entertainment with intuitive commands entirely controlled from a remote control. Dell announced that it would start producing flat-screen TVs, a historic move into CE for a company that previously had made more than 80 percent of its revenues from sales to enterprises.[31]

The driving force for these companies was the belief that consumers were willing to manage and manipulate their digital content instead of merely viewing it. Microsoft and others saw the need for software as a major driver in CE. Microsoft's vision was summarized by Rick Thompson, senior vice president of Microsoft's Windows Extended Platforms Group:

> Since the release of Windows XP and the rich media experiences it enables, we've seen an explosion of growth in digital media. As more consumers acquire, manage and enjoy photos, videos and music, they are looking for new ways to access this content both in the home and on a variety of devices. The efforts of the Digital Home Working Group will increase interoperability between PCs and these consumer electronics devices to create tremendous opportunities for exciting new consumer products and services.[32]

For Microsoft, the need for interoperability was paramount. The Redmond giant was releasing products that would allow the Xbox to be used for karaoke and remixing music.[33] It had organized about 50 focus groups on consumer attitudes regarding remote controls and managing digital information stored on different devices.[34]

To be successful, IT companies needed to reproduce the PC industry model to apply to home appliances. They were critical of the belief propagated by CE manufacturers, that CE products were too complicated to follow a horizontal model. Novelty and innovation were fostered by open standards. The IT-leaders were looking for a wave of innovation to create demand for their products. According to Louis Burns, vice president and general manager of Intel's Desktop Platforms Group: "Collaborating and applying open industry standards to speed up development of interoperable products will dramatically increase the pace of convergence and innovation, and is going to bring huge benefits to consumers with products that are easy to set up and operate and will share digital content."[35]

The CE Vision

Consumer electronics manufacturers saw a potentially huge market that might escape them. Consumer electronics were adopting an interoperability model but had moved quickly to secure the most valuable layers of the architecture to keep control over product design. Even more importantly, they were promoting a vision where there would be no center in the digital home, but rather a constellation of interconnected devices coexisting with different functions. Cesar Vohringer, CTO of Philips Consumer Electronics explained this vision: "The establishment of open standards and home networking interoperability, we believe, will unleash a rich digital media environment of interconnected devices that enable us all to experience our favorite content and services wherever and whenever we want."

The view was shared by Keiji Kimura, corporate senior vice president of Sony Corporation: "With the rapid advances in broadband networking technology, it is of paramount importance that CE products be able to connect with each other as well as with personal

---

[31]Cathy Booth Thomas, "Dell Wants Your Home," *Time*, October 6, 2003, p. 48.

[32]Digital Home Working Group, "17 Leading Companies Form Working Group," http://www.dhwg.org/news/2003_06_24 (April 21, 2004).

[33]Don Clark, Robert Guth, and Nick Wingfield, "Microsoft and Intel Lay Siege to the TV," *The Wall Street Journal Europe*, January 4, 2004, p. A1.

[34]Robert Guth, "Microsoft Takes On Consumer Electronics with New PC," *The Wall Street Journal*, September 30, 2003, p. B1.

[35]Digital Home Working Group, loc. cit.

computers and deliver the rich experience and benefits of a digital home."

Sony, Samsung, Philips, and others were investing large amounts of money in chip plants to make traditional stereos or televisions more like PCs. Matsushita had plans to spend $1.2 billion on a new chip factory. Cooperation within the industry or with IT giants was spreading. But CE manufacturers also propagated their vision that the PC would never be as easy to use, as enjoyable, and as fashionable as a television. Andy Parsons, senior vice president of Pioneer, explained: "When you consider that a very large group of consumers could never figure out how to program their VCR, it seems overly optimistic to expect that the mass market segment will ever be able to install a media center PC as it is currently defined."[36] According to Ken Kutaragi, executive deputy president of Sony Corporation and president and CEO of Sony Computer Entertainment, PCs will never equal CE in quality: "I don't mean to put down the PC, but it's sort of like fast food."[37]

The Mobile Vision

Convergence was also shaking the mobile industry. Nokia's position had been evolving from the peak of the 2G era, when Jorma Ollila, Nokia's CEO, argued that "the convergence of Internet to mobile phone will not lead to one single player becoming master of the universe. We're likely to see a horizontal value chain, like in computers." In early 2002, Nokia announced that their business model would be "hardware, software and services." In a contradictory move, in February 2002, Nokia used the 2004 3GSM World Congress[38] to announce an initiative aimed at making it easier for operators to mix hardware and software from different vendors. This was called the "Open IP Base Station Architecture," whose goal was to lead to modular devices with open internal interfaces. The most significant part of this initiative was the emphasis put on Symbian.

If software were to grow separately from hardware, Nokia potentially could be in a difficult position. In hardware, margins could erode while cell phones became boxes that no-brand manufacturers produced at lower costs. In addition, companies like Samsung could replace them as the company with the most fashionable products because they were selling both cell phones and many other consumer electronic goods.[39] Last but not least, in software, the popularity and sophistication of Microsoft's products could force Nokia to use Microsoft standards and pay royalties to Microsoft on each shipped cell phone.

Nokia was acknowledging that they might have to give up some layers of the smart devices stack to horizontalization. According to Pertti Korhonen, executive vice president, Nokia Mobile Software: "As the world leader in mobile communications, Nokia's mission is to provide easy-to-use products that are an integral part of people's everyday life at home and on the move. The backbone of these products and services is built on open standards and interoperability."[40]

While looking to build standards and interoperability, Nokia and its allies were arguing that cell phones and cell phone components were too complex to be commoditized. Handsets manufacturers and carriers were still looking for differentiation as a source of competitive advantage. David Levin explained: "We do not believe there will be a commoditization of handsets. There is too much complexity in manufacturing. Each model must be able to run on up to 600 different wireless networks. Manufacturers cannot compete only on low costs and rapid production."

The Content Provider Vision

Content providers had been suffering from their investments in the convergence, as exemplified by the unsuccessful merger of AOL and Time Warner. Major studios were cautious of any further venturing into the IT world. But they were also courted by IT companies who saw the richness of content as a major lever in their penetration strategy. Microsoft, for example, had hired Warren Lieberfarb, the former head of Time Warner's home-video division, to help promote Windows Media format as a standard.

Hollywood's studios were also worried about protecting digitized movies from unauthorized copying in the home. Time Warner was working with Matsushita and Intel on a copyright protection system. Despite

---

[36]Adam Morstad, "No Direction Home?" *Emedia the Digital Studio Magazine*, August 1, 2003, p. 22.

[37]Don Clark, Robert Guth and Nick Wingfield, "Microsoft, Intel Enter Living Room," *The Asian Wall Street Journal*, January 6, 2004, p. A1.

[38]The 2004 3GSM World Congress had been held in Cannes, France, on February 23–26, 2004.

[39]Nokia's brand value was number six globally, at 29.44 billion dollars, while Samsung ranked number 25 at 10.85 billion. Samsung's brand appreciation was however much faster. For more information, see Gerry Khermouch and Diane Brady, loc. cit.

[40]The Digital Home Working Group, loc. cit.

EXHIBIT 11 |
Global Mobile Phones
Market Share in 2003

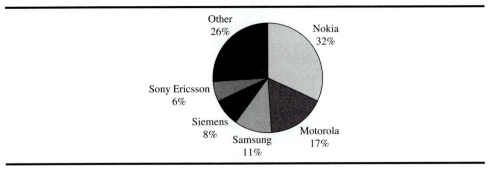

Source: Compiled from Datamonitor, *Global Mobile Phone Industry Profile,* op. cit. p. 12.

extensive efforts, a widespread endorsement of Internet technologies by content providers was still out of the question unless contents would circulate on private, closed distribution channels like those of cable TV, where pirating of movies and songs, although still possible, was easier to trace and fight.

Samsung's Strategy: Leading the Digital Convergence Revolution

Samsung's vision was to become a worldwide reference in bringing to market products and concepts for all digital devices, within the general framework of creating a "high tech way of life" referred to as the DigitAll paradigm.[41] Samsung wanted to be a single location to shop for the devices that would create a "high tech way of life:" the company fundamentally appreciated the nature of the connected consumer's entertainment experience and was driving convergence in parallel to all their product segments.

As explained by Eric Kim, the effort to sponsor the box-office success *Matrix Reloaded* was motivated by the connection with the consumer experience Samsung was creating: "The Matrix fits with our brand perfectly. The target audience is young—in their 20s and 30s—and it conveys a very cool lifestyle message." This goal of creating a lifestyle was extremely vast, ambitious, and long-term oriented. According to Paul Jackson, analyst at Forrester research: "Phones opened a lot of doors for Samsung. It is almost the only phone company that makes consumer products as well. People who have a Samsung phone and are happy with it become better disposed to buying its DVD players."[42]

Ahead of its competitors, Samsung had already started to deliver its vision. The company had unveiled home network frameworks and was aggressively negotiating deals with construction companies to provide a home networking system to apartment complexes. In the United States and Japan, in particular, the company was seeking to team up with solution providers, while marketing products that aggressively targeted house builders. Initiatives such as "Homepad," the Digital Fridge or Samsung's "World Best," a new air conditioner with cutting-edge technology that controlled hazardous indoor germs, were at the leading edge of the company's product management and marketing. So far, those products had remained prototypes or marketing tools to draw admiring gasps from the showroom's audience.

Samsung's Strategy in the Industry Struggle

As a diversified giant both in the CE and the handset worlds (see Exhibit 11 and Exhibit 12), Samsung could endorse any of the industry models. Its wide scope and long-term horizon allowed Samsung to be more pragmatic than its rivals in focusing on one layer of the industry model. At the beginning of 2003, Samsung announced its first Windows-powered phone:

> Microsoft and Samsung Electronics officially unveiled the Samsung Windows-Powered MITs (Mobile Intelligent Terminal) SGH-i700. This "smart" device is a result of Microsoft and Samsung's commitment to collaborate and develop a portfolio of Windows-Powered smart, wireless devices that address diverse customer requirements and design preferences.[43]

---

[41]For more information, see Samsung "DigitALL", http://www.samsung.com/DigitAll/ (May 19, 2004).

[42]Maija A. Pesola, "From Microwaves to the Matrix," *Financial Times*, September 11, 2003, p. 8.

[43]PRNewswire, "Microsoft and Samsung Reveal Windows Powered Pocket PC for GSM/GPRS Networks," February 17, 2003, http://www.prnewswire.co.uk/ (April 21, 2003).

Samsung's
competitors—Global
Consumer Electronics
in 2003

Company	Sales (billion dollars)
Sony	27.8
Matsushita Electric Industrial Co., Ltd.	17.7
Koninklijke Philips Electronics N.V.	9.1

Source: Compiled from Datamonitor, *Global Consumer Electronics Industry Profile*, op. cit. p. 11.

The same day, it announced its equity participation in Symbian: "Samsung Electronics Co. took ownership of 5 percent of Symbian for 17 million pounds (18.35 million dollars), its first minority investment outside of South Korea and a move that some analysts said helps assure the British group's systems will be a major force in the next generation of phones."[44] Samsung was also one of the early adopters of Palm OS for Smartphones, with Palm Powered Smartphones, and was considering a participation in MontaVista, a provider of Linux for Smartphones.

Samsung did not develop software internally for any of its applications. The company licensed or outsourced developments. It was also very pragmatic in buying components from outside vendors, with the exception of their core component capability in memories (DRAM and flash). Although Samsung had the capability to produce chips for television or cell phones, it used the services of engineering companies, while maintaining control of strategic, added-value chip developments. Although Samsung was outsourcing hardware projects worth several hundred million dollars,[45] it also identified critical components and developed them in-house. In particular, Samsung took steps to become less dependent on Qualcomm Inc. for semiconductors. Samsung's new CDMA 2000 handsets contained Samsung's own semiconductors.[46]

Samsung was also prompted to embrace industry standardization initiatives. For Smartphones, the main standardization body was the Mobile Industry Processor Interface (MIPI) Alliance. The MIPI was an industry initiative established to define and promote open standards

for interfaces to mobile application processors.[47] For digital devices, Samsung was part of the Digital Home Working Group (DHWG), a task force of the world's largest electronics makers that had agreed on common standards to make it easier for consumers to swap songs and pictures at home.[48]

Direct cooperation with competitors was not uncommon. In January 2004, Philips Electronics and Samsung Electronics agreed on a single software standard for chips used in devices such as digital televisions. The standard was called Universal Home Application Programming Interface (UH-API) and aimed at convincing software makers, system integrators and device vendors to write applications for their TVs and DVD players (electronic programming guides, shopping applications, and music and video stores, etc.).[49]

In April 2004, however, Samsung Electronics and Sony set up a joint venture liquid crystal display (LCD)[50] company with Sony, thus directly targeting Philips, the world's largest LCD maker. Samsung was to invest in kind, while Sony would put up funds of an equal worth.[51]

[44]Victoria Shannon, "Samsung Joins Symbian Mobile Phone Group," International Herald Tribune, February 18, 2003, p. 11.

[45]Adrian Baschnonga, "Agere Systems Signs US$200m Chipset Deal with Samsung," *World Market Research Center Daily Analysis*, February 2, 2004, http://www.wmrc.com/ (April 21, 2003).

[46]David Pringle, "Samsung to Use Its Own CDMA Chip," *The Wall Street Journal*, April 14, 2003, p. B5.

[47]In this MIPI Alliance, members included Agilent Technologies, Infineon Technologies, Marvell International, Philips Electronics, Seiko Epson, Siemens AG, Sony Ericsson Mobile, Symbian, Synaptics, Toshiba, and others. The founding members were ARM, Nokia, ST Microelectronics, and Texas Instruments. http://www.dhwg.org/home (April 21, 2004).

[48]Promoter members were Fujitsu, Hewlett-Packard, IBM, Intel, Kenwood, Lenovo, Microsoft, NEC, Nokia, Panasonic, Philips, Samsung, Sharp, Sony, ST, and Thomson. http://www.dhwg.org/home (April 21, 2004).

[49]Lucas van Grinsven, "Philips and Samsung Agree on Chip Software for TVs," *Reuters*, January 6, 2004.

[50]A screen type, used most often in laptops, that uses electric current to align crystals in a special liquid.

[51]Organization of Asia-Pacific News Agencies, "Samsung-Sony Joint Venture," OANA Newswire, September 22, 2003, http://www.oananews.com/ (April 21, 2004).

Samsung's Product Strategy

Frenzy of New Products   In Samsung's massive product line strategy and trial-and-error strategy, it was essential to be able to supply the world with innovative products faster than its competition, both in handsets and CE. Sung Kyu Lee, president and chief executive officer of Pantech,[52] one of Samsung's competitors in Korea, benchmarked the industry efficiency by comparing his company, Samsung and LG,[53] another competitor: "We want to develop one product within seven months, almost half of others' development time. It takes Samsung about six months or less to develop a new product, while LG takes between 10–12 months."[54] Nokia planned to launch 40 handsets in 2004, while Samsung planned to launch 130, 98 percent of which would have a color screen, and over half of which would have cameras.[55]

Focus on Very High End and on the Power of the Brand: The Accelerator   In 2004, Samsung Electronics had high brand awareness, and was associated with innovation and quality, which could be traced back to Samsung's interest in the premium market beginning in 1997. As the Asian economic crisis started to rage, Samsung saw its profits erode dramatically. As Samsung was already a low-cost manufacturer, the situation became quickly intolerable and improving margins became imperative. To do this, the company focused on premium markets, where they could sell products for higher prices, and increased its product design capabilities. The company doubled its number of designers to 300, opened design bureaus in the United States, Europe, and Japan and began to pick up design awards. Since 1998 it had won 17 awards at the Industrial Design Excellence Awards sponsored by the Industrial Design Society of America[56]—a performance equaled only by Apple. Four years later, after a high-profile advertising push linked to the Matrix films and Olympic sponsorships, the company's brand perception had changed dramatically.

The strategic focus was the premium market and high margins. Phones that retailed for $300 or more in the United States were no longer Nokia's exclusive domain. Samsung made the expensive camera phone that a young consumer wanted to brandish.[57] To sell premium products, Samsung was launching premium concepts. The bar-format phone (Samsung SGH-X600) was one of many examples. It was designed and marketed for people "who lived for the night." Like the popular Samsung, it came in a midnight blue and silver trim. As described in Samsung's brochure: "It will fully satisfy your appreciation of the beauty in your world and delivers the wonders of convenience as well. With the SGH- X600 integrated flash and night mode, you can forget blurry night shots. The LED flash installed in the device captures your special moments even in the darkness."[58]

Changing public perception was the work of Eric Kim, head of global marketing operations. When he joined in 1999, the Samsung name barely registered outside its home country except as a maker of cheap microwave ovens and television sets. According to Kim, the change was promoted through three qualities: "wow," simplicity, and exclusivity:

> Each department has a quota for how many "wow" products it must create each year. This year's "wow" products include a Dick Tracy-style wristwatch phone and the ultra-light and thin X10 notebook personal computer. Although we aim for the top end of the market, there is a desire to put across a message of inclusivity. Samsung's slogan is "DigitALL: Everyone's invited."[59]

Globalization, with Priority Given to India and China   Samsung was trying very hard to reinforce its domination in those markets, using its geographical proximity. Internally, efforts were made to recruit Chinese graduates from top American business and engineering schools; externally, Samsung directly invested in production lines and marketing towards China in the hope of selling $10 billion of products by 2005, or 20 percent of 2003 sales.[60] For 2003, Samsung's investment in China represented $3.1 billion.[61]

---

[52]Pantech, http://www.pantech.com/ (May 5, 2004).

[53]LG Electronics, http://www.lge.com/index.do (May 5, 2004).

[54]Yun-Hee Kim, "South Korea Pantech Sees Swing to Net Profit In 2004," Dow Jones International News, February 5, 2004.

[55]Carlo Longino, "Nokia Slips as Samsung Steals Share," April 16, 2004, http://www.thefeature.com/article?articleid=100534 (April 21, 2004).

[56]A consortium seen as a reference in the industrial design profession. http://www.idsa.org (April 28, 2004).

---

[57]John Gapper, "Nokia and the Insistent Ringing of Competition," Financial Times, April 20, 2004, p. 21.

[58]Samsung Electronics, "SGH-X600 an Amazing Rotating Camera," Products 2003, http://www.samsung.com/Products/MobilePhone/GSM/MobilePhone_GSM_SGH_X600.htm (April 21, 2004).

[59]Maija A. Pesola, loc. cit.

[60]James Brooke, "Koreans Look to China, Seeing a Market and a Monster," The New York Times, February 10, 2004, p. 1.

[61]"Samsung Invests $ 3.1 Billion in China in 2003," SinoCast China Business Daily News, December 5, 2003.

Samsung also planned to set up a chip research and development center in Suzhou. The ambitious move aimed to turn China into Samsung's second-largest chip-producing location after Korea, underscoring the chipmaker's resolve to ride on the wave of China's greater role in the global industrial sector.[62]

Samsung owed its expansion in China to the penetration of smuggled handsets and the nice handset appearance design. Interestingly enough, as a proof of their long-term commitment to leadership in China, Samsung offered warranty services to both dealer-smuggled handsets and regular ones.

Control of critical components One key to Samsung's cell phone success had been its ability to roll out new features faster than its rivals. One of the first makers outside of Japan to use color screens in phones, Samsung had moved on to loading them with MP3 players, TV remote controllers, and camcorders. This was possible because of the integration within Samsung of a powerful semiconductors arm. Samsung was the second largest semiconductor manufacturer in the world in 2004, with 5.9 percent market share, compared to 16.7 percent for Intel, in a market worth $168 billion.[63] The availability within the group of DRAM and flash memory, essential in digital cameras and flat screens, gave Samsung's products improved integration and shorter time to market.[64] In 2004, Samsung Electronics climbed to the top of the global market for flash memory chips, achieving a dominant market share of 20 percent, at $615 million for the third quarter of 2004, up 50 percent from the same quarter last year. Intel made $416 million in sales, for the fourth-largest share of 13.5 percent, while Intel was number one in flash memory in 2002 but lost ground after an unfortunate decision to raise flash memory prices in early 2003.[65]

Samsung's Rivals Samsung had been dubbed "the New Sony." Its market value of about $88 billion made Samsung Asia's most valuable technology company, at almost twice Japan's Sony, whose profits in PlayStation were used to support its consumer-electronics business. Yet, in both internal and external literature, Samsung was compared to Sony. On the other end, Sony's president, Kunitake Ando, had set up an expert task force designed to monitor Samsung's strategic moves and requested a weekly update about its competitor.[66] Sony's operating margin for 2004 was estimated at 2.3 percent, compared to 17 percent for Samsung.[67]

It was not Sony, however, but Nokia that was suffering the most from Samsung's progresses. In 2004, for the first time, the Finnish group's market capitalization fell below Samsung's. In April 7, 2004, when Nokia announced its quarterly results, Nokia's shares lost 8.2 percent, while Samsung's shares rose by 9 percent.[68]

Samsung's Manufacturing

Before the marketing effort that created Samsung's new prosperity, the company's main competitive advantage was superb manufacturing in a number of areas. Samsung was known to launch products quicker than its competitors, with higher standards of quality. Samsung's manufacturing was also extremely flexible and scalable. This was primarily due to the quality of the people. Senior engineers, for example, were "encouraged" to stay after their office hours to give lectures to a class of junior engineers. Job rotation was prohibited (changing from DRAM to microprocessors or from one plant to another one) in order to accelerate the development of a knowledgeable engineer corps. On-the-spot task force teams would mobilize any time a problem occurred in production. Both R&D and production engineers were located at the same place, living in Samsung's campuses.[69] This allowed production to start with limited knowledge. Anytime a critical issue was detected, the group would gather day and night to solve it.

Field management was considered a priority ("treasures come from the field"). Even the highest ranking engineer was located close to the production line and was supposed to spend time with the operators, working on inspection, quality control, and the like. Although this was changing with the new priority given to marketing,

[62]Yang Sung-jin, "High-tech Players Eager to Use China as Base for Production and Exports," *The Korea Herald*, July 8, 2003.

[63]Datamonitor, *Global Semiconductors—Industry Profile*, Datamonitor, May 2004, p. 12.

[64]Hae Won Choi, "Samsung Weds Gloss with Wizardry—Focus on 'Premium' Phones May Help Korea Firm Grab Market Share From Nokia," *The Wall Street Journal Europe*, 15 April, 2004, p. A6.

[65]Choi Hong-seop, "Samsung Ranks as Top Flash Memory-Chip Maker," *The Chosun Ilbo Co.*, November 22, 2003.

[66]Cliff Edwards, Moon Ihlwan, and Pete Engardio, "The Samsung Way," *BusinessWeek*, June 16, 2003, p. 56.

[67]Masahiro Ono, "*Sony—Do Global Earnings Justify Brand Strength?*" (Tokyo: Morgan Stanley, December 2003), p. 7.

[68]Christopher Brown-Humes, "Samsung Mounts Challenge to Nokia," *Financial Times*, April 17, 2004, p. 1.

[69]Plants such as the Suwon plant, the Giheng plant or the Onyang plant covered several square kilometers and employed tens of thousands.

EXHIBIT 13 | Samsung Electronics' Investment in Property, Plant and Equipment

$ Million	Land	Building and Structures	Machinery and Equipment	Construction in Progress	Others	Total
Balance at December 31, 2002	$ 1,628.43	$ 2,661.80	$ 6,388.45	$ 1,103.23	$ 482.08	$ 12,263.99
Acquisition	$ 1.05	$ 16.73	$ 198.39	$ 5,262.33	$ 374.61	$ 5,853.11
Transfer	$ 51.93	$ 560.87	$ 4,689.13	$ (5,179.89)	$ (122.04)	$ –
Disposal	$ (7.16)	$ (7.49)	$ (61.97)	$ –	$ (4.79)	$ (81.41)
Depreciation	$ –	$ (167.33)	$ (2,871.00)	$ –	$ (143.87)	$ (3,182.20)
Others	$ –	$ –	$ –	$ (34.67)	$ –	$ (34.67)
Balance at December 31, 2003	$ 1,674.25	$ 3,064.58	$ 8,343.01	$ 1,150.99	$ 585.98	$ 14,818.81

Source: Compiled from Samsung, "Audited Financial Statements," 2003,
http://www.samsung.com/AboutSAMSUNG/InvestorRelations/FinancialInformation/downloads/2003_end04_eng_note.pdf (May 19, 2004).

many key positions in general management were still filled with former production engineers. Historically, this had created a culture of "assembly line," pervasive up to the higher level of management.

In the product design, manufacturing engineers and assembly line managers participated right at the beginning, along with R&D engineers. Plant construction started before the final development of the product. Samsung carried out 24-hour rush work and nonstop construction so that the plant could start producing on Day One of the product validation.

Investment in manufacturing had been a priority within Samsung Electronics, even during the dark years. In 2003, Samsung invested 6.8 trillion Won (5.8 billion dollars) to extend manufacturing capabilities (see Exhibit 13). In 2004, Samsung Electronics announced its intention to spend 1.2 trillion Won (1 billion dollars) to build a memory-production line to produce chips using cutting-edge technology.[70] The line, Samsung's thirteenth, would allow more chips to be produced from a single silicon wafer, boosting output and lowering production costs per chip. Total capital spending was 6.4 billion dollars.[71] Out of those, Samsung planned to invest 2.74 trillion Won (2.3 billion dollars) in its seventh-generation LCD production line and 4.1 billion dollars in DRAM and LSI, to produce large panels for television sets and monitors beginning in 2005.[72]

Conclusion

Samsung was following a very ambitious strategy. The target was to become the reference in the digital home through mobile phones and CE. Samsung had based its strategy on products particularly fashionable and appealing to trendy customers. But on the road to convergence they had to play not only with companies such as Nokia and Sony, but also with IT giants such as Intel and Microsoft. And Samsung, an increasingly sophisticated product designer and marketer, was still adapting leading trends rather than pioneering them. Samsung was creating products, but was still struggling to invent a concept in the way Sony invented the Walkman in 1979 or the world's first CD player in 1982.[73]

This new competition took place in a very immature industry. The digital home was looking for a model and for customers. Despite industry attempts to standardize formats and components, the quality of products was still unsatisfactory and it was unclear what customers' needs really were. Would Samsung be able to make the good bets and satisfy those new needs?

---

[70]The leading technology in the sector was the 12-inch, or 300-millimeter wafer.

[71]Lehman Brothers, Technology, *Semiconductors Capital Spending Budget Survey*, April, 19, 2004, p. 19.

[72]Yun-Hee Kim, "Samsung to Add Production Lines For LCDs, Chips," *The Wall Street Journal*, January 14, 2004, p. B4.

[73]Datamonitor Company Profiles, *Sony Corporation—History*, (New York: Datamonitor, February 2004).

Case 4.4

The New, New HP in 2004 (A): Leading Strategic Integration

To be recognized as the leading technology company in the world, we have to now move up to system-level management and innovation.[1]

—Carleton "Carly" S. Fiorina, chairman and CEO,
Hewlett-Packard Company

Introduction

The past five years had been eventful for Hewlett-Packard. When new CEO Carleton S. "Carly" Fiorina arrived at the company in mid-1999, the technology industry was nearing the peak of a bull market. HP, however, had failed to benefit much from the buoyant market. Soon after her arrival, Fiorina set out to reorganize HP, streamlining and centralizing decision making in order to face a rapidly changing environment with increasingly demanding customers. Within a year of her tenure, the technology market crashed, exacerbating the need for further change. Fiorina, by then chairman and CEO, and HP's board of directors decided that radical strategic change was necessary, leading to the far-reaching move to acquire computer rival Compaq. After a dramatic proxy fight, the acquisition took effect in May of 2002.

A merger as big and bold as Hewlett-Packard's $19 billion acquisition of Compaq Computer had never taken place before in the technology industry. Fiorina called it an "historic" event.[2] She believed it was the right move for HP; a key element in her mission to make HP, in her words, "the leading technology company in the world." The integration went more smoothly than anybody outside of the HP and Compaq executive suites predicted.[3] Integration targets were met and ambitious cost-saving estimates were exceeded. During 2003, HP had been able to sustain or improve its strategic position in its core businesses.

In early 2004, with the organizational integration of the Compaq acquisition mostly completed, top management was looking toward capitalizing on the potential competitive advantages of the strategic integration of both companies in order to achieve the goal of becoming the leading technology company in the world. Top management had to make sure that HP would achieve superior profitable growth with its portfolio strategy. (See Exhibit 1 for selected HP financial data.) This would require high performance from its individual businesses in increasingly competitive environments,[4] the development of new strategic leadership skills to capitalize on opportunities for strategic integration across the organization, and continued significant innovation.

The New Corporate Strategy: Driving Strategic Integration

The successful organizational integration of Compaq was a Herculean task. Fiorina decided, in her own words, to "overgun it." Overgunning meant spending well over $100 million and pulling 2,500 of HP's and Compaq's key employees away from their jobs to plan every detail involved in executing the merger—from designing a new organization structure, to deciding

---

[1]All quotes from Carleton S. "Carly" Fiorina are from the author's interview on September 26, 2003 unless otherwise cited. Subsequent quotes from this interview will not be cited.

[2]Letter from Fiorina to HP employees, September 4, 2001.

[3]For more detail on the organizational integration challenges associated with the HP and Compaq merger see, Robert A. Burgelman and Philip E. Meza, "HP and Compaq Combined: In Search of Scale and Scope," Stanford Graduate School of Business, SM-130.

[4]For an overview of the strategic challenges faced by HP's individual businesses, see Robert A. Burgelman and Philip E. Meza, "The New New HP (C): Winning in the Core Businesses," Stanford Graduate School of Business, SM-125C.

Professor Robert A. Burgelman and Philip E. Meza prepared this case as the basis for class discussion rather than to illustrate either effective or ineffective handling of an administrative situation. This case can be used in conjunction with "HP and Compaq Combined: In Search of Scale and Scope," SM-130, "The New New HP in 2004 (B): Winning in the Core Businesses," SM-125B, "The New HP Way," SM-72 and "HP, Compaq and the New PC Landscape," SM-72B, each by Burgelman and Meza.

EXHIBIT 1 | HP Selected Financial Data 1999–2003 ($ million)

	October 31, 2003	October 31, 2002	October 31, 2001	October 31, 2000	October 31, 1999
Revenue					
Equipment revenue	58,939.0	45,969.0	37,498.0	41,653.0	36,113.0
Service revenue	13,657.0	10,165.0	7,325.0	6,848.0	5,960.0
Financing income	465.0	454.0	403.0	369.0	298.0
Total revenue	73,061.0	56,588.0	45,226.0	48,870.0	42,371.0
Cost of equipment	43,689.0	34,189.0	28,863.0	30,343.0	25,436.0
Cost of services	9,959.0	7,414.0	4,396.0	4,470.0	4,284.0
Financing interest	209.0	189.0	236.0	233.0	168.0
Research/development	3,652.0	3,369.0	2,724.0	2,627.0	2,440.0
Selling/general/ administrative	11,012.0	8,763.0	6,950.0	6,984.0	6,225.0
Restructuring charge	800.0	1,780.0	384.0	102.0	0.0
In-process R&D	1.0	793.0	35.0	0.0	NA
Acquisition-relelated charges	280.0	701.0	25.0	0.0	NA
Amortization of goodwill/ intangibles	0.0	107.0	174.0	86.0	NA
Amorization of intangibles	563.0	295.0	NA	NA	NA
Litigation settlement	0.0	(14.0)	400.0	0.0	0.0
Total operating expense	70,165.0	57,586.0	44,187.0	44,845.0	38,553.0
Interest/other, net	21.0	52.0	171.0	356.0	345.0
Losses on divestitures	0.0	0.0	(53.0)	203.0	0.0
Investment losses	(29.0)	(75.0)	(455.0)	41.0	31.0
Net income before taxes	2,888.0	(1,021.0)	702.0	4,625.0	4,194.0
Provision for income taxes	349.0	(118.0)	78.0	1,064.0	1,090.0
Net income after taxes	2,539.0	(903.0)	624.0	3,561.0	3,104.0
Net income before extraordinary items	2,539.0	(903.0)	624.0	3,561.0	3,104.0
Discontinued operations	NA	NA	0.0	136.0	387.0
Extraordinary item	NA	NA	56.0	0.0	0.0
Accounting change	0.0	0.0	(272.0)	0.0	0.0
Net income	2,539.0	(903.0)	408.0	3,697.0	3,491.0

Source: Company reports.

NB: Consolidated statement includes results of Agilent Technology prior to its spin-off on June 2, 2002. Consolidated statement includes results from Compaq as of May 3, 2002, its date of acquisition.

Revenue by Business Segment and Region for Fiscal Year 2003

Business Segment		Region	
Imaging and Printing Group	$22.6 billion	United States	$29.2 billion
Personal Systems Group	$21.2 billion	Europe, Middle East, Africa	$28.5 billion
Enterprise Systems Group	$15.4 billion	Asia Pacific (exc. Japan)	$8.0 billion
HP Services	$12.3 billion	Americas (exc. U.S.)	$4.3 billion
HP Financial Services	$1.9 billion	Japan	$3.1 billion
Corporate Investments	$0.3 billion		

Source: Company reports.

NB: Segment and region totals to not equal due to rounding.

EXHIBIT 1 | Selected Combined HP/Compaq Financial Data by Group 2001–2002 (cont.)

Imaging and Printing Group—Combined Company Results

For the following years ended October 31	Combined Company Results	
Dollars in millions	2002	2001
Net revenue	$20,326	$19,470
Earnings from operations	$3,248	$1,876
Earnings from operations as a percentage of net revenue	16.0%	9.6%

Personal Systems Group—Combined Company Results

For the following years ended October 31	Combined Company Results	
Dollars in millions	2002	2001
Net revenue	$21,962	$26,800
Loss from operations	$(532)	$(977)
Loss from operations as a percentage of net revenue	(2.4)%	(3.6)%

Enterprise Systems Group—Combined Company Results

For the following years ended October 31	Combined Company Results	
Dollars in millions	2002	2001
Net revenue	$16,449	$20,486
(Loss) earnings from operations	$(912)	$279
(Loss) earnings from operations as a percentage of net revenue	(5.5)%	1.4%

HP Services—Combined Company Results

For the following years ended October 31	Combined Company Results	
Dollars in millions	2002	2001
Net revenue	$12,411	$12,846
Earnings from operations	$1,443	$1,586
Earnings from operations as a percentage of net revenue	11.6%	12.3%

HP Financial Services—Combined Company Results

For the following years ended October 31	Combined Company Results	
Dollars in millions	2002	2001
Net revenue	$2,088	$2,126
(Loss) from operations	$(133)	$(164)
(Loss) from operations as a percentage of net revenue	(6.4)%	(7.7)%

Source: Company reports.

which products to keep, which thousands of employees to let go, and how to integrate company e-mail and replace signage. The company set and met an ambitious target: Be ready by day one. Since that day in early May 2002, the critical challenge was to achieve the competitive advantage made possible by the strategic integration of the two companies. To do so, Fiorina changed the organization structure to effectively pursue a new vertical-and-horizontal operating model, created a new leadership framework, emphasized the importance of exploiting HP's new scale and scope in all operations, strengthened corporate marketing, and redirected the company's considerable R&D efforts toward focused innovation.

Restructuring for Strategic Integration

Reconsidering the Organization Structure   Upon her arrival in July 1999, Fiorina had quickly decided to change HP's silo structure, which allowed the business units maximum strategic freedom (Exhibit 2). She wanted

EXHIBIT 2 |

Schematic of HP's
Organizational Model
in 2000 (4 x 16)

Under this organizational structure, all functions and activities have been consolidated into 16 product categories across four geographical regions.

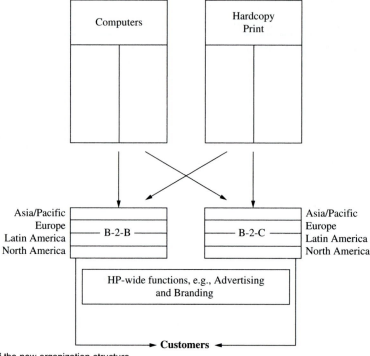

Source: Authors' sketch of the new organization structure.

Note: HP has separate sales organizations for B-2-B and B-2-C.

Additional View of HP's Organization Structure in 2000

Front-End or Customer-Facing

Business Customer Organization	Consumer Business Organization	
Responsible for worldwide sales of HP's products and services and worldwide marketing and delivery of HP products to large and medium-size businesses	Responsible for marketing, distribution, sales and support activities for HP's entire range of consumer products	
20,000 employees headed by Harry (Webb) McKinney.	5,000 employees headed by Pradeep Jotwani.	**HP Services**
		Responsible for HP's services businesses, including consulting, outsourcing, support, etc.
		30,000 employees headed by Ann Livermore

Back-End or Product-Facing

Computing Systems	Imaging and Printing Systems	Embedded and Personal Devices	HP Labs
Responsible for computer products and systems for business customers. Products include servers, software and storage	Responsible for printing, scanning and digital camera platforms	Responsible for personal digital assistants and handheld products, wireless and Internet services, personal storage appliances, embedded software, commercial	Responsible for providing technological leadership and inventing new technologies.
13,000 employees headed by Duane Zitzner.	15,000 employees headed by V. J. Joshi.	1,450 employees headed by Iain Morris.	850 employees headed by Dick Lampman.

Note: HP Services has characteristics of both front end and back end organizations

Source: HP, London, Simon, "HP's Pragmatic Mother of Invention," *The Financial Times,* August 22, 2001.

to reduce the number of product lines and move decision making closer to the customer. Her goal was to take the complexity that the customer faced in dealing with HP and move it inside the company. Fiorina had reassigned the four groups (Peripherals comprising InkJet and LaserJet printers, Personal Systems that included Intel-based PCs, Enterprise Systems of UNIX-based systems, and Services) that aggregated over 80 lines of business into two broad groups: Go-to-Market (front- or customer-facing) and Product Generation (back- or product-facing). Business groups that handled sales and marketing—front- or customer-facing groups—were organized according to customer type. Research, development, and elements of manufacturing—back- or product-facing groups—were organized by product or technology type. There were two customer-facing divisions—Business Customer Organization (BCO) and Consumer Business Organization (CBO)—and three product-facing groups—Computing Systems, Imaging and Printing, and HP Labs. Later in 2001, a fourth back-end division, Embedded and Personal Technology, was added. A separate services division was also created to satisfy the needs of large customers for outsourcing and information technology consulting. This group straddled the customer-facing and product-facing groupings. The creation of this unit followed HP's abandoned attempt to buy the consulting arm of PwC in November 2000.[5] All of the groups were given worldwide scope.

In practice, the customer-facing group presidents were responsible for the revenues and sales and marketing costs. The product-facing group presidents controlled the R&D and manufacturing costs. The product-facing groups were primarily responsible for the P&L beyond 12 months; the customer-facing groups were responsible for the P&L within 12 months. The customer-facing groups were responsible for sales and profits of existing products and extensions of existing products; the product-facing groups were more responsible whenever new products were introduced. The product-facing groups were also responsible for cost-of-goods-sold. Top management believed the new structure would eliminate waste from duplication of marketing and development (which would previously have been held in its old divisional silos) and would encourage the invention of products that integrate technologies.

With this structure, HP could more easily see information in three ways: by product category, by customer view, and by region. Before, HP thought of customers in terms of products. [HP had 85 product lines, which it sold through four to five distinct sales groups.] Under the changed structure, it tried to know buyers as customers. This allowed HP to develop sales strategies and price and service structures that were better tailored to help customers meet their objectives. Critics, however, pointed out that design engineers housed in back-facing units tended to become cut off from customers. Other technology companies such as Xerox, Motorola, IBM, and Fiorina's previous company, Lucent, had experimented with similar models, with varying degrees of success. One key issue was the lack of clarity about responsibilities.

In late 2003, Fiorina looked back on the lessons she had learned from her initial reorganization. She said:

I think it was a necessary step for us to take for two reasons.

One: because we had to take the organization through the process of understanding that we had to serve our customers the way they wanted to be served and have one sales force.

Two: it was important for the back end as well as the front end. What happened on the back end was equally important because we got to this notion of leverage and reuse by putting businesses together into big product development organizations that had not been together in the past. We put together imaging and printing businesses that had never been together before. It was a huge deal to say InkJet and LaserJet are one printing business. People were wildly emotional about this at the time. Those were important steps we had to take to move down the path converging over 80 different businesses into one company, by means of leverage and reuse.

The lessons I think we learned from our experience with this is we did not manage the change with enough rigor. That is a clear lesson I took with me later going into the Compaq integration. In our earlier reorganization, there wasn't enough programatic management and disciplined inspection of effective change. I learned when people feel they no longer have accountability for and connection to customers, you lose something really important. Our product-focused organizations felt disconnected from customers, like it wasn't their job any more, and that was a big issue. Another lesson I learned from our experience reorganizing our front-end/back-end structure was that in order to get the value out of our portfolio, in order to really deliver this value proposition, we have to acknowledge and internalize and

---

[5]Simon London, "HP's Pragmatic Mother of Invention," *Financial Times*, August 22, 2001.

EXHIBIT 3 | HP
Operating Model
(October 2003)

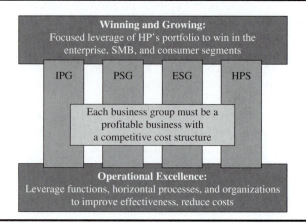

Source: HP.

Note: This is the operating model prior to changes in organization structure proposed for 2004, e.g., reduction from 4 to 3 separate P&Ls. The essence of the operating model, for example the interrelationships of responsibilities, remained the same.

organize around the fact that we are a systems business. And we can't walk away from that. And so any organization structure that breaks a system up into piece parts ultimately isn't going to work.

Taking to heart the lessons learned from the first major reorganization, Fiorina also designed a new organization structure for the company to facilitate implementation of the corporate strategy.

Establishing a New Operating Model Wanting to capitalize on the potential competitive advantage associated with HP's broad business portfolio, Fiorina decided on a new operating model as the foundation for HP's corporate strategy moving forward. This resulted in four lines of business: Imaging and Printing (IPG); Personal Systems Group (PSG); Enterprise Systems Group (ESG); and HP Services (HPS) (Exhibit 3). These lines of business could be thought of as verticals, or stacks; each was run by an executive vice president with ultimate responsibility for the success of the group. Running across these four stacks, like the weft of a woven fabric, were responsibilities for channels and customer segments. For example, the executive vice president running ESG had ultimate responsibility for these activities as far as his domain was concerned. Where there was strong overlap in channels and customer segments, as with IPG and PSG, responsibility for channels and customer segments was shared.

Harry "Webb" McKinney co-led the HP/Compaq integration effort. McKinney was a longtime HP veteran

who had managed the Business Customer Organization (BCO) group, responsible for all business customers, and covering supply chain and customer-facing systems and P&Ls, as well as sales and marketing to these customers. McKinney discussed the evolution of the new organization structure:

> You could take the strategy HP had in 2001 as the starting point. At that time, we were having operational issues around what I would call "one face" to the customer.
>
> When we considered how to structure the new company post merger, we had the same goal. We basically wanted to organize around our major customer segments. We wanted to ensure that we had very strong [market] ownership in those dimensions while continuing to be competitive in front of the customer, whether they want to buy a complex solution or just a printer.
>
> That work continues. Right now we have stronger alignment in the product dimension than the model HP had in 2001 and quite a bit stronger alignment than Compaq had. We have four product groups, which was true before, so the product group structure is quite similar. What we have done that is a little different is, we asked three of the four product group managers to also be responsible for a customer segment.[6]

---

[6]All quotes from Harry "Webb" McKinney are from the author's interview on August 20, 2003. Subsequent quotes from this interview will not be cited.

EXHIBIT 4 | HP's Interrelated Structure 2003—Until May 2004

	Blackmore*	Livermore	Joshi*	Zitzner*
	Enterprise Systems	HP Services	Imaging & Printing	Personal Systems
Areas of focus	• Servers • Storage • Software • Solutions	• Customer support • Managed services • Consulting and integration • Domain expertise	• Consumer/ commercial printing • Digital imaging • Digital publishing	• Desktops • Workstations • Notebooks • Handhelds • Digital entertainment
Channel	Enterprise	Public Sector	Consumer	Commercial Direct
Managing on Behalf of HP	*Enterprise	Enterprise SMB	*Consumer SMB	*SMB Consumer

Source: HP.

McKinney explained how the new structure calls for cross-responsibilities; with overlap in responsibilities between groups (Exhibit 4):

> Peter Blackmore, who is responsible for the enterprise hardware business, is also responsible for enterprise customers. Duane Zitzner is responsible for small/medium business customers. And he runs the PC business organization. Vyomesh Joshi ("VJ") runs the imaging and printing business and is responsible for the consumer business. Each of those leaders has two major responsibilities. One is to make sure their product category is managed well and the other is to make sure that a set of customers is served well. For the corporate accounts, for example the top 100 or so accounts, we have teams of people focused on each customer just like we did before. There will be product specialists on those teams, whatever that particular customer needs. That account manager for that corporate account will report into Peter Blackmore's organization. So he'll be held accountable. We call it Managing on Behalf of HP or "MOBO" for short.

This structure applied to all of HP's operations in 178 countries around the world (Exhibit 5). The company divided the globe into four regions: Americas; Europe, Middle East, Africa (EMEA); Asia Pacific; and Japan. Each business group had a separate management structure within each region and each country had a business group manager, one of whom served as the lead country manager. Determining the specific roles and responsibilities of country managers was a project that McKinney and his team had been working on. The group was trying to find the right balance of local autonomy and speed, empowerment versus centralized governance from headquarters, and support for the global strategy.

The New Leadership Framework

Having learned from her first attempt at developing the "New HP" that "we've got to manage change with massive inspection and discipline. Everyone has to feel a connection to the customer and it's a systems business and we can't get away from it," Fiorina wanted to provide a common foundation for exercising personal leadership throughout the new, large and complex post-merger HP organization. To do so she introduced a new "Leadership Framework" that was to be rigorously followed; that is, all employees in all positions had to examine their decisions and actions against four key elements.

EXHIBIT 5 | HP's
Regional Structure

HP Regional Structure

Americas	ESG	HPS	IPG	PSG	
EMEA					
AP					AP and Japan
Japan					

- Capabilities in 178 countries
- Four regions: Americas, Europe, Middle East, Africa (EMEA), Asia Pacific (AP), Japan (IPG and PSG treat AP and Japan as one region)
- Each business group has separate management structure within each region
- Each country has a business group manager, one of whom serves as the lead country manager
- Smaller countries may be grouped into a subregion, which will act as a large country

Source: HP.

The first element of the framework was the new *Strategy*, which included the corporate objectives, operating model (see below), and value propositions. HP's overall value proposition encompassed three elements: high-tech, low cost, and best total customer experience. For its enterprise and public sector customer segments, HP intended to offer the best return on information technology (RoIT), more agility and more accountability. For the small and medium customer segment, HP wanted to offer more reliability, more service and support, and more local expertise—all at a competitive price. For the consumer segment, HP intended to offer simple and rewarding experiences by making technologies work better together. The strategy also required leaders to achieve a world-class cost structure for their part of the operations. Finally, the strategy was to engage in focused innovation: to invest in technology and business practices where HP could make a valued contribution and to work with partners for the rest. With this, Fiorina said: "We have laid out a winning strategy."

The second element of the leadership framework was *Structure and Processes*. Here Fiorina emphasized the importance of effective alignment and governance of the vertical and horizontal dimensions of the operating model. She wanted to streamline the company to facilitate collaboration, efficiency, and the leveraging of HP's new scale and scope. While reporting P&L statements for HP's various (vertical) businesses, she underscored the importance of both the vertical and the horizontal dimensions. The third element was *Metrics, Results, and*

Rewards. An important part of this was the introduction of the balanced scorecard to increase accountability, reward performance, and cultivate operational excellence. The fourth and final element was *Culture*. This involved shared values and standards of conduct (Exhibit 6). According to Fiorina, "We recognize that how we do things is as important as what we do; that character counts."

Fiorina emphasized: "So every time we're dealing with a problem or an opportunity or any one of these organizations is thinking about what they have to do, they're required to go around this frame: What's my strategy, what's my value proposition, how do processes help me, what are my metrics? And what we're trying to do is obviously not only operate more effectively as a system, but train people to think in a systems way. And it's hard, and I think it is the secret sauce."

Exploiting Scale and Scope

HP intended to realize large synergies from its operating model. The company created a new group called Global Operations and tasked it to find and wring synergies from the expanded company. Fiorina assigned the group to Jeff Clarke, executive vice president of Global Operations and formerly the chief financial officer of Compaq. Clarke was responsible for HP's global supply chain, procurement, logistics, e-business, and customer operations. As such, he touched each and every group at HP.

EXHIBIT 6 | HP's
Leadership
Framework

> Strategy
> • Our corporate objectives
> • Our corporate strategy
> • Our value proposition
>
> Values and   Structure and
> behavior   processes
> • Our shared values   • Our operating model
> • Our standards of conduct
>
> Metrics, results
> and rewards
> • Our balanced scorecard

Source: HP.

Clarke pointed out that one important result of the HP-Compaq merger was that the resulting company became an 800-pound. gorilla for suppliers. He said:

> All of a sudden we became 40 percent of the consumption of the industry. So when I go and talk to my contract manufacturers, I say, I'm your anchor store (using the analogy of a shopping mall). I will get subsidized rent—in fact you'll pay me to fill your lines and then the other traffic will come. This may not be sustainable over the long term, but right now the advantage we have with our size and scale is to get the preeminent position, not only on cost, but also on security of supply. When the market heats up again, I will want those extra line starts. And when the market softens, I want the best terms for letting off.[7]

Although Clarke thought HP's supply chain efficiencies offered the company a source of sustainable competitive advantage, he also looked to HP's size to provide real leverage with suppliers. Clarke said, "When we go out to negotiate with large DRAM makers, we're doing it for HP, we're not doing it for supply chain A, supply chain B, region A, region B, product line A, product line B. It's one HP going out there. In terms of logistics, when we fill a truck up it's got printers, handhelds, servers, and PCs as necessary. So that utilization is an advantage against a one-trick pony, a company that is 80 percent PCs in the North American market."

The buyer power that HP acquired from its merger with Compaq extended beyond component and OEM purchasing, said Clarke:

> When it comes off the factory line, we've got the largest scale from the shippers because of our logistics capabilities. One of the things critics ridiculed about our merger was our size in PCs. Contract manufacturers build both PCs and printers. The fact that HP builds 50 million printers a year and between 20 and 30 million PCs a year, depending on how our direct mix goes versus our contract manufacturing mix, versus an IBM that will build somewhere around 15 million PCs a year, gives us a huge advantage.

Mike Winkler, executive vice president and chief marketing officer, who came from Compaq and was previously executive vice president of operations in the early stage of the merged companies, explained further how HP had been able to achieve major cost savings across the four businesses:

> Appointing a horizontal function that had empowerment for the total chain spend of the company, horizontally across all the business groups and with teeth behind it to enforce new standards, processes, suppliers . . . enabled us to get that billion-and-a-half dollars savings. There would be supply chain heads in each of the individual business groups who had dual reporting relationships. So, rather than only answering to their bosses in the business groups, I now write half of their individual performance appraisals. This ensured cross-organization collaboration. The second thing was that we had to get a common set of values and objectives against which we

---

[7]All quotes from Jeff Clarke are from the author's interview on September 18, 2003 unless otherwise cited. Subsequent quotes from this interview will not be cited.

were all measured. We also formed a supply council, which met virtually on a weekly basis . . . working in a noncontentious spirit toward the common goal. Carly also helped. Whenever we ended up with some disagreements . . . Carly would invariably rule on the side of the horizontal function.[8]

In late November 2003, HP announced that Clarke had resigned. The move was unexpected. HP declined to discuss details but said Clarke's resignation was "mutually agreed to and appropriate." Press reports said that Clarke left because he had wanted the CFO position and quoted Clarke as saying, "That was the job I wanted and that position was unavailable."[9]

Strengthening Corporate Marketing

The success with integrating the supply chains across the company led Fiorina to appoint Mike Winkler as chief marketing officer (CMO), which was a new position to HP. According to Winkler:

Marketing was not strong in the HP culture. Technology and engineering were. Some would say that marketing as a discipline was, if not undervalued, disrespected. So we made it an objective to put marketing on a more analytical basis. Every marketing activity now has a quantifiable return and a measurable metric associated with it.

We formed the CMO office and all of the marketing people in the business groups have dual reporting lines into me. We've taken out about 15 percent of the total marketing cost of the company in the last year. We benchmarked ourselves. We were spending about 5.5 percent of revenue on marketing. IBM spends 6 percent and Dell less than 5 percent. We set for ourselves a benchmark of 4.5 percent. Our spending ratio of people to programs was much too high relative to any industry standard in some cases 60 percent on people, 40 percent on programs. The benchmark is 20 percent on people and 80 percent on programs. So, we had to take a lot of marketing people out but we reinvested most of that money in demand creation, advertising, brand development, and other areas of the marketing mix that we believe have greater payback for us.

We engaged in a massive brand campaign, spending about $400 million on an annual basis in November of 2002. We have had the first feedback from the campaign and it's really quite astonishing. The Interbrand survey of *BusinessWeek* said that HP went from 14 to 12 in its ranking of the world's most valuable brands. And in conjunction with promoting the brand, we implemented a program which we called "Operation One Voice." Previously we had a distributed marketing budget and advertising across various business groups and regions. There was an entirely inconsistent look and feel about what HP was about in the messaging. We dropped our advertising agencies from close to 100 down to 2. So we not only saved $120 million on an annual rate, we also got so much more impact and power from the investments that we were making.

Focused Innovation

Following the merger with Compaq, Shane Robison, executive vice president and chief technology officer, who came to HP from Compaq where he had been senior vice president and chief technology officer of strategy and technology, was responsible for shaping HP's overall technology agenda and for leading the company's strategy and corporate development efforts including mergers, acquisitions, divestitures and partnerships. He led HP's technology and strategy councils as well as the development of future technology road maps, working closely with HP's business units and HP Labs.

Robison discussed the role of innovation and information sharing at HP: "We've had some enlightened leadership in the R&D space and we've had a lot of help from Carly in terms of encouraging people to be transparent. We have a process whereby people have realized that this is not a punitive process. This is a process where we're genuinely trying to figure out how to make the right investment choices."[10] Robison described how his office manages technology innovation at HP:

There are some initiatives that span the business groups. For example, mobility. Mobility touches PSG, IPG, ESG, and Services and you need participation and contribution from all of those groups to have a successful mobility solution. So I drive that through the combination of the chief technology officers and the chief marketing officers, from each of the groups. And we have

---

[8]All quotes from Mike Winkler are from the author's interview on September 17, 2003. Subsequent quotes from this interview will not be cited.

[9]Scott Morrison, "Hewlett-Packard Executive Makes a Sudden Departure," *Financial Times*, November 26, 2003, p. 17.

---

[10]All quotes from Shane Robison are from the author's interview on September 18, 2003. Subsequent quotes from this interview will not be cited.

strategic plans around that—I bring it into Carly's staff meetings for reviews and that helps a lot because you get people's attention. We've got four of those initiatives: management software, mobility, rich media, and security. They touch multiple groups and we've got teams behind them and road maps [business plans] behind them and commitments that we expect from all the businesses. Given that different pieces roll up in different groups and numbers, now we face the challenge how do you measure whether you're making progress?

Keeping in mind that most of the R&D work that goes on at HP takes place not at a central group, that is, HP Labs, but within the individual businesses, it seemed that managing the process could be particularly challenging. Robison said:

> We have 25,000 people in the company who do technology R&D. Performance measures vary radically from group to group. But overall, for the development teams it's easy, you either meet your commitments and hit your deadlines, or you don't. For the research side, it is pretty much the same. Perhaps a little more subjective, and I think a little harder, but the group is smaller and so you've got a much more intimate view of what's going on and so you can tell—based on many years of experience—whether you're making progress. But the milestones are different and the metrics are different.

Robison's office was a source of protection for new ideas that did not yet fit within a specific business in the company. He said:

> We have an incubation process for things that are really outside of our four business groups that are potentially large businesses. We keep it here in my group because the machinery is so heavy in the big business groups that unless it is a concept that is fairly well aligned with their normal thinking, it takes too long to develop. We've got one project, which is fairly mature right now, that we call Procurve. It is a networking business. It generates several hundred million dollars a year and double-digit growth. It is very profitable and we manage it carefully, like a jewel. It's small, but by any other standard it's a pretty good business.
>
> I get ideas from all over the company. People send e-mails with stuff and I've got business development teams to look at them and analyze the potential and run the numbers. If it looks like there is real potential, we'll do something with it. So that's the one-offs.

One of HP's most famous assets is its highly respected HP Laboratories (HP Labs), the company's central R&D group, directed by Richard H. Lampman, senior vice president of research. Lampman, a 32-year veteran of HP, reported to Shane Robison and was responsible for the research activities in seven research labs around the world, with the dual objectives of providing leading-edge technologies to HP's current businesses and creating new technology-enabled opportunities for HP.

HP Labs created technology for the various businesses within the company. Lampman described it as "a network model instead of the old model of vertical integration. It puts us in the position of selling both technology and strategies that are enabled by technology."

Lampman described how HP's strategy of using HP-owned technology while leveraging the technologies of their partners would affect HP Labs. He said:

> If you look at the PC business or the lower end server products in the company, we fully exploit all of the assets available in the industry to participate in those segments, but in our services business and vertical industry segments, such as Imaging and Printing, and in our high-end computer systems offerings, there's a lot of HP-unique technology there.
>
> From an R&D standpoint, what that means is that we are going to fully leverage and exploit what we can through various partnerships in the industry and we're going to pick where we can bring those unique values. That's the heart of our R&D strategy.
>
> We leverage investments that come out of the copier industry in our laser business and in ink-based printing we have a vertically integrated technology stack. We feel we gain a lot out of both of those strategies, but that means that you have to have flexibility to pick what's the best answer.[11]

With HP's new strategy, the largest program in HP Labs was Utility Computing (the Adaptive Enterprise—see below). This involved research on computer systems and architecture problems; rethinking which resources were most critical. Lampman said the typical data center was a very complex mix of hardware, software, and expensive professionals. To try to find solutions around these costs, Lampman issued a challenge to his researchers:

[11]All quotes from Richard H. Lampman are from the author's interview on September 11, 2003, unless otherwise indicated. Subsequent quotes from this interview will not be cited.

EXHIBIT 7 | Six Planks of HP Lab's Strategy as of September 2003

- The first one concerned "Computer Systems": Where does innovation go as we move toward industry standard building blocks? This area involves Utility Computing (Adaptive Enterprise); grid computing extended to enterprises.
- The second plank was focused on "Printing and Imaging": How can you expand this franchise into new areas? In the early 1990s, we had big efforts into digital photography, and more recently into digital publishing.
- The third plank involved "Industry-Based Vertical Industries": Our view is they will be more important. We will pick a few areas to build intellectual property with partners. The largest is mobility. We are also looking at the life sciences, and telecom. These latter vertical industries will require thousands of machines running in concert.
- The fourth plank concerned "Technologies for Services": Developing technologies to make services delivery more cost-effective.
- The fifth focused on "Consumer Systems": This used to be about PCs with peripherals. It now includes the Web and Web services. For example, downloading software to make a new device, automatic toner cartridge ordering, etc. Another example was using a Nokia phone to print something, thus making an interoperable consumer world. HP Labs aimed to contribute pieces to open-source platforms to drive adoption.
- The sixth plank involved "Emerging and Disruptive" technologies, such as nanotechnology, high-performance computer system breakthroughs, extending Moore's Law (it will run out soon because the barrier is running into limitations imposed by physics). How about a computer attached to a molecule, put in a drug?

Source: As described by Dick Lampman, Senior Vice President of Research, Director of Hewlett-Packard Laboratories in author's interview.

"What would it take to build and operate a 50,000-computer data center? What would that look like? At the time, the biggest centers had about 5,000 computers and were very complex, with PhDs running the systems, which were complex and not robust."

Lampman described the challenges of the past as about "managing computers," and those of today as about "managing large collections of computers with fewer people." In the near future, he thought that the most pressing challenges would stem from "organic computer management, to provide features such as efficient disaster recovery." In the more distant future, Lampman thought challenges would come from "market-based models for information," because as systems get more complex, the algorithms that control them will reach their limits, and there will be a need for a self-organizing capability.

Lampman also described what he called the "six planks" of HP Labs' strategy going forward (Exhibit 7). Lampman summarized his challenge in directing research at HP Labs: "We want to be intentional, but not so intentional that we choke out creativity."

Asked to compare the focused innovation approach to the approach of the old HP, which had, after all, produced company-transforming innovations such as printers, Carly Fiorina said:

> The short answer is it will be different. And yes, HP wasn't a printing company and then it became a printing company—but fundamentally what happened was HP existed within an incredibly stable operating model, which was: Engineers go off and invent standalone

products and when something gets successful enough to be a relatively large business, you create a division. Then what happened? Well, all of a sudden a networked world. The 1990s was not coincidentally the time when HP started to slow down. At that same time, the world was becoming networked and connected and everything now suddenly had the possibility of being digitized.

The new things that are most interesting are not point products, although we do a lot of those and that's good stuff. But the new things that are most interesting are things like security across—I mean real fabric innovations, real security across this incredibly complex system of interconnected devices and applications and processes and systems; or rich media; or mobility; or management of incredibly heterogeneous, complex environments. Example: Our software road map. We're not trying to do database software, application software, middleware. But what we're trying to do, where we're innovating . . . is to go from element management to environment management to application management to business process management, heterogeneous business process management with service level agreement. That's a huge innovation. But it's a system-level, fabric-level innovation, not a point product in the same traditional way.

Customer Perspectives on Postmerger HP Innovation

Some external observers, however, remained somewhat skeptical about HP's new approach to innovation. The chief information officer (CIO) of one leading telecommunications company with well over $50 billion in annual revenue and a large customer of HP, said:

> HP has done a good job integrating Compaq rapidly. They have taken costs out. Tactically, they have done a fine job, making it work so far. The question is, where are they headed strategically, beyond the merger integration? They have tried to change HP, make it more market driven, but HP has a legacy of breakthrough innovation, and that part has been significantly de-emphasized. Some great technical people have left the company. HP is becoming more like IBM Global Services. Selling ink and services is fine, but they have de-emphasized innovation (in spite of using words like "Invent").
>
> Long-term the issue is whether they can continue to keep their traditional breakthrough innovative thinking. The issue is real, because in the computing space they don't have architectural control of programming languages, not in operating systems, hardware, application servers, or storage. So it's hard for me as a CIO to feel that they can credibly do things that are "game changing." When a tech guru gets up, people move toward that. I am not sure HP has them do [really innovative things] anymore; or surfaces them. They have de-emphasized capturing the mind share of the CIO.
>
> HP has good people. They try hard. They fight hard for accounts. On the business side, they have squeezed IT costs down; they know how to do that. But as CIO, they only get my attention if they screw up. I not only expect great (economic) value, but also want to be able to view them as a strategic partner in helping me drive innovation within my company. Long-term it will be tough not to have extreme creativity, especially if you don't have control points.[12]

Other analysts and CIOs credited HP with making strides in innovation and agility.[13]

> Entertainment company DreamWorks, the movie and television production company responsible for cutting-edge computer animated hit films such as *Shrek* was a strategic partner of HP. Prior to the merger, DreamWorks

purchased many of its computer products from HP, ranging from desktops to high-end servers. However, as computer animation increased in importance to the studio and became a faster changing industry, DreamWorks set out looking for a technology partner instead of just a technology supplier. DreamWorks' Chief Technology Officer (CTO) Ed Leonard said, "Computer-generated animation is a young and dynamic industry. A lot of technology gets developed in the course of each film that DreamWorks makes. So, we are as much an innovation and technology company as we are a film company."[14] The speed of change in computer animation was increasing in part because the industry was moving away from proprietary technologies and toward open standards. Leonard explained, "Our industry has shifted from high-end, proprietary software and hardware to open standards applications run on Intel-based Linux x86 architecture. Five years ago, almost everybody in this business used Silicon Graphics workstations to produce computer-generated animation. Today nobody does that anymore. It's mostly done on Intel/AMD-based Linux systems."

According to Leonard, these were areas in which HP excelled. He said, "HP's strategy focus aligns with what we care about. They are leaders in using Linux for high-end applications and in graphics applications. They have a deep pool of 3D graphics expertise. They really care about making Linux work for graphics. This is important to us."

Since DreamWorks did not buy as large a volume of equipment from HP as many of HP's other customers, there was some concern on the part of the studio that it could get lost in the shuffle as HP underwent its merger integration with Compaq. Leonard said his fears were quickly put to rest:

> We soon realized that HP had a clear plan for our relationship with them at the outset of its merger with Compaq. This made us much more comfortable. There were some hiccups, or speed bumps, along the way. For example, some product lines we used and were comfortable with got axed in HP's consolidation. But HP was smart about its choices. While we were too small of an account to have any direct influence in deciding which product lines HP kept and which it discarded, we were quickly made happy with the product lines that were new to us.

---

[12]Source: author's interview of the CIO of a leading telecommunications company on March 15, 2004.

[13]See various analysts' reports, such as Gartner research notes by B. Igou et al., "Magic Quadrant: Server Vendor High-Availability Services, 2003," 29 October 2003 and Kristen Noakes-Fry and Trude Diamond "HP Business Continuity and Availability Services," 20 January 2004 for discussions of HP innovation and agility in serving the corporate market.

[14]All quotes from Ed Leonard are from the author's interview on 1 July 2004. Subsequent quotes from this interview will not be cited.

While DreamWorks may not be one of HP's biggest customers from the standpoint of sales, the studio was definitely on the cutting edge of technology applications. As such, the two companies worked together even at the level of R&D. Leonard said:

> Something that is particularly important to us in our strategic relationship with HP is our direct interface with HP Labs and other R&D areas in the company. Key engineers from DreamWorks and HP get together a couple of times a year to exchange ideas and challenges. We tell them what we are working on and they give us their points of view about technology advances and changes. Sometimes a gem falls out of this interaction and we find that HP has a solution to a problem DreamWorks is facing. One example of this is utility rendering services (URS): The idea that computing is a utility and a resource that can change with demand. We used this in making the film *Shrek 2*. We experienced a technology capacity problem making that film, so we ended up using URS to do a significant amount of rendering [computer-generated animation] offsite. This was the first time we had done anything like that. We formed a new business model with this.

> We have become a working lab and test bed for HP. It is very symbiotic. HP gets innovation out of the lab faster, and DreamWorks gets the technology first.

In working with HP since before its merger with Compaq, Leonard noticed changes in the company. He said, "I have noticed a clear shift in the feel and texture of who HP is as a company. I cannot point to the Compaq merger and say that is the reason, but where HP always had rock-solid engineering, as a company, it did move slower. It was slower to get ideas out of the lab. Now, HP still has terrific engineering, but the company is more fleet. HP has the spirit of urgency."

Continuing the Pursuit of Strategic Integration in 2004

Further Refining the Operating Model

After having stabilized the core businesses, Fiorina and the Executive Council (a group of HP senior executives that works with HP's chairman and CEO to set strategy for the company) felt that the organization needed some further fine-tuning to better pursue the corporate strategy, particularly in the areas of customer focus, simplification, and profitable growth. Having learned from the acquisition integration that effectively managing change

requires rigorous planning and a holistic approach encompassing all the moving parts, Fiorina wanted to further apply these new "best practices," such as program management, appropriate metrics, and focused teamwork. With Webb McKinney having recently retired, Arun Chandra, in charge of strategy and operations for the CMO, was asked to take on the job while simultaneously continuing to fulfill his senior marketing executive duties. Chandra saw the job as a short-term assignment. He saw his task as a logical further extension of executing the corporate portfolio strategy.

After several weeks of talking to all the members of Fiorina's staff about the major work streams that needed to be improved in order to implement the corporate portfolio strategy of "pulling all of HP's offerings in front of the customer,"[15] Chandra formed seven major teams to do all the work. Different teams focused on the end-to-end value chain, the end-to-end financial processes, the design of a Customer Solutions Group, the design of a Technology Solutions Group, the combination of the commercial and enterprise channels into one, customer segment–driven marketing, and growth initiatives. Team members were senior people drawn from the staffs of the Executive Council members. Having learned from the acquisition integration, Chandra made sure to involve people from the different regions from day one in order to facilitate implementation.

Technology Solutions Group In December 2003, HP announced changes to its organization structure, starting in May 2004, that would recombine and reduce its four principal lines of business, with distinct profit and loss (P&L) statements, to three (Exhibit 8). The Enterprise Services Group (ESG), which had been led by Peter Blackmore would be folded into a new entity called Technology Solutions Group (TSG) which would be run by Ann Livermore. This new group would encompass systems (servers and storage), software and services. HP said it would report the P&L statements for systems, software, and services separately, to increase transparency.

Customer Solutions Group HP also created the Customer Solutions Group (CSG), under the direction of Peter Blackmore. This group would sell the entire portfolio of HP products and services to enterprise,

---

[15]All quotes from Arun Chandra are from the author's interview on February 4, 2004. Subsequent quotes from this interview will not be cited.

EXHIBIT 8 | HP Organization Chart (October 2003)

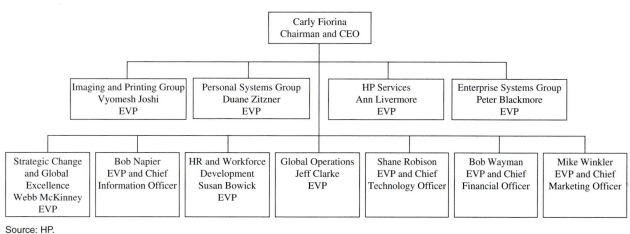

Source: HP.

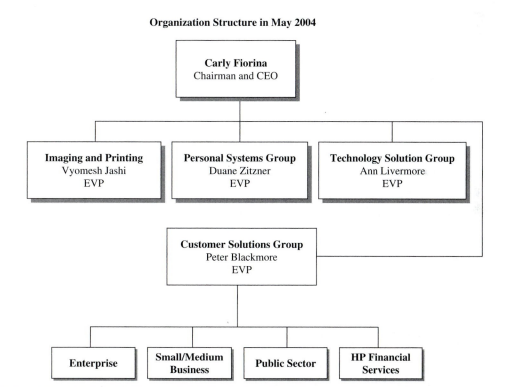

Source: Authors' reconstruction.

public sector, and small/medium business customers. Chandra explained: "If you go back to the operating model, we had horizontal things at the bottom, we talked about operational excellence, IT, global operations. What in effect we've done now is create a horizontal component on the top. So CSG is focused on sharpening our customer focus, bringing in the entire portfolio and finding opportunities for growth that we would otherwise overlook." The small and medium business segment of this group, which in the old model reported to Duane Zitzner, now reported to Peter Blackmore. For enterprise companies CSG would focus on finance, manufacturing, telecommunications and retail. New segments were added to Public Sector including Education and Healthcare, in addition to Law Enforcement, Defense and Security. HP Financial Services (the leasing company) also reported to Blackmore. However, the CSG group would not constitute a separate P&L.

Combining the Commercial and Enterprise Channels
The company combined its multiple channels organizations into a single channel team under the dual control of Zitzner, who led HP's indirect sales channels, and Blackmore, who led the direct sales channels. IPG continued to drive the retail channel on behalf of the entire company and in addition will pick up responsibility for the direct customer contact for the customer segment.

Customer Segment–Driven Marketing   Arun Chandra said that "The direction is to look at marketing by customer segment as opposed to marketing by product. Companies like Sony have done that very effectively. A Sony advertisement will show at least two products, if not three. And they will have a theme tied to it as opposed to saying "here's my camera." We must tell a story of the "home" as opposed to a story about "products."

Growth Initiatives   Blackmore's CSG was also accountable for developing new business for all of HP, with a particular emphasis on increasing HP's share of enterprise and government IT spending. With Blackmore running the global sales force, there was an expectation of focusing on growth opportunities in the various geographies, such as new markets like Russia and other parts of Eastern Europe and continued emphasis on India and China.

In addition to the above, HP combined the Operations and IT teams under executive vice president Gilles Bouchard. The company wanted to simplify the organization in order to increase speed and accountability and provide clearer responsibility for the customer contact. As a result of these changes:

- CSG would drive the direct customer contact for Enterprise, SMB and Public Sector customers.

- PSG would drive the indirect/channel contact for business customers.

- IPG would drive all the customer contact for consumers.

Chandra was quite aware of the tensions that naturally existed in a portfolio of businesses that had traditionally pursued strategies based on different market disciplines: product leadership versus operational excellence versus customer intimacy.[16] He felt that the operating model would allow HP to actually drive against each of these disciplines:

> The bottom part of the operating model has always been about very large operations and finding a balance between what needs to be done once and centrally versus what needs to be done individually in the businesses, and thereby achieve operational excellence whilst maintaining product innovation, for instance. The formation of the CSG and the focus on segment-based marketing is an effort to get higher customer experience and to achieve greater customer intimacy. So that's the belief set. And as always with things like this, and that's why we write cases, time will tell. But I am very clear in my mind and the organization is very clear in its mind about what we're trying to do—increase our customer focus, simplify our organization and processes, and drive profitable growth.

Small/Medium Business: Serving the "Fortune 500,000" and Beyond

The effects of the merger were seen in HP's efforts to market to small and medium-sized businesses (SMB). These were companies that HP liked to refer to as the "Fortune 500,000"; firms that ranged from, say, a handful of lawyers or architects sharing an office to fairly sizeable organizations. It was a diverse (and diffuse) market, but also very large. HP estimated that SMBs worldwide represented a $440–$550 billion market for IT and IT-related goods and services. Of this, HP thought about $200–250 billion worldwide was addressable by the company. This was a group of customers that HP had long served. HP estimated it sold $20–$21 billion each year to the SMB market. HP was spending $750 million to reach this segment.

Discussing HP's success in the SMB market heretofore, John Brennan, senior vice president, Small and Medium Business Segment—the executive in charge of SMB segment operations—said, "We got here because we have good products and the right channel strategies."[17]

---

[16]For more on this subject, see Michael Treacy and Fred Wiersema, *The Discipline of Market Leaders,* Persus Books, 1995.

[17]All quotes from John D. Brennan are from the author's interview on March 31, 2004. Subsequent quotes from this interview will not be cited.

However, in the wake of the merger with Compaq, Brennan's goal was to fundamentally change the way in which HP reached and served the SMB market. Brennan said: "We came out of the merger with a great portfolio of products and services. But that portfolio was not consciously targeted and brought to the SMB market. We want to go from being a leader in fact, to owning the consciousness of the market. We want to sustain, broaden, and strengthen our position in SMB. It's value proposition, channel strategy, sales strategy, marketing, and product positioning."

Brennan said that the economics of servicing the SMB market were unique from those that governed the Enterprise or Public Sector, which along with SMB, were the three markets that were served by distinct sales and marketing processes. Brennan said:

> To serve SMB, we have had to build a different marketing capability, distinct from say, Enterprise, where you can 'name'—identify and preselect—accounts, where it's one-to-one selling.
>
> With SMB, it's high-volume, closed loop marketing. High-volume because there are 28 million SMB customers in the US alone; closed loop because we want our marketing efforts to yield measurable results.

This requires a different posture and set of capabilities; more quantifiable than we had in the past. Now, marketing teams know they have to open presentations with marketing financials and performance statistics. We test, measure, and improve. We look for reproducible results.

Reaching the SMB in a substantial way is a challenge. You have to wrestle with the cost to reach and the potentially poor per-customer economics [of such a diverse market]. How do you reach and serve these segments effectively? It is a battle of return on sales and marketing dollars; return per customer over the cost to acquire and maintain. I make sure sales and marketing dollars deliver adequate growth in revenue and gross margins. With this structure, I have a perspective about what trade-offs we can make, for example, pricing.

Because of the way that HP had structured the sales and marketing organizations, Brennan felt he was in a position to see the totality of the SMB market for HP as a whole, and to make decisions that reflected the best interests of the company with respect to the SMB market, instead of just representing a single product line. Brennan controlled the entire sales and marketing effort for SMB. He reported to Peter Blackmore and sat on Mike Winkler's staff (Exhibit 9). Brennan said, "You

EXHIBIT 9 |

Examples of Individual Subprofit and Loss (P&L) Silos

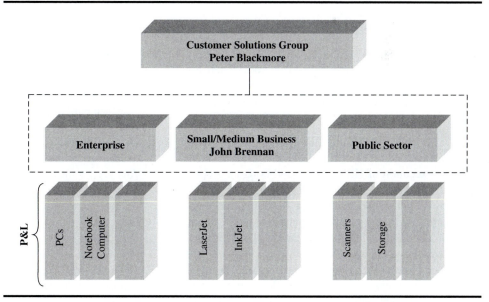

Note: Responsibilities for sub P&L silos, such as PC's Notebook Computers, etc. for the Enterprise group, stay within each group. Sub P&Ls are distinct from overall P&Ls, such as those associated with the three P&L groups that HP will report in May 2004 , IPG, PSG and Technology Solutions Group (TSG).

Source: Author's reconstruction.

risk homogenizing P&Ls if you move them to a front-end organization. In a multiportfolio company it's important to acknowledge the business and P&L dynamics of very distinct categories."

The scope of SMB was so large that Brennan worried about all competitors. The easiest for him to identify were Dell and IBM in the United States, and Legend Computer in China.

The width of the viewpoint that HP's integrated structure gave Brennan helped him think of the SMB market as a whole and create products and services that meet the unique needs of the SMB market. Brennan said, "I have banished the word 'bundle.' It is attractive to some customers, but not to most of the SMB market. Instead, we use 'soft bundling' such as if you buy something you can get a discount or benefit if you buy something else later. Its temporal bundling, you unlock it over time." Brennan explained:

> I want SMB to be relevant to customers in terms of products and/or solutions. We do this through demand generation, where HP runs ads featuring several of our product lines and categories, instead of just one, and soft bundling [described above]. We have not had a mechanism for doing this before. There had been only ad hoc efforts in the past.
>
> We want our SMB efforts to embrace and support all our routes to market. Specifically, it's important to understand that our large network of VARs is an asset in serving this market.

There was no single tack that HP would take in reaching and serving the SMB market. Brennan said, "I tell my people, stop wishing for a pure channel strategy, it doesn't exist and it won't."

The Role of the CEO: Deciding Which Syllable to Emphasize

Effective execution of HP's vertical-and-horizontal operating model and the systems perspective that drove it required uniquely sophisticated and demanding personal leadership skills on the part of its senior executives. At any given time, these leaders had to carefully balance the imperatives of their business-level strategies—in part determined by what their direct competitors were doing—against the imperatives of the corporate-level strategy and the associated responsibilities of managing on behalf of HP—the so-called MOBO directive. While, in principle, the underlying system perspective should inspire and

facilitate higher-level integration of the vertical and horizontal strategies rather than compromising or neglecting one or the other, in the real world of immediate pressures, limited resources and energies, and bounded rationality, difficult trade-offs would likely impose themselves. In addition, these senior executives also had to be able to drive their intended "balanced" strategies down through several levels of management in a timely fashion—a nontrivial challenge given the size and complexity of the organization.

Ultimately, the CEO had to provide strategic direction to help senior executives make the right tradeoffs. Fiorina seemed clearly aware of this role. She said:

> For example, in the trade-offs we now have to make, timing is everything. I was just in Houston talking to all our employees and I said sometimes it's all about what "syllable" you put the emphasis on. The first year after the acquisition, the emphasis was on the vertical syllable because we had to get product lines integrated, organizations integrated, cost structures put in place. And so if you ask people where's the biggest leverage, it was in the vertical one.
>
> Today (September 2003), the bigger leverage is the horizontal syllable. And so, you see us now shifting our external value proposition and how we go to market and how we talk internally from this to consumer solutions, SMB solutions, enterprise solutions. All last year we talked about imaging and printing and PCs. But since May we have launched our "Adaptive Enterprise" value proposition; we have launched our consumer value proposition with 158 digital imaging and digital entertainment products; and we just launched our "Smart Office" initiative for the small and medium business. And those value propositions and solutions and strategies are less about the vertical businesses and more about the horizontal segments. And people are working much more now to deliver those. And next year as well, as we drive the supply chain to get the next billion dollars out and we deliver the next generation of customer knowledge management in our IT organization. So now the measures have to shift as well. We just took a decision a week and a half ago that we are changing the emphasis in people's metrics around what they get paid on for our fiscal 2004, which begins in November, so that more of a weight is on the horizontal syllable and less on the vertical one.

Addressing the issue of how quickly top management can drive a changing strategic emphasis and associated changes in performance measurement deep into the large, complex HP organization, Fiorina said:

> I think as organizations develop muscles for change they can do it faster and faster, but not overnight. So, can we do it faster today than we could do it four years ago? Absolutely. People don't freak out now. It's not a big emotional "Oh what are you talking about, we're doing different metrics." . . . Organizations become more adaptable. Sustainable success requires adaptability. That is a skill. Just like collaboration is a skill. So we're trying to learn and institutionalize the skill of adaptation. But you cannot swing pendulums wildly in organizations because change has a huge tail in an organization, it's complex. And what we decide as a senior team realistically isn't fully understood, much less executed way out in South Africa say, for at least three months and probably more like six. So, that's why rigorous inspection is necessary, so you know how long is the tail: Is it getting executed? Is our execution or adaptability accelerating or is it decelerating? And it's not a steady pace. Sometimes it speeds up and then it slows down.
>
> So there is a difference between adaptability and swinging the pendulum wildly. I think people have to see a roadmap that makes sense to them and that's why frameworks are important. So, this [Leadership] Framework has been important to us, because now when we say to people we're going to shift the emphasis from vertical to horizontal, and now you're going to see more of your metrics getting focused on consumer, enterprise, and small-and-medium business, they understand the journey we've been on. It's not all of a sudden some brand-new idea. You have to kind of prepare the organization in advance. So, for example, I started talking a lot to senior leaders about changing the emphasis and put programs in place to support it in June. We won't change metrics until November. So now people have six months—first we started talking about it, then we started laying out

value propositions, then we introduced products into the market, then we changed the metrics. So people kind of know where you're going.

Conclusion

By early 2004, HP had managed to defy its critics who predicted the wheels would fall off the company before it left the starting line. Less than two years after the merger closed, HP proudly reported huge cost reductions and managed to hang on to or even increase market share in its most important businesses. This was remarkable, considering the scope and scale of its organizational integration challenges.

Now, however, the strategic integration, captured in the new vertical-and-horizontal operating model, had to be forcefully and effectively executed. HP had to deliver more if it were to become the "leading technology company in the world." HP really would have to be "Better Together" if it was going to beat its very powerful rivals, Dell and IBM, to name two. It would also have to negotiate the forces that would shape the markets in the future. For Fiorina, the strategic challenges ahead seemed clear:

> I think the strategic direction is set, the change management agenda is set, and the frameworks we have in place can sustain us for quite some time. So now we have to leverage what we've put together and really execute against what is a complex systems model and deliver higher and higher-order innovation and value.
>
> We have set a large ambition. We want to be the leading technology company in the world and be recognized as such. I think we can be. And when I say the leading technology company in the world, it's more than just being number one or two in the verticals. To be recognized as the leading technology company in the world, we have to now move up to that systems-level management and innovation. So, that's what you should look for in the future.

Case 4.5

The New, New HP in 2004 (B): Winning in the Core Businesses

In order to get the value out of our portfolio, in order to really deliver this value proposition, we have to acknowledge and internalize and organize around the fact that we are a systems business. We can't walk away from that. Any organization structure that breaks up a system into piece parts ultimately isn't going to work.[1]

—Carleton "Carly" S. Fiorina, Chairman and CEO, Hewlett-Packard Company

Introduction

Hewlett-Packard's $19 billion acquisition of Compaq Computer in May 2002 was a key element in CEO Carleton "Carly" Fiorina's mission to make HP "the leading technology company in the world." The organizational integration went more smoothly than anybody outside of the HP and Compaq executive suites had predicted.[2] Integration targets were met and ambitious cost-saving estimates were exceeded. The ability of the combined HP and Compaq to be "Better Together," in the words of an HP slogan after the merger—the strategic integration of the two companies capitalizing on the entire corporate business portfolio—would be the real test of the merger.[3]

At the same time, however, the "new, new HP" would have to be able to continue to compete effectively in its different core businesses against entrenched and highly aggressive competitors. Premerger HP competed against Compaq, Dell, IBM, Sun, EDS, Canon, Lexmark, Epson, and others. Postmerger the new new HP, girded with selected assets from Compaq but run by many of the same premerger HP senior executives (e.g.,

Fiorina and the three executive vice presidents who ran HP's three lines of business), faced mostly the same groups of competitors. During 2003, HP had been able to sustain or improve its strategic position in its core businesses. (Exhibit 1 shows HP's financial results for the past five years.) But as before, each of HP's core businesses would have to compete against very strong competitors, and these companies had not stood still while HP digested Compaq. The question was whether it was possible to maintain winning competitive business strategies on so many different fronts and whether the corporate emphasis on strategic integration—the "horizontal syllable" as Fiorina liked to put it—would ultimately interfere with the varying strategic logics of the different vertical business groups.

The Competitive Environment in Early 2004

In early 2004, HP faced a rapidly changing competitive environment. The information technology industry was still recuperating from a prolonged downturn and might have changed for good, with customers expecting more for less from their vendors. Also, digitization had triggered convergence—or collision, depending on one's vantage point—between the computing, consumer electronics, telecommunications, imaging, and entertainment industries. And future convergences driven by digitization, with the life sciences for instance, were looming on the horizon. Given the scope of HP's business portfolio, the company needed to compete against

---

Professor Robert A. Burgelman and Philip E. Meza prepared this case as the basis for class discussion rather than to illustrate either effective or ineffective handling of an administrative situation. This case can be used in conjunction with "HP and Compaq Combined: In Search of Scale and Scope," SM-130, "The New New HP in 2004 (A): Leading Strategic Integration," SM-125A, "The New HP Way," SM-72 and "HP, Compaq and the New PC Landscape," SM-72B, each by Burgelman and Meza.

---

[1]All quotes from Carleton S. "Carly" Fiorina are from the author's interview on September 26, 2004 unless otherwise cited. Subsequent quotes from this interview will not be cited.

[2]For more detail on the organizational integration challenges associated with the HP and Compaq merger, see Robert A. Burgelman and Philip E. Meza, "HP and Compaq Combined: In Search of Scale and Scope," SM 130, Stanford Graduate School of Business.

[3]For more detail on the strategic integration challenges, see Robert A. Burgelman and Philip E. Meza, "The New New HP in 2004 (A): Leading Strategic Integration," SM-125A, Stanford Graduate School of Business.

EXHIBIT 1 | HP Selected Financial Data 1999–2003

$ millions	October 31, 2003	October 31, 2002	October 31, 2001	October 31, 2000	October 31, 1999
Revenue					
Equipment revenue	58,939.0	45,969.0	37,498.0	41,653.0	36,113.0
Service revenue	13,657.0	10,165.0	7,325.0	6,848.0	5,960.0
Financing income	465.0	454.0	403.0	369.0	298.0
Total revenue	73,061.0	56,588.0	45,226.0	48,870.0	42,371.0
Cost of equipment	43,689.0	34,189.0	28,863.0	30,343.0	25,436.0
Cost of services	9,959.0	7,414.0	4,396.0	4,470.0	4,284.0
Financing interest	209.0	189.0	236.0	233.0	168.0
Research/development	3,652.0	3,369.0	2,724.0	2,627.0	2,440.0
Selling/general/ administrative.	11,012.0	8,763.0	6,950.0	6,984.0	6,225.0
Restructuring charge	800.0	1,780.0	384.0	102.0	0.0
In-process R&D	1.0	793.0	35.0	0.0	NA
Acquisition-relelated charges	280.0	701.0	25.0	0.0	NA
Amortization of goodwill/ intangibles	0.0	107.0	174.0	86.0	NA
Amorization of intangibles	563.0	295.0	NA	NA	NA
Litigation settlement	0.0	(14.0)	400.0	0.0	0.0
Total operating expense	70,165.0	57,586.0	44,187.0	44,845.0	38,553.0
Interest/other, net	21.0	52.0	171.0	356.0	345.0
Losses on divest.	0.0	0.0	(53.0)	203.0	0.0
Investment losses	(29.0)	(75.0)	(455.0)	41.0	31.0
Net income before taxes	2,888.0	(1,021.0)	702.0	4,625.0	4,194.0
Provision for income taxes	349.0	(118.0)	78.0	1,064.0	1,090.0
Net income after taxes	2,539.0	(903.0)	624.0	3,561.0	3,104.0
Net income before extraordinary items	2,539.0	(903.0)	624.0	3,561.0	3,104.0
Discontinued operations	NA	NA	0.0	136.0	387.0
Extraordinary item	NA	NA	56.0	0.0	0.0
Accounting change	0.0	0.0	(272.0)	0.0	0.0
Net income	2,539.0	(903.0)	408.0	3,697.0	3,491.0

Source: Company reports.

NB: Consolidated statement includes results of Agilent Technology prior to its spin-off on June 2, 2002. Consolidated statement includes results from Compaq as of May 3, 2002, its date of acquisition.

Revenue by Business Segment and Region for Fiscal Year 2003

Business Segment		Region	
Imaging and Printing Group	$22.6 billion	United States	$29.2 billion
Personal Systems Group	$21.2 billion	Europe, Middle East, Africa	$28.5 billion
Enterprise Systems Group	$15.4 billion	Asia Pacific (exc. Japan)	$8.0 billion
HP Services	$12.3 billion	Americas (exc. U.S.)	$4.3 billion
HP Financial Services	$1.9 billion	Japan	$3.1 billion
Corporate Investments	$0.3 billion		

Source: Company reports.

NB: Segment and region totals to not equal due to rounding.

(continued)

EXHIBIT 1 | Selected Combined HP/Compaq Financial Data by Group 2001–2002 (Cont.)

Imaging and Printing Group—Combined Company Results

For the following years ended October 31 Dollars in millions	Combined Company Results	
	2002	2001
Net revenue	$20,326	$19,470
Earnings from operations	$3,248	$1,876
Earnings from operations as a percentage of net revenue	16.0%	9.6%

Personal Systems Group—Combined Company Results

For the following years ended October 31 Dollars in millions	Combined Company Results	
	2002	2001
Net revenue	$21,962	$26,800
Loss from operations	$(532)	$(977)
Loss from operations as a percentage of net revenue	(2.4)%	(3.6)%

Enterprise Systems Group—Combined Company Results

For the following years ended October 31 Dollars in millions	Combined Company Results	
	2002	2001
Net revenue	$16,449	$20,486
(Loss) earnings from operations	$(912)	$279
(Loss) earnings from operations as a percentage of net revenue	(5.5)%	1.4%

HP Services—Combined Company Results

For the following years ended October 31 Dollars in millions	Combined Company Results	
	2002	2001
Net revenue	$12,411	$12,846
Earnings from operations	$1,443	$1,586
Earnings from operations as a percentage of net revenue	11.6%	12.3%

HP Financial Services—Combined Company Results

For the following years ended October 31 Dollars in millions	Combined Company Results	
	2002	2001
Net revenue	$2,088	$2,126
(Loss) from operations	$(133)	$(164)
(Loss) from operations as a percentage of net revenue	(6.4)%	(7.7)%

Source: Company reports.

strong competitors in many of these industries as well as be quick to spot and exploit opportunities created by their convergence.

The Computer Industry

IBM   When it came to scope and scale, HP had a natural competitor: IBM. Fiorina thought that IBM was a terrific competitor to have, at least so far as it helped galvanize HP's employees to understand and meet the task (Exhibit 2). Fiorina said:

IBM and HP are the only alternatives for the scope and scale problems. But we approach it very differently, with very different portfolios. IBM has a more vertically integrated strategy than they did in the 1980s. It is a totally vertically integrated approach. It is a very successful model, but one that is under strain, in my judgment, because they are trying to compete against so many players in that stack. It is a less flexible and less cost-effective model both for them and their customers. We have growth opportunities they don't have in the

EXHIBIT 2 | Selected Financial Information for IBM Fiscal Years Ended 1999–2003

	31-Dec-03	31-Dec-02	31-Dec-01	31-Dec-00	31-Dec-99
Reported in $ millions					
Global services	42,635.0	36,360.0	34,956.0	33,152.0	32,172.0
Hardware sales	28,239.0	27,456.0	30,593.0	37,777.0	37,888.0
Software	14,311.0	13,074.0	12,939.0	12,598.0	12,662.0
Global financing	2,826.0	3,232.0	3,426.0	3,465.0	3,137.0
Enterprise inv.	1,120.0	1,064.0	1,153.0	1,404.0	1,689.0
Total revenue	89,131.0	81,186.0	83,067.0	88,396.0	87,548.0
Cost of revenue	56,113.0	NA	NA	NA	NA
Global services	NA	26,812.0	25,355.0	24,309.0	23,304.0
Hardware	NA	20,020.0	21,231.0	27,038.0	27,591.0
Software	NA	2,043.0	2,265.0	2,283.0	2,240.0
Global financing	NA	1,416.0	1,693.0	1,965.0	1,821.0
Enterprise inv.	NA	611.0	634.0	747.0	1,038.0
Sell./Gen./Admin.	17,852.0	16,891.0	17,048.0	17,535.0	16,294.0
Research & development.	5,077.0	4,750.0	4,986.0	5,374.0	5,505.0
Unusual (SGA)	NA	1,847.0	NA	NA	NA
Other (unusual)	NA	494.0	NA	NA	NA
Total operating expense	79,042.0	74,884.0	73,212.0	79,251.0	77,793.0
Intell./Devel. Inc.	1,168.0	1,100.0	1,476.0	1,728.0	1,506.0
Other income	(238.0)	267.0	353.0	1,008.0	848.0
Interest expense	(145.0)	(145.0)	(234.0)	(347.0)	(352.0)
Net income before taxes	10,874.0	7,524.0	11,450.0	11,534.0	11,757.0
Provision for income taxes	3,261.0	2,190.0	3,304.0	3,441.0	4,045.0
Net income after taxes	7,613.0	5,334.0	8,146.0	8,093.0	7,712.0
Net income before extraordinary items	7,613.0	5,334.0	8,146.0	8,093.0	7,712.0
Discount. ops.	(30.0)	(1,755.0)	(423.0)	NA	NA
Net income	7,583.0	3,579.0	7,723.0	8,093.0	7,712.0

Source: Company reports.

(continued)

consumer space. We are the largest consumer technology company in the world. IBM made a decision to exit the consumer business.

But in the printing space in particular, if you think about every physical process becoming a digital process, document management in a business is a huge deal. So now IBM is actually looking around in the marketplace for a printing partner with domain expertise on document management. I've been asked would IBM ever consider repurchasing Lexmark? And I said, well isn't that interesting. And you know everybody thought it was so brilliant that they spun off Lexmark, it created great shareowner value for a decade, but it may not create shareowner value for the next decade. Lexmark is under huge pressure as a standalone printing player and IBM will have difficulty getting at the document management market.

If HP continued along its trajectory, it would compete more and more against IBM. Both companies were looking for an increasing piece of the highly fragmented services market; indeed, IBM sought to provide customers "e-business on demand." This emphasis on services had increased under the leadership of Sam Palmisano, who took over the chairmanship and CEO position in 2002 from Lou Gerstner, the man widely credited with reinvigorating the company and saving it from a self-inflicted breakup after years of desultory performance.

Within a year in his new role, Palmisano set IBM on a course toward services. In 2001, IBM had 100,000 people in the higher-end professional consulting. In July 2002, the company paid $3.5 billion to acquire the consulting arm of PwC, the company HP nearly purchased in

EXHIBIT 2 | Additional IBM Financial Data

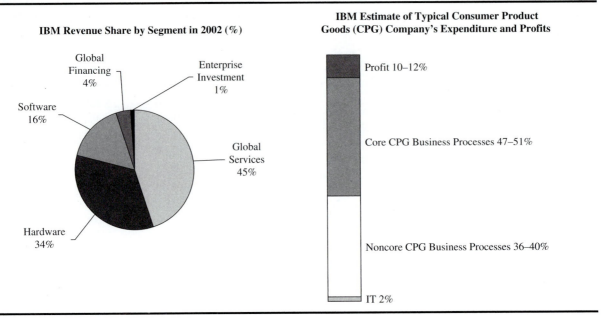

IBM Revenue Share by Segment in 2002 (%)

Global Financing 4%
Enterprise Investment 1%
Software 16%
Global Services 45%
Hardware 34%

IBM Estimate of Typical Consumer Product Goods (CPG) Company's Expenditure and Profits

Profit 10–12%
Core CPG Business Processes 47–51%
Noncore CPG Business Processes 36–40%
IT 2%

Source: Company Reports, *Financial Times.*

2000. The 30,000 consultants would be deployed to support IBM's efforts to grow its business process consulting services. Palmisano said, "Clients are not only looking for innovative ideas to improve their businesses, they are seeking a partner with deep business expertise and the ability to exploit leading, open standards–based technology to turn these ideas into bottom-line business benefits. This acquisition underscores our commitment to this strategy. Our consulting and services professionals will provide a powerful capability, beginning with business innovation and extending through implementation, to help clients improve their competitiveness and drive sustained growth and profitability."[4]

This expansion in services was coupled in late 2003 with Palmisano's vision for "self-healing" computing systems and networks. The vision would leverage IBM's research capabilities to create technologies that can form systems and networks "to detect, analyze, correlate, and resolve IT problems and automatically diagnose the root cause of a problem in complex systems." IBM was working with Cisco and Toshiba to develop the technology.

The vision seemed to resemble the "Adaptive Enterprise" framework espoused by HP (see below).

In late 2003, IBM announced that, beginning in January 2004, it would reorganize its software business around 12 industry sectors. The software business at IBM had failed to break out of a narrow range of annual revenue, earning between $12.6 billion and $13.1 billion in each of the past four years. The business had been largely dependent upon mainframe software leasing, a steady, but slowly declining, market. Scott Hebner, vice president of IBM Software said, "This strategic shift is on the same scale as our decision to exit the software applications market in 1998." Hebner was referring to IBM's focus on so-called middleware, software that links together large, important applications from various vendors. When IBM exited the applications market, other developers such as PeopleSoft and Siebel no longer viewed IBM as a competitor and began developing products that ran on IBM middleware, creating a profitable business for the company. Along with the planned reorganization, IBM also announced that it would spend hundreds of millions of dollars in a campaign to attract software companies to develop products to run on IBM's middleware. This could mean that IBM would try to strengthen its relationships with system

[4]"IBM to Acquire PwC," IBM press release, July 30, 2002.

integrators such as Accenture and others. These relationships were strained when IBM purchased PwC and became a direct competitor. According to Steve Mills, head of IBM Software, "There was a cooling off in our relationships with some of the system integrators following the PwC acquisition last year . . . but those relationships have come back."[5]

IBM was the company that really stoked the PC revolution with the launch of its 5150 PC in August 1981. In 2001, IBM abandoned the PC retail market, selling instead through value-added resellers (VARs) and the IBM direct sales force. In January 2002, IBM announced that it would no longer manufacture desktop PCs. In order to reduce costs, IBM sold its desktop PC manufacturing operations in the United States for an undisclosed sum to Sanmina-SCI, a San Jose, California–based OEM PC manufacturer. As part of the transaction, IBM awarded Sanmina-SCI a $5 billion three-year contract to build desktop PCs that would be sold under the IBM label. The company planned to continue with its own design and marketing operations for the NetVista line of desktop PCs and continued to manufacture its ThinkPad laptops at a company plant in Guadalajara, Mexico. Under the deal with Sanmina-SCI, the OEM would assume management of IBM's outsourced PC operations in Scotland, which manufactured IBM-labeled PCs for Europe, the Middle East, and Africa.

IBM did not intend to exit the PC business entirely. The company wanted to be able to offer a full range of computers, yet reduce its costs. Bob Moffatt, general manager of IBM's Personal & Printing Systems Group, said the outsourcing deal ". . . will allow us to further lower our costs, while we continue to develop and deliver a full line of PC products and services for our customers. . . . PCs are an important part of IBM's e-business infrastructure offerings. We've been executing a strategy to make this business even more competitive. This agreement supports that strategy, which is to leverage the skills of the industry where it makes sense to improve our costs, and focus more of our own investments on areas that deliver the highest value to our customers."[6]

IBM's PC operations had been performing poorly. For the third-quarter 2001, the company reported that revenue from desktop sales declined 30 percent compared to the same period in the previous year. At the time of the transaction, IBM's Personal and Printing Systems Group experienced a year-over-year decline in pretax income of 180 percent for the period.[7]

Sun Microsystems   Sun provided network computing infrastructure solutions comprising computer systems including hardware and software, network storage systems, and support services. Sun's products were used to build and operate important (so called mission-critical) network computing environments. Sun, one of the dominant forces in the computing industry, continued to sell hardware based on its own microprocessor and operating system, a version of the Unix system called Solaris. Sun's services business was entirely geared toward selling and supporting Sun's hardware.

Since the dot-com bust, Sun had been having problems. Its growth had slowed sharply, and its annual revenue was less than half that of its main competitors IBM and HP (Exhibit 3). Sun's main hardware products, high-end by industry standards, were facing increased competition from lower-priced computers that used Intel chips and Microsoft software. In the past, Sun had used it popular and innovative software to sell its hardware. In late 2003, it adopted a new strategy. Sun launched a new software business model in which it bundled together various pieces of infrastructure software together in sets of suites, and sold them as integrated sets, upgraded once a quarter, for an annual per employee license fee.[8] For example, the Java Office desktop software, a replacement of Microsoft's Office suite of applications, would cost companies only $50 per employee per year if they also purchased the Java Enterprise stack of applications, or $100 on its own. Microsoft's offering was much more expensive. This action along with others was seen by some as part of a larger strategy for Sun to move away from providing only discrete technology hardware solutions and more toward systems integration, much like IBM did in the 1990s.

Dell Inc.   As HP looked in one direction and saw IBM, when it looked in the other direction, it could not miss its other natural competitor: Dell, Inc. Much of Dell's

---

[5]Tom Foremski, "Big Blue Bets on a Coming Revolution," *Financial Times*, December 1, 2003, p. 19.

[6]"Sanmina-SCI to manufacture IBM NetVista desktops in U.S., Europe," IBM press release, January 8, 2002.
http://www.ibm.com/news/us/2002/01/08.html

[7]Paul McDougall, "IBM Exits PC Manufacturing; Awards $5 Billion Outsourcing Contract," *InformationWeek*, January 8, 2002.
http://www.informationweek.com/story/IWK20020108S0003

[8]"Sun Resets Software Industry with New Java Enterprise System Priced at $100 per Employee with Infinite Right to Use," press release, September 16, 2003.

EXHIBIT 3 | Selected Financial Data for Sun Microsystems Fiscal Years Ended 1999–2003

	30-Jun-03	30-Jun-02	30-Jun-01	30-Jun-00	30-Jun-99
Reported in $ millions					
Products	7,793.0	9,093.0	15,015.0	13,421.0	10,171.0
Services	3,641.0	3,403.0	3,235.0	2,300.0	1,635.0
Total revenue	11,434.0	12,496.0	18,250.0	15,721.0	11,806.0
Cost of products	4,342.0*	5,506.0	7,961.0	6,096.0	4,696.0
Cost of services	2,150.0	2,074.0	2,080.0	1,453.0	974.0
Research & development	1,837.0	1,832.0	2,016.0	1,630.0	1,280.0
Sell./gen./admin.	3,329.0	3,806.0	4,445.0	4,065.0	3,196.0
Restructuring charge	371.0	517.0	75.0	0.0	NA
Goodwill amortization	NA	0.0	285.0	72.0	19.0
In-Process R&D	4.0	3.0	77.0	12.0	121.0
Impair GW & intangibles	2,125.0	6.0	NA	NA	NA
Total operating expense	14,158.0	13,744.0	16,939.0	13,328.0	10,286.0
Equity investment	(84.0)	(99.0)	(90.0)	208.0	0.0
Interest income	166.0	243.0	405.0	250.0	NA
Interest expense	(43.0)	(58.0)	(100.0)	(84.0)	NA
Interest expense, net	NA	NA	NA	NA	85.0
Gain mkt. debt secs.	32.0	114.0	58.0	4.0	NA
Net income before taxes	(2,653.0)	(1,048.0)	1,584.0	2,771.0	1,605.0
Provision for income taxes	776.0	(461.0)	603.0	917.0	575.0

Source: Company reports.

success stemmed from its low prices. Its low-price leadership was supported by a relentless focus on costs. By combining its efficient build-to-order system and tightening its supply chain, Dell cut inventory levels from 40 days to 17. Dell's gross margins hit 22 percent (Exhibit 4).

In 1997 Dell opened its Internet sales channel. Within a few months of going online, the company sold $1 million worth of computers per day online; this with a staff of 30, compared to the 700 people it would have taken to handle that much business over phones. Riding the Internet boom, by 1999 Dell's sales reached $18 billion while driving inventory to record lows. Dell also managed to gain 13 percent share of market in servers.

During the downturn of 2001, when computer sales slipped industrywide, Dell launched a price war. Dell's gross margins dropped from 21.3 percent in October 2000 to 17.5 percent in July 2001. Even with reduced margins, Dell managed to earn $361 million in profits due to cost cuts, while rival computer makers lost $1.1 billion. In 2002, when global PC shipments increased by a sluggish 2.7 percent, Dell reported 21 percent revenue growth year-over-year in the fourth quarter of 2002. All

regions, product revenues, and customer segments reported double-digit increases in revenue during a quarter that had been difficult for the industry. In early 2002, Dell reported its lowest ever level of operating expenses, at 10.2 percent of revenues, compared to 18.3 percent at Compaq and 20.6 percent at HP.[9] In late 2003, according to research firm Gartner Group, Dell had 15 percent of the worldwide PC market, compared to HP with 14.3 percent. In the United States the situation was reversed, Dell had 16.8 percent of the PC market compared to HP with 18.8 percent.[10]

Dell spent only about 1.5 percent of revenues on research and development, compared to 5 percent spent by most competitors. It relied on suppliers, such as Intel and Microsoft, to do research. Dell offered standardized technologies suited to high-volume production. John Medica, vice president of client products at Dell and a former executive at Apple Computer, said, "At Apple,

[9]Caroline Daniel, "Inside Dell," *Financial Times*, April 2, 2002.
[10]"Preliminary 4Q03 and 2003 Worldwide PC Results: Happy Holidays!" Gartner Market Analysis, January 2004.

EXHIBIT 4 | Selected Financial Data for Dell, Inc. Fiscal Years Ended 2000–2004

	30-Jan-04	31-Jan-03	01-Feb-02	02-Feb-01	28-Jan-00
Reported in $ millions					
Net revenue	41,444.0	35,404.0	31,168.0	31,888.0	25,265.0
Total revenue	41,444.0	35,404.0	31,168.0	31,888.0	25,265.0
Cost of revenue	33,892.0	29,055.0	25,661.0	25,445.0	20,047.0
Sell./gen./admin.	3,544.0	3,050.0	2,784.0	3,193.0	2,387.0
Research/dev./engin.	464.0	455.0	452.0	482.0	374.0
Special charges	NA	0.0	482.0	105.0	NA
Purchased R&D	NA	NA	NA	NA	194.0
Total operating expense	37,900.0	32,560.0	29,379.0	29,225.0	23,002.0
Investment & other	NA	NA	NA	NA	188.0
Gain/loss investment	NA	67.0	(277.0)	307.0	NA
Interest/inv. income	NA	154.0	314.0	305.0	NA
Interest expense	NA	(17.0)	(29.0)	(47.0)	NA
Other	180.0	(21.0)	(66.0)	(34.0)	NA
Net income before taxes	3,724.0	3,027.0	1,731.0	3,194.0	2,451.0
Provision for income taxes	1,079.0	905.0	485.0	958.0	785.0
Net income after taxes	2,645.0	2,122.0	1,246.0	2,236.0	1,666.0
Net income before extraordinary items	2,645.0	2,122.0	1,246.0	2,236.0	1,666.0
Extraordinary item	NA	0.0	0.0	0.0	0.0
Accounting change	NA	0.0	0.0	(59.0)	NA
Net income	2,645.0	2,122.0	1,246.0	2,177.0	1,666.0

Source: Company reports.

demand is created through innovative products. At Dell, our innovation is around the business model. We are not positioned as a market maker."[11] Dell founder, chairman, and CEO Michael Dell said in an interview, "If we look across the whole $800 billion IT market, we see that there is a kind of standardization and commoditization occurring across many different product areas, so we have tried to understand what the best opportunities are for us to deliver value."[12]

Those opportunities seemed to relate to unparalleled mastery of the supply chain and manufacturing processes. Dell concentrated its R&D on improving its manufacturing model. Dell's efficient build-to-order model reduced costs and allowed the company to squeeze prices while maintaining profitability, even as PC growth turned negative. More than half of Dell's orders were placed over the Internet. Orders translated onto the factory floor

as a spool of bar-coded stickers, which designated which parts were needed. Assemblers scanned the code and a green light flickered in front of containers of the requisite parts. The factories held four hours' worth of inventory,[13] compared to more than four weeks for many rivals.[14] Dell's model gave the company "negative float"—its customers paid Dell before parts were ordered from suppliers, but Dell did not have to pay its suppliers for another month or so. Dell continued to refine its manufacturing model. In 2000, Dell had 3 million square feet of manufacturing space. By the middle of 2002, it had 1.5 million square feet, but produced 30 percent more.[15] In addition, this lean and information-rich structure seemed to give Dell real-time market intelligence. Dell said, "When we launch a new product, we know within 48 hours whether or not it is going to work."[16]

[11]Caroline Daniel, op. cit.

[12]Geof Wheelwright, " Bytes to Order: Understanding Supply Chain Execution Supplement," *Financial Times*, November 26, 2003, p. 15.

[13]Geof Wheelwright, Ibid.

[14]"The Dell Model: How Well Will It Travel?" Knowledge@Wharton, March 12, 2003.

[15]Caroline Daniel, op. cit.

[16]Geof Wheelwright, op. cit.

346 Part Five   Convergence or Collision—Take I: Computing Meets Cellular Phone and Consumer Electronics

Competitors, such as Gateway, tried to emulate aspects of the Dell build-to-order model, but with only limited success. Dell created a streamlined supply chain and established relationships with suppliers that offered reliable delivery of high-quality components. The extremely efficient manufacturing processes produced quality products integrated with a customer order-taking system that customers valued and for which they were often willing to pay some premium. Dell's products were often not the lowest-priced alternatives for customers.

Dell was profitable in PCs. HP had not always been profitable in the category. Jeff Clarke, the former CFO of Compaq who later became executive vice president of global operations at HP after the merger, said HP was profitable in PCs for two of the past three quarters [1Q and 2Q 2003] and drew a finer distinction:

> Publicly, Dell states that it makes about 8 percent operating profit. They say they make somewhere around 5 percent in PCs. But that includes services and it includes printing and it includes options, which are the richest part. If you include everything we sell to consumers, we make great profit. That includes printing and services. Our services business is over 10 percent bottom-line profit—richer than any publicly stated profit from Dell. And our printing business at 14 percent profit is far richer, perhaps double anything from Dell. So be careful when you try to compare the figures, they're just not always the same.

> Dell's business is 80 percent PCs and 70 percent in the North America market. They have a very rigid, inflexible supply chain, which restricts them from entering into other markets, and it shows. We, in turn, have a very different business: 27 percent of our business is PCs and 60 percent of that is international. We have the same procurement costs for items we outsource, and that's about 80 percent of the cost of the PC. In some regions we have lower manufacturing costs, because we are utilizing contract manufacturing in lower wage regions, compared to Dell, which is manufacturing in the comparatively higher wage North American region.[17]

Clarke discussed the differences between HP and Dell in the important area of notebook computers, one of the few bright spots of the PC industry where sales were growing and margins remained strong. Clarke said:

HP has 18 percent market share compared to Dell's 16 percent—both companies are profitable in notebook computers. [In the second quarter of 2003] the notebook market grew an incredible 22 percent. HP grew 48 percent while Dell grew 31 percent. Toshiba grew 9 percent. We grew at twice the rate of the market and faster than Dell for a second straight quarter. Even Dell makes its notebooks now through contract manufacturing. In notebooks, Dell loses an important feature of their supply chain: configurability, the ability to build to order, e.g., put a different size drive, etc. Because if you start opening that thing up, all of a sudden the quality goes down. Even Dell now has moved subscale to contract manufacturers for that.

Nevertheless, for much of the 1990s, Dell's revenue increased about 40 percent annually. More than half of its revenues come from desktop PCs. As the market for PCs—and IT in general— slowed, some thought that the years of phenomenal growth were, necessarily, behind it. The company was said to be considering acquisitions, but also looked for more organic growth. In 2002, Dell's President and Chief Operating Officer Kevin Rollins surmised, "There's a lot of large companies out there and we have about 3 per cent market share within the total IT industry today and that's pretty small. . . . So we look at that and say, 'well, that's a pretty nice playing field to run on to.'"[18]

To underscore its move into products beyond PCs, Dell changed its name in July 2003 to Dell, Inc. In 1996, Dell launched a line of Intel-standard servers and now sells more of those servers than any other company. However both HP and IBM are ahead of Dell in server revenue, on the strength of their higher value Unix-based servers.[19] By the end of 2002, Dell still made the most of its revenue by selling PCs in the United States. Around 70 percent of Dell's revenues were derived from United States sales in 2002. Servers and storage accounted for only about 20 percent of its revenues. Dell had been focused on the small and medium enterprise (SME) market while competitors such as Compaq and IBM enjoyed strength in the larger enterprise market. A Dell spokesman said, "The main strategic areas we are pushing are servers, storage, and services for large- and medium-sized corporations."[20] Dell tried

---

[17]All quotes from Jeff Clarke are from the author's interview on September 18, 2003. Subsequent quotes from this interview will not be cited.

[18]Caroline Daniel, op. cit.

[19]"New Worlds To Conquer; For Michael Dell to Double the Size of His Company, He'll Need to Move into New Markets Held by Rivals That Promise Tough Competition," op. cit.

[20]"The Dell Model: How Well Will It Travel?" op. cit.

to sell enterprise customers a strategy it called "scale out," in which businesses would use clusters of inexpensive Intel servers as the foundations of their IT infrastructure. Michael Dell said, "What we're talking about is aggregating all the computing power and being able to dynamically allocate resources amongst a pool of shared servers. . . . Scale out is really leveraging the high-volume, industry-standard economics of microprocessor chipsets, high-volume disk drives, and other components built in hundreds of millions of units per year to run large databases and applications."[21] While scale out would feature industry-standard servers, some analysts thought that Dell would need to invest more in software and services in order to really crack the enterprise server market.

Another new area of growth for Dell was printers. In March 2003, Dell introduced four new printers for customers ranging from individual consumers to corporations. The printers featured ink and toner management systems, which displayed ink or toner levels during every print job and proactively prompted users to order replacement cartridges. When cartridges began to get low, the status window delivered a message alerting users to order a replacement cartridge from Dell. One mouse click led to Dell's online imaging supply store, which recognized each user's printer model and offered the appropriate replacement ink or toner cartridge. The printers were priced from $139 to $838. Replacement cartridges started at $29.99 for black ink and ranged to $74.99, with standard shipping included in the price.[22]

Dell planned to introduce additional ink-jet and laser printers in North America later in 2003. The program was the result of Dell's work with printer maker Lexmark, which had 18 percent of the market in 2002, to develop Dell-branded printers and ink and toner cartridges. Lexmark was the largest rival to printer giant HP, which had 52 percent of the market in 2002. Dell's partnership with Lexmark led some observers to speculate that Dell would not look to undercut pricing in the printer market, but rather use its direct-sales model to compete on convenience and service. Dell sold over 2 million third-party printers in 2002.[23] The global inkjet business was estimated at $21 billion in 2002.[24]

Jeff Clarke was sanguine about the competition Dell offered HP in printers. He said:

Dell's supply chain is built around configurability. You don't configure a printer. Think of how cars used to be built. You used to select from a host of options, such as FM radio, leather seats, rear wipers, etc. Toyota changed all that. They said everybody gets an FM radio, everybody gets air conditioning, everybody gets intermittent wipers. They changed the configurability of the car industry and I believe that is happening to the PC industry now. I believe that Dell's core advantage of configurability of flexibility in how you build a PC is no longer germane to the typical consumer or the typical business.

Where scale did play a part in the printer business, Clarke thought the advantage was with HP. He said, "We make 50 million printers a year compared to maybe 2 million made by Dell. We make 500 million InkJet cartridges, all with the same capital intensity and same basic fabrication."

While Dell was clearly a major competitive force for HP to reckon with, Jeff Clarke said in late 2003 that HP's multiple supply chains would turn out to be a major competitive advantage:

We spend many times more than them on our supply chain. We have five supply chains [that allow us to be in multiple businesses]. If I wanted to only be in one business, I could have a very low-cost supply chain. But instead we want to be in broad businesses and our strategy is that there is up-sell [opportunity].

My argument against Dell is that the rigidity of their supply chain has limited their ability to go into new markets, it's limited their ability to go international, it has allowed them to be a great one-trick pony in that supply chain. The rigidity of that supply chain is going to end up being a problem for them. The flexibility of our supply chains allows us to go into markets and the new scale of HP allows us to go into them with dominance.

Clarke recognized that Dell was several years ahead of HP with its direct model, but believed that it would be

---

[21]"New Worlds To Conquer; For Michael Dell to Double the Size of His Company, He'll Need to Move into New Markets Held by Rivals That Promise Tough Competition," op. cit.

[22]"Dell Direct Simplifies Purchasing of Printers, Replacement Cartridges; Company Offers Recycling of Used Printers," Dell press release, March 25, 2003.

[23]Scott Morrison, "Dell Takes on Printer Market," *Financial Times,* March 25, 2003, p. 22.

[24]Keith Bradsher, "Chinese Computer Maker Seeks Aggressive Global Growth," *New York Times,* February 22, 2003.

possible for HP to catch up with them. As HP moved to sell more through its growing direct channel, it would likely face conflicts with retailers, who remained a critical channel for the company, particularly with printers and ink, products from which HP derived most of its profits. Clarke said:

> It's customer choice. Customers will end up choosing the form of distribution they prefer. So if a customer wants to pay for the retail, they will buy retail. If they aren't willing to pay for the retail, then they will buy on the Web and so we will offer on the Web a different set of products or different price points. We can also offer a hybrid channel, a kiosk in retail stores that allows a customer to walk into the store and yet get that configurability of choice at the store.
>
> Dell, by the way, tried that and failed miserably. Just an example of how their model is so rigid. So you may have noticed about a year ago they came out with a kiosk program that made the front pages of *The Wall Street Journal* and they had a big launch and they have quietly exited that. So they continue to try for results outside their model, but they miss.

Legend   In China, HP and Dell faced that country's dominant PC maker, Legend (Exhibit 5). The company dominated the fast-growing Chinese PC market, with a 27.7 percent share in 2002. Legend's nearest competitor, another Chinese PC maker, Founder, only had a 9.4 percent share. HP's share of the market for PCs in China had fallen from around 10 percent in 1999 to around 4 percent by 2002. During that same period, Dell had increased its share of the market from around 1 percent to 6 percent.[25] Legend was reported to enjoy good brand value in China, known for high quality, good service and value, as well as innovations geared specifically for the Chinese market. In the first half of the fiscal year ending in September 2003, Legend's revenues were HK$10.37 billion (US$1.3 billion), up 20 percent from the same period the previous year.

The Chinese government started Legend in 1984. The company's Hong Kong and other foreign operations were partially spun off in 1994, with the subsidiary becoming listed on the Hong Kong stock exchange. The state-owned parent group sold its important Beijing operations to the Hong Kong subsidiary in 1997, and in 2001 the Chinese government awarded large blocks of stock and options in the company to its senior management.

The result of all these deals was that the Chinese government owned 65 percent of the parent company, which in turn owned 57 percent of the Hong Kong operations, said Mary Ma, chief financial officer of the Hong Kong unit.

China's PC market was growing so quickly that it was slated to outpace Japan and become the world's No. 2 market in the first few years of the 21st century. Legend's strengths have enabled it to grow market share as well as sheer units: where the market as a whole grew 20 percent year-on-year during the third quarter of 2002, according to company figures, Legend's sales grew 21 percent.

Opportunities for HP in China were a particular interest of longtime HP-veteran Harry "Webb" McKinney. McKinney had run worldwide sales and marketing for HP's enterprise accounts and later helped manage the HP-Compaq merger integration. He was subsequently tasked with driving change across post-merger HP. McKinney was keenly focused on China. He said: "We felt we have been too fragmented, we showed up too much as four product groups and not one company. The China manager doesn't work for me. But I have someone who I've hired at the VP level who is very experienced in Asia who is now working with the Asia/Pacific team . . . making sure we're executing, getting that in front of the Executive Council."[26] (The executive council was a group of HP senior executives that worked with HP's chairman and CEO to set strategy for the company.)

As Dell, HP and other foreign companies were looking at China, Legend was looking overseas for growth. The company wanted to increase its foreign sales from the current 7 percent to 25–30 percent by 2006. Ma said, "Our focus will still be on China in the coming few years. We will be exploring international markets in the meantime. Selling PCs in Hong Kong is certainly an example of a market test."[27]

The New Consumer Electronics Industry

Formerly as distinct from computing as an office from a living room, the consumer electronic industry and the computing industry were increasingly overlapping. This shift blurred the boundaries that formerly separated the industries; now computer makers were aiming for consumers' living rooms and the consumer electronics

---

[25]Data from Gartner and Dataquest.

[26]All quotes from Harry "Webb" McKinney are from the author's interview on August 20, 2003. Subsequent quotes from this interview will not be cited.

[27]"The Dell Model: How Well Will It Travel?" op. cit.

EXHIBIT 5 | Selected Financial Data for Legend Computing Systems

Reported in millions of HKD (as of 15 March 2004 $1 = HKD 7.8)

	31-Mar-03	31-Mar-02	31-Mar-01	31-Mar-00	31-Mar-99
Reported in millions of HKD					
Turnover	20,233.3	20,853.3	27,219.2	17,449.6	11,633.6
Total revenue	20,233.3	20,853.3	27,219.2	17,449.6	11,633.6
Change in inventory	NA	NA	NA	NA	12.7
Cost of goods sold	17,234.7	18,070.8	23,911.2	15,237.7	10,053.8
Selling expense	379.8	382.4	492.3	340.0	212.2
Advertising	425.1	397.4	542.9	249.8	126.9
Staff costs	688.5	674.9	835.7	644.7	441.0
Other operating	490.6	461.9	589.8	374.1	402.0
Depreciation	NA	NA	NA	93.3	72.2
Amortized goodwill	NA	0.0	580.9	NA	NA
Amortized intangible	15.2	NA	NA	NA	NA
Impair loss goodwill	NA	0.0	165.6	NA	NA
Interest income	(77.2)	(67.4)	(103.2)	(16.4)	(13.6)
Write-off	NA	NA	NA	NA	0.0
Exchange loss	NA	NA	NA	NA	0.0
Total operating expense	19,156.9	19,920.0	27,015.2	16,923.3	11,307.2
Interest w/in 5 Yrs.	0.0	(11.0)	(32.0)	(31.3)	(45.3)
Interest over 5 Yrs.	NA	NA	NA	NA	0.0
Interest/financing Leases	NA	0.0	(0.1)	(0.5)	(1.0)
Other interest	0.0	(0.8)	(1.4)	(9.6)	0.0
Disp. subs/secs.	(26.8)	164.2	(1.3)	NA	NA
Gain of associated	(34.8)	8.5	0.0	NA	NA
Associated companies	13.8	(13.0)	(6.6)	2.8	0.4
Net income before taxes	1,028.7	1,081.2	162.6	487.7	280.5
Provision for income taxes	26.0	23.1	19.2	(3.2)	5.0

Source: Company reports.

activities associated with that space, and consumer electronics companies were including more computation power and applications in their products.

This shift was vividly illustrated by computer maker and seller Gateway. In 2003, Gateway changed its business model, for the third time in three years, to increase the sales of non-PC digital products such as digital cameras and plasma screen televisions. The company closed all of its non-U.S. outlets and almost half of its U.S.-based stores to focus on selling consumer electronics in remaining outlets.

Shelf space in Gateway stores was reallocated, with PCs only accounting for 20 percent (down from 80 percent) of the inventory, with the rest taken by Gateway-branded digital electronics items. Gateway would also increase its in-store inventory to allow shoppers to carry out their purchases. This was another change, where Gateway's original model (much like Dell's with its retail "demo" kiosks) was to make the sale in the store and then build the unit for shipment to the buyer from a central warehouse. The new delivery policy increased the amount of cash tied up in inventory. Gateway founder and CEO Ted Waitt said, "Because we have our own stores, we can sell these products direct to customers for up to 25 percent or 30 percent or 40 percent lower than the competitors and still make more money than we make on a PC."[28]

---

[28]"Gateway Counts on Digital Media Future, De-emphasizes PC Retail Market," *Online Reporter,* August 30, 2003.

EXHIBIT 6 | Selected Financial Data for Sony Corporation

Reported in millions of Japanese Yen (as of 15 March 2004 $1=Yen 108.8)

	31-Mar-03	31-Mar-02	31-Mar-01	31-Mar-00	31-Mar-99
Net sales/overseas	6,916,042.0	7,058,755.0	6,829,003.0	6,238,401.0	6,415,418.0
Insurance/financing	512,641.0	483,313.0	447,147.0	412,988.0	339,368.0
Other operating	44,950.0	36,190.0	38,674.0	35,272.0	49,396.0
Total revenue	7,473,633.0	7,578,258.0	7,314,824.0	6,686,661.0	6,804,182.0
Cost of sales	4,979,421.0	5,239,592.0	5,046,694.0	4,595,086.0	4,633,787.0
Sell./gen./admin.	1,819,468.0	1,742,856.0	1,613,069.0	1,478,692.0	1,500,863.0
Insurance/finance	489,304.0	461,179.0	429,715.0	389,679.0	321,320.0
Devaluation secs.	23,198.0	18,458.0	4,230.0	2,015.0	NA
Total operating expense	7,311,391.0	7,462,085.0	7,093,708.0	6,465,472.0	6,455,970.0
Interest income	14,441.0	16,021.0	18,541.0	17,700.0	23,313.0
Royalties	32,375.0	33,512.0	29,302.0	21,704.0	NA
Foreign exchange	1,928.0	0.0	0.0	27,466.0	2,895.0
Sale of secs. inv.	72,552.0	1,398.0	41,708.0	28,099.0	7,645.0
Iss. stk. equity inv.	0.0	503.0	18,030.0	727.0	58,698.0
Other income	36,232.0	44,894.0	60,073.0	50,603.0	60,354.0
Interest expense	(27,314.0)	(36,436.0)	(43,015.0)	(42,030.0)	(48,275.0)
Foreign exchange loss	0.0	(31,736.0)	(15,660.0)	0.0	NA
Other expense	(44,835.0)	(51,554.0)	(64,227.0)	(61,148.0)	(75,151.0)
Net income before taxes	247,621.0	92,775.0	265,868.0	264,310.0	377,691.0
Provision for income taxes	80,831.0	65,211.0	115,534.0	94,644.0	176,973.0
Net income after taxes	166,790.0	27,564.0	150,334.0	169,666.0	200,718.0
Minority interest	(6,581.0)	16,240.0	15,348.0	(10,001.0)	(12,151.0)
Equity in affiliates	(44,690.0)	(34,472.0)	(44,455.0)	(37,830.0)	(9,563.0)
Net income before extraordinary items	115,519.0	9,332.0	121,227.0	121,835.0	179,004.0
Accounting change	0.0	5,978.0	(104,473.0)	0.0	NA

Source: Company reports.

Perhaps no company was as seemingly well positioned to exploit the melding of computing and consumer electronics as Sony. (See Exhibit 6 for Sony selected financials.) With its computers, televisions, and stereos as well as recording and movie studios, the Japanese technology powerhouse had a major presence in both industries. In 1999 the company was restructured to make it less dependent on manufacturing television sets, video recorders, and personal stereos. By 2003, the company earned half of its profit from its PlayStation 2, a market leader in the video game industry. Sony also continued at the forefront of digital recording technology. The company had the goal of linking Sony devices together to provide a networked home-entertainment system. The company also produced copious amounts of content from games to music and movies. However, Sony had been taking a hit in profitability over the past few years, due in part to the company's high cost base. In October 2003 Sony announced new restructuring plans that would shed 20,000 jobs to make it leaner and perhaps better able to compete and lead in the consumer-electronics industry.

The Imaging and Printing Industry

It is tempting to say that HP prints money—its imaging and printing businesses are so profitable. At the time of HP's merger with Compaq, imaging and printing products accounted for 133 percent of the company's earnings from operations.[29] HP's printers were only

[29]Imaging and printing activities earned $410 million from operations while total segments earned only $309 million from operations in 2Q 2001.

marginally profitable; it was products such as toner and ink which generated 93 percent of total imaging operating profits and 118 percent of operating profits overall. Indeed, Michael Dell said his biggest mistake was "not getting into printers sooner."[30]

It was with HP's over $20 billion printer business in its sights that Dell launched its bid to enter the printer market. Formerly a seller of the company's printers, when HP merged with Compaq, Dell launched its own line of printers. Dell met with early success, selling an estimated 1.5 million printers in its first nine months in the business in 2003. Some analysts estimated that Dell would sell over 4 million printers in 2004. By the second quarter of 2004, Dell had already earned more than $1 billion in revenue from printers and ink cartridges, which was the fastest rate of revenue growth of any product category in Dell's 20-year history.[31] Still, HP would be hard to beat, as the company accounted for 40 percent of the worldwide printer market in 2003, but that did not stop Dell and others from trying. Industry sales were trending away from black-and-white laser printers, where HP had 70 percent of the market and toward color printers and all-in-one devices that could print, fax, scan, and copy—markets where HP faced tougher competition from Canon, Lexmark, and Xerox.

Such devices stood to benefit from the boom in digital photography. Some estimated that over 50 billion digital photos were taken in 2003,[32] creating a potentially enormous market for photo printing. While few of these digital photos were actually printed, HP accounted for 50 percent of the market for such photos that were printed from home.[33] Consumers tended to use all-in-one devices, some of which could also serve as photo printers, much more frequently than they used single purpose printers. The boom in this area did not extend to traditional imaging and printing markets. For example, most of Xerox's growth in recent quarters had come from multifunctional printers as opposed to the traditional corporate printing market. Jim Firestone, Xerox's chief strategist said, "The market is strengthening, but there are no indications of robust corporate replacements."[34] Xerox exited the consumer printer business

when it restructured in the face of deep financial problems in the summer of 2001. That left the bulk of the consumer market to companies such as HP, Lexmark, Canon, and Seiko Epson. HP and Lexmark were the leaders, with 58 percent and 21 percent, respectively, of the U.S. market for multifunctional printers. HP dominated the market for inkjet photo printers, with two-thirds of the U.S. market, followed by Epson and then Lexmark. Still, HP was the giant of the industry; its $20 billion in imaging and printing revenues towered over the less than $4.8 billion earned by Lexmark in 2003.

Dell's entrance in the printer market highlighted the basic difference in strategy between the company and HP. Dell relied on other companies to develop technologies and products, usually getting involved with its own R&D to refine products. Tim Peters, Dell's vice president and general manager of imaging and printing said, "Your reach can be extended enormously if you reach beyond your own backyard."[35] Dell partnered with Lexmark, Samsung, Fuji, Xerox and Kodak, which represented a mix of expertise in office printing and digital photo printing technologies. HP stayed mostly in its own expansive research "backyard" designing the microprocessor that controlled the printer laser and developing the software that drove most of its printers. However, HP relied on Canon to provide printer engines and toner cartridges for laser printers (as opposed to digital photo printers). Commenting on the fundamental difference between Dell and HP, Michael Dell said, "A better business model . . . will beat a better technology . . . The days of engineering-led technology companies are coming to an end."[36]

Strategic Leadership of the Core Businesses in 2004

While the corporate-level strategy naturally emphasized the horizontal dimension of the operating model—the cross-business leveraging of the entire portfolio—each of the vertical business groups still needed to be able to develop a winning business-level strategy against its clear and distinct competitors. Pursuing a winning "vertical" business strategy whilst simultaneously supporting the "horizontal" dimension of the operating model would require very strong and somewhat novel and rare strategic leadership skills on the part of HP's senior executives.

[30]Steve Lohr, "The Innovator versus the Distributor," *The New York Times*, May 24, 2004.

[31]Ibid.

[32]Ibid.

[33]Ibid.

[34]Olga Kharif, "Printing a Record of Growth," *BusinessWeek*, February 17, 2004.

[35]Steve Lohr, op.cit.

[36]Ibid.

Imaging and Printing Group (IPG): Leading with Big Bangs

Vyomesh "VJ" Joshi, a 23-year veteran of the company, ran HP's Imaging and Printing Group (IPG) group. IPG was a cash-generating machine for the company. This group earned 28 percent of HP's revenue in 2002 and contributed 105 percent of the company's operating profits that year, which meant some of HP's other groups lost money. In 2003, imaging and printing accounted for 79 percent of HP's total profits. This financial performance stemmed from IPG's market strength. The company enjoyed 70 percent of the market for black-and-white laser printers. Its main competition came from all-in-one devices that combined printers with fax machines and scanners. In this market, HP competed with Canon (the maker of many of HP's printer engines), Lexmark (the former printer group within IBM), and the troubled Xerox. Printers represented something of an annuity for HP. Most customers spent twice the printer's purchase price on ink cartridges over the lifetime of the product. Ink cartridges brought 35 percent margins and earned HP $2.2 billion, or 70 percent of the company's earnings in 2002.[37]

Before the merger was announced, Joshi had already started a quiet revolution at IPG, fundamentally changing the structure and strategy of the group that earned most of the company's profits. The revolution had two phases, which Joshi called "Big Bang 1" and "Big Bang 2." Joshi said, "Big Bang 1 was an implosion, fundamentally altering the strategy and structure that IPG used to design and develop new innovations in printing. Big Bang 2 was an explosion into new markets and technologies."

Big Bang 1   Big Bang 1 was ignited in 2001. Where IPG had been organized around its core products, InkJet and LaserJet printers, Joshi focused on markets. IPG organized around five groups: personal printing, shared printing, digital imaging, digital publishing, and supplies. Speaking in late 2002, Joshi said, "I felt that if you focus on market and really say how do we go to market and how do we really meet the customer needs from that, then we will be able to use appropriate technology in making that happen. So that's a much better way to look at that."[38]

For years, HP's printer group used a "waterfall" model for development where innovation was directed toward the high end of the market and products cascaded over time to the lower end. Joshi explained:

> We have our own Moore's Law here: InkJet technology has been doubling speed, measured in drops per second, every 18 months. And, we have also been building a big installed base every year. It took us 15 years to build the first 100 million printers shipped and it took just under three years to ship the next 100 million.

> The beauty of this is you could do this waterfall, where high-end products cascade down over time to lower-end markets. So over time product prices will fall from $500 to $400 or $300 to $100 dollars. We will generally design a cartridge and a printer together as a system so we can improve the quality and improve the speed and the basic fundamental structure.

However, by 2001 IPG experienced disturbing sales trends. HP was far and away the dominant player in printing, but it had been losing share and sales to low-end makers, in particular to competitor Lexmark, a printer company that had been spun off from IBM in 1991. HP experienced unfamiliar slippage in printer sales; by the middle of 2001, sales, while still very robust, were declining by 9 percent a quarter. Between 2001 and 2002, HP's market share for printers in the U.S. had slipped from 51.5 percent to 47.1 percent. Lexmark, always in HP's sights, actually slipped a little in the same period, going from 17.8 percent share to 17.4 percent.[39] Much of this lost share as well as the growth in the market had been captured by smaller printer makers during that period.

In response to this change, Joshi turned IPG's waterfall development model upside down. He explained, "In your earlier case study ["The New HP Way"[40]] you show how Lexmark was gaining market share. By 1999, it was clear to me that we needed to be really successful in the lower end of the market, because they were getting a lot of market share. We asked, can

[37]Ben Elgin, "Can HP's Printer Biz Keep Printing Money?" *Business Week*, September 1, 2003, p. 80.

[38]All quotes from Vyomesh "VJ" Joshi are from the authors' interview on September 19, 2003. Subsequent quotes from this interview will not be cited.

[39]InfoTech Trends. NB: According to InfoTech Trends. Epson and OKI Data also lost share, but a group of printer makers designated as "Others" (i.e., not HP, Lexmark, Epson, or OKI Data) increased share from 4.8% to 24.4% between 2001 and 2002.

[40]By Robert A. Burgelman and Philip E. Meza, Stanford Graduate School of Business, SM-72.

we design for the low end through innovation, and then go up?" Joshi explained the new strategy:

> What we wanted to do was completely change the cost structure around our waterfall model. If you want to design for the low end with the idea of migrating upwards, you need to build a complete platform for that. The problem with this is you can't do just one piece. You need to completely change the portfolio. So you had to come up with a way where you design a new platform and then add value to new, differentiated products.
>
> This had never been done before in any big, high-technology market. There was tremendous resistance to this plan. People said, you can't do that, this is just not going to work, it's very risky. It was also very expensive. It turned out that there was more innovation involved in the low end than one might imagine. High-end products used to have 50 patents, however, low-end products that sell for $49 are covered by 100 patents.

Joshi said HP spent more than $1 billion changing its innovation strategy at IPG. Thinking in terms of platforms allowed IPG to better leverage its innovation. In a separate interview, Carly Fiorina highlighted one of the benefits of IPG's platform model. She said, "Whereas in your first case[41] InkJet and LaserJet were different platforms, now we have common drivers, common software across our printing products."

These products were also designed to be parts of imaging systems. IPG now thinks in terms of imaging platforms. Joshi said, "This requires working all the way from design, to manufacturing, to go to market. This forced us to really think about leverage across the technology. So the conversation happened now across the InkJet and LaserJet to say how do we really build a personal printing business and how can we appropriately apply that technology."

While IPG's grip on consumer imaging seemed firm, the group looked for new growth in the high-end digital publishing business. At the same time, the HP/Compaq deal was announced, HP also announced a much smaller acquisition of an Israeli company called Indigo. The deal for $700 million did not attract the same attention as the Compaq merger, but was important to IPG. According to Fiorina:

> The Indigo decision really was reflective of the fact that we had concluded (a) that we wanted to keep the portfolio

together, because as every process becomes digitized, we knew we needed imaging, computing, services, and networking. But (b) it was reflective of a belief, a decision, that we could beat the analog companies and the analog models—that we could beat them fairly quickly, and so we were going to put all our efforts into the digital alternative.

Big Bang 2   Big Bang 2 involved using HP's entire portfolio as a weapon against competitors. It sought to ride the wave of convergence amongst consumer electronics, computing, imaging, and printing. IPG had an $18 billion business in consumer markets. Joshi estimated that IPG's products were in over 110,000 retail outlets, 10 percent of all retail outlets in the world. Big Bang 2 involved leveraging IPG's huge installed base, along with HP's other assets to "enable consumers to enjoy more of life by delivering simple and rewarding experiences." In particular, Joshi aimed at digital photography and digital entertainment. As he explained, "The customer wants simplicity. The customer wants choice, the customer wants convenience and the customer wants control. We have to figure out how to use the building blocks we have to deliver these things."

Joshi teamed up with Duane Zitzner, the executive vice president running PSG, to develop a new type of digital imaging and entertainment experience. For example, Joshi described how working together, IPG and PSG developed a new digital camera with advanced intelligence, developing software that allowed users to take better photographs in a variety of conditions, such as when the subject being photographed was standing in front of a bright glass window. HP's software, embedded in the camera, would perform the corrections necessary to capture a good picture. This camera was part of a system; HP produced a docking station for PCs that enabled users to plug in their cameras and manage their images, including one-touch printing to (IPG hopes) an HP printer. Joshi said, "Our approach is to build our consumer strategy and add in entertainment functions. We are already in the consumers' home offices; we also want to be in their living rooms. So our strategy is to create entertainment."

Stephen Nigro, senior vice president, Imaging and Printing Group Technology Platforms, who leads the 3,600-person IPG Technology Platforms Organization, provided an example of innovation cutting across IPG and PSG. This was an innovation announced in January 2004:

> We have a new imaging and labeling technology for optical drives, called LightScribe, which actually came out of our new business creation process that we have in

---

[41]Ibid.

our organization. But for us to fully utilize the idea and to get at the market, we had to leverage the assets that we had inside of PSG. And so we were able to come together and basically define a program that brings in the buying power of PSG, the optical drive expertise of PSG, the chemistry and imaging expertise of IPG, and the high volume expertise that we have to define a breakthrough in optical drives and optical discs. If we were only a printing company it would have been more difficult, if not impossible, to drive that sort of innovation. And this innovation will actually show that it is possible to invent in the PC space. It is going to give HP a competitive advantage in PCs for some time. Eventually, this will become an industrywide standard—at least that's our business model.

Putting that together was not easy. So, early on, we had to work through who's going to get the credit, who gets the revenue credit, who gets profit credit. And that's where it is up to the leadership to really embrace and understand the operating model. And if they can, then they'll see how to work through it. So, the leadership of PSG and we just said this is 50/50. I'm not going to sweat with we should get 60 percent and they should get 40 percent. At the end of the day, it's all HP, and so let's just come up with something that allows us to quickly get through.[42]

HP had technical muscle and it also had tremendous retailer clout. It used this clout to introduce the products of Big Bang 2 to the consumer world. Joshi said:

> We went to our retailers and resellers and said we want to create an "experience center." We went to Circuit City, J&R, Best Buy and [convinced them of the concept]. Now when customers come into the stores and say, "Hey I want to do digital imaging," they will see our cameras and printers, and they'll learn [how they can make them work together easily]. We introduced 158 products between PSG and IPG. Nobody else can come close to this.
>
> Big Bang 1 was the platform strategy, moving up from the low end. Big Bang 2 was the go-to-market approach.

Longtime HP executive Mary Peery, senior vice president of IPG's Digital Imaging and Publishing Organization gave an example of the benefits IPG had seen with the new operating model's horizontal emphasis on the customer segment:

For the past four years, I worked hard trying to connect PSG with IPG in the area of digital imaging. And I tell you for the first two years it was really tough. Part of it was we probably weren't as clear as we should have been on a strategy. Part of it was just resource constraints. Part of it was the vertical mentality. But as we've moved in the last 12 to 15 months, it's become very clear that it's critical we provide truly integrated solutions and experiences to the customer. Getting sponsorship from VJ and Duane around the importance of this work has brought down all kinds of barriers. What we've been able to achieve in the last 12 months in the digital imaging space in working across PSG and IPG far exceeds what I was able to do in the two-and-a-half years prior to that.

For example, in our latest product introduction, out in early Fall 2003, there was a set of products around the media center PC which has software that was co-developed with IPG and PSG. There is an integrated docking station for our camera on the PC that is the product of careful joint work between the two groups. We worked on a common user interface across multiple of our products between PSG and IPG, so that to the customer the look and feel was exactly the same as they went from product to product to product, whether they chose to use them independently or as an integrated solution. We found ways to do this expeditiously because we had a common goal of introducing a new consumer experience in a given time window. We have a long way to go yet, but it's a great first step. We found ways to allocate resources differently, to split the bill, so to speak, of funding it differently that we were not able to do before.[43]

Chris Morgan, vice president, IPG Sales & Marketing in charge of worldwide marketing for IPG, described the effects of the operating model on his approach:

> So, how it affects me day-to-day is that I'm looking at all of the imaging and printing needs and I'm also looking across the consumer segment. But my real emphasis is to make sure that as a company we are doing the right thing for the customer, so I spend a lot of time on integrating strategies, for instance from our Personal Systems Group. In August we rolled out our consumer strategy. Two years ago, if HP had done that there would not have been the integration of the PC stuff with the

---

[42]All quotes from Stephen Nigro are from the author's interview on November 14, 2003.

[43]All quotes from Mary Peery are from the author's interview on November 20, 2003.

printing stuff. We actually not only had very integrated messages and good marketing activities, but even the products themselves had capabilities that were formally integrated, such as camera docks in the PC, the same digital photography software—a product called HP Image Zone—for the PC and the printer products. So, we achieved a much more formal integration of the solution, what we call "Better Together." We actually made that strategy real.[44]

Joshi felt future opportunities for IPG would stem from successfully penetrating new horizontal customer segments. For example, he had his sights set on television sets. "Because the displays are becoming digital and once you have digital display [it moves into HP's area of expertise]. Getting the power horizontally by customer segment is where we need to go. This is very different than the way we used to work in HP."

This was another area, however, where HP would face competition from Dell. In late November 2003, HP announced plans to launch its own line of flat-screen TV monitors, a move that would take the company into the living rooms of its customers. At the same time, Dell announced that it too would begin selling its own 17-inch flat-panel LCD television monitor. The devices were rapidly gaining popularity. Japanese manufacturer Sharp projected the market for LCD TVs to double to 3 million units by the end of 2003. Pioneer, a maker of the higher-quality flat plasma display panels, predicted the market for those devices would also double from 637,000 units to 1.43 million units sold by March 2004.[45] Dell reportedly thought of the LCD monitor as more of a PC peripheral than a consumer electronics product, and was thus ripe for selling through its Internet and telephone channels. Others disagreed, thinking that consumers would want to see and touch the product before buying it (something Dell pointed out was also said about the other products that the company successfully offers over the Web and over the phone). If this proved to be the case, HP's relationships with a worldwide network of 110,000 stores in 167 countries could be especially helpful in selling these devices.[46]

Looking ahead, Joshi outlined several strategic challenges for IPG. He emphasized the importance of excellent execution at all the levels, and the need for individuals to overcome the tendency to wear an IPG hat or a consumer hat. He also saw a need to get better measurement systems, especially the tools and processes necessary to measure a consumer P&L, because "what you can't measure, you can't control." He also saw a need to strive for 100 percent compatibility: "We must work with all systems, but we can offer 150 percent with all-HP components." Finally, Joshi felt that IPG would have to be able to integrate profitably, though this challenge could prove the most difficult:

> I do believe there was something there in having a vertical approach and doing business management by business model. However, the challenge stemmed from the fact that these things have very different business models. So, you have to balance the vertical and horizontal approaches for the good of HP. We need to have very tight customer metrics so we focus on customers rather than just IPG or PSG. That's the winning formula. These are new territories for us. I don't want to claim that we already know for certain how to do this.

In 2003, HPs imaging supplies business generated $15 billion in revenue; as a whole, the imaging and printing group generated $22.6 billion in revenue in that year. Given the company's reliance on the profits made from imaging and printing, and in particular, printing consumables (such as toner and ink cartridges)—most of HP's operating income in the past few years has come from such consumables—HP had to look closely at anything that threatened that rich source of revenue. It was thought that HP made little profit from printers themselves, and instead made most of its profit from printer cartridges, which it sold, depending upon the printer, for under $20 to as much as $300. As printer prices declined over the past few years, the prices for cartridges increased. Indeed, antitrust authorities of the European Commission, the same group that carried on the Microsoft antitrust enquiries in spite of the matter more or less being settled in the United States, was also looking into HP's and competitor Lexmark's marketing practices in the very lucrative printer consumables business. In particular, regulators were investigating the use of technologies such as smart chips. Such devices told consumers when they were running low on toner (the dry ink used in laser printers), but also made it harder for users to substitute cartridges with lower-priced generic or remanufactured alternatives, which often cost half the

---

[44]All quotes from Chris Morgan are from the author's interview on November 17, 2003.

[45]Michiyo Nakamoto, "Dell to Take On Japanese Market with TV Launch," *Financial Times*, November 27, 2003, p. 18.

[46]Scott Morrison and Richard Waters, "HP Planning to Launch Own Flat Screen," *Financial Times*, November 27, 2003, p. 18.

price (but did not always match the printing quality) of those offered by leading printer manufacturers. Generic or remanufactured cartridges made up around 27 percent of the market in 2002, but were growing at 12 percent per year, almost twice the growth rate for consumables offered by leading printer makers.[47]

Personal Systems Group (PSG): Playing Well with Others at HP

HP's Personal Systems Group (PSG) developed and manufactured commercial and consumer personal computers, technical workstations, personal digital assistant and handheld products, wireless and Internet services, personal storage appliances and embedded software. Products within this group had razor-thin margins. For example, HP made an operating profit in PCs of just .1 percent in fiscal year 2003, earning $22 million. This total was dragged down by a particularly challenging third quarter in 2003, in which the PC group represented 29 percent of HP's sales, but showed an operating loss of $56 million with –1.1 percent operating margin for the quarter. By the first quarter of 2004, things had improved somewhat and operating margin had become positive again at 1 percent, earning $62 million. HP thought the group would be a steady earner over time, perhaps generating between 2 percent and 3 percent operating profit margins in the future. The group was run by Duane Zitzner, executive vice president Personal Systems Group and a 14-year veteran of HP. Prior to the merger with Compaq, Zitzner had been president of HP's Computing Systems organization and had formerly run HP's PC business.

In many ways, the PC business was where HP and Compaq competed the hardest against each other. The industry had become cutthroat as Dell relentlessly lowered prices and HP and Compaq had to fight Dell and each other to maintain share. Given the history of bruises that they inflicted on each other in PCs, one might think that the respective PC teams would have proven the most difficult to merge peacefully. However, Zitzner said that he experienced "no competitive tensions between HP employees and former Compaq employees in PSG. The decisions around which brands and lines of business to keep were straightforward and nonpolitical, which may have prevented tensions from developing."[48] The choices

of which lines to keep and which to drop were dictated by market position. PSG kept HP's products in high-end workstation and consumer PCs; it kept Compaq's businesses in commercial PCs, notebook computers, and handhelds.

Zitzner said

PSG had a four-part strategy, which involved

1. Developing and maintaining world class cost structure and processes;

2. Creating innovative products that offer a great experience;

3. Commanding reach and breadth of channels (i.e., retail, commercial and direct selling); and

4. Leveraging the strength of HP.

Achieving this strategy depended on other groups at HP. Cost structure and processes related to the supply chain management described earlier. PSG's innovation and customer experience was often twinned with IPG. For instance, "Big Bang 2," described earlier, also relied on PSG. Zitzner explained:

With Big Bang 2 we released 158 new products. The hit at Big Bang 2 was the HP DVD+ movie writer product. You can take any analog format, so let's say you take your camcorder or your VCR, you hook it up to the computer and it will take that analog format and copy it to DVD+. You can then play it in your DVD player, you can play it in your PC. Put it on a DVD+, and you can have it for 50 years, unlike tape and regular CDs which start to deteriorate after about 10 years. And, by the way, now it's in your computer, you can do anything you want with it.

That's an example of what I'm talking about. It doesn't mean innovation for innovation's sake, but in the PC space there are tons of innovation HP can do. Look at the media center PC that we came up with. We integrated a TV tuner and DVD+ into this unit so it's sort of a real cool PC. HP worked with Microsoft on it. It's twice as expensive as a normal PC and yet we couldn't keep them on the shelves at the holiday season last year. Everybody wanted one.

As for reach and breadth, Zitzner felt that these products demanded multiple sales channels. He said:

If you think about something like a DVD movie writer or a media center PC, consumers aren't going to spend money unless they can see it and touch and feel it. The same is true with notebook computers. People like to

---

[47]Pui-Wing Tam, "Ink-Cartridge Knock-Off Artists Give Full-Price Competition Fits," *The Wall Street Journal*, September 25, 2002.

[48]All quotes from Duane Zitzner are from the author's interview on September 19, 2003, unless otherwise indicated. Subsequent quotes from this interview will not be cited.

touch and feel it, because there's a different feel to them. So, we've got to be able to deal both with direct and indirect [retail] channels. We're going to deal with the conflict that is going to occur—it's important that you adapt to the customer.

To help make HP "better together," PSG also worked with Ann Livermore's HP Services group. Zitzner said: "We are linked into Ann's organization. When she goes in and sells a managed services platform, we want to be able to have tools and capabilities that if you have an all-HP solution, it's going to allow her to do a better job."

HP Services (HPS): A New Growth Engine

HP looked to its services group to be a main engine for growth in the future. The merger with Compaq doubled the size of the group to 65,000 professionals, 40,000 of them in customer support, while the balance was in the consulting and fast growing outsourcing segment. The company believed that in one way or another, HP Services (HPS) would touch on many facets of the new HP, presenting them in a valuable package to a wide variety of enterprise customers. In the second quarter of 2003, the group represented 18 percent of HP's sales and earned operating income of $337 million, with a 10.9 percent operating margin. Ann Livermore, executive vice president of HP Services and a 21-year veteran of HP, ran the group.

The merger of HP and Compaq created, in Livermore's words, "the number one leader in services at the IT infrastructure level. Period, the end."[49] By some estimates, IT services comprise a $600 billion-per-year industry. However, it was highly fragmented, and industry leader IBM had less than 10 percent of the market. Before the merger, neither HP nor Compaq had enough services operations to make much of an impact in the huge but highly fragmented services industry. After the merger, Livermore felt that the new company would create a force in services, rivaling service giant IBM. HPS, however, had a different approach to services compared to IBM. HPS would work in IT Infrastructure services, targeting only selected applications services and systems integration consulting.

Also, after HP's aborted attempt to acquire Price Waterhouse Coopers (PwC) in late 2000 and IBM's subsequent purchase of PwC for $3.2 billion, CEO

Fiorina had come to the conclusion that it would be very difficult for a high-cost, people-intensive services strategy to be profitable: "We think the high-priced consultant model is a value proposition of the past and will not translate well into the future." For the same reason, Fiorina had decided that HP would not try to buy EDS: "It is a backward-looking value proposition in the sense that we don't think it is any longer about throwing people at technology to make it less complex. We think it is about using technology to make technology less complex. And therefore, we think it's a huge deal that our managed services business is attached to a technology business. In fact, we think about managed services as a technology business, not a people business. "

In April 2003, HPS entered the scene in a dramatic way. HP announced that its services group won a $3 billion, 10-year IT outsourcing bid from consumer products giant Procter and Gamble (P&G). The contract had HP taking over P&G's data center operations, PC support, help desk and some software development and maintenance as well as business continuity services. HP was also buying some of P&G's data center assets and would hire 2,000 P&G employees who worked in these functions. It had been reported that IBM and Electronic Data Systems (EDS) had also been contenders for the P&G contract won by HP. Indeed, in 2002 EDS had captured nearly all of P&G's IT outsourcing, valued at $7 billion. However, EDS's dramatic earnings shortfall gave P&G reason to be worried about the health prospects of their would-be partner. Dan Talbott, a senior director in HPS and one of the leading figures in securing the P&G deal, who worked 23 years for EDS and about 4 years for IBM before joining HP, explained HP's different approach:

> EDS is out there saying we will make [your IT operations] run better and cheaper than anybody you know. IBM is saying we will help you run your business better than you can yourself—we'll tell you how to do it. HP is out there saying, we will give you better information so that you can run your business—we'll give you the tools so that you have faster access, faster reactions, so that you can make the business decisions.[50]

Talbott also described how IBM tries to use prospective customers' access to their R&D labs as a major

[49]All quotes from Ann Livermore are from the author's interview on September 8, 2003. Subsequent quotes from this interview will not be cited.

[50]All quotes from Dan Talbott are from the author's interview on November 14, 2003.

differentiator, something that EDS cannot compete with, but HP can. He underscored the importance of this in the P&G case:

> So, I was looking into our labs and . . . for instance, our imaging and printing group spends a lot of energy on getting "flesh tones" right, which is very difficult, because flesh has a texture and different variations, so our labs spend a tremendous amount of energy trying to analyze skin tones and reproduce them accurately. P&G is a huge cosmetics company . . . they got excited when they saw some of this stuff.

HP followed up the P&G deal with another outsourcing win from Swedish telecom company, LM Ericsson.

Outsourcing deals of this size required winners to pay large upfront expenses and often did not pay off until years into the contract. However, the two deals represented an important debut for HPS. Livermore explained: "One of our very important strategic choices was [that] we were going to selectively pursue and win some really mega contracts during the first year. To be a tier-one services player, you have to demonstrate that you could win and manage such deals."

Becoming a tier-one services player puts HPS in direct competition with services giant IBM. A key difference between the two companies was that HP depended upon partners to provide services that it chose not to deliver. IBM tended to be more of a one-stop shop. Livermore discussed the differences in structure and strategy between HPS and IBM:

> We use partners to augment and extend our capabilities. I don't think you see IBM doing this. We believe that having other services providers look at HPS as a partner and look at IBM services as a competitor is good for us. This is part of HP's broader strategy: we want to be able to create ecosystems of partners that are powerful. This is a corporatewide objective that we have consistently implemented also inside services. We are very aggressively trying to partner at the company level, companies like Microsoft, Oracle, SAP, BEA, Accenture, and Deloitte as important solution partners. There are services partners in that mix as well as software partners.

> It's also a bet on what customers prefer. And we believe that what customers want is a well-integrated solution, but we believe that when you look at their environment, it is so heterogeneous that you have to be able to help them deal with that environment. There is no big customer who's homogeneous. So we're taking advantage

of that customer reality. Customers have to deal with that reality, so we think we have to, too.

Partnerships can be difficult to maintain. Livermore said that she thought partnering was a skill HP has had for a long time. She said, "It was a premerger skill that we have maintained. We have always partnered very well with a number of corporate resellers in the services business. We've used them to help us deliver warranty services, we've used them to help us deliver services around the printing and PC spaces. But over the past two years, we put a lot of effort around teaming some of the big systems integrators. And it's basically because we believe we win more against IBM when we do that."

Still, in a fast-changing industry such as IT services, the borders are bound to be fluid. HPS found that from time to time, it runs into its partners as competitors. Livermore described how HPS handled this touchy situation: "We have found that you have to be very, very clear with your partners where you are going to play and then you have to be consistent. And if you pick new areas that you're going to expand, you need to tell them. So a lot of this is basic relationship management that we do with our partners, where we communicate with them, we tell them what we're going to do, we do it, the consistency is really important."

Livermore felt that relying upon partners did not reduce HPS's scope of opportunities. The market was so big and fragmented, Livermore felt there were plenty of opportunities for both parties. Livermore described a situation when HPS complemented the capabilities of a key partner, Accenture:

> Our manufacturing customers find it interesting and exciting to learn from and adopt a lot of the practices we have developed and use inside HP. A lot of our growth in providing services to the manufacturing sector is coming from taking what we have done inside HP and doing it for them; for example, with supply chain management. We have great capabilities and expertise in supply chain management and in manufacturing engineering. We take our knowledge in these areas and offer it to manufacturing customers. Our internal best practices are a nice complement to the deep business process expertise of Accenture in manufacturing solutions.

There can be a fine line between complements and competitors. Sometimes HPS possessed and sold some of the same expertise as was available from HPS's partners.

According to Livermore, HPS's strategy of using partners was a facet of the company's larger strategy and structure. Referring to HP's organization structure of four vertical groups [HPS, IPG, ESG, and PSG] Livermore said, "A completely vertically integrated strategy like IBM's may be simpler, but we think that a partnering strategy is more sustainable over a long period of time because we believe fundamentally in the technology industry [that] you have to be able to partner to have a sustained value proposition. Livermore said HP hoped to use its partnership strategy to create a universe of other players (an ecosystem) whose "interest is served by playing with you, so in order to keep that together you must keep, I suppose, winning deals together."

This strategy meant that HPS would leverage both its vertical sister organizations and the horizontal functions they all shared: namely HP's supply chain, human resources and finance functions. Livermore said: "We think that the secret sauce is leveraging the power of the portfolio from a customer perspective to win and grow, doing things with our portfolio that other companies can't do."

For example, Livermore said that HPS worked with HP's Personal Systems Group (PSG) to deliver warranty services. While this function might not come immediately to mind for most people, Livermore explained it was the largest point of overlap between the two groups in terms of financial commitment and number of transactions: "We team with PSG as they put together the products and determine the warranty terms and conditions. We work with them to do the delivery of the warranty services. And we will work with them and decide where we team and do the delivery, and where we use channel partners to team and do some of the delivery."

HPS also worked with the Enterprise Systems Group (ESG) to deliver solutions to enterprise customers. Livermore said, "More and more large corporate accounts don't care about buying the PC. They care about the whole life cycle, including the procurement of the product, the installation of the product, the moves, the ads, the changes. They care about help desk, they care about onsite support and all of that together is the life cycle. And they also care about how the PCs are managed from the servers over the network." HPS could manage this process for ESG's customers, using the resources of PSG. Livermore said: "This is one of the great advantages we have against Dell. They do not have the capability to do big global services deals. They just flat out cannot do it."

HPS had ambitious growth targets. Livermore said: "You know the thing that is our most important challenge today is not growing too fast in the managed services

business. So it all has to do with not taking on more than you can do. So in the managed services business when you have a really hot market segment, the most important thing is making sure that you have the processes, the capacity, the capability to take on all the deals that you have. The most important choices are the deals that you don't take."

Some critics suggested that HPS might be losing money on high-profile deals in order to establish a foothold for the group. Livermore said there was a disciplined and structured process around deciding which deals to take. She described HPS's SOAR (Solution Opportunity Approval and Review) process that brought together the opportunity team and management to formally review and approve new customer opportunities and significant changes to existing projects:

> Part of the SOAR process is looking at the profitability of the deal over its lifetime. Since the merger, we won about 250 managed services deals, ranging from very small ones to very large ones. We do these reviews on each one. During the review process, we look at what it takes to deliver, and make sure that we have the resources lined up and ready to go.

> Depending on the deal size, it may be that the country manager in the U.K. can sign off on the deal, or it may be that my European services manager signs off, or it may be that it needs to come up and get my review, along with [that of] the chief financial officer for our business. Some deals require Bob Wayman's [CFO] review, some deals require Carly and the board's review, depending on the size of the deal. When you look at big managed services deals, such as our contracts with Ericsson or P&G, they have a lot of the characteristics of an acquisition. The level of commitment that is required of HP to execute such a deal is sufficiently high that the board needs to be informed.

Joe Hogan, vice president of worldwide marketing, strategy and alliances (MSA) for HP Services' Managed Services group elaborated:

> If we have a client opportunity that requires a platform that PSG or IPG can provide, we would all be in that SOAR review so that we could look each other in the eye and say, "OK we agree, this is how we're going to price so we're going to price by the account, by the portfolio, we agree this is the margin and we agree that these are things we have to do, people we have to provide to the project manager or to the lead business unit to get this thing done and to go ahead and win it."

Once the client accepts the proposal, the negotiations begin. We then have a preliminary meeting about where we think we want to be. Once negotiations are complete prior to signing, it's been reviewed again and then if it is big enough, it will go to the Executive Council for approval. After the project is started, we use the quarterly review process and the total customer experience measurements to make sure you are hitting the mark. These are usually done jointly with the client.[51]

Looking forward, Livermore had her eyes set on selectively moving "up the stack" of IT services. She explained, "We're not staying just at the IT infrastructure level. We are selectively adding more capabilities in the application space and the business process outsourcing space." Livermore wanted to be choosy about the deals HPS took on: "The most important thing is to continue to grow the accounts you already have rather than just winning new ones; really staying focused on taking care of very large customers and every single day absolutely delighting them with what you do. And continuing to expand the business we do with Procter & Gamble, expand the business we do with Ericsson, because they are so pleased with our relationship. That's more important than just winning more accounts."

Enterprise Systems Group (ESG): Spanning Both Ends of the Market

Until May 2004, HP's Enterprise Systems Group (ESG) was run by Peter Blackmore, executive vice president, Enterprise Systems Group. Blackmore was responsible for development, manufacturing and customer engagement for the company's enterprise products and solutions, which included a full range of solutions, servers, storage and software products. Blackmore was also responsible for the worldwide enterprise field organization. Prior to the merger with HP, Blackmore was Compaq Computer Corporation's executive vice president of Sales and Services.

ESG was perhaps the most troubled of HP's four business groups. In the second quarter of 2003, the group represented 21 percent of HP's sales, but earned an operating loss of $70 million with a negative 1.9 percent operating margin. The group was in the uncomfortable position of facing competition from both Dell on the low end and IBM on the high end. ESG also faced

competition from Sun Microsystems, but that company's troubles made it less worrisome to HP. ESG earned about $16 billion in revenue in 2003, around $15 billion from hardware and about $800 million from software. ESG's products ran Unix, Windows, and Linux operating systems. It also sold storage.

Throughout the merger and through 2003, ESG had managed to maintain its share of market, accounting for about 30 percent of worldwide server sales.[52] During this time, the group cut 8,000 employees, and now operated with a force of 32,000 people. Revenue remained flat for most of the year, at around $3.9 billion per quarter in 2003. However, the group met its goal of achieving profitability by the fourth quarter of 2004, reporting operating profit of $109 million on revenues of $4.07 billion.

Blackmore believed there would be more consolidation in the server industry. He said, "I've got a great belief that if you look at this consolidation of the market, one of the server vendors is going to end up with 50 to 60 percent share and the other two or three, whoever remains, are going to then fight amongst themselves. And we want to be the one with the dominant share." Blackmore explained, "Customers do not want too many strategic suppliers any more. It's hard to do. So they're very happy to say I'll take the two full-range parties, which are IBM and us. And that doesn't mean they won't stop using Dell, but it's not strategic, it's tactical. So I look at the two competitors, not like over here and us in the middle, I look at us in front and the other two have got to polarize towards us which I think—given industry standard technologies—there's only one end point."[53]

Blackmore thought that the consolidation would be a function of the drive to industry-standard building blocks in servers. In late 2003, 55 percent of ESG's revenue came from industry-standard servers. He said:

> If you look at what's happened in the hardware business, it's moving to industry-standard building blocks. That means the cost paradigm changes fundamentally. We are ahead of the game in that transformation because we have the IA 32 and market leadership there. We have closed the gap on Dell in pricing to a large extent by getting our cost base right. You then have IA 64, which

---

[51]All quotes from Joe Hogan are from the author's interview on November 14, 2003.

[52]Pui Wing Tam, "The Man on the Hot Seat at HP's Enterprise Unit," *The Wall Street Journal*, August 19, 2003.

[53]All quotes from Peter Blackmore are from the author's interview on September 11, 2003. Subsequent quotes from this interview will not be cited.

is the replacement of all the RISC architectures. We are way ahead of the market; we are the only ones that have put a stake in the ground and said "that's where we're going." IBM has the capacity to be in four or five different architectures because they are a huge company, but the economics are not in their favor.

So, if you look this time next year, we'll be the only hardware manufacturer with two chip sets, IA 32 and IA 64. We will have much simpler operating systems, we'll have one Unix, one Windows, and one Linux. This will give us a cost base advantage and ability to grow faster than anybody else. And you can trust that Dell will have a good IA32 system, but it's not clear to me they'll have IA64 systems at the same level. They also do not have the things that make those systems sexy, such as virtualization management software, which helps enterprises really make use of all of their boxes by utilizing thousands of blade servers[54] and a rack. It's not simple and it takes a lot of virtualization and other management software to do it right.

Regarding the fate of HP's old mainline product PA-RISC, Blackmore said, "You put it into maintenance mode. You never want your customers not to have one if they need one and all computer systems have a very long tail. The tail is actually very profitable, so you don't want to cut the tail off, but that's not where your R&D dollars go, that's not where your marketing dollars go."

Discussing potential tensions associated with offering systems that ran Microsoft's Windows and the open source operating system Linux, Blackmore said:

> At the moment it's very manageable unless something happens in the market. Linux is attacking Unix, not Windows. So there is hardly any loss of Windows customers to Linux. There's a huge shift in Unix customers to Linux. So, we have to be brave though to say—we're not going to sell you a Unix box, we're going to sell you a Linux box. Frankly, the cost of the box is pretty much the same. So from a hardware and profitability point of view, there isn't a gap. We actually have a very good business model for Windows, so by default have a very good business model for Linux.

The Unix market tends to then gravitate towards the higher-end systems, where Linux doesn't give the scalability and clustering, security, etc. But it is very good on the low end. Now that's very good for us. It doesn't work for a company like Sun because they've never developed a Windows business model and only had the high-end Unix business model, so we were fortunate that we had the industry standard business model existing already. We had the RISC business model and the industry standard business model and Linux actually fits very nicely on the industry standard business model, so we're fine.

The thing you have to do then is make sure the services ecosystem gets the profitability it used to get on Unix. Because then the company owns the same amount of profit. So that's what we're working on. But Linux in itself is actually good and we actually have the leading market share in Linux and the leading market share in Windows and the leading market share in Unix.

Blackmore also discussed the challenge ESG faced moving to industry-standard servers. He said:

> You don't pass Go unless you've got that low cost. So you have to teach the engineering teams not to over-engineer the products, but to really differentiate through genuine value-add. There are plenty of places to differentiate even with industry standard building blocks such as blade technology and managements software. Another example, we can sell Superdome [a high-end server] with virtualization software and soft partitioning. It's not something you build into the hardware, it's all software. You don't buy these capabilities from Intel or Microsoft; you build them. And then the high customer satisfaction is self-evident; that is always the biggest barrier to entry.

Blackmore described how ESG worked with other business groups on pricing customer deals:

> The base pricing is done competitively versus your competition. If you're on a major bid, then frankly, it's always negotiated. And what you do there is you can look at negotiating it internally within the business groups, so you can more effectively compete with the portfolio. And what you tend to do is negotiate with the customer across the portfolio. So if we've got X hundreds of millions of dollars a year in some account, we'll say "yeah, we could have a lower margin on this product," because overall the margin on the account is great. That is just good business sense. But what you don't want to do is subsidize one group with another because there is something wrong with the competitive

---

[54]Blade servers use modular architecture that places the server on a single board (or blade). Each blade includes microprocessors and memory. The blades can then be stacked in a rack where they can share a common high-speed bus. Blade servers can address the needs of large-scale computing centers to reduce space requirements for application servers and lower costs.

EXHIBIT 7 | HP Organization Chart (October 2003)

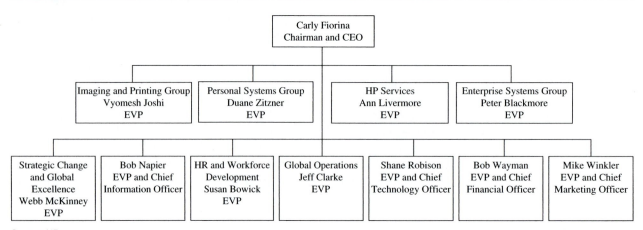

Source: HP.

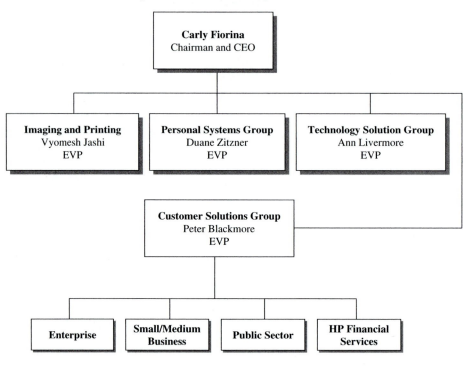

Source: Authors' reconstruction.

basis of that group. Basically, we don't do cross-subsidies. It flows through for the price you set it at, so it goes into the individual group P&L as is. So if you really take a low margin, it flows through as a low margin. Now, what we'll do is then look at the overall margin across the groups and say that's good for HP.

Refining the Model   In December 2003, HP announced changes to its organization structure, starting in May 2004, that would recombine and reduce its four principal lines of business, with distinct profit and loss (P&L) statements, to three (Exhibit 7). The Enterprise Services Group (ESG), which had been led by Peter Blackmore would be folded into a new entity called Technology Solutions Group (TSG) which would be run by Ann Livermore. This new group would encompass systems (servers and storage), software, and services. HP said it would report the P&L statements for systems, software and services separately, to increase transparency.

HP also created the Customer Solutions Group (CSG), under the direction of Peter Blackmore. This group would sell the entire portfolio of HP products and services to enterprise, public sector and small/medium business customers. Arun Chandra, in charge of strategy and operations for Mike Winkler, the chief marketing officer (CMO), explained: "If you go back to the operating model, we had horizontal things at the bottom, we talked about operational excellence, IT, global operations. What in effect we've done now is create a horizontal component on the top. So CSG is focused on sharpening our customer focus, bringing in the entire portfolio and finding opportunities for growth that we would otherwise overlook."[55] The small and medium business segment of this group, which in the old model reported to Duane Zitzner, now reported to Peter Blackmore. For enterprise companies CSG would focus

on finance, manufacturing, telecommunications, and retail. New segments were added to Public Sector including Education and Healthcare, in addition to Law Enforcement, Defense, and Security. HP Financial Services (the leasing company) also reported to Blackmore. However, the CSG group would not constitute a separate P&L.

Conclusion

Prior to its merger with Compaq, HP depended upon profits from its wildly successful imaging and printing business to support the company's far less successful computer businesses. Two years after the merger, HP still relied on its printing business (albeit less heavily) for most of the company's profits. Fiorina said that HP was a "systems business," not just an imaging and printing company, and she thought the merger helped HP become more competitive in the elements of that system, including the PC, enterprise computing, and services businesses. In mid-2004, the challenges facing each of HP's core businesses warranted the serious attention of top management; in particular the issue of balancing HP's horizontal (cross-business) and vertical (multibusiness) strategic considerations would have to rank high on the agenda.

---

[55]All quotes from Arun Chandra are from the author's interview on February 4, 2004. Subsequent quotes from this interview will not be cited.

PART 6

Convergence or Collision—Take II: Do Digits Defeat Pen and Plastic?

"Electronic Arts in 2002" continues to be a highly successful horizontal (software only) creator, marketer, and distributor of video games for consoles and PCs. Throughout the 1990s, EA has been able to create a unique combination of distinctive competencies supported by an equally unique strategic leadership culture. These competencies include those of a Hollywood-like studio system to create compelling content and manage creative risk, a highly sophisticated marketing and distribution company able to manage market risk, and a strong technical company able to manage the technology risk associated with evolving hardware platforms (various consoles and the PC). Since the late 1990s, the company has also begun to create digital content for online gaming and has invested heavily in the Internet-based channel, but so far with mixed results. Key questions facing the company in 2002 are how to proceed in this new channel and, more broadly, how to achieve its stated intent to become the "number one entertainment company in the world."

Important discussion topics for this case are (1) managing key uncertainties and risks, (2) the links between culture and strategy, (3) strategic challenges of online gaming, and (4) winning as a pure content player in the converging computing and entertainment industries. In terms of our three key themes, this case offers an example of the challenges of extending *P*-controlled change as industries converge; it offers a nice example of aligning strategy and strategic action; and it provides another opportunity to examine how a successful company could transform itself in advance of having to in order to better exploit new opportunities arising from industry convergence.

"Disney in a Digital World: Disney in 2001—Distributing the Mouse" and "Disney in a Digital World (D): A Digital Decade? Disney in 2003 and Beyond" help examine the strategic challenges that the company faces as it confronts the consequences of the digitization of content and distribution. Having acquired the ABC TV network in the mid-1990s, and having been less than successful at becoming an entertainment force on the Internet, the company was still struggling with the question of how much and how broad its control over distribution should be. The company also had been less than successful in its efforts so far to develop video games, and its traditional characters faced competition from new ones developed by video game makers, such as Nintendo. In addition, it was still relying on traditional "pen"-based animation competencies for much of its traditional film making. The success of digital animation films and Disney's dependence on Pixar for digital animation had taken on strategic importance. The widely publicized divergence of views of Disney CEO Michael Eisner and Pixar CEO Steve Jobs concerning what the U.S. Government should do to protect intellectual property rights from technology-facilitated "piracy" added urgency to considering this strategic dependence.

Important discussion topics for this case are (1) anticipating and managing strategic inflection points, (2) the role of autonomous strategic action, (3) managing competence-based dependency, and (4) maintaining brand identity in a changing world. In terms of our three key themes, this case offers an example of *P*-independent change that might morph into runaway change; it shows how external forces may drive strategy and action apart and the difficulties of finding a basis for a new realignment; it also raises the question of how to transform a company late in the game when it may face more threats than opportunities.

"Universal Music Group in 2003" is the world's largest recording company and part of the troubled Vivendi Universal conglomerate. The company was the market leader in the music recording industry, which was in the third year of a severe downturn by 2003. UMG and its competitors have had to contend with challenges presented by free online distribution services (such as Napster and KaZaa) that are rapidly replacing consumption of music in the form of "plastic"—CDs—containing fixed sets of songs, many of which are often less than memorable. By 2003, it is clear that in spite of forceful and somewhat successful efforts of the RIAA to stem the piracy tide, the music companies will have to come up with new strategies to protect their profitable growth opportunities in the face of inexorable technological change. These new strategies will have to be formed in light of the rapidly changing and consolidating oligopolistic structure of the recording industry.

Important discussion topics for this case are (1) the interplay of technological and cultural change, (2) the collision of "communal property" and "private property" values, (3) the role of collective strategy in defending industry interests, (4) turning a threat into opportunity, and (5) anticipating the structure of the digital entertainment industry. In terms of our three key themes, this case offers an example of runaway change; it shows how quick and radical changes in what it takes to win put enormous pressure on companies' ability to cope with what they've got and actually force them to reconsider what the most important elements are of what they've got and how to put those to better use in the changed conditions. It also raises the question again of how to transform a company that is late in the game when it faces more threats than opportunities.●

Case 5.1

Electronic Arts in 2002

We want to be the number one entertainment company in the world.

—John Riccitiello, President and COO, Electronic Arts[1]

Introduction

Over the past decade, Electronic Arts (EA) negotiated both technological uncertainty and fickle consumer tastes to become a leading maker of video games for consoles and personal computers (PCs). In August 2002, EA's president and COO, John Riccitiello discussed several elements that had contributed to the company's success. He firmly believed that ultimately the company's success derived from EA's team. Riccitiello stressed that the management team—comprised of several executives including himself—formed the strategy and provided the leadership that guided the company. Riccitiello added:

> We nailed distribution. Our internal studio model works. We stopped marketing small games and became better at selecting games on which to bet big. Our marketing presence is stronger than anybody else's. We articulated a clear strategy: We focused our efforts on the Play Station (Sony) and not on Dreamcast (Sega); we redirected our online efforts but did not kill them. We focused on our people. We have made mistakes in the past, but our strength is that we can stop them and learn.

---

[1]All quotes from John Riccitiello are from the author's interview on 21 August 2002.

Frederic Descamps (MBA 2003) prepared this case under the supervision of Professor Robert A. Burgelman and Philip E. Meza as the basis for class discussion rather than to illustrate either effective or ineffective handling of an administrative situation. This case can be used in conjunction with "Electronic Arts in 1995" SM-24A and "Electronic Arts in 1999" SM-24B, Stanford Graduate School of Business.

Looking forward, Riccitiello said that EA would try to achieve its vision of becoming the "greatest entertainment company in the world" by focusing on just a few key strategic challenges. EA needed to remain the number one content provider for console, personal computer (PC), and online games. The company also needed to continue its success with attracting and developing talented people. Riccitiello showed a three-page presentation laying out the six areas critical to EA realizing its vision (Exhibit 1).

In 2002, however, EA had to contend with a series of new threats and opportunities that would affect its ability to realize its vision. Some challenges were technological, for example, online gaming, while others stemmed from the fast-changing developments among potential collaborators and competitors. Software giant Microsoft entered the market with its Xbox console at the same time that the once dominant, but more recently beleaguered, console and game maker Sega abandoned the console hardware business to focus solely on creating games. Since 1995 Sony had been the undisputed leader of the last generation consoles. Sony would try to extend its dominance in the 128-bit console market with its PlayStation 2, while Microsoft would likely prove to be a fierce competitor. Nintendo seemed relegated to third place, yet maintained a stranglehold on the market for younger audiences. Meanwhile, online gaming emerged as the fastest growing trend in the industry, but few companies had managed to generate profits out of it.

To go beyond its current success, EA had to find new sources of growth. Would online gaming ever be profitable for EA? What would it take to lead in this segment? What is the nature of the threat and challenge to EA represented by Microsoft and its Xbox, and the new generation of 128-bit consoles? What skills, competencies, and resources did EA need to compete?

General Industry Trends

Overall, the video game market was thriving. The industry had grown at an average rate of 12 percent per year over the last six years in the U.S. alone.[2] Moreover, the introduction of a new generation of 128-bit consoles

---

[2]"Fast Facts: Historical U.S. Sales Figures," The Interactive Digital Software Association (IDSA): http://www.idsa.com/ffbox7.html.

EXHIBIT 1 |

Electronic Arts Goals

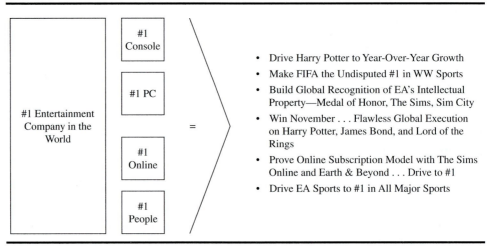

Source: John Riccitiello

initiated a new cycle of growth for the industry.[3] The video game industry generated revenues exceeding Hollywood's ticket sales, reaching $6.35 billion[4] in the United States alone and over $20 billion worldwide[5] in 2001 (Exhibit 2). In the same year, over 225 million units of games were sold in the United States, more than 11 times the number of tickets sold to National Basketball Association (NBA) and National Hockey League (NHL) games combined and about 14 times the number of National Football League (NFL) tickets sold in the 2000 season.[6] Some analysts predicted the video game industry would achieve household penetration of over 50 percent in the United States and

35 percent in Europe by 2005.[7] The entire industry experienced a 20 percent increase in sales for the first half of 2002, with analysts forecasting a similar performance for the second half of the year.[8] The industry was expected to grow by 40 percent in the United States by 2006.[9]

Video games had come a long way. No longer the realm of boys playing alone in their rooms, the PC and console game industry had grown into one of the largest and most dynamic segments of the entertainment industry. New gaming techniques such as massively multiplayer

---

[3] A new generation of more powerful consoles is released approximately every five years. Traditionally, the processing power increases greatly with each new generation. The last generation was based on 32-bit and later 64-bit processors, whereas the current generation is based on 128-bit processors.

[4] "2001 Game Industry Sales Data & Graphs," IDSA: http://www.idsa.com/2001SalesData.html.

[5] "Video Game Market Thriving Despite Economic Slowdown," *Los Angeles Times,* November 11, 2001. NB: Other sources estimated that movie box office revenue accounted for 14 percent ($8.26 billion) of the $59 billion spent on entertainment in 2001. Video and DVD sales and rentals accounted for 28 percent ($16.52 billion) in 2001. (Source: "Numbers," *Business 2.0,* September 2002, p. 38 citing ACNielsen; Kagan; Veronis Suhler.) While the issue of which was larger, video games revenue or box office receipts, may be important for bragging rights, the close content relationship between video games and movies, as well as the fact that movie rental/sales were double the size of box office receipts could bode well for the video game industry.

[6] "2001 Game Industry Sales Data & Graphs," IDSA: http://www.idsa.com/2001SalesData.html.

[7] "The Multimedia Markets in North America and Europe," p. I, Executive Summary, International Development Group, March 2002.

[8] NPD Funworld Press Release, August 20, 2002.

[9] "The U.S. Market for Video Games and Interactive Electronic Entertainment," Press Release, DFC Intelligence, February 2002.

EXHIBIT 2 | Dollar Sales for United States Video Game Industry PC and Console Software, 1997–2001

Year	Annual Sales
2001	$9.4 billion
2000	$6.6 billion
1999	$6.9 billion
1998	$6.2 billion
1997	$5.1 billion

Source: "First Quarter 2002 Video Games Fact Sheet", NPD Funworld: http://www.npdfunworld.com/funServlet?nextpage=trend_article1.html.

EXHIBIT 3 | Demographics of PC and Console Game Players by Percent of Total

PC	1997	1998	1999	2000	2001
Male	55%	62%	57%	59%	61%
Female	45%	38%	43%	41%	39%
Under 18	28%	30%	31%	28%	32%
18–35	35%	31%	29%	30%	28%
36+	38%	39%	40%	42%	39%
Consoles					
Male	73%	70%	65%	70%	74%
Female	27%	30%	35%	30%	26%
Under 18	54%	44%	46%	42%	43%
18–35	34%	36%	35%	37%	36%
36+	13%	20%	19%	21%	21%

Source: Interactive Digital Software Association (IDSA), 2001.

online gaming, dynamic content creation, community-driven modification, and persistent-state worlds added to the excitement (see below). Content continued to improve and titles originally developed for games, such as the popular "Mario Bros." and "Tomb Raiders" franchises, were extended into motion pictures. With more technology advances on the horizon, growing online game revenue opportunities, and increasingly advanced artistry and creativity by developers, the video game industry was likely to gain even more importance in the overall entertainment industry in the coming years.

In the 1980s, the core age demographic of gamers was 12–18 and overwhelmingly male. At that time, there were around 20 million people falling within that age group in the United States. By 2002, the core age demographic of video game players expanded to 10–45 for men and 10–35 for women, with a population of around 96 million people in those age ranges in the United States. By 2006, the population of these demographics could reach 120 million people.[10]

The range of game titles expanded to meet the needs of this older demographic. Many games were developed that featured more mature content, advanced game play and sports-oriented themes. This in turn attracted new audiences from among adults who previously had not been gamers. By 2000, 60 percent of all Americans, or about 145 million people, played console or PC games on a regular basis. The majority of console game players

were 18 and older.[11] Meanwhile, media franchises marketed to children such as Pokemon, Monsters Inc., and Disney, systematically added video games to their portfolios of intellectual property. The video game industry was now considered by many to be another form of mainstream entertainment—as important as movies and television (Exhibit 3).

The Console Market: A Cyclical but Predictable Industry

The console market was highly cyclical. The growth cycles were determined by the release of each new generation of consoles, which had occurred approximately every five years for the last two generations of consoles. Hardware and software cycles were closely intertwined in a relationship described by the "tie ratio," the average number of games sold for each console sold. The video game industry was one of the very few industries that knew in advance about the transitions it was going to experience and could therefore anticipate peaks and troughs in demand for content. The industry experienced well-defined and regular cycles over the life of any given platform (Exhibit 4).

The Transition Years: End of a Cycle and Market Anxiety

A few years into a generation of consoles, manufacturers start announcing work on the next new generation of more powerful consoles. As the release dates of the new

---

[10]"The Online Game Market 2002," DFC Intelligence, Press Release, June 2002.

[11]2000 Survey by Peter Hart Research for the IDSA, "State of the Industry—Report 2000–2001," P7, IDSA.

EXHIBIT 4 |

Gaming Console
Installed Base:
Cumulative Hardware
Unit Sales (U.S.)

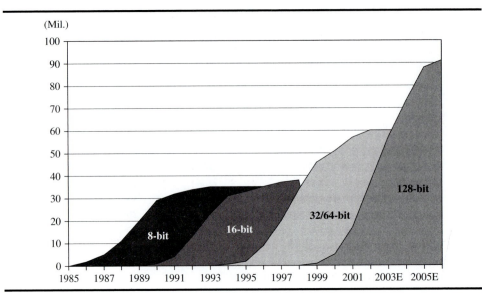

Source: "Content is King— An In-depth Look at Interactive Entertainment Software," P18, Wedbush Morgan
Securities, May 2002.

generation become nearer, sales of current generation consoles slow down. In turn, sales of the then-current generation software slow down dramatically, decreasing revenues for game companies. At the same time, game developers need to allocate resources to the production of new and updated titles for the next generation of consoles.

The Introduction of the New Generation (1st Year) New platforms, even when introduced simultaneously by competitors, usually commanded premium pricing. This helped companies recoup upfront investment in development, sales, and marketing. In the past, new consoles were usually first introduced in Japan followed by the United States and then other markets such as Europe and elsewhere in Asia up to six months later. Going forward, some believed that consoles would be first introduced in the United States. New platforms were purchased by early adopters; hard-core gamers who often own one or more consoles of the previous generations and are somewhat price insensitive. It was critical for each console manufacturer to feature star titles to help jump-start console sales. Console makers hoped to develop or attract software that was exclusive or otherwise unique in order to draw audiences to the new platform. Most console makers also act as game developers, creating game titles for the launch of their

consoles and also striking deals with third-party publishers such as EA, Activision, THQ, or Namco.

The Price War (1st and 2nd Years) After each console maker introduces their new platforms, competition heats up among the manufacturers, prompting them to lower the prices of their hardware. Price cuts are generally initiated by the manufacturer who first introduced its new console in the market. The other console manufacturers follow suit and reduce their prices. Most of them sell the platform hardware at a loss, hoping to make money on the sales of software and licensing fees to third party publishers. The reduction in console prices attracts a broader wave of gamers resulting in a surge in hardware and software sales.

Maturity and Mass Market (3rd and 4th Years) At this stage, console prices are further reduced, making the consoles accessible to more gamers. Games become more sophisticated as developers are now accustomed to the technical specifications of the consoles. In addition, they are able to publish more games due to streamlined development processes and reduced production costs. Game prices decrease. Console manufacturers reduce their first-party publisher activities, on the current generation, to focus on managing third-party publishers and investing in developing titles for the next generation of consoles.

The End of the Cycle—Market Anxiety (5th Year)

A couple of years before the beginning of a new cycle, console manufacturers announce their plans for the next generation of consoles. Core gamers refrain from buying games and systems in anticipation of the forthcoming generation. As the release dates for new consoles near, prices of the current generation machines drop further, making them a commodity. Soon, a new cycle begins and older generation consoles are slowly phased out.

The End of the 32-Bit/ 64-Bit Generations: One Clear Winner by Knockout

For Sega and Sony, their 32-bit console cycles began in 1994 with the introduction of the 32-bit Sega Saturn and Sony PlayStation in Japan. In 1995 Sega and Sony launched their 32-bit consoles in the United States. Later in 1995, Nintendo made a false start with its proposed 64-bit console. In 1996 Nintendo finally launched its 64-bit N64. During the 32-bit/64-bit cycle, Sony supplanted Nintendo as the leading console manufacturer and relegated Sega to third place. With double-digit growth, 1999 was a record-breaking year for the game industry. During 2000, the transition year, sales did not plummet but remained flat at $6 billion. Some thought this attested to a new level of durability and maturity for the overall market.

Sony emerged as the clear winner of the 32-bit/64-bit console generation battles. The company achieved an installed base of 90 million PlayStation Ones (PS1), compared to 18 million for Nintendo's N64 and a mere 9 million for Sega's Saturn.[12] The PS1 also benefited from a significantly broader software library. Unlike the existing Sega and Nintendo systems, the PlayStation platform (PSX) relied heavily on third-party software to generate hardware sales. Sony managed to appeal to nontraditional gamers such as young adults and adults, whereas its competitors appealed mainly to younger audiences. PlayStation became a significant line of business for Sony, at times accounting for more than a third of electronic giant's operating profit. (Exhibit 5).

Nintendo took second place with its strong positioning among kids and teenagers. It was also almost at par with Sony in Japan, their home market. Nintendo's strategy was to sell its hardware cheaper than its competitors, marketing their console more like a traditional toy, targeted toward the 8- to 16-year-old demographic. Sales of Nintendo's games followed the same seasonal pattern as toys, selling the most during holiday seasons. Nintendo managed to develop and perpetuate over the years strong properties such as "Mario Bros.," "Pokemon," and "Zelda" that had been tremendous successes among kids since its first console, the Nintendo Entertainment System (NES) debuted in the 1980s. Some of these properties managed to keep their appeal to gamers as they grew into young adults and adults. In 2001, Nintendo released the GameBoy Advance, a handheld console with the power of 32-bit generation consoles (Exhibit 6).

At the end of 2000, Sega retreated from the console market to focus exclusively on its strong software business. This decision came after several months of heavy losses incurred by its Dreamcast, the first of the 128-bit consoles. After having finished third behind Sony and Nintendo in the 32-bit/64-bit generations, Sega hoped to get a significant market advantage by launching its 128-bit console ahead of its competitors. The platform never achieved the sales needed to make a profit. Dreamcast did not attract the market's attention, which was anticipating the release of the PlayStation 2 (PS2). Sega raised the bar quite high by integrating a modem and a browser into the Dreamcast to enable multiplayer online gaming. Sega bet heavily on advanced technological features as well as on online gaming. In 1995 Sega was the first console manufacturer to develop and maintain an online gaming infrastructure, years ahead of its competitors. However, the manufacturing and infrastructure costs associated with the Dreamcast proved prohibitive in the end. Sega slowly phased out support for its Dreamcast console and became a third-party publisher like Electronic Arts (Exhibit 7).

Sega hoped to leverage competencies it had developed over the years as both a console manufacturer and software publisher. Sega benefited from popular proprietary intellectual property (IP), with titles such as "Sonic: The Hedgehog," that it had developed for its platforms and was now porting to Sony and Xbox platforms. Sega also decided to focus on professional sports titles, one of the most popular game genres. The pro sports genre had long been dominated by Electronic Arts, which owned the leading titles for most of the major professional sports. Sega also took aim at developing

---

[12]"The Multimedia Markets in North America and Europe," International Development Group, March 2002. Source of installed base for Sega Saturn (as of 1997): http://www.sega-saturn.com/saturn/other/news-jan.htm.

EXHIBIT 5 | Selected Financial Data for Sony Corporation (millions of Yen)

	31-Mar-2002	31-Mar-2001	31-Mar-2000	31-Mar-1999	31-Mar-1998
Sales—core business	7,542,068	7,276,150	6,651,389	6,754,786	6,715,866
Sales—other	36,190	38,674	35,272	49,396	45,138
Total sales	**7,578,258**	**7,314,824**	**6,686,661**	**6,804,182**	**6,761,004**
Cost of goods sold	5,700,771	5,476,409	4,984,765	4,955,107	4,889,696
Sales, general and administrative expenses	1,742,856	1,613,069	1,478,692	1,500,863	1,345,584
Unusual income / expenses	0	0	0	0	0
Total expenses	**7,443,627**	**7,089,478**	**6,463,457**	**6,455,970**	**6,235,280**
Interest expense	(36,436)	(43,015)	(42,030)	(48,275)	(62,524)
Other expenses	(5,420)	83,537	83,136	77,754	(3,937)
Pretax income	**92,775**	**265,868**	**264,310**	**377,691**	**459,263**
Income taxes	65,211	115,534	94,644	176,973	214,868
Income after taxes	**27,564**	**150,334**	**169,666**	**200,718**	**244,395**
Minority interests	16,240	15,348	(10,001)	(12,151)	(16,813)
Miscellaneous earnings adjustments	(34,423)	(44,455)	(37,830)	(9,563)	(5,514)
Net income (excluding extraordinary items and depreciation)	**9,381**	**121,227**	**121,835**	**179,004**	**222,068**
Accounting change	5,978	(104,473)	0	0	0
Net income (including extraordinary items and depreciation)	**15,359**	**16,754**	**121,835**	**179,004**	**222,068**

Note: The U.S. dollar ranged between 116.2–127.6 yen in 2001 and 117.9–133.7 yen in the first nine months of 2002.

Source: OneSource.

games for wireless devices with its Sega Mobile Division, which rolled out its first wireless games in August of 2002.

The Beginning of a New Cycle: The 128-Bit Generation

The new generation console cycle was kicked off in October of 2000 with the launch of Sony's PS2 in Japan, North America, and Europe. In 2001, the console market turned lukewarm, as gamers awaited the arrival of the Microsoft's Xbox and Nintendo's GameCube. The new generation console was based on 128-bit technology. In an unprecedented move inside the industry, Sony decided to make the PS2 backward compatible with PS1 games. The PS2 was an immediate success and Sony took the lead by

establishing a strong position in the market.[13] In December 2001, one year after its inception, the installed based of PS2 was around 20 million in Japan, the United States, and Europe.[14] The PS2 was also an attempt by Sony to reach beyond the game market. The PS2 was meant to be a

---

[13]Sony did not have adequate supply of PS2 consoles at launches. In its 10k report issued on 14 August 2001, EA noted that, "At launch, Sony shipped only half of the number of PlayStation 2 units to retailers in North America than it had originally planned, and it shipped significantly fewer units than planned at launch in Europe as well. [Console] shortages were announced as being caused by shortages of components for manufacturing. Due to these shortages, our results of operations for fiscal 2001 were adversely affected."

[14]"The Multimedia Markets in North America and Europe," Executive Summary, PV, International Development Group, March 2002.

EXHIBIT 6 | Selected Financial Data for Nintendo Corporation (millions of Yen)

	2002	**2001**	**2000**
Net sales	554,886	462,502	530,340
Cost of sales	334,620	278,462	289,638
Gross margin	**220,266**	**184,040**	**240,702**
Selling, general, and administrative	101,114	99,342	95,361
Operating income	**119,151**	**84,697**	**145,341**
Other income			
Interest income	22,904	39,133	23,119
Foreign exchange gain (loss)	43,419	66,335	(62,486)
Other	2,391	3,600	
Total other income	68,715	109,069	
Other expenses			
Total other expenses	**1,248**	**1,520**	NA
Income before income taxes and extraordinary items	**183,023**	**168,651**	NA
Provision for income tax and enterprise tax	74,351	93,710	46,675
Income taxes deferred	2,445	(21,358)	
Minority interests income	(218)	(303)	338
Net income	**106,444**	**96,603**	**56,061**

Note: NA indicates data was unavailable for the category. The U.S. dollar ranged between 116.2–127.6 yen in 2001 and 117.9–133.7 yen in the first nine months of 2002.

Source: Company reports.

family entertainment center, capable of playing DVDs and CDs, as well as video games. By being first on the market, Sony managed to get a head start over Microsoft's Xbox and Nintendo's GameCube. In April of 2002, 18 months after it introduced the PS2, Sony dropped its console price to $199. Microsoft and Nintendo dropped their prices to $199 and $149, respectively.

Traditionally, each new growth cycle increased technological innovation and sales revenues. In the past, the console market grew by 50 percent or more with each new generation of technology. EA estimated that the 128-bit generation consoles would develop an installed base of between 180–200 million systems worldwide by 2006, compared to the 125 million units of the previous generation console sold by 2002[15] (Exhibit 8).

By the end of 2002, Sony was expected to reach an installed based of slightly under 30 million PS2s in

North America and Europe, trailed by Microsoft and Nintendo with 10 million and 8 million units, respectively. In the battle for second place, Microsoft was ahead of Nintendo, which had strong market share in Japan and was popular among younger gamers. Sony already leaked its ambitious plans for the PS3, poised for release around 2005. Microsoft was said to be considering launching a midgeneration console, which would be an enhanced version of its Xbox, or even contemplating a leap straight to the next generation.

The PC Market

In 2001, the PC game market reached revenues of $1.5 billion in the United States and $1.2 billion in Europe.[16] (Exhibit 9) The market was currently dominated by four

---

[15]Ibid, p. 13.

[16]"The Multimedia Markets in North America and Europe," p. 7, International Development Group, March 2002.

EXHIBIT 7 | Selected Financial Data for Sega Corporation (millions of Yen)

	31-Mar-2001	31-Mar-2000	31-Mar-1999	31-Mar-1998	31-Mar-1997
Sales	242,913	339,055	266,194	331,605	432,826
Total sales	**242,913**	**339,055**	**266,194**	**331,605**	**432,826**
Cost of goods sold	218,235	290,492	201,819	270,710	347,325
Sales, general and administrative expenses	76,697	88,917	62,287	63,043	72,320
Total expenses	**294,932**	**379,409**	**264,106**	**333,753**	**419,645**
Interest expense	(2,414)	(3,226)	(2,175)	(3,719)	(2,768)
Other expenses	(1,060)	151	(32,563)	(10,628)	4,801
Pretax income	**(55,493)**	**(43,429)**	**(32,650)**	**(16,495)**	**15,214**
Income taxes	(792)	1,531	10,573	3,165	9,105
Income after taxes	**(54,701)**	**(44,960)**	**(43,223)**	**(19,660)**	**6,109**
Minority interests	2,971	2,080	342	339	108
Miscellaneous earnings adjustments	0	0	0	(16,314)	(4,185)
Net income (excluding extraordinary items and depreciation)	**(51,730)**	**(42,880)**	**(42,881)**	**(35,635)**	**2,032**
Net income (including extraordinary items and depreciation)	**(51,730)**	**(42,880)**	**(42,881)**	**(35,635)**	**2,032**

Note: Sega FY 2002 results unavailable as of September 2002. The U.S. dollar ranged between 116.2–127.6 yen in 2001 and 117.9–133.7 yen in the first nine months of 2002.

Source: OneSource.

publishers: Electronic Arts, Vivendi Universal Games, Infogrames Entertainment, and Microsoft. These publishers represented 64 percent of the retail market.

There were a few important differences between the console and the PC game markets. The PC platform changed more rapidly than did platforms for consoles. New PC processors were put on the market every quarter and 3D accelerating video cards every six months or so. Consequently, PC games were usually more advanced than their console counterparts since they took advantage of the more powerful machines. In 2002, top of the line PC's featured over 2GHz processors with 512MB of RAM and GeoForce 4 video cards, whereas consoles were equipped with processors running around 300 MHz. In addition, PCs were easily networked and connected to the Internet, whereas consoles were not. Online gaming drove the sales of numerous titles. Valve Software's best-selling title "Half-Life," for instance was still selling well a few years after its inception in 1998 thanks to "Counter-Strike," a free multiplayer modification that was exclusively played online.

PC games could be very attractive to developers since there were often no console-related royalties to pay, leading to greater margins for software producers. In addition, there were no console cycles to deal with, while PCs offered a continuously improving hardware platform. Yet, it was still a very difficult business. Over the last four years, PC game sales continued to grow steadily. Another complication to the PC market was the increasing competition from console games. Traditionally, the two markets used to cater to slightly different demographics and gaming genres. As consoles became more technologically advanced, certain genres such as strategy, role-playing, or adventure games, that used to be found only on PCs, also became available on consoles.

EXHIBIT 8 | Console Hardware Market Data

Console Hardware Unit Sales, North America and Europe, 1999–2005 Est.

(in 000 units) Total North America	1999 18,315	2000 15,273	2001 21,060	2002E 27,261	2003E 28,146	2004E 24,609	2005E 17,465
Nintendo 64	3,900	2,694	1,053	107	N/A	N/A	N/A
Nintendo GameCube	N/A	N/A	1,290	4,320	5,292	5,076	3,564
Sony PlayStation	6,265	3,410	2,376	1,391	535	N/A	N/A
Sony PlayStation 2	N/A	1,144	6,552	8,000	8,367	6,848	4,415
Microsoft Xbox	N/A	N/A	1,492	5,243	6,527	6,420	4,066
Game Boy/Color	8,150	8,025	2,996	1,540	N/A	N/A	N/A
Game Boy Advance	N/A	N/A	5,301	6,660	7,425	6,265	5,420
Total Europe	**12,163**	**10,475**	**11,981**	**17,205**	**20,794**	**22,435**	**21,365**
Nintendo 64	1,090	612	275	115	N/A	N/A	N/A
Nintendo GameCube	N/A	N/A	N/A	2,335	3,165	3,905	4,510
Sony PlayStation	6,768	3,395	2,054	980	630	355	N/A
Sony PlayStation 2	N/A	658	4,363	6,120	7,810	7,630	6,230
Microsoft Xbox	N/A	N/A	N/A	2,595	3,630	4,485	5,275
Game Boy/Color	4,305	5,810	2,419	650	N/A	N/A	N/A
Game Boy Advance	N/A	N/A	2,870	4,410	5,559	6,060	5,350
Total	**30,478**	**25,748**	**33,041**	**44,466**	**48,940**	**47,044**	**38,830**
Total (in 000s of US$)	**2,122,422**	**1,690,901**	**4,908,515**	**6,772,107**	**6,406,709**	**5,279,600**	**4,195,525**

Source: "The Multimedia Markets in North America and Europe," p. 12, International Development Group, March 2002.

Console Hardware Installed Base, North America and Europe, 1999–2005 Est.

(in 000 units) Total North America	1999 64,717	2000 79,990	2001 101,058	2002E 128,319	2003E 98,762	2004E 92,230	2005E 109,695
Nintendo 64	14,578	17,272	18,325	18,432	N/A	N/A	N/A
Nintendo GameCube	N/A	N/A	1,290	5,610	10,902	15,978	19,542
SonyStation	23,429	26,839	29,215	30,606	31,141	N/A	N/A
SonyStation 2	N/A	1,144	7,696	15,696	24,063	30,911	35,326
Microsoft Xbox	N/A	N/A	1,500	6,743	13,270	19,690	23,756
Game Boy/Color	26,710	34,735	37,731	39,271	N/A	N/A	N/A
Game Boy Advance	N/A	N/A	5,301	11,961	19,386	25,651	31,071
Total Europe	**45,915**	**56,390**	**68,471**	**85,676**	**70,224**	**92,659**	**87,070**
Nintendo 64	5,090	5,702	5,987	6,102	N/A	N/A	N/A
Nintendo GameCube	N/A	N/A	N/A	2,335	5,500	9,405	13,915
SonyStation	19,560	22,955	24,989	25,969	26,599	26,954	N/A
SonyStation 2	N/A	658	5,131	11,251	19,061	26,691	32,921
Microsoft Xbox	N/A	N/A	N/A	2,595	6,225	10,710	15,985
Game Boy/Color	21,265	27,075	29,494	30,144	N/A	N/A	N/A
Game Boy Advance	N/A	N/A	2,870	7,280	12,839	18,899	24,249
Total	**110,632**	**136,380**	**169,529**	**213,995**	**168,986**	**184,889**	**196,765**

Source: "The Multimedia Markets in North America and Europe," p. 13, International Development Group, March 2002.

(continued)

EXHIBIT 8 | Console Software Market Data (cont.)

Console Software Unit Sales, North America and Europe, 1999–2005 Est.

(in 000 units) Total North America	1999 121,400	2000 126,441	2001 137,803	2002E 157,199	2003E 179,896	2004E 178,919	2005E 152,284
Nintendo 64	28,500	29,141	14,605	1,080	N/A	N/A	N/A
Nintendo GameCube	N/A	N/A	3,639	19,476	29,900	36,233	30,294
SonyStation	66,500	60,900	49,118	23,868	6,048	N/A	N/A
SonyStation 2	N/A	2,812	31,665	52,909	74,358	65,664	51,188
Microsoft Xbox	N/A	N/A	4,926	26,068	37,830	46,522	37,902
Game Boy/Color	26,400	33,588	23,759	8,448	1,960	N/A	N/A
Game Boy Advance	N/A	N/A	10,091	25,350	29,800	30,500	32,900
Total Europe	**58,261**	**66,172**	**69,610**	**67,294**	**93,589**	**119,569**	**143,380**
Nintendo 64	7,201	6,173	3,233	1,139	N/A	N/A	N/A
Nintendo GameCube	N/A	N/A	N/A	7,315	13,758	20,795	32,330
SonyStation	41,843	40,926	32,798	11,610	6,420	2,588	N/A
SonyStation 2	N/A	1,390	14,475	26,865	38,940	46,682	47,840
Microsoft Xbox	N/A	N/A	N/A	6,981	15,535	23,149	34,140
Game Boy/Color	9,217	17,683	14,921	2,564	N/A	N/A	N/A
Game Boy Advance	N/A	N/A	4,183	10,820	18,936	26,355	29,070
Total	**179,661**	**192,613**	**207,413**	**224,493**	**273,485**	**298,488**	**295,664**

Source: "The Multimedia Markets in North America and Europe," p. 18, International Development Group, March 2002.

Wireless Games

Games that traditionally had been played on PCs and consoles were reaching other platforms such as the Internet and wireless devices or personal digital assistants (PDAs). Though still limited in size and scope, these markets were growing quickly and were expected to contribute incremental revenue in the latter end of the current game console cycle and into the next. These channels could constitute a new attractive market for video game companies. As telecom operators deployed next-generation 2.5G and 3G wireless networks, some looked to games to provide compelling advanced applications to help speed customer adoption. In 2000, there were 7.3 million wireless data subscribers in the United States, but some analysts expected this market to grow dramatically. One report projected the number of wireless data subscribers to increase to 137.5 million by 2005.[17]

There were several barriers to the development of wireless gaming. Wireless handset manufacturers used closed, proprietary operating systems in their phones.[18] Further, most wireless devices were not browser-enabled and could accommodate only very limited services such as text messaging. This constrained the quality and quantity of games available for wireless devices. The small size and poor quality of the video display available on next-generation wireless devices further inhibited game attractiveness and the limited data storing capacity of these devices increased demand on network bandwidth—an expense that the small base of users could not support. In 2002, EA had made only small investments in this market.

The Online Gaming Phenomenon

By 2002, three types of online gaming emerged: multiplayer online games, massively multiplayer online games in persistent state worlds, and portal games.

---

[17]"Efiles: Games without Frontiers," Gartner Group Eweek, July 2, 2001.

[18]NB: In June 1998, leading mobile phone makers Nokia, Motorola, and Ericsson and handheld computer maker Psion formed a joint venture called Symbian to develop software to run mobile phones and devices. By 2002, Nokia was known to sell its software cheaply to other mobile phone producers.

EXHIBIT 9 | PC Data

Multimedia Home PC Installed Base, North America and Europe, 1999–2005 Est. (000)

	1999	2000	2001	2002E	2003E	2004E	2005E
Total North America	51,190	58,932	65,023	70,946	76,536	81,671	86,360
Total Europe	36,218	44,648	51,722	58,171	64,874	71,673	78,530
Total	**87,408**	**103,580**	**116,745**	**129,117**	**141,410**	**153,344**	**164,890**

Software Sales Data

PC CD-ROM Software Unit Sales 1999–2005 (in 000s)

	1999	2000	2001	2002E	2003E	2004E	2005E
Total North America	88,744	91,503	89,210	91,886	94,940	98,596	102,529
Total Europe	48,735	53,492	56,008	59,125	62,563	65,755	68,925
Total	**137,479**	**144,995**	**145,218**	**151,011**	**157,503**	**164,351**	**171,454**

PC CD-ROM Software Sales 1999–2005 (in 000s of US$)

	1999	2000	2001	2002E	2003E	2004E	2005E
Total North America	2,106,157	1,920,642	1,867,924	1,925,866	1,941,295	1,924,581	2,001,876
Total Europe	1,717,955	1,590,300	1,516,343	1,556,605	1,584,043	1,623,130	1,665,496
Total	**3,824,112**	**3,510,942**	**3,384,267**	**3,482,472**	**3,523,140**	**3,545,924**	**3,665,579**

Entertainment PC CD-ROM Software Unit Sales 1999–2005 (in 000s)

	1999	2000	2001	2002E	2003E	2004E	2005E
Total North America	59,199	66,332	68,795	72,095	76,259	80,382	84,896
Total Europe	36,892	41,757	44,512	47,770	51,360	54,790	58,100
Total	**96,091**	**108,089**	**113,307**	**119,865**	**127,619**	**135,172**	**142,996**

Entertainment PC CD-ROM Software Sales 1999–2005 (in 000s of US$)

	1999	2000	2001	2002E	2003E	2004E	2005E
Total North America	1,439,849	1,410,438	1,496,641	1,562,549	1,599,514	1,610,024	1,697,285
Total Europe	1,271,584	1,238,909	1,208,915	1,262,653	1,299,610	1,353,972	1,407,413
Total	**2,711,433**	**2,649,347**	**2,705,556**	**2,825,202**	**2,899,124**	**2,963,996**	**3,104,698**

Source: "The Multimedia Markets in North America and Europe," p. 2 and pp. 4, 5, 6, and 7, International Development Group, March 2002.

Multiplayer gaming, the first type of online game to appear, was introduced to the mass market in 1991. Early titles such as "Doom" and "Duke Nukem" were among the first games to be published with a multiplayer-option and played over local area networks (LANs) or direct dial-up connections. With the massive adoption of the Internet, online gaming became one of main trends to shape PC games over the past decade. The most popular genres were first-person shooters, real-time strategy, and more recently, role-playing games. An increasing number of games were played exclusively online. With hundreds of thousand of gamers playing online at any given moment throughout the world, online games opened a new universe of possibilities both for gamers and game makers. Instead of merely battling their computers, players now tested their skills against human counterparts, who were unpredictable by nature. This constant reservoir of players endlessly expanded the possibilities of games. In addition, these games did not have any specific endings and could be played indefinitely.

A new subset of online games called massively multiplayer online games (MMOG) or persistant-state world games emerged. These games staged persistent worlds, that is, games that subsist independently of the players on a continuous basis and can host simultaneously hundred of thousands of players. These new types of games featured continuously developing original story lines, and some actually reached out to players into the physical world through cell phones, instant messaging, pagers, or fax machines.

Portal games were different from the two others types of online gaming. They were played almost exclusively on the Web via portals that offered a wide variety of games. The types of games played were simpler, more traditional games such as backgammon, chess, and card games. They appealed to a much broader audience of casual gamers. This audience was drawn to free, easy-to-play games offered by a range of portals and pure-play online game sites. Yahoo!'s Games and EA's Pogo portals were among the most visited. In 2002, there were between 4,000 and 5,000 online gaming sites worldwide, with more than 30 million people in the United States playing an online game at least once per month.[19] Casual web gaming represented half of the time spent on broadband entertainment.[20]

By 2006, 114 million people were predicted to play online worldwide and 23 million people playing via consoles.[21]

Opportunities in Online Gaming

For game makers, the development costs of multiplayer online games were higher than for traditional games. Still, online multiplayer features became standard, and the vast majority of PC games shipped in 2002 had this capability. For game publishers, the challenge associated with online games was keeping players interested. One way of doing that was to introduce new content into the game on a regular basis. For instance, they staged events, introduced new quests, and hired players to play roles or trigger events such as natural catastrophes in their virtual worlds. The role of managing content was new to publishers who, like other consumer software vendors, were used to simply releasing their products and then issuing add-ons and patches and selling expansion packs. With online multiplayer games, the life cycle of games was extended beyond purchase and launch.

To finance the development and maintenance costs of online games, game makers adopted subscription-based business models. After purchasing a game, players had to pay a monthly fee to access the corresponding online content. Many online services that were originally free started to require paid subscriptions, typically ranging from $10 to $20 per month for unlimited game time. With hundreds of thousands of paying players, popular online computer games such as "EverQuest" and "Ultima Online" generated steady revenue streams and were envied by other segments of the software and entertainment industry. For instance, Sony's "EverQuest" had attracted about 400,000 subscribers worldwide, and generated $5 million in revenue every month with a gross-profit margin of over 40 percent.[22] Yet the majority of online gamers were still reluctant to pay to play. In 2002, pay-based online games attracted only hard-core gamers. As with other media, video game publishers had to educate their customer base about this new model and justify the premium they required by offering attractive content that would keep players coming back and paying. These business models were far from perfect however; while Sony's "EverQuest" had been a success, Electronic Arts decided to close the doors on its "Majestic" online offering. Some predicted that total United States revenue from online gaming in 2002 would reach approximately $280 million, and grow at a rate of 25 percent to 30 percent each year until 2005.[23] Analysts thought advertising could account for one-third of these revenues while the bulk would come from subscriptions. With "The Sims Online" coming out in November 2002 and "Star Wars Online" slated for launch in 2003, a real test of the mass market popularity of online gaming may have been at hand.

The Challenges of Online Gaming

Online gaming presented many challenges to developers. Online computer games required higher up-front investments than traditional games. The game engines were more complex because they had to process interactions among players over networks, which increased their development costs. Also, game publishers had to make significant investments in the server infrastructure necessary to host games. Dedicated high-availability servers were needed to insure persistent play and a high quality of service, a prerequisite if companies wanted their players to continue paying subscriptions.

These games also required continued investment after the launch. As opposed to traditional games,

[19]"Interactive Entertainment—Hitting the Cycle's Sweet Spot," Credit Suisse First Boston, May 15, 2002.

[20]"Can Broadband Save Internet Media?" *McKinsey Quaterly,* no. 2, 2002.

[21]"The Online Game Market 2002," Press Release, DFC Intelligence, June 2002.

[22]Geoff Keighley, "The Sorcerer of Sony," *Business 2.0,* August 2002, http://www.business2.com/articles/mag/0,1640,42210,FF.html.

[23]"The Multimedia Markets in North America and Europe," Executive Summary, p. I, International Development Group, March 2002.

online game makers needed to dedicate entire creative teams to support the service after the game's launch. This turned video game companies into service providers, with requisite demands for competencies such as customer relationship management capabilities (24 hours/seven days per week). Other challenges to surmount included the lower than expected penetration of broadband and the necessary consumer education on pay-for-play gaming.

Online Console Gaming

Microsoft planned to launch its online console gaming service, called "Xbox Live," in Fall 2002. Microsoft announced it would spend over $2 billion over the next few years to build out the Xbox Live network and develop the next generation of its game console. From the start, Microsoft had looked toward online gaming, making its Xbox the only 128-bit console to integrate a cable modem. Microsoft developed a proprietary network infrastructure that favored the "walled-garden" or closed network, with Xbox gamers able to connect to each other only through the Microsoft-maintained Xbox Live system. Microsoft would even control bandwidth used to run titles from third-party publishers. The system would include games from Microsoft and third-party publishers. Microsoft planned to sell a $50 Xbox Live starter kit that included a headset, microphone, a one-year subscription to the service and software that allowed the Xbox to tap into an existing broadband Internet connection.

Nintendo planned to release its online gaming peripheral in Fall 2002. Selling for around $34, the device would feature both a dial-up and broadband adapters. Nintendo's online gaming strategy was the most conservative among the three console manufacturers. Nintendo would leave the management of online gaming to publishers. Game publishers themselves would be responsible for operating the online networks on which their games ran. Nintendo would neither collect any additional revenue from GameCube online games nor would it charge an access fee. Sony announced the launch of its online gaming service in August 2002. Unlike Microsoft, Sony left it to individual game publishers to do the back-end work of maintaining servers and other infrastructure, while Sony would provide the software to make it work. The PS2 was not equipped with online capabilities. Sony sold a $40 adapter that supported both analog and digital Internet connections.

Despite the flurry of activity, the general sense among console makers was that online console gaming would not see a major uptake during this generation of consoles. Many analysts thought that online game investments would not pay off before the next new generation of consoles, expected in 2006, when broadband penetration in households likely would be higher. Also, game consoles had mass-market appeal because they only required a television set, compared to the expensive broadband Internet connections (ranging between $34–$54 per month in the United States) plus a monthly subscription for game content.

Electronic Arts Maintains Industry Leadership

In 2002, Electronic Arts was the leading publisher of both PC and third-party console titles (Exhibit 10). In the last quarter of FY2002 EA had three of the top 10 titles for both Sony's PS2 and PS1, as well as Microsoft's Xbox consoles. EA produced top-selling games in most of the existing genres. With the 128-bit cycle in full swing worldwide, EA enjoyed double-digit revenue growth in all of its geographic regions during FY2002. At a time when corporate balance sheets were under intense scrutiny, EA offered investors an unleveraged company with almost $1 billion in cash. In the fourth quarter of FY2002 alone, EA added over $300 million to its cash reserve (Exhibit 11).

EA Went Long on PlayStation

Since the middle of the 1990s, EA made three strategic decisions that accounted for most of its continued success. According to Frank Gibeau, vice president of North America sales and marketing, "the most important decision EA made over the last years was the single-minded deliberateness with which we bet on Sony's PS1 and then PS2." As it did during the 32/64-bit generation consoles with the PS1, EA bet that Sony's PS2 would become the dominant platform in the next generation. Gibeau said:

> We evaluate the potential of platforms by asking three questions: Does the underlying technology enable us to develop advanced entertainment? [Beyond this] What is the probability of success in the three major markets: Asia, the United States and Europe? For Microsoft, the answer was negative in Asia and to a lesser extent negative in all markets because of Microsoft's lack of reputation as a console gaming company. The response was neutral for Sega and positive for Nintendo and Sony. Finally, does each manufacturer have the capital and corporate will to support its console business?

EXHIBIT 10 | U.S. Market Share Per Publisher

United States Market Overview
Top 10 Entertainment PC CD-ROM Publishers 2001 (Ranked by Value)

Publisher	Dollar Sales	Unit Sales	# of SKUs	Market Share (by $)	Market Share (by units)	ARP
Electronic Arts	$312,359,172	12,763,748	281	22%	20%	$24
VUG	$266,055,440	10,717,601	371	19%	17%	$25
Infogrames	$210,249,940	11,773,327	471	15%	18%	$18
Microsoft	$121,942,997	3,575,843	75	9%	6%	$34
Activision	$73,387,008	3,759,944	252	5%	6%	$20
Ubi Soft	$53,456,544	1,617,807	97	4%	2%	$33
Take-Two	$49,090,979	2,065,259	181	3%	3%	$24
Disney	$33,220,369	2,033,554	76	2%	3%	$16
Valusoft	$27,822,531	2,199,364	79	2%	3%	$13
Eidos	$22,084,396	895,793	55	2%	1%	$25
Top 10 total	**$1,169,669,377**	**51,402,241**	**1,938**	**83%**	**79%**	**$23**
Ent. CD-Rom Total	**$1,413,026,071**	**64,857,223**	**3,278**	**100%**	**100%**	**$22**

Source: "The Multimedia Markets in North America and Europe," International Development Group, March 2002.

United States Market Overview
Top 10 Console and Handheld Publishers 2001 (Ranked by Value)

Publisher	Dollar Sales	Mkt Share by $	Unit Sales	Mkt Share by Unit	ARP
1. Electronic Arts	$730,376,846	16%	18,394,255	13%	$40
2. Nintendo	$710,479,261	16%	19,843,015	14%	$36
3. Activision	$366,792,950	8%	11,295,702	8%	$32
4. Sony	$358,021,304	8%	11,878,606	8%	$30
5. THQ	$284,058,201	6%	8,819,582	6%	$32
6. Take-Two	$204,587,897	4%	6,475,495	5%	$32
7. Konami	$173,642,109	4%	4,406,766	3%	$39
8. Infogrames	$159,432,835	4%	7,248,952	5%	$22
9. Sega	$157,916,167	3%	5,334,590	4%	$30
10. Acclaim	$148,959,220	3%	5,466,486	4%	$27
Top 10 Total	**$3,294,266,790**	**72%**	**99,163,449**	**70%**	**$33**
Market Total	**$4,547,095,791**	**100%**	**140,986,669**	**100%**	**$32**

Source: "The Multimedia Markets in North America and Europe," International Development Group, March 2002.

The answer was negative for Sega so EA decided to support the PS2 over the Dreamcast.[24]

EA concentrated its development efforts on the PS2 and supported its launch aggressively by releasing their best-selling titles on it. Gibeau explained, "From our standpoint, it is like a military battle: the winner is the one who gets there first and with the most numerous forces."

EA even passed Sony as the number 1 publisher of titles for the PS2 with 28 percent market share and 5 of the top 10 titles in the United States in fiscal year 2002.[25]

Why EA Learned to Love Transitions

Most game developers dreaded the transition years between two generations of consoles. For the majority of game companies that derive lot of their revenues

---

[24]All quotes from Frank Gibeau are from the author's interview on 16 August 2002.

[25]2002 Annual Report.

EXHIBIT 11 | Selected Financial Data for Electronic Arts

	Year Ended March 31, 2001			
	EA Core (excl. EA.com)	**EA.com**	**Adjustments and Eliminations**	**Electronic Arts**
Net revenues from unaffiliated customers	$1,280,172	$ 42,101	$ —	$1,322,273
Group sales	2,658	—	(2,658)	—
Total net revenues	1,282,830	42,101	(2,658)	1,322,273
Cost of goods sold from unaffiliated customers	640,239	12,003	—	652,242
Group cost of goods sold	—	2,658	(2,658)	—
Total cost of goods sold	640,239	14,661	(2,658)	652,242
Gross profit	642,591	27,440	—	670,031
Operating expenses:				
Marketing and sales	163,928	12,475	8,933	185,336
General and administrative	93,885	10,156	—	104,041
Research and development	248,534	77,243	63,151	388,928
Network development and support	—	51,794	(51,794)	—
Customer relationship management	—	11,357	(11,357)	—
Carriage fee	—	8,933	(8,933)	—
Amortization of intangibles	12,829	6,494	—	19,323
Charge for acquired in-process technology	—	2,719	—	2,719
Total operating expenses	519,176	181,171	—	700,347
Operating income (loss)	123,415	(153,731)	—	(30,316)
Interest and other income, net	16,659	227	—	16,886
Income (loss) before benefit from income taxes and minority interest	140,074	(153,504)	—	(13,430)
Benefit from income taxes	(4,163)	—	—	(4,163)
Income (loss) before minority interest	144,237	(153,504)	—	(9,267)
Minority interest in consolidated joint venture	(1,815)	—	—	(1,815)
Net income (loss) before retained interest in EA.com	$ 142,422	$(153,504)	$ —	$ (11,082)

BALANCE SHEET DATA AT FISCAL YEAR END	**2002**	**2001**	**2000**	**1999**	**1998**
Cash, cash equivalents and short-term investments	**$ 796,936**	$ 466,492	$ 339,804	$312,822	$374,560
Marketable securities	**6,869**	10,022	236	4,884	3,721
Working capital	**699,561**	478,701	440,021	333,256	408,098
Long-term investments	**—**	8,400	8,400	18,400	24,200
Total assets	**1,699,374**	1,378,918	1,192,312	901,873	745,681
Total liabilities	**452,982**	340,026	265,302	236,209	181,713
Minority interest	**3,098**	4,545	3,617	2,733	—
Total stockholders' equity	**1,243,294**	1,034,347	923,393	662,931	563,968

Source: Company reports

(*continued*)

EXHIBIT 11 | Selected Financial Data for Electronic Arts (cont.)

Net Revenues by Region for Fiscal 2002 and 2001

	2002	2001	Increase	% change
North America	$ 1,093,244	$ 831,924	$ 261,320	31.4%
Europe	519,458	386,728	132,730	34.3%
Asia Pacific	53,376	51,039	2,337	4.6%
Japan	58,597	52,582	6,015	11.4%
International	631,431	490,349	141,082	28.8%
Consolidated Net Revenues	$ 1,724,675	$1,322,273	$ 402,402	30.4%

Source: Company reports.

Worldwide Net Revenues by Product Line for Fiscal 2002 and 2001 (in thousands)

	2002	2001	Increase/(Decrease)	% change
EA Studio:				
PlayStation 2	$ 482,882	$ 258,988	$ 223,894	86.4%
PC	456,292	405,256	51,036	12.6%
PlayStation	189,535	309,988	(120,453)	(38.9%)
Xbox	78,363	—	78,363	N/A
Nintendo GameCube	51,740	—	51,740	N/A
Game Boy Advance	43,653	—	43,653	N/A
Game Boy Color	38,026	—	38,026	N/A
Advertising	38,024	6,175	31,849	515.8%
Online Subscriptions	30,940	28,878	2,062	7.1%
License, OEM and Other	24,762	20,468	4,294	21.0%
N64	18,152	67,044	(48,892)	(72.9%)
Online Packaged Goods	3,296	3,198	98	3.1%
	1,455,665	1,099,995	355,670	32.3%
Affiliated Label:	269,010	222,278	46,732	21.0%
Consolidated Net Revenues	$ 1,724,675	$1,322,273	$402,402	30.4%

Source: Company reports.

from the console market, it meant plummeting sales and profits. In 2001, the industry had seen rough times. Several companies including Sega, Electronic Arts, and Infogrames eliminated jobs to trim expenses. A number of small game studios shut their doors or looked for buyers because they could not cover development costs.

EA's CFO Stan McKee described how the company handled platform transitions.

> Having lived through several console generations, we have learned to adapt through the difficult console transition period. Actually, we see the transition years between two generation of consoles as an opportunity for us to get fit and lean. One year before the transition

starts, EA starts trimming. Last year was the middle of a transition period for us, but we managed to keep operating expenses in the low single digits while revenues were up 30 percent, which levered income up by 100 percent.

> We clamp down on "science projects" among studios, i.e., small development efforts that we don't know about that consume an enormous amount of resources when you multiply one or two of these across all of our studios. We'll watch expenses and sometimes make the studios more responsible for sticking to budgets. No area is sacred and immune to this approach. However, the key franchises such as "The Sims" or our sports titles are not going to get starved.

In parallel, EA mitigates the lower console revenues associated with the transition by getting more revenues out of the PC market as well as by beefing up its global distribution capability.

This practice is now deeply ingrained in the company's tactics and will be used again for the next transition. In short, we say that transition is our friend.[26]

Managing Risks and Making Hits

At the heart of EA's hits are hit-making studios. In 2002, EA operated 11 studios in four countries. Studios were responsible for conceiving and developing games. The studios housed a mix of game developers and programmers.

John Riccitiello described how the role of studios inside EA evolved over the years as they learned to collaborate more with other parts of the organization:

> Studios are traditionally at the center of the organization—they are the heroes—however the marketing function is increasingly equally responsible for the success of games. This creates creative friction. For instance, there will be debates concerning the complexity of a game versus the size of the market. It is critical to find the key thing that will make a game a success. Together, the studio and marketing teams partner to ensure we create a great gaming experience that is well targeted and extremely focused on a specific gameplay experience.
>
> In other cases, the issue is uphill marketing, which is the extra marketing effort that is sometimes necessary to make a game a success. The publishing organization often does not want to do it, so this requires being able to decide which are the truly worthy titles. To be able to do this requires teamwork, which depends on the mutual respect that exists between the key executives heading our studios and the publishing division. There are many personal bonds between these two groups.

Rusty Rueff, senior vice president of human resources for EA, outlined the company's studio strategy:

> We see our system of studios as a family: you can have siblings with immensely different personalities but still they share the same values stemming from their familial education. Likewise, when we acquire a new studio, we look for a baseline set of values but then we encourage different personalities to coexist.

Our pipeline of creativity is one of our top competitive advantages. This stems from three elements. First, EA has the top talents in the industry. Our people have track records of creating hit games and are recognized by their peers in the industry. Many have lived through several technology cycles and transitions and have learned to adapt quickly to new technology.

Second, we are investing significant efforts in training and development to make sure our people are ahead of the curve in terms of technology. The only way to be the number one on current and next-generation consoles is to have top mastery of the technology.

Third, today we enjoy a strong culture of knowledge-sharing among our studios. This is also key to our success: People share tips, tricks, code, development tools and technical breakthroughs on a regular basis across our studios.

The next challenge is to grow the next generation of creative leaders in our studios. In Hollywood, people who can direct a $100 million movie project are very few. This is because the people who finance such projects only trust a limited number of people with the appropriate skills. The video game industry is becoming similar with production budgets increasing more and more. A few years ago, one person could be responsible for multiple franchises. Now, we assign one creative leader per project, sometimes on multiple platforms. The development cycle of a game is around 2 years and can require a team of over 60 people. Who do you trust for such projects? It is therefore key for EA to be able to nurture our creative managers and help them grow to handle such responsibilities.[27]

EA has also learned to better allocate its resources to maximize the market potential of its games. John Riccitiello explained:

> Last year, barely any of the products we launched lost money. This stems from two facts. First, we are not afraid to kill products, even just before their launch, if we think they are not going to make it big. We stopped marketing small games. The winning formula for us is to have fewer SKUs (stock-keeping units) and invest more per title. We get a better payoff by letting certain products die and by putting twice as much money behind other products. Five years ago, we used to ship between 65 and 70 SKUs a year. This year, we are shipping 58 SKUs. This means

[26]All quotes from Stan McKee are from the author's interview on 7 August 2002.

[27]All quotes from Russell Rueff are from the author's interview on 21 August 2002.

we are getting better at what we are doing. It is like a diet. This is easy to understand why it is good for you, but conceptually hard to do.

In turn, we are betting more on big games. We go big on each of our launches. We do not have any stealth launches. In the creative industry, it is important to go big, to get the marketplace to know what you are doing. EA is expert at moving audiences and creating hits.

Feeding and Milking the Video Cash Cow

Electronic Arts developed several lines of successful franchise products including "FIFA Soccer," "Madden NFL," "NHL Hockey," "Triple Play," and "The Sims." In 2002, EA established a dominant position in most of the gaming genres. This was achieved year after year by producing a broad type of "A" titles. For instance, in 2001 "Harry Potter" was EA's most successful title launch ever, with sales of more than 7 million units on four platforms. EA managed to create new genres with games like "The Sims." In March 2002, EA announced that it had shipped over 6.3 million copies of "The Sims" worldwide and over 12 million units including "Sims" expansion packs, making it the best-selling PC game of all time. Still, no title made up more than 10 percent of EA's total revenues, eliminating dependencies on any single brand or release. Unlike many of its competitors, EA could afford to have a portfolio strategy: exploring both strategic and risky avenues. Risky projects were financed by titles that were more predictable, such as sequels to hits. Smaller video game companies did not have this luxury since they relied on fewer titles and had to consider breakeven economics on a title-by-title basis.

EA can afford to not break even quickly on a few titles or suffer a few lackluster years developing a title franchise. Stan McKee said, "EA's business is not entirely based on hit picking," adding:

> Actually, I would argue that 80 percent of our revenues are predictable. We have a lot of recurring revenues from iterations of existing licenses. For example, sports games, which generate approximately 45 percent of our revenues, are mostly simple iterations over the years. Likewise, Sims' expansion packs sell approximately 2 million units on average.

Over the last 10 years, an important trend in games had been licensed brands and sequels. As video games moved into the mass-market, brands and sequels began to dominate. The company's popular franchises in the sports genre and leading non-sports products like "*007*,"

"The Sims," "Medal of Honor," and others give EA a level of sales predictability found nowhere else in the industry.

Betting on EA Sports

Thanks to top-of-the-line sports games, grassroots marketing techniques and massive amounts of TV advertising during major sports events, EA Sports was becoming one of the most recognized sports brands in the United States. EA Sports game franchises dominated their respective markets worldwide. EA aspired to become one of the top sports brands, on par with Nike, ESPN, or *Sports Illustrated*.

Since its beginning in the 1990s, EA Sports had been able to fend off serious competition in the sports genre, in particular from Microsoft and Sega. Sega publicly stated that it was aiming for EA Sports. With sports games representing 25 percent of the industry and growing at 25 percent per year, some at EA were unsure why Sega would target the leviathan of the industry instead of focusing on building its own franchises. Even Microsoft, as yet, failed to make a dent into EA's sports franchises. John Riccitiello said:

> On football, EA enjoys 75 percent market shares against Sony, Sega, and Microsoft, three of the biggest electronic entertainment companies in the world. EA outsells Microsoft 9 to 1 on their own platform in sports games. Microsoft said a few years ago that they would knock us off on PC sports games. It got us scared at first, but we continued to focus on producing great games. Microsoft was reducing their prices to compete against us. It didn't work and they exited because they could not build any continuity.

EA Vice President of Marketing and Brand Innovation, Don Transeth, who was part of the original team that launched the EA Sports brand discussed EA's success in the sports genre:

> From the very beginning, we pinned our ambitions on becoming a major sports brand with benchmarks such as Nike, ESPN, *Sports Illustrated* and the like. We have always seen ourselves as a sports company that makes video games. While our competitors focus exclusively on creating sports games, we have managed to make our games part of the sports world. Cyberstrator [a device for using Madden graphics to demonstrate plays on TV broadcasts] is a prime example of our strategy. We offered the most prominent TV sports programs, such as *Monday Night Football*,

the use of our Madden NFL game engine to simulate and create views of the games to support their pre- and postgame commentaries. All the while, our brands and our technology are prominently displayed to the large audience.[28]

Grassroots Marketing Strategy: The Example of Madden NFL 2003

Aside from creating content, EA's success in the sports genre stemmed from its extensive marketing efforts. To support its sports brands, EA used a variety of approaches to marketing. Those ranged from traditional media advertising, PR events involving big-name athletes such as golf pro Tiger Woods and pro basketball player Jason Kidd, co-promotion partnerships with selected top brands, event sponsorship, promotional events around major sports venues like the Super Bowl, syndicated TV programming, and numerous grassroots initiatives.

John Riccitiello pointed to "Madden NFL 2003" as exemplifying EA's approach to marketing:

> First, we work hard at generating very positive word of mouth from key purchase influencers through grassroots marketing strategies. In the purchase process, most people ask others about what games they should buy. They also look at Web sites and magazines. The gamer population can be segregated into three groups: at the top of the pyramid, there is the core audience of hard-core gamers. In the case of Madden, those are NFL players, football players, fraternity guys, football fans. At the bottom of the pyramid is the mass-market.

> Every other company does a good job at reaching mass-market gamers. Yet, we are second to none at reaching the top of the pyramid. We put a lot of emphasis on grassroots marketing for journalists, Web sites, beta-testers, EA campus representatives, trade magazines, by being present at football games, by going directly to football players. Our goal is that when one of these core influencers is asked about a game, he has been hit a dozen times by our marketing message and will therefore recommend our game.

> EA Campus Reps initiative is a great example of how we excel at reaching key influencers. Every year, EA Sports enlists over 30 campus representatives selected among students to promote our games on university

campuses all over the United States. We bring them to our headquarters to train them and expose them to our brand. They then become peer marketers, whose mission is to create a buzz about EA Sports on campus. They in turn look for trendsetters and taste makers on campus and get our products in their hands.

> The second part of our marketing strategy is advertising. We consider that the war starts months before the launch of the game. As such, our advertising efforts start between 6 and 12 months before the actual launch. For instance, we were advertising for Madden on the NFL draft five months before the actual launch of the game. We run commercials with rookies during programs that typically get low viewers' rating but are watched by super hard-core football fans. Sports writers wrote about our commercials and that also helped us spread the word. In the end, we have created this omnipresent presence in the market even before our game has arrived.

> Third, we invest a lot in our distribution operations to make sure our games arrive on time at the thousands of stores that carry our products.

EA's Publishing and Distribution Strategy[29]

EA was the first company in the video game industry to develop a direct distribution system. As early as 1984, the company chose to make direct distribution a cornerstone of its strategy. Ted Judson recounts the four historical steps EA took to build its top-notch distribution system:[30]

> In 1984, we were the first company to sell direct to Egghead [a national computer products retailer] and the mom-and-pops [small retailers]. It was controversial for a $25 million company, as we were at that time, but it forced us to create a sales organization. The second turning point was when we entered the console market in 1988 with games for the Nintendo console. This enabled us to develop broader distribution relationship with specialized retailers. The most important breakthrough came at the beginning of the 1990s when sales of our games for the Sega 16-bit system exploded and were

[28]All quotes from Don Transeth are from the author's interview on 23 August 2002.

[29]For information concerning EA's distribution strategy in the mid 1990s, see Burgelman and Meza, "Electronic Arts in 1995," SM-24A. A revision of "Electronic Arts in 1995" SM-24, Stanford Graduate School of Business by Carrie C. Oliver, David Bartenwerfer, Jeff Skoll, Lindsay Van Voorhis and John Wright and Professor Robert A. Burgelman.

[30]All quotes from Ted Judson are from the author's interview on 28 August 2002.

even driving hardware sales. This gave us the clout necessary to create relationships with large retailers such as Target, Wal-Mart and K-Mart.

This boom in the console business had a profound structural impact on our distribution system. It drove the development and redesign of our distribution capacity, our sales force, our back-end system and our point of sale marketing strategy. In 1996, as the game market had become more mature, we started seeing our large accounts having two buyers: for PCs and consoles, respectively. In 1997, we decided to split our sales force to reflect this evolution. Actually, the two markets have quite different dynamics. The console market is TV driven and based on volume. The PC market is more sophisticated, there is more product selection, and the audience is older.

In 2002, EA had a direct salesforce in North America and international subsidiaries in 27 countries. From the warehouse it built in Louisville, Kentucky, in 1996, EA manufactured, packaged, and distributed titles created by its studios, as well as those created by some third-party game developer partners in 75 countries. By distributing its products directly to retailers, EA competed more effectively for shelf space and deployed better point-of-sale promotions. Direct distribution also enabled EA to better manage inventory levels and to respond to market trends more rapidly. Typically, EA had a worldwide time to market of two weeks once a game was finished. In 2001, EA won the prestigious Wal-Mart Vendor of the Year Award, competing against major electronics and entertainment corporations.

Ted Judson outlines how EA's current distribution system constituted a competitive advantage: "Our system is capable of handling massive numbers of orders of all sizes. We have real time reporting capabilities of our sales performance, which allows us to better manage our inventory and track demand. We know exactly how our business is doing and our market shares. [Because of this] retailers have learned to lean on us for their purchasing strategy of our games."

Frank Gibeau said:

The efficiency and extensive international scope of our distribution system has also enabled us to pick up business from video game companies with no publishing and distribution activities such as game development studios. EA's distribution business took one of three forms:

- Distribution only in which the partnering game companies did their own production and advertising and EA distributed their titles. This earned the least amount of money for EA.

- Co-publishing, where companies produced the games and EA marketed and published them. EA receives 20 to 30 percent in royalties. EA has these relationships with Disney, Fox Interactive, and Lego Interactive.

- Development plus publishing where EA found third-party titles produced by independent studios and did all testing, marketing, and distribution. The margins EA earns depends on the size of the deal and the nature of the companies involved.

Despite being the worldwide leader in its industry, EA still did not enjoy the same dominance in Asia. The main Asian market for EA was Japan, which with the United States and Europe were the world's three main geographical markets in terms of video game sales. While its shares in Australia, New Zealand, South Korea, and Singapore were similar to those attained in the United States, its shares in console markets were lower in Japan. The company was also the number 2 maker of PC games in Japan, but number 1 in online gaming in that important Asian country. One of the main barriers to EA's development in Asia was piracy, especially in mainland China and neighboring countries.

Other Avenues for Growth

Beyond extending its franchises, EA looked for growth through licensing relationships and acquisitions. EA sought to license IP with potential for series development (e.g., "James Bond" titles, "Lord of the Rings," "Harry Potter," and the like). The company tried to be very conservative about striking such deals. EA would license only material that had proven popularity and durability. It would not take a chance on licensing an unproven property. The company also prided itself on its discipline in avoiding bidding wars for material.

EA tried to exercise similar fiscal discipline in its acquisitions. EA looked to acquire IP or brands that it could extend into new markets. Any company it considered buying also had to have good management in place and be culturally compatible with Electronic Arts. Further, EA eschewed many of the distractions that acquisitions often entailed. Stan McKee said:

We buy only the precise assets we want. For example, we paid twice the price to buy just Westwood Studios, which was a part of Virgin Interactive, than what Viacom wanted for the whole Virgin Interactive property.

There was a lot of duplication in distribution and titles and studios between EA and Virgin and we figured it would cost us $30–$40 million in management distraction to dispose of the assets we did not want. In the end, it was worth it to us to pay $120 million for only the part [Westwood Studios] that we wanted. We didn't want the distraction of closing studios and dismantling distribution chains across the globe.

These acquisitions were paid for with a currency that the company jealously guarded: shares. EA viewed its share price as a strategic asset, allowing the company to fund acquisitions while inoculating itself against unwanted advances from would be acquirers. Over the past few years there had been speculation that EA would make a good acquisition target for a Hollywood studio. Indeed, games benefit from better economics than movies since they are more profitable. For example, "Madden NFL" cost around $10 million to develop on all platforms and sold 4.5 million units, which generated approximately $190 million in revenues. On average, EA games generated 54 percent gross margins. EA's "Harry Potter" game sold 9 million units that generated approximately $270 million. Some studios tried to enter the video game market but met little success. Viacom and Disney both had prominent failures in games. McKee observed, "The gap between EA and traditional entertainment companies is narrowing."

The Online Challenge for EA

Since 1998, EA made significant investments in developing a solid online infrastructure through its EA.com business unit. EA.com was launched in October 2000 to house all the company's online gaming initiatives, including Web-based gaming as well as multiplayer games. EA.com's business model was to generate revenues from both subscriptions and advertising. With the economic downturn beginning 2001 and the dramatic decrease in Internet advertising, EA.com had been experiencing significant financial losses. Still, in 2002, EA considered its online group to be a major strategic investment (Exhibit 12).

EXHIBIT 12 | U.S. Online Gaming

PC Online Gaming Households in the United States

Data in millions, unless otherwise stated

	1999	2000	2001	2002	2003	2004	2005
Total U.S. households	100.4	103.2	104.3	105.5	106.6	107.7	108.8
U.S. online PC gaming households	20.71	24.8	29.16	34.19	40.33	45.36	48.19
Penetration %	21%	24%	28%	32%	38%	42%	44%
Average number of online PC gamers/household	1.5	1.65	1.7	1.7	1.67	1.65	1.65
Total number of U.S. online PC gamers	31.06	40.91	49.58	58.12	67.35	74.84	79.51

Source: IDC, CSFB Technology Group Estimates.

Console Online Gaming Forecast

	2001	2002	2003	2004	2005
U.S. households with online game consoles (%)	1.10%	4.80%	11.80%	16.70%	18.70%
U.S. households online via consoles (%)	0.00%	1.40%	5.60%	10.30%	13.10%
Annual online console gaming revenue ($M)	3	293	1,022	1,788	2,322
Average spending for online gaming/ household ($)	58	196	167	156	157

Source: GartnerG2, CSFB Technology Group estimates.

In November 1999, EA.com partnered with AOL in a 5-year $85 million marketing agreement to provide the game channel for all of the AOL brands and services. AOL was responsible for ad sales and marketing the site to its users. EA.com's business model included revenue from advertising, sponsorships, and subscriptions.

The objective of the deal was to marry AOL's traffic with EA's content. The deal exposed EA to two expensive challenges. EA had to come out of the gates with both diverse content and infrastructure in place to accommodate, from day one, traffic sent from AOL. The service had to be capable of handling the visitors it attracted from AOL's base of then 25 million subscribers. At the outset, 8 million to 10 million visitors were expected. After some growing pains, the service became the fourth most visited site on the Internet after AOL, Yahoo, and MSN. In May 2002, the service attracted 13 million unique visitors who spent 5 billion minutes there. The site accounted for 44 percent of market share in game sites in May 2002.

EA acquired the casual gaming site, Pogo.com, in early 2001. Pogo.com and EA.com have one of the most recognized brands in the online gaming space, and brought over 15 million subscribers to the EA.com site.

Free Web gaming not withstanding, EA had not made significant inroads in subscription-based multiplayer gaming. In 2001 and 2002, EA launched "Majestic" and "Motor City Online," two sophisticated pay-for-play initiatives that both folded a few months after their inceptions. In 2002, EA counted on the releases of major online-only massively multiplayer games such as "The Sims Online," and "Earth and Beyond," to start recouping its investments in EA.com. EA looked to "The Sims Online," an online sequel to all-time bestseller "The Sims" to provide a proof of concept for subscription-based online gaming. If "The Sims Online" did not turn out to be profitable, what would work? The success of "The Sims Online" could validate online pay-for-play for mass-market customers, beyond those hard-core gamers who, as yet, comprised the only paying audience for online games.

Conclusion

By carefully selecting platforms and dominating the genres in which it decided to compete, Electronic Arts successfully navigated the complex marketplace for game software. The company married creative and technical skills—a competency that eluded many entertainment companies such as Hollywood studios—to produce market-leading content for game consoles and PCs. The conservative management of EA's resources brought the company to its current level of success. However, EA was now exposed to new and powerful forces as it looked for future growth and pursued its mission to be "the number 1 entertainment company in the world."

COO John Riccitiello was thinking particularly hard about several strategic leadership issues:

> First, the strategic chess game of resource allocation to different technological platforms: Which partners can we trust? Who will able to execute? Second, the identification of new intellectual properties that could be turned into multihundred million franchises: How many? How to get the right ones? How to make them bigger? Third, capability development: Good ideas are numerous in our organization, but what is important is to be able to select and develop them. We have lots of good people who can deliver, but there are not enough of them to execute all the ideas we have. We need to constantly invest in training programs to develop people, teach them and cull them. Fourth, our culture: A single-purpose entertainment company has never been developed before.

In addition to the internal challenges EA faced, several external opportunities and threats existed in 2002. Would Internet gaming, which had proved to be an electronic boneyard for many others, be profitable for Electronic Arts? What role would Microsoft play in EA's future? That company was famous for successful second tries; what if it also picked up on Sega's challenge to "Beat EA?" Could Electronic Arts resist such an onslaught?

Case 5.2

Disney in a Digital World: Disney in 2001—Distributing the Mouse

I am nervous of the monumental pressure of the L.A. Times and The New York Times and Variety [asking] "How come Disney is not buying Telemundo?" "How come Disney is not buying NBC?" "How come Disney doesn't own 12 million cable homes?" "Why doesn't Disney buy AT&T Broadband and get in the pipe business?"

I'm nervous that we'll all—including me—lose sight. . . . I have to tie myself to the vision and I have to say to myself, 'What is Disney?'

   —**Michael Eisner speaking about Disney's reluctance to buy distribution assets in an interview with** *The New York Times,* July 2, 2001.[1]

Introduction

Disney's efforts to move beyond content have met with mixed success. In January 2001, the company layed to rest its much-touted Go.com network Internet portal. In doing so, Disney had to write down over $900 million. Before the company announced its $5.2 billion purchase of News Corp's cable network Fox Family Worldwide in July of 2001, Disney was sitting on over $14 billion in cash and unused bank lines of credit.[2] In addition, the company's operations generated tremendous amounts of money. Going into 2002, Disney expected to generate $2 billion in free cash flow (Exhibit 1).

Disney's financial strength notwithstanding, the 1990s had been bumpy. Disney began the decade seeming to avoid the moves some of its competitors were making into distribution. Disney's longtime CEO Michael Eisner stated as much in 1993 when he strongly underscored Disney's commitment to content, adding, "If we have one concern, it is only that no one business entity be allowed to control access to the new [entertainment delivery] systems."[3]

Nevertheless, Eisner spent the remainder of the decade adding delivery systems to the Disney empire. Before its ill-fated foray with Go Networks—cobbled together from its purchase of search engine Infoseek and other Internet assets—Disney paid $19 billion to purchase the broadcast television network ABC in 1996. Meanwhile, traditional Disney competitors such as media giant Viacom and a new powerhouse on the scene, AOL Time Warner, built a portfolio of content assets that in many cases were beating Disney in head-to-head competition, while also investing heavily in distribution assets (Exhibit 2). To be successful against these increasingly powerful media competitors—who possessed both content and distribution assets—Disney would either have to make huge investments in distribution, where it had not been strong in the past, or trust that compelling content would always find an audience.

Does Disney Need to Own Pipes?

Disney and indeed all media companies struggled with the question of whether content producers, such as movie studios, needed to own distribution infrastructure such as physical cable or satellite transmission (often referred to as "pipes") into homes in order to ensure distribution. Or, could compelling content always find profitable distribution and thus relieve successful content producers of the risk and distraction of owning expensive distribution infrastructure, which required a different set of management skills to operate than those needed for content creation.

Different camps formed with different opinions as to the answer. Jean-Marie Messier, the chief executive

---

[1]Seth Schiesel, "For Disney's Eisner, the Business Is Content, Not Conduits," *The New York Times,* July 2, 2001. NB: Telemundo is a Miami-based Spanish language broadcast television network owned by Sony Pictures Entertainment and Liberty Media. It was purchased by General Electric's broadcaster NBC for $2.7 billion on 11 October 2001.

[2]Ron Grover, "The Glittering Prizes on Disney's Shopping List," *BusinessWeek,* May 25, 2001. The purchase was for $5.3 billion in cash and assumption of $2.3 billion in debt.

[3]Michael Eisner Letter to Shareholders Disney 1993 Annual Report.

Professor Robert A. Burgelman and Philip E. Meza prepared this case as the basis for class discussion rather than to illustrate either effective or ineffective handling of an administrative situation. This case can be used with "Disney in a Digital World," SM-29A Stanford Graduate School of Business by Burgelman and Meza.

EXHIBIT 1 | Selected Financial Data for Disney

Consolidated Results

In millions, except per share data)	Pro Forma (unaudited)		As Reported		
	2000	1999	2000	1999	1998
Revenues:					
Media networks	$ 9,615	$ 7,970	$ 9,615	$ 7,970	$ 7,433
Studio entertainment	5,994	6,166	5,994	6,166	6,586
Parks and resorts	6,803	6,139	6,803	6,139	5,532
Consumer products	2,608	2,777	2,622	2,954	3,165
Internet group	392	348	368	206	260
Total revenues	$ 25,412	$ 23,400	$ 25,402	$ 23,435	$ 22,976
Operating income (1)					
Media networks	2,298	1,580	2,298	1,580	1,757
Studio entertainment	110	154	110	154	749
Parks and resorts	1,620	1,479	1,620	1,479	1,288
Consumer products	454	567	455	600	810
Internet group	(396)	(208)	(402)	(93)	(94)
Amortization of intangible assets	(1,351)	(1,362)	(1,233)	(456)	(431)
	2,735	2,210	2,848	3,264	4,079
Restructuring charges	—	(132)	—	(132)	(64)
Gain on sale of Ultraseek	153		153	—	—
Gain on sale of Fairchild	—	—	243	—	—
Gain on sale of starwave			—	345	—
Total operating income	2,888	2,078	3,244	3,477	4,015
Corporate and other activities	(103)	(131)	(105)	(140)	(164)
Gain on sale of Eurosport	93	—	93	—	—
Equity in Infoseek loss	—	—	(41)	(322)	—
Net interest expense	(554)	(595)	(558)	(612)	(622)
Income before income taxes and minority interests	2,324	1,352	2,633	2,403	3,229
Income taxes	(1,385)	(941)	(1,606)	(1,014)	(1,307)
Minority interests	(107)	(88)	(107)	(89)	(72)
Net income	$ 832	$ 323	$ 920	$ 1,300	$ 1,850

Source: Disney

officer of media conglomerate newcomer Vivendi Universal observed, "What are the groups which are building direct relationships with customers and which are not? I think you have clearly in one camp AOL Time Warner and Vivendi Universal, building these direct customer relationships. And on the other side you have another group which is not doing it, where you find Disney, where you find Viacom. And you have someone in the middle, which is News Corp."[4] Viacom's CEO Sumner Redstone often proclaimed the power of content, yet Viacom recently built a new network, UPN, which complemented its acquisition of broadcast network CBS. In addition, Viacom owned the powerful video rental chain Blockbuster. (See below.) In 2001, News Corp. was bidding for the DirecTV satellite system owned by Hughes Electronics, a division of General Motors. Any deal for DirecTV would likely cost in the neighborhood of $30 billion. In 2001, distribution assets were very expensive, yet Disney was increasingly alone in its strategy of eschewing these assets.

[4]Seth Schiesel, "Vivendi Tries a Strategy That Is Largely Untested," *The New York Times,* August 27, 2001.

EXHIBIT 1 | Selected Financial Data for Disney (cont.)

Balance Sheet Assets

(In millions)	2000	1999
Assets		
Current assets		
Cash and cash equivalents	$ 842	$ 414
Receivables	3,599	3,633
Inventories	702	796
Film and television costs	3,606	3,598
Deferred income taxes	623	607
Other assets	635	679
Total current assets	10,007	9,727
Film and television costs	2,895	2,962
Investments	2,270	2,434
Parks, resorts, and other property, at cost		
Attractions, buildings and equipment	16,610	15,869
Accumulated depreciation	(6,892)	(6,220)
	9,718	9,649
Projects in progress	1,995	1,272
Land	597	425
	12,310	11,346
Intangible assets, net	16,117	15,695
Other assets	1,428	1,515
	$45,027	$43,679

Source: Disney.

(continued)

Time Warner Pulls the Plug on Disney

Disney largely relied on the pull created by the quality of its content to ensure distribution. In April 2000 it learned how risky such a strategy could be when Time Warner pulled Disney's ABC from seven metropolitan markets including New York and Los Angeles for almost 48 hours. The dispute came at a crucial time for ABC. It was the beginning of May 2000 "sweeps," the period during which a network's ratings are measured to set advertising rates for the coming months. Some 3.5 million viewers were affected by the blackout. The two companies had been haggling over terms ever since their previous agreement ran out December 31 1999.[5]

According to published news reports, Disney insisted that if Time Warner wanted to continue to carry ABC, it also had to carry Disney's cartoon and soap opera networks and shift the Disney Channel from a premium offering, for which subscribers paid extra, to the basic cable lineup. Time Warner claimed that Disney's demands would cost the cable company an additional $300 million a year. In response, Time Warner pulled Disney programming from its cable programming.

Within two days, the Federal Communications Commission (FCC) became involved announcing that Time Warner had violated federal rules that prohibited deletion of a local commercial television station during a sweeps period. The companies reached an agreement soon thereafter. Still, the incident illustrated how customer demand alone may not be sufficient to ensure distribution. Indeed, ABC programs such as the highly popular *Who Wants to Be a Millionaire,* and sports programming from Disney's successful ESPN network had been dropped for a time.

Time Warner owned the cable system that ran into subscribers' homes. Disney owned the content that was

[5]"Disney Duels with Time Warner," *The Newshour with Jim Lehrer,* May 2, 2000.

EXHIBIT 1 | Selected Financial Data for Disney (cont.)

Balance Sheet Liabilities

(In Millions)	2000	1999
Liabilities and Stockholders' Equity		
Current liabilities		
Accounts and taxes payable and other accrued liabilities	$ 5,161	$ 4,588
Current portion of borrowings	2,502	2,415
Unearned royalties and other advances	739	704
Total current liabilities	8,402	7,707
Borrowings	6,959	9,278
Deferred income taxes	2,833	2,660
Other long-term liabilities, unearned royalties, and other advances	2,377	2,711
Minority interests	356	348
Stockholders' equity		
Preferred stock, $.01 par value		
Authorized—100 million shares, issued—none		
Common stock		
Common stock—Disney, $.01 par value	9,920	9,234
Authorized—3.6 billion shares, issued— 2.1 billion shares		
Common stock—Internet Group, $.01 par value	2,181	—
Authorized—1.0 billion shares, issued— 45.3 million shares	12,767	12,281
Retained earnings	(28)	(25)
Other accumulated comprehensive income	24,840	21,580
	(689)	(605)
Treasury stock, at a cost, 31 million Disney shares		
Shares held by TWDC Stock Compensation Fund II, at cost		
Disney—1.1 million shares as of September 30, 2000	(40)	—
Internet Group—0.9 million shares as of September 30, 2000	(11)	—
	24,100	20,975
	$45,027	$43,679

Source: Disney.

delivered over those cables. Their business arrangement, like all arrangements between broadcast stations and their local cable systems, was governed by the 1992 Cable Television Act. The broadcaster had a choice. It could opt for the act's so-called "must carry" provision, under which the cable operator must transmit the broadcaster's signal, but pay no fee, or it could opt for the act's so-called "retransmission consent" provision, which set up a negotiation between the two.

Under retransmission consent, the cable system did not have to carry the local station's programs, but if it did, it had to pay a mutually agreed price. Most large broadcasters, including ABC, opted for the latter arrangement.[6,7]

---

[6]Ibid.

[7]Federal Communications Commission Cable Television Fact Sheet, July 2000.

EXHIBIT 2 | Selected Industry Rankings by Competitor Disney Industry Position

	Broadcast TV	Cable TV Programming	Amusement Parks	Movies	Consumer Products	Internet
	ABC has not found a new hit since Who Wants to Be a Millionaire?	Disney owns 50 percent of Lifetime and a stake in A&E and others. It also owns 80 percent of ESPN.	Worldwide Visitors	Industry Total Jan 2–June 3, 2001 U.S. and Canada box office revenue $3.0 billion. NB: Disney owns Miramax.	Industry Total 2000 world-wide retail entertainment licensing revenue, estimated $69 billion	Disney's Websites include the popular ESPN, ABC and NFL.com sites.
	U.S. primetime avg. viewers Oct 2'00 May 23'01 season	U.S. weekend cable avg. viewers Jan 1–June 24 '01	Estimated visitors in 2000	Box office revenue	Ranked by licensing revenue individual amounts not available	U.S. visitors, May 2001
	Share	Millions	Million	Millions Shares		Millions

Broadcast TV

			Share
1.	CBS	12.5	12%
2.	ABC	12.5	12
3.	NBC	11.6	12
4.	FOX	9.6	9
5.	WB	3.8	4
6.	UPN	3.7	4
7.	PAX	1.4	1

Cable TV Programming

		Millions
1.	Nickelodeon	2.3
2.	Lifetime	1.9
3.	Turner Broadcasting	1.6
4.	Cartoon Network	1.5
5.	TNT	1.4
6.	Disney Channel	1.2
7.	USA Network	1.1
8.	HBO	1.1
9.	MTV	0.8
10.	ESPN	0.7

Amusement Parks

		Million
1.	Walt Disney	89.3
2.	Six Flags	48.8
3.	Universal Studios	23.8
4.	Anheuser-Busch Parks	20.2
5.	Cedar Fair	14.0
6.	Paramount Parks	12.0
7.	Grupo Magico Internacional	8.3
8.	Blackpool Pleasure Beach	7.8
9.	The Tussauds Group	7.7
10.	Alfa Smartparks	6.2

Movies

		Millions	Shares
1.	Paramount	$373.9	12.5%
2.	Sony/Columbia	332.9	11.1
3.	Warner Brothers	304.8	10.2
4.	Buena Vista	285.8	9.5
5.	Miramax	273.5	9.1
6.	Universal	256.1	8.5
7.	MGM/UA	230.1	7.7
8.	DreamWorks	217.0	7.2
9.	Fox	203.1	6.8
10.	New Line Cinema	142.0	4.7

Consumer Products

1.	Disney
2.	AOL Time Warner
3.	Viacom
4.	Vivendi Universal
5.	Sesame Workshop
6.	Lucas Film Entertainment
7.	HIT Entertainment (Lyric Studios)
8.	News Corporation (Fox)
9.	Seban Entertainment
10.	Sony

Internet

		Millions
1.	AOL Time Warner sites	70.0
2.	Microsoft sites	61.4
3.	Yahoo	57.6
4.	Lycos	32.9
5.	X10.com	28.6
6.	Excite Network	28.2
7.	About	25.7
8.	Infospace	20.2
9.	Amazon	20.0
10.	Disney Internet Group (DIG)	19.9

Source: *The New York Times*; Authors.

NB: A&E is Disney's Arts and Entertainment Network.

(continued)

EXHIBIT 2 | Assets of Selected Media Companies (cont.)

	Disney	AOL-Time Warner	Viacom	Vivendi-Universal	News Corp.	Sony[a]
Broadcast TV stations	•	•	•		•	
Broadcast TV network	•	•	•		•	
Cable distribution systems		•				
Cable networks	•	•	•		•	•
Satellite TV				•	•	•
Film production	•	•	•	•	•	•
Film library	•	•	•	•	•	•
Movie theaters				•		•
Music	•	•		•		•
Radio	•		•			
Publishing	•	•	•	•	•	
Internet	•	•	•	•	•	•
Theme parks	•	•		•		
Retailing	•	•	•	•		
Audio/video players						•
2000 Revenues ($ bil)	$25.4	$36.2	$20.0	$17.7[b]	$14.2	$10.0[c]

Source: *The Economist*; annual reports; Standard & Poor's; One Source; Bloomberg; Harvard Business School; Authors

[a]Sony Corporation of America.

[b]Includes only the media portions of the company. The total was $48.4 billion.

[c]Includes only the media portions of the company. The total was $64.5 billion.

Regarding the dispute, Disney President Robert Iger said, "On Time Warner's side, it's about using their power as a monopolist. As an unbelievably strong gatekeeper, it has a choke hold of sorts on the consumer, in terms of controlling television access to their home—using that power in an abusive way, to essentially drive the economics of a business arrangement in their favor." Joseph Collins, chairman and CEO of Time Warner Cable saw it differently. He said, "We don't feel that we're using anybody to achieve corporate goals . . . we want our customers

EXHIBIT 2 | Top Ten Media Competitors by Revenue (cont.)

Company	Revenue 2000–01 ($ billion)	Revenue 1999–00 ($ billion)	Percent Change
1. AOL-Time Warner	36.200	32.500	11%
2. Walt Disney	25.400	23.400	9
3. Viacom	23.400	21.700	8
4. Vivendi-Universal	22.100	19.300	14
5. Bertelsmann	19.100	15.400	24
6. News Corp.	13.800	14.100	−2
7. Sony	9.300	11.300	−18
8. Comcast	8.400	7.600	11
9. AT&T Broadband	8.200	5.000	62
10. Cox Enterprises	7.800	6.000	30

Source: *Variety* August 27, 2001.

NB: NBC was 11th with $6.8 billion, a 17 percent increase.

EXHIBIT 3 | Selected Financial Data for AOL Time Warner

	Six months Ended June 30
	2001 actual
Revenues:	(millions)
Subscriptions	$7,915
Advertising and commerce	4,331
Content and other	6,036
Total revenues	18,282
Costs of revenues	(9,828)
Selling, general and administrative	(4,698)
Amortization of goodwill and other intangible assets	(3,556)
Gain on sale or exchange of cable television systems	—
Merger-related costs	(71)
Operating income (loss)	129
Interest income (expense), net	(671)
Other income (expense), net	(1,105)
Minority interest income (expense)	(180)
Income (loss) before income taxes and cumulative effect of accounting change	(1,827)
Income tax provision	(276)
Income (loss) before cumulative effect of accounting change	(2,103)
Cumulative effect of accounting change, net of $295 million income tax benefit	—
Net income (loss)	(2,103)

Source: AOL Time Warner.

(continued)

to have ABC, we've never said anything differently than that, and we think they should have ABC—but we don't think ABC should be using the retransmission consent rules to extract things from our customers"[8] (Exhibit 3).

While the dispute involved money, for example the amount in fees that Time Warner would pay Disney to carry ABC, it also involved a large portion of competitive jockeying. Disney attempted to force retransmission and better positioning of programs that directly competed with Time Warner properties such as its Cartoon Network and Soap Opera Network. In this case, Disney relied on legislation to get its programs back into the cable. In the end, an agreement between ABC and Time Warner was signed in which the cable company added several Disney channels to its standard package lineup.

Still, it was a rude awakening for a company long accustomed to the protection afforded by the market power generated by its rich content.

Disney's Strategy in 2001

In the summer of 2001, Disney management outlined a five-point plan for the company. Disney wanted to own more content, own more cable channels, invest in new distribution technologies, make the most of theme park management fees, and continue building direct-to-retail relationships for its consumer products so it could rely less on its own costly stores.[9] While Disney was clearly the undisputed leader in some of these areas, such as theme parks, the company faced more competition in

[8]"Disney Duels with Time Warner," *The Newshour with Jim Lehrer,* May 2, 2000.

[9]Disney second quarter earnings call.

EXHIBIT 3 | AOL Time Warner Inc. Consolidated Balance Sheet (cont.)

	June 30, 2001 actual
(millions, except per share amounts)	
ASSETS	
Current assets	
Cash and equivalents	$ 1,357
Short-term investments	—
Receivables, less allowances of $1.446 billion, $1,725 billion and $97 million	5,106
Inventories	1,644
Prepaid expenses and other current assets	1,987
Total current assets	10,094
Noncurrent inventories and film costs	7,248
Investments, including available-for-sale securities	11,313
Property, land and equipment	11,973
Music catalogues and copyrights	2,942
Cable television and sports franchises	27,629
Brands and trademarks	10,750
Goodwill and other intangible assts	126,618
Other assets	2,255
Total assets	$ 210,822
LIABILITIES AND SHAREHOLDERS' EQUITY	
Current liabilities	
Accounts payable	$ 1,976
Participations payable	1,153
Royalties and programming costs payable	1,450
Deferred revenue	1,620
Debt due within one years	20
Other current liabilities	5,824
Total current liabilities	12,043
Long-term debt	20,457
Deferred income taxes	12,622
Deferred revenue	1,212
Other liabilities	4,920
Minority interests	3,481
Mandatorily redeemable preferred securities of a subsidiary holding solely debentures of a subsidiary of the Company	—
Shareholders' equity	
Series LMCN-V Common Stock, $.01 par value, 171.2 million shares outstanding at June 30, 2001 and December 31, 2000 pro forma	2
AOL Time Warner (and America Online, as predecessor) Common Stock, $.01 par value, 4,273, 4,101 and 2,379 billion shares outstanding	42
Paid-in capital	156,371
Accumulated other comprehensive income, net	48
Retained earnings	(376)
Total shareholders' equity	156,087
Total liabilities and shareholders' equity	$ 210,822

other areas, such as in cable channels and to some extent in the creation of new kinds of content, from Web-based entertainment to new forms of digital animation.

Disney's Cable Assets

In order to gain more distribution outlets, some analysts expected Disney to bid for AT&T's cable TV unit, AT&T Broadband. But on October 3, 2001, Disney president Bob Iger said an investment by Disney in broadband communications was unlikely and that the corporation was well-positioned as an entertainment-focused company in a rapidly consolidating marketplace. "An investment in broadband pipe is highly unlikely. We don't need to buy into pipe to grow our businesses. It's more important for our content to be strong and in demand."[10] Perhaps recalling Disney's troubles with Time Warner, Iger also said his company saw a "potential problem" in companies owning both content (e.g., TV shows) and broadband pipe (e.g., cable TV delivery) if those owners began to discriminate against shows from rival content providers. Iger added, "We would be extremely wary, and watch closely, if there was extraordinary ownership of both distribution and content. If we see any discrimination against content not owned by the pipe owners, we would probably be very vocal in Washington."[11] While Disney executives had often expressed their faith in the pull of good content, the almost $40 billion price tag may have dissuaded Disney from bidding.

As Iger mentioned above, Disney did plan to acquire more cable channels. The company recently purchased Fox Family Worldwide Cable Network, which it was to rename Disney Family Network. Fox Family Channel was one of the most widely available cable networks in the United States, reaching 80 million households.[12] The Family Channel targeted an older audience than either the Disney Channel or Disney's cartoon channel Toon Disney attracted. Of course, Disney owned broadcaster ABC and its host of cable assets such as ESPN. Disney's consolidated cable networks represented about 28 percent of the company's overall asset value, compared with 11 percent for the ABC Television Network and TV stations, 12 percent for the film and television production operations, 4 percent for radio, 21 percent for theme parks, and 7.5 percent for consumer products. Morgan Stanley Dean Witter estimated Disney's overall asset value at roughly $85 billion.[13]

Disney's existing cable networks (including ESPN and The Disney Channel) generated 22 percent of the company's annual cash flow, or more than $1 billion. Even in a challenging advertising year as was experienced in 2001, analysts estimated the ABC-owned TV stations would generate nearly 10 percent of Disney's overall cash flow, or about $483 million on nearly $1 billion in revenues.

By comparison theme parks contributed an estimated 43 percent of Disney's overall $5.3 billion in annual cash flow. However they required at least $1 billion in annual reinvestment. Thus, although the theme parks generated twice as much cash flow as Disney's media networks, they required five times more capital.[14]

Disney on the Web

By the second quarter of 2001, Disney's Internet group reported a 17 percent year-on-year decrease in revenues to $38 million. On March 30, Disney reabsorbed its Internet unit, converting outstanding shares of Walt Disney Internet Group stock, and issuing 8.6 million of Disney common stock. Operating losses for the Internet group were stemming by the second quarter of 2001, improving 47 percent over the previous year's second quarter to $31 million. The company attributed the improved losses to better operating performance and cost reduction efforts at Disney-branded and ESPN-branded sites, as well as to the shutdown of Toysmart.com. Disney-branded sites brought in additional revenue through licensing deals and ticket sales for its theme parks.

Go Goes Away   In January 2001, Disney closed Go.com and eliminated its Disney Internet Group tracking stock. A year earlier, Disney decided to back away from using its Go.com Web site as a portal, repositioning it to deliver entertainment content instead. The site lost money since its creation. Commenting on his decision to close Go.com, Michael Eisner said, "The advertising community has abandoned the Internet."[15]

---

[10]"Disney Iger Says Broadband Deal Unlikley," *The New York Times,* October 3, 2001.

[11]Ibid.

[12]Sallie Hoffmeister, "Walt Disney to Acquire Fox Family," *Los Angeles Times,* July 21, 2001.

[13]Diane Mermigas, "Disney Is Primed to Start Buying," *Electronic Media,* September 03, 2001.

[14]Ibid.

[15]Christopher Parkes and James Harding, "Disney May Cut Jobs and Abandon Go.com," *Financial Times,* January 28, 2001.

By late 2001, Disney's Internet strategy seemed uncertain. Bob Iger, president and COO, said the company was focused on "establishing integration between TV properties and Web sites."[16]

New Distribution Technologies— Eliminating the Gatekeepers

New distribution technologies promised to disrupt the traditional value chains that defined entertainment distribution. As the above-mentioned Time Warner/Disney dispute illustrated, the company that controlled the transmission assets owned the relationship with the customer and influenced how that customer consumed the content, for example deciding what programming was offered and where on the "dial" that programming appeared—in the popular single-digit real estate or the relative Siberia of double or even triple-digit channels. The power of the new distribution technologies, particularly broadband Internet, to disrupt markets came from the way it broke down these links in the value chain and created additional avenues of access. For content firms like Disney, broadband Internet offered the company a way to establish a direct relationship with the customer, while bypassing the existing gatekeepers such as cable operators. However, more than cable operators stood between Disney and a paying audience. One large gatekeeper that Disney would like to bypass was the ubiquitous Blockbuster video rental chain.

Blockbuster and the Video Rental Gatekeepers

The relationship between studios and video rental chains—particularly Viacom's Blockbuster chain—was complex. It resembled two people shaking hands, both clinching knives in their other hands held behind their backs. This is not surprising given the relationship started with a lawsuit. In the early 1980s, a group of studios fought home VCR pioneer Sony to the U.S. Supreme Court to prevent the sale of Sony-made videocassette recorders in the United States. Studios claimed that VCRs would promote copyright infringement. The studios never perceived that consumer VCRs would support an important new distribution channel for films. Sony eventually triumphed with a 1984 decision that allowed consumers at home to record whatever was being shown

on their TV screens. Studios soon had an extremely profitable new channel for their content, but did not become a force in video distribution and rental. By 2001, the largest player in the U.S. video rental industry was Blockbuster, bought in 1994 by Viacom for $8 billion. In 2001, Blockbuster had almost 5,000 stores in the United States. and counted 42 million U.S. households as active Blockbuster members[17] (Exhibit 4).

For much of the 1990s, Blockbuster and many other video rental companies were not doing well financially. Rental companies paid studios very high prices for cassettes, using fixed-fee contracts, and kept the rental revenue. In 1998, Blockbuster and other large chains initiated revenue-sharing contracts, consisting of an upfront fee per tape (ranging from nothing to $8 dollars) and a revenue-split paid on the basis of rental revenue. Studios typically earned between 40 percent and 60 percent of rental revenues.[18]

The revenue sharing was profitable for both video rental chains and the studios. In 2000, studios collected more than $14 billion from videocassette sales and rentals. That figure represented 45 percent of studio revenues, making it their largest single cash source. Still studios grew to resent sharing revenue with the video rental chains and feared their power as intermediaries between studios and the public. Studios perceived that it was the rental chains that had the relationship, or the potential for a relationship, with the movie-consuming public. Disney's chief strategy officer Peter Murphy said, "We want to have that relationship. We want to know their name and what they like to watch. If you like Ben Affleck, we want to tell you we have another Ben Affleck film coming out. If you like action films, we want to tell you about an action film you might not have already seen." Murphy estimated that Americans spent about $2 billion a year renting Disney videos but that Disney received only 30 to 35 percent of that.[19]

Blockbuster was also moving into alternate distribution channels. The company signed deals with studios for new distribution rights. Specifically, if a studio wanted Blockbuster to carry its videos and DVDs, it would have to allow Blockbuster to distribute its films over the Internet as well. Karen Raskopf, a spokeswoman for the

---

[16]Disney third quarter 2001 call.

[17]www.blockbuster.com.

[18]Julie Holland Mortimor, "The Effects of Revenue-Sharing Contracts on Welfare in Vertically-Separated Markets: Evidence from the Video Rental Industry," January 10, 2001. www.bol.ucla.edu/~hollandj/.

[19]Seth Schiesel, "For Disney's Eisner, the Business Is Content, Not Conduits," *The New York Times,* July 2, 2001.

EXHIBIT 4 | Selected Financial Data for Viacom

Income Statement

(In Millions)	2000	1999	1998
Revenues			
Cable networks	$ 3,895.0	$ 3,045.5	$ 2,607.9
Television	$ 5,381.7	$ 2,352.0	$ 2,271.4
Infinity	$ 2,764.7		
Entertainment	$ 2,758.3	$ 2,665.9	$ 2,914.3
Video	$ 4,960.1	$ 4,463.5	$ 3,893.4
Publishing	$ 596.0	$ 610.7	$ 564.6
Online	$ 100.7	$ 29.8	$ 13.7
Intercompany eliminations	($ 412.8)	($ 308.6)	($ 169.2)
Total revenues	$20,043.7	$12,858.8	$12,096.1
Operating income (loss)			
Cable networks	$ 1,250.0	$ 932.4	$ 744.3
Television	$ 431.2	$ 143.4	$ 262.4
Infinity	$ 589.4		
Entertainment	$ 209.7	$ 231.1	$ 235.5
Video	$ 75.7	$ 127.9	($ 342.2)
Publishing	$ 49.6	$ 54.3	$ 53.2
Online	($ 256.7)	($ 64.5)	($ 7.5)
Segment total	$ 2,348.9	$ 1,424.6	$ 945.7
Corporate expenses/eliminations	($ 950.5)	($ 177.3)	($ 194.1)
Residual costs of discontinued operations	($ 77.5)		
Total operating income	$ 1,320.9	$ 1,248.3	$ 751.6

Source: Viacom.

(continued)

video chain said, "We want to distribute their content in every place a consumer might want to get it."[20]

Movies over the Internet

The Internet held the promise of providing one direct avenue from the studios to consumers. In September 2001, Disney and Rupert Murdoch's News Corporation formed an alliance to deliver feature films over the Internet. The joint venture, called Movies.com, would compete with MovieFly, an initiative headed by five major studios, MGM, Paramount, Sony, Universal, and Warner Brothers, for a similar service.

Executives said Movies.com would launch in early 2002 and would differ from MovieFly in a few important ways, most notably in that it would not only distribute movies on demand over the Internet but would also reach consumers with enhanced TV cable systems capable of receiving on-demand content. The TV channel was expected to look very much like the Web site, where trailers and behind-the-scenes footage will be featured free and where movies may be ordered for about $4 each, with rewind, fast-forward, and pause capabilities. Peter Levinsohn, executive vice president of worldwide pay television and pay-per-view at 20th Century Fox said, "We're very bullish on the Internet long term, but we have to be realistic. There are fewer than 10 million broadband connections in the U.S. That's why we'll take the business to cable television also."[21] Disney's Eisner predicted, "In the very near future, anyone with a broadband connection will have the option of paying, say $3, to rent a movie directly through movies.com rather than driving to a video store." Disney and News Corp. did not have plans to release films at Movies.com before their video release,

[20]Ibid.

[21]Paul Bond, "Net Film Deal Pairs Studios," *Hollywood Reporter,* September 11, 2001.

EXHIBIT 4 | Selected Financial Data for Viacom (cont.)

Balance Sheet Assets (In Millions)

	As of December 31,	
	2000	**1999**
ASSETS		
Current Assets		
Cash and cash equivalents	$ 934.5	$ 680.8
Receivables, less allowances of $246.2 (2000) and $109.5 (1999)	3,964.1	1,697.4
Inventory	1,402.0	1,959.5
Other current assets	1,531.8	860.7
Total current assets	7,832.4	5,198.4
Property and equipment		
Land	731.8	450.3
Buildings	837.1	660.1
Capital leases	852.5	881.9
Advertising structures	2,076.5	--
Equipment and other	4,505.8	3,263.6
	8,985.7	5,255.9
Less accumulated depreciation and amortization	2,383.9	1,830.6
Net property and equipment	6,601.8	3,425.3
Inventory	3,632.9	2,829.5
Intangibles, at amortized cost	62,004.1	11,478.9
Other assets	2,574.9	1,554.3
Total assets	$82,646.1	$24,486.4

Source: Viacom.

(*continued*)

though both left that option open. Disney's Murphy was direct in his assessment of Movie.com's potential impact, "We intend to be Blockbuster."[22] Such a strategy would put Movies.com in more direct competition with video rental chains. Fox's Levinsohn said, "Blockbuster is an extremely important client. That being said, we need to explore new opportunities to enhance consumer choice."[23]

Pipe Dreams?

Another way around gatekeepers was through hard-drive devices such as Tivo's personal video recorders, which enabled simultaneous recording and playback of TV programs. Disney's Murphy was working on a plan to use a television broadcast spectrum to transmit movies overnight to these hard-drives. Murphy called this "data-casting" and hoped to start preliminary service sometime in 2002. Murphy said, "We see movies as the Trojan horse. Once you have a relationship with the customer and you have a big hard-drive in their house, there's all sorts of different data you can put on there. It can be music, it can be TV, it can be text."[24]

For Disney and other content producers, another major goal was video on demand (VOD) service via the Internet. However, in 2001, some thought high-quality Internet-based VOD services were still a decade away. In 2001, the active capacity of the Internet's backbone in North America was capable of handling 500 gigabits per second (gbps). Current streaming media applications, such as RealPlayer or Windows Media Player, with their 3 inch by 3 inch, low-resolution images, required a unique 300 kilobit per second (kbps) data stream to be allocated for the duration of the transmission to each user. Under current technology, for the picture quality to be improved to that used by a VHS video recorder, the transmission requirement increased to 500 kbps. To provide

[22]Ron Grover, "Power Lunch," *BusinessWeek,* March 19, 2001.
[23]Ibid.

[24]Ibid.

EXHIBIT 4 | Selected Financial Data for Viacom (cont.)

Balance Sheet Liabilities

(In Millions)	As of December 31,	
	2000	**1999**
LIABILITIES AND STOCKHOLDERS' EQUITY		
Current liabilities		
Accounts payable	$ 1,261.1	$ 544.4
Accrued expenses	2,790.2	1,431.2
Deferred income	605.9	371.4
Accrued compensation	642.0	473.3
Participants' share, residuals, and royalties payable	1,220.3	1,087.2
Program rights	709.8	196.9
Income taxes payable	305.0	1.0
Current portion of long-term debt	223.9	294.3
Total current liabilities	7,758.2	4,399.7
Long-term debt	12,473.8	5,697.7
Pension and postretirement benefit obligation	1,636.8	245.0
Other liabilities	5,770.2	1,765.5
Commitments and contingencies		
Minority interest	7,040.2	1,246.5
Stockholders' equity		
Class A common Stock, par value $.01 per share; 500.0 shares authorized; 138.0 (2000) and 139.7 (1999) shares issued	1.4	1.4
Class B common Stock, par value $.01 per share; 300.0 shares authorized; 1454.7 (2000) and 606.6 (1999) shares issued	14.5	6.1
Additional paid-in capital	50,729.9	10,338.5
Retained earnings	1,431.8	2,247.9
Accumulated other comprehensive loss	(152.5)	(30.2)
	52,025.1	12,563.7
Less treasury stock, at a cost; 1.4 (2000 and 1999) Class A shares and 96.3 (2000) and 47.1 (1999) Class B shares	4,058.2	1,431.7
Total stockholders' equity	47,966.9	11,132.0
Total liabilities and stockholders' equity	$82,646.1	$24,486.4

Source: Viacom.

a picture quality as good as DVD (digital video disc), the data rate increased to 750 kbps.[25]

Consider a 30-second clip of content that 100,000 people in the U.S. choose to view at the same time. Even at the low resolution used by current streaming media applications, the capacity required to transmit the piece of content was 30 gbps, or 6 percent of the entire Internet backbone capacity in North America. With the size of audiences that Disney and others hoped to attract, for example popular television shows in the U.S. attracted up to 20 million viewers at a time, even modest use of Internet-based VOD for mainstream content seemed unlikely under current backbone capacities.[26]

Edge servers, also known as content delivery networks (CDN), provided by companies such as Akamai addressed this need. Using a television metaphor, CDNs

[25]"Reality Check for Video on Demand," *The Economist,* July 21, 2001.   [26]Ibid.

could be thought of as repeaters, stationed strategically to help manage the Internet traffic by avoiding the backbone or by finding efficient routes through it. Thus, large audiences trying to view popular content would be divided among a number of CDN sites where a copy of the content would be stored. However, CDNs had their own limitations. They worked best in cases where the Internet usage was predictable. CDNs were less helpful when many users wanted to choose from a wide range of content. CDNs were less capable of distributing the load for "many-to-many" distribution, such as would be the demand for much of Disney's repurposed content.

Nor could Disney or others take much comfort from estimates that in 2001 the United States. was approaching an Internet bandwidth glut. Such a glut referred to "unlighted" optical cable. Lighting the optical cable would require a commitment from Internet Service Providers (ISPs) who were not certain to recoup their investments without profitable services such as compelling VOD. But without the increased capacity made possible by lighting more cable, content providers were uncertain there would be sufficient capacity to handle VOD.

The economics of Internet-based VOD were different from those of broadcast or cable television. Broadcasters were fixed-cost producers; the more viewers a network attracted, the cheaper it became to add each new viewer. Also, as viewership increased, broadcasters could obtain higher advertising rates for its fixed-cost content, leading to larger profit margins. The same is not true for streaming video. With each additional user comes an additional cost, and at present there is no advertising model in place to offset those costs. For example, under current costs, content owners paid approximately one cent to stream one megabyte of video. The size of even a modest-sized movie was at least 1,000 megabytes. Thus it could cost $10 or more to deliver one movie to one viewer.[27]

Technology and telecommunications firms were working to improve distribution efficiencies. Copyright issues remained. Neither the technological, and thus economic issues, nor the legal questions were insurmountable, but Internet-based VOD seemed far off.

Teaching an Old Mouse New Tricks

Disney Borrows Content from Pixar

The first time in its history that Disney released an animated movie sequel in theaters—instead of the less profitable direct-to-video market—was in 1999 with the

hugely popular *Toy Story 2*. This feature, like its predecessor, *Toy Story*, was not created by Disney at all. Instead it came from the computers and proprietary software of Pixar Animation Studios in the San Francisco Bay Area. Pixar was acquired from Lucasfilm by Steve Jobs in 1986. *Toy Story 2,* which was created by Pixar and distributed by Disney, grossed $360 million worldwide (with a production budget of $90 million) and was sold on over 22 million videocassettes in the United States. This sequel was the world's second highest grossing animated feature, behind Disney's homegrown traditional animation 1994 hit *The Lion King,* which earned $312 million in the United States alone.

In 1991, Pixar entered into an agreement with The Walt Disney Studios for the creation and production of up to three full-length feature films using Pixar's advanced, three-dimensional computer animation technology as well as the company's creative story and animation talents. *Toy Story* was the first film made under this agreement. In 1997, Pixar announced a new agreement with Disney to replace the previous three-film deal. Pursuant to the new agreement, the two studios would be equal partners on five upcoming movies (including the remaining two films under the old agreement) and all related merchandise. Disney purchased 1 million shares of Pixar's common stock. Disney also had warrants to purchase an additional 1.5 million shares of Pixar common stock. If the warrants were exercised, Disney would have a combined total of approximately five percent of Pixar.[28]

Computer Animation Becomes More Popular and Crowded

Pixar proved to be technically adept and creative. By 2001, the company won eighteen Academy Awards in both technical and creative categories. The creative force behind the *Toy Story* series and other Pixar hits was the company's Executive Vice President—Creative, John Lasseter. Steve Jobs said, "John Lasseter is the closest thing we have to Walt Disney today." Peter Schneider, president of Walt Disney Feature Animation also made the comparison: "Look at Walt Disney's legacy: he told great stories, with great characters, and he pushed the boundaries of animation. With *Toy Story* and *A Bug's Life,* Lasseter has astounded us twice."[29]

Lasseter trained as a traditional animator and began his career at Disney in 1979. He was intrigued by Disney's

[27]Ibid.

[28]"Corporate Backgrounder" Pixar.com.

[29]Cathy Booth, "The Wizard of Pixar," *Time,* December 14, 1998.

three-dimensional computer work used in its groundbreaking feature, *Tron.* However, Lasseter grew frustrated by Disney's lack of further interest in digital animation and left to work for George Lucas's special-effects company in 1983. There he worked hard developing computer skills and creating effects for movies that often did not do well at the box office. Lasseter remembered, "You'd kill yourself on effects, but no one remembered the films."[30]

Computer generated films generally cost less to make, usually around $50 million compared to twice that for high-quality traditional animated features. Technical problems could cause costs to escalate in either discipline. Traditional and digital animation used many of the same technical and creative skills. Yet Disney had not produced the same kind of success in digital animation as had been achieved by Pixar or Disney's rival DreamWorks. Further, many of Disney's traditionally animated features earned less than digitally animated releases. The digital animation feature, *Shrek,* produced by DreamWorks' PDI computer-animation shop in Palo Alto, California, grossed more than $362 million worldwide by August 2001. *Atlantis,* a traditional animation feature and Disney's only animated feature released in the summer of 2001, earned around $100 million.[31]

Other companies were moving into digital animation features. In March 2002, News Corp's 20th Century Fox was preparing to release *Ice Age,* a 3-D computer generated animated feature. Meanwhile, DreamWorks

was establishing a Los Angeles annex of its PDI computer animation studio. About the increasing competition from digital animation, Disney feature group chairman Richard Cook said, "We're going to continue to do what we've been doing for the past 70 years. We are not in any way standing pat (but) I don't think there's anything in particular we're going to change."[32]

Playing Games

In September 2001, Disney formed the Buena Vista Game Entertainment Studio to handle the company's line of video games. The unit was established to expand the company's game offerings to include broadband, wireless, and online games as well as those that already existed for video consoles and PCs. Disney's president and COO Robert Iger said, "Technological changes are rapidly sweeping the game industry. This new business unit will position the Walt Disney Co. to take full advantage of this evolving landscape by consolidating our existing game activity and aggressively and creatively pursuing new opportunities in entertainment."[33] Disney estimated that industrywide retail sales of entertainment game software would reach $15 billion in 2001. That included increasingly popular Internet-based games, which allow people to play regardless of geography or language[34] (Exhibit 5).

[30]Ibid.

[31]Carl Diorio, "Computers Rule Toon Town," *Variety,* August 7, 2001

[32]Ibid.

[33]Ann Donahue, "Disney Puts Games in One Basket," *Video Business,* September 13, 2001.

[34]Jesse Hiestand, "Disney's New Game Unit Playing Away From Base," *Hollywood Reporter,* September 20, 2001.

EXHIBIT 5 | Selected Data for Videogames

U.S. Computer Games Market Share August 2000–July 2001

Rank	Company	Market Share
1.	Electronic Arts	22%
2.	Vivendi Universal	17%
3.	Infogames Entertainment	17%
4.	Microsoft	9%
5.	Activision	5%
6.	Interplay	4%
7.	Ubisoft	3%
8.	**Disney**	**3%**
9.	Valusoft	2%
10.	Eidos	2%

Source: *Screen Digest,* September 2001.

(continued)

EXHIBIT 5 | Selected Data for Videogames (cont.)

U.S. Videogame Software Sales Data

Year (est.)	Units Sold (M)	Software Spending ($ M)	Average Unit Price
2000	134.5	4,640	$34.50
2001	162.0	5,630	$34.75
2002	193.5	6,782	$35.05
2003	221.6	7,834	$35.35
2004	249.5	8,912	$35.72

Source: "GameCube: Mighty Mite," *Video Business*, August 28, 2000.

Annual Expenditure in the U.S. on Various Entertainment Activities in 1999

Activity	Amount Spent ($ bil)
Video/audio/computer equipment	81.4
Casino gambling	26.3
Home video rentals/sales	18.6
Lotteries	16.5
Recorded music shipments	14.6
Amusement park receipts	9.1
Movie box office gross	7.5
Videogame/entertainment software sales	**6.9**
Spectator sports	6.3
Cable TV subscriptions	3.6

Source: "How Americans Spend Time, Money," *Research Alert*, December 1, 2000.

NB: For all of the above, category definitions and sales figures vary by source.

The game studio was to be a standalone business unit, with its president, Jan Smith who remained in charge of Disney Interactive, reporting to Iger. Disney Interactive, part of the consumer products division, developed video games and learning titles for PCs and such consoles as Sony's PlayStation 2 and Microsoft's upcoming Xbox.

Conclusion

Disney's traditional content remained compelling. The company enjoyed success in broadcast and cable television. Its theme parks, populated by old and new characters and attractions ranging from Mickey Mouse to the new *A Bug's Life* ride continued to draw visitors in droves. In 2001, however, it was not clear that Disney would enjoy similar success in creating new types of content, such as Web-based entertainment or digital animation. Nor were the nascent distribution technologies Disney was exploring certain to effectively bypass entrenched gatekeepers like AOL Time Warner or Viacom's Blockbuster. Would Disney still be able to avoid buying expensive distribution assets, relying upon the power of its content to find audiences? Also, how risky was it for Disney to effectively rent and not own the skills behind the new film-making technologies that created the *Toy Story* series and others? While Disney's corporate coffers were deep, they were not infinite, so the company would have to make trade-offs. Distribution assets were costly to purchase and operate. Would those content producers who bought expensive distribution assets come to regret spending their money and attention on pipes that had nothing to do with content creation? Or would Disney again be held hostage by gatekeepers interested in promoting their own content?

Case 5.3

Disney in a Digital World (D) A Digital Decade?: Disney in 2003 and beyond

. . . We are once again at the beginning of a vast and exciting period of opportunity . . . what we expect will be a Digital Decade for us at Disney. We have already implemented a number of initiatives to place our company in the forefront of the digital transformation of the entertainment industry.

We realize that everyone does not share our view, seeing the digital revolution as a threat to the established analog way of doing things . . . and many are paralyzed by a fear of digital piracy.

Indeed, we are a conflicted industry. Hollywood studios spend enormous sums of money encouraging people to see its films and TV shows and then spend more money devising ways to control and limit how people can see its films and TV shows.

—**Michael Eisner, Chairman and CEO, Walt Disney, Inc., in remarks to the National Association of Broadcasters, April 7, 2003**

Introduction

Until recently, Disney had not been conflicted in its approach to the digital revolution. The company was a vocal opponent of digital distribution technologies, comparing the companies that produced such technologies to sword suppliers to pirates.[1] In 2003, as Disney embarked on what it called its "digital decade" the company had to contend with significant challenges—both external and

---

[1]Amy Harmon, "Piracy, or Innovation? It's Hollywood vs. High Tech," *The New York Times,* March 14, 2002.

Professor Robert A. Burgelman and Philip E. Meza prepared this case as the basis for class discussion rather than to illustrate either effective or ineffective handling of an administrative situation. This case can be used with Robert A. Burgelman and Philip Meza, "Distributing the Mouse: Disney in 2001," SM-29C, Stanford Graduate School of Business.

self-induced. A poor economy and fear of terrorist activities reduced travel and negatively impacted Disney's theme parks and resorts. Other problems were internal to the company. For example, the issues of corporate governance resonated at the company where the board of directors had long been considered by some critics to be less than independent and not always qualified.[2]

The company's collection of assets, including media networks, theme parks, studios, and consumer products were turning in mixed results. Disney's ABC broadcast network struggled, but its film group performed well. However, the company generated cash flow at a terrific rate. Some analysts estimated that Disney would earn $900 million in free cash flow by the end of 2003.[3] With that kind of performance, nothing had to change soon. Since Disney's share price had been cut in half over the past several years, cash was an increasingly important currency to the company. But if Disney was indeed to embark on a digital decade, what assets would it need and which, if any, should it shed? Was cash flow itself enough to see the company to success, or would fundamental changes in strategy need to occur before Disney could go digital? How could the company that pioneered so many entertainment concepts in the last century compete in the next?

Disney in 2003

The Walt Disney Company was a diversified worldwide entertainment giant with operations in four business segments: Media Networks, Parks and Resorts, Studio Entertainment and Consumer Products (Exhibit 1). Disney's Media Networks group oversaw the company's television and radio networks, including cable and satellite as well as international broadcast operations. The company's Parks and Resorts group ran Walt Disney World Resort and Disney Cruise Line in Florida, the Disneyland Resort in California, and ESPN Zone restaurants, and licensed Tokyo Disneyland Resort in Japan and licensed and operated the Disneyland Resort Paris, in France. Disney's Studio Entertainment group produced live-action and animated motion pictures, television animation

---

[2]Laura M. Holson, "Eisner Faces Difficult Year at Disney," *The New York Times,* March 17, 2003.

[3]Jill Krutick and Suk Han, "Disney: ABC and Parks Hold the Keys to the Kingdom," Citigroup Smith Barney, May 1, 2003.

EXHIBIT `1 | The Walt Disney Company and Subsidiaries

(In millions)	As Reported			Pro Forma (unaudited)		
	2002	2001	2000	2002	2001	% Changes
Revenues						
Media networks	$ 9,733	$ 9,569	$ 9,36	$ 9,763	$10,157	(4%)
Parks and resorts	6,465	7,004	6,809	6,465	7,004	(8%)
Studio results	6,691	6,009	5,918	6,691	6,009	11%
Consumer products	2,440	2,590	2,762	2,441	2,620	(7%)
	$25,329	$25,172	$25,325	$25,360	$25,790	(2%)
Segment operating income						
Media networks	$ 986	$ 1,758	$ 1,985	$ 990	$ 1,949	(49%)
Parks and resorts	1,169	1,586	1,615	1,169	1,586	(26%)
Studio results	273	260	126	273	260	5%
Consumer products	394	401	386	394	419	(6%)
	$ 2,822	$ 4,005	$ 4,112	$ 2,826	$ 4,214	(33%)

Source: Company reports.

programs, musical recordings, and live stage plays. The company's Consumer Products group licensed Walt Disney characters and other properties and operated retail, direct mail, and online stores selling products based on characters and films. The group also published books, magazines, and comics worldwide and produced and licensed computer software and video games.

One area the company was no longer involved in was Major League Baseball. In April 2003, the company sold its Anaheim Angels baseball team, whose stadium was located just down the street from Disneyland, to an Arizona businessman for $182 million. Despite winning the 2002 World Series, the team lost $10 million that year, and was projected to lose another $9 million in 2003. Disney bought 25 percent of the team in 1996 for $30 million and the rest in 1998 for $110 million after its principal owner, entertainer Gene Autry, died. Disney spent $100 million more to renovate the team's stadium, which continued to be owned by the city of Anaheim.[4] Disney had reportedly been seeking a buyer for the Angels since 2000, asking $250 million for them.[5] Disney still owned

the National Hockey League team The Mighty Ducks of Anaheim. It seemed likely that it too would be sold. The other high-profile team-owning media companies, AOL Time Warner and News Corp., were reputedly trying to find buyers for their respective professional sports teams.

Disney also made news with its announced plan to pilot a new DVD technology that would allow play for 48 hours before a special coating oxidized, rendering the disk unplayable. The technology for these disposable DVDs was aimed at the rental market, and perhaps at competing media conglomerate Viacom's Blockbuster, which was being sued by Disney in a dispute over revenue sharing of rental/sales DVDs. In 1998, Blockbuster and other large chains initiated revenue-sharing contracts, consisting of an upfront fee per tape (ranging from nothing to $8 dollars) and a revenue-split paid on the basis of rental revenue. Studios typically earned between 40 percent and 60 percent of rental revenues.[6] The revenue sharing was profitable for both video rental chains and the studios. In 2000, studios collected more than $14 billion from videocassette sales and rentals. That figure

[4]Frank Ahrens, "Disney Finds Buyer for Anaheim Angels," *Washington Post,* April 16, 2003, p. E01.

[5]"Take Me Out the Ballgame: Disney Unloading Angels," *Hollywood Reporter,* April 22, 2003.

[6]Julie Holland Mortimer, "The Effects of Revenue-Sharing Contracts on Welfare in Vertically-Separated Markets: Evidence from the Video Rental Industry," January 10, 2001, (www.bol.ucla.edu/~hollandj/).

EXHIBIT 1 | The Walt Disney Company and Subsidiaries Consolidated Statements of Income (cont.)

	Year Ended September 30,		
(In millions, except per share data)	**2002**	**2001**	**2000**
Revenues	$25,329	$25,172	$25,325
Costs and expenses	(22,924)	(21,573)	(21,567)
Amortization of intangible assets	(21)	(767)	(1,233)
Gain on sale of businesses	34	22	459
Net interest expense and other	(453)	(417)	(497)
Equity in the income of investees	225	300	208
Restructuring and impairment charges	—	(1,454)	(92)
Income before income taxes, minority interests and the cumulative effect of accounting changes	2,190	1,283	2,633
Income taxes	(853)	(1,059)	(1,606)
Minority interests	(101)	(104)	(107)
Income before the cumulative effect of accounting changes	1,236	120	920
Cumulative effect of accounting changes:			
Film accounting	—	(228)	—
Derivative accounting	—	(50)	—
Net income (loss)	$1,236	$ (158)	$920
Earnings (loss) attributed to Disney common stock[1]	$1,236	$ (41)	$1,196
Earnings per share before the cumulative effect of accounting changes attributed to Disney common stock:			
Diluted	$0.60	$ 0.11	$0.57
Basic	$0.61	$ 0.11	$0.58
Cumulative effect of accounting changes per Disney share:			
Film accounting	$ —	$ (0.11)	$ —
Derivative accounting	—	(0.02)	$ —
	—	$ (0.13)	$ —
Earnings (loss) per share attributed to Disney common stock:			
Diluted	$0.60	$ (0.02)	$0.57
Basic	$0.61	$ (0.02)	$0.58
Average number of common and common equivalent shares outstanding for the Disney Common stock:			
Diluted	2,044	2,100	2,103
Basic	2,040	2,085	2,074
Loss attributed to Internet Group common stock	N/a	$ (117)	$ (276)
Loss per share attributed to Internet Group common stock (basic and diluted)	N/a	$ (2.72)	$ (6.18)
Average number of common and common equivalent shares outstanding for the Internet Group common stock	N/a	43	45

(1) Including Disney's retained interest in the Internet Group, Disney's retained interest in the Internet Group reflects 100% of Internet Group losses through November 17, 1999, approximately 72% for the period from November 18, 1999 through January 28, 2001 (the last date prior to the announcement of the conversion of the Internet Group common stock) and 100% thereafter.

Source: Company reports.

(*continued*)

EXHIBIT 1 | The Walt Disney Company and Subsidiaries Geographic Segments (cont.)

(In Millions)	2002	2001	2000
Geographic Segments			
Revenues			
United States and Canada	$20,770	$20,895	$21,036
Europe	2,724	2,599	2,745
Asia Pacific	1,325	1,232	1,150
Latin America and other	510	446	394
	$25,329	$25,172	$25,325
Segment Operating Income			
United States and Canada	$1,739	$3,045	$3,332
Europe	499	533	471
Asia Pacific	545	437	320
Latin America and other	39	(10)	(11)
	$2,822	$4,005	$4,112
Identifiable Assets			
United States and Canada	$47,241	$41,961	
Europe	2,355	1,428	
Asia Pacific	329	292	
Latin America and other	120	129	
	$50,045	$43,810	

(1) Identifiable assets include amounts associated with equity method investments, including notes and other receivables, as follows:

Media networks	$860	$792
Parks and resorts	$459	$408

(2) Includes goodwill and other intangible assets totaling $19,360 in 2002 and $14,351 in 2001.

(3) Primarily deferred tax assets, other investments, fixed and other assets.

Source: Company reports.

represented 45 percent of studio revenues, making it their largest single cash source.

Media Networks

The Media Networks division contained Disney's television and radio networks. It also operated the Walt Disney World Resort and Disney Cruise Line in Florida, the Disneyland Resort in Anaheim, California, and the ESPN Zone restaurants. Disney licensed the operations of Tokyo Disneyland in Japan, and both licensed and managed the Disneyland Resort Paris, located just outside of the French capital. The division's Studio Entertainment group produced live-action and animated motion pictures, television animation programs, musical recordings, and live-stage plays. Also within the division, the Consumer Products group licensed Walt Disney characters and other intellectual property to manufacturers, retailers, show promoters, and publishers worldwide.

Walt Disney operated the ABC television broadcast network and the ABC radio networks, along with a group of television and radio stations in the United States. Disney also owned cable, satellite and international broadcast operations including ESPN-branded networks, the Disney Channel, Disney Channel Worldwide, SOAPnet, Toon Disney, ABC Family Channel, and Fox Kids channels in Europe and Latin America. Disney also partially owned through joint ventures other media properties including A&E Television Networks, Lifetime Entertainment Services and E! Entertainment Television. The Media Networks division also produced original television programming.

Disney's television efforts offered a mixed picture throughout 2002 and into 2003. The television operations enjoyed strong sales but also experienced a surge in expenses, much of which were attributable to the war in Iraq. At the broadcast division, revenue increased

EXHIBIT 1 | The Walt Disney Company and Subsidiaries Consolidated Statements of Cash Flows (cont.)

	Year Ended September 30,		
(In millions)	**2002**	**2001**	**2000**
Net income (loss)	$1,236	$(158)	$920
Operating items not requiring cash			
Depreciation	1,021	987	962
Amortization of intangible assets	21	767	1,233
Gain on sale of businesses	(34)	(22)	(489)
Equity in the income of investees	(225)	(300)	(208)
Restructuring and impairment charges	—	1,247	92
Minority interests	101	104	107
Cumulative effect of accounting changes	—	278	—
Film and television costs	(97)	(13)	(210)
Other	364	402	164
	1,151	3,450	1,651
Change in working capital			
Receivables	(535)	279	223
Inventories	(35)	54	65
Other assets	(86)	6	36
Accounts and taxes payable and other accrued liabilities	225	(435)	436
Television costs	404	(149)	402
Deferred income taxes	(74)	1	22
	(101)	(244)	1,184
Cash provided by operations	2,286	3,048	3,755
Investing activities			
Investments in parks, resorts and other property	(1,086)	(1,795)	(2,013)
Acquisitions (net of cash acquired)	(2,845)	(480)	(34)
Dispositions	200	137	913
Proceeds from sale of investments	601	235	207
Purchases of investments	(9)	(88)	(82)
Investments in Euro Disney	—	—	(91)
Other	(37)	(24)	9
Cash used by investing activities	(3,176)	(2,015)	(1,091)
Financing activities			
Borrowings	4,038	3,070	1,117
Reduction of borrowings	(2,113)	(2,807)	(2,494)
Commercial paper borrowings, net	(33)	(186)	(741)
Exercise of stock options and other	47	177	482
Repurchases of common stock	—	(1,073)	(166)
Dividends	(428)	(438)	(434)
Cash provided (used by financing activities)	1,511	(1,257)	(2,236)
Increase (decrease) in cash and cash equivalents	621	(224)	428
Cash and cash equivalents, beginning of year	618	842	414
Cash and cash equivalents, end of year	$1,239	$ 618	$842
Supplemental disclosure of cash flow information:			
Interest paid	$674	$625	$583
Income taxes paid	$447	$881	$1,170

Source: Company reports.

(continued)

EXHIBIT 1 | The Walt Disney Company and Subsidiaries Business Segment Results (cont.)

(In millions)	Pro Forma (unaudited)		As Reported
	2002	**2001**	**2000**
Revenues			
Broadcasting	$5,064	$ 5,945	$6,327
Cable networks	4,699	4,212	3,509
	$9,763	$10,157	$9,836
Segment Operating Income			
Broadcasting	$ (36)	$ 783	$ 970
Cable networks	1,026	1,166	1,015
	$ 990	$ 1,949	$1,985

Source: Company reports.

13 percent to $1.4 billion, but operating losses increased from $13 million to $105 million in the first quarter of 2003. These revenue numbers were hurt by the fact that ABC was fourth in the ratings for broadcast networks in prime time during the 2001–2002 season.[7] Revenue from Disney's cable operations (principally ESPN and ABC Family) increased by 13 percent to $1.1 billion, but operating income rose just 5 percent to $337 million in the first quarter of 2003. Loss of advertising due to the war in Iraq was expected to cost Disney's television operations up to $70 million in the first quarter of 2003. Disney felt that it retained pricing power by announcing that ESPN would take its annual 20 percent increase in license fees beginning in August 2003. The company offered to strike deals for lower fees if cable and satellite operators signed on for longer term commitments with other ESPN programming offered by the cable network.[8] In 2003, there were four domestic ESPN networks and 87 million people in the United States interacted (i.e., watched, read the magazine, visited the Web site) with an ESPN media brand every week. ESPN International reached 120 million homes in 147 countries and territories. *ESPN The Magazine*, launched in 1998, had 1.7 million subscribers.[9]

Better news came from the Disney Channel, a cable network featuring children's entertainment, which celebrated its 20th anniversary in 2003. The Disney Channel more than tripled its revenue over the past 10 years, earning $736 million in 2002. It was the only commercial-free basic cable network for children, yet it generated $411 million in cash flow in 2002. The channel commanded premium subscription fees, with carriers paying around 75 cents per subscriber, well above the industry average of 25 cents per subscriber and far above Disney Channel's main competitors, AOL Time Warner's Nickelodeon, which charged 33 cents, and Viacom's Cartoon Network which charged 13 cents.[10] By 2003, there were 19 Disney Channels, four Toon Disney channels (featuring all-animation programming), and three Playhouse Disney channels (featuring programming for preschoolers) reaching 80 million households in the United States and 18 million internationally in 69 countries.[11]

The Disney Channel offered the kind of synergies that made the company rich in the past. In May 2003, Disney produced a popular movie based on a character from its popular live-action (i.e., nonanimated) *Lizzie McGuire* program, a hit with the 9- to 14-year-old audience. It was the first feature film Disney had released based on a live-action

---

[7]David Jefferson, "Finding Disney," *Newsweek,* June 2, 2003.

[8]"Disney Gets Slammed on the TV Side: War, Sports Rights and Unpaid Bills Take a Toll on Broadcast and Cable," *Broadcasting & Cable,* May 5, 2003.

[9]Robert A. Iger, president and COO, in prepared remarks for the shareholder meeting on March 19, 2003.

[10]Kimberly Speight, "Winning Ways: Disney Channel Celebrates 20 Years in the Business by Giving the Competition a Run for its Money," *Hollywood Reporter,* April 15, 2003.

[11]Michael Eisner in prepared remarks for the shareholder meeting on March 19, 2003.

TV show since the 1950s. The success of this franchise led the company to develop a new strategy toward programming on the channel. Disney Channel President Rich Ross described the company's strategy for its cable television programming as a "hammock." He said the company wanted to create a hammock that would span two important demographic groups: 2- to 8-year-old children and 9- to 14-year-old adolescents.[12] The Disney Channel, which had lacked programming for older children, seemed to be finding the hammocks that kept children viewing as they grew out of short pants.

Beyond hammocks, Disney was, as always, interested in merchandise. Robert Iger, president and chief operating officer of the Walt Disney Company said: "A major initiative of Disney Consumer Products is to work more closely with Disney Channel to develop merchandise for some of its popular programming. . . . One of the important benefits of this strategy is that successful TV shows are sustainable properties that last for years and therefore offer long life cycles for associated merchandise."[13]

Consumer Products

Disney's consumer products group offered mixed results over the past several years. The company was steadily reducing the number of stores it operated in the United States from 522 to 387 over the past three years. The company was also considering selling its chain of around 110 international retail stores, which was making a loss for the company. Such stores were being closed as the leases expired on their spaces.[14]

The store reduction seemed to be part of a strategy to forge direct links with retailers. The company was also expanding its line of Disney-branded merchandise to include foods (such as breakfast cereals and fruit drinks) as well as consumer electronics. The effort marked a change in Disney's past efforts at merchandising. Whereas the company had been content to let others create products that they licensed from Disney, now the company developed new merchandising ideas in collaboration with retailers. The president of Disney Consumer Products group estimated that the annual retail value of Disney-branded merchandise was $13 billion dollars.[15] That was a market too important for Disney to leave to others.

Among the new categories was consumer electronics. Disney announced that it would launch Disney-branded video and audio products. The products included a 13-inch color television, DVD player, personal digital radio, stereo CD boombox, personal CD player, and clock radio. The products were created with an outside design house and would be manufactured and distributed by Memcorp Inc., makers of Memorex consumer electronics. All products were specifically designed for ages 6 and older. The new Disney Electronics would initially be available at Circuit City, Sears, and Target.

Beyond new categories, Disney was repackaging its traditional wares. The company introduced a "Princesses" line of products for girls. The merchandise would feature characters such as Snow White and Sleeping Beauty from Disney's heritage, and Ariel from *The Little Mermaid*, from Disney's more recent movies. The company thought that the line would earn $1.4 billion at retail in 2003.[16]

It's a Rough World After All

Perhaps the most troubled group in 2003 was the company's Parks and Resorts division. Disney operated the Walt Disney World Resort in Florida, which included the Magic Kingdom, Epcot, Disney–MGM Studios and Disney's Animal Kingdom; 13 resort hotels; a retail, dining, and entertainment complex; a sports complex, and conference centers, campgrounds, golf courses, water parks, and other recreational facilities. In addition, Disney Cruise Line was operated out of Port Canaveral, Florida. The Disneyland Resort in California included Disneyland, Disney's California Adventure, three resort hotels, and Downtown Disney. Disney's Regional Entertainment group operated the ESPN Zone chain of sports-themed restaurants. Disney earned royalties on revenues generated by the Tokyo Disneyland Resort, which includes two theme parks and two Disney-branded hotels near Tokyo, Japan, and is owned and operated by an unrelated Japanese corporation. Walt Disney also had an investment in Euro Disney S.C.A., a publicly held French company that operated Disneyland Resort Paris, which included the Disneyland Park and the Walt Disney Studio Park; seven themed hotels and two convention centers; the Disney Village; a shopping, dining, and entertainment center; and a 27-hole golf facility. The company earns royalties on Disneyland Resort Paris revenues. A subsidiary of Walt

---

[12]Kimberly Speight, op. cit.

[13]Robert A. Iger, president and COO in prepared remarks for the shareholder meeting on March 19, 2003.

[14]Christopher Parkes, "Walt Disney Considers Sale of Its Retail Stores Chain," *Financial Times*, May 23, 2003, p. 18.

[15]Ibid.

---

[16]Christopher Parkes, "Interview: Andy Mooney, Walt Disney, Transformer of a Mickey Mouse Outfit," *Financial Times*, May 28, 2003, p.10.

Disney also receives management fees from Euro Disney. The company's Walt Disney Imagineering unit designs and develops new theme park concepts and attractions, as well as resort properties. Walt Disney also manages and markets vacation ownership interests in the Disney Vacation Club. This division also ran the company's NHL franchise.

Domestic and international park attendance was reduced by a combination of poor economy in the United States, reduction of travel in the period surrounding the war in Iraq and fear of severe acute respiratory syndrome (SARS) in various countries in Asia (although not Japan, home of Tokyo Disney) and Toronto, Canada. This was on top of a lackluster year in 2002, in which attendance was down 1 percent to 170.7 million in all major amusement parks in the United States.[17]

Disney predicted total profits for the fiscal year ending September 30, 2003 would be up 25 percent, which fell short of the 35 percent gain it reported in fiscal 2002. Disney lost attendance in most of its Orlando parks, but attendance grew 5 percent at Disneyland in California.[18] The company reduced costs in all of its parks. Parks and Resorts spent less than $650 million for fiscal 2002, more than $600 million below fiscal 2001. The company expected to hold down capital expenditures to similar levels in 2003.[19]

While holding down the costs at the parks, the company still planned to mine them for synergies with other division. For example, Disney planned two live-action movie releases in 2003, based on Disneyland attractions: *Pirates of the Caribbean* and *Haunted Mansion*.

Studio Entertainment

The Studio Entertainment segment produced live-action and animated motion pictures, television animation programs, musical recordings, and live-stage plays. Disney distributed its studio entertainment content through Walt Disney Pictures, Touchstone Pictures, Hollywood Pictures, Miramax, and Dimension studios. By the end of March 2003, films from Disney's various studios accounted for 25 percent of the domestic box office receipts in the first three months of 2003.[20]

In the early 1990s, Michael Eisner became famous for holding down movie production costs. It was a practice the company tried to continue. Two recent Disney films, *Bringing Down the House* and *Sweet Home Alabama* each cost a modest (by Hollywood standards) $35 million to produce. (In 2003, the average film in Hollywood cost $60 million to produce.)[21] *Sweet Home* generated over $125 million in domestic box office receipts, and by March 2003 was well on its way to selling over 8 million units in home video. The company expected the film to earn a total profit of over $130 million. *Bringing Down the House* looked as though it could meet or exceed *Sweet Home*'s box office total and should be a strong video title as well. However, Disney opened wide its wallet for the aforementioned *Pirates of the Caribbean* and *Haunted Mansion* movies, spending about $140 million and $90 million, respectively. Home video sales were an important source of revenue for the company. In 2002, Disney DVD unit sales increased by more than 50 percent over the prior year.[22]

Ironically, Disney's animated film department, where the company had made its name, was more of a worry. Most of Disney's animated feature successes in recent years had come from their partnership with Pixar, a studio that specialized in computer-generated animation, with Disney playing the distributor and taking profits. Disney had a deal with Pixar in which it paid or shared the production cost for seven films; in return, Disney took about 62 percent of the profits and retained ownership and sequel rights.[23] Disney's previous four animated films (not produced by Pixar) earned $357 million compared to the $856 million earned by Pixar's previous four releases, which included hits such as the *Toy Story* films, *A Bug's Life*, and *Monsters Inc.*[24]

---

[17]Wayne Friedman, "Attendance Down: Theme Parks Face Tough Summer," *Advertising Age,* April 28, 2003.

[18]Ibid.

[19]Thomas O. Staggs, senior executive vice president & CFO, prepared remarks for the shareholder meeting on March 19, 2003.

[20]Michael Eisner in prepared remarks for the shareholder meeting on March 19, 2003.

[21]Claudia Eller, "Disney Banking on Lower Cost Films," *Los Angeles Times,* April 6, 2003.

[22]Thomas O. Staggs, senior executive vice president & CFO, prepared remarks for the shareholder meeting on March 19, 2003.

[23]In the original deal with Pixar, Disney paid 100 percent of the production cost for the first feature (*Toy Story*), with an option for two additional pictures, and kept 80–90 percent of the profits along with IP rights. With the success of the initial Pixar features, the companies renegotiated and extended their agreement through 2006. Now they evenly split the production costs and Disney's share of the profits was about 62 percent, with Disney still retaining IP rights to the features. After the release of *Finding Nemo* in 2003, two additional features remained under the agreement. Source: Michael Eisner's comments at the Sanford C. Bernstein & Co. 19th Annual Strategic Decisions Conference, June 3, 2003.

[24]Jefferson, op.cit.

Pixar's success continued in the summer of 2003, with its release of *Finding Nemo,* which earned $70.3 million in less than a week, breaking box office earnings records for an animated feature. Buoyed by its success, perhaps chafing at the terms of its deal with Disney, and with only two films left in its Disney contract which ran to 2006, Pixar began discussions with other studios for future distribution deals. Michael Eisner expressed his confidence that Disney and Pixar would continue to do business together, but with perhaps a less rich deal. He said, "I suspect we will change the kind of relationship we have with Pixar, but I am fairly confident we will continue to be in business with them."[25] With the success of competing studios with an interest in digital animation, such as DreamWorks, Pixar did not lack for interested parties. For its part, Eisner said Disney had all of the assets in place to continue producing its own digital animation features. The company had eight such films under development by the middle of 2003. However, Eisner pointed to one asset that Disney lacked: "What Pixar has that we don't have is John Lasseter [Pixar executive vice president and director of the company's highly successful features]. . . . Every once in awhile a genetic accident falls into place; and John Lasseter *is* the unique thing at Pixar. (Emphasis Eisner.) Yes, their technology is a little ahead, but not that far ahead, you can buy a lot of the 3-D technology off the shelf. It is his ideas, sense of humor and inventiveness. . . . He is unique."[26] Prior to co-founding Pixar in 1986, Lasseter worked as an animator at Disney.[27]

In light of this important source of revenue, Disney speeded up its release cycle of the so-called platinum collection limited-release classic films. Such films are released for the home video market with great fanfare. After a year in release, the videos are "locked away" for a period of 10 years. The purpose was to impose a sense of urgency around ownership of classic titles. Eisner was quoted: "We determined we don't have to go to 10 [years moratorium]. . . . That increased the number of films that can go out. In addition, we want to go through our entire library by 2007 on DVD, because we believe that [midway through] 2007, we'll be looking at high-definition DVD, which gives us the

ability to start over again."[28] Left unsaid was the impact of popular file-sharing services on such a release strategy.

Disney's digital distribution strategy seemed uncertain by mid-2003. The company was in talks with cable, satellite, and IT providers to weigh the possibilities of video-on-demand services.

Further, the company was two years in the making with a plan to digitally stream movies via the unused portion of a station's spectrum to set-top boxes for an on-demand pay-TV service. In early 2003, the company announced it would conduct tests of a proposed service it called "Moviebeam." The service will offer 100 Disney movies from both current and library product.[29]

Putting Together a Digital Decade

Eisner pointed to several steps Disney undertook to put the company on the road to its Digital Decade. Disney content was appearing on advanced third-generation cell phone systems in Japan and Europe. The ABC broadcast network was the only network in the United States broadcasting in true high definition, including Dolby 5.1 digital surround sound. Eisner also held out the promise of new interactive features to accompany its traditional content. He called this "a strategy of offense that will help combat the problem of piracy as effectively as defensive legislative and encryption strategies."[30] Eisner told shareholders:

> The changes enabled by the digital revolution will go to the core of what entertainment—especially Disney entertainment—is all about . . . emotional connection with audiences. For example, fans of our animated characters will be able to relate to them in new ways as these characters take on a new dimension, both literally and figuratively . . . transformed into the hyper-reality of 3-D animation. Where this takes our company going forward has no limits, whether talking about new and original content or redistributing or remaking of content from the phenomenal Disney library.
>
> As a company, we are committed to aggressively pursuing the opportunities of the digital world. The ones

[25]Michael Eisner comments at the Sanford C. Bernstein & Co. 19th Annual Strategic Decisions Conference, June 3, 2003.

[26]Ibid.

[27]http://www.pixar.com/companyinfo/aboutus/mte.html.

[28]"Disney on Platinum Push for Earnings: Roster of Classic Films Grows as Rotation Quickens Through 2007," *Video Business,* May 5, 2003.

[29]"ABC's On-Demand 'Moviebeam' Gets a Test: Without Fanfare, Network Experiments with Streaming Service," *Broadcasting & Cable,* April 14, 2003.

[30]Michael Eisner in prepared remarks for the shareholder meeting on March 19, 2003.

who benefit the most will be the ones who are first to embrace this new way to connect with audiences. It offers opportunities we can only begin to imagine as we are just at the beginning of this digital decade.

Conclusion

The Disney Corporation was, by any definition, a formidable entertainment conglomerate. The company pioneered and continued the practice of successfully earning more money in new ways from the IP it created. With its films, broadcast, and cable television, amusement parks, live-action plays, and other channels, Disney possessed myriad ways to pull money from consumers. The development of those channels was the hallmark of what Michael Eisner called the "Disney Decade." However, during that decade, Disney's hold on animated features, or more specifically digital animation, slipped. Now that he wanted the company to embark on a "Digital Decade," what would Disney need to do?

Case 5.4

Universal Music Group in 2003

Several factors are combining to debilitate the current business model. File sharing, illegal copying of music, the easy availability of CD burners, dedicated retail consolidation, retail outlets that are getting killed, a generation of people who have never had to buy music, the shrinking number of distributors, and increased competition from video games and other forms of entertainment for the loose change in consumers' pockets. . . . This is the perfect storm that we must battle.

— Tom Sturges, EVP Creative Affairs, Universal Music Publishing Group[1]

Introduction

2003 was a critical time for the recording industry. For all of its glamor, the business of making and selling recorded music had become staid, with an oligopoly of companies using well-established business models to produce the same products in the same ways. But within the span of just a few years, a series of forces hit the industry and threatened to change it forever.

Sales of recorded music had declined globally and in the United States for each of the past three years. In addition, the industry was struggling to deal with the twin forces of digitization of music and efficient and easy Internet distribution of digitized content. Increasingly powerful and useful personal computers (PCs) that played and copied all types of content, widely available broadband Internet connectivity, and popular and easy-to-use

---

[1]All quotes from Tom Sturges are from the author's interview on February 27, 2003. Subsequent quotes from this interview will not be cited.

Lewis Fanger, MBA '03, and Cecilia Goytisolo O'Reilly, MBA '03, prepared this case under the supervision of Professor Robert A. Burgelman and Philip E. Meza as the basis for class discussion rather than to illustrate either effective or ineffective handling of an administrative situation.

file sharing services created unprecedented threats and opportunities for the recording industry. By 2003, the industry had had a couple of years to come to terms with these forces. As the largest of the big five recording companies, Universal Music Group (UMG) had a lot at stake. How should UMG respond to changes in the industry? What were the biggest challenges to UMG's current business model and where would the biggest opportunities be in the future? With the International Federation of the Phonographic Industry (IFPI), the organization representing the international recording industry, projecting a further 5–7 percent drop in music sales in 2003, it was imperative that UMG start finding solutions soon.

History of Universal Music Group

The history of Universal Music Group goes back to the days of the silent nickelodeon theaters of the early 1900s. Originally consisting of a single theater showcasing short films in Chicago, Illinois, Universal's precursor company, the Independent Moving Picture Company owned by pioneer filmmaker Carl Laemmle, soon expanded to include film distribution and production to avoid onerous licensing fees charged by studios and their distribution arms. In 1915, Laemmle moved his company to Universal City, California, and renamed it Universal Film Manufacturing Company. It operated the world's first self-contained filmmaking community. In 1952, music label Decca Records purchased a controlling interest in Universal.

Also originally based in Chicago, the Music Corporation of America (MCA) was founded in 1924 by Jules Stein as an agency that booked bands for various clubs. The now legendary Hollywood executive Lew Wasserman joined the company in 1936 and, through the development of both film and television production businesses, led the company into the forefront of recorded entertainment. In 1962, after several years of sharing space on the Universal lot, MCA officially merged with Universal by purchasing Decca Records, then Universal's parent company.

Beginning in the 1960s, Wasserman sought to diversify MCA/Universal beyond film and television by investing more in music and live entertainment assets. In 1964, the company purchased Leeds Music and Duchess Music, and MCA's Music Publishing arm began taking shape. Several other music acquisitions occurred over the ensuing years, including ABC Records (1979), Chess Records (1985), and Geffen Records (1990).

EXHIBIT 1 |

Revenue Distribution
for Vivendi Universal
by Business Unit
(In Millions)

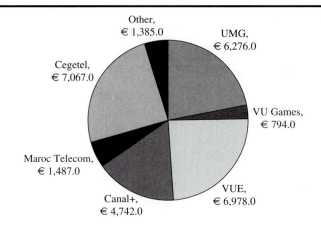

Universal Music Group (UMG)—The largest recorded music business in the world, UMG acquires, manufactures, markets, and distributes recorded music in 63 countries. Key recording artists include Eminem, Ashanti, Shania Twain, and U2. The company also manufactures, sells, and distributes music videos and DVDs, and owns mail-order music/video clubs.

Vivendi Universal Games—VU Games develops, markets, and distributes games for both the worldwide PC and console gaming markets.

Vivendi Universal Entertainment (VUE)—Based in the United States, VUE focuses on the film, television, and theme park markets. Universal Pictures Group produces and distributes motion pictures; Universal Television Group produces and distributes television programming (including *Law and Order* and *The Jerry Springer show*) and owns four U.S. cable television networks (including USA Network and the Sci Fi Channel); and Universal Parks and Resorts operates theme parks and resorts in the U.S., Japan, and Spain.

Canal+ Group—In addition to serving as a leading European studio for film and television, the Canal+ Group is the leader in the production and distribution of digital and analog pay-TV in France.

Marco Telecom—Maroc Telecom is the incumbent fixed line and leading mobile telecom operator in Morocco.

Cegetel Group—Through two majority-owned subsidiaries, SFR and Cegetel, this group is the second largest mobile telecom and second largest fixed line operator in France.

Source: Company reports.

The 1990s marked a period of larger corporate ownership for the company, when Japanese technology conglomerate Matsushita Electric Industrial Company purchased MCA in 1991 for $6.6 billion. Less than four years later, the Seagram Company (known for its spirits business) acquired 80 percent of MCA in 1995 for $5.7 billion and soon thereafter renamed it Universal. Under the leadership of Edgar Bronfman, Jr., whose family closely controlled Seagram, Universal Music Group was transformed into the largest music label in the world, through purchases of Interscope Records and Polygram (A&M, Def Jam, and Island Records).

In June 2000, Seagram sold the Universal entertainment assets (which also included motion picture and television studios and theme parks) to the French conglomerate Vivendi, forming Vivendi Universal (VU). By early 2002, VU was staggering under the tremendous debt it built up buying various assets such as Universal. With a management coup and several board defections, Universal Music Group's fate with Vivendi Universal was unclear in April 2003. Universal Music Group was one of six business units, representing 23 percent of total revenues in 2002. The five other business units were Cegetel Group, Vivendi Universal Entertainment, Canal+ Group, Maroc Telecom, and Vivendi Universal Games (Exhibit 1).

EXHIBIT 1 | Selected Financial Data for Vivendi Universal (cont.)

(In € Millions)	Actual			Pro Forma	
	2000	**2001**	**2002**	**2001**	**2002**
French GAAP					
Revenue	41,580	57,360	58,150	27,733	28,729
Revenue, excluding Vivendi Environnement	15,286	28,266	28,112	27,733	28,729
Operating income	1,823	3,795	3,788	2,113	2,037
Net financial expense	(762)	(1,928)	(4,742)	(1,108)	(4,068)
Income before exceptional items, taxes, goodwill Amortization, equity interest, and minority interest	1,061	1,867	(954)	1,005	(2,031)
Net income (loss)	2,299	(13,597)	(23,301)	(13,228)	(24,108)
Net income (loss) excluding goodwill amortization and impairment	2,933	1,606	(3,582)	729	(4,626)
Revenue segment data					
Cegetel Group	5,129	6,384	7,067	6,384	7,067
Universal Music Group	495	6,560	6,276	6,560	6,276
Vivendi Universal Entertainment	194	4,938	6,270	6,874	6,978
Canal+ Group	4,054	4,563	4,833	4,563	4,742
Maroc Telecom	—	1,013	1,487	1,351	1,487
Vivendi Universal Games	572	657	794	657	794
Holding & Corporate	—	—	—	—	—
Other	2,667	1,289	1,385	1,344	1,385
Total revenue	13,111	25,404	28,112	27,733	28,729
EBITDA segment data					
Cegetel Group	—	1,705	2,329	—	2,329
Universal Music Group	—	1,158	961	—	961
Vivendi Universal Entertainment	—	653	1,197	—	1,334
Canal+ Group	—	571	224	—	253
Maroc Telecom	—	540	786	—	786
Vivendi Universal Games	—	132	171	—	171
Holding & Corporate	—	(261)	(483)	—	(483)
Other	—	(105)	(19)	—	(20)
Total EBITDA	—	4,393	5,166	—	5,331
U.S. GAAP					
Revenues, excluding Vivendi Environnement	11,961	28,259	28,012	27,726	28,629
Net income (loss)	1,908	(1,172)	(44,467)	—	(44,447)
Net income (loss) excluding goodwill amortization and impairment	2,607	534	(4,518)	—	(4,518)

Note: Pro forma results reflect the acquisition of the entertainment assets of USA Networks (May 2002), the acquisition of Maroc Telecom (April 2001), and MP3.com (May 2001)—and the disposition of certain interests in Vivendi Environnement (through December 2002) and VU Publishing (December 2002)—as if these transactions had occurred at the beginning of 2001.

Source: Company reports.

EXHIBIT 2 | Major Releases for Universal Music Group, 2002 and 2003

Artist	Units Sold (mm)
1Q 2002	
Now That's What I Call Music Vol. 9	2.2
Devdas OST	2.0
O Brother OST	1.9
Aach Mujhe Achche Lagne OST	1.4
Nickelback	1.3
2Q 2002	
Eminem	7.6
Nelly	2.7
Ashanti	2.2
Sheryl Crow	2.1
Papa Roach	1.3
3Q 2002	
Eminem	3.4
Nelly	3.0
Bon Jovi	1.9
Toby Keith	1.8
Enrique Iglesias	1.0
4Q 2002	
Shania Twain	8.1
8 Mile OST	6.1
U2	5.2
Nirvana	3.8
Eminem	2.9

Source: UMG.

Upcoming Artist Releases

1H 2003	2H 2003
Limp Bizkit	U2
Method Man	Enrique Iglesias
Mary J. Blige	Ja Rule
Ludacris	Ronan Keating
Metallica	No Doubt
Stevie Wonder Tribute	Ashanti
Florent Pagny	Sting
The Cardigans	Nine Inch Nails
Ryan Adams	Blink 182
Marilyn Manson	Dr. Dre
Musiq	Jay Z
Brian McKnight	Diana Krall
Terri Clark	Nelly Furtado
Lucinda Williams	Sophie Ellis Bextor
	Tupac
	India Arie
	Puddle of Mudd
	Vanessa Carlton
	Texas
	Noir Desir
	Zucchero (Live)
	Johnny Hallyday (Live)
	DMX

Source: UMG.

Consisting of both recorded music (the various record labels, including Geffen, MCA, Motown, Verve, Polydor, Decca, and Island Def Jam) and music publishing (Universal Music Publishing Group), UMG was arguably the most successful music company in 2002, with operations in 63 countries and making one of every four albums sold worldwide. In addition to having the most successful album of 2002 (Eminem's *The Eminem Show* sold 12 million units), the company also won 31 Grammy Awards at the 2003 ceremony. Additionally, Universal Music Publishing Group (UMPG) increased its library to over 1 million copyrights as of year-end 2002, including songs by Prince, U2, Shania Twain, and No Doubt.

Although the global market for CD sales fell by 7 percent during 2002, UMG revenues declined by only 2 percent and the company's worldwide market share actually increased. Management believed its focus on a well-diversified artist portfolio combined with its long-term artist contracts, which indirectly forced management to focus on artist development for the long-term, helped abate some of the "perfect storm" forces affecting the industry. (For a summary of UMG's best-selling albums of 2002, as well as its top outlooks for 2003, see Exhibit 2.)

Traditional Music Label Business Model and Industry Dynamics

Every year, an estimated 7,000 nonclassical albums are released.[2] These releases are issued by companies commonly known as record labels. Record labels manufacture

---

[2]Harold L. Vogel, *Entertainment Industry Economics,* Cambridge University Press (Cambridge: 2001), p. 163.

EXHIBIT 3 | Manufacturing Costs for CDs, Circa 1990

Revenues per unit	$8.75
Cost per unit	
Raw media	$0.90
Pressing/recording costs	0.80
Jewel box/plastic casing	0.40
Package	0.35
Printed material	0.10
	$2.55
Gross profit per unit [(1)]	$6.20

(1) Gross profit before royalties and overhead (including write-downs of unsuccessful albums) and marketing costs.

Source: Harold Vogel, *Entertainment Industry Economics*, Cambridge University Press (Cambridge: 1990), p. 144.

(*continued*)

and market CDs, tapes, digital downloads, and other media of music. Record labels can also engage in music publishing. Although production, distribution, and publishing are often a part of the same corporate family, they need not be.

Music Labels

The music labels earned revenue solely off of the sales of CDs, tapes, legal digital downloads, and other related music media. Production costs, paid upfront by the label, for a typical album were approximately $125,000, but could reach upwards of $300,000. With only 5–10 percent of new album releases ever becoming a hit and reaching gold status (500,000 units sold in the United States) and the average artist lasting only three albums, music labels assumed a sizable amount of risk for each new artist they signed and each album they authorized for recording (Exhibit 3).

Radio stations, which represented a good source of promotion for recording artists, added only three or four songs to their playlists in any given week. Thus, record labels spent considerable sums for promotion. Posters, in-store displays, radio/television commercials, press kits, free records to radio stations, and numerous other marketing items were quite expensive. For a standard release, typical marketing expenses ran to $100,000 per album and could exceed $500,000 for a major artist release. Additionally, music videos were typically produced at an additional cost, ranging from $70,000 to $100,000 for new and midlevel artists: all for the extremely *un*likely chance of creating a hit record.

For example, during 2001, MCA Records spent over $2.2 million to produce and market *Ultimate High,* an album by 18-year-old recording artist Carly Hennessy. Part of this cost included a $100,000 advance to Hennessy, in addition to living expenses of $5,000 during album production and $500,000 for promotional appearances. With such high costs, Hennessy needed to sell between 500,000 and 700,000 units for MCA to break even. The company was confident that it was possible, however, given Hennessy's prominence in her native Ireland as both a character in the musical *Les Miserables* and a spokesmodel for a brand of sausage. Three months after the album's release, though, *Ultimate High* had sold only 378 units for total revenues of only $4,900.[3]

Because the up-front cost of recording (but not releasing) an album is relatively small compared to the costs of marketing and distributing a CD, record labels traditionally have a large catalog of unreleased albums. This large pool of unreleased albums allows record labels to quickly diversify their portfolio of bets on new releases, as the trends in hit albums can change unexpectedly.

After an album was finally approved for release and manufactured, it still had to be distributed for sale. The physical distribution process was difficult to manage. Since the probability of achieving a hit was so small, an unexpected hit record required the quick replenishment of inventories in countless retail outlets across the country. It was important that a distribution company be large enough to stock and ship hundreds of thousands of units on short notice, a requirement that forced many large record labels to handle their own distribution. Smaller independent labels, lacking the capital to distribute products on their own, often used the distribution arms of major labels as their distribution network. To reach "mom and pop" retail record stores and smaller towns, record labels turned to independent distributors. These regional distributors, using their knowledge of the local market, targeted specific products to each niche outlet (Exhibit 4).

Music Publishing

Music publishers coordinate the licensing of songs, whether to record labels for inclusion on an album, to radio stations for play on the radio, or to film/television/advertising companies in commercials and soundtracks

---

[3]Jennifer Ordonez, "Behind the Music: MCA Spent Millions on Carly Hennessy," *The Wall Street Journal*, February 26, 2002, p. A-1

EXHIBIT 3 |

Major Divisions of a
Typical Record Label
(cont.)

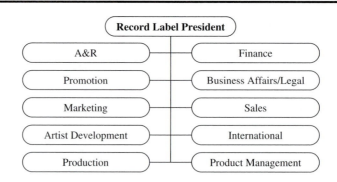

The typical record label includes many divisions in addition to distribution. They include:

A&R (Artists & Repertoire)—Through its own talent scouts and other sources, the A&R department is constantly looking for new talent to sign and develop.

Promotion—Promotion handles relations with radio stations and focuses on getting more time for the label's singles.

Marketing—This department handles artwork for albums, promotional merchandise (including promotional videos), in-store displays, advertising, and publicity.

Artist Development—This department helps artists out with tour efforts, including promotions in each of the cities visited and the ample stocking of record stores with the touring artist's CDs.

Production—This department covers basic factory functions such as manufacturing, assembling, and shipping of CDs, tapes, etc.

Finance—Finance overlooks many of the accounting/budget aspects of the music business, such as the computation of royalties and the number of units that an artist sells.

Business Affairs/Legal—This department negotiates and drafts legal contracts with artists, record clubs, foreign licensees, etc.

Sales—This department focuses on stores, ensuring that albums are making their way onto store shelves.

International—Employees in this department oversee the release of albums outside of the United States, often coordinating the actions of the same departments as listed above, but in other countries.

Product Management—This division coordinates the efforts of all the other departments to create the best-possible marketing push for an artist's new album, hopefully resulting in large sales.

Source: Reprinted with the permission of Simon & Schuster Adult Publishing Group from *All You Need to Know About the Music Business* by Donald S. Passman. Copyright © 1991, 1994 1997 by Donald S. Passman.

(Exhibit 5). Unlike record labels, which essentially only earn revenues from the sale of CDs (or other media), the typical music publishing company has a more diversified revenue stream. These revenue sources, totaling approximately $2 billion in the United States and $7 billion worldwide in 1999, are comprised of:

- *Mechanical Royalties*—A record company must pay songwriters and music publishers for the use of every song on an album. The payment for these rights is called a mechanical royalty. Typically, a record label pays $0.08 per song on an album (called the statutory mechanical rate), with 75 percent of

the royalty paid to the songwriter and the remainder paid to the publishing company. For new bands, mechanical royalties are often only $0.06 to compensate for the additional risk to the record company of introducing an unknown artist. Record companies also usually add a cap or ceiling of 10 or 11 songs per album.[4]

- *Performance Income*—Performance income stems from the payment for the right to play songs on the radio, on television, in concert, in nightclubs, and

---

[4]Figures per phone conversations with Tom Sturges.

EXHIBIT 4 | Music Industry—Current Distribution Process Flow

Major Record Company Distribution

The above diagram shows how most records are distributed to stores. A record label creates and manufactures the CD and distributes the CD through a network that it owns.

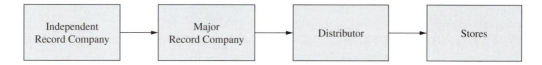

Independent Record Company—Distributed by a Major Record Label

The above diagram shows one possible way for independent labels to distribute their music to stores. The major record labels allow the use of their distribution networks, although the independent records may not get the same attention to detail as the major labels' products.

True Independent Record Company Distribution

The above diagram shows another possible way for independent labels to distribute their music to stores. Using independent distributors located regionally around the United States and world, independent labels can more easily target niche music stores—because these regional players are more wired into local music scene—and "mom and pop" shops too small to be efficiently handled by the major label distribution outfits.

Source: Reprinted with the permission of Simon & Schuster Adult Publishing Group from *All You Need to Know About the Music Business* by Donald S. Passman. Copyright © 1991, 1994, 1997 by Donald S. Passman.

so on. Instead of handling these payments on an individual basis, performing rights societies such as BMI and ASCAP coordinate payments to the publishing companies. For radio play, publishing companies typically split 5 percent of a radio station's total advertising revenue.

- *Synchronization/Transcription Fees*—These licenses are payments for the use of music in films, television shows, filmed commercials, etc. (called "synch licenses" because the music is synchronized with visual images) and radio commercials (transcription licenses). Typical television licenses can earn between $1,000 and $3,000 for the use of a song in a television program, while typical film fees range from $15,000 to $75,000 and higher, and typical television commercial fees go from

$25,000 to $500,000 and higher. However, these fees can vary widely depending on the popularity and current market value of a song. For example, Madonna recently earned approximately $4 million for the use of her song "Ray of Light" in one year's worth of Microsoft television commercials.[5] Other artists, such as the group Coldplay, refuse to license their songs to commercials in order to maintain artistic independence.

- *Print/Publishing*—Print/publishing consists of sheet music (e.g., for pianos) and folios (an entire book of songs). Sometimes a folio consists of a varied collection of songs, called a mixed folio, while a matching folio includes all of the songs of

[5] Ibid.

EXHIBIT 5 |

Revenue Distribution
for a Typical Music
Publishing Company

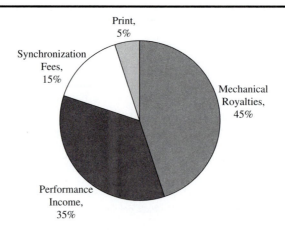

- Music publishing companies focus on the business of the music industry and handle the licensing of songs to other parties. Some of the major publishing companies include Warner/Chappell and Universal Music Publishing Group (UMPG), although they need not be affiliated with a major label. Note that many songwriters will have their albums manufactured and marketed by one label (e.g., Virgin/EMI) while keeping their publishing rights at another unaffiliated company (e.g., UMPG).

Source: Company estimates.

a particular album. Publishing companies typically receive 20 percent of the retail price for sheet music to a single song, or approximately 15 percent of the retail price for a folio.

Tom Sturges, executive vice president for creative affairs of Universal Music Publishing Group, commented on the ability of other publishing revenue streams to make up for declining revenue from reduced mechanical royalties: "Publishers have the advantage of multiple income streams. As we see the decline in mechanical royalties, we've made additional efforts in our other areas, like synchronization fees."

Industry Structure

As of early 2003, the global market for recorded music, valued at roughly $33.7 billion, was dominated by five major players: Universal Music Group, Sony, Warner Music Group (WMG) EMI, and BMG. These "big five" together accounted for roughly 74 percent of the industry in 2002 (Exhibit 6). UMG led the big five, with 23 percent of the market. This oligopoly structure was the result of several years of consolidation, motivated by the desire to create synergies from combining record company assets, from production to distribution, under one roof in order to better compete globally.

Further, these recording heavyweights—all except EMI, which was a pure play in recorded music—were nestled into highly diversified portfolios of companies. For example, industry market share leader UMG belonged to the troubled media conglomerate, VU. In 2002, UMG represented 22 percent of total VU revenues. The other major labels represented smaller portions of their parent company's total revenues and were often dwarfed by other business units (Exhibit 7). The big five record labels that were owned by media conglomerates had been referred to as mere "duchies in large media empires with other, often conflicting priorities."[6] Indeed, Sony Electronics represented a whopping 70 percent of Sony Corporation's total revenues while Sony Music represented only 8 percent. Similarly, AOL Time Warner was refocusing on high-speed Internet services (one common use of which is downloading free music) much to the reputed distaste of its Warner Music subsidiary.[7] Elsewhere, two main music executives at BMG resigned in outrage at parent company Bertelsmann's investment in Napster.

VU was not the only empire unwinding its portfolio. In February of 2003, WMG was officially in play. Parent

[6]Charles C. Mann, "The Year the Music Dies," *Wired Magazine,* February 2003, pp. 90–93.

[7]Ibid.

EXHIBIT 6 | Market Shares in the Global Recording Industry 2000–2002E

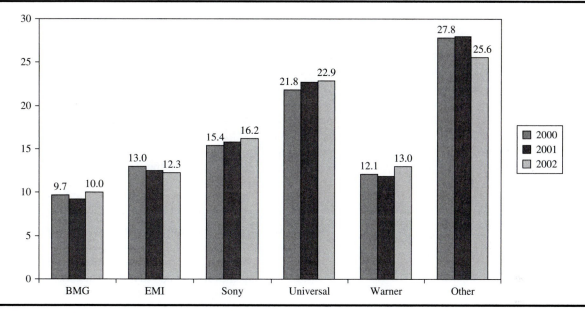

Note: 2002 data are Morgan Stanley Research Estimates, May 8, 2002.

Source: Company data, IFPI, Morgan Stanley Research.

company AOL-Time Warner entered into preliminary talks about selling a majority stake in Warner Music to rival music company EMI. Corporate leadership was also in flux. In January 2003, Howard Stringer, chairman and chief executive of Sony Corporation of America, replaced Sony Music's high-profile leader Tommy Mottola with Andrew Lack, former president of NBC and an outsider to the music industry. Stringer said, "The industry has been run from the beginning by A&R (artists and repertoire) people and at this point we needed a better view."[8] Meanwhile, EMI stated in its 2002 annual

---

[8]Tim Burt, "Films and Music at the Centre of a Revolution," *Financial Times,* February 11, 2003.

EXHIBIT 7 | Music Revenues and Operating Profit as a Percentage of Parent Company's Revenues and Operating Profit

		Revenues			Operating Profit		
		Music	**Parent**	**%**	**Music**	**Parent**	**%**
Music Entity	**Parent**						
Universal Music	Vivendi-Universal	6,276	28,729	21.8%	556	1,877	29.6%
Sony Music	Sony Corporation	4,833	56,979	8.5	152	1,012	15.0
EMI	EMI	3,504	3,504	100	273	273	100
Warner Music	AOL Time Warner	3,929	38,234	10.3	419	9,656	4.3
BMG Entertainment	Bertelsmann	3,324	17,998	18.5	(5)	1,084	−0.5
Other	n/m	11,276	n/m	n/m	n/m	n/m	n/m
Total		32,779					

Note 1: All figures given in $mm except Vivendi Universal, given in €mm.

Note 2: UMG, WMG FYE 12/31; Sony, EMY FYE 3/31, and BMG FYE 6/30.

Source: Company year-end reports.

report that it had made "a number of senior level appointments" to drive the company's long-term transformation from a "record company to a more broadly based music business."

Several industry insiders hinted that the parent company's short-term focus on earnings had caused pressure on the music labels to achieve short-term returns in the development of its artists, where traditionally the music labels preferred to invest more time in the development of each of its roster artists. Jim Guerinot, manager to popular acts such as No Doubt and Beck, argued against the "Wall Street mentality" that he saw plaguing record labels once larger conglomerates took rein:

> No longer do we have guys running their labels from a creative point of view. Instead it became like running a public company. The expectation for growth and profit transformed our business into much more of a traditional business, but this is not a traditional business. You are dealing with artists and creativity. The delivery of albums on time, for example, can be hard. What happens between an expected release date of October and the actual pushed-back release date of January? An artist wakes up in the morning and comes up with the greatest song that he's ever written. That's the delay. The creative process is the delay. You can't put a time on that. Executives at the top—outside of the label—have taken a business model of making the best record to get the best sales and turned it into a corporate model of looking for earnings growth.[9]

The Music Industry Since 2001

After the demise of Napster in 2001, other free file-sharing programs quickly emerged to take its place. Napster, a hybrid peer-to-peer (P2P[10]) service with centralized servers, had been easy to shut down. The next generation of file-sharing networks, such as Gnutella (an open source network shared by users of the software programs written for it—Morpheus, BearShare, LimeWire, and FastTrack (a proprietary network[11] hosting the users of Grokster, Kazaa, and iMesh)—were true P2P programs, operating without central servers. With true P2P software, users could search for music files residing directly on other users' computers without being directed by a centralized server. This network structure made responsibility for illegal music files (and litigation targets) more diffuse. Most of the P2P networks sustained themselves for a time through advertising revenue, but litigators increasingly tied these companies up in court. Although the labels became savvier about otherwise preventing their content from being shared illegally, providing for legitimate subscription-based download services as an alternative, and companies and universities began limiting file-sharing activity, P2P networks continued to thrive. Compared to a February 2001 estimate of Napster's number of concurrent users (1.6 million users[12]), the ever popular P2P, Morpheus, had 1.08 million average concurrent users in February 2002.[13] Following an aggressive attack on Morpheus[14] later that month, Kazaa and the FastTrack network reached estimated concurrent user levels of 2.78 million by October 2002.[15]

Subscription Services

Simultaneously, the record labels launched their initial efforts to provide legitimate alternatives to the P2P networks. In December 2001, Pressplay (a joint venture

---

[9]All quotes from Jim Guerinot are from the author's interview on March 19, 2003. Subsequent quotes from this interview will not be cited.

[10]Peer-to-peer (P2P) refers to a class of applications that uses resources such as storage, processing cycles, content (e.g., digitized music or video files), etc., available on PCs and servers connected to the Internet. Because accessing these decentralized resources means operating in an environment of unstable connectivity and unpredictable IP addresses, P2P nodes must operate outside the DNS system and have significant or total autonomy from central servers. (Source: Clay Shirkey, "What Is P2P and What It Isn't," O'Reilly & Associates' OpenP2P.com.) DNS is short for domain name system (or service), an Internet protocol that translates domain names into IP addresses.

[11]FastTrack was designed by a Dutch company known as Consumer Empowerment. The company used this technology to build Kazaa and then licensed it to MusicCity.com, which built Morpheus (which later switched to Gnutella), and Grokster, Ltd., which built Grokster.

[12]Antonette Goroch, "Neo-Napsters Proliferate in the Wake of Napster's Demise," *Broadband Week,* August 20, 2001.

[13]Report on FastTrack network user by Redshift Research, Inc. "Kazaa Use Grows by Nearly 70% in Two Months as Morpheus Fades," May 1, 2002, http://www.redshiftresearch.com/pressrelease3.asp.

[14]Cade Metz, "The File Swap Flip-Fop," *PC Magazine,* March 28, 2002. On February 26, 2002 Morpheus clients stopped working. Though reasons are unclear, it is generally accepted that Morpheus came under a denial of service attack from the FastTrack network, Morpheus client machines' registries were altered, and users received a message encouraging and helping them to migrate to Kazaa.

[15]Redshift Research, Inc., http://www.redshiftresearch.com/P2PUserStats.asp.

between Sony and UMG) and MusicNet (a joint venture between AOL Time Warner, Bertelsmann AG, EMI) were launched. Both offered a monthly subscription service in exchange for different tiers of access to online songs. Subscription rates ranged from $9.95 to $14.95 per month. These first incarnations of subscription services received mixed reviews from users who could not access as many songs as were available on P2P networks. However, over the past couple of years the labels increased the number of songs available on these services. They have also embarked upon various other digital distribution services via third-party agreements (such as UMG's distribution agreement with TowerRecords.com and other click-and-mortar retail distributors to sell digital tracks online).

By early 2003, the industry had begun launching version 2.0 of its online subscription services. Tom Sturges, executive vice president of creative affairs at Universal Music Publishing Group, reflected on the industry's initial inability to capitalize on file-sharing. "This was the first time that the music business did not take advantage of a new technology. When we moved from LPs to cassettes, sales grew. From cassettes to CDs, sales grew. Some major players believe we lost the digital distribution opportunity altogether by not embracing Napster. They had collected 45 million users. These were centralized users—not distributed over P2P networks in multiple places. They loved music and, who knows, might have paid for the service Napster had to offer." While some music industry executives continued to compare file sharing to theft, seeing it as a threat, Sturges saw parallels with the business's other marketing efforts, "What is MTV? What is radio? They were fantastic marketing and promotion vehicles via which the industry introduces its talent to the world. And what was Napster? Why was it so different and why were we unable to see the potential benefits?"

As early as 1999, some people were predicting the demise of traditional retail distribution for music. One particularly sanguine investment report at the time postulated that by 2003, consumers would rarely if ever drive to Tower Records for their music.[16] Instead they "would tap into a vast cloud of music on the Net. This heavenly jukebox, as it is sometimes called, will hold the contents of every record store in the world, all of it instantly accessible from any desktop."

So what was taking so long for music companies to construct their heavenly jukeboxes, and come out with competitive offerings for digital distribution? It wasn't that easy, explained Amanda Marks, senior vice president, Universal Music Group/e-Labs. Once the labels began to recognize the potential for digital distribution, they had a gargantuan task ahead of them, especially those like UMG with aggressive digital distribution plans. "We are the biggest music company with the most to lose, so it is incumbent upon us to transform all our business processes for digital distribution."[17] Specifically, the company undertook massive efforts to digitize and metatag (code that describes the content of the work so that full attribution is available for recovering royalties) on a track-by-track level, thus adding new infrastructure while converting legacy systems and feeding these into the company's new digital distribution support system. These steps were necessary to make track-by-track sales a reality. For example, said Marks, "We had to tag each track with unique identifiers so each could flow through the royalty system, paying artists accordingly. For instance, on a Billie Holliday Greatest Hits album there could be three different versions of the same song, and a different trail of royalty participants for each, with different payment setups for the different producers and musicians on each different track."

Moreover, the scale was enormous since the company had committed itself to making its entire active catalog (110,000 tracks, which excluded classical, which were not in the legacy systems) available to customers via á la carte downloads. By March 2003 UMG had approximately 70,000 tracks online. Marks recounted the strides e-Labs had made:

> We're proud of having already made over 70,000 tracks available to the marketplace through 30 or so affiliate sites and services—the largest volume seen so far—and aiming for the full active catalog by end of 2003. Also, we were the first to come out with tens of thousands of tracks at a $0.99 price-point, a price we thought would be in the consumers' sweet spot.

UMG and the other labels continued their steady progress toward robust digital distribution catalogs, but their efforts were haunted by structural challenges in certain segments. One problem was efficient handling of micropayments (small charges) for online music consumption.

---

[16]Sanford C. Bernstein & Co. Investment Research Group report, as cited in Charles C. Mann, "The Heavenly Juke Box," *The Atlantic,* December 15, 1999, http://www.theatlantic.com/issues/2000/09/mann.htm.

[17]All quotes from Amanda Marks are from the author's interview on March 5, 2003. Subsequent quotes from this interview will not be cited.

EXHIBIT 8 | Music Consumer Profile, 1992–2001

Consumer Profile by Age

	1992	1993	1994	1995	1996	1997	1998	1999	2000	2001
10–14 Years	8.6%	8.6%	7.9%	8.0%	7.9%	8.9%	9.1%	8.5%	8.9%	8.5%
15–19 Years	18.2	16.7	16.8	17.1	17.2	16.8	15.8	12.6	12.9	13.0
20–24 Years	16.1	15.1	15.4	15.3	15.0	13.8	12.2	12.6	12.5	12.2
25–29 Years	13.8	13.2	12.6	12.3	12.5	11.7	11.4	10.5	10.6	10.9
30–34 Years	12.2	11.9	11.8	12.1	11.4	11.0	11.4	10.1	9.8	10.3
35–39 Years	10.9	11.1	11.5	10.8	11.1	11.6	12.6	10.4	10.6	10.2
40–44 Years	7.4	8.5	7.9	7.5	9.1	8.8	8.3	9.3	9.6	10.3
45+Years	12.2	14.1	15.4	16.1	15.1	16.5	18.1	24.7	23.8	23.7

Consumer Profile by Gender

	1992	1993	1994	1995	1996	1997	1998	1999	2000	2001
Male	47.4%	49.3%	47.3%	47.0%	49.1%	51.4%	51.3%	49.7%	49.4%	51.2%
Female	52.6	50.7	52.7	53.0	50.9	48.6	48.7	50.3	50.6	48.8

Source of Purchase

	1992	1993	1994	1995	1996	1997	1998	1999	2000	2001
Record store	60.0%	56.2%	53.3%	52.0%	49.9%	51.8%	50.8%	44.5%	42.4%	42.5%
Other store	24.9	26.1	26.7	28.2	31.5	31.9	34.4	38.3	40.8	42.4
Tape/record club	11.4	12.9	15.1	14.3	14.3	11.6	9.0	7.9	7.6	6.1
TV/newspaper/magazine ad/ 800 number	3.2	3.8	3.4	4.0	2.9	2.7	2.9	2.5	2.4	3.0
Internet[1]	NA	NA	NA	NA	NA	0.3	1.1	2.4	3.2	2.9

(1) Does not include record club purchases made over the Internet.

Source: Recording Industry Association of America.

For example, teenagers, who are traditionally the most avid music buyers, do not typically possess credit cards, the primary method of payments for subscription services. The labels had invested heavily to develop teen recording stars, but the teen segment could not always follow through to purchase for this reason. Not surprisingly, the well-respected market research firm Ipsos Insight reported that, "Total file-sharing remains constant, with teens driving adoption," as illicit downloaders of titles by those same teen stars.[18] (See Exhibit 8 for demographic and point-of-purchase profiles.)

Several of the initial proprietary attempts at subscription services received criticism from users. Both MusicNet and Pressplay were criticized for their overly complex software, confusing price schemes, limited inventory (rolling out only a small number of tracks at launch date), limited song portability (the inability to copy songs to portable devices), and difficulties moving memberships and music from one computer to another. Some services provided only tethered downloads, limiting use of a track to the duration of the user's subscription. This characteristic irked those consumers who for so long had been accustomed to "owning" the music once purchased through traditional retail distributors. Critics said it seemed that these services were overseen by executives more concerned with "locking down" content than distributing it.[19]

EMusic, the first all-MP3 subscription download service (launched initially in 1998 and acquired by

[18]Data from "TEMPO: Keeping Pace with Digital Music Behavior," (an Ipsos-Insight quarterly digital music study conducted in December 2002) as referenced in "File-Sharing and CD Burning Remain Steady In 2002," February 20, 2002, and Ipsos release, http://www.ipsos-pa.com/dsp_displaypr_us.cfm?id_to_view=1743.

[19]Jimmy Guterman, "Music to Fans' Ears; Finally, a Legit Online Music Service That Delivers What Consumers Really Want," *Business* 2.0, November 20, 2002.

EXHIBIT 9 | The Paid Service Landscape, as of May 2003

Service	Sponsors	Songs	Features	Monthly Pricing	Paying Subscribers
Pressplay	Sony & UMG joint venture (launched 12/01)	250,000 • from big 5 plus indie labels • proprietary format (not MP3s)	11/14/02 - first service to allow consumers to buy and "burn"	$9.95 for unlimited tethered downloads and streaming, 40 digital radio stations. $17.95 adds 10 portable downloads per month. $179.40/year adds 120 portable downloads on day 1 (only) of service. Extra packs of portable downloads for $0.50–1.19 per song (packs of 5, 10, 20 songs).	Not disclosed.
MusicNet	RealNetworks (40%), AOL Time Warner, Bertelsmann AG, EMI and Zomba joint venture (launched 12/01)	250,000+ • from big 5 plus indie labels • Available only on RealNetworks' RealOne service		$3.95 online plays, 20 tethered $8.95 unlimited on both $17.95 also allows burning 10 songs to CD	35,000+
MusicNow (formerly Full Audio)	Content licensed from the five majors	200,000+		$4.95 radio channels $9.95 adds unlimited tethered downloads and streamed songs $0.99 to download a track	Not disclosed.[a]
Rhapsody (Listen.com)	Content licensed from all majors (launched 12/01)	292,000	Streaming-only	$4.95 for 58 radio stations, can make custom radio stations; $9.95 adds unlimited streamed songs and access to burn songs to CD for $0.99 per track	Not disclosed ("tens of thousands"[a])
EMusic	Vivendi Universal	250,000+ • all MP3 • mostly independent labels	#1 MP3 subscription service in 2000	$9.99 (one-year commitment) or $14.99 (three-month commitment) brings unlimited access tracks that can be streamed, burned and downloaded to both PCs and portable digital music devices.	70,000[b]
iTunes	Apple	250,000+	Music store integrated in jukebox software	No monthly subscription fee $0.99 per track Essentially unlimited downloads and ability to stream songs through network to up to 3 other computers	2 million songs downloaded in first 16 days

[a]John Borland and Stefanie Olsen, "RealNetworks—Listen Make Online Music Noise," CNET News.com, April 22, 2003. On April 21, 2003, RealNetworks agreed to pay $36 million in cash and stock for the privately held Rhapsody, in which it had already acquired a minority stake in February 2003. The companies declined to state exactly how many paid subscribers Rhapsody had at the time, alluding only to "tens of thousands."

[b]Eric Hellweg, "Subscription Music Services Heat Up ," *MIT Technology Review,* April 16, 2003. This is an end of year 2002 EMusic company estimate.

Vivendi in 2000) and Listen.com's Rhapsody (a privately held online music subscription service launched in December 2001) instead focused on ease of use and diversity in their music offerings, prompting the other services to follow suit. The subscription services had come a long way despite initial difficulties in the consumer experience (Exhibit 9). In the process, they learned that the right to burn single tracks could be especially important in the United States market, where the market for singles, usually priced at $5, had collapsed.

The $1 price point (of which an estimated $0.60 paid for song licenses/royalties) could catalyze the return of the market for singles and continue to fulfill the purpose of the singles market: to draw new customers nearer to a larger purchase.

By the middle of 2003, the labels, and a new entrant onto the scene, Apple Computer's iTunes music download service, had begun to make real headway in providing reasonably priced and comprehensive music download services. Still, an estimated 1.2 million unique tracks were available through file-swapping services, and market research firm Ipsos estimated that 20 million Americans had engaged in file-sharing during December 2002 alone.[20]

Troubling Trends for the Recording Industry

By the first half of 2002, world sales of recorded music had fallen by 9.2 percent in dollar value and unit shipments were down 11.2 percent (Exhibit 10).[21] In 2002, the worldwide recording industry suffered its third straight year of declining sales. Sony told investors it expected music revenues to fall an additional 13–15 percent in 2003.[22] In the United States, sales had also declined steadily over the past three years, with sales of recorded music falling 8.2 percent in dollar value and 11.2 percent in unit shipments. (Prior year sales are shown in Exhibit 11).

During the same 2002 period, the Recording Industry Association of America (RIAA), the industry's trade group and lobby, reported that seizures for counterfeit CDs had risen by 69.9 percent.[23] CD drives that could record (burn) as well as play CDs were standard issue on even the most inexpensive PCs, enabling millions of consumers to potentially bypass bootlegging middlemen and duplicate their own CDs.

The major recording labels and their industry associations blamed piracy for an estimated $5 billion loss in 2002. As mentioned earlier, MP3 file-swapping via P2P services such as Kazaa and others was still rampant despite the much publicized legal action that shut down Napster. According to CNet's Download.com, over 211 million copies of Kazaa's P2P software had been downloaded as of April 2003, growing by an estimated 3 million per week. Even though this number included upgrades and multiple copies downloaded by individual users, the figure dwarfed the estimated 70 million copies downloaded by the Napster community. The recording industry feared that the precedent—or worse, tradition—of free downloadable music had been established for some consumers.

The industry also worried about fast-changing information processing technologies, such as increasingly powerful processors, CD burners on PCs, and consumer broadband Internet connectivity. Consumers could now make perfect digital copies of recordings and trade them around the world effortlessly. With a broadband connection, it took only a few minutes to download MP3 files and burn them onto a CD or pass them on to others.

---

[20]They also estimate that 40 million individuals had engaged in file-sharing to date, as of the survey date (December 12–16, 2002).

[21]"Global Sales of Recorded Music Down 9.2% in the First Half of 2002," IFPI, October 10, 2002, www.ifpi.org.

[22]Peter Thal Larsen and Tim Burt, "Sony Music Braced for 15% Sales Drop," *Financial Times*, March 20, 2003.

[23]"RIAA Releases Mid-Year Snapshot of Music Industry," RIAA Press Release, August 26, 2002, www.riaa.com.

EXHIBIT 10 | Recent Global Music Industry Sales, 1998–2002

	1998	1999	2000	2001	2002
Industry revenues ($bn)	38.7	38.5	36.9	33.7	32.0
% Change		−0.5%	−4.2%	−8.7%	−5.0%
Units shipped (bn)	4.1	3.8	3.5	3.3	3.1
% Change		−8.1%	−6.7%	−5.0%	−8.0%

Note: Numbers in bold were given in releases. 2001 reported figures do not match decline percentages. One possible reason is that base 2000 figures were adjusted downward ex post or 2001 dollar values were adjusted to include newer media, such as DVD-Audio.

Source: IFPI.com year-end press releases.

EXHIBIT 11 | Historical Music Industry Sales in the US, 1976–2002

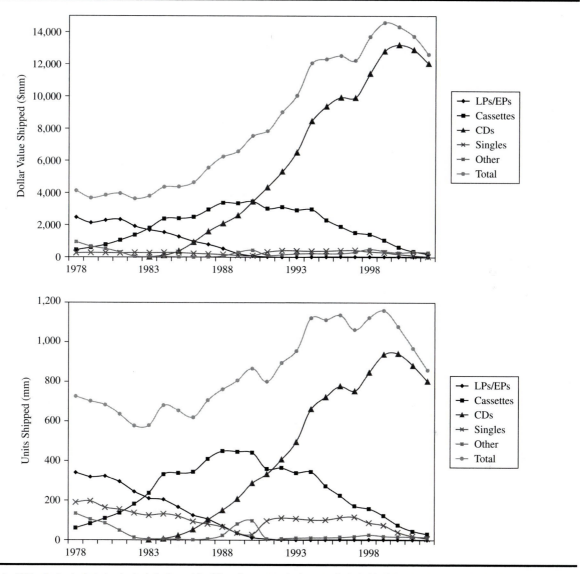

Note: Prior to 1991, singles included only vinyl singles, while CD and cassette singles were included in Other. Beginning in 1991, all sales of singles are included under Singles. Other also includes DVD-Audio sales and music video sales.

Source: Recording Industry Association of America.

Information processing advances continued to outpace not only the music industry's attempts to safeguard content, but also to find a business model that still allowed consumers many of the "fair use"[24] activities of the past,

such as the ability to transfer songs onto portable devices.

While piracy was a major concern for the labels and the economic downturn in the United States may have added to the industry's headaches, some industry executives looked for problems within the industry itself. The music industry in general was saddled with the problem of redeeming itself in the eyes of consumers, who seemingly harbored disgust for the sustained high level of CD

[24]Fair use is a concept in copyright law under which certain activities such as reproducing copyrighted material, without paying additional copyright charges, for educational purposes was deemed acceptable or "fair use" of such material. It was a fungible concept, subject to changing interpretation.

prices and often characterized the industry as greedy. Tom Sturges said, "I think when you can buy a DVD with tons of extra features for less than the price of a new CD, something is wrong." Howard Stringer, chairman and CEO of Sony Corporation of America was quoted as saying, "In the music business, the problem is easy to see. We alienated music people; we alienated the consumer when we cranked up CD prices too high, and we alienated retailers for the same reason. There was dissatisfaction at the number of tracks on a CD that were any good. We upset the artists because they felt they were being ripped off. And device manufacturers were confused about it all."[25]

Record Labels' Response to Strategic Challenges

Record labels took various actions to fight the strategic challenges represented by technological changes. Some were aimed at limiting the threat from piracy, while others tried to leverage opportunities created by the technical forces that caused the industry, and its established business model, so many problems.

Several actions undertaken by labels to fight piracy are listed below.

Litigation   Recording industry lawyers brought suits claiming copyright violations in cases such as *RIAA v. Napster*, *RIAA v. Audioglaxy* and *RIAA v. Kazaa*, attempting to outright quash the services or at least tie up those P2P networks in court to drain their funding. Unfortunately for the labels, after one service closed, others sprouted like Medusa's hydras. (See "We'll See You in Court" below.)

Legislation   Before it adjourned at the end of 2002, the 107th Congress was considering two bills that would strengthen the labels' position. The Consumer Broadband and Digital Television Promotion Act (S. 2048, a.k.a. CBDTPA), introduced in the Senate by Sen. Ernest Hollings (D-SC) on March 2002, essentially was a technology mandate requiring makers of digital media devices to include government-approved copyright protection standards into their products. The P2P Piracy Prevention Act (H.R. 5211) introduced in the House by Rep. Howard Berman (D-CA) in 2002 stated that copyright holders would have the right to disable,

interfere with, block, or otherwise impair a peer-to-peer node that they suspect is distributing their intellectual property without permission. Versions of these and other copyright-related bills were expected to be introduced in the 108th Congress (2003). The RIAA made $42,500 in contributions to lawmakers in both parties in the 2001–2002 political cycle.[26]

Copy Protection   Several labels tried encrypting data on CDs that would prevent their being played on PCs (and thus copied). This action was unpopular with consumers who felt they had the right to play legally purchased CDs on their computers. In addition, such measures often proved ineffective since they could be overcome by users.

Watermarking   EMI stated that it was digitally stamping each song on advance/prerelease CDs in order to identify the sources of illegal copies of advance releases. Several labels followed suit. This was more of a psychological deterrent to prevent reviewers from copying (ripping) the CD and sharing the files for fear of being identified by the labels. Despite watermarking, prereleased music continued to make its way to P2P networks.

Listening Parties   Several labels revived the tradition of having listening parties to promote new releases in order to prevent reviewers from obtaining the tracks themselves. The group Radiohead promoted their album *Kid A* this way, but unfortunately somehow all the tracks were reconstructed and uploaded to the networks after a European prerelease party.

Cassette Prereleases   This method was far more effective than watermarking or listening parties because an MP3 recorded from a cassette is of sufficiently low sound quality to make downloading them pointless.

Value-added CD Buying   The provision of outtakes, video clips, live tracks, and the occasional free T-shirt was applauded by critics as a more effective way to stimulate retail CD sales than the piracy-deterrent techniques. The labels were also moving toward more value-added formats such as Super-Audio CDs (SACDs) and DVD-Audio, which offer greater storage capacity

---

[25]Tim Burt, "Films and Music at the Centre of a Revolution," *Financial Times*, February 11, 2003.

[26]Federal Election Commission, www.fec.org.

and quality of sound[27]. Recently the labels have brought down the pricing of these formats to the same level as CDs and were reissuing classic albums like Pink Floyd's *Dark Side of the Moon* on SACD.[28]

Spoofing This technique placed dummy files containing noise, a chorus loop, or some promotional message in files intentionally mislabeled on P2P networks. It proved only mildly annoying to users of the networks since downloaders could easily find good copies of the music they were seeking. Record executives would not comment on engaging in these activities, but one spoofing company claimed that labels paid it $10,000 per month per album to carry out spoofing campaigns.[29] Companies associated with these activities include Overpeer and Media Defender.

Interdiction This involved identifying peers (i.e., individual users) on the networks with lots of files to share and bombarding them with enough requests to deny other downloaders access to that peer's files—essentially a denial-of-service attack. While the labels flatly denied using interdiction, one P2P metrics company reported witnessing such activity on the networks, and a rate card submitted by one spoofing company to labels included interdiction as a service.

We'll See You in Court

The Recording Industry Association of America (RIAA) handled many of the industry's important lawsuits, including current cases targeting all of the file sharing services, such as Kazaa and Morpheus. It was the

RIAA's lawsuit that resulted in the shutdown of Napster. Hilary Rosen, chairman and CEO of the RIAA, commented on her group's litigation against the P2P networks: "We knew we were losing the PR battle. It was a tsunami. But instinctively, I always thought that people thought we were right. They thought it was a free ride, and boy was it fun, but it would never last. So while I knew [the labels'] political strategy was drawing blood, I knew we'd win."[30]

More recently in 2003, the RIAA successfully sued phone company Verizon Communications, forcing it to identify a customer who had shared (uploaded) over 600 music files via a peer-to-peer service. Citing the right to be anonymous online, Verizon argued that it should not be forced to identify which of its consumers were using their broadband connections to illegally share music files. However, U.S. District Judge John Bates wrote in his opinion that Section 512 of the Digital Millennium Copyright Act used "language that is clear," allowing copyright owners to subpoena service providers for information about users without seeking a judge's approval first.[31] Although awaiting appeal, the ruling would allow the RIAA to identify, without filing a lawsuit first, thousands of music pirates at a time. The decision also further allowed the RIAA to target individual alleged pirates in their homes.

It was not the casual downloader the RIAA was after, since few of these individuals ever uploaded files to share with others. With just 3 percent of online users providing 97 percent of illegal music on the file sharing services, it was this 3 percent that the labels hoped to target to help curb piracy problems.[32] UMG's Amanda Marks stated: "Music pirates are no different than bootleggers on the street corner, except they're not getting any compensation for downloaded songs. We are always concerned about negative public relations, but it's hard for it to get any worse than it is. We are less worried about what music pirates think of us. Pirates are not our paying consumers."

In addition to handling most of the lawsuits related to piracy, the RIAA had undertaken an aggressive education

---

[27]CD offers 16-bit data, 44.1 kHz sampling, two-channel data, while DVD-Audio offers 24-bit data, with a sampling rate of 96 kHz for six-channel audio, or 129 kHz for two-channel stereo. DVD-Audio also offers a storage capacity of up to seven times as great (approx. 4.7 GB of data) as that of current CD technology. The additional capacity can be used for advanced resolution quality sound, or for longer recordings, plus visual content accessible via television or PC-liner notes, song lyrics, artist bios, photo galleries, or video clips. SACD (backed by Sony and Philips), on the other hand, increases the resolution of music even more than DVD-Audio by recording music at a much higher sampling frequency—approximately 2.8224 MHz—and converting it to 1-bit data. The result is sound that is theoretically superior to DVD-Audio sound. SACD offers up to six times the storage capacity of the current CD format.

[28]Wilson Rothman, "Beyond the CD: A Bid to Burnish Records' Sheen," *New York Times,* March 13, 2003.

[29]Jeff Howe, "Dirty Dozen: 12 Ways the Record Labels Fight Back," *Wired Magazine,* February 2003, p. 98.

---

[30]Matt Bai, "Hating Hilary," *Wired Magazine,* February 2003, page 99.

[31]Declan McCullagh, "RIAA Wins Battle to Identify Kazaa User," CNet News.com, January 21, 2003. Signed into law in 1998, the Digital Millennium Copyright Act (DMCA) sought to protect digital content by making it illegal to circumvent antipiracy measures built into commercial software.

[32]Matt Bai, "Hating Hilary," *Wired Magazine,* February 2003, p. 97.

EXHIBIT 12 | Alternate Approach to Recovering Revenues: Charging the ISPs

Jim Guerinot, manager of musical acts such as No Doubt and Beck, agrees with the idea of taxing Internet providers. "The goal should be to monetize this large group of free music downloaders while making them more active customers. A solution that restricts access and makes the process more difficult will only continue to shrink revenues. There are many channels on cable television that one may not have paid for on a pay-per-view basis but have become essential fare and created further programming opportunities. There are many drivers with good driving records paying for insurance so that all drivers can share the road. A friend of mine refers to this as charging on an actuarial basis rather than an actual basis. I think that is a good template of how to view this new model."

In the table below, Guerinot outlines a simple model for arriving at a rough estimate of what to charge ISPs. "The most shocking part of this," notes Guerinot, "is how little the music industry would need to charge to recover 100 percent of their revenues leaving the CD brick-and-mortar business fully incremental. . . . The numbers would need to be anticipated at something other than 100 percent of all Internet users. However, since this identical service is presently available to the consumer for free it would not be a horrible notion to glean $1.99 per month from a 70-million-person user base, the number of registered Napster users. That would give us $1.671B per year, 35 percent of the full 2001 revenues and 100 percent of new Internet income."

2001 Recorded Music Revenues (IFPI)

$13,411,700,000	Total gross revenues, U.S. 2001
$1,117,641,667	Total monthly gross revenues
278,058,881	U.S. population
$48.23	Gross revenues per cap. annually
$4.02	Gross revenues per cap. monthly

Net Revenues per Month (through online distribution)

$18.98	Retail price
$12.00	Wholesale price
36.78%	Retail margin
$0.90	Manufacturing cost
$0.60	Distribution fee (5% of wholesale price)
44.68%	Total retail, manufacturing and distribution
20.00%	Percent of shipped overstatement by IFPI
64.68%	Total extra percentage in IFPI number if distributed online
$1.42	Net revenues per cap. monthly

Per Month Subscriber Fee

$1,117,641,667	Total gross revenues (per month)
$394,766,582	Total monthly net revenues
278,058,881	U.S. population
166,835,329	U.S. population that uses the Internet
$2.37	**The magic number**
	This is what is required to charge each Internet user to equal 2001 net revenues.

Source: Jim Guerinot.

campaign. With evidence that many users conducted their downloading from their office or university-owned lines, the RIAA warned companies and schools about copyright infringements taking place with their hardware and networks. In March 2003, the RIAA sent 300 letters to companies warning: ". . . In short, your computer network and resources are being used to illegally distribute copyrighted music on the Internet. . . . We strongly urge you to take immediate steps to prevent the continued infringement of our members' sound recordings on your corporate network. These acts of infringement could expose your employees and your company to significant legal damages."[33]

---

[33]"Piracy Warning Targets 300 Companies," CNET News.com, March 17, 2003.

The RIAA has also encouraged labels to ease licensing restrictions, develop digital copy protections for music, and invest more in online subscription services, focusing on the long-term potential instead of short-term losses. Rosen also proposed a levy paid by ISPs to labels for allowing consumers free access to file sharing services. In her keynote speech, Rosen said, "Let's face it. They [the ISPs] know there's a lot of demand for broadband simply because of the availability [of file sharing]."[34] (See Exhibit 12 for a sample revenue model for ISP levies.)

Creating Solutions

During 2002, the record labels and technology companies began to resolve some of their disputes. Both Microsoft and RealNetworks, the developers of the two competing leading media player software, inched closer to Hollywood by promising to include additional content safeguards in their technologies. Previously, the general attitude at some technology companies had been to access content with little regard for copyright protection. Amanda Marks excitedly anticipated the day when consumers could have secure, easy access to their music files: "Ultimately, we would love to have CDs with preripped second session files so that, with the click of a mouse, you could easily transfer music tracks to a computer or a portable device. Right now, though many are working on finding a solution, none of the various technology companies have yet provided something that is really viable. No one thinks you can stop CD piracy 100 percent, but stopping 70 to 80 percent of casual piracy would be nice."

All of the labels were reconsidering CD pricing. Some recent releases, such as Bruce Springsteen's latest album, *The Rising*, had been listed at $9.99 in pricing experiments. While these lower prices received praise from consumers, and retailers such as Best Buy had been pushing for a lower MSRP for CDs, record labels tended to focus instead on adding value to the CDs listed at higher price points. In addition to adding music videos to CDs, other ideas being offered include offering free T-shirts with a CD purchase and first-access to concert ticket sales. Indeed, according to one recent RIAA survey, only 3 percent of polled consumers thought CD prices were too high.

Some likened the music industry's reliance on the CD to the putative soft drink industry, where cola was only sold in two-liter bottles instead of in cans, from soda fountains, etc. The RIAA and others pushed record labels to embrace MP3s as an additional retail form, before the idea was popular with individual labels. Now, in addition to online tracks, the RIAA was pushing for the adoption of new physical forms such as SACD and DVD-Audio. Although these two new standards competed with each other, many new players coming onto the market were equipped to play both forms. These higher-quality recordings would likely target audiophiles and more affluent consumers, offering high-resolution audio and surround sound capability. "When I first heard surround sound I said, 'the perfect environment is in the car,'" said Elliot Sheiner, a Grammy-winning mixing engineer adapting the Steely Dan and REM catalogs for the new formats. "You get DVD-Audio in the car, and people listen to surround sound for the first time, they will want it in their home."[35]

With the firing of Tommy Mottola as chairman of Sony Music, the unit was planning a fundamental restructuring of its global music operations. The review, expected to examine the unit's entire structure, would focus on artists' contracts, CD manufacturing, digital rights management, and distribution.

One example of the marriage of those synergies was the creation of a "custom CD" Web site for a popular Sony-produced television show, *Dawson's Creek*. At the site, fans can create their own custom CD of 14 tracks, from an initial database of 75 songs heard on the show's soundtrack, for $14.95. In addition to building fan loyalty for the television show, executives hope the custom CDs will expose viewers to a new range of artists.

BMG, meanwhile, lowered costs by avoiding bidding wars for high-priced talent and eliminating many of the lavish perks associated with the industry, such as fresh flowers on every floor. "Years ago, we might have said, 'Let's sign Mariah [Carey], let's be hot,'" said Rolf Schmidt-Holt, Chairman of BMG. "But times have changed. I don't put my company at risk for one contract. . . . We can't do business as we did two years ago, five years ago or ten years ago."[36] BMG has also tried to change the culture of the music unit by adding clauses into artist contracts that levy financial penalties if albums are delivered late.

---

[34]"RIAA: ISPs Should Pay for Music Swapping," CNET News.com, January 18, 2003.

[35]Wilson Rothman, "Beyond the CD: A Bid to Burnish Records' Sheen," *The New York Times*, March 13, 2002.

[36]Martin Peers, "New BMG Chief Tightens Reins on Costs, Perks and Gets Results," *The Wall Street Journal*, March 17, 2003.

EMI had trimmed its roster of artists as a way to lower costs, cutting 400 artists during 2002. With only 5–10 percent of music releases ever recouping production costs, and far fewer ever making a profit, executives at EMI were instead focusing more on developing talent in the long term and concentrating more marketing dollars on a smaller number of artists. Their plan was to bet bigger with fewer acts. For example, EMI sought to build artist brands, similar to that of singer Robbie Williams, whose most recent album sold over 5 million copies by March 2003 and who was recently signed to an estimated £80 million contract. EMI has financially committed itself to the long-term success of Robbie Williams, as the company will not record a profit from the six-album deal until total album sales top 18 million units.

As labels invested more money in their "stable of brands," popular artists increasingly found themselves faced with the decision to remain at a label (if they were not cut) or do things independently. Recently, some artists, including Aimee Mann, Todd Rundgren, and Prince, have ventured down this path of independence. Mick Hucknall, former front man for the band Simply Red, summed up his dislike of record label contracts:

> The contract was basically immoral. Like many artists, my deal meant I paid for the cost of recording the music. I paid for the marketing. And I didn't get any royalties until those costs had been incurred. But despite this, the contract stated that the master recordings still belonged to the record company. I don't know any other business where you pay for something and then someone else owns it. If there was some way of saying it was illegal I would say it, but it's certainly immoral.[37]

Another well-established artist, Natalie Merchant, said she left her record label to bypass label censorship and create less commercial albums. Merchant noted, "I've been writing things that are much more obscure and sort of shelving them, thinking I can't get this past a corporate boardroom and I won't even try. . . . I thought, why fight an uphill battle for attention?"[38]

For Merchant, a modest recording budget and the ability to inexpensively market her new album on her personal Web site—thus eliminating promotion costs of $1 million alone—dramatically lowered the number of unit sales required for breakeven. According to Gary Smith,

Natalie Merchant's manager, "We're not trying to recoup some enormous debt. The economics of making this record are very prudent. When we sell 200,000 copies, we'll be standing on our chairs, hollering. If we released this record with these kinds of goals on a major label, we would look like a failure. At Elektra, if you just sell 1.5 million, everyone goes around with their heads down."

However, without 17 years of radio and in-store promotion from Elektra Records to build her brand name and recognition, it would have been difficult for Merchant to brave the music landscape alone. According to artist manager Jim Guerinot, the marketing efforts of the record labels were very valuable, especially to newcomers. Guerinot argued, "Labels are needed for their marketing. Their marketing helps make the artist brand. I wouldn't want to do it without the labels, and I don't think we need to do it without them."

UMG Actions Thus Far

As executives from UMG began to consider new options in the battle to reverse declining music revenues, they thought it would first be best to review the company's major initiatives thus far.

One of the first steps taken by UMG in 1999 was the creation of e-Labs, a 40-person division devoted entirely to the company's burgeoning digital initiatives. According to Amanda Marks, the group strives to license UMG's music content widely to not only UMG-backed sites such as Pressplay, but also "to anyone with a sustainable business model and a secure technology platform for our content." Some beneficiaries of UMG's licensing policy include MusicNet, Rhapsody, FullAudio, and Streamwaves, as well as three subscription radio services, Musicmatch, Launchcast, and RCS.

Subsequent to the creation of e-Labs, UMG began investing heavily in digital distribution. In May 2001, Vivendi Universal, UMG's parent, purchased MP3.com for $372 million as "a big step forward for Vivendi Universal's priority to develop and implement an aggressive, legitimate, and attractive offering of our content to our consumers."[39] According to a VU press release, MP3.com's music distribution technology and data tracking systems were the chief reasons for the acquisition.

It is this aggressive action that helped speed the formation of Pressplay, the company's online music subscription service with Sony. This technology also probably

---

[37]Sathnam Sanghera, "Mick Hucknall," *Financial Times,* March 27, 2003.

[38]Jon Pareles, "Natalie Merchant, No Strings Attached," *The New York Times,* March 13, 2003.

[39]Jean-Marie Messier, Vivendi Universal Press Release, May 21, 2001.

helped the company efficiently digitize and metatag its active catalog, resulting in over 70,000 singles available for à la carte download (through TowerRecords.com and about 30 other affiliates) and easily outpacing its competition.

UMG has also actively supported the RIAA in its legislative actions and piracy lawsuits. However, the company has additionally filed lawsuits of its own. In April 2003, UMG joined with EMI in a copyright infringement lawsuit not against Napster, but against Napster's financial backer, Hummer Winblad Venture Partners. The other three major labels did not join in this lawsuit, probably because of the technology ties of both Warner Music (AOL) and Sony Music (Sony) and Bertelsmann's own attempts to purchase Napster's assets.

The company was also bracing for the next generation of physical media, with plans to release albums in the DVD-Audio format beginning in the autumn of 2003. While UMG executives stated in our interviews that they did not believe DVD-Audio would fully make up for the decline in CD sales, it should help when combined with online subscription services, à la carte downloads, ring tone licenses for cell phones, increases in synchronization revenues, and other developing revenue streams.

Conclusion

As the leading company in the music industry, Universal Music Group had a lot a stake in how well it navigated the "perfect storm" that had hit. While the storm may have been caused by technology forces outside of industry, labels struggled to find business models that would serve themselves, their parent companies and consumers within the new technological framework that had emerged. With labels, their parents and particularly their technology company complementors in varying degrees of financial distress, much was at stake—both for listeners and investors.

PART 7

Convergence or Collision—Take III: IP Meets Telephony

"The U.S. Telecommunications Industry (B): 1996–1999" describes key developments since the passage of the Telecommunications Act of 1996. During this period, the industry saw considerable merger activity, increasing intensity of competition, the continued convergence between voice and data networks, and a number of technological innovations. In the wake of the act long-distance service providers were attempting to enter local markets, while local carriers sought to provide long distance and other services. Moreover, telephone and cable companies were entering the market for high-speed data services, including Internet access, with telephone companies investing in digital subscriber line (DSL) technologies and cable companies investing in cable modems. The importance of Internet protocol (IP) technology and the viability of Internet telephony had become manifest. Wireless services continued their rapid growth, and new forms of wireless service were introduced, including broadband wireless.

Important discussion topics for this case are (1) government regulation/deregulation driving industry evolution, (2) the role of predators and prey, (3) unanticipated consequences of strategic intent, (4) micro rationality and macro irrationality, and (5) finding new sources of customer value. In terms of our three key themes, this industry note is an example of runaway change; it shows again the pressures that industry change puts on the alignment of strategy and action; but it also shows that the speed at which companies can transform themselves—if the transformation is based on sound strategic insight—determines who the winners and losers are likely to be in runaway change.

"Slouching Toward Broadband: Revisited in 2005" discusses the situation of broadband availability and its prospects in the United States. The note offers, first, the opportunity to get a better understanding of how broadband actually works, and second, a quick overview of the regulatory environment. The note also provides the opportunity to examine the strategic situation from the perspective of the local service, cable, Internet service provider, cellular, satellite, and power-line companies, as well as from the perspective of the entertainment companies. Understanding the stakes that these various companies have in the advent of universal broadband access helps one better understand the reasons for the slower than expected adoption in the United States (compared to some other nations). The note also offers the opportunity to look at the situation from the perspective of the U.S. government. Some view relatively poor regulatory oversight, and as a function of this, the high cost of broadband services, as the reasons for slow adoption. Others blame the slow adoption on a lack of popular broadband products, the so-called killer applications, which would drive consumers to broadband. However, new wireless broadband technologies (such as Wi-Fi and WiMax) are emerging that may pose a disruptive threat to the wireline-based technologies.

Important discussion topics for this case are (1) diverse strategic interests and the prisoner's dilemma, (2) unanticipated consequences of regulation, (3) market challenge versus market failure, (4) strategic inertia, and (5) likely winners and losers in the broadband market segment. In terms of our three key themes, this case offers examples of P-controlled change (by the government) turning into runaway change; the different inertial forces that lead different companies to experience in different ways a divergence between what it takes to win and what the company has got; and it offers the opportunity again to examine who the players are that seem to be the fastest at transforming themselves in order to be winners in the broadband market segment by 2010.

"Hanging Up the (Old) Phone: IP Communications in 2004" discusses the impact of Internet protocol (IP) communications, specifically voice over Internet protocol (VoIP), on the existing telephony market. Like broadband, the change to VoIP telephony fundamentally affected a variety of companies in different market segments. By 2004, start-up companies, as well as large, established phone companies and cable TV providers, offered VoIP calling plans that could substitute many of the phone services sold by the same or other established providers. The case offers, first, the opportunity to understand better how VoIP actually works, the fundamental differences between VoIP and the public switched telephone network (PSTN), and the implications of recent Federal Communications Commission (FCC) decisions. It also offers the opportunity to discuss the strategic situation from the perspective of the different players (incumbents and new entrants), as well as from the perspective of the telecommunications equipment suppliers.

Important discussion topics for this note are (1) the technology adoption life cycle, (2) "community interest" focused attackers and "profit protection" focused defenders, (3) the business model of the start-up VoIP providers, (4) optimal timing for incumbent strategies, and (5) likely winners and losers in the VoIP market segment. In terms of our three key themes, the case offers an example of P-independent change that could potentially turn into P-controlled change or runaway change for the incumbents; it allows again examination of the different inertial forces that lead different companies to experience in different ways a divergence between what it takes to win and what the company has got; and it offers again the opportunity to examine who the players are that seem to be the fastest to be able to transform themselves in order to be winners in the VoIP market segment by 2010.●

Case 6.1

The U.S. Telecommunications Industry (B): 1996–1999

Part B of this note describes key developments in the U.S. telecommunications industry since the passage of the Telecommunications Act of 1996. During this period, the industry saw considerable merger activity, increasing intensity of competition, the continued convergence between voice and data networks, and a number of technological innovations. In the wake of the act, long-distance service providers were attempting to enter local markets, while local carriers sought to provide long distance and other services.

Moreover, telephone and cable companies were entering the market for high-speed data services, including Internet access, with telephone companies investing in digital subscriber line (DSL) technologies and cable companies investing in cable modems. As voice and data networks continued to converge, the importance of Internet protocol (IP) technology and the viability of Internet telephony had become manifest. Wireless services continued their rapid growth, and new forms of wireless service were introduced, including broadband wireless.

Impact of Regulatory Change

Passage of the Telecommunications Act (on February 8, 1996) set up three major battlefronts within the industry. First, it opened the $108.3 billion (1998 revenues)[1] market for local phone service to its first serious competition: AT&T, the nation's largest telecommunications company, was now permitted to get back into the local phone business, which it had been forced to leave 12 years earlier.

Second, the act allowed the incumbent local exchange carriers (ILECs) to enter the long-distance business, both within and outside of their service region:

they could offer in-region long-distance only after demonstrating that they had opened their local markets to competition, but they were free immediately to offer out-of-region long distance, without any precondition.

Third, the act shifted cable companies into a new strategic position: Like ILECs, cable companies have wires into customers' homes—the coveted "last mile." Though the idea of cable telephony had been around for years, cable operators had been prohibited from offering phone service; the Telecommunications Act gave new life to the prospect of cable-based telecommunications.

RBOCs

Regulators and legislators presumed that, as a result of the Telecommunications Act, the RBOCs would attempt to compete in each other's regions. But as a sector, the RBOCs' initial strategic reaction instead was to consolidate. In 1997, Pacific Telesis merged into SBC Communications (a $16 billion deal), while Bell Atlantic acquired Nynex for $25.6 billion. Moreover, further consolidation is in the works: Bell Atlantic is planning to acquire GTE (for $53 billion), and SBC wants to buy Ameritech (for $62 billion). Both deals await government approval. Meanwhile, cross-region competition among RBOCs has been virtually nonexistent. The major exception was SBC's acquisition of Southern New England Telecommunications for $5 billion in 1998, which gave the company a position in Bell Atlantic's territory.

Only two RBOCs—BellSouth and US West—had not merged with other companies, but in July 1999 US West agreed to be acquired for $35 billion by Denver-based Qwest Communications. Qwest, a long-distance company founded in 1988, has nearly completed an 18,815-mile fiber-optic network connecting 150 cities. If the deal goes through, BellSouth (which owns a 10 percent stake in Qwest) will be the only RBOC not to have entered the consolidation game. For Qwest, the US West acquisition would immediately provide a customer base to which it could market services on its state-of-the-art fiber system.

The RBOCs all have their eyes on the $104-billion long-distance market, but as of August 1999—more than three years after passage of the Telecommunications Act—no RBOC had received FCC approval to offer long-distance service in its region. (That situation may soon change, however: Some observers expect that Bell

---

[1] *Preliminary Statistics of Common Carriers, 1998 Edition,* Federal Communications Commission, 5/99.

This note was prepared by Eric Martí, under the supervision of Professor Robert A. Burgelman and Dr. Andrew S. Grove, for use as a basis for class discussion. It draws upon earlier industry notes prepared by John W. Foster, Alva H. Taylor, and Raymond S. Bamford, MBA '96.

Atlantic may be granted permission to offer long-distance in New York sometime this year.) And though the RBOCs were immediately free to provide local and long-distance service outside of their regions, as a group they have pursued these opportunities only to a limited degree.

All of the RBOCs operate significant wireless businesses in their regions (as beneficiaries of the original cellular licenses that the FCC granted to the ILECs in 1984, plus additional licenses won in subsequent auctions). Moreover, since permitted by the Telecommunications Act of 1996, they now offer data services such as high-speed lines (e.g., T1, T3)[2] and Internet access.

A key area of RBOC vulnerability is their dependence on access fees, which accounted for 22.5 percent of their 1998 revenues.[3] The FCC is forcing the ILECs, over time, to reduce these rates toward the actual cost of providing access. Though there is some disagreement between the ILECs and IXCs over the true cost of access, the figure is significantly less than the 3–4 cents per minute that they now charge. (AT&T estimates the cost is .5 cent per minute.)[4] In any case, that revenue source is being eroded both by the FCC reduction mandate and by IXC strategies to bypass RBOC networks.

GTE

Unlike the five Baby Bells, the Telecommunications Act of 1996 freed GTE immediately to enter any market—including long distance—without restriction. GTE built its own long-distance capabilities, and by the end of 1998 it had captured 2.7 million customers. With 1998 revenues of $25.5 billion, GTE has a strong position in each of the important telecom sectors, including local (23.5 million lines in 28 states), wireless (4.8 subscribers in 17 states), online services, and long distance.

In August 1997, GTE completed its acquisition of BBN, the Internet service provider credited with designing the Internet (and establishing the @ sign), for $616 million. AT&T had held a minority interest in BBN, and had been rumored as a potential acquirer of BBN. GTE also is investing billions of dollars to build a private, 17,000-mile nationwide data network and has invested $485 million for

a 20 percent share of Qwest's new network. GTE started to roll out high-speed DSL service in its region in June 1998, with plans to offer the service in 16 states.

As noted above, GTE has agreed to merge with Bell Atlantic. The combination would create the country's largest provider of local phone service (with 65.1 million lines), operating in 39 states and 76 of the top 100 markets nationwide. It would also become the largest wireless provider, with 11.4 million subscribers.

Long-Distance Carriers

In contrast to the RBOCs' reluctance to compete outside their regions, the long-distance players—AT&T, MCI WorldCom, Sprint, and others—have aggressively pursued strategies to expand the scale and scope of their operations. Their moves are aimed both at enhancing their positions in long distance and at entering new markets, particularly the local-service business and the fast-growing market for "broadband" data services. Strategically, these companies are trying to develop the capability to offer customers a wide array of telecommunications services—one-stop shopping. AT&T is the most dramatic example of this strategy—the ultimate success of which remains to be seen. But it took a bold new CEO—C. Michael Armstrong, recruited in late 1997 from Hughes Electronics Corp.—to pull it off.

AT&T   With Armstrong at the helm, AT&T embarked on a string of major acquisitions, beginning with the purchase of Teleport Communications Group for $11.3 billion[5] in January 1998, which gave it access to local service in 85 markets. As a result of the deal, AT&T expected to save about $1.25 billion in 1999 due to financial synergies and reduced local network access fees. Shortly after, the company struck a deal to acquire cable operator TCI—the nation's largest, with 13.5 million subscribers—for $58 billion (renaming the unit AT&T Broadband & Internet Services). Later that year, in October 1998, AT&T announced its $1.5 billion acquisition of Vanguard Cellular Systems, one of the largest cellular operators in the United States. Vanguard provided services to approximately 625,000 customers under the Cellular One brand name. This was followed in December 1998 by AT&T's $5 billion acquisition of IBM's Global Network Services, a data network service for corporations. Then, in May 1999, AT&T announced its bid to acquire number-three cable operator

---

[2]T1 and T3 refer to circuits capable of transmitting data at 1.5 megabits per second and 45 megabits per second, respectively.

[3]In 1998, the five RBOCs had combined revenues of $113 billion (from all sources); of that amount, $25.5 billion came from access fees. Data from annual reports.

[4]"Plain Talk on the Future of Communications," speech by AT&T Chairman C. Michael Armstrong, 9/29/1998.

---

[5]Note: AT&T paid approximately 22 times revenue.

EXHIBIT 1 | Selected Financial Data for RBOCs and GTE, 1990–1998
All figures are in millions of dollars, except for Return on Average Equity (percentage)

	1998	1997	1996	1995	1994	1993	1992	1991	1990
AMERITECH									
Revenues	17,514	15,998	14,917	13,428	12,570	11,710	11,153	10,818	10,663
Net income (loss)	3,606	2,296	2,134	2,008	(1,064)	1,513	(400)	1,166	1,254
Cash flow from operating activities	4,810	4,510	3,743	3,557	3,430	3,189	3,288	2,804	2,886
Capital expenditures	2,982	2,641	2,440	2,120	1,877	2,092	2,237	2,152	2,116
Total assets	30,299	25,339	23,707	21,943	19,947	23,428	22,818	22,290	21,715
Stockholders' equity	10,897	8,308	7,687	7,015	6,055	7,845	6,992	8,097	7,732
Return on average equity (%)	36.20	28.71	29.03	30.72	16.84	20.39	17.84	14.73	16.26
BELL ATLANTIC									
Revenues	31,566	30,368	13,081	13,430	13,791	12,990	12,647	12,280	12,298
Net income (loss)	2,965	2,455	1,882	1,858	(755)	1,403	1,341	(223)	1,313
Cash flow from operating activities	10,071	8,859	4,416	3,981	3,753	4,234	3,930	3,756	3,535
Capital expenditures	7,447	6,638	2,553	2,627	2,648	2,517	2,560	2,545	2,747
Total assets	55,144	53,964	24,856	24,157	24,272	29,544	28,100	27,882	27,999
Stockholders' equity	13,025	12,789	7,423	6,684	6,081	8,224	7,816	7,831	8,930
Return on average equity (%)	22.97	24.29	24.66	29.17	19.60	18.47	17.67	15.89	14.98
BELLSOUTH									
Revenues	23,123	20,633	19,040	17,886	16,845	15,880	15,149	14,446	14,345
Net income (loss)	3,259	3,261	2,863	(1,232)	2,160	880	1,618	1,472	1,632
Cash flow from operating activities	7,741	7,039	5,863	5,443	5,172	4,786	4,947	4,390	4,527
Capital expenditures	5,212	4,858	4,455	4,203	3,600	3,486	3,189	3,102	3,191
Total assets	39,410	36,301	32,568	31,880	34,397	32,873	31,463	30,942	30,207
Stockholders' equity	16,110	15,165	13,249	11,825	14,367	13,494	13,799	13,105	12,666
Return on average equity (%)	20.60	23.02	22.84	11.94	15.50	7.58	12.33	11.69	12.66
GTE									
Revenues	25,473	23,260	21,339	19,957	19,944	19,748	19,984	19,621	18,374
Net income (loss)	2,172	2,794	2,798	(2,138)	2,451	900	(754)	1,580	1,541
Cash flow from operating activities	5,890	6,244	5,899	5,033	4,740	5,277	4,832	4,784	3,744
Capital expenditures	5,609	5,128	4,088	4,034	4,192	3,893	3,909	3,857	3,453
Total assets	43,615	42,142	38,422	37,019	42,500	41,575	42,144	42,437	33,769
Stockholders' equity	8,766	8,038	7,336	6,871	10,556	9,677	10,171	11,417	9,210
Return on average equity (%)	27.30	36.35	39.39	29.27	24.47	10.00	16.92	15.31	18.07

Sources: Standard & Poor's, Market Guide, company reports.

(continued)

EXHIBIT 1 | Selected Financial Data for RBOCs and GTE, 1990–1998
All figures are in millions of dollars, except for Return on Average Equity (percentage) (cont.)

	1998	1997	1996	1995	1994	1993	1992	1991	1990
NYNEX*									
Revenues			13,454	13,407	13,307	13,408	13,155	13,250	13,585
Net income (loss)			1,477	(1,850)	793	(394)	1,311	601	949
Cash flow from operating activities			3,689	3,648	3,700	3,655	3,506	3,246	2,875
Capital expenditures			2,905	3,188	3,012	2,717	2,450	2,499	2,493
Total assets			27,659	26,220	30,068	29,458	27,714	27,503	26,651
Stockholders' equity			7,059	6,079	8,581	8,416	9,724	9,120	9,149
Return on average equity (%)			20.49	14.59	9.33	(3.00)	13.92	6.58	10.25
PACIFIC TELESIS**									
Revenues			9,588	9,042	9,274	9,244	9,935	9,895	9,716
Net income (loss)			1,142	(2,312)	1,159	(1,504)	1,142	1,015	1,030
Cash flow from operating activities			2,592	2,769	2,947	2,727	3,053	2,659	2,760
Capital expenditures			2,454	2,002	1,631	1,800	2,056	1,867	1,937
Total assets			16,608	15,841	20,139	23,437	22,516	21,838	21,581
Stockholders' equity			2,773	2,190	5,233	7,786	8,251	7,729	7,401
Return on average equity (%)			42.60	28.24	17.45	2.38	14.29	13.42	13.47
SBC									
Revenues	28,777	26,681	13,898	12,670	11,772	10,690	10,015	9,332	9,113
Net income (loss)	4,023	1,674	2,101	(930)	1,649	(845)	1,302	1,076	1,101
Cash flow from operating activities	8,381	7,596	4,824	4,021	3,967	3,441	3,615	2,893	2,671
Capital expenditures	5,927	6,230	3,027	2,336	2,350	2,221	2,144	1,826	1,778
Total assets	45,066	44,836	23,449	22,003	26,005	24,308	23,810	23,179	22,196
Stockholders' equity	12,780	10,520	6,835	6,256	8,356	7,609	9,304	8,859	8,581
Return on average equity (%)	34.53	14.75	31.22	24.18	20.66	16.97	14.33	13.26	13.00
US WEST									
Revenues	12,378	11,479	11,168	9,484	9,176	10,294	10,281	10,577	9,957
Net income (loss)	1,508	1,527	1,501	1,184	1,150	(2,806)	(614)	553	1,199
Cash flow from operating activities	3,927	4,191	3,614	2,719	2,509	3,338	3,292	3,030	2,822
Capital expenditures	2,672	2,168	2,444	2,462	2,254	2,449	2,261	2,654	2,559
Total assets	18,407	17,667	16,915	16,585	15,944	20,680	27,964	27,854	27,050
Stockholders' equity	755	4,367	3,917	3,476	3,179	5,861	8,268	9,587	9,240
Return on average equity (%)		29.08	32.87	35.58	25.44	6.74	13.21	5.88	13.85

*Acquired by Bell Atlantic in 1996.

**Acquired by SBC in 1996.

Sources: Standard & Poor's, Market Guide, company reports.

EXHIBIT 2 | Selected Financial Data for Major Long-Distance Carriers, 1990–1998
All figures are in millions of dollars, except for Return on Average Equity (percentage)

	1998	1997	1996	1995	1994	1993	1992	1991	1990
AT&T									
Revenues	53,223	51,319	52,184	79,609	75,094	67,156	64,904	63,089	55,977
Net income (loss)	6,398	4,638	5,908	139	4,710	(3,794)	3,807	522	2,735
Cash flow from operating activities	10,217	8,353	6,867	9,690	8,956	7,129	7,874	6,015	5,463
Capital expenditures	7,981	7,143	6,339	6,411	5,304	3,942	4,183	3,979	3,667
Total assets	59,550	58,635	55,552	88,884	79,262	60,766	57,188	53,355	43,775
Stockholders' equity	25,522	22,647	20,295	17,274	17,921	13,850	18,921	16,228	14,093
Return on average equity (%)	25.30	20.83	29.85	0.79	29.65	24.25	21.66	3.44	20.39
MCI*									
Revenues		19,653	18,494	15,265	13,338	11,921	10,562	9,491	7,680
Net income (loss)		149	1,202	548	795	582	609	551	299
Cash flow from operating activities		3,488	3,144	2,979	2,355	1,978	1,726	1,271	1,549
Capital expenditures		3,828	3,347	2,866	2,897	1,733	1,272	1,377	1,274
Total assets		25,510	22,978	19,301	16,366	11,276	9,678	8,834	8,249
Stockholders' equity		11,311	10,661	9,602	9,004	4,713	3,150	2,959	2,340
Return on average equity (%)		1.36	11.86	5.89	11.58	15.93	19.29	19.71	12.46
QWEST									
Revenues	2,243	697	231						
Net income (loss)	(844)	15	(7)						
Cash flow from operating activities	45	(36)	33						
Capital expenditures	1,413	346	57						
Total assets	8,068	1,398	264						
Stockholders' equity	4,238	382	9						
Return on average equity (%)		7.425	na						
SPRINT									
Revenues	17,134	14,874	14,045	12,765	12,662	11,368	9,230	8,780	8,345
Net income (loss)	415	953	1,184	395	891	55	457	368	309
Cash flow from operating activities	4,255	3,379	2,404	2,729	2,472	2,136	2,018	1,565	1,201
Capital expenditures	4,231	2,863	2,434	1,857	2,016	1,595	1,151	1,244	1,566
Total assets	33,231	18,185	16,953	15,196	14,936	14,149	10,188	10,464	10,553
Stockholders' equity	12,448	9,037	8,532	4,671	4,554	3,949	2,839	2,545	2,324
Return on average equity (%)	3.86	10.85	18.08	20.58	20.87	14.19	15.93	15.16	14.01

*Acquired by WorldCom in 1998.

(*continued*)

EXHIBIT 2 | Selected Financial Data for Major Long-Distance Carriers, 1990–1998 (cont.)
All figures are in millions of dollars, except for Return on Average Equity (percentage)

	1998	1997	1996	1995	1994	1993	1992	1991	1990
WORLDCOM									
Revenues**	17,678	7,351	4,485	3,640	2,221	1,145	801	263	154
Net income (loss)	(2,669)	384	(2,213)	268	(122)	104	(6)	18	10
Cash flow from operating activities	4,085	1,318	798	616	261	151	84	42	27
Capital expenditures	5,418	2,645	657	356	192	36	58	19	13
Total assets	86,401	22,390	19,862	6,635	3,430	2,515	870	337	169
Stockholders' equity	45,003	13,510	12,960	2,187	1,827	1,622	343	100	39
Return on average equity (%)	(9.12)	2.70	(28.91)	12.49	(8.70)	9.77	(1.16)	25.39	28.66

**WorldCom completed its acquisition of MCI on 9/14/98 and accounted for the transaction as a purchase; accordingly, the operating results of MCI are included from the date of acquisition.

Sources: Standard & Poor's, Market Guide, company reports.

MediaOne—which had already negotiated a deal to be acquired by number-three cable operator Comcast. In the end, Comcast and AT&T worked out an agreement, with AT&T getting MediaOne—with 5 million customers—for $62 billion. The deal still awaits FCC approval (most analysts agree that it will be approved).

Having spent some $126 billion on these deals—plus $11.5 billion to acquire McCaw Cellular in 1994—AT&T is making one of the boldest gambits in U.S. corporate history. The reason is clear: its core business—long distance—is no longer a significant source of growth. The long-distance market, now rife with competition, has grown at an average annual rate of only 5.5 percent overall since 1990. Meanwhile, competition has cut AT&T's share of that sluggish market to 44.5 percent in 1997 (from 90 percent in 1984).[6] Nonetheless, AT&T relied on long-distance for 86 percent of its 1998 revenues. So, even though the local phone market has grown at an average annual rate of just 5.6 percent over the last 5 years, nearly 100 percent of those revenues have gone to the ILECs: taking share from the ILECs is at the heart of AT&T's game plan.

Driving AT&T's cable-acquisition strategy are two key motives. First, cable systems have wires directly into customer homes, thereby enabling AT&T to bypass the ILECs' local loops (or "last mile") and to avoid paying access charges. In 1998, AT&T spent $15.3 billion in access fees paid to local phone companies, which

represented nearly 34 percent of its long-distance revenues of $45.6 billion. Second, coaxial cable is a broadband medium—it has the capacity to carry content at high speed, such as graphics, video, and audio. Based on this combination of bypass and bandwidth, AT&T hopes to build a nationwide system offering businesses and consumers a complete bundle of telecom services: local and long-distance phone service, cable, high-speed Internet access, and other advanced services (e.g., movies on demand).

Including the MediaOne acquisition, AT&T's cable network would pass 25.5 million homes (about a quarter of the nation's households), to which it could market cable phone services. Moreover, AT&T has agreements with Time Warner and Comcast (the number two and three cable operators, respectively), to market AT&T phone services to their cable customers. This would extend the potential reach of AT&T's cable phone service to 60 percent of all households. AT&T is now testing cable phone service in several U.S. markets.

However, the job of creating a full-blown, advanced telecommunications network from a patchwork of cable systems is neither simple nor cheap. Most cable networks require significant upgrading in order to serve as two-way communications systems. According to *Fortune* magazine, upgrading systems to handle voice costs about $500 per subscriber, and $700 to $1,200 for upgrades to carry high-speed data traffic.[7] And *Teletechnology* newsletter estimated that, as of the

---

[6]*Long Distance Market Shares*, Federal Communications Commission, 3/99.

[7]*Fortune*, 7/5/99.

beginning of 1998, only 17 percent of cable infrastructure was ready for two-way communication.[8]

Cable networks, in their current state, are deficient as telecommunications systems in several ways. For example, the traditional "tree and branch" network architecture upon which most cable systems were originally based makes them very vulnerable to service outages: damage suffered at any point on the network interrupts traffic for all customers downstream. By contrast, the star or ring architectures employed by the ILECs provide redundant channels to minimize network outages. Moreover, while coax cable is capable of maintaining speed and data integrity over a relatively long distance from the trunk to the home, the trunk portion of the system, which carries traffic from the head-end to the distribution branches in neighborhoods, would have to be upgraded to fiber-optic.

The most important disadvantage to the cable infrastructure is that it was designed to provide one-way delivery of video, and systems must be retrofitted with switches and signal relays to allow for two-way transmission, as well as head-end equipment that can both send and receive transmissions. Other obstacles for the cable operators have been a lack of industrywide standards for key technical components such as servers and network transmission protocols which have hampered software development in such critical areas as billing and traffic monitoring systems, vital aspects of delivering high-quality customer service.

Cable operators also face significant organizational hurdles in attempting to convince users to entrust their mission-critical telephony needs to a cable provider. Cable operators must overcome the monopolist mindset with which they have run their cable networks and for which they have earned a reputation for providing poor customer service while steadily increasing rates. In addition, cable operators lack network-management experience, and have traditionally viewed themselves as participants in the entertainment business, focused on acquiring content and reselling it.

MCI WorldCom As AT&T pursued its growth strategy, the other IXCs were not standing still. In late 1997, for example, number two long-distance provider MCI announced that it would merge with the much smaller number four provider, WorldCom, for $37 billion—a move that took the industry by surprise. The deal closed in September 1998, and the combined entity was renamed MCI WorldCom. GTE and British Telecom had also made runs at MCI, and in early 1997 MCI appeared to have been sold to BT for $20 billion. However, GTE upset that deal with a cash offer of $28 billion, and WorldCom bested GTE with an all-stock counteroffer initially worth $30 billion.

Prior to the MCI deal, WorldCom had approximately 5.5 percent of the U.S. market, including many highly profitable business customers. MCI added 22 million long-distance customers, which were also considered among the industry's most profitable.[9] The combined MCI WorldCom had 25 percent of the long-distance market and operations in 65 countries.

The MCI deal was the dramatic continuation of an aggressive acquisition strategy that WorldCom had been pursuing since the early 1990s. It had already acquired MFS (in 1996) and Brooks Fiber (in 1997), two large fiber-based CLECs. Combining MCI's local service with its MFS and Brooks Fiber operations, the company spanned 100 of the top local markets. Previously, MCI had been struggling to build local networks in 30 cities, with losses of approximately $800 million on revenues of $500 million in 1997.[10] After the merger, MCI would leverage WorldCom's local networks rather than continue building its own.

MCI WorldCom planned to utilize its own local infrastructure, rather than RBOC service. According to Tim Price, CEO of MCI WorldCom's U.S. subsidiary, "We are going to be an absolute power. . . . Our local strategy has always been built upon infrastructure. . . . If most of my revenue came from residential customers, I would do resale. But most of my revenue comes from business-to-business sales."[11] MCI WorldCom is well-positioned to attract business customers: a high percentage of companies are concentrated in central cities, where MFS and Brooks Fiber had laid their networks, and the company's high-speed fiber infrastructure can handle corporations' growing data-traffic needs.

While domestic long distance accounted for two-thirds of MCI WorldCom's 1998 revenues of $30.4 billion, the company's major sources of growth lie elsewhere. In 1998, for example, revenues from domestic long distance grew by less than 9 percent from their 1997 level, versus far higher rates of increases in other

---

[8]*Teletechnology,* 7/10/98.

[9]*Fortune,* 11/10/1997.

[10]*Fortune,* 10/27/1997.

[11]*Fortune,* 3/2/98.

segments: local services (80 percent), Internet services (69 percent), international services (59 percent), and data (28 percent).[12]

One noticeable gap in MCI WorldCom's offerings is wireless. The company has no significant cellular or PCS operations, while its chief rivals lead these markets—AT&T in cellular and Sprint in PCS. This lack impinges on MCI WorldCom's ability to sell itself as a single source for corporate telecommunications needs. Most of MCI WorldCom's efforts in wireless are focused on data services. In the first half of 1999, MCI WorldCom announced deals to acquire SkyTel (the number-two paging service), as well as CAI Wireless and Wireless One (both providers of broadband wireless services).

Sprint   Sprint, the number-three long-distance company with about a 10 percent share of the U.S. market, has not pursued an all-out acquisition strategy like AT&T and MCI WorldCom.[13] But it, too, has its eyes on local service and the growing data market. The company had 1998 revenues of $17.1 billion, two-thirds of which came from its long-distance operations. It also offers local service, with 7.6 million lines in 18 states. And Sprint PCS, a wholly owned unit, operates the nation's largest PCS system, with more than 3 million subscribers. PCS revenues in 1998 were $1.23 billion (though the unit actually incurred a net loss of $2.64 billion).[14]

In December 1998, Sprint launched an entirely new network infrastructure, called ION (Integrated On-demand Network), optimized to carry voice, video, and data. According to Sprint CEO and Chairman William Esrey, ION is Sprint's strategy to grow its data services business and to expand into local markets. The new network employs packet-switched, asynchronous transfer mode (ATM) technology and supports the Internet protocol (IP). The company has invested $2 billion developing this network, and plans to spend an additional $400 million over the next two years. It expects

improved efficiencies from the ION network to save the company $1 billion over the next five years.[15] Sprint ION services currently are available in a handful of cities to large businesses, which connect to the backbone via high-bandwidth lines (e.g., T1 or T3). Residential service in several markets is scheduled for the fall of 1999. The company will use a combination of digital subscriber line (DSL) service—via agreements with various CLECs that are now rolling out this service—and fixed wireless technologies[16] to provide high bandwidth for the "last mile" connecting residences to the ION network.

According to Sprint, ION offers "virtually unlimited bandwidth over a single existing telephone line for simultaneous voice, video calls, and data services."[17] Using the new network, Sprint predicted that the cost to deliver a typical voice call will drop by at least 70 percent, and will allow full-motion video conferencing to be offered at lower cost than a typical long-distance call today.

In August 1998, Sprint launched a phone-to-phone Internet telephony service, called Callternatives, in Atlanta, Dallas, Los Angeles, San Francisco, and Seattle. The service allows calls throughout the United States—for 7.5 cents a minute—and to numerous international locations at rates of up to 75 percent less than circuit-switched service.[18] "I cannot say it clearly or loudly enough: Sprint is fully, completely committed to IP," said CEO Esrey.[19]

Qwest   In January 1998, Qwest Communications purchased long-distance carrier LCI in a $4.4 billion stock deal, which made Qwest the fourth-largest IXC in the United States, after AT&T, MCI WorldCom, and Sprint. For most of its history, Qwest had supplied network capacity and construction services to larger phone companies. But with the near completion of its fiber-optic coast-to-coast telecom network, the company is now competing to provide service to end users. Headed by Joe Nacchio, formerly the number-three executive at AT&T, the company has become an aggressive player in long-distance and data services.

---

[12]MCI WorldCom 1998 Annual Report.

[13]One notable exception is Sprint's acquisition of several wireless cable TV companies in early 1999, including People's Choice TV (for $420 million), American Telecasting (for $167.8 million), Videotron USA (for $180 million), and Transworld Telecommunications (for $30 million). The acquisitions provide Sprint with broadband access to homes, enabling it to bypass ILEC access fees. (Sources: *The Wall Street Journal*, 4/28/99, 5/4/99, 5/6/99; *Network World*, 5/10/99).

[14]Sprint 1998 Annual Report.

[15]Sprint 1998 Annual Report.

[16]DSL and fixed wireless technologies are explained later in this note; see section on "Technological Developments" below.

[17]Sprint press release, 6/02/1998.

[18]*Business Communications Review*, 1/1/99.

[19]Cnet (news.com), 7/16/1998.

EXHIBIT 3 | Selected Quarterly Financial Data for Several Emerging Data-CLECs
(All figures are in millions of dollars)

	30-Jun-99	31-Mar-99	31-Dec-98	30-Sep-98	30-Jun-98	31-Mar-98
COVAD COMMUNICATIONS						
Revenues	10.8	5.6	2.8	1.6	0.8	0.6
Net income	(41.9)	(28.9)	(19.9)	(16.6)	(8.9)	(2.8)
Total assets	593.8	577.2	139.4	144.6	146.5	na
Total debt	353.8	358.5	142.9	138.0	133.1	na
Stockholders' equity	172.0	187.4	(24.7)	(6.4)	8.1	na
NORTHPOINT COMMUNICATIONS						
Revenues	2.5	1.3	0.5	0.2	0.1	0.04
Net income	(37.9)	(23.4)	(15.9)	(7.8)	(3.3)	(1.9)
Total assets	503.1	131.0	60.5	na	na	na
Total debt	58.3	56.1	51.9	na	na	na
Stockholders' equity	425.0	47.6	(6.5)	na	na	na
RHYTHMS NETCONNECTIONS						
Revenues	1.6	0.7	0.3	0.2	0.1	0.01
Net income	(42.9)	(23.9)	(15.3)	(11.9)	(6.8)	(2.4)
Total assets	789.3	245.5	171.7	174.0	na	na
Total debt	494.3	163.7	158.2	152.9	na	na
Stockholders' equity	239.1	41.6	(6.7)	8.2	na	na

Sources: Market Guide, company reports.

Qwest, along with a new generation of telecommunication companies (including Level 3, IXC, and Williams), focuses on applying the latest communications technologies to the telecom industry. Qwest's state-of-the-art network is designed to deliver both voice and data packets at high speed. According to Nacchio, "People ask if we're telecom guys or Silicon Valley guys. I like to say that we are a Silicon Valley company on the other side of the Rockies. . . . The incumbents are not poised for data growth. They are plagued by proprietary technology and a collapsing pricing structure."[20]

The weak link in Qwest's position, however, is its lack of local access to end users. In 1998 Qwest tried to solve that problem by signing marketing deals with US West and Ameritech allowing Qwest to offer long-distance services to US West's and Ameritech's local customers. Qwest had signed up many customers for this service. However, AT&T and MCI sued, arguing that the arrangement violated the 1996 Telecommunications Act. The FCC agreed, and in September 1998 rejected the deal.

The company launched three new initiatives to reach end users. First, the US West acquisition would give Qwest immediate access to US West's 16 million customers, 50,000 of whom now subscribe to high-speed DSL service. Second, it recently invested $90 million for a 19 percent stake in Advanced Radio Telecom Corp., which is building a broadband wireless network in more than 40 U.S. markets. Finally, the company has local-access agreements with two CLEC start-ups—Covad Communications and Rhythms NetConnections—which are rolling out high-speed DSL services to an increasing number of markets.

CLECs

Since passage of the Telecommunications Act of 1996, activity among CLECs has moved into high gear. The overall number of CLECs jumped from 57 in 1995 to 146 in 1998[21]—many of them started directly in the wake of the Telecommunications Act. Their 1998 revenues were $3.3 billion (compared to $1.9 billion in

---

[20]*Fortune*, 6/8/1998.

[21]*Trends in Telephone Service*, Federal Communications Commission, 2/99.

1997),[22] and they had 5.6 million lines in service, up from 1.6 million in 1997.[23] And by early 1999, CLECs' interconnections with ILECs numbered nearly 5,500—double the number from the year before.[24]

While some CLECs focus on opportunities to buy ILEC service at wholesale rates—which the Telecommunications Act requires ILECs to offer competitors—and resell it at a mark-up, most are installing some combination of their own lines (usually fiber-optic) and switches that interconnect with ILEC exchanges. Only the leanest of operators can make money on pure resale of ILEC facilities, because the gross margin is only about 15 percent. A facilities-based CLEC, however, can earn margins of 50 percent to 80 percent. (AT&T, MCI, and Sprint had all tried the resale game as an initial foray into local service, but they quit because none could make a profit. Indeed, AT&T lost an average of $3 per month on each subscriber.)[25]

Most CLECs focus on small to midsize business customers, who occupy urban office buildings and suburban industrial parks. Revenues from these dense clusters of high-volume customers are enough to justify the expense of installing lines to customer premises and laying the fiber-optic rings that transport traffic to interconnections with ILEC or IXC exchanges. CLECs are especially aggressive in providing high-speed lines to businesses: according to *Telecommunications* magazine, "CLECs now get more than half of their profits from T1 service." Moreover, by some industry estimates, CLECs may control 40 percent of all T1 business by 2002.[26]

The CLECs remain highly fragmented, with a large number of small but growing players. But, just as AT&T acquired Teleport and WorldCom acquired MFS and Brooks Fiber, more consolidation in this sector can be expected.

Technological Developments

While the effects of the Telecommunications Act on competition are being played out, technology is also bringing dramatic change to the industry. There are many recent

innovations, but they can generally be divided into two categories: wireline technologies that enable high-speed transmission of content, and new wireless technologies—including broadband—that provide further alternatives to wireline service.

Chief among the first category—the wire-based "broadband" technologies—are digital subscriber line (DSL), cable modems, and dense wavelength division multiplexing (DWDM).

DSL

Digital subscriber line (DSL) enables high-speed transmissions over the twisted-pair, copper telephone wire that is standard in most homes and residences. Many different variants of DSL have been developed, but the most common is ADSL (asymmetric DSL). It enables upstream communication (i.e., transmission from the customer premises) at a rate of 64–640 kilobytes per second (Kbps) and downstream rates of up to 1.5 megabytes per second (Mbps). Faster variants of DSL can achieve speeds of up to 52Mbps. By comparison, today's fastest consumer dial-up modems operate at a maximum of 56Kbps.

Though developed in the late 1980s and early 1990s, DSL technology was not commercially deployed until 1997. It requires customers to have a DSL modem connected to their equipment (typically connected to a computer), and the phone company also must have special DSL equipment at its switching facilities. One major limitation of DSL is that, for technical reasons, it is available only to customers located within a few thousand feet of the phone company's switching office (beyond that distance, the signal degrades). With the current state of the technology, as much as 40 percent of the population does not have access to DSL.

Cable Modems

Cable modems are another innovation addressing the broadband issue. Though first introduced in the early 1990s—Zenith was one of the original developers of the technology—only in recent years have cable modems been installed in significant numbers. But with the arrival of the Internet in full force, residential demand for high-speed Internet connections has spurred usage of cable modems. Moreover, cable systems were originally designed for one-way transmission only; cable modems at the customer premise, therefore, cannot be deployed until the cable system is upgraded to accommodate two-way communications.

---

[22]*Monitoring Report*, Federal Communications Commission, 6/99.

[23]*Business Communications Review*, 6/99.

[24]Interconnection statistic cited by US West CEO Solomon Trujillo in his speech "Assessing the Telecommunications Act of 1996: Is America Getting What Americans Want?" 1/1/99.

[25]*Telephony*, 3/16/98.

[26]*Telecommunications*, 4/99.

Cable modems can theoretically provide connections up to 10Mbps. However, due to cable's tree-and-branch architecture—by which the system effectively is a large local area network—connection speed degrades as more people in the system are online at the same time. (DSL technology does not have this drawback, because each subscriber's connection is a dedicated line to the phone company's exchange.) Even so, cable-modem connection speeds exceed by many times the 56Kbps rates of today's standard modems.

The race is on between DSL and cable modems to deliver high-speed connections to residences and small businesses. So far, cable modems have the lead. In 1998, there were 500,000–700,000 cable-modem users, versus 200,000–300,000 DSL subscribers nationwide (estimates for both technologies vary). Many analysts forecast this trend to continue. For example, research firm Jupiter Communications predicts that by 2002, cable-modem users will outnumber DSL subscribers, 6.8 million to 3.4 million.[27]

Dense Wavelength Division Multiplexing (DWDM)

Another technology addressing wire-based broadband is dense wavelength division multiplexing (DWDM). Just as DSL technology enhances the capability of copper phone wire, DWDM does something similar for fiber-optic cable: It increases the transmission capacity of a fiber strand by dividing the light passing through it into many waves, each of which can carry a signal. Currently, DWDM can increase fiber-optic transmission by 80 times,[28] and further improvements are expected soon. (In its laboratories, Lucent Technologies has divided the light in a single fiber into 100 beams, each traveling at 10 billion bits per second—10 times today's usual rate; the resulting capacity—1 trillion bits per second—is more than sufficient to handle all of North America's telecommunications needs.)[29] This is a great advantage to owners and developers of fiber-optic systems, because DWDM enables them to increase the effective capacity of existing fiber at far less expense than laying more fiber underground.

DWDM and other innovations have dramatically expanded the transmission capacity of fiber-optic networks. Indeed, Qwest—which has nearly completed construction of an 18,500-mile network—claims that its system has enough bandwidth to transmit the equivalent of the entire contents of the Library of Congress coast to coast in 20 seconds.[30] Moreover, Qwest is just one of five companies building extensive fiber-optic networks throughout the country: Frontier, IXC, Williams, and Level 3 have projects of similar scale in various stages of completion. All of this is in addition to the fiber-optic networks that AT&T, MCI WorldCom, and Sprint have in place, as well as the RBOCs' and CLECs' regional fiber backbones. This surge in fiber supply has spurred predictions of an imminent bandwidth glut. For example, Forrester Research, a market research firm, says the glut will start next year and will extend until 2005 or later.[31] Worldwide Renaissance, a consulting firm, comes to a similar conclusion: "within two years, the United States will have 400 times more telecommunications capacity than it had in 1998"—enough to handle 54 trillion simultaneous phone calls—yet "demand for space on networks to carry computer traffic, video and voice calls will grow only 20 times."[32] In April 1999, *Forbes* reported that since June 1998, "the wholesale spot price of bandwidth is down 35 percent, thanks to ample supply."[33] And according to a recent MIT study, 83 percent of the bandwidth on AT&T's international fiber network goes unused.[34]

The new fiber firms, on the other hand, state their belief that demand will be virtually infinite, as new bandwidth-hungry applications reach businesses and consumers: video on demand, video teleconferencing, and consumer videophones, TV-style programs on the Internet, and other multimedia-based communications. "I don't see a glut," said IXC CEO Benjamin Scott. "I see a big wave of demand."[35] Level 3 CEO James Crowe answers the glut predictions with this analogy from the computer industry: "Did Intel glut the microprocessor market by coming out with generation after generation of more powerful and cheaper microprocessors? Of course not. Demand just took off and sucked up the supply."[36] Of the five new fiber companies, Williams Communications is alone in its strategy of offering

---

[27]*Cable World*, 5/24/99.

[28]*Technology Review*, 3/1/99.

[29]*BusinessWeek*, 12/7/98.

[30]*Denver Rocky Mountain News*, 2/14/99.

[31]*Fortune*, 3/15/99.

[32]*Boston Globe*, 7/10/99; *Dallas Business Journal*, 7/2/99.

[33]*Forbes*, 4/19/99.

[34]*Data Communications*, 5/7/99.

[35]*Investor's Business Daily*, 3/3/98.

[36] *Barron's*, 6/14/99.

bandwidth only at wholesale; all the other firms offer—or will offer—services to end-users.

Fixed Wireless

In the wireless area, a technology referred to as "fixed wireless" or "wireless local loop" (WLL) offers another option to conventional wireline service. Rather than lay down cable and install wire into customer premises—a very expensive undertaking—providers of fixed wireless services mount receiving and transmitting equipment on the customer's rooftop at far less cost. This equipment sends and receives signals to and from a central tower, which serves as the switching facility that ties into the public phone system. There are several variants of this technology, distinguished primarily by the radiowave spectrum used and bandwidth capacity.

In recent years, the FCC has auctioned off licenses to different portions of spectrum for wireless services. An alphabet soup of technologies[37] has appeared:

- LMDS (local multipoint distribution system) operates in the 28-GHz and 31-GHz spectrum and provides transmission speeds ranging from 1.54Mbps (T1 rate) to 45Mbps (T3 rate).

- MMDS (multichannel multipoint distribution service) was originally designed to deliver cable TV programming over a wireless network (so-called "wireless cable"); it operates in the 2.5-GHZ to 2.7-GHz spectrum and provides bandwidth of 128Kbps to 3Mbps.[38]

- DEMS (digital electronic message service) operates in the 24-GHz and offers bandwidth up to 1.54Mbps (Teligent is the leader in this area).

- Finally, broadband services are also available in the 39-GHz spectrum; WinStar and Advanced Radio Telecom lead the field. WinStar's "Wireless Fiber" service, for example, offers T1-level bandwidth of 1.54Mbps.

---

[37]Data on various fixed wireless technologies from "Annual Report and Analysis of Competitive Market Conditions with Respect to Commercial Mobile Services," Federal Communications Commission, 6/24/99.

[38]This is the technology, for example, employed by the four wireless cable companies that Sprint acquired in early 1999. The FCC distributed MMDS licenses as early as 1984; but operators did not deploy MMDS for two-way communications, as Sprint and others now intend to use the technology. (Source: *Network World*, 5/10/99.)

Internet Telephony

Another active development area is Internet telephony, particularly the use of the Internet for long-distance voice communications. The appeal is mainly economic: Calls made over the Internet—whether voice or data—are not subject to the access fees that local phone companies charge for terminating standard long-distance calls. Given that long-distance companies now pay out a third of their revenues in access fees, avoiding those charges means huge cost savings.

But there are a few drawbacks to Internet telephony. The main one is the inferior audio quality of Internet calls versus conventional phone calls over circuit-switched networks. In order to be transmitted over the Internet, the speaker's voice first must be digitized (turned into bits of data) and arranged in packets, then transmitted like any other data packets through the Internet's switches. But packet-switching technology was not designed for voice communication: Packets do not travel together in a steady stream along a single conduit—as does the signal in a standard analog call over the phone—and any single packet can be momentarily delayed at any switch on its path, or it can be dropped altogether. Such delays and losses cause the call to sound choppy or broken.

Though currently less than 1 percent of voice calls are carried over the Internet, analysts predict that figure to grow dramatically. One research group projects that by 2002, Internet-based voice calls will be a $9.4 billion market.[39] A number of companies have been started to exploit the cost advantage of Internet telephony. However, until the technology is developed to solve the audio quality problem—an area that's being actively researched—Internet telephony is likely to remain a minor niche. Nonetheless, all the major carriers—from AT&T and MCI WorldCom to the RBOCs—are investigating Internet telephony, and some now even offer this service in a limited way (e.g., Sprint's "Callternatives" service).

In a recent test of international call audio quality, IDT Corp.'s Net2Phone Direct—a service that allows phone-to-phone calling over IDT's proprietary packet-switched network—scored 3.69, on a scale of 1 to 5, versus 4.10 for AT&T's conventional circuit-switched service. This result suggests a narrower quality gap than many industry observers had expected. But the price gap was enormous: the IDT calls cost just 10 cents per minute, compared to $1.90 per minute for AT&T's peak business rate.[40]

---

[39]*Network Computing*, 3/8/99.

[40]*Network Computing*, 3/8/99.

The biggest bet on Internet telephony is being made by two young companies, Qwest and Level 3. Each is spending billions to build its own high-speed, packet-switched network based on Internet protocols. Level 3, for example, plans to spend $10 billion to build a 16,000-mile system connecting major U.S. cities and selected foreign markets (10 percent of which had been completed by mid-1999). Both firms believe that technological improvements will soon solve the quality issues of Internet telephony, leaving them with enormous cost advantages over circuit-switched competitors. Those advantages are driven primarily by the swift pace at which router and fiber-optic technologies—two key elements of the new-generation networks—are increasing their price performance. Routers double their price performance every 20 months, while advances in optical technologies (e.g., DWDM) double fiber network performance every 10 months.[41] Level 3 chief executive James Crowe believes that the company will be able to offer prices 20 percent below those of established companies like AT&T and MCI WorldCom. But that's only the beginning. "We see no reason," Crowe recently told the press, "why we won't be able to drop our prices by 50 percent or more each year, once we get going."[42] Indeed, Level 3 claims it will be able to carry calls over its all-packet network for less than 4 percent of the cost of circuit-switched service.[43]

Explosive Growth of Data Traffic

In addition to deregulation and technology, a third major trend is also driving change in the telecommunications industry: the explosive growth of data traffic and the consequent demand for broadband services. Data traffic includes transmission of fax, text, graphics, video, audio, and other nonvoice content. According to one research group, in 1999 data will have surpassed voice as a percentage of worldwide telecommunications content (when measured as bits transferred) and, by 2002, will account for 92 percent of worldwide content.[44] Faxes, for example, now account for some 40 percent of all long-distance telephone traffic.[45]

Alan Taffel, VP of business development for UUNet Technologies, Inc. (a subsidiary of MCI WorldCom that provides Internet access), told *Upside* magazine: "The load customers are placing on our network is doubling every three and a half months, and in some periods faster than that, which is equivalent to 1,000 percent per year."[46]

At the root of the data explosion is the information revolution: automated business processes such as electronic data interchange (EDI), for instance, generate large volumes of data that must be shuttled from party to party. Moreover, the tremendous rise in World Wide Web activity and Internet usage for e-mail, newsgroups, and other communications translates into increased traffic over phone lines and Internet backbones.

Broadband

The dramatic growth in data traffic is driving another key trend in telecommunications: the growing demand for broadband services. Multimedia content—which is rich in graphics, audio, and video—requires far more bandwidth for its transmission than do ordinary voice calls (see Exhibit 4). While the backbones of today's phone networks (which are primarily fiber-optic cables) can handle the broadband needs of multimedia content, the bottleneck comes at the "last mile": the twisted-pair copper wire that runs into the home or business.

Much of what is happening today in the telecommunications industry centers on the problem of delivering broadband capability to the home or office. AT&T's push into cable, for instance, is as much an effort to provide broadband service to consumers as it is to win their local phone business: The company wants to bundle high-speed Internet access along with cable-TV and local phone service.

Several other developments on the broadband front deserve mention. One is the emerging new class of "data CLECs." These firms primarily focus on offering DSL service to small and midsize businesses, as well as the home-office customer. Taking advantage of surging demand for high-speed Internet connections—and the ILECs' slow pace in serving these customer segments—recent start-ups like NorthPoint Communications, Covad Communications, and Rhythms NetConnections have rolled out service throughout the country. Covad, for example, now offers service in 20 major markets.

---

[41]*Barron's*, 6/14/99.

[42]*Barron's*, 6/14/99.

[43]*InformationWeek*, 6/21/99.

[44]*America's Network*, 5/15/98; data cited are from Insight Research Corp. (Parsippany, NJ).

[45]*Business Communications Review*, 4/99; statistic cited is from research firm IDC.

[46]*Upside*, 7/98.

EXHIBIT 4 | Infrastructure Bandwidth Requirements

Media Transmitted	Required Bandwidth	Transmission Infrastructure Required[7]
Styled text	2–10Kbps	Twisted pair wire, coax cable, fiber optics
Speech graded audio[1]	32–64Kbps	Twisted pair wire, coax cable, fiber optics
Still images	10–128Kbps	Twisted pair wire, coax cable, fiber optics
Low-quality compressed video[2]	100Kbps–1.5Mbps	Twisted pair wire, coax cable, fiber optics
High-fidelity audio[3]	176Kbps–1.5Mbps	Twisted pair wire, coax cable, fiber optics
Medium quality compressed video[4]	1.5–6Mbps	Twisted pair wire, coax cable, fiber optics
High-quality compressed video[5]	6–24Mbps	Coax cable, fiber optics
Visualization[6]	50–100Mbps	Coax cable, fiber optics

[1]Speech graded audio (SGA) refers to audio that accompanies video, rather than ordinary voice telephony. SGA requires higher bandwidth due to the necessity of synchronizing audio with the video which it accompanies.

[2]Used in such applications as current digital videophone, low-quality video typically saves bandwidth by transmitting 15 frames per second (vs. 30 fps for broadcast video), resulting in jerky images, and by using a very small display window often only 25 percent of the full screen size.

[3]High-fidelity audio requires increased sampling rates to eliminate delays and gaps.

[4]Transmits 30 frames per second, providing better quality images and motion, but still limited to small display windows in uses such as delivery of CNN to a window on the users PC, etc.

[5]Required for very high resolution workstations used in collaborative engineering and scientific design and research in networked configurations.

[6]Involves 3-D imaging of complex structures or designs, such as solid modeling and 3-D animation, which must be performed in real time.

[7]Achieving high speed transmission rates on twisted pair wire requires use of digital technologies such as DSL.

Source: Computer Technology Research Corp.

The company partners primarily with Internet service providers, who sell Covad's DSL service bundled with Internet access.

These data CLECs have experienced rapid growth. For the three months ended 3/31/99, Covad's revenues totaled $5.6 million, up from $186,000 in the same period in 1998; NorthPoint's revenues totaled $1.3 million, up from $35,000; and Rhythms NetConnections' revenues totaled $660,000, up from $10,000.[47] Moreover, the stock market has favorably viewed the growth prospects of these firms, as evidenced by the recent market values of their stocks: $4.1 billion for Covad, $4.9 billion for NorthPoint, and $4.7 billion for Rhythms NetConnections (all as of July 14, 1999).

While the data CLECs typically focus on the broadband needs of business customers, high-speed cable networks have emerged to provide broadband to the home. The two leading services are At Home and Roadrunner, both of which were started within the last few years. At Home was founded in 1995 as a joint venture that included cable operators Comcast, Cox, and TCI. AT&T's acquisition of TCI gave it 26 percent ownership of At Home (and a controlling share of votes). At the end of 1998, At Home had 331,000 subscribers;

Roadrunner, which is owned by Time Warner and began offering service in 1995, had 180,000 subscribers. Together, the two services accounted for nearly three-quarters of the estimated 700,000 subscribers to high-speed cable service.[48]

Also on the broadband scene are companies building wireless networks capable of high-speed transmission. In a fixed wireless system, a radio transmitter mounted on the customer's premises communicates with a central antenna site, which serves as the gateway to the phone system or Internet. The two most prominent entries in the broadband wireless arena are Teligent and WinStar. Like the data CLECs, they are targeting small and midsize businesses in major markets. Teligent, for example, which was founded in 1996, has entered 28 markets covering 83 million people and plans to enter 12 additional markets by the end of 1999. In addition to high-speed data services, Teligent also offers local and long-distance service. Headed by former AT&T president Alex Mandl, Teligent has licenses to operate in 74 markets nationwide, all of which it plans to enter by the end of 2001.[49]

[47]Revenue data from the companies' annual reports and SEC filings.

[48]*Quarterly Cable Statistics,* Bear Stearns, 4/30/99.

[49]Teligent data from company's Web site, www.teligent.com, 7/99.

WinStar's strategy in broadband wireless has been to contract with owners of corporate real estate to secure access rights to buildings. By March 1999, the company had access rights to more than 4,800 commercial buildings, with plans to increase that number to 8,000 by year's end. It has licenses in more than 160 major markets, including all of the top 50 cities. The company now offers service in the top 30 U.S. markets, and had 380,000 lines in service as of March 31, 1999. It will add 10 more U.S. markets by the end of 1999. The eventual network will cover more than 60 percent of the nation's small to medium-sized businesses.[50]

An interesting development on the broadband wireless front is the planned purchase, by AT&T unit Liberty Media Group, of Associated Group, Inc., which is Teligent's largest shareholder. If completed, the $3 billion deal would give AT&T a 41 percent stake in Teligent—and another weapon to bypass RBOCs in the battle for local phone business.

Developments in Satellite-Based Communications

Iridium

Iridium, the Motorola-led global phone venture, is to date the most ambitious effort in the satellite-based sector. Thus far, the results have been dismal. When the company launched its service on November 1, 1998, it promised to sign up 52,000 subscribers over the next five months and have revenues of $30 million; but by March 31, 1999, it had only 10,300 users and sales of just $1.45 million. Moreover, the company has quarterly payments of $100 million on $3.4 billion in debt, which it has been unable to meet.[51] In August 1999, Iridium filed for bankruptcy.

Iridium initially promoted its service as an alternative to cellular: The target market was globe-hopping businesspeople, some 5 million strong and growing. These folks, the thinking went, would use a single Iridium satellite phone to replace the several different cell phones required for each continent on which they traveled. But that plan did not work out, for several reasons. The Iridium phone itself—which is 7 inches long, weighs 1 pound, and originally cost around $3,000—is much larger and heavier than today's palm-size cell phones. Moreover, it requires a line of sight to one of Iridium's 66 satellites, which means that it doesn't work indoors. And at $2 to $7 per minute, the usage charges were high. In June 1999, in response to market resistance, Iridium reduced the per-minute fees to between $1.59 and $3.99, and lowered the handset cost to $1,495.[52]

Moreover, the company appears to have based its business plan on assumptions that did not hold up over time. For example, it had originally projected a cost of $2.5 billion to build the system, but that ballooned to $5 billion. Meanwhile, as Iridium was building the system, cellular service—against which Iridium was positioning itself—expanded rapidly, while its price declined. By the time Iridium became operational, the competitive landscape had shifted. As of this writing, Iridium's current management faces the challenges of working out a solution with its creditors and developing a revenue stream that has a hope of meeting operating expenses.

Teledesic

Iridium's problems notwithstanding, privately held Teledesic is marching ahead with its plans to build a satellite-based "Internet-in-the-Sky." Cost is perhaps the largest hurdle Teledesic must overcome in implementing its plans. Under its original plan to launch 840 satellites—when each satellite would have run $100 million to build and launch—the cost was prohibitive. Teledesic scaled back the number of satellites in its system to 288, and it has pushed back the targeted starting date for service to 2004. The company thus far has raised some $1.5 billion in equity investment, against a total projected development cost of $9 billion. In 1999, Teledesic signed agreements with Motorola as the prime contractor and with Lockheed Martin as the prime launch service. Motorola also is an investor in Teledesic.

Though Teledesic plans to offer voice capabilities over its system, its main focus is to provide wireless broadband service enabling computers to connect to the Internet and corporate intranets. Customers will have compact low-power terminals and antennas mounted on their rooftops, which will connect inside to a computer network or PC. Most users will have an uplink connection

[50]WinStar data from company's Web site, www.winstar.com, 7/99.

[51]Data on Iridium's problems from *Forbes,* 6/14/99.

[52]Data on new pricing structure from the company's Web site, www.iridium.com, 7/99.

of up to 2Mbps and a downlink connection of up to 64Mbps; connection at 64Mbps in both directions will be possible using special high-speed terminals.[53]

In contrast to Iridium's premium pricing strategy, Teledesic foresees end-user rates comparable to those of wireline broadband services such as DSL or cable modem. However, Teledesic service will be marketed through a network of service partners, and these resellers will set rates for the areas they serve.

Teledesic will not be a lone player in the satellite-based broadband business—and it may not be the first. SkyBridge LP, a U.S.-based company led by French communications equipment giant Alcatel and other international partners, is building a system of 80 LEO satellites to offer broadband connectivity. It plans to have service available by 2001. Another potential entrant is Astrolink, a $3.5 billion venture led by Lockheed Martin that would employ four high-orbit satellites; start of service is scheduled for mid-2002. Hughes Electronics Corp. is also working on a broadband service called Spaceway, which would use eight high-orbit satellites to provide global Internet connectivity and which it plans to have in service by 2003.

Intersection of Telecommunications and IT Industries

In 1999, telecommunications and information technologies are converging. A prime example, discussed above, is Internet telephony, which uses packet-switching technology (originally intended to connect computers) to carry voice conversations. This convergence is bringing IT companies—hardware and software developers alike—into various aspects of the telecommunications business. One of the most visible IT companies moving into the telecom arena is Microsoft.

Microsoft's first major foray into telecommunications came in June 1997, when it put up $1 billion for 11.5 percent of cable operator Comcast. Microsoft chairman Bill Gates described the investment as part of his "vision of linking the PC and TV" to offer advanced "capabilities to deliver video, data and interactivity to the home."[54] Then, in December 1998, Microsoft invested $200 million for a 1.3 percent stake in Qwest. Qwest will offer hosting services, built on Microsoft

platforms, over its high-speed network.[55] In May 1999, the software giant bought $5 billion of AT&T convertible securities and warrants (equivalent to equity of 3.4 percent). In return, AT&T agreed to license an additional 2.5 million copies of Microsoft's Windows CE software for its digital cable set-top units, with an option for 2.5 million more. This is in addition to an earlier 5-million unit commitment made by TCI in 1998 before being acquired by AT&T.[56] Also in May, Microsoft invested $600 million for a 4.25 percent stake in Nextel Communications, a provider of wireless services in 50 U.S. markets. Nextel customers will be able to use digital phones to access Microsoft's MSN Web portal as their gateway to a customized set of Internet services.[57] Microsoft has also made a number of moves overseas in telecom. In May it paid $120 million to acquire the Swedish firm Sendit, which provides a service that enables customers to view and send messages on their cell phones using Internet browser software. In addition, Microsoft invested more than $500 million in two U.K. cable operators, Telewest and NTL Inc., who are rolling out interactive, broadband service over their networks. And a $300-million investment for a 7.8 percent stake in United Pan-Europe Communications,[58] Europe's second-largest cable company, will put Windows CE software on digital set-top boxes in UPC's 3.4 million homes across Europe beginning next year.[59]

Trends for the Future

The future of the U.S. telecommunications industry will likely extend and amplify the trends in place today. The SBC-Ameritech, Bell Atlantic-GTE, and US West-Qwest mergers, if approved, will consolidate a significant segment of the industry, placing pressure on BellSouth—the only RBOC not in a merger deal—to find a growth strategy. More consolidation is also likely in both the wireless and cable sectors, in which hundreds of small and mid-size companies operate. RBOCS will experience greater competition for local service as the CLECs continue to cherry-pick business and home-office customers from the ILECs and as AT&T rolls out local phone service over its cable network.

---

[53]Teledesic data from company's website, www.teledesic.com, 7/99.

[54]*Chicago Sun-Times*, 6/9/1997.

[55]Dow Jones Business News, 12/14/98.

[56]Deutsche Bank Research, 5/10/99.

[57]Dow Jones Business News, 5/28/99.

[58]Reuters English News Service, 7/26/99.

[59]*New Media Markets* (London), 6/3/99.

Convergence of telecommunications and information technology will increasingly bring traditionally non-telecom companies—such as Microsoft, Cisco, 3Com, and others—into telecom-related businesses. For example, the operating-system battle between Microsoft's Windows CE and 3Com's Palm OS in handheld computers—in which 3Com enjoys a lead[60]—is extending into new generations of cell phones and wireless devices designed to take advantage of the emerging broadband services to connect to the Internet.

The growth of wireless services will continue to outpace growth in the wireline sector. The market penetration rate of cellular and PCS services in the United States at 26 percent is far less than in many other industrialized nations, such as Italy (36 percent), Japan (37 percent), and Finland (58 percent).[61] One research group forecasts a penetration rate of 54 percent by 2004.[62]

Another area certain to continue its rapid growth is the demand for high-speed Internet access, via technologies such as DSL, cable modems, and broadband wireless. Much of that growth will come from small-business and residential customers, for whom such services are only now becoming widely available. As expanded services and increased competition force prices down over the next few years, this market may experience explosive growth similar to that of cellular and PCS services in the 1980s and 1990s.

Finally, the market for Internet telephony will likely be another major growth area. As both audio quality and service improve, the dramatic cost savings will drive the market. As noted earlier, already the quality difference between circuit-switched and packet-switched calls (at least over IDT's IP network) is relatively small, while the price difference is enormous.

All of these trends add up to an increasingly competitive telecommunications industry. The predictable effects—as in all competitive marketplaces—will be a greater variety of offerings and declining prices. The two major wild cards are technological innovation and government regulation.

---

[60]*Business 2.0,* 8/99.

[61]*BusinessWeek,* 5/3/99.

[62]*Mobile Computing & Communications,* 6/99; the research report cited is "US Wireless Voice Market Forecast Update (1999–2004)," Strategy Analytics (Boston).

Case 6.2

Slouching toward Broadband: Revisited in 2005

Introduction

At a time when many things Americans consumed were "supersized," Internet access in the United States was decidedly sparing. Instead of using always-on broadband to gulp down Internet access, most Americans sipped the Web through slow dial-up connections.[1] For unfortunates using dial-up, the World Wide Web became the "World Wide Wait" as it took several minutes for a graphic-rich and therefore bit-intensive Web page to download at those speeds. More advanced Internet applications, such as Web phone calls, video-on-demand, or Web broadcasts of music or television were haltingly slow or completely impractical at nonbroadband speeds. The full benefits of the Internet as a delivery channel for much consumer-targeted advanced e-commerce or entertainment applications would have to wait until broadband became ubiquitous.

In contrast to the United States, many other countries were making broadband penetration a national priority, and their citizens were fast becoming more wired than those in the United States. For example, while by 2004 the United States still led the world in the total number of broadband access lines in use, the country fell off the list of the top 10 nations measured by broadband lines per capita (Exhibit 1). The reasons for the slower-than-expected adoption of broadband in the United States varied according to viewpoint. Some pointed to either insufficient or excessive regulatory oversight and, as a function of this, the high cost of broadband services as the reason for slow adoption. Others blamed the slow adoption of broadband on a lack of popular broadband products, the so-called killer applications, which would drive consumers to broadband. Another important factor contributing to lower broadband penetration in the United States compared to a country such as South Korea, was the large size of the United States and its comparatively unconcentrated population. Lower population concentrations in the United States made it more expensive to build out the necessary infrastructure, which added to the start-up problem. Still, as the then chairman of the United States Federal Communications Commission (FCC) Michael Powell pointed out in late 2001: "Combined broadband availability [in the United States] is estimated to be almost 85 percent. The intriguing statistic is . . . only 12 percent of these households have chosen to subscribe."[2] By early 2005 the penetration of broadband had improved in the United States, to the point where around half of residential users accessed the Internet via broadband, but that was woefully short of other countries such as Japan where more than 90 percent of residential users accessed the Internet with broadband.

A form of broadband known as digital subscriber line (DSL) was offered by established telephone companies and smaller companies competing with them. A different form of broadband was offered by cable television service providers. Many aspects of competition for telephone companies were prescribed in the Telecommunications Act of 1996, which was meant to

---

[1]Because broadband vehicles such as DSL or cable could deliver high-speed Internet access and voice telephone service or cable television signals at the same time, the user's connection to the Internet could be left on without interrupting these other services. This, and the better, richer experience given through broadband, was the reason broadband users spent more time on the Internet compared to dial-up users. The FCC defines broadband as the ability to download (receive bits) and upload (transmit bits) at speeds of 200,000 bits per second (200 Kbs). However, most basic streaming media applications needed download speeds approaching 1,000,000 bits per second (1Mbs). Most cable service providers approached or exceeded this download speed by the end of 2004. Most DSL services featured download speeds of around 800 Kbs at the end of 2004. Dial-up offered data transfer rates of 56 Kbs or slower.

Professor Robert A. Burgelman, Les Vadasz, and Philip E. Meza prepared this case as the basis for class discussion rather than to illustrate either effective or ineffective handling of an administrative situation. It is a revision of SM-98 by Burgelman and Meza.

---

[2]Michael K. Powell, Chairman, FCC, at the National Summit on Broadband Deployment, Washington, D.C. October 25, 2001 (http://www.fcc.gov/Speeches/Powell/2001/spmkp110.html).

EXHIBIT 1 |

Worldwide Broadband
Penetration by
Country

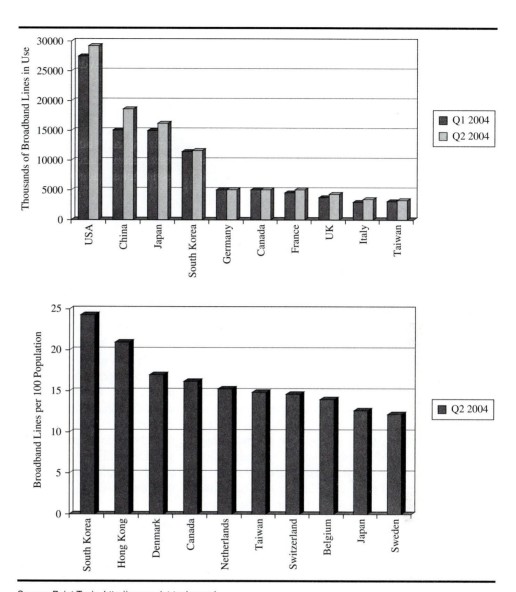

Source: Point Topic. http://www.point-topic.com/

content/dslanalysis/Q2+04+numbers+analysis.htm. Used with permission.

spark competition among local and long distance telephone service providers. (Cable companies did not
bear the same level of regulation-enforced competition
as did phone companies.) At the time of the 1996 Act,
telephone companies and cable companies did not
overlap much in their services or revenue models. By
the end of 2004, this was changing. Many considered
the 1996 Act flawed. For example, broadband Internet
access did not figure prominently in it, and established
phone companies, spun-off from the former telephone
monopoly AT&T, now known as regional Bell operating

companies (RBOCs),[3] continued to lobby Congress
and the FCC to roll back many of the Act's provisions,
particularly those dealing with broadband service. By
late 2004, these efforts were meeting with some
success.

---

[3]RBOCs, also known as incumbent local exchange carriers (ILECs),
compete against competitive local exchange carriers (CLECs) for
consumer and business local telephone services provided over
switched telephone networks.

EXHIBIT 2 |

Worldwide Broadband
Penetration by Type

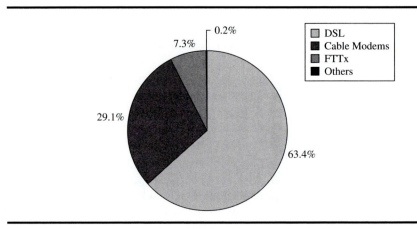

Source: From Point Topic. http://www.point-topic.com/content/dslanalysis/Q2+04+numbers+analysis.htm. Used with permission.

In the late 1990s, in the fog of uncertainty that followed the 1996 Act, cable companies pushed ahead in investing upwards of $100 billion over eight years to upgrade their networks in order to offer enhanced services, particularly video-on-demand and telephony service. During this time, many RBOCs held off investing much in their networks, and instead lobbied Congress to roll back various provisions of the 1996 Act. Luckily for the cable companies, the same network upgrades they made with video and telephony service in mind also enabled them to offer cable broadband to consumers. After initially failing to invest much in DSL services, RBOCs had since been playing catch-up in the United States.

DSL penetration continued to lag cable penetration in the United States and Canada, making North America the only region in the world where cable was the broadband leader (Exhibit 2). Making things worse for RBOCs was the fact that their core business, providing local phone service via the public switch telephone networks, was shrinking fast—a victim of competition from wireless telephone services, and more recently the phenomenon of telephone service provided over the Internet, known as voice over internet protocol (VoIP).[4] Salvation for the RBOCs could lie in the holy grail that they and cable companies were both pursuing in a broadband world: the so-called "triple play" of services (television transmission, telephony, and Internet access). Through

high-speed Internet access, either RBOCs or cable companies could provide this triple play, a market estimated to exceed $134 billion in 2004.[5]

By the end of 2004, new technologies and infrastructure were emerging—available to both cable companies and telephone companies—that promised to upset the balance between DSL and cable and offer consumers more choices for broadband access. What were the forces involved in broadband in the United States and how did they influence its deployment? In turn, could companies and industries influence those forces to their own advantage?

Flavors of Broadband

Broadband through cable and DSL was achieved by augmenting long-existing technologies. There were several methods currently available to deliver broadband to homes. In general, they provide bandwidth through standard telephone lines (copper wire twisted pair) already installed in homes, through cable TV coaxial cable, or via satellite. Each of these modes was originally designed for other purposes, for example voice telephone service or transmission of television signals. Cable and DSL were by far the most advanced technologies for delivering broadband to the home.

For a while, among the most economically developed nations in the world—mostly members of the Organization

[4]For more on VoIP, see Burgelman, Vadasz, and Meza, "Hanging Up the (Old) Phone: IP Communications in 2004," SM-127, Stanford Graduate School of Business.

[5]Market size estimate from the Yankee Group, cited in Catherine Yang, et al., "Cable vs. Fiber," *BusinessWeek,* November 1, 2004, p. 36.

for Economic Cooperation and Development (OECD)—cable led DSL in consumer broadband penetration. In 1999, 84 percent of consumer broadband subscribers used cable versus 16 percent with DSL. By the end of 2000, cable slipped to 55 percent versus 45 percent with DSL. By June 2001, cable edged out DSL by 51 percent to 49 percent.[6] However, by the middle of 2004, DSL had far outpaced cable in most regions around the world, except North America, as noted above.

Broadband over Cable TV Lines

A cable television service provider is a company that lays and services coaxial cable and presents programming that is transmitted through the coaxial cable that runs into subscribers' homes and screws into their TVs or set-top boxes.[7] Cable television system operators are distinct from cable networks, which provide programming. However, some multiple systems operators (MSOs), or their parent companies, also own cable networks.

The same coaxial cable that runs into each cable subscriber's home is capable of delivering broadband Internet access as well as telephone service (Exhibit 3). To access the Internet, the subscriber must have a cable modem, a device that attaches to the cable just like a TV converter box but decodes and manipulates data rather than television signals. Beginning in the late 1980s, many cable companies began upgrading their networks with high-capacity fiber-optics to support delivery of enhanced, two-way services such as interactive television, which did not win broad consumer support, and video on demand (pay per view), which fared better. Broadband Internet access offered a new, rich market for this transmission capacity. By the mid-1990s, some cable companies introduced broadband Internet services for their subscribers.

High-capacity optical fibers connected the cable operator's central facility (the "head end") to each neighborhood area (the "node"), which typically encompassed about 1,000 homes, each a potential customer. In an HFC system, the data channel was shared among the homes linked by coax to the end of the local fiber-optic line. Thus, the actual data rate achieved in any individual home depended on the number of users sharing the channel at a given time.[8] Most cable broadband customers experienced download speeds of 1 megabit per second (mbs). There was also a lower-speed channel in the reverse direction to carry data from the home back to the Internet, which uploaded data at around 200 Kbs.

Broadband over Phone Lines

By 2004, most broadband over telephone lines used a variety of DSL technology, which taken together were often abbreviated xDSL.[9] In the United States, DSL service was provided by incumbent local exchange carriers (ILECs) and competitive local exchange carriers (CLECs). However, by 2000, four years after the Telecom Act meant to spur competition between ILECs and newcomers, four of the leading five DSL providers were still ILECs.

There were several ways available to transmit data at high rates over the twisted pair of copper wires designed to convey phone calls and in place in almost every home in the United States. The twisted pair of copper telephone wires typically ran to the local exchange carrier's central office containing a switch. A switch was a complex piece of equipment that routed telephone calls to other switches or phones as necessary. DSL service did not use such switching equipment. Instead, DSL switches were installed in the central office to exploit the full data-carrying capacity of the wires, which normal phone calls did not use. This allowed DSL subscribers to simultaneously use the same twisted-pair wire for telephone calls and data transmission (Exhibit 4).

DSL services could be provided to homes within a 4 to 5 kilometer radius from the telecommunication exchange or central office. The most widely deployed version was asymmetric DSL, or ADSL. It typically delivered data at speeds of under 1 Mbs, with upload speeds of around 200 Kbs. Subscribers who resided closer to the RBOC's central offices (where the phone company's equipment was located) experienced somewhat faster download transmissions. Much faster transmission speeds, operating at 1.544 mbs, were also available from T1 lines, initially developed to enable multiple voice connections

---

[6]Sam Paltridge, "The Development of Broadband Access in OECD Countries," Organization for Economic Cooperation and Development (OECD), 29 October 2001. (http://www.oecd.org/pdf/M00020000/M00020255.pdf).

[7]An organization that owns two or more cable television systems is known as a multiple system operator (MSO). Prominent examples of MSOs include Comcast, TimeWarner Cable, and Cox Communications.

---

[8]Milo Medin and Jay Rolls, "The Internet Via Cable," *Scientific American,* October 1999.

[9]Asymmetric DSL (ADSL) and Symmetric DSL (SDSL) are the most popular forms of DSL in the world. In addition, other types of DSL include high-data-rate DSL (HDSL) and very-high-rate DSL (VDSL).

EXHIBIT 3 |

Schematic of Cable
Broadband

Hybrid Fiber-Coax System

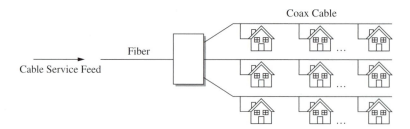

Cable Modem in the Home

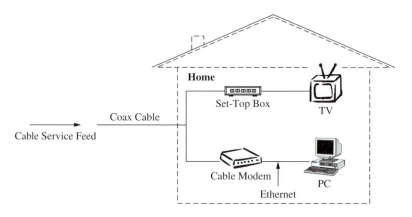

Frequency Utilization

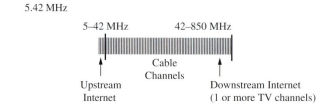

Source: Authors.

using a single line. T1 has traditionally been priced for commercial voice access, which cost more than most people could afford for data access.

Satellite

For customers not offered broadband services by cable companies or ILECs (typically customers in rural areas where sparse populations and long distances from infrastructure made them unprofitable to service), broadband access was possible without going through cable or phone companies. These consumers looked to satellite or wireless broadband for high-speed access. Satellite and wireless broadband offered the newest modes for delivery of broadband Internet access to consumers. By the end of 2004, these modes accounted for barely 1 percent of all consumer broadband in the United States.

Satellite systems were the most widely used wireless broadband system. By early 2002, two companies, DirecPC and StarBand, provided two-way satellite-based Internet access of around 500 kbs, or approximately 10 times the speed of dial-up modems. This transmission rate was expected to improve within the next few years.

EXHIBIT 4 |
Schematic of DSL

Digital Subscriber Line

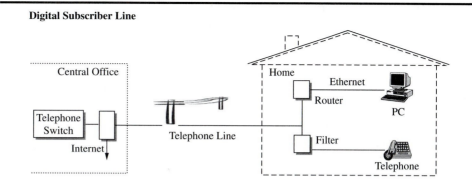

DSL on Telephone Line

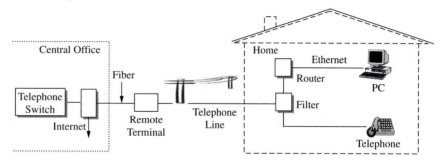

Frequency Utilization

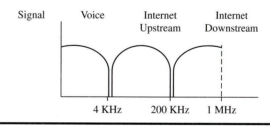

Source: Authors.

These companies used geostationary satellites that orbit the earth 36,000 kilometers (22,000 miles) above the equator at the same speed as the earth's rotation (and thus appeared from the ground to be stationary) to communicate with fixed-orientation dish antennas attached to customers' homes. They used advanced signal processing to compensate for transmission delays caused by the great distances their radio signals traveled. As with satellite TV, trees and heavy rains could affect reception of the Internet signals. Another drawback was the satellite's higher latency (a measure of the time it takes for a packet of data to get from one designated point to another), which made it less than ideal for real time Internet applications. The services were generally aimed at consumers who could not receive DSL or cable broadband services.

Coming Attractions

Most newer broadband technologies required new infrastructure. Whereas cable and DSL both used existing infrastructure, other methods of broadband delivery required the build-out of expensive systems and networks.

However, the advantages in terms of transmission speed and ubiquity of service could make them worthwhile.

Broadband over Power Lines (BPL)

This technology employed the electric wires already bringing electricity to homes to carry high-speed Internet access. Because electricity travels at a lower frequency than Internet transmissions, the two could coexist on the same line without interference, as is the case with DSL and voice transmissions over phone lines. With the advent of new semiconductors that could make power line broadband transmission feasible, BBL was gaining attention. Power lines were already in place and reached more homes than either cable systems or even telephone lines.

The BPL method promised the enormous benefit of using the extant and ubiquitous infrastructure that brought electricity to every room in almost every home, to bring broadband service at a fraction of the cost of building new connections. The technology overcame the so-called last mile problem: the cost of extending connections from trunk lines to the consumer's premises. It also held the hope of using the electric wires that girded homes and turning them into wired local area networks (LANs)

Some of the biggest proponents of BPL were AT&T and other local phone companies, such as competitive local exchange carriers (CLECs), which supported the technology because it did not rely on the local phone networks owned by regional Bell operating companies (RBOCs) such as SBC Communications, BellSouth, Verizon Communications, and Qwest Communications.

In late 2004 BPL was still considered unreliable and very expensive. At this point, there were about two dozen trials of the technology underway throughout the United States. While BPL could be attractive, there were many hurdles for the technology to overcome. For example, signals, which degraded over distance, needed boosting and could also create interference. Additional infrastructure might also be needed for practicable BPL service, which would make the technology more costly than initially hoped. For these reasons, some thought BPL was destined to become a niche method of access, as satellite was proving to be.

WiFi: A Potential Hot Spot for Broadband

For several years network enthusiasts toyed with applications emerging from a technical standard designated 802.11b, but more commonly called wireless fidelity or WiFi. This networking protocol (standard) governed

wireless local area networks that could transfer data at speeds of up to 11 megabits per second, faster than the less than 1 megabit per second that DSL provided, and far faster than the 144 kilobit per second data transmission rates (but within a much shorter range) that third-generation (3G) mobile service providers planned. Other versions of the 802.11 protocol could download data at 54 Mbs and work was being conducted on versions that could download at 100 MBs. Users communicated with WiFi transmitters or base stations, known as "hot spots," via small antennas connected to devices such as desktop or laptop computers and personal digital assistants. For example, a DSL subscriber could connect a DSL modem to a WiFi hot spot, in this case a base station, and enjoy wireless broadband access (for multiple devices) within a range of 150 feet or so, using small, easy-to-install equipment bought for between $100–$300. While some hoped that WiFi would make broadband more attractive to consumers, others noted that it was easy to share WiFi connections, even between residences such as apartments, and observed that the networking standard raised the specter of broadband piracy, especially in densely populated areas. However, this problem was likely to be reduced with new security capabilities.

Providers emerged offering subscription-based WiFi broadband Internet access via a growing network of hotels, coffee shops, airports, and other facilities. For example, by 2002, the ubiquitous Starbucks equipped 530 of its stores with hot spots and planned to offer WiFi access in 70 percent of its 3,200 stores in North America.[10] Subscription rates varied, but some plans offered unlimited high-speed wireless Internet access to networks of WiFi stations across the country for around $70 per month. Since WiFi applications operated in unlicensed airwave spectrums, the frequencies used by devices such as baby monitors, these service providers did not face the same large costs as 3G cellular providers in acquiring their spectrum. There was no free lunch: The expense of 3G stemmed from spectrum costs and the build-out of a network of infrastructure to support ubiquitous access. The drawback to WiFi was its very limited coverage area.

By 2004, some cities were considering creating a series of municipal hot spots to provide their residents free or low-cost wireless broadband access via WiFi. The City of Philadelphia was planning to privately raise

---

[10]Amey Stone, "Special Report: The Wireless Net," *BusinessWeek,* April 1, 2002.

$10 million to pay for a program to install and operate hot spots (probably on light poles that the city already owned) to serve Philadelphia's 1.5 million residents. The city hoped wireless connections would speed economic development in areas where businesses could not afford to pay $800 to $1,500 monthly for high-speed T-1 lines, as well as benefit education. Diana Neff, the chief information officer for Philadelphia said: "The reason we won't just let the market do this is that there are societal needs that aren't inherently part of the capitalist system. We need to be sure no communities in Philadelphia are excluded, whether there's an R.O.I. or not."[11]

Other cities were considering similar plans. In general, residents would have to spend between $75 and $150 to purchase WiFi receivers for PCs. Wireless cards for notebook computers cost about $40—but these were increasingly standard equipment on notebook computers. Some cities thought that the service could be paid for by advertising, which would appear when a user logged on to the network. In contrast to Philadelphia, New York City recently awarded contracts to six wireless contractors, who paid a total of $23 million for the right to use 3,000 city light poles as bases for cellular and, possibly, wireless Internet service for paying customers.[12]

One worry was that a newer wireless technology, such as WiMax, which transmits broadband access signals 30 miles instead of the 300 feet range of WiFi, would consign such municipal WiFi projects to an early obsolescence.

WiMax   Companies such as Intel, Nokia, and AT&T were hopeful that this wireless data protocol for high-speed, long-range transmission of data would take off. Most importantly, WiMax represented a high-speed, low-cost wireless last mile. Instead of using the RBOC's last mile or the RBOC's or cable companies' expensive fiber, consumers could surf the Web at high speeds via wireless transmission between distant WiMax broadcast equipment and a WiFi base station or modem in their homes. Another potential market for WiMax would be high-speed Internet access to rural consumers who were bypassed by DSL and cable services.

By the end of 2004 WiMax was just getting underway. Although it was a fixed technology, Intel planned to make WiMax a standard feature in laptop computers over the next few years, when it hoped a mobile version of the protocol would have been agreed. WiMax-capable mobile phones could also follow, in which WiMax operators could compete with established cell phone service providers.

There were big roadblocks on the path to a WiMax world. Service operators could face a start-up problem, hesitant to commit themselves to WiMax until the technology and services were better proven. Perhaps the biggest problem was airwave real estate: Few operators had the spectrum to dedicate to WiMax. Further, mobile WiMax would compete with a different mobile broadband standard known as 802.20, which was already in development. Proponents of this standard noted that it required a narrower spectrum than WiMax and worked in moving cars and trains, which WiMax would not.[13] However, WiMax was likely to occur both in licensed and unlicensed bands. Providers using a licensed spectrum could probably charge higher fees to users because they could likely deliver higher quality of service on their licensed spectrum.

Fiber (Fiber-to-the-X, FTTx)

This was a technology that particularly interested the RBOCs, most of whom had failed to make broadband infrastructure investments at a level commensurate with their cable company competitors. With fiber, RBOCs could catch up with their cable competitors. Optical fiber carried data at superfast speeds compared to the copper wires owned by RBOCs or the coaxial cable owned by cable companies. With fiber, RBOCs could offer extremely high-speed Internet access, telephone service, video-on-demand, and even high-definition television service. Fiber promised to wipe out the differences between cable companies and RBOCs by allowing both to offer voice, data (Internet access) and television services—the "triple play" of consumer services that providers thought would keep subscribers from switching (churning) their service providers.

Fiber-to-the-curb, a system of optical fiber to a local phone hub accompanied with improved copper phone lines extending to homes, was estimated to cost around $300 per household to install. RBOC SBC planned to roll out the service to 18 million homes by the end of 2007. Monthly fees to consumer were estimated to be

---

[11]Bob Tedeshci, "Big WiFi Project for Philadelphia," *The New York Times,* September 27, 2004.

[12]Ibid.

[13]"WiFi's big brother," *The Economist,* March 11, 2004.

similar to cable's FTC systems. This technology transmitted data at speed of around 25 Mbs. An even faster
system, called fiber-to-the-home, in which optical fiber
lines were installed directly into consumers' homes,
offered speeds of 30 mbs. It was estimated that FTH
would cost around $800 per household to install.
Monthly fees were estimated to be similar to those
charged by fiber-to-cable or fiber-to-curb systems.

An ISP Looks at Broadband

In the go-go days of the Internet in the late 1990s, the
United States teemed with Internet service providers
(ISPs), companies that faced the customers as they
surfed the Web. By the end of 2004, however, most of
these ISPs consolidated or were driven out of business.
One large independent ISP remained: EarthLink.
Founded in 1994, EarthLink was the third largest ISP in
the United States. By the end of 2004, EarthLink had
5.5 million subscribers—1.4 million of whom were
broadband subscribers—and about $1.4 billion in annual
revenue. The company was also making a profit.
EarthLink provided Internet dial-up (narrowband) and
broadband access via DSL and cable. The company also
provided various other Internet services including Web
site hosting, Internet advertising, domain name registration, and e-mail. Most (62 percent) of EarthLink's total
revenue was derived from narrowband access fees. Of its
total revenue, 32 percent came from broadband access
fees charged to its broadband customers. Web hosting
and advertising accounted for the remainder of the company's revenue (about 6 percent).

EarthLink considered itself practically the only
large independent ISP left. The company had roughly 7
percent of the total ISP market by the end of 2004. Other
independent ISPs combined had around 5 percent.[14]
Almost 90 percent of the market was controlled by Time
Warner's AOL, Microsoft's MSN and other large players
such as cable MSOs and RBOCs (with the latter two
groups dominating the market for broadband).
EarthLink's customers dealt directly with EarthLink,
which in turn leased access lines from ILECs (synony-
mous with RBOCs) or cable companies.

Broadband access was a big problem—and chief
expense—for EarthLink. ILECs did not like being
forced by Title II regulation to share their pipes when

cable companies, which were not subject to the same
regulation, did not have to share their lines. Some of the
problem may have stemmed from the mindsets of
ILECs. For example, EarthLink paid one large ILEC
$21 per month for DSL access. That same ILEC charged
its own customers $19.95 for retail DSL when bundled
with other premium voice services. One major ILEC
surmised that wholesale DSL was its most profitable
business, estimating that it took only two months to pay
back investments in that market compared to 14 months
to pay back for a retail DSL customer. It would seem that
an ISP such as EarthLink would make a very nice channel for an ILEC.

But, according to Garry Betty, president and CEO
of EarthLink: "ILECs don't think about the channel conflict that they are causing. For example, EarthLink pays
between $125 million and $150 million each year for
access to the four largest ILECs. But that figure is still
too small to get their attention. They continue to make
decisions about pricing without consulting us."[15]

Even more challenging for EarthLink than negotiating access deals with ILECs had been the problem of
obtaining access to cable facilities in the United States.
Betty felt his company had benefited from the United
States Department of Justice's review of the AOL/Time
Warner merger back in 2000 (when Time Warner's vast
cable network came under closer regulatory scrutiny and
it was keen to minimize its apparent power). EarthLink
now had access throughout the Time Warner cable
system; however the ISP had difficulty completing
agreements with other cable system operators, which
inhibited EarthLink's growth.

Still, on an operating basis, EarthLink had had more
success buying access from cable companies rather than
ILECs. It had been easier and cheaper for EarthLink to service its cable access customers. For example, cable companies generally provided the cable modem to their
broadband customers.[16] By comparison, it cost around $75
for EarthLink to supply a DSL customer with preinstall
work and modem subsidy. However, by the end of 2004
cable was generally somewhat more expensive, since the
ADSL access charges EarthLink paid were falling.

For EarthLink, the richer surfing experience provided
by broadband helped spur demand for the company's

---

[15]All quotes from Garry Betty are from the author's interview on
4 November 2004. Subsequent quotes from this interview will not
be cited.

[16]According to one estimate, DSL modems cost around $38.

additional value-added services. To make money, EarthLink had to price its service $10–$15 over the lowest price offered by ILECs or cable companies. To keep customers paying this premium, EarthLink offered around-the-clock customer support and a host of value-added services. For example, EarthLink was the first ISP to offer pop-up blocking, spyware blockers, and spam controls. By the end of 2004, the company had moved into Internet calling services (VoIP). EarthLink offered a free VoIP service called Free On Net Calling to EarthLink customers, enabling them to make VoIP calls to other EarthLink subscribers (and to subscribers to another free VoIP service called FreeWorld Dial-up). Early next year, EarthLink will offer a premium service that would enable VoIP calling that can terminate to regular phone lines, known as the public switched telephone network (PSTN). This will be offered at a price similar to competing VoIP services that terminate to the PSTN, perhaps around $20–$25 per month.

Yahoo! and Its Allies

For Internet consumer and business services company Yahoo! broadband offered a way to get closer to consumers. Three years ago, the company embarked on an alliance with RBOC SBC to provide co-branded DSL access to customers. The idea was to lend the cachet of the Yahoo! brand to the RBOC, while SBC took care of provisioning and maintaining the physical network and billing customers. SBC handled the traffic and Yahoo! handled the experience once the traffic was brought to its Web site. Broadband offered crucial avenues of growth to both companies. Steve Boom, senior vice president for broadband access and bundled services at Yahoo! said, "With broadband, Yahoo! can get closer to the consumer. It enables us to offer more robust features, such as video services, and other premium services."[17] Of course, consumers needed to get to Yahoo! via a broadband connection to be able to use these services.

Boom explained how Yahoo! came to these alliances, "The narrowband world was dominated by players other than telcos, for example Internet service providers such as AOL. However, broadband changed the strategic landscape. RBOCs saw broadband as an opportunity to take away business from AOL and others." Increasingly, broadband was being used as a centerpiece of a multiservice

strategy for both RBOCs and cable companies. Boom said, "Our alliance with RBOCs such as SBC and Verizon make up an important part of the RBOC's 'triple play' [data, fixed voice, and video] which, when you add wireless service, becomes a 'quadruple play' or 'Grand Slam.'" This put Yahoo! and broadband access providers at the center of each others' strategies. Boom commented, "For a while, the only advantage providers offered customers for buying a bundle of services was a discount when they signed up for the bundle. However, soon these services will all employ Internet protocol, so offering a layer of value-added services which integrate across networks will become crucial as a point of differentiation."

The business model for Yahoo! and its broadband partners was similar to that of cable TV operators and content providers such as cable programmers. Boom said, "Yahoo! bundles some premium services to end users at no extra charge; this is like a basic cable television service. Just as Comcast pays a monthly fee to ESPN for its content, so too do the alliance partners pay monthly fees to Yahoo!." The financial value to Yahoo! was in the monthly subscriber fee. In addition, Yahoo! found that broadband alliance users were more engaged with other Yahoo! services. Boom said, "We are able to monetize these users through Yahoo!'s traditional monetization techniques, such as media, sponsored search, and à la carte premium services, which our experience shows SBC Yahoo! customers are more likely to use. Yahoo! shares this incremental revenue stream back with its alliance partners, creating a mutually aligned incentive structure around customer engagement."

Yahoo! was basically agnostic about the choice of broadband delivery technology: DSL, cable, WiMax, it did not really matter. The company had alliances with RBOCs and, in Canada, with Rogers Cable. In the United States, most cable companies were trying to develop their broadband solutions on their own, so Yahoo! focused on DSL, which, outside of North America, was the dominant broadband access method.

Regulatory Issues

Incumbents cited regulatory uncertainty as a major source of inertia in the rollout of broadband in the United States. Much of this uncertainty stemmed from attempts to stimulate competition in the Telecommunications Act of 1996. Under the 1996 Act, RBOCs were required to share their central office facilities with competitive telecommunications service providers. This opened the

---

[17]All quotes from Steve Boom are from the author's interview on 18 January 2005. Subsequent quotes will not be cited.

market for others to offer DSL service as well as local phone service to customers. In the wake of the 1996 Act, RBOCs focused on defending themselves against competition from CLECs. RBOCs did whatever they could to undermine CLECs in consumer broadband, making it difficult for rival DSL service start-ups to interconnect to the RBOC's equipment, and going so far as to bar rivals' technicians from bathroom facilities at switches.[18] Other RBOCs became less aggressive about expanding DSL service into new regions, instead focusing on offering the service to areas they already served. Analysts estimated that it took RBOCs two years to recover the costs associated with installing and servicing a consumer DSL account. In addition, DSL service often eliminated the need for a second residential telephone line—a lucrative source of revenue for RBOCs. With the high-profile closures of many DSL start-ups, the RBOCs had the field largely to themselves by 2004.

The cable industry, which was not regulated as a common carrier, escaped many of the changes that RBOCs found most onerous. In response to the ruling, many RBOCs underinvested in DSL while they continued to fight the 1996 Act. Meanwhile, cable companies, which had monopolies in their regions, spent heavily to upgrade their networks to offer video-on-demand and voice telephony as well as broadband. As mentioned above, while DSL was the most popular way for consumers to receive broadband Internet access in most regions of world, more consumers in the United States obtained their broadband access through cable than via DSL.

Broadband, along with voice over internet protocol (VoIP), coexisted awkwardly with the Internet, access to which straddled two highly regulated industries, cable companies and RBOCs, which themselves were undergoing fundamental regulatory and technological changes. These changes were driven by the fact that the Internet fundamentally undermined a complex system of subsidies—totaling around $20 billion each year—generated from calls made by and to RBOCs. Business users subsidized consumers, long-distance callers subsidized local calling, urban areas subsidized rural areas and so on. In 2004, long-distance carriers MCI, Sprint, and AT&T wrote down a total of $19 billion of phone assets. Some RBOCs were considering selling their local phone networks in order to focus on wireless and broadband. Indeed, the RBOCs' revenue from local phone services declined by $15 billion between 2001 and 2004, falling 7 percent a

year.[19] (See Exhibit 5 for a comparison of key financial data for selected cable companies and RBOCs.)

In late 2004, RBOCs received a victory from the FCC, which decided not to force the Bells to share (unbundle) their new fiber networks with rivals on regulated terms and conditions. The ruling applied to fiber-to-the-home loops, fiber-to-the-curb loops, the packetized functionality of hybrid copper-fiber loops, and packet switching. Packet switches allow carriers to provide advanced services over fiber networks. A majority of FCC commissioners found that consumers would benefit by making RBOCs more vigorous competitors to cable companies, which play "a significant role in the current broadband market." The FCC concluded that its action "furthers the Congressional goal of encouraging broadband deployment under Section 706 of the [1996] Act."[20]

In a vehement dissent from the above ruling, FCC Commissioner Michael J. Copps noted that the U.S. had fallen from 4th in the world to 13th in broadband penetration. Copps wrote:

> While the country experiences broadband freefall, the [FCC] has embarked on a policy of closing off competitive access to last mile bottleneck facilities. . . .
>
> The facts are clear. This Commission's most recent report on high-speed services shows that the residential and small business market is a duopoly. Our data show that new satellite and wireless technologies—exciting though they are—together serve only 1.3 percent of this market. Broadband over power line does not yet even register. Yet the majority chooses to ignore the Commission's statistics, preferring instead sweeping rhetoric about regulatory relief and broadband competition.
>
> The Commission's approach to broadband . . . amounts to a regulatory policy of crossing our fingers and hoping competition will somehow magically burst forth. With the international economy increasingly dependent on broadband facilities, faith-based approaches to advanced telecommunications are insufficient. We cannot afford to wait. . . . The country must create vigorous competition to drive the low prices and high speeds that can usher in a prosperous broadband economy."[21]

---

[18]Stephanie N. Mehta, "How To Get Broadband Moving Again," *Fortune*, December 10, 2001.

[19]Revenue figure from UBS Warburg, cited by Catherine Yang et al., "Cable vs. Fiber," *BusinessWeek*, November 1, 2004, p. 38.

[20]"Federal Communications Commission Further Spurs Advanced Fiber Network Deployment," FCC press release, October 22, 2004.

[21]Statement of Commissioner Michael J. Copps, Dissenting, Memorandum Opinion and Order (WC Docket Nos. 01-338, 03-235, 03-260 & 04-48).

EXHIBIT 5 | Comparison of Annual Revenue and Growth for Selected Cable Companies and RBOCs

	2003 Annual Revenue ($M)	3-Year Growth Rate
Cable Companies		
Comcast	18,348	30.0%
Time Warner Cable*	7,699	27.7
Cox Communications	5,759	16.2
Charter Communications	4,819	15.3
Cablevision Systems	4,177	2.1
RBOCs		
Verizon	67,752	1.5
SBC	40,843	−7.4
BellSouth	22,635	−4.7
Qwest	14,288	0.3

*Includes only Time Warner Cable revenue

Source: Company reports.

Perhaps the root of the regulatory problem lay in the fundamental differences between the present rules governing telecommunications, and those likely to be effective for the near future and beyond. Current telecommunication regulation was more effective in governing a telecommunications world anchored by physical switches and geography—and in which there were meaningful differences between RBOCs and cable companies. If real high-speed broadband becomes ubiquitous in the United States, the distinctions that characterized RBOCs and cable companies fall away, and a new regulatory regime will be needed.

The Importance of Broadband

Big Bucks from Broadband, but for Whom?

In 1987, economist Robert Solow coined the Solow Paradox saying, "You can see the computer age everywhere but in the productivity statistics." For much of the 1990s, businesses and economists were at a loss to find evidence that gains in information technology (IT) performance contributed much national economic growth. However, the second half of the 1990s saw marked productivity gains that many attributed in part to IT. In the first half of the decade, gross domestic product (GDP) grew at an annual rate of 2.4 percent, compared to 4.1 percent annual growth in the second half of the

decade. During the second half of the 1990s, the estimated rate of price decline for computers more than doubled from 15.1 to 32.1 percent.[22]

Many economists pointed to networking as the crucial link between increased IT performance and productivity gains. Networks, essentially any connection between two or more computers, are made far more robust by broadband. Others pointed to broadband as an important potential catalyst for general economic growth in the United States. A Brookings Institution study conducted in July 2001 estimated that broadband could add $500 billion per year to the United States economy.[23]

---

[22]Dale W. Jorgenson, "Information Technology and the U.S. Economy," *American Economic Review* 91, no. 1 (March 2001).

[23]Robert W. Crandall and Charles L. Jackson, "The $500 Billion Opportunity: The Potential Economic Benefit of Widespread Diffusion of Broadband Internet Access," The Brooking Institution, July 2001. (www.criterioneconomics.com/documents/ Crandall_Jackson_500_Billion_Opportunity_July_2001.pdf). The authors conclude that universal adoption of broadband in the United States (universal defined as equal to the 94 percent of U.S. households with at least one phone line) could provide consumers with economic benefits of up to $400 billion per year while producers of network equipment, household computers, ancillary equipment, software, and producers and distributors of entertainment products could benefit by as much as $100 billion per year (p. 2). It should be noted that this study was commissioned by the New York–based RBOC Verizon.

The study found consumers would benefit from enhanced online home shopping and entertainment services as well as from a variety of additional services. The researchers estimated that $400 billion per year could be derived from such services while an additional $50 billion to $100 billion per year could be added to the economy from broadband-related gains experienced by manufacturers of computers, software, and entertainment products.

In the fourth quarter of 2001, e-commerce generated an estimated $25 billion in revenue worldwide.[24] The United States accounted for over 46 percent of that market. A mere 10 years earlier that figure was close to zero. A May 1999 survey by Mercer Management Consulting in Washington, D.C. showed that people with high-speed access searched for information and made purchases online at approximately double the rate of those with lower-speed analog modems.[25] In 1990, around 15 percent of U.S. households owned a computer. By 2000, more than 50 percent of U.S. households owned a computer and by 2001 a similar percentage of households had access to the Internet. From 1996 to 2001, the average hours of Internet use per person soared in the United States. However, the growth in the average number of hours per person spent on the Internet was declining even as Internet applications increased. Similarly, the rate of consumer spending (in nominal dollars) on personal computers in the United States was declining over the previous five years. Some suspected that this decline was the result of consumer frustration with narrowband access for increasingly broadband applications.[26]

A National Imperative?

Some technology industry leaders had been increasingly vocal about the need for the United States to increase the penetration of consumer broadband in the country. Large technology companies such as Cisco, Intel, and Microsoft, as well as prominent technology investment bankers and venture capitalists, banded together to form TechNet, a technology industry advocacy group. TechNet, and prominent technology industry leaders, have framed the issue of consumer broadband penetration as a matter of national strategic importance.

John Chambers, president and CEO of networking giant Cisco, said: "Broadband should be a national imperative for this country in the twenty-first century, just like putting a man on the moon was an imperative in the last century. . . . In order to stay competitive, educate the workforce, and increase productivity, the United States must have ubiquitous broadband." Intel's CEO Craig Barrett said: "It is critically important for the United States to adopt a national broadband policy that encourages investment in new broadband infrastructure, applications, and services—particularly new last-mile broadband facilities. . . . Regulatory policies should encourage all companies to deploy these expensive and risky facilities."[27]

Such leaders are promoting a set of decidedly non–laissez-faire government policies to promote consumer broadband in the United States. These included asking the government to offer tax credits to help companies defray the costs of bringing broadband to poor and rural areas, and exempting new RBOC broadband investments from federal regulation. Some observers noticed how strange it was for technology companies with large financial stakes in broadband deployment and traditionally critical of RBOC foot dragging to support exempting RBOCs from federal regulation. FCC Chairman Powell seemed unsure whether such a national policy was warranted, saying: "I caution, however, that we have to distinguish between a true market failure, and what is simply hard or challenging. . . . In struggling through the challenge it will be common for some to want to try and leap ahead by securing government assistance. Market failure might demand a government response, but market challenges should be left to market players."[28]

Conclusion

For all of the promise of new broadband delivery technologies, such as WiFi, WiMax, and BPL, for the near future it seemed that most Americans who purchased broadband access would use cable or DSL. At the same time, like continents formerly separated by an

---

[24]Michael Pastore, "New Records Predicted for Holiday E-Commerce," *E-Commerce News,* October 21, 2001.

[25]P. William Bane and Stephen P. Bradley, "The Light at the End of the Pipe," *Scientific American,* October 1999.

[26]Crandall and Jackson, "The $500 Billion Opportunity," July 2001.

[27]"TechNet CEO's Call for National Broadband Policy," TechNet Press Release, January 15, 2002 (http://www.technet.org/issues/updates//2002-01-15.69.phtml).

[28]Michael K. Powell, Chairman, FCC, at the National Summit on Broadband Deployment, Washington, D.C. October 25, 2001 (http://www.fcc.gov/Speeches/Powell/2001/spmkp110.html).

ocean, the cable and ILEC industries were undergoing seismic shifts that brought them closer together. However the regulatory regimes that governed these industries were not keeping up with these changes. Similarly, neither the cable industry nor the ILEC industry seemed to be developing business models that would fully exploit the fundamental changes that were taking place.

Until broadband became ubiquitous, the service triple play would remain out of reach for everybody. Would the triple play, which destroyed the foundations that supported the vast ILEC and cable industries, provide sufficient economic benefit to justify the disruption it wrought? What, if anything, could ILECs or cable companies do to help shape their futures and speed the consumer adoption of broadband? Was that really in their interests? Ubiquitous broadband was certainly in the interests of companies such as Intel, Microsoft, EarthLink, and countless others. What could they do to catalyze the arrival of consumer broadband? What, if anything, should the United States government do to make its citizens more wired?

Case 6.3

Hanging Up the (Old) Phone: IP Communications in 2004

If you're a big incumbent, and you enjoy the competitive advantages of being the owner of that kind of infrastructure system, you, in my opinion, ought to be terrified. You ought to be terrified because we are lowering the barriers in which people can effectively reach consumers and offer them alternatives that look a lot like what you have a massive infrastructure dedicated to providing.

—**Michael K. Powell, Chairman, United States Federal Communications Commission (FCC) speaking about the impact of IP communications on established telecommunications companies.[1]**

Introduction

Internet protocol, often abbreviated as simply IP, refers to the method that governs the way data is exchanged over the Internet. IP is the *lingua franca* that allows for communication via the Internet by a variety of devices. Phones (with special modems), computers, personal digital assistants (PDAs), or other so-called IP-enabled devices can use the Internet for voice communications. Such devices, connected to the Internet, can offer a type of phone service called voice over Internet protocol (VoIP).[2] This can take place computer-to-computer, in which case existing telephone systems may or may

not be completely bypassed; telephone-to-computer, computer-to-telephone, or telephone-to-telephone, any of which would use only some elements of traditional telephony infrastructure and the Internet (Exhibit 1). When applied to phone calls, IP communications could enhance—or supplant—traditional telephone services.

For over 120 years, phone service has been a utility, like water and electricity, central to our daily lives, and as such was highly regulated at both the state and federal levels. In the United States alone, the value of the telecommunications business was nearly $302 billion in 2001. The industry was comprised of companies with hundreds of billions of dollars invested in the infrastructure used to provide phone services, from creosote-covered telephone poles strung with copper wires, to central offices full of circuit switching equipment, to undersea fiber-optic cables and satellites circling the earth. VoIP offered a different way of making calls and exchanging data—one that would impact both established telecommunications companies and the government by shifting or eliminating tens of billions of dollars paid in fees and taxes. Estimates for the uptake, traffic, and revenue generation of VoIP varied widely. Some analysts expected VoIP service providers, such as the established companies and start-ups discussed in this note, to generate $4 billion in revenue by 2007. Other analysts thought that the market for communications equipment for VoIP, valued at $1 billion in 2002, could reach over $4 billion by 2006.[3]

The fundamental change to telephony service that VoIP portended affected a number of constituencies. Start-up companies, as well as large, established phone companies and cable television providers, offered VoIP calling plans that could substitute many of the phone services sold by the same or other established providers. These same providers might also benefit from VoIP by using it to enter new markets. Other companies that previously had nothing to do with telephony could become VoIP telephone service providers: For example, the necessary software codes to make VoIP calls had been written into Microsoft's XP operating system through its instant messaging feature. However, IP communications represented a fundamental challenge to the complex web

---

[1]Michael K. Powell, "Conversation with NCTA President Robert Sachs," National Cable & Telecommunications Association Convention, New Orleans, LA, May 4, 2004, http://www.fcc.gov/commissioners/powell/mkp_speeches_2004.html.

[2]Some pronounce VoIP by enunciating the letters, "v.o.i.p."; others pronounce the acronym as a word, "voype."

Professor Robert A. Burgelman, Les Vadasz, and Philip E. Meza prepared this case as the basis for class discussion rather than to illustrate either effective or ineffective handling of an administrative situation.

---

[3]Source: Boardwatch, cited in "Time to Redial: VOIP (Voice over Internet Protocol) Makes a Comeback," *Knowledge@Wharton,* January 28, 2004.

EXHIBIT 1 |

Modes of Voice over
Internet Telephony

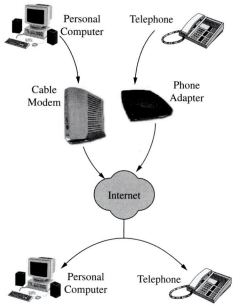

Source: http://www.fcc.gov/voip/

Four Flavors of VoIP

In 2004, there were four general ways in which users could make VoIP calls. Using just a land-line telephone or a computer (or other digital device capable of high-speed Internet access) a user could access at least one of the four types of VoIP listed below.

- *Computer-to-computer.* Users downloaded software (a client) available from several VoIP companies. With this software, calls could be made using the computer's microphone, speakers, a sound card and, to be practicable, a high-speed Internet connection. Users of such services could make calls for free to other computers with the same software client.

- *Computer-to-telephone.* This method allowed users to call any telephone from their computer. Like computer-to-computer calling, it required a software client. The software client was usually available for free, but the calling party usually incurred a small per-minute charge paid to the VoIP service provider.

- *Telephone-to-telephone.* With this method, users could connect directly to any telephone in the world. Several companies offered this service. The user dialed a special number to reach one of the company's gateways, and then entered the telephone number they wanted to reach. The company connected the call through its IP-based network and the Internet.

- *Telephone-to-computer.* This was a less popular method of VoIP telephony. In this method, a company provided special numbers that allowed a standard telephone user to initiate a call to a computer user. The computer had to have the company's software client running to receive the call.

Source: Authors.

of federal and state regulations that governed telephony. Because VoIP telephony was not tied to physical telephony networks in specific geographic regions, it raised the question of whether federal or state regulators would have jurisdiction over VoIP services and how jurisdiction would be exercised. Some worried that long-cherished societal benefits known collectively as universal service, which provided telephone access to rural, handicapped, or indigent consumers, paid for by tariffs on telephone traffic on the current telephone system, could be threatened if VoIP became ubiquitous.

I'll Call You: Old-Fashioned Phone Service[4]

Traditional telephone service, provided by circuits, switches, and telephones connected by copper wires, was greatly expanded in the early part of the twentieth century in the United States under a government-granted monopoly. Before this time, the telephone business was highly competitive with many small companies competing to provide service and not always interoperating with other networks. Some customers had to maintain two phones, one for local service and one for long distance because their local telephone company would not interconnect to the long-distance provider (or vice versa). In addition to this low-simmering industry chaos, rural areas were often neglected by any telephone company, their populations too sparse to be profitably served.

In the interest of wiring as much of the country as practicable and making phone service available and affordable to the majority of consumers, both urban and rural, in 1913 the U.S. government gave one company, American Telephone and Telegraph (AT&T) a monopoly on the provision of local and long-distance telephone service and equipment. Prior to this, the market for telephone service in the United States had been chaotic, with hundreds of small telephone companies offering local service, and AT&T, by far the market leader, relentlessly consolidating by acquiring small telephone service companies in the most profitable regions. In exchange for its government-granted monopoly, AT&T agreed to stop acquiring competing telephone service companies, and to use monopoly rents from long-distance and business services to help subsidize those

remaining competing telephone companies that were serving otherwise unprofitable rural areas. AT&T's monopoly rents would also subsidize technological research and development.

AT&T and its Bell Telephone equipment subsidiary became such a monolith and so pervasive in everyday life, it became known as "Ma Bell."[5] This monopoly held until the so-called Carterfone decision in 1968 in which the FCC determined that non-AT&T equipment could be attached to the PSTN as long as it did not harm the network. A later decision in the late 1970s required that all terminal equipment be connected to the telephone network through standard plugs and jacks, and that technical information be provided to independent suppliers on the same terms as subsidiaries of telephone companies. These two decisions broke AT&T's monopoly in telephone equipment.

The government had also been attacking the AT&T monopoly in the courts, going after AT&T's Western Electric equipment monopoly and later taking on the company's long-distance monopoly. In 1974, MCI, a long-distance competitor to AT&T that slipped through the monopoly, filed an antitrust suit against AT&T. The U.S. Justice Department pursued the case, and in 1982 AT&T settled, resulting in the break-up of its near monopoly in telephony service in the United States. The purpose of the government action was to separate local exchanges, where the government felt natural monopolies were appropriate, from those parts of AT&T, such as long-distance, manufacturing, research and development, where it felt competition was appropriate. The AT&T divestiture agreement with the Justice Department—known as the Modification of Final Judgment (MFJ)—became effective on January 1, 1984. On this day arose the new AT&T and seven regional Bell operating companies (RBOCs). The RBOCs were chartered with providing local telephone service in their designated regions. They were prohibited from offering long-distance and information services, and also from manufacturing telecommunications equipment for domestic use (though they could manufacture and sell equipment overseas through separate subsidiaries). AT&T remained in business as a long-distance provider, using the long-lines assets it retained following its break-up. AT&T also kept its Bell Laboratories research

---

[4]For more information on telecommunications deregulation in the United States, see Robert A. Burgelman, Andrew S. Grove, and Eric Marti, "The Telecommunications Industry: A&B," SM-5A and SM-5B, Stanford Graduate School of Business.

---

[5]AT&T was dropped from the Dow Jones Industrial Index (DJII) in April 2004. The company was added to the DJII in 1939. As of April 2004, two RBOCs, Verizon and SBC, were included in the DJII.

arm and its equipment maker, Western Electric.[6] An important provision of MFJ stipulated that AT&T was prohibited from owning any portion of the RBOCs.

In 1996, the telecommunications industry underwent a third regulatory shock with passage of the Telecommunications Deregulation Act by the U.S. Congress. This act provided major changes in laws affecting telecommunications and cable television. The main purpose of the law was to stimulate competition in telecommunications services, which had grown to encompass much more than simple telephone calls. Among its provisions, the law specified how local telephone carriers could compete, the price at which RBOCs had to lease their lines to their competitors, known as competitive local exchange carriers (CLECs), and how and under what circumstances companies could provide long-distance services. The 1996 Telecommunications Act did not result in as much competition as legislators had hoped. For several reasons, including foot-dragging in interconnection by RBOCs, also known as incumbent local exchange carriers (ILECs), and the burst of the dot-com bubble in 2000, which also dragged down investments in telecommunications, CLECs did not take off as expected. By December of 2002, CLECs provided only 13 percent of the 188 million phone lines in use in the United States, up from 11 percent in June of 2002.[7] Some cable television companies offered telephone service via the coaxial cables running into subscribers' homes, but cable companies did not compete against ILECs as seriously as some supporters of deregulation had hoped. Consolidation among RBOCs subsequent to the act left only four RBOCs: BellSouth, Qwest, SBC and Verizon.

By 2002, the average monthly household telecommunications expenditure in the United States was $83: $36 for local exchange; $12 for long-distance; and $35 for wireless service. In the 15 years from 1984 to 2001, the average cost of long-distance calling dropped from 32 cents per minute to 10 cents per minute. The price of 10 cents per minute represents a mix of international calling (averaging 35 cents a minute) and domestic interstate calling (averaging 8 cents per minute).[8] (In 2002,

Americans spent $9.8 billion on international calls.[9] see Exhibit 2).

Throughout the 1990s, cellular telephone service gained in popularity. By the end of 2002, cell phone users spent, on average, more time talking on their cell phones than they did on their land-lines. Some cell phone users, called "cord cutters" in industry vernacular, were even dropping their land-line service altogether. There still were not many cord cutters in 2004, but with the advent of wireless number portability, the size of this group was expected to increase.[10]

Even with the increasing popularity of wireless, there was tremendous value in owning the physical connection to a home. Whether they were made up of a phone company's copper wire or a cable company's coaxial cable, these so-called last mile connections were the conduits through which phone, cable, and high-speed Internet access flowed from provider to consumer. (In the United States in 2003, cable provided about 60 percent of broadband access, compared to under 40 percent for DSL.)[11] Last mile-connections were expensive to deploy and jealously guarded by their owners. In an age when cable companies could provide phone service and high-speed Internet access, and an ILEC's installed copper lines could be used to provide high-speed Internet access in addition to plain old telephone service, the last mile became increasingly valuable. For all the talk about deregulation increasing competition in phone service, service providers such as IXCs and others still had to reach the customer—and the expense of connecting to a customer's premises (installing a new last mile) proved too large to overcome.

Anatomy of a Phone Call

To understand the impact of VoIP telephony, it is important to first understand the established telephony structure. VoIP was based on software, which was easily written and changed. Traditional digital telephone systems were based

[6]These latter two interests were combined, renamed Lucent Technologies, and spun off in 1996.

[7]Source: "FCC Releases Study on Telephone Trends," FCC press release, August 7, 2003, http://www.fcc.gov/Bureaus/Common_Carrier/Reports/FCC-State_Link/IAD/trend803.pdf.

[8]Source: "FCC Releases Study on Telephone Trends," op.cit., http://www.fcc.gov/Bureaus/Common_Carrier/Reports/FCC-State_Link/IAD/trend803.pdf.

[9]FCC, "Trends in Telephone Service," http://www.fcc.gov/Bureaus/Common_Carrier/Reports/FCC-State_Link/IAD/trend504.pdf.

[10]http://www.cellular-news.com/story/8773.shtml.

[11]Source: "FCC Trends in Telephone Service," op.cit. The FCC estimated that as of June 2003, coaxial cable provided 58.3 percent, ADSL 32.7 percent, other wireline 5.2 percent, fiber 2.5 percent, satellite or fixed wireless 1.3 percent. NB: Other wireline includes symmetric DSL; fiber is optical fiber to customer's premises.

EXHIBIT 2 | Selected U.S. Telephony Data

Telecommunications Revenues by Type of Carrier in 2001

Type	Revenue in 2001 ($M)
Total telecommunications industry revenue	$301,800
Incumbent local exchange carriers (ILECs)	$117,885
Interexchange carriers (IXCs)	$81,272
Competitive access providers and competitive local exchange carriers (CAPs and CLECs)	$12,998

Note: Total includes all telecommunications services, including wireless and pay phones.

Source: FCC Industry Analysis and Wireline Competition Bureau, August 2003.

Average Monthly Household Telecommunications Expenditures By Type of Provider

Year	Local Exchange Carriers ($)	Long-Distance Carriers ($)	Wireless Carriers ($)	Total ($)
1996	30	21	9	60
1997	32	25	11	68
1998	33	23	14	69
1999	34	21	17	72
2000	35	18	23	75
2001	36	15	29	79
2002	36	12	35	83

Source: FCC Trends in Telephone Service.

Method of Obtaining Local Service

Type	Lines in 2003 (millions)
Incumbent local exchange carriers (ILECs)	151.8
Competitive local exchange carriers (CLECs)	29.6
Mobile wireless	157.0
Cable (television) telephony	3.2

ILEC and CLEC Lines 1999–2003

Date	ILEC Lines (millions)	CLEC Lines (millions)	Total (millions)	CLEC Share (%)
December 1999	181.3	8.2	189.5	4.3
December 2000	177.6	14.9	192.6	7.7
December 2001	172.0	19.7	191.7	10.3
December 2002	162.7	24.8	187.5	13.2
December 2003	151.8	29.6	181.4	16.3

Source: "Local Telephone Competition: Status as of December 31, 2003," FCC Industry Analysis and Technology Division, Wireline Competition Bureau, June 2004.

on a blend of hardware and software.[12] For most of the past 120 years, when people made a phone call, they did so over a dedicated wire line. A typical customer was a subscriber who used a telephone in his premises to initiate or receive a call. That call was transmitted over a circuit from the subscriber's premises to a nearby local exchange switch. If it was a local call, the transmission was switched at a phone company facility called a central office to the proper local subscriber line. If the call was long-distance, the local switch sent the transmission to an interexchange switch; the call was then sent over long-distance lines (known as long lines) to the appropriate local exchange switch, and there it was finally connected to the proper subscriber line for completion. For most of its history, telephony has used a network of physical circuits and switches. The collection of these systems around the world, both government-owned and privately-owned, but for public use, are referred to as the public switched telephone network or PSTN.[13]

The MFJ settlement drew the geographic boundaries for local access transport areas (LATAs), which defined the distinction between local and long-distance calls. Each of the local exchange carriers' (LECs) regions were carved up into multiple LATAs. LECs were permitted to offer intra-LATA service (i.e., calls within a particular LATA in their region), while inter-LATA service (i.e., calls between two LATAs, whether in the same or different regions) was reserved for the interexchange carriers (IXCs), such as AT&T, MCI, and other long-distance companies.

CLECs and IXCs had to pay RBOCs an access fee for every call that the local carrier transmitted along its local loop into the customer's premises. In most cases, local access was purchased from the RBOCs at a standard rate that the RBOCs were required to offer to all carriers. (These fees could add up. In 2003, AT&T paid $10.8 billion in access fees to local carriers, out of total revenues of $34.5 billion in that year.) These so-called incumbent LECs (or ILECs)[14] enjoyed virtual monopolies on wireline service in their regions, receiving nearly 100 percent of local-service revenues.

---

[12]Digital telephone systems started coming into use in the 1980s. These systems replaced electromechanical telephone systems that did not use software.

[13]The system is also sometimes referred to as "plain old telephone service" or POTS.

[14]Confusingly, the acronyms LECs, ILECs and RBOCs can be used to describe the same company. Today, the four ILECs that have consolidated from the so-called Baby Bells (RBOCs) following deregulation are often referred to as "The Bells."

What Is Voice over Internet Protocol Telephony?

VoIP allows users to make telephone calls using a computer network, primarily the Internet. Calls made entirely over the Internet were not subject to the access fees that local phone companies charged for terminating standard long-distance calls. Given that long-distance companies paid out a third of their revenues in access fees, avoiding those charges meant huge cost savings. Importantly, VoIP also offered enterprises and consumers a wider variety of telephony services compared to regular telephony.

How VoIP Works

VoIP technology can use the Internet to transmit calls. With VoIP, telephone voice calls are packetized, broken down into unique units, and addressed as "packets" using Internet protocol (IP), the protocol or method by which data is sent from one computer to another on the Internet. This protocol uses packet switching for shuttling data over the network. There is no continuing physical connection between the end points that are communicating. Each packet that travels through the Internet is treated as an independent unit of data without any relation to any other unit of data. Depending upon the VoIP service, the call may touch the PSTN physical network at some point or may completely bypass it. This contrasts with traditional land-line telephony: instead of using a circuit switch network to transmit the call, a physical path is obtained for and dedicated to a single connection between two end-points in the PSTN for the duration of the call. During that time, no one else can use the lines involved. (See Appendix: How VoIP Works.)

Because a VoIP call is not completely tied to the PSTN, unlike a regular call, it can be handled in a wider variety of ways compared to a traditional voice call. This enables VoIP to offer users much more flexible and valuable services, giving greater functionality. Because a VoIP call is less tied or not at all tied to the PSTN physical network, it presents challenges to the regulatory bodies that govern these networks.

No central authority has governed the standards used in IP communications. The technical standards that govern VoIP have evolved from various standards bodies, the most prominent being the International Telecommunications Union (ITU) and the Internet Engineering Task Force (IETF). To the extent that these standards bodies do not address a specific need or want of a VoIP service, individual companies modify their

EXHIBIT 3 | PC and Broadband Consumer Penetration in the United States

U.S. Household PC Growth and Penetration

Year	Number (millions)	Percent
2001	71.1	67
2002	74.1	69
2003 est.	77.5	71
2004 est.	80.8	73
2005 est.	84.1	75
2006 est.	86.7	77
2007 est.	88.7	78

NB: Years 2003–2007 projected.

Source: Jupiter Research. Cited in Infoplease.com.

Growth in High-Speed Line Penetration in the United States

	December 1999	December 2000	December 2001	December 2002	June 2003
Total High-Speed Lines	2,754,286	7,069,874	12,792,812	19,881,549	23,459,671

NB: High-speed defined as exceeded 200kbps in at least one direction.

Source: FCC, "Trends in Telephone Service."

systems to make the desired enhancements and then sometimes go back to the ITU or IETF to try to make their changes part of the accepted standard.[15]

VoIP Needs Broadband   VoIP was first introduced in 1995, but early versions had limited utility: poor quality calls were possible only between computers, not phone-to-phone, and parties on each end had to have compatible hardware and software. VoIP, to be effective, required broadband connections to the Internet (low-speed narrowband connections do not transfer enough data quickly enough to allow for calls of acceptable quality). Few consumers had these elements—especially broadband Internet access—in the 1990s (Exhibit 3). By 2004, things were different. In the United States, over 29 million consumers (a little less than 20 percent of households) had broadband Internet access, and their numbers were growing.[16] VoIP growth was tied to

broadband penetration. As stated above, growth estimates varied widely. Estimates for the number of VoIP users in 2003 varied between 100,000 and 150,000, and some expected up to 400,000 individual consumers to use VoIP in the United States by the end of 2004. This was tiny compared to the over 107 million households in the United States that had traditional land-line telephone service.[17] However, many expected VoIP services to soon catch on with consumers and businesses in the U.S., and some analysts estimated that more than 17 million users, approximately 16 percent of homes in the United States, would use VoIP by 2006.[18] As more consumers had broadband Internet access, the potential market for VoIP grew. AT&T expected 47 million households to have some kind of broadband access by 2007.

VoIP users could dispense with their land-lines completely and still make (VoIP) phone calls as long as they

---

[15]Source: Jeff Pulver.

[16]Written Statement of Michael K. Powell, chairman, Federal Communications Commission on Voice over Internet Protocol (VoIP) before the Committee on Commerce, Science, and Transportation, United States Senate, 253 Russell Senate Office Building, Tuesday, February 24, 2004, p. 4.

[17]Number of land-lines as of November 2003. Source: FCC, "Trends in Telephone Service," May 6, 2004, http://www.fcc.gov/Bureaus/Common_Carrier/Reports/ FCC-State_Link/IAD/trend504.pdf.

[18]Estimate of consumer adoption of VoIP from Stephanie N. Mehta, "The Future Is on the Line," *Fortune,* July 26, 2004, p. 122. Statement that enterprises would adopt VoIP services at a faster rate than consumers is the estimation of the authors.

maintained high-speed Internet access. (DSL users would still need the land-line DSL connection since high-speed access is needed to use VoIP.) Still, there were some prominent disadvantages with VoIP compared to traditional land-line telephony. Some Internet voice services would not work during power outages; it was difficult for some Internet voice services to seamlessly connect with the 911 emergency dispatch centers or identify the location of Internet voice 911 callers; and some VoIP companies did not offer listings in telephone directories.

Peering   Other problems with VoIP services would likely prove more troublesome. Since different VoIP providers used slightly different (and sometimes incompatible) technical standards, direct interconnection between VoIP services was largely impossible; they had to use the public phone system as a go-between. A process called peering, in which network operators made small technical adjustments enabling them to directly exchange data with other networks, overcame this problem. If VoIP networks peered with each other, they could directly exchange calls without using the PSTN as a go-between. Some VoIP networks freely peered with other VoIP services. Others peered with only a few and still others refused to peer at all or charged a fee to peer. If a VoIP network did not wish to peer, there was little that other VoIP networks could do. In this event, the users of the two VoIP services would not be able to directly connect using only VoIP (they would have to use the PSTN as a go-between).

Regulatory Issues of VoIP

In 2004, there was tremendous uncertainty surrounding the regulatory outlook of VoIP in the United States and elsewhere. For example, it was not clear whether the FCC alone had jurisdiction or whether individual states and their various bodies that regulated telephony in their regions would have a say. VoIP challenged the definitions that governed telephony in the United States. These definitions were established in the Telecommunications Deregulation Act of 1996, which made distinctions between three classes of telecommunications. One class was known as Telecommunications, in which there is no change in content or form, such as through a company's internal network. These activities were subject to light regulation. The next class was known as Telecommunications Service, which was offered to the public for a fee and subject to common carrier tariffs. Another class was called Information Service, which could include transmission processing, changing content or form, storage, forwarding,

and other activities. Such services were not regulated in the same way as a Telecommunications Service, and were not subject to economic pricing or economic regulation.[19]

An earlier law had already made distinctions between "basic" telecommunications service and "enhanced" information services. Voice calls carried over the PSTN were considered a basic telecommunications service and subject to common carrier regulation, which brought with it a host of laws and taxes.[20] Conversely, some information services, such as those provided by Internet service providers (ISPs) were defined as enhanced services and not subject to Title II regulation. Thus enhanced services escaped the regulations and taxes imposed upon so-called common carriers, such as LECs, IXCs, and others.[21]

Led by Senator Ted Stevens and others, the FCC's 1997 budget passed by Congress included the provision that the FCC explore the impact that VoIP would have on universal service. In 1998, the FCC's so-called Stevens Report pointed out that Internet service providers (ISPs), the gateways at both ends of a VoIP transmission, supported universal service with tens of millions of dollars of revenue because, as end users, ISPs paid fees on the connections they purchased from phone companies. The FCC also determined that computer-to-computer VoIP services were not viewed as a telecommunications service and thus were not subject to common carrier regulations. However, the FCC determined that phone-to-phone VoIP might be treated as a telecommunications service, and thus would be subject to the stringent common carrier regulation, under a variety of circumstances, including if the provider claimed to provide voice telephony service, if the phone equipment was the same as that used to place calls over the PSTN, and if the service transmitted [data] without net change in form or content.[22] Also in 1998, the European Commission made similar findings about how EC regulations would likely differentiate between computer-to-computer versus phone-to-phone VoIP models.[23]

[19]FCC 98-67, p. 16.

[20]Common carriers were defined under Title II of the Communications Act of 1934 (47 U.S.C. 201 et seq.).

[21]Definitions from Russ Hanser and Jennifer McKee, "FCC Treatment of Voice Over IP," FCC Wireline Competition Bureau, http://www.fcc.gov/voip/presentations/fcc-wcb.pdf.

[22]These were the findings of the FCC Report to Congress CC Docket No. 96-45, 1998, "Stevens Report."

[23]J. Scott Marcus, "IP Telephony: An Innovative Service That Has Largely Flourished in an Unregulated Environment," FCC Office of Plans and Technology, January 21, 2003, http://www.fcc.gov/osp/iptelephony-marcus.pdf.

With VoIP, as with regular telephony, both telephone and cable companies would be able to provide phone service. The cable companies that offered regular phone service faced similar regulatory hurdles and tariffs as those faced by phone companies. However, some RBOCs worried that it would be difficult for them to compete in VoIP against unregulated Internet-based VoIP companies while they, the RBOCs, faced stiff regulation. Other RBOCs were less worried and charged ahead with VoIP plans of their own. Many cable companies too were entering the market for VoIP.

Complicating the regulatory picture was the fact that telecommunications services were heavily regulated at both the federal and state levels. States were concerned that classifying VoIP as an information service, and hence exempting it from much regulation and most state-level taxes, could leave state treasuries with massive financial shortfalls in the event that VoIP services substituted for regulated and taxed circuit-switched telephony services. In August 2003, the telephony regulator of the state of Minnesota ruled that VoIP company Vonage should be subject to state telecoms regulations. A U.S. District Court judge in Minnesota overruled the decision, but there were 49 other shoes maybe waiting to drop. There was also the possibility of having VoIP ruled as a hybrid service—part telecommunications service, part information service—as a federal appeals court ruled about cable broadband. The FCC was also staking a claim to administer the regulations that would apply to VoIP. While a host of state courts were getting involved in adjudicating rules and regulations surrounding VoIP in their jurisdictions, the FCC argued that, since the Internet crossed state lines, VoIP was an interstate matter; hence, VoIP regulation would fall within the purview of the FCC (a federal entity) and not the individual states. Indeed, in November of 2004, the FCC ruled in favor of a petition submitted by VoIP service provider Vonage to declare the company's product an interstate service, giving the FCC regulatory control.[24] The ruling still left plenty of dust unsettled. For example, the FCC did not take up the broad issue of whether VoIP constituted an "information" service instead of a telecom service. As an information service, VoIP calls would be exempt from various tariffs and fees paid by telecom companies on their calls. Nor did the FCC rule on specific aspects of VoIP service, such as a requirement for VoIP

911 (E911) emergency call tracing or provisions for VoIP Universal Service, which would subsidize VoIP services for rural and poor or handicapped (e.g., deaf) customers.

The FCC Wrestles with VoIP

At the FCC, much of the work concerning VoIP policy was headed by Dr. Robert Pepper, chief of policy development. Pepper and his colleagues at the FCC wrestled with the political, technological, and social issues raised by VoIP. A key concern of the FCC, lawmakers, and individual state regulators was the impact of VoIP on important telecommunications-related social goals, such as universal service. Pepper said, "While the goal of universal service does not change, the traditional way of collecting money for it—implicit subsidies embedded within tariffs—will not be sustainable going forward because of changes in industry technology, market structure, and the players. This gets at an important policy question: Is VoIP an intrastate or interstate service? Is it an information service or a telecommunications service? If a call terminates to the PSTN, should it incur interstate access charges or should it only pay a local termination charge?"[25] There was more at stake than semantics. Pepper explained, "The price for local call termination is between .1 cent and .2 cents. If VoIP calls were deemed an interstate access call, the termination would be .55 cents to .6 cents—more than a five-fold price difference."

The flexibility of VoIP communications, particularly compared to calls generated through the PSTN system, highlighted some of the problems of applying tariffs and regulations designed for PSTN traffic to VoIP. Pepper gave an example that he heard from a state telecommunications commissioner.

> Say you have just landed at San Francisco International Airport and you get into a cab and ask, "I want to go to Union Square; how much is it going to cost me?" The cabbie says, "It depends on where you came from." You respond, "That doesn't make any sense, it's the same mileage for you." The cabbie says, "I'm sorry, that's the law. If you came from Chicago, it will cost $10, if you came from Los Angeles, it will cost you $25, if you flew in from Oakland, I'll pay you $2."

Pepper continued, "It makes no sense. But that's what we have in termination pricing in telephones." According

---

[24]"FCC Finds That Vonage Not Subject to Patchwork of State Regulations Governing Telephone Companies," FCC press release, November 9, 2004. http://hraunfoss.fcc.gov/edocs_public/attachmatch/DOC-254112A1.doc.

[25]All quotes from Robert Pepper are from the authors' interview on June 29, 2004 unless otherwise cited. All subsequent quotes from this interview will not be cited.

to Pepper, VoIP required a different set of metrics: "Voice is no longer the relevant product or service and, in the broadband IP world, the minute is no longer the appropriate metric [on which to base tariffs and regulation]." The industry would struggle to determine what would be the best metrics in an IP communications world.

A major source of regulatory uncertainty was which regulator(s)—federal (FCC) or states—had jurisdiction? The implications of split jurisdictions could be dire for some start-up VoIP services. Pepper said, "The jurisdiction for regulating VoIP-to-PSTN has not yet been resolved and there are still individual states that want to regulate VoIP companies. If VoIP companies are required to undergo regulation in each and every state, it becomes a lawyer's game, not a high tech game and not an Internet game, and the incumbent phone companies win because they have lawyers in every state."

For the FCC and Congress, the biggest concern around VoIP was making sure that important social and public goals, such as accessibility, 911 emergency calls, and law enforcement's ability to perform lawful taps on VoIP communications were still available with VoIP services. In the past, tariffs on the economic components of PSTN service, such as voice call, and minute metering (similar to traditional utility regulation) were combined with social policies to achieve and fund the social goals listed above. Pepper said, "These do not have to be combined. They have been in the past, because that was the easiest way to achieve the social policy. What we are trying to do for analytical and discussion purposes is separate the utility and economic components from social policies. The social policies do not change. The ways we achieve these goals in an IP-based environment will change, but they are all possible in the VoIP world."

The impact of VoIP was roiling an already turbulent regulatory environment. Widespead consumer adoption of mobile telephone service by late 2004 had fundamentally changed the economics of subsidy structures in telephony. The impact from mobile telephony had been largely unforeseen in the 1996 act. VoIP promised to heap even more stress on the already shaky regulatory foundation for telephony.

Two Important FCC Decisions in 2004: Pulver and AT&T

In 2004, the FCC issued two important decisions that gave a little more regulatory clarity to VoIP. These were the Pulver Decision issued in February 2004 and the AT&T declaratory ruling issued in April 2004.

In February 2003, VoIP entrepreneur Jeff Pulver petitioned the FCC to find that his VoIP service called Free World Dialup (FWD) (see below) was neither a "telecommunications service" nor "telecommunications," as described above. Several entities encouraged the FCC to find against Pulver. In particular, some incumbent telecom providers lobbied against the petition as did both the U.S. Department of Justice (DOJ) and the Federal Bureau of Investigation (FBI); the latter two groups worried about the ability of law enforcement agencies to monitor VoIP calls. Few organizations lent their support for the petition. Still, within 12 months, by February 2004, the FCC made its decision, announcing that "FWD was neither 'telecommunications' nor 'telecommunications service.'" It further declared that FWD was an "unregulated 'information service' subject to the Commission's jurisdiction."[26] The FCC's Robert Pepper said, "One of the really important implications of the Pulver Decision was not just the finding that it was an information service, but that it was an *interstate* information service, and that the FCC gets to decide what it is, and not the [individual 50] states."

Soon after the Pulver decision, in April 2004 the FCC ruled against AT&T in a declaratory ruling the company requested in October 2002 to determine whether AT&T would have to pay interstate access charges to connect certain VoIP calls.[27] (AT&T wanted to avoid interstate fees on the origin and termination of the call.) At issue were interexchange calls initiated in the same manner as traditional interexchange calls, by an end user who dialed 1 + the called number from a regular telephone. When the call reached AT&T's network, AT&T converted it from its existing format into an IP format and transported it over AT&T's Internet backbone. AT&T then converted the call back from the IP format and delivered it to the called party through the LEC's local business lines. AT&T hoped the FCC would rule that such calls were not subject to interstate access fees to the LECs of call recipients. This format was different from AT&T's CallVantage VoIP service (see below) which was similar to other VoIP services and not subject to this ruling.

The FCC found that under the current rules, the service described above was subject to interstate access charges. The FCC sought to limit this interpretation, and hence the applicability of access charges, to a class of what might be thought of as a hybrid VoIP call.[28] In

---

[26]FCC 04-97, p.18.

[27]FCC 04-97.

[28]IP-Enabled Services, WC Docket No. 04-36, FCC 04-28, para. 61.

effect, the FCC distinguished between "pure" VoIP calls that never touched the PSTN (which were not subject to connection fees) from calls that originated and terminated on the PSTN, but may have been carried over the Internet at some point during the duration of the call.

The VoIP Marketplace in 2004

There is a famous cartoon of a dog typing at a PC keyboard above the caption, "On the Internet, nobody knows you're a dog." Internet-based VoIP companies such as Free World Dialup and Vonage may have been counting on the fact that on the Internet, nobody knew (or cared) that they were a start-up and not a well-established phone company. Indeed, VoIP called into question the premise of what it took to be a phone company. (See Exhibit 4 for selected financial data for public companies discussed in this section.)

Low Barriers to Entry

VoIP service did not require the massive infrastructure investments that PSTN voice services needed. VoIP pioneer Jeff Pulver said: "These days the real barrier to entry to the VoIP service market is the underlying know-how to make something work and keep it working rather than the creation of the platform itself. Much of the underlying software is open source or otherwise available for free. But knowing how to pull the pieces together and make it work—that is what creates and maintains the barriers." Pulver explained (only somewhat jokingly), "On the surface, a powerful desktop server running Linux and the time needed to configure one of these platforms was the only real cost. Throw in money for an operations staff and a budget for marketing and some money for co-location at the ILEC and you too can join the growing list of people offering voice over broadband services."[29]

For example, would-be VoIP start-ups could buy access to software, ready-made Web sites and fiber-optic networks from wholesalers such as Covad Communications for as little as $25,000 for a basic set of services needed to start an Internet phone business. One Covad customer, Unity Business Networks LLC of Denver, which has been selling Internet calling services since March 2003 and operated with only 20 employees,

had about 70 small businesses as customers by August 2004. Bob Paulsen, Unity's co-founder and president commented, "It's unbelievable how much we can offer for such a small investment." Unity had revenue of roughly $750,000 and said it turned cash flow positive earlier in 2004.[30]

In 2004, several VoIP companies were up and running, offering services to consumers and enterprises with a variety of plans, most charging between $15 and $40 for various time amounts (up to unlimited) of local and long-distance calling. Many different types of companies offered VoIP services. RBOCs, cable companies, VoIP start-ups and AT&T all offered VoIP services. Given the seemingly low barriers to entry, many wondered how VoIP services would differentiate themselves in the increasingly crowded marketplace. Some of the smaller VoIP players worried that ISPs could be able to identify and potentially discriminate against some VoIP traffic, giving scope for ISPs to suggest their networks were somehow optimized for their brand of VoIP service. It was thought that the FCC and other regulators would prohibit such behavior if it could be proven.

Impact of VoIP on the Bells

Since the end of 2000, RBOCs lost 28 million local lines, a drop of over 18 percent. Some of these lines were lost due to cell phone "cord cutters," others went due to competition from cable telephony, but an increasing amount were victims of VoIP services. This drop in local lines was unprecedented; it was the first time since the Depression in the early 1930s that phone companies had seen the number of their local lines decline. By 2004, the Bells were losing 4 percent of their residential lines each year. The loss in local lines underscored the weakness of the Bells' basic business model: selling a high-priced commodity—voice calls—in a market that was now highly competitive and becoming more so with the advent of VoIP. Symptomatic of this problem, credit rating agency Standard & Poor's put three of the four RBOCs (BellSouth, SBC Communications and Verizon) on "credit watch" for a possible downgrade.[31]

---

[29]Quotes from Jeff Pulver in this paragraph are from an exchange with the authors on 24 August 2004.

[30]Ken Brown and Almar Latour, "Heavy Toll: Phone Industry Faces Upheaval as Ways of Calling Change Fast," *The Wall Street Journal,* August 25, 2004, p. A1.

[31]Ken Brown and Almar Latour, "Heavy Toll: Phone Industry Faces Upheaval as Ways of Calling Change Fast," op. cit.

EXHIBIT 4 | Selected Financial Data

AT&T Selected Data from 2003 Income Statement

	2003 ($ millions)
Revenue	
AT&T Business	25,075
AT&T Consumer	9,400
Corporate and Other	54
Total revenue	**34,529**
Operating Expenses	
Access and other connection	2,698
Costs of services and products	2,011
Selling, general, and administrative	1,921
Depreciation and amortization	1,186
Net restructuring and other charges	4
Total operating expenses	**7,820**
Operating income	**1,166**
Net income	**571**

Source: AT&T 2003 Annual Report.

Comcast Selected Data from 2003 Income Statement

	2003 ($ millions)			(millions)
Revenue				
Video	12,096		Video subscribers	21,468
High-speed Internet	2,255		High-speed Internet	
Phone	801		Subscribers	5,284
Advertising Sales	112		Phone subscribers	1,267
Other	619			
Franchise fees	608			
Total revenue	17,491			
Operating expenses				
Programming expenses	3,909			
Other operating, selling, general and administrative	7,232			
Operating income before depreciation and amortization	6,350			
Net income	3,240			

Source: Comcast 2003 Annual Report.

(*continued*)

EXHIBIT 4 | Selected Financial Data (cont.)

Verizon Selected Data from 2003 Income Statement

	2003 ($ millions)
Revenue	
Domestic telecom	39,602
Domestic wireless	22,489
Information services	4,114
International	1,949
Corporate & other	(402)
Consolidated revenues	**67,752**
Operating expenses	
Cost of services and sales	21,783
Selling, general and administrative expense	24,999
Depreciation and amortization expense	13,617
Sales of businesses, net	(141)
Consolidated operating expenses	**60,258**
Pro forma net income	**2,906**

Source: Verizon 2003 Annual Report.

Nortel Selected Data from 2002 Annual Report

	2002 ($ millions)
Revenue	
Wireless Networks	4,211
Enterprise Networks	2,582
Wireline Networks	2,254
Optical Networks	1,465
Other	48
Total revenue	**10,560**
Cost of revenues	**6,953**
Gross profit	**3,607**
Operating expense	
Selling, general and administrative	(2,675)
Research and development	(2,230)
Amortization of acquired technology	(157)
Stock option compensation	(91)
Special charges	(2,298)
Gain (loss) on sale of business	(40)
Loss from continuing operations before income taxes	**(3,804)**

Source: Nortel 2002 Annual Report.

One example of the trouble RBOCs faced was exemplified by Qwest Communications. Qwest had lost 3 million lines since the end of 2000, including 200,000 in the second quarter of 2004 alone. Some estimated that Qwest was losing around $200 million in high-margin revenue each year due to the loss of local lines and ancillary services. The company laid off 10,000 people in the past two years. In response to the threat posed by VoIP, Qwest became the first Bell to start its own VoIP service in 2003. "It has become one big communications sector. People really haven't grasped that. . . . The trouble is, the Bells have such high overhead that the upstarts can easily underprice them," said Qwest CEO Richard Notebart.[32]

For RBOC Verizon, the move to offer VoIP was about getting customers locked in to broadband. Bob Ingalls, president of Verizon retail markets acknowledged that VoiceWing could cannibalize the company's residential phone business, but thought that the risk "was a reality of the market we are in," adding, "We are not worried about cannibalization; we see this first and foremost as an opportunity to grow the broadband market."[33]

Still, for the time being, RBOCs had lots of cash and were looking for ways to spend it. In late 2003, BellSouth considered buying AT&T. It later backed off, but many believed that the Bells would try to buy the remaining big long-distance companies, AT&T (see below) and MCI (formerly called WorldCom).

Cable "Triple Play"

RBOCs and cable companies hoped to have success in bundling various services, such as phone, TV, Internet access and wireless service. Investment bank Goldman Sachs estimated that VoIP services would take 7 percent of residential phone lines from RBOCs by 2006 and that cable companies would be able to get 10 percent of their customers to sign up to cable-based VoIP services in the first year of availability, 20 percent in two years and 30 percent after four years. One motivation for the Bells and cable companies to offer VoIP was to enable them to offer a very desirable "triple play" of television, Internet access, and voice to their customers.[34] If cable companies

---

[32]Ken Brown and Almar Latour, "Heavy Toll: Phone Industry Faces Upheaval as Ways of Calling Change Fast," op.cit.

[33]Paul Taylor, "Verizon Launches VoIP Service," *The Financial Times,* July 23, 2004, p. 20.

[34]The Bells could emulate the cable "triple play" by teaming up with satellite television companies, offering packages of phone, broadband, and TV service.

EXHIBIT 4 | Selected Financial Data (cont.)

2003 Income and Cash Data for Selected Companies

	Type of Company	2003 Net Revenue ($M)	2003 Cash and Marketable Securities ($M)
AT&T	Telecommunications	34,529	2,459
BellSouth	RBOC	22,635	4,556
Comcast	Cable	17,491	1,550
Cox Communications	Cable	5,759	84
EarthLink	ISP	1,402	439
Qwest	RBOC	14,288	1,756
SBC	RBOC	40,843	4,806
Time Warner	Media (including cable and ISP)	39,565	3,040
Verizon	RBOC	67,752	699

Source: Company reports.

became this central to the lives of their customers, churn was likely to decline. In May 2004, Comcast, the largest cable television company in the United States, announced that it would enter the market for VoIP service. In doing so, it joined cable rivals Time Warner Cable, Cablevision Systems Corp., and Cox Communications, Inc., all offering cable television and phone service through their installed lines. Cablevision offered telephone service to all its 2.9 million subscribers. Cox Communications, which already offered phone service based on circuit switch technology to nearly 1 million customers, began Internet-based phone service in Roanoke, Virginia in late 2003. Time Warner Cable, a unit of Time Warner Inc., said it would offer telephone service to all of its 11 million customers by the end of 2004.[35]

The use of IP was one thing that all companies in the VoIP business had in common; however, other than that, different companies used different methods to transmit the voice and data components of calls. Some touched the PSTN at the beginning and/or end of the call while others completely bypassed the PSTN.

Skype: P2P Phoning

One VoIP company, Skype, was launched by the two co-founders of the phenomenally popular peer-to-peer (P2P) file sharing service called KaZaA. Skype used P2P technology to transmit its calls. It completely bypassed the PSTN and connected only with other Skype users. Skype claimed that their P2P telephony solved many of the problems that have prevented VoIP from attaining mainstream acceptance, for example, creating code in their software clients to overcome the low call completion rates due to firewalls on users' PCs.[36]

A major limitation for Skype was the fact that calls could only be made between the PCs of parties that were both signed onto the free Skype service; that is, they were connected to the Internet with their computers switched on. This led some critics to call it a closed system, but its supporters underscored Skype's very easy-to-use interface and high call quality. With Skype calls were free, but the company planned to make money by charging for services such as voice mail. By July 2004, people all over the world had downloaded 17.5 million Skype clients. In July 2004, the company announced plans for a prepaid service, called SkypeOut, that would enable Skype users to terminate calls via the PSTN to land-lines or cell phones. Skype also announced plans for a service called SkypeIn to allow non-Skype users to call Skype customers.[37]

---

[35]"Comcast to Offer Phone Service by 2006," Reuters, May 27, 2004.

[36]Ibid.

[37]Erika Morphy, "Skype Signs On Four Carriers in Preparation for New Pre-Pay Service," www.newsfactor.com, July 27, 2004.

Free World Dialup

As its name suggested, Free World Dialup (FWD) was a free service that enabled users to circumvent the PSTN by connecting voice calls over the Internet using a PC or an IP-enabled telephone. Operated by a staff of eight people, FWD provided the ability for two or more people connected via broadband to the Internet to call and talk to each other.

When users communicated via FWD, their calls did not touch the PSTN. Because of this, FWD users could not communicate with anybody outside of the FWD system. However, once users were set up with their own FWD number, they could also obtain, for free, a U.S. or international direct-inward-dial (DID) number mapped to their FWD number. With a DID number, users could receive direct-dial phone calls. Companies existed that offered free phone numbers to users. These phone numbers could be registered with FWD, which would forward the call, via the Internet, to the FWD account holder. One such company was IPKall, which issued users a free phone number in Washington state. A FWD user could register an IPKall-issued Washington state PSTN phone number with FWD. Callers to that number would incur the costs associated with making a PSTN call to that Washington number. However, that call would be routed over the Internet to the FWD user who could receive the call anywhere in the world. Thus, the caller incurred the costs associated with a PSTN call to Washington state but could reach and speak to the FWD user wherever in the world he or she happened to be, provided the FWD user was connected to the Internet (via broadband) at the time the call was made. If the FWD user was not connected to the Internet at the time of the call, or did not pick up, the call went into voice mail and messages were sent to the user's e-mail as a WAV sound file. Other companies existed that could issue London, England–based PSTN numbers.

Like most VoIP services, FWD offered a rich set of features. FWD customers were in reach wherever there was high-speed Internet access; a user's net-connected phone rang regardless of where in the world the user was physically located. FWD offered three-way calling capability, and the company peered with over 50 other service providers, so FWD customers could easily call the subscribers of most non-FWD Internet telephone services (e.g., Vonage, Packet8, and others). FWD also offered conference or bridge lines in which users could set up and control their audio conferences.

Making Money from Free VoIP

Free World Dialup was founded in 1995 by VoIP pioneer Jeff Pulver as a hobby project. Between 1995 and 2002, Pulver experimented with various iterations of FWD, adjusting the software and engineering specifications of the service. The attention Pulver gave to FWD ebbed and flowed, subject to the demands of his day jobs and family obligations. However, by the end of 2002, FWD was becoming a robust service and quickly attracting users. While FWD was a free service, Pulver owned and operated a successful VoIP industry conference called VON (voice on the net), which drew several thousand participants, along with sponsors, each year. Pulver used proceeds from the conference to subsidize FWD. In May 2004, Pulver said, "I use about $2 million a year from VON to help support FWD."[38] For Pulver, FWD, while clearly a passion of his, was the equivalent of a razor for which he used other ventures to provide blades. Pulver was involved in several for-profit companies and ventures centered on IP communications. He also engaged in strategy consulting through Pulver.com consulting.

Pulver said: "When I first started FWD in 1995, I got a small write-up in *The Times* of London. I showed it to my dad and he said, 'That's great, but do you think you can commercialize it?' I told him I thought I could somehow."

In answer to his father's concerns about his ability to commercialize FWD, Pulver had several for-profit interests that complemented FWD. For example, Pulver sold IP-enabled phones that allowed users to make VoIP calls without a computer or PDA. (The phones, which resembled ordinary cell phones, needed to be connected via broadband to the Internet.)

Pulver's FWD users constituted a market for potential VoIP-related, for-profit services. In the 1990s, people spoke about the importance of "eyeballs" to a Web site, hoping that if people visited the site, it could somehow make money from the traffic through advertising or transactions. Pulver had similar hopes that he could make money from FWD's users. Pulver said, "Our users are prequalified to use VoIP, which can be valuable to Vonage and others. In addition, there are other services that we are only now beginning to imagine: Voice IM (instant messaging); chat; multiparty conferencing; social network applications, such as dating services, buddy lists, etc., all done with IP communications, are some likely revenue-generating services."

---

[38]All quotes from Jeff Pulver are from the authors' interview on May 27, 2004, unless otherwise cited. Subsequent quotes from this interview will not be cited.

By the middle of 2004 according to Pulver, FWD had 200,000 registered users and was growing by about 600 registered users per day.

Ma Bell Gets into VoIP

In the same way that people began taking personal computers seriously after IBM entered the market, a similar milestone occurred for VoIP in March 2004, when AT&T launched "CallVantage," its much promoted VoIP service. AT&T had dipped a toe into the enterprise VoIP market as early as 1997, but all of its efforts in the VoIP market, prior to CallVantage, had been services geared for the enterprise market and managed by AT&T. With CallVantage, AT&T plunged completely into the market for consumer local and long-distance VoIP service. Now AT&T offered VoIP services for both enterprises and consumers.

AT&T shipped subscribers a small piece of hardware called a telephone adapter (TA). Users plugged their phones or PCs into the TA, which in turn was plugged into a DSL or cable modem. (Like other VoIP services, CallVantage required high-speed Internet access.) CallVantage users could often connect their current phone numbers to the service or select a new number from a fast-growing selection of area codes. By September 2004, the service was available in 170 markets (MSAs) in 39 states.[39] Callers to CallVantage subscribers would have to pay to make the call to the selected area code; thus, if most of a user's callers were likely to be located in the 415 area code, a user could select a CallVantage number with that area code.

The Background to AT&T's Entry into VoIP

AT&T's big move into VoIP was spearheaded by its chairman and CEO David Dorman. Dorman described the background of AT&T's involvement in VoIP. Dorman said, "The kernel of our VoIP program was AT&T's $1.4 billion investment for 32 percent [controlling interest] of VoIP company Net2Phone made under AT&T's former chairman and CEO Michael Armstrong in August 2000. We made the investment because we were worried about the ability of AOL to annex voice service on top of narrowband Internet access."[40]

[39]"AT&T Adds More Advanced Calling Features to AT&T CallVantage Service," AT&T press release, September 15, 2004.

[40]All quotes from Dave Dorman are from the authors' interview on June 18, 2004, unless otherwise cited. Subsequent quotes from this interview will not be cited.

For AT&T, VoIP was not just another service. Dorman viewed it as an essential element for the company's competitive well-being. Dorman said: "We view the Internet [and VoIP] along with wireless [cellular] as access technologies." Since deregulation, AT&T had been separated from its residential customers by RBOCs, who owned the local loop. As mentioned above, AT&T had to pay access charges to use those local loops, or the so-called last mile to their customers' premises.

VoIP (as well as cellular telephony) offered AT&T a way to bypass the last mile and connect directly with residential customers again. Dorman said: "We see VoIP as the perfect way to create more [access] choice for ourselves for both retail and wholesale customers."

Bundles of Joy   In addition to consumer access, AT&T thought that VoIP gave the company the important ability to bundle service. Dorman said, "The 'Holy Grail' in this business is the service bundle." AT&T was offering customers bundles including local phone, long-distance, Internet access, and wireless (i.e., cellular). However, AT&T could not directly offer, but had to buy, Internet access and local phone service. Dorman explained, "If you have to buy them from others, it is usually more expensive. However, VoIP gives us the ability to offer residential customers our own local and long-distance voice over IP." It seemed that the ability to bundle a more complete service offering was every bit as important to AT&T as unfettered access. Dorman said, "Bundles greatly reduce customer churn. Churn is our biggest cost. Think of it this way, if you have customer acquisition costs of say, $400 (to pick a number), and 36 percent churn, and several million customers, you can see the impact that churn has on your costs." Dorman thought that bundling VoIP services with local, long-distance, and wireless could reduce churn. He said, "If a customer has three or four different services with you, it is very difficult for competitors to hive off one or two of those services."

The importance of the consumer bundle to AT&T greatly diminished after the company announced in July 2004 that it would focus on the enterprise market (see below).

The VoIP Challenge to RBOCs

According to Dorman, VoIP threatened the fundamental business model of RBOCs. These companies made little or no money on basic phone service. Instead, they made money on features that they could bolt onto basic phone service, such as caller ID and other value-added services. Most VoIP services, including CallVantage, Skype, and Free World Dialup offered these features, and many others unavailable with traditional telephony, for free or at a much cheaper price than those charged by RBOCs. Dorman said:

> The Bells have $150 billion in capital dedicated to the voice, which has long been the killer application of telecommunications. However, VoIP allows for the extraction of voice from the service. No costly central offices, with floors and floors of dedicated switches are needed with VoIP. Instead, you use Intel-based or other standardized servers and software code, which are cheap to scale. The Bells and cable companies want to sequester voice into their models. But you cannot legislate/regulate voice packets differently from data packets.

As AT&T battled telecom providers in the United States and elsewhere, Dorman felt that the company had overcome its own aversion to change. The company had been famously slow moving, with little of its renowned inventiveness translating to superior services. Something like CallVantage would probably not have been possible in the AT&T of old. But the company had changed, according to Dorman.

> Something like VoIP has to be raised up by the CEO. Every week, we review our VoIP efforts; we look at the hot list of impediments and blow up anything that gets in the way. We are giving this kind of attention to VoIP, wireless, and IP services.
>
> You need a critical mass of like-thinking managers. It goes from the officers of the company to the next layer down. It is not the rank-and-file that stops efforts like VoIP; it's the middle and senior managers that are the sticking points. When I became CEO, we had 14 layers of management between me and line employees. Now we have only seven to eight layers. We had 120 officers in the company. Now we have 49, each with more fulsome responsibilities and more accountability. Of these 49 company officers, 30 came from outside of AT&T and the remaining officers were the revolutionaries of the company.
>
> Now at AT&T, it is OK to try and fail, but it is not OK not to try.

AT&T was trying hard. The company thought its biggest obstacles to CallVantage were broadband penetration and inertia. AT&T was targeting the 18- to

30-year-old demographic and wanted to be the dominant provider for this group.

The company was aggressive about servicing partners. Being "access agnostic," it worked with cable operators to provide VoIP to customers. Dorman said AT&T could get a cable operator set up to offer its own customers (AT&T provided) private-labeled VoIP services in only 30 days, with AT&T drop shipping the telephone adaptors and providing the sales and customer support functions. Thus AT&T was trying to become both a private-label and an end-user provider.

AT&T De-emphasizes Traditional Residential Services

AT&T's push into VoIP came at a time when the company was particularly troubled. In early August 2004, bond rating agency Standard & Poor's announced it was reducing AT&T's debt rating to "junk," citing concerns about AT&T's declining revenue and profitability. Its core long-distance business was suffering from a large decline in revenue, evidenced by the fact that overall revenue fell 11 percent to $8 billion in the first quarter of 2004, compared to $9 billion at the same period in 2003.

In late July 2004, AT&T announced that it would stop marketing traditional telecommunications services, such as consumer local and long-distance services, and instead focus exclusively on marketing telecommunications services to businesses and residential VoIP. At the time of the announcement, AT&T provided local and long-distance phone service to 29 million U.S. subscribers, making it the largest long-distance company in the country and the single largest competitor to the four RBOCs in their core local consumer markets.[41]

Despite its strong consumer brand (AT&T spent about $1.8 billion a year marketing consumer services),[42] 75 percent of AT&T's revenue came from business services, and the majority of its traffic from business long-distance traffic came from long-distance wholesalers who purchased lower-priced wholesale long-distance minutes rather than the more profitable

[41]"AT&T Exits $63 Billion Dollar Consumer Market—Will There Be More?" IDC press release, July 29, 2004.

[42]Paul Taylor, "Ma Bell Loses Its Status as Domestic Icon: AT&T Strategy Shift Highlights Task It Faces in Markets It Once Dominated," *Financial Times,* August 27, 2004, p. 26.

business retail minutes.[43] Operating margins for AT&T's business division were around 3 percent and revenue was falling. In the consumer local and long-distance market, AT&T competed against other legacy long-distance companies, RBOCs (recently allowed to provide long distance), CLECs, and VoIP start-ups. In June and August of 2004, the FCC issued rules that would allow ILECs—owners of the last mile—to raise by an average of 15 percent the prices they charged to long-distance carriers (and other carriers) to lease local lines.[44] (It was necessary for AT&T and CLECs to lease local lines from ILECs in order to offer local service.) Here, AT&T earned margins of nearly 12 percent, but margins were trending downward. Given these developments, some analysts expected other long-distance providers to also eventually exit the consumer long-distance market. While AT&T would continue to serve its existing consumer base, the company's market share amongst this group was expected to wither over time.

Vonage

Established in 2001, Vonage was the oldest continuously run VoIP company in operation.[45] It boasted features and ease of use that made it a popular choice for consumers and enterprises. As with AT&T's CallVantage, Vonage users received a welcome package that included a digital phone adapter, and setup was easy. It used the Internet to initiate, route, and terminate calls. Once users

were set up, they had access to a rich variety of free services such as three-way calling, call forwarding, and many others that PSTN services charged extra for or could not offer. Users could manage their accounts online through a Web-based screen called a "Dashboard" which displayed a list of the most recent incoming and outgoing calls, provided service announcements, and offered links to billing configuration screens. Voice mail notifications could be sent to the user's e-mail address, or the received voice messages could be converted into a sound (WAV) file and forwarded to the user's e-mail address where they could be heard. Vonage offered e-mail answers for installation and technical support, customer service, and billing, as well as a toll-free, 24/7 Vonage help phone or fax line.

While the company was expanding its presence in the United States and Canada, as of August 2004, Alaska, Hawaii, Idaho, Iowa, Montana, West Virginia, and Wyoming and six provinces in Canada had no available area codes in the Vonage system. This meant that users could not select an area code and phone number within those regions. Thus, a user in Alaska could still use the Vonage service, but would not be reachable with an Alaska-based area code and phone number. The company expected to add these states as it expanded its service.

Vonage equipment was sold directly through the company's Web site and via retail partners such as Amazon.com, RadioShack, Best Buy, Circuit City, Staples and Office Depot. Wholesale partners such as the ISP EarthLink, Coral Springs, Florida, cable company Advanced Cable Communications, and others resold Vonage broadband phone service under their own brands. In August 2004, Vonage had more than 235,000 lines in service and added more than 25,000 lines per month to its network, and at that time, over 5 million calls per week are made using Vonage.[46]

Equipment Suppliers

For all of the media focus on VoIP in the consumer market space, enterprises were the biggest early adopters of VoIP services. In 2004, companies such as Cisco Systems, Nortel Networks, and Avaya expected to sell up to $2 billion worth of IP-based PBXs (public branch exchanges)—equipment that allowed enterprises to use

---

[43]In 2Q 2004, AT&T reported "consolidated revenue of $7.6 billion, which included $5.6 billion from AT&T Business and $2.0 billion from AT&T Consumer. Consolidated revenue declined 13.2 percent versus the second quarter of 2003, primarily due to continued declines in LD voice revenue. . . . Long-distance voice revenue decreased 17.6 percent from the prior-year second quarter, driven by continued pricing pressure as well as a continued mix shift in volume from retail to wholesale. Volumes were flat on a quarter-over-quarter basis, with growth in wholesale volumes offset by a decline in retail volumes." Source: "AT&T Announces Second-Quarter 2004 Earnings, Company to Stop Investing in Traditional Consumer Services; Concentrate Efforts on Business Markets," AT&T press release, July 22, 2004.

[44]Paul Taylor, "FCC Unveils Line Charging Rules," *Financial Times,* August 21/22, 2004, p. 9. The FCC's decision to allow the price increases was controversial. One FCC commissioner (Michael Copps) warned that this and other recent decisions put the FCC "on track to butcher the pro-competitive vision of the 1996 [Telecommunications Deregulation] Act."

[45]Starting as a hobby project, Free World Dialup had not been continuously operated since its founding in 1995.

[46]"Vonage and Linksys Team Up to Redefine the Telecommunications Marketplace," Vonage press release, August 24, 2004.

their data networks to process voice calls.[47] Some analysts thought that IP communications reached an important tipping point in 2004 and that enterprises were more likely to install VoIP telephone equipment rather than traditional PSTN-based equipment. For example, in late September 2004, Bank of America, the third-largest bank in the country, said it would begin deploying 180,000 Internet phones throughout the United States Bank officials said the move to VoIP would let them replace 362 traditional telephone switches (PBXs) and give employees more resources for mixing telephone calls and data.[48]

According to one research firm, by 2006, sales of IP PBXs were expected to exceed those of traditional PBX equipment.[49] Indeed, the market for traditional telephony equipment was declining in the face of IP communications, falling by an estimated 11.5 percent in the first quarter of 2004 and by 21.4 percent in 2003.[50] As mentioned earlier, the market for VoIP equipment, estimated at $1 billion in 2002 was expected to reach over $4 billion by 2006.[51] Some thought the market for VoIP equipment could reach $30 billion by 2008.[52]

IP communications, at least in enterprises, was not just a North American phenomenon. The Asia/Pacific region was the fastest growing market for IP telephony equipment sales, reporting sales increases of 43 percent in the first quarter of 2004. The North American market increased 18 percent while the European market grew by 8 percent over the same period.[53]

IP communications represented a burgeoning new category for equipment makers, a much-needed bright spot for the equipment industry after the years of declining sales that marked the dot-com bust of 2000. For some equipment makers, developing new VoIP systems meant incurring higher costs, which they could not pass on to extremely cost-conscious buyers. However, many equipment makers hoped to improve their margins by developing and selling new VoIP software products to create valuable applications for new VoIP systems, features not possible with traditional telephony.

Companies were attracted to IP telephony because it offered cost savings as well as additional features, such as video and other multimedia applications as well as seamless forwarding of calls regardless of location, which were not available through traditional telephony. Importantly, IP communications and an enterprise's already installed traditional telephony assets were not mutually exclusive. By 2004, companies were using IP communications as a binding network that could efficiently overlay already-installed traditional telephony networks that had been added over time as companies grew and developed or acquired locations with different telephony networks.

The Nortel Perspective

Nortel Networks, a Canada-based telecommunications equipment maker with $9.8 billion in revenue in 2003 was a major presence in the market for IP communications equipment. It focused on providing equipment that helped enterprises to bridge between traditional telephony and IP communications. Vickie Marvich-McGovern, director, Enterprise Multimedia Solutions, Nortel Networks said:

> Today, the VoIP market is mostly comprised of enterprises that are migrating to IP communications, or "greenfield" users, such as new branches of established companies building on sites without an existing telecommunications infrastructure. We do not see many large enterprises using only VoIP. They are migrating their infrastructure as it makes sense for the business to do so. And we have seen some very large customers that were early adopters of our competitors' VoIP systems rip them out because they had failed to live up to expectations. In the earlier days of VoIP, customers had to compromise on functionality to go pure VoIP; that is no longer the case.[54]

For Nortel, at least in 2004, the best IP communications solutions bridged and augmented traditional telephony systems. Marvich-McGovern said, "The real value of IP communications, for equipment makers,

---

[47]Eric J. Savitz, p. 19.

[48]Scott Thurm, "Cisco Gets Internet-Phone Pact from Bank of America for U.S.; Sign of How Technology Is Becoming Mainstream, Replacing Older Systems," *The Wall Street Journal,* September 28, 2004. p. A.2.

[49]Source: Yankee Group cited in "Infonet Embraces Convergence," *Light Reading,* April 6, 2004, http://www.lightreading.com/document.asp?doc_id=50610&site=lightreading.

[50]Paul Taylor and Rob Budden, "Save a Packet on Phone Calls," Financial Times, FT-IT Review, July 21, 2004, p. 1.

[51]Source: Boardwatch, cited in "Time to Redial: VOIP (Voice over Internet Protocol) Makes a Comeback," op. cit.

[52]Paul Taylor and Rob Budden, "Save a Packet on Phone Calls," op. cit.

[53]Paul Taylor and Rob Budden, "Save a Packet on Phone Calls," op. cit.

[54]All quotes from Vickie Marvich-McGovern are from the authors' interview on 6 July 2004. Subsequent quotes from this interview will not be cited.

service providers, and customers comes from applications such as collaborative capabilities or instant messaging, which are more easily deployed over an IP network."

Conclusion

When telecommunication deregulation was put into place in the mid-1990s, cable television services were thought to offer the spur of competition in the local telephony market. It did not happen that way. Neither did CLECs gain much of a foothold. However, IP communications may offer a substitute to these well-entrenched elements of telephony. It could also offer a complement to many of these same companies. The force of IP communications seemed compelling, too compelling for service providers, equipment vendors, and others to wait for regulatory certainty. What forces should companies evaluate as each of the industry elements thought about the impact of IP communications?

Appendix

How VoIP Works

Regular telephone service via the PSTN uses a dedicated circuit between the caller and the local office of the telephone carrier. The dial tone indicates that the circuit has been established. When the caller dials the number they wish to reach, the call is routed through a switch at the carrier's local office to the local office of the carrier used by the callee, where it is transmitted through a switch and sent to the callee's phone. During the entire time of the telephone call, the circuit is continuously open between the two phones. This circuit cannot be used to carry other voice calls. (NB: DSL works at a different frequency from voice calls, which is why DSL users can talk and access the Internet at the same time using the same physical connection.)

Like other data networks, VoIP does not use circuit switching (as is used by the PSTN); instead it uses packet switching. The transmission (including voice calls, e-mails, or anything else sent or received via the data network) is broken into small pieces called packets. Each packet contains the IP address of its intended recipient. These packets are sent over the network (e.g., the Internet) and reassembled in the correct order.

Packet switching used by VoIP provides several advantages over circuit switching. One big difference is efficiency; whereas PSTN calls take up a dedicated circuit for the entire time of the call, packet switching allows several telephone calls to occupy the amount of space occupied by only one in a circuit-switched network.

VoIP is proving popular with enterprises. Companies that use VoIP for multiple telephones will typically operate a digital private branch exchange (PBX). A PBX is essentially a switch used to connect a number of phones (extensions) to each other and to one or more outside phone lines. Most digital PBXs can convert the standard circuit-switched signal from each phone into digital data that can be sent over a packet-switched, IP-based network.

In this scenario, the caller hears a dial tone sent by the PBX, which indicates that the connection is ready. The caller dials the phone number. The PBX determines to what IP address to map the number. (In mapping, the number is attached to the IP address of another device called the IP host. The IP host is typically another digital PBX that is connected directly to the phone system of the number dialed.) In some cases, particularly if the callee is using a computer-based VoIP client, the IP host is the system to which the callee wishes to connect. Calls to non-VoIP numbers are transmitted in the regular way.

A session is established between the caller's PBX and the other party's IP host. The systems will implement two channels, one for each direction, as part of the session. For the time of the session, the caller's PBX and the callee's IP host transmit packets back and forth when there is data to be sent. The PBX at the caller's end keeps open the circuit between itself and the callee's phone extension while it forwards packets to and from the IP host at the other end. When the caller hangs up, the circuit is closed, freeing the line. The caller's PBX sends a signal to the callee's IP host that it is terminating the session. The IP host terminates the session too.

Follow the Money

Follow the Money: Where Fees and Tariffs Are Applied.

Who Pays/ Receives?	Caller	RBOC	Tariff Agents	CLEC	ISP	VoIP Service
Type of Call						
PSTN→PSTN	Pays phone bill	If caller subscribes to RBOC, it receives monthly fee. Caller's RBOC or CLEC pays access charge to callee's RBOC. Interstate and intrastate long-distance fees are paid by RBOC or CLEC.	Caller's and callee's PUC receives tariff based on per-minute charges.	If caller subscribes to CLEC, the CLEC pays access fees to the callers and callee's RBOCs.	Not applicable.	Not applicable.
VoIP→PSTN	Pays VoIP service (unless free service).	VoIP company pays access fee to callee's RBOC.	Only callee's PUC receives tariff based on per-minute charges.	Not applicable.	Caller must have high-speed Internet access.	Pays callee's RBOC access fee. Receives fee from caller (unless free service).
VoIP→VoIP	Pays VoIP service (unless free service).	None.	No tariffs paid.	None.	Caller and callee must have high-speed Internet access.	No charges paid (unless peering charges apply). Receives fees from sub-scribers (unless free service(s)).
PSTN→VoIP	Pays phone bill.	If caller subscribes to RBOC, it receives monthly fee.	PUC receives tariff on access to caller's RBOC.	If caller subscribes to CLEC, it receives monthly fee. CLEC pays access to caller's RBOC.	Callee must have high-speed Internet access.	Receives fees from sub-scribers (unless free service(s)).

NB: Free VoIP services were usually only available for free when calling other users within the network. VoIP calls within a network did not touch the PSTN and thus did not incur RBOC access fees for originating or terminating calls.

Source: Authors.

Schematic of a VoIP Call

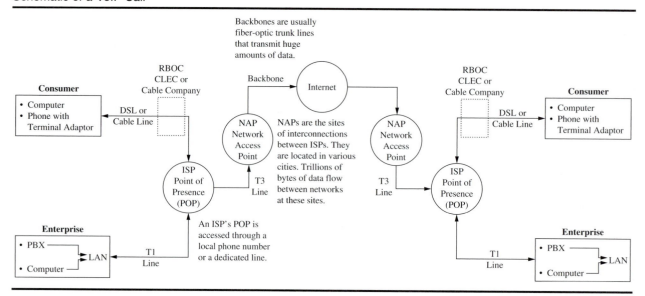

Source: Authors.